WORKS ISSUED BY

THE HAKLUYT SOCIETY

MISSIONS TO THE NIGER I

SECOND SERIES
No. CXXIII

ISSUED FOR 1962

HAKLUYT SOCIETY

PATRON
H.R.H. THE DUKE OF GLOUCESTER, K.G., P.C., K.T., K.P.

COUNCIL AND OFFICERS, 1963-64

PRESIDENT
SIR ALAN BURNS, G.C.M.G.

VICE-PRESIDENTS

Professor E. G. R. TAYLOR, D.Sc.
J. N. L. BAKER, Esq., M.A., B.Litt.

JAMES A. WILLIAMSON, Esq., D.Litt.
Professor D. B. QUINN

COUNCIL (WITH DATE OF ELECTION)

W. E. D. ALLEN, Esq., O.B.E., F.S.A. (1961)
Professor C. R. BOXER, F.B.A. (1960)
G. R. CRONE, Esq., M.A. (1961)
E. S. DE BEER, Esq., D.Litt. (1961)
Professor G. S. GRAHAM (1960)
Sir PHILIP HAY, K.C.V.O., T.D. (1963)
G. W. B. HUNTINGFORD, Esq., D.Litt. (1963)
Sir HARRY LUKE, K.C.M.G., D.Litt. (1961)
F. B. MAGGS, Esq., F.S.A. (1962)

J. W. S. MARR, Esq. (1960)
General Sir JAMES MARSHALL-CORNWALL (1963)
G. P. B. NAISH, Esq., F.S.A. (1960)
J. H. PARRY, Esq., C.M.G., M.B.E., Ph.D. (1962)
Royal Geographical Society (Sir GILBERT LAITHWAITE)
Miss ALWYN RUDDOCK, Ph.D., F.S.A. (1962)
Lieut. Cdr. D. W. WATERS, R.N. (1959)

TRUSTEES

J. N. L. BAKER, Esq., M.A., B.Litt.   E. W. BOVILL, Esq., F.S.A.
Sir GILBERT LAITHWAITE, G.C.M.G., K.C.B., K.C.I.E., C.S.I., Hon. LL.D.

TREASURER
J. N. L. BAKER, Esq., M.A., B.Litt.

HON. SECRETARIES

R. A. SKELTON, Esq., B.A., F.S.A., F.R.Hist.S., British Museum, London, W.C.1.
Miss EILA M. J. CAMPBELL, M.A., F.S.A., Birkbeck College, London, W.C.1.

HON. SECRETARIES FOR OVERSEAS

Australia: G. D. RICHARDSON, Esq., M.A. The Public Library of N.S.W., Sydney, N.S.W.
Canada: Professor J. B. BIRD, McGill University, Montreal.
India: Dr. S. GOPAL, Historical Division, Ministry of External Affairs, New Delhi.
New Zealand: C. R. H. TAYLOR, Esq., M.A., Box 52, Tawa.
South Africa and Central Africa: DOUGLAS VARLEY, Esq., Private Bag 167 H, Salisbury, S. Rhodesia.
U.S.A.: W. M. WHITEHILL, Esq., Ph.D., F.S.A., Boston Athenaeum, Boston, Mass.

Publisher and Agent for Sale and Distribution of Volumes:
CAMBRIDGE UNIVERSITY PRESS,
Bentley House, 200 Euston Road, London, N.W.1

The annual subscription to the Society is £2 2s. sterling ($6 U.S. currency) payable on 1st January. There is no entrance fee.

Members are entitled to all volumes issued by the Society (other than those of the Extra Series) during the period of their membership. As a rule, two volumes are produced each year.

Applications for membership may be addressed to any of the Honorary Secretaries. No proposer is necessary.

Plate I. Major Alexander Gordon Laing
After the engraving by S. Freeman

MISSIONS TO THE NIGER

VOLUME I

THE JOURNAL OF
FRIEDRICH HORNEMANN'S TRAVELS
FROM CAIRO TO MURZUK
IN THE YEARS
1797–98

★

THE LETTERS OF
MAJOR ALEXANDER GORDON LAING
1824–26

Edited by

E. W. BOVILL

CAMBRIDGE
Published for the Hakluyt Society
AT THE UNIVERSITY PRESS
1964

PUBLISHED BY
THE SYNDICS OF THE CAMBRIDGE UNIVERSITY PRESS
Bentley House, 200 Euston Road, London, N.W.1
American Branch: 32 East 57th Street, New York 22, N.Y.

©
THE HAKLUYT SOCIETY
1964

*Printed in Great Britain
by Robert MacLehose & Company Limited
at the University Press, Glasgow*

PREFACE

The Council of the Hakluyt Society hopes to publish a short series of volumes on the exploration of the Niger following its discovery by Mungo Park.

This volume, being the first of the series, naturally begins with the travels of Friedrich Hornemann. It then leaps a quarter of a century to the great journey of Alexander Gordon Laing, regardless of the earlier work of G. F. Lyon and Oudney, Denham and Clapperton in the same field. This unfortunate departure from chronological order has been imposed by financial considerations. While Hornemann's journal is too short for a single volume, Lyon's is too long for less than a volume; and Denham and Clapperton will require two or more. It was, however, found just possible to present Hornemann and Laing in a single volume. This has now been done, but they have been treated as two separate works, Book I and Book II, with a common Preface and a common Index.

Book I, on Hornemann's travels, takes the conventional form of a Hakluyt Society publication — an edited text preceded by an introduction.

Book II, on Laing, is, apart from the introduction, far from conventional. This is because its stirring and romantic story has had to be built up from miscellaneous material drawn from a variety of contemporary sources. This material has had to be welded together with editorial matter far in excess of the Society's custom. All the more important contemporary documents, whether in Laing's or in other hands, have been printed exactly as they were written but they do not suffice to tell the whole story. Because of their repetitive nature, many other records, notably the less important letters by Laing or by those closely associated with him, and many official dispatches, have been omitted. But there are few of these other records which do not contribute something to the Laing story. The fragmentary material drawn from these unpublished documents is the substance of the editorial interpolations without which it would not have been possible to build up a coherent and concise account of the Mission to Timbuktu.

Not the least of the problems which have harrassed me, as editor, has been what to print and what to leave out. In every case the responsibility for the decision rests solely on my shoulders.

But my task would have been far harder had not many kind friends — some of them unknown to me personally — generously responded to my importunate demands for help. The footnotes record most of the assistance I have received, but no mere footnote could do justice to the excessive kindness of some of those who have helped me.

Foremost among the latter is my valued friend Dr. L. Cabot Briggs of Harvard on whose great knowledge of the peoples of northern Africa I have constantly drawn. But my indebtedness to Dr. Cabot Briggs goes much further than that. Without his encouragement — perhaps insistence is the right word — I would never have had the temerity to offer to edit Laing, a task for which Dr. Cabot Briggs himself was so much better qualified.

The kindness with which that great authority on the Sahara, Professor Théodore Monod, responded to the frequent claims I made on him is only part of my great debt to him. He has also been tireless in his search for material, in both France and Africa, which he thought might help me. My regret is that considerations of space have not permitted me to make full use of the fruits of his disinterested researches. With characteristic modesty, and unknown to me, another great French scholar, Monsieur Raymond Mauny, joined with Professor Monod in helping to provide information I needed. With the bitter feelings between France and England which the loss of the Laing journals provoked much in my mind, I find great pleasure in recording the very generous assistance I have received from these distinguished French scholars.

I have also received much help from various quarters nearer home. Miss Maboth Moseley, the author of an unpublished work on Laing, not only lent me a copy of her book but allowed me the use of the notebooks she had compiled from the Laing records. Few authors would have been so generous to so unwelcome an interloper.

Those good friends of the Hakluyt Society, the staff of the Royal Geographical Society, have repeatedly helped me with both Hornemann and Laing. I have particularly in mind Mr. G. R. Crone and his two assistants Mr. G. S. Dugdale and Mrs. E. M. Molloy.

My ignorance of Arabic would have hampered my work but for ready assistance from my friend Professor C. F. Beckingham who never spared himself in answering my many questions.

I also gratefully acknowledge the help I have received from certain other friends, each in his or her particular field of learning. Amongst them are Lady Brogan, the Rev. Dr. A. J. Arkell, Mr. Seton Dearden and Mr. Robin Hallett.

I must also record the unfailing courtesy and helpfulness I have invariably received in the Public Record Office and in the library of the Royal Society for which I am very grateful. Unpublished Crown-copyright material in the Public Record Office has been reproduced by permission of the Controller of H.M. Stationery Office. Manuscript material in the library of the Royal Society is published by permission of the Society, in whose possession the copyright of the original remains.

In common with every other Hakluyt Society editor over many past years, I am deeply indebted to the Hon. Secretary, my valued friend Mr. R. A. Skelton. Like many others, I am bewildered by his capacity for combining uncompromising insistence on the strictest adherence to the editorial rules of the Society with a profound understanding of, and sympathy for, an editor's problems. This volume has been completed under the lash of his merciless whip, but at least I have been solaced by the kindly help of Miss Eila M. J. Campbell, to whom also I am deeply grateful.

E. W. BOVILL

CONTENTS

PREFACE   page v

THE JOURNAL OF FRIEDRICH HORNEMANN'S TRAVELS

EDITOR'S INTRODUCTION

    i. The Search for the Niger   3
    ii. Friedrich Conrad Hornemann   8
    iii. Paris to Cairo   19
    iv. Cairo to Murzuk   25
    v. Murzuk to Bokani   31
    vi. Hornemann and the Niger   38

BIBLIOGRAPHICAL NOTE   40

The Journal

INTRODUCTION   45

PREFACE, containing some Account of F. Horneman; of the Preparations for his Voyage; and of Events previous to his leaving Cairo   52

CHAPTER

  I Voyage from Cairo to Augila
    i. To Ummesogeir   58
    ii. Observations on the Desert; passing from the Valley of Natron to the Mountains of Ummesogeir   62
    iii. Ummesogeir, and further Journey to Siwah   64
    iv. Siwah   66
    v. Antiquities of Siwah   70
    vi. Departure from Siwah; Journey to Schiacha; and Danger which the Traveller there incurred   75
    vii. Departure from Schiacha; Arrival at Augila   80

  II i. Augila, and further Progress to the Confines of Temissa   84
    ii. Observations on the Region of the Harutsch   88
    iii. Arrival at Temissa, and further Journey   92
    iv. Of Zuila   94

v. Further Journey, and Arrival at Mourzouk, the Capital
　　　　of the Kingdom of Fezzan　　　　　　　　　　*page* 95

　　III Some Account of Mourzouk, and of the Kingdom of Fezzan　　98

APPENDIX

　　I Some Account of F. Horneman, after his Arrival at Mourzouk　　　　　　　　　　　　　　　　　　　　　　　　108

　　II A Memoir, containing various Informations respecting the Interior of Africa; transmitted from Mourzouk in 1799, by F. Horneman　　　　　　　　　　　　　　　　　　111

* * *

THE LETTERS OF
MAJOR ALEXANDER GORDON LAING

ABBREVIATIONS　　　　　　　　　　　　　　　　　　124

INTRODUCTION
　　i. The Materials　　　　　　　　　　　　　　　　125
　　ii. The Problem of the Niger　　　　　　　　　　　129
　　iii. Alexander Gordon Laing: The Soldier　　　　　132
　　iv. Laing and the Niger　　　　　　　　　　　　　138
　　v. The Road to Timbuktu　　　　　　　　　　　　145
　　vi. Yūsuf Karamanli　　　　　　　　　　　　　　　149
　　vii. Colonel Warrington　　　　　　　　　　　　　151
　　viii. Clapperton and Laing　　　　　　　　　　　　161
　　ix. Hatita　　　　　　　　　　　　　　　　　　　164
　　x. The Story of Timbuktu　　　　　　　　　　　　168
　　xi. Alexander Gordon Laing: The Explorer　　　　173

ITINERARY　　　　　　　　　　　　　　　　　　　　183

The Letters

CHAPTER
　　I Preparations　　　　　　　　　　　　　　　　　185
　　II Tripoli: Laing and the Bashaw　　　　　　　　194
　　III Tripoli: Emma Warrington　　　　　　　　　206

IV	Farewell to Laing	page 214
V	Tripoli to Ghadames	228
VI	Ghadames	241
VII	In Salah	273
VIII	The First Attack	296
IX	Timbuktu	308
X	The Search for Laing	319
XI	The Missing Journals	330

APPENDIX

I	Journal of Major A. Gordon Laing	342
II	Laing's *Cursory Remarks on the course and termination of the Great River Niger*	366
III	Laing's *Notes on Gadamis*	374
IV	Emma Gordon Laing	386
V	*The Report of Laing's Death published in* L'Étoile *of 2 May 1827*	389

BIBLIOGRAPHY 391

INDEX 395

ILLUSTRATIONS

PLATES

I Major Alexander Gordon Laing. After the engraving by S. Freeman	*Frontispiece*
II Tripoli: The Old English Consulate	*facing page* 154
III Tripoli: The English Garden	*facing page* 158
IV Ghadames: The Asnam. After a sketch by Laing	*facing page* 264

MAPS

I Hornemann's probable route	*facing page* 31
II The route of Mr. Frederick Hornemann from Aegypt to Fezzan, compiled by J. Rennell, 1802	*facing page* 58
III Hornemann's map of Hausa	*page* 116
IV Laing's Map of his route from Tripoli to Ghadames	*facing page* 228
V Laing's probable route to Timbuktu	*facing page* 273
VI (*a*) Laing's sketch map of the middle Niger (*b*) Laing's sketch map of the upper Niger (*c*) Laing's sketch map illustrating his theory that the Volta was the Niger's outlet to the sea	*facing page* 367

THE JOURNAL OF
FRIEDRICH HORNEMANN'S TRAVELS
FROM CAIRO TO MURZUK
IN THE YEARS
1797–98

EDITOR'S INTRODUCTION

i. *The Search for the Niger*

The deep interest in Africa which the early Portuguese voyages down the Guinea coast had aroused in the fifteenth century had soon been lost. The discoveries of America and the Cape route to the East had opened up untapped sources of wealth which quickly absorbed all the interest of Europe in oversea exploration. Nevertheless, the African trade had continued. Every creek and anchorage along the broken coasts of Barbary and Guinea was known to traders from half the nations of western Europe, so when, in the second half of the eighteenth century, enquiring minds turned once more to the unexplored continent that lay so close at hand, it was to the merchants and traders who knew the coasts so well, that geographers first looked for information about the wholly unexplored interior. These enquiries, prosecuted with the greatest diligence, proved unfruitful because one of the cardinal principles of the inland trade had always been to guard against interlopers. As the European merchants were compelled to confine their trading activities to their *fonduks*, factories and trading beaches, so were the African merchants with whom they traded, the coastal middlemen, forbidden to penetrate the interior. Consequently the mass of information so industriously gathered was for the most part worthless. Indeed, it was worse; all of it being at second or third hand it was so inaccurate and contradictory that it only added to the confusion in men's minds. Consuls and merchants on the Barbary shore knew no more about the origins of the gold, ivory, ebony, pepper and 'morocco' leather which toiling caravans poured into their ports from the remote interior, than did the Guinea traders about the sources of the slaves, gold, ivory and gum on which they grew rich. To them, to the Barbary consuls and merchants and the Guinea traders, rich countries like Bornu, Hausa and Bonduk, and the great entrepôts of Agades, Katsina and Timbuktu, were mere names which they could not place on a map with greater accuracy than the geographers of the day of Leo Africanus in the early sixteenth century. They even believed that the ancient kingdoms of Mali and Ghana still survived. Above all they did not know, because Leo had failed to notice, whether the Niger flowed from east to west, as Herodotus had said, or westwards, as El Edrisi had declared in the twelfth century.

Happily, in England there was a small group of men, of whom Sir Joseph Banks, President of the Royal Society, was the leader, who regarded the continued ignorance about the interior of Africa as a reproach on their age which must be resolved by more resolute methods.

'Notwithstanding the progress of discovery on the coasts and borders of that vast continent', they declared, 'the map of its interior is still but a wide extended blank, on which the geographer, on the authority of Leo Africanus, and of the Xeriff Edrissi the Nubian author, has traced, with a hesitating hand, a few names of unexplored rivers and of uncertain nations.

'The course of the Niger, the places of its rise and termination, and even its existence as a separate stream, are still undetermined. . . .

'Sensible of this stigma, and desirous of rescuing the age from a charge of ignorance, which, on other respects, belongs so little to its character, a few individuals, strongly impressed with a conviction of the practicability and utility of thus enlarging the fund of human knowledge, have formed the plan of an Association for Promoting the discovery of the interior parts of Africa.'[1] Thus was founded, on 9 June 1788, the African Association.

It seems probable that the Association came into being just when it did because the services of two promising explorers had suddenly become available. These were John Ledyard and Simon Lucas. Ledyard was an American with 'an invincible desire to make himself acquainted with the unknown, or imperfectly discovered regions of the globe'. After spending several years amongst North American Indians studying 'the means of obtaining the protection, and of recommending himself to the favour, of Savages . . . [he] had made, with Captain Cook, the Voyage of the World'. Financed by Joseph Banks, he had explored, rather unprofitably, little-known parts of North America, Russia and Siberia, whence, after being expelled, he had returned destitute to England. No sooner had the African Association been formed than it engaged Ledyard to traverse Africa 'from East to West, in the latitude attributed to the Niger, the widest part of the Continent'.

Simon Lucas had spent three years of his youth as a slave in Morocco to which he had been carried by a Sallee rover. Soon after his release he had returned to Morocco as British Vice-Consul, and sixteen years later had returned to take up the post of Oriental Interpreter at the Court of St James. Attracted by his considerable knowledge of Arabic and the Moslem way of life, the Association had sought and secured his

[1] *Proceedings*, 1, 6–8.

services. To him it allotted the task of crossing 'the Desert of Zahara, from Tripoli to Fezzan; for they had learned from various information, that with this kingdom, which in some measure is dependent on Tripoli, the traders of Agadez and Tombuctou, and of other towns in the Interior of Africa, had established a frequent and regular intercourse'. From Fezzan Lucas was to make his way home 'by the way of the Gambia or by that of the Coast of Guinea'.

The Association raised £430 to equip and finance these two 'Geographical Missionaries' the first of whom, John Ledyard, left for Egypt only three weeks after the founding of the Association. On arrival in Cairo, where he was befriended by the Venetian Consul, Charles Rosetti, he lodged in a Christian monastery and at once began enquiring about the interior, among merchants and in the slave market. He found that Cairo was trading with Senaar, Darfur and Fezzan, and through Fezzan with Timbuktu, and he heard Wangara talked of 'as a place producing much gold'. The high hopes raised by the good impression his reports made on his employers were quickly shattered by the news of his death in Cairo from a 'bilious complaint . . . attributed to the frowardness of a childish impatience'.[1]

Simon Lucas was also a disappointment to the Association. Arriving in Tripoli in October 1788, he secured the Bashaw's permission to travel to Fezzan on the plea that he wished to see its 'Roman antiquities' and to collect 'a variety of medicinal plants that are not to be found in Europe'. But the disturbed state of the desert, where the nomads were in revolt against the Bashaw, made his early departure impossible. His prospects improved when two Shereefs of Fezzan arrived in Tripoli with their caravan of slaves and senna. They consented to take him under their protection and to answer for his safe arrival in Fezzan. In February he accompanied them eastwards, travelling along the coast, to the little port of Misurata whence they intended to start for the interior. But the revolt in the desert had continued and the caravan routes were still too unsafe for travel. When March arrived, with the hot season at hand and the revolt unabated, the Shereefs decided to remain in the north until November. Thereupon Lucas returned to Tripoli and made his way back to England where he arrived in July, and left the Association's service. Later he was appointed Consul-General in Tripoli where we shall meet him again.

During his long stay in Tripoli and Misurata Lucas had collected a good deal of unreliable information about the interior. Its publication

[1] *Proceedings*, I, 41.

by the Association, who were naturally unaware of its many inaccuracies and gross mis-statements, served only further to confuse geographers.[1] It did, however, suggest that, as later proved to be true, the crossing of the Sahara was more hazardous than travelling in the remote countries of the south. It was encouraging that one of the Shereefs 'with the utmost cheerfulness and confidence of safety, proposed to accompany and conduct Mr. Lucas, by the way of Fezzan and Cashna [Katsina], across the Niger, to Assenté [Ashanti], which borders on the coast of the Christians'.[2]

At this time the Hausa city of Cashna or Katsina was scarcely less famous than Timbuktu. It was certainly the most important market of the west-central Sudan, a position it was soon to yield to its neighbour Kano. Lucas's reports had led the eminent geographer Major James Rennell to regard Katsina 'as the central kingdom of the great body of Africa'.[3] It was the city which Shabeni, one of the Association's Arab informants,[4] had called Hausa and described as equalled only by London and Cairo. The wealth and grandeur of its empire exceeded 'those of any kingdom he had seen, England alone excepted'. 'The existence of the city of Houssa', reads the Association's *Proceedings*, 'and of the empire thus described by Shabeni, was strongly confirmed by the letters which the Committee received from his Majesty's Consuls at Tunis and Morocco, and with this additional circumstance of information from them, that both at Tunis and Morocco the eunuchs of the Seraglio were brought from the city of Houssa.'[5] The Niger, at this time, was believed to run westwards, south of the kingdom of Cashna, towards Timbuktu.[6]

Meanwhile the Association, possibly disappointed at the financial response to their purely scientific appeal, had begun to hint at the com-

---

[1] *Proceedings*, I, 47–205.   [2] Ibid., I, 126.   [3] Ibid., I, 220.
[4] Shabeni, or Aseed el Hage Abd Salam Shabeeny, was a native of Tetuan. At the age of fourteen he accompanied his father to the Sudan where he remained for twelve years, two of which he spent in Hausa and the rest in Timbuktu. When he was twenty-six he returned to Tetuan where he established himself as a merchant. In 1795, returning from a business trip to Hamburg, the English ship in which he was travelling was captured at sea and taken to Ostend where Shabeni found himself a prisoner of war. Having secured his release through the good offices of the British Consul, he resumed his journey and was put ashore at Dover. From there he appears to have made his way to London. Either there or in Dover he was closely interrogated about the interior of Africa, the interpreter being Simon Lucas who had known Shabeni's father and mother in Tetuan (J. G. Jackson, *An Account of Timbuctoo and Housa*, London, 1820, p. v).
[5] *Proceedings*, I, 241. On account of their good looks, intelligence and industry, Hausa slaves had long commanded a premium in the slave markets of the Maghreb.
[6] Ibid., I, 220.

mercial advantages that might accrue from geographical discovery. With Timbuktu and Hausa in mind, they suggested that the exploration of the Niger 'might possibly open to Britain a commercial passage to rich and populous nations'. So when, in 1790, they engaged Major Houghton, late of the 69th Regiment, who had served on the West African coast, to seek the Niger by way of the Gambia they instructed him also to visit 'the cities of Tombuctoo and Houssa'. Reaching the mouth of the Gambia in November, Houghton made his perilous way to Bambuk; thence he crossed the Falemé and Senegal rivers, and, when last heard of was fully expecting to reach Timbuktu.

The news that Houghton had reached Bambuk, to which hitherto, it was thought, no European had penetrated, gave great satisfaction to the Association, but his conclusions regarding the course of the Niger were sensational. The chief of these were that it rose to the east of Bambuk and that it flowed from west to east.

In spite of the then widely-held belief that the Niger's course was to the west, Houghton's conclusions were readily accepted because they accorded with much that the Association had learnt from natives of Africa both in London and in Tunis where it had a valuable correspondent in the British Consul, Mr Magra. The acceptance of Houghton's conclusions called for a complete revision of current ideas regarding the main course of the river and its termination. Houghton had been told by a much-travelled African, Shereef Mamadu of Timbuktu, that the Niger 'receives several considerable streams from the west, before it reaches the neighbourhood of Tombuctoo, where ... it divides into two branches, the smallest of which passes close to Tombuctoo, whilst the main branch proceeds to Houssa, a very considerable city, situated ... a few days journey from Tombuctoo'.[1] This found acceptance in the critical eyes of James Rennell but he rejected — on sound scientific grounds — Houghton's suggestion that the source of the Niger would ultimately be found to be also that of the Nile. Having satisfied himself from other sources that, correctly enough, Hausa was a country and not a city, and, incorrectly, that Katsina also was a country, Rennell's final conclusion about the middle course of the Niger, was that 'the great river, designed by us under the name of Niger, communicates with the country of Cashnah, as well as that of Tombuctoo, and Houssa'.[2] Thus the precise situation of the Hausa city of Katsina became the subject of keen speculation among geographers. To discover Katsina, they believed, was to discover the middle course of the Niger.

[1] *Proceedings*, I, 282.   [2] Ibid., 286.

A measure of the excitement caused by the new light Houghton had thrown on the most perplexing geographical mystery of the age is the extraordinary flights of fancy which were formally recorded in the stately *Proceedings* of the Association. 'That in some of the cities of these insulted empires', they read, 'the knowledge and the language of ancient Egypt may still imperfectly survive, is not an unpleasing supposition: nor is it absolutely impossible that the Carthaginians, who do not appear to have perished with their cities, may have retired to the southern parts of Africa; and, though lost to the world in the vast oblivion of the Desert, may have carried with them to the new regions they occupy, some portion of those arts and sciences, and of that commercial knowledge, for which the inhabitants of Carthage were once so eminently famed.'[1]

The next heard of Houghton, who was confidently expected to reach Timbuktu and discover the Niger, was a report of his death near Nioro at, it was believed, the hands of an assassin. His success in penetrating so far inland convinced the Association that the Gambia was the most promising gateway to the interior of Africa and the discovery of the upper reaches of the Niger. But it was more than four years after Houghton's death before they found someone to explore further the trail he had blazed. The man of their choice was young Mungo Park who was to fulfil the high hopes to which Houghton's work and his own character had given rise. Arriving on the Gambia in May 1795 he vanished into the interior to win for himself, more than a year later, lasting fame as the discoverer of the Niger.

ii. *Friedrich Conrad Hornemann*

Long before any news had been received from Mungo Park — indeed, before he had discovered the Niger — the African Association had received, and accepted, the offer of a young German, Friedrich Conrad Hornemann,[2] to enter their service as an explorer.

Hornemann was the son of Friedrich Georg Hornemann, pastor of Hildesheim in Saxony. We do not know the date or place of his birth,

---

[1] *Proceedings*, I, 258. Similarly in 1817 Commander W. H. Smyth, R.N., reported from Tripolitania 'several remarkable conversations relative to the existence of certain Christian tribes in the interior of Africa; and, it would appear, in the neighbourhood of Wangara and Gooba [Gobir]' (*The Mediterranean* (London, 1854), 481).

[2] Although in their Minutes the African Association spelt Hornemann's name correctly, Sir Joseph Banks, in his letters, always refers to him as Horneman, the anglicized form of his name under which the Association later published his *Journal*.

but as he was baptized at Hildisheim on 20 September 1772 he was probably born there shortly before that date. In 1791 he matriculated as a theological student at Göttingen University, but he appears to have had no vocation for the church for thereafter he devoted himself to the study of African geography and to preparing himself for a career as an explorer. In the summer of 1795 he sought a recommendation to the African Association from Dr Johann Friedrich Blumenbach, an anatomist and anthropologist of Göttingen, a Fellow of the Royal Society, and a friend of Sir Joseph Banks.[1]

Blumenbach appears to have done as the young man wanted for in the course of the next few months the Association made some sort of an offer to Hornemann. But it was not till the following summer that his name appeared in the official records. The following is from the minutes of a meeting of the committee held on 3 June 1796:

> Read a Letter from Professor Blumenbach to Sir Joseph Banks, dated Göttingen and Sir Joseph's Answer.
> Read also the following Letter from Professor Blumenbach to Sir Joseph Banks dated Göttingen, May 4th 1796, enclosing the Proposals from Mr. Hornemann.
>
> Göttingen, May 4th 1796
>
> Sir,
> After having returned you my most obliging and most hearty thanks for the highly interesting Mineralogical curiosities you were so kind to favor me with, I come directly to Mr. Hornemann's Proposal.
> As soon as I received your Letter I enquired for the most particular information about his character, Talents, circumstances etc. and now after all what I have learned I may say, that there will be hardly a Man better qualified for the purpose in question than he is.
> He is universally known by all his acquaintances as a Man of an excellent character, and besides other good qualities, as a very good Economist, who, tho' in a very moderate circumstances (having lost his father, a clergyman, who left a widow with several children) yet has always managed his Economical arrangements in such a way, that he lived decently without ever incurring the least Debts. etc.
> He is a young robust man of an athletic bodily constitution, infatigable [sic] but always taking great care and good precaution for preserving his health.

---

[1] This is all we know of Hornemann's upbringing, and we owe it to Adolf Pahde, *Der Erste Deutsche Afrikaforscher (Fr.K. Hornemann, geb. 1772, gest. 1801)* (Hamburg, 1895).

After having received the contents of your last favors, he made a trip to Göttingen to confer with me.

As he wishes to become as useful as possible to the Association, he thinks it very convenient, or rather necessary to pass some months before his departure here in Göttingen for his better preparation.

My brother-in-law, Professor Heyne, F.R.S.,[1] First Librarian of the University, who takes the greatest interest in that matter, will with all his heart give him all information and hints in his power.

The same promised to me in the most liberal way another Relation of mine, Professor Heeren[2] (Prof. Heyne's Son in Law) the author of the work on the Trade of the Ancients, of which the second volume just now is published.

That I will furnish Mr. Hornemann with such notices of Natural History which may make his Expedition the more useful, as for instance, with the Geographical part of Mineralogy etc., I need not to tell you.

But besides this, he would spend his time principally with Our Orientalists, for the Arabian Language etc — with our Mathematicians and Astronomers etc.

In the mean time, he will also acquire some necessary practical knowledge of Domestic Medicine and Surgery, and employ a part of his time for perfectionning [*sic*] himself still more in drawing etc.

All this will be done in a few months and I should think that if the Association would allow him for this preparative Residence Eight pounds Sterling *per month* it would be a moderate Sum, but sufficient for him as an excellent economist, and of which he will I am sure dispose in the most proper way.

In regard to the other conditions, it would be impossible for *him* to propose them in detail. But however he has on my advice, though in haste, set down some of the Principal articles. As I am myself, just now in a great hurry, I am sorry that I cannot translate them in English, but I enclose an Extract of his Paper in German.

The only thing about which he wishes to learn as soon as possible the resolution of the Association is, his coming to Göttingen for some months.

I have the honor to be etc. etc.

(sgd) Jno Fredk Blumenbach.

Translation of the *Proposals from Mr. Hornemann* enclosed in the preceeding Letter.

1. I cannot at present ascertain the expences of My Journey to Alexandria; but I will enquire how much the passage from Leghorn to that place costs, and then I will make an estimate — It shall be as reasonable as possible, and the African Society will certainly not disapprove of it.

---

[1] C. G. Heyne, 1729–1812, was a distinguished classical scholar.
[2] A. H. L. Heeren, 1760–1842, a classical scholar and historian with a particular interest in North Africa.

2. As to the Equipment, I will be as economical concerning it as the circumstances will admit, partly that I may travel with the greater ease, and partly to prevent the quantity of Baggage giving me the appearance of a Rich man, and affording a pretence for Treachery. By Equipment, I mean the necessary weapons, some mathematical Instruments, Telescopes and the like. I wish to be allowed to chuse those articles myself, and if Professor Blumenbach will permit, to shew him the accounts of them. But should it be the practice of the Society, to allow a stated Sum for fitting out, I shall be equally satisfied with that; I only beg to be apprized of it.

3. I request the Society will send me to this place, if not all, yet some of the recommendatory Letters for Alexandria and Cairo, in order that, if some accident were to prevent the arrival of those that shall be forwarded by other means, I shall not however, arrive without some introduction.

4. As in my journey from Cairo to Kashna [Katsina][1] I shall perhaps touch at Moursouck [Murzuk], where there are two Shereefs with whom Mr. Lucas[2] had got acquainted; I much wish to have an Arabic introductory letter of the said Mr. Lucas to those Shereefs *Founad* and *Imhammed*, as one of them in particular, being Son in law to the King of Fezzan, may be of great use to me.

5. Might not, by means of the Turkish Ambassador now in England, a Firman be obtained for me? If I dont mistake, the African Society have already endeavoured to obtain one for Mr. Lucas.

6. On my arrival at Moursouk, I will endeavour to send copies of my Journals which will contain my progress from Cairo to Fezzan — I shall forward them by Mesurata and Tripoli to London; and for this purpose I request an address to some Trusty person either at Mesurata or Tripoli.

7. I wish the African Society would promise to interest itself in my favor on my return, which at all events must afford some illustrations concerning the State of the Interior parts of Africa, that I may not, after having struggled with innumerable difficulties, be left in a dismal situation. This mediation might operate either by an application to the King for an adequate Civil Employment, or by obtaining from the Public a reasonable recompense, as Sir Joseph Banks seems to intend.

8. Should I, during my residence of one or two years at Kashna, be able to obtain the confidence of the Inhabitants so far as to induce one of them to venture a Journey into Europe with me, which in that case would be an inducement for me to undertake a second journey, the Society will engage to maintain this Native in Europe, until I again set off with him.

9. Should I unfortunately meet with my fate in this Enterprise I request the Society, that the recompence which it is intended to obtain for me, if my Services should be found of sufficient magnitude, be transmitted to my Mother and Sisters: and at all events, should I perish on my Journey, to remit

---

[1] The route he was to follow had evidently been decided before his proposals came before the Association officially.

[2] This was Simon Lucas, now Consul-General in Tripoli.

to these, my nearest Relations, a moderate Sum at the option of the Society, since my death would occasion, not an irreparable, but certainly a considerable loss to them.

Should the Members of the African Society agree, at least to the most essential parts of this Proposal, They may on my part depend on the most punctual execution of their Instructions, in as far as they may be rendered practicable without obstructing the general plan. Prepared, as I shall be by my residence at Göttingen, I shall be able to observe many objects, and I hope to form very accurate opinions of them. The following will be the chief points I shall attend to: The manner of Travelling in Africa — The conduct of Travellers — Trade on the Journey — Names of Places — The Longtitudes and Latitudes of the principal places and great Mountains — Views — Observations on the Manners of the Natives through whose countries I shall travel — Drawings of their Dress — Observations on the nature of the Soils — its fertility and cultivation — on population — Examination of the Minerals.

During my stay at Kashna The Language, — Religion — Government — relation between the subject and the Emperor or Ruler — Customs and Manners — Trades, Employments and manner of living of the Inhabitants — Commerce — Slave Trade — Intercourse with neighbouring States — Arms and Tactics — Climate — Dimensions — fertility — produce — in general, the Natural History of the Country. Researches concerning the course of the Niger — possibility of a communication between the Interior of Africa and the Coast. — Geographical determination of places — Drawings of all remarkable objects etc.

Resolved

That the Committee do approve of the character of Mr. Hornemann and are of opinion that he is likely to make an useful Traveller in their Service.

That the Proposal he has forwarded to them be answered article by article; and in the event of his acceding to their terms, that they will allow him, on account of the Association, the Sum proposed by Professor Blumenbach to maintain him during a Six months Residence at the University of Gottingen.

That the Committee feel themselves much indebted to Professor Heyne, Professor Blumenbach and Professor Heeren, for their liberal offer of Instructing Mr. Hornemann in such things as they think will be useful to him during his Travels in Africa; and will report their opinion of the obligation conferred by these learned Professors on the Association, at the next General Meeting.

Answers to Mr. Hornemann's Proposals.

1. The Committee have no doubt, from the Character they have heard of Mr. Hornemanns Economy, that he will not in any part of his Travels put them to unnecessary expence; They are therefore as confident as Mr.

Hornemann is, that they shall accede to his Estimate when it is sent to them.

2. Respecting Equipment, they wish Mr. Hornemann to be furnished with such things as may appear on due consideration likely to be useful in his Journies, and are not solicitous to economise in that article. They request Mr. Hornemann to furnish them with a List of the articles he shall fix upon with the concurrence of Professor Blumenbach, which they will take into immediate consideration.

3. Mr. Hornemann shall certainly be furnished with Letters of Recommendation both to Alexandria and Cairo before his departure; and it is not impossible that the Association may wish him to take England in his way, in order that they may be enabled to confer with him in person.

4. Mr. Lucas being dead, it is impossible the request can be complied with.[1]

5. The Association never have applied for a Firman for any Traveller; but application will be made to the Turkish Ambassador resident in London, in order that one may be obtained for Mr. Hornemann, if on due consideration the utility of it to that Gentleman is likely to countervail the difficulty of obtaining it. The Committee however are not very sanguine on the subject of its utility, because the moment Mr. Hornemann really commences his Travels in their Service, he will depart from all countries in which the authority of the Porte is admitted.

6. The Committee will furnish Mr. Hornemann with Letters to the British Resident at Tripolis; but they have many doubts whether he will find it possible to join the Caravan which proceeds by the Rout of Moursouk to Cashna, as they are not able to learn that any Christian has hitherto been allowed to travel with it a single days journey.

7. The African Association will certainly Interest themselves in Mr. Hornemann's favor on his return, and have little doubt of procuring for him some Establishment proportioned to the Services he may have performed — having already procured from Government a Pension for the widow of Major Houghton.

8. How far the Society might chuse to encumber themselves with the maintenance of a Native of Cashna, is more than the Committee can take upon themselves to determine, but they will at a fitting opportunity take the opinion of the Association on that subject.

9. The Society have made it a Rule never to pledge themselves in any shape to the maintenance of the Kindred of Persons who may die in their Service — their funds are wholly insufficient to answer contingencies of so extensive a nature, but as they have procured a Pension for Mrs. Houghton, after having for some time given money to her support, it is certainly probable that in the case of Mr. Hornemann's decease in their

---

[1] Simon Lucas, far from being dead, was, as we have seen, Consul-General in Tripoli, where, in due course, he and Hornemann were to meet.

Service, they will make his Mother and Sisters some acknowledgement proportioned to the benefit that they have received from his Discoveries, and the actual situation of their funds at the time.

Respecting the Temple of Jupitor Ammon, the Committee incline to believe that an attempt to discover that would not be so eligible as an Undertaking to proceed into the distant Interior.[1] A Mr. Brown,[2] an Englishman, has lately made a trial, in which he nearly lost his life. He found that Sewah is an Oasis, answering tolerably well to the Great Oasis where the Temple is said by Ancient Writers to be situated; but he saw no ruin in the Town — a mile from it he found a Building about 30 feet long, 14 wide and 10 high, decorated with Egyptian Sculpture, which was probably a Sacellum to the Great Temple. The discovery of his being a Christian rendered it however necessary for him to make a precipitate retreat from the Country.

Although the Committee of the Association had accepted Hornemann's services and had decided on the route of his 'proposed journey', the *Proceedings* do not record what his assignment was. The first we hear of this is in a letter Hornemann wrote to Banks some months later.

Confident that what little doubt remained about the source and upper reaches of the Niger would soon be resolved by Park or some other traveller, the Committee had turned their minds to the problem of the middle course of the great river. They had decided, it will be recalled, that the key to this problem was the discovery of the Hausa city of Katsina about whose situation there were many divergent views. The best overland route to Katsina was, as the Committee had been told, the old Garamantian road running south from Tripoli through Fezzan. Nevertheless, perhaps mindful of Simon Lucas's sorry failure to penetrate inland from Tripoli, they decided that the next attempt should be made from the east. Their instructions to Hornemann were to proceed, after the completion of his training, to Cairo and from there to make his way to Fezzan and Katsina. Wholly ignorant of the countries they were directing him to traverse and equally so of the perils of desert travel, they little realized the magnitude of the task they had set him.

On 7 December Hornemann wrote to Banks from Göttingen thanking him for the opportunity to satisfy his childhood's 'desire to travel in unknown parts of the world ... which are increased with

[1] As no mention of this famous temple was made in Hornemann's written proposals, the reference here must be to another occasion, perhaps to some verbal proposal.
[2] W. G. Browne, who had visited Siwah in 1792.

growing age, having the best constitution and being always in a good humour, and also in possession of some skill to recommend myself to the favour of uncultivated people'. At Göttingen he has applied himself to the study of 'Natural History and Arabic, and the ancient and modern geographers ... and of finding the Longitude and Latitude'. He expresses his gratitude to his professors, especially to Professor Dr Blumenbach 'who succours me in the most effectual manner with his counsel and learning'.

He enquires whether it is 'still fixed that I shall set out from Cairo to Kashna, if the Committee will that I go from here to Venice, or if I shall set out to London, for obtaining in person my instruction for my Tour'. His training in Göttingen should be completed by the end of January, and he wants to arrive in Egypt as soon as possible after that 'for using the time before my travels from Cairo to Kashna to acquaint myself with the manner of living and with the climate, and to perfection me in the language of these Regions'.[1]

Banks decided that Hornemann must come to London, and he sent Blumenbach £30 for his travelling expenses. 'I confess', he wrote in his covering letter, 'I have great hopes that this young man will succeed: he seems to have been born for some enterprise of Travel that will do him honor in the eyes of his contemporaries'.[2] On the same day, 7 January, he wrote to Hornemann that in spite of the difficulty he would have in travelling from London to Cairo, now that the French were 'masters of the Mediterranean', it was the Committee's wish that he should do so. 'The advantages you will receive', he wrote, 'by conferring with persons here who are well acquainted with Egypt, will be sufficient to compensate the inconvenience of passing through France, & as you are the native of a neutral country, they have no doubt you may do it without danger of detention'. The £30 he has sent him through Blumenbach is 'a sum considerably larger, according to my calculation, than you will spend if you meet with no accident or delays'. He is advised to take the packet from Cuxhaven. 'Wherever she lands, you will find a Stage Coach which will bring you to London, where you will find me in Soho Square.'[3]

Hornemann arrived in London in the middle of March and attended a meeting of the Committee of the Association on the 20th of that month, held at the house of the Earl of Moira, a member of the Committee.

'Mr. Horneman', read the minutes of the meeting, 'the German

[1] *D.T.C.*, x (1), 91, 92.   [2] *D.T.C.*, x (2), 24.   [3] Ibid., 25.

Gentleman whose proposals to Travel in the Service of the Association had been considered and answered by the Committee on the 3rd June 1796, ... attended.'

The Committee resolved that while Hornemann was in London the Treasurer should pay his landlord 12s. a week for lodging, and that he should be allowed for his maintenance and personal expenses $1\frac{1}{2}$ guineas a week. It was also agreed that he should be authorized to purchase, at the expense of the Association, the following instruments for use during his travels: a small Hadley's sextant with stand and an artifical horizon (£14 14s. od.), a 3 feet schromatic telescope and stand (£7 17s. 6d.), a time keeper (£26 5s. od.), two pocket compasses, a few necessary books and a 'Memorandum Book, with Ivory leaves'.

The Committee then resolved:

That it be recommended to him to proceed from hence to Cairo, and on his arrival at the Town to fix his Residence either with the Father of the Propaganda or in some other convent, and to live there quietly, without divulging his intentions of Travelling, to the English Resident or to any other European.

That he is advised to remain at Cairo as long as he shall think proper, and to Employ his time during his Residence there in acquiring an intimate knowledge of the Arabic Language, and of such others as he may think likely to be of use to him in his Travels: also, in learning the Manners & Customs, not only of the Natives, but also of all such strangers as may arrive there from the interior Country.

That he do on all occasions, when Strangers from the interior are Resident in Cairo, use his utmost endeavours to become acquainted with them, and to ingratiate himself in their favour; and that whenever he finds an opportunity of accompanying such Strangers to their Native Country, which in his opinion is a suitable and proper one, he do proceed with them, and that he do more especially prefer to accompany Strangers whose Country is near to the situation where Cashna is supposed to be; if in other respects his Chance or ultimate success in the journey is, in his own opinion, equal.

That the Treasurer be empowered to offer to Mr. Horneman, as a Compensation for his Services, an Annuity of £200 a year, to commence from the time when he arrives at Cairo, to which place all his Expenses are to be defrayed by the Association; this Annuity to be payable in case of his death to his Assigns half a year beyond the date of the last Letter that has been received from him by his Employers. This agreement to last for five Years after his arrival at Cairo, and longer if the Association shall at the End of that time be satisfied with his Services, and he shall chuse to continue them.

That Sir Joseph Banks be requested to make application to the Government of France for a Passport for the use of Mr. Horneman, to enable him to Travel with Security to some of the French Ports in the Mediterranean from whence he may with the most ease procure a passage to Egypt.[1]

The Committee's final resolution requesting Banks to apply to the government of France, with which Britain was then at war, for a passport for Hornemann did not present the difficulties that might have been expected. This was because in the previous year Banks had placed Jean Charretié, the French Commissioner in London for the exchange of prisoners of war, under an obligation to him by generously returning to France the botanical collection of a French scientist who had been taken prisoner by the British. Through Charretié's good offices a passport was issued to Hornemann.

At a meeting of the Committee of the Association held on 23 June 1797:

The following Instructions to Mr. Frederick Hornemann were Read:

Instructions from The Committee of the
African Association to Mr. Frederick
Hornemann.

The Committee having received from Mons. Charretié, by direction of the French Government, a Passport for Mr. Hornemann permitting him to Travel through France to Marseilles, it is their wish that he do proceed to Paris without delay, and from thence to Marseilles; from which port he will embrace the first opportunity that offers of a vessel to Alexandria to proceed thither. That from Alexandria Mr. Hornemann do proceed, in a way that may appear to him most convenient, to Grand Cairo; in which city he will fix his residence either with the father of the Propaganda, or in some other Convent, and live there quietly, without divulging his intentions of travelling to the English Resident, or to any other European.

The Committee recommended to him to remain at Cairo as long as he shall think proper, and that he employ his time, during his residence there, in acquiring an intimate knowledge of the Arabic Language, and of such other Languages as he may think likely to be of use to him in his Travels; also in learning the Manners and Customs, not only of the Natives, but also of all such Strangers as may arrive there from the Interior Country.

That on all occasions when Strangers from the Interior are Resident in Cairo, Mr. Hornemann do use his utmost endeavour to become acquainted with them, and to ingratiate himself in their favor; and that whenever he finds

[1] *D.T.C.*, x (2), 27–9.

an opportunity of accompanying such Strangers to their Native Country, which in his opinion is a suitable and proper one, he do proceed with them; and that he do more especially prefer to accompany Strangers whose country is near to the situation where *Cashna* is supposed to be, if, in other respects, his chance of ultimate success in the Journey is in his own opinion equal.

It appears to the Committee, after a careful perusal of Mr. Ledyard's Journal, and Letters, that it is a very doubtful matter if a Christian will ever be permitted to join a Mahometan Caravan: and finding there are Pagan Black Merchants who Trade from *Bournou* to Egypt, The Committee are inclined to think that Mr. Hornemann will find it safer and more convenient to put himself under the protection of some of the Pagan Nations.

As from the concurrent accounts received by the Committee respecting the course of the River Niger, they have reason to think that it runs Eastward, and terminates in an immense Lake or Mediterranean Sea; it becomes a matter of extreme importance that Mr. Hornemann should collect all the information possible on this subject.

Should Mr. Hornemann fortunately be able to extend his Travels as far as the supposed situation of Cashna, the inhabitants of which consist in a mixture of Pagans and Mahometans; it may be a matter deserving his serious consideration, whether he ought not to endeavour to make his way from that Country in a South west direction to the Bite of Benin, or some part of the Gold Coast, where he will find Ships from most of the European Nations, and may return to Europe in one of them by the West Indies.[1]

The particular route, however, by which Mr. Hornemann will proceed from Cairo to the Interior Countries of Africa, or that by which he will return to Europe, must be left to his own discretion; but the Committee will feel the strongest solicitude to receive, by every possible opportunity, an account of his proceedings.

Whatever observations Mr. Hornemann's journey may enable him to make on the Animal, Vegetable or Mineral productions of the Inland Countries of Africa, The Committee will be happy to receive; and they are not without hopes, that the various Caravans which traverse the Continent of Africa in all directions, as well as the communication of the Slave Dealers with the Gambia and the Gulph of Guinea, may render opportunities frequent of receiving Letters or Dispatches from him; and that the expedient of drawing a Bill of *Five Pounds* on the cover of each Letter may ensure the safety of the Conveyance.

When Mr. Hornemann has occasion to write to his friends in Germany, it is expected that he will cautiously avoid mentioning to them, any thing relative to his progress or discoveries in Africa that may anticipate the publications of the Association.

---

[1] Most of these ships were engaged in the West Indian slave trade.

Resolved:

That the preceeding Instructions be approved of, and that the Secretary be requested to deliver a copy signed by him to Mr. Hornemann.

That Sir Joseph Banks be requested to furnish Mr. Hornemann with Sixty Pounds for his Journey to Alexandria; Mr. Charrettié having obligingly engaged to supply Mr. Hornemann with Louis d'ors and Bills of Credit on Paris to that amount; which is deemed sufficient for his Journey.

That Sir Joseph Banks be requested to apply to the Secretary of State for a Letter to Mr. Baldwin, recommending Mr. Hornemann to his good offices, as His Majesty's Consul at Alexandria.

That Mr. Edwards be requested to write Letters to the following eminent Professors, Thanking them for the assistance they afforded Mr. Hornemann during his residence at Gottingen, and requesting their acceptance of the Proceedings of the Association, — to — Professor Blumenbach — Professor Heeren — Professor Hoffman[1] — Professor Heyne — and Professor Tychsen.[2]

On 26 June Hornemann wrote to Banks, returning Rennell's 'instructions for taking or determining distances', and concluding 'I wish, Sir, I could explain you my feelings in this last time I am in London, chiefly the great esteem I have for you'. With the letter he enclosed a memorandum recording his wishes regarding the payment of his salary of £200 a year. He wished his mother in Hildescheim to be paid an annuity of £60 which, in the event of his death, should be paid to Blumenbach for his relations. The rest of his salary was to be retained by the Association to meet such drafts as he might draw on it while in Africa. In the event of his death any balance standing to his credit was to be dealt with in the same way as the annuity.[3]

iii. Paris to Cairo

Hornemann must have set off on his travels very soon after this for the next we hear of him is in Paris where, on 12 July, he wrote to Banks reporting his safe arrival some days previously after crossing the Channel in a neutral vessel from Dover to Calais. In Paris he had been warmly welcomed by two Fellows of the Royal Society, the astronomer Joseph Lalande and the botanist Pierre Broussonet. Through them he had made many acquaintances with African con-

---

[1] Probably the botanist F. G. Hoffman, 1761–1826.
[2] Probably O. G. Tychsen, 1734–1805, an orientalist who published an Arabic Grammar in 1792.
[3] *D.T.C.*, x (1), 154–6.

nections, but none had proved so helpful as a Turkish merchant from Tripoli who happened to be in Paris.[1] 'Never shall I forget', he wrote, 'the kindness & complaisance of this bearded Gentleman. He reprehended the plan to penetrate in the interior of Africa from Cairo, & told me the only possible & the most easy way for a christian was by *Tripoli & Faizzan*. He offered me to send me by his recommendations so secure to Fezzan, as he thought to travel from here to Marseilles. I answered him that I was obliged by my instructions to go to Cairo, but I hoped he would notwithstanding this procure me some recommendation for Cairo. He answered that time nothing — but to day he surprized me in a very pleasant manner, giving me a letter of recommendation to one of his friends at Cairo, whom he told to be in acquaintance with a great number of Merchants out of the interior of Africa. In this letter written in Arabic "he begs his friends to assist me in every way, to shew me the town ... to make me acquainted with such merchants out of Africa; whom he knew as good & brave men, to assist me when I should like to go in the interior, chiefly to Fezzan ... & should not permit that I traveld with bad people — he should do me all the pleasures as to himself, his old friend". He described me in his letter as a young Englishman, and said I applied me to the Trade & therefore I was curious to see the world, & *I was his friend*. I have not necessary to explain how useful this recommendation may perhaps be for me, & I think it is good & favourable to make the acquaintance of Mahomedans by Mahomedans.'[2]

Hornemann intended to leave as soon as possible for Lyons from where he would proceed to Marseilles in the hope of finding a ship to Alexandria.

In August he wrote to Bryan Edwards, the Secretary of the Association, that he was in Marseilles and finding difficulty in continuing his journey. There were ships bound for Leghorn, Smyrna and Cyprus but 'vessels for Egypt are not here'. He had therefore decided to sail for Cyprus in the *Adelaide*, Captain Baizetil, 'a Frenchman of good repute ... the vessel is going in some days'. The constant delays in reaching Africa were proving irksome to the impetuous young man. 'I think very often', he wrote, 'that it perhaps may be easier for me to go in the Interior of Africa than to Egypt.'[3]

---

[1] This man was probably Sidi Mohammed D'Ghies, a much-travelled Tripolitan merchant who knew Europe well and was to become the Bashaw's Foreign Minister. See p. 151 below.

[2] *D.T.C.*, x (1), 163–5.   [3] *D.T.C.*, x (2), 111–12.

He got away on 11 August, and on the 31st reached Lernica where he heard of a large Venetian vessel lying at Limassol which was to sail shortly for Egypt. He boarded her and, on 9 September, sailed for Alexandria which he reached four days later. He spent ten days there under the hospitable roof of George Baldwin, the British Consul-General, whom the traveller W. G. Browne, in 1792, had also found very helpful. 'Is it by my conduct, or is it his Character?' he ingenuously enquired of Banks, 'he has shewed me so many services, and given me so many advises, as I could ever ask of him, if he was a member of your Association.'[1] He sent Banks a detailed account of his expenses to date from which it is evident that he was being very careful with his employers' money. 'You gave me £60 to Marseilles, with the advice to pay the passage to Egypt in Alexandria,' but he expects it to cover his expenses as far as Cairo. After some difficulty he negotiated a draft for £53 'a sum certainly not large for the first, where I have to pay so much for New Dresses in the Custom of the Country'. Direct communication with London not being possible owing to the war, he will send his letters by way of Trieste to the British Ambassador in Vienna, for forwarding.

He travelled to Cairo by way of Rosetta, where he had to change boats, carrying letters of introduction given him by Baldwin. Among these letters was one to Charles Rosetti, the Venetian Consul and Chargé d'Affaires for the English Consul, 'whose acquaintance is indispensably necessary for me, by what I have heard here in a Convent from a German Monk'.[2]

The beauty of the Nile fascinated the young traveller but his enjoyment of it was clouded by the poverty of the people. 'Great ... was my regret', he wrote, 'when I reflected that these delightful Fields, as in general the whole Country, which by its fruitfulness & situation might be rendered one of the happiest in the world, is possessed by a people groaning under Governors whose despotism oppresses & where anarchy must destroy it.'[3]

Thanks to Baldwin's letter to Rosetti and to a fortunate meeting with another German from Göttingen, Hornemann soon settled down in Cairo, where he had arrived on 4 October. All the convents being full, he took lodgings, hoping later to move into the Convent of the Propaganda[4] with the monks of which he had made friends. He at once set

---

[1] *D.T.C.*, x (1), 179. [2] Ibid., 183. [3] Ibid., 196.
[4] This was doubtless the convent where Ledyard had lodged and which he described as consisting 'of missionaries sent by the Pope to propagate the Christian faith, or at least to

about collecting what information he could gather about the interior. He found the other Europeans curiously uninterested in the reason for his being in Cairo which made the ban of secrecy imposed on him by the Association easy enough. In a letter to Bryan Edwards, however, he admitted having mentioned the object of his journey to George Baldwin, 'requesting him and his family not to divulge it, to which they have faithfully kept...'. 'I have sometimes conversed', his letter continued, 'with the Monks of the Propaganda at Alexandria about the interior of Africa, the best mode of penetrating into it &c, but they always directed me to Mr. Rosetti. When I arrived at Cairo, I soon perceived that all the Monks here were in a manner dependent upon this man, & that he possessed great influence. I found likewise that his opinion of the African Association was, that they were connected merely by commercial interests... I have not been able to gain any well founded intelligence respecting Caravans coming from the interior. Thus much however appears certain that one Caravan comes from Sennaar which is joined by the Caravans from Darfour, & another from Siwah joined by those from Gódemsch [Ghadames] & Fásān [Fezzan].[1] But not one of the persons whom I have consulted know any thing of Caravans from Burnu [Bornu] & Kashna.' He hopes to glean more information as soon as he has mastered Arabic sufficiently to converse with Arabs from the Maghreb. He was in fact making the study of Arabic, under a Greek Roman Catholic, his principal occupation.[2]

This letter, dated 18 October, reached London in January and brought a prompt reprimand from Banks. The Committee, he wrote, 'do not complain of your having forgot the advice you so frequently received, against connecting yourself in any shape with Baldwin or Rosetti, but they are seriously sorry you have done so.[3] The only advice I ever gave to you in strong language was to avoid by all means suffering either of these Gentlemen to know your intention of Travelling. I

---

give shelter to Christians. The Christians here are principally from Damascus: the convent is governed by the Order of Recollects: a number of English, as well as other European travellers, have lodged there' (*Proceedings*, I, 27). The Sacred Congregation *de Propaganda Fide*, officially the Sacra Congregatio Christiano Nomini Propagando, is charged with the spread of Catholicism and with the regulation of ecclesiastical affairs in non-Catholic countries. So great was the authority of the Cardinal Prefect of Propaganda that he became known as the 'Red Pope'.

[1] According to W. G. Browne these caravans, from Sennar, Darfur and Fezzan brought slaves, gold dust, ivory, rhinoceros horns, ostrich feathers, gums and drugs.

[2] *D.T.C.*, x (1), 196–8.

[3] Nevertheless, Hornemann had been officially commended to Baldwin. See p. 19 above.

cannot, however, but feel gratitude to them for the hospitality they have shewn to you'.

Baldwin and Rosetti combined their consular duties with their business as merchants. In advising Hornemann to avoid them both the Association evidently feared that if they got wind of the object of his journey they would conclude it was an attempt to interfere with their trade with the interior and do their best to frustrate it.[1] How unjustified they were in their suspicion, for which presumably Ledyard had been responsible, is clearly shown by the assistance the two consuls so readily gave to Hornemann, though both regarded his undertaking as foolhardy, and said so.

The rest of Banks's letter made more agreeable reading. 'The Committee, as well as myself', it read, 'are well contented with your conduct & the alacrity you have shewn in proceeding diligently to the place of your destination; they wish you to remain quietly where you are, & by no means to move until you have attain'd a fluency in the Arabic Language & a competent knowledge of the Customs of the Mograbins &c.[2] They are well aware that a detention of considerable length in the place where you now are, is likely to facilitate very much the ultimate object of your Mission.'

The letter concluded with some sensational news which can hardly have failed greatly to encourage a young man setting out for the mysterious interior of Africa. 'Mr. Parke', it read, 'has return'd from his expedition to the interior of Africa by the Gambia; he penetrated till within 14 days of Tombouctoo, & might have enter'd that Town could he have pass'd for a Mahometan; but he desisted from the attempt on being told by all the persons he met that the Mahometans, who have the Rule of the Town, would certainly put him to death as a Christian, if he entered it.

'Mr. Parke discovered the Jaliba [Joliba], or Niger River, running to the Eastward, & trac'd it for 200 miles, at the end of which course near Jennie [Jenne] it is a large & navigable River: he was uniformly well treated by the Pagan Negroes, whose hospitality never failed to relieve him; not ill treated by the Mahometan Negroes, but they seem'd to hate him for being a Christian; & he was always very ill received & twice taken prisoner & plundered by the Arabs, who spar'd his life, but

---

[1] Rosetti, the Venetian Consul, was of course chiefly interested in the bead trade which his countrymen had carried on with Africa for centuries past. He had shown Ledyard samples of 1,500 different kinds of beads.
[2] The people of the Maghreb.

took all he possess'd even his instruments: he is, however, well, & will make a most interesting publication of his Travels.'[1]

In Cairo Hornemann's luck was running out. Events which were seriously to menace his plans were about to supervene. In April, shortly before his planned departure for Fezzan, there was an outbreak of plague which compelled him to remain where he was, and confined him to his house. His next attempt to leave Cairo was frustrated by unexpected inability to negotiate a draft on London to provide finance for the journey. A French commercial house, on whom he had no sort of claim, came to his rescue with a generous offer of unsecured credit to the full extent of his needs. But at this juncture, just when all his initial difficulties had been overcome, the caravan with which he was to travel had suddenly to disperse in the panic into which the whole country had suddenly been thrown. On 2 July 1798 Bonaparte had seized Alexandria and, announcing that he had come only to destroy the Mamlukes, whose oppressive rule had so moved Hornemann on his first arrival, was advancing on Cairo. The populace naturally turned on the Europeans in their midst who were only saved from the fury of the mob by being taken into protective custody by the authorities, not, we may be sure, out of regard for the Christians, but to avoid inflaming the invaders by their massacre.

On 25 July, four days after the Battle of the Pyramids, Bonaparte occupied Cairo. With the destruction of his fleet by Nelson a week later, he had to content himself with establishing French rule and culture in a land which corruption and oppression had brought to ruin. Thus circumstances which had gravely threatened Hornemann's prospects turned in his favour. He was introduced to Bonaparte who, with characteristic magnanimity, promised him every assistance, even offering any cash he might require, and undertaking to forward his letters to London subject only to their being written in French. This happy turn in his fortunes he reported to London at the end of August when he was also able to announce his expected departure for Fezzan a few days later with a caravan of pilgrims returning from Mecca.

Disguised as a Moslem trader, he was setting out full of confidence in the success of his mission. He intended to spend eight or nine months in Fezzan before continuing his journey to Katsina. He hoped to return to England in two and a half or three years' time either by way of Senegambia or, rather surprisingly, Mecca. It seems probable that this unexpected suggestion sprang from his conviction that it would be

[1] *D.T.C.*, x (2), 165–7.

easier to preserve his disguise in the cosmopolitan company of pilgrims than in a caravan of merchants. He had in mind a third alternative, that of returning through Tripoli which, perhaps as the result of his meeting with the friendly Tripolitan Turk in Paris, he seems to have had every intention of visiting if he could. His request to Banks, on the eve of leaving Cairo, for a letter of credit for £100 or £150 to be sent to the British Consul in Tripoli clearly points to this. He also well knew that, as both the Turk in Paris and his friends in Egypt had told him, but contrary to what the Association believed, Fezzan was far more easily reached from Tripoli than from Cairo. Should he be compelled to retreat, withdrawal should be easiest through Tripoli, but there is no hint in his letters of any such contingency having entered his mind. On the contrary, they reflect a wholly admirable resolve to overcome all obstacles that might stand between him and his goal, and great confidence in his ability to do so. He hoped anyway to do better than Park to whom he adopted a rather patronizing attitude which ill became so young and inexperienced a traveller.[1]

He was in one respect setting out under more agreeable circumstances than he had any reason to expect. He had had the good fortune to engage as his interpreter another German. This man, Joseph Frendenburgh, had been a Mamluke who, under Egypt's new rulers, had unexpectedly recovered his freedom and had been persuaded to abandon his intention of returning to Germany in order to accompany Hornemann. A Mohammedan, with three pilgrimages to Mecca to his credit, and a complete master of both Turkish and Arabic, he was exceptionally well qualified to aid Hornemann in his undertaking.

iv. Cairo to Murẓuk

Hornemann joined the Fezzan caravan on 5 September, and the following day they set out along the pilgrim road to Siwa. This ran westwards below the escarpment of the Maghra Hills, at the foot of which fresh-water springs were abundant. On the 15th they arrived at the little village of Ummesogeir (Un Sogeir or Qara) through which W. G. Browne, also bound for Siwa, had passed in 1792. Here they rested for a few days before resuming their journey to Siwa which they reached on 21 September. Hornemann devoted much of the eight days

---

[1] 'La méfortune de M. Parke', he wrote to Banks, 'je plains: j'espère réussir mieux que lui.' He goes on to point out how much more sensible Park would have been to travel, like him, disguised as a Moslem (*D.T.C.*, xi, 67).

they spent here to examining the ruins of the famous Temple of Jupiter Ammon, and in exploring the catacombs. Like Browne before him, he found the Siwans very suspicious of this unaccountable interest in the ancient 'works of Infidels', and he was in some fear of their penetrating his disguise.

On the fourth day out on the road to Aujila, while they were camping at Scheibat (part of the oasis of Jaghbub), the caravan was assailed by a band of 300 Siwans who had been sent to seize Hornemann and Frendenburgh of whose true identity they had become convinced. 'You are the new Christians from Cairo', they declared, 'and come to explore our country.'[1] Hornemann's resource and diplomacy rescued them from a very dangerous situation. Frendenburgh had greatly aggravated it by treacherously showing their assailants Hornemann's French passport (issued to him by Bonaparte), obviously to save his own skin. They were, however, able to resume their journey next day with the whole caravan still convinced that they were Moslems.

On 6 October the caravan arrived at Majabra, one of the principal oases of Jalo of which Aujila was the capital. Hornemann went on to Aujila but, if we may judge by his very superficial account of it, he appears not to have realized its importance as an ancient centre of the caravan trade.

Since leaving Cairo the caravan had gathered more travellers and camels at its various stopping places. At Aujila, where it was joined by merchants from Benghazi and elsewhere, it attained such a size that its headman adjudged it unwise to continue the journey to Murzuk without first making sure that there would be enough water for so many on the last but most perilous stage of their journey. Accordingly, soon after their arrival, a man was sent ahead to report on the situation. On his return, twelve days later, fully satisfied that there was enough water for so large a caravan, the journey was resumed. Seven days after leaving Aujila they entered the dreaded Harug, a rugged waterless plateau very difficult for camels, and extending almost to Tmessa, a walled village where they arrived on the sixteenth day out from Aujila. Here, having entered the kingdom of Fezzan, they received a warm welcome typical of its kind-hearted negroid inhabitants. The following day they reached Zuila, a former capital of Fezzan, and still a town of some importance. Pursuing their journey down the Hofra, through Hammera and Traghen, they arrived at Murzuk on 17 November, where

[1] *D.T.C.*, xi, 266.

the pilgrims and merchants were received in state by the Sultan, a Karamanli from Tripoli.

Hornemann had arrived in Murzuk to find that a caravan bound for Hausa was to set out in a very few days. On learning that it was likely to be attacked by Tuareg and that it 'consisted wholly of black traders' (doubtless Hausa merchants) who, he feared, were not sufficiently influential to 'facilitate his friendly reception with the Moors of interior Africa', he decided not to travel with it. He hoped, however, not to be long delayed in Murzuk as a big caravan from Bornu, which he would be able to accompany on its return journey, was expected shortly.

Soon after their arrival in Murzuk Hornemann and Frendenburgh were 'seized with the country fevers', of which the latter died.[1] On his recovery Hornemann learnt that the Bornu caravan was not, after all, due for some months. So he decided, rather than 'stay in such a miserable place as Fezzan, which is, after the Caravans are sett off, the most disinteresting Town I ever saw',[2] he would seize the opportunity for his projected visit to Tripoli in order to forward to the Association a report on his travels to date. He left in the middle of June and two months later arrived in Tripoli where he had the good fortune to be befriended by Dr Bryan McDonogh, the medical officer attached to the British Consulate who was at this time acting for the Consul-General, Simon Lucas, then on leave.[3] McDonogh was, wrote Hornemann to Banks on 19 August, 'exactly that Gentleman I wanted. He is liked by the present Basha, & can give me assistance more than any Turk in town: he is a literate man, & knows to esteem the undertakings of the Society, & is acquainted with many members of it. I arrived here considered of the Furds as a man of doubtful character; but he puts me now by his assistance & credit in a very good situation. He can procure me recommendations of the Basha for my Travel, which are absolutely necessary in this time in this country, because every stranger is taken a *Spy of the French.*

'I think, Sir, Mr. McDonogh deserves the thanks of the Committee; & I beg you, when you write to him, at least to tell him that I feel gratitude for what he has done for me.'[4] In the same letter he gave a

---

[1] Malaria. Hornemann attributed his recovery to 'the continued use of Kina' (quinine) (*D.T.C.*, XI, 268).
[2] Ibid.
[3] We later hear of McDonogh acting as chargé d'affaires for the Portuguese Consul-General.
[4] Ibid., 270. There was a third Briton in Tripoli at this time, Peter Lisle, a renegade Scot who commanded the Tripolitan fleet and now called himself Murad Rais. The U.S.

summary of the information he had collected in Murzuk about the interior.[1]

Simon Lucas returned to his post in Tripoli in October. It was hardly to be expected that the unsuccessful explorer of former years would find the self-confident, and possibly patronizing, young German — just returned from a perilous journey which he himself had refused to attempt — a welcome visitor. Hornemann, reporting the return of the Consul-General, commented to Banks, 'I dont know if the Committee believes his excuses for his returning to England, or if they give them so little a credit, as I do myself; but I took it my duty to settle all my affairs, before he was acting with Dr. McDonogh his assistance, whom I mentioned in my former letter, and whose real services I can not recommend you enough.

'Of the British Consul of this place I have now nothing to request. I live amongst the Arabs of the town and in a Karavanserey (or Fanduck) that is in a public Inn, where any young foreigner without family is living, and where I lived the whole time I am here.'[2] Later, however, after the friendly McDonogh ('He ... will do more for me than 10 consuls') had left Tripoli, Hornemann did turn to Lucas for help in negotiating a draft, and was refused. Nevertheless, Lucas had the grace to report well on Hornemann to Banks. 'From my knowledge of his person and abilities', he wrote on 12 April 1800, 'during his short residence here, I perceived that you could not have fixed upon a more proper person for such an undertaking and I doubt not if God spares his health he will prove himself worthy the choice of your respectable Society. I did all I could to forward him on the expedition with proper recommendations and a supply of cash, of which he began to run short.'[3] It is probable that in the end Lucas became more helpful for on Hornemann's return to Murzuk he wrote thanking him 'for the friendship you shewed me and the real services you did to the African Society in recommending & protecting me during my residence in Tripoli'.[4]

But Hornemann had secured the friendship of more influential people than the British Consul. Among them was his old friend the

---

Consul, James Leander Cathcart, 'blamed much of the American difficulty in Tripoli', we read, 'upon this satanic Scot who had married the Pasha's daughter and was much given to drink and boasting. Murad, Dr. Bryan McDonogh, and another Englishman named Lucas made up a drunken triumvirate who delighted in plotting ways to gall the Yankee consul' (L. B. Wright and Julia H. Macleod, *The First Americans in North Africa*, Princeton, 1945, p. 89).

[1] See p. 111 below.   [2] *D.T.C.*, XI, 294.   [3] *D.T.C.*, XII, 65.
[4] Ibid., 66. He signed this letter 'F. Hornemann call'd Juset ben Abdallah'.

Turk to whom he had babbled in Paris. But his indiscretion on that occasion appears to have served him well in Tripoli. 'The Basha of this place', he wrote to Banks on 29 November,

a sensible man, & a good friend of all what is English, is acquainted in a good manner with my undertakings; it must be so, because I found here again that Turk I mentioned in my letter of Paris 1797.

He has given me a very strong recommendation like a passe-porte, wherein he calls me by my adopted Turkish name — calls me one of his men he liked chiefly ... he beg'd leave me to go where I should like &c. The Basha gave me these letters in the last audience — I went alone to him: he call'd me before all the people by my Turkish name, & treated me like so. I thank my good progresses on that account to the happy conjuncture to have three headmen of this Country for my friends.

My plan in going from here is yet the same I wrote you in my first letter from here, — to go to Fessan, from there immediately to Agades to Kashna. To make from there the excursus 'untill Cabi [Kebbi] & Nyffé [Nupe] at the left of the River Niger, (of this side of the Niger). To go from Sudan to Tombuctu from where I shall return by that way I shall think the most proper for the Society & for my own honour, not only as an enterprising, but also as a prudent man.

I look upon my Travels done, as upon the work of an apprentice: — now I think I have the experience at least of a young Master. It is a new plan to travel as a Mohamedan in these Countries, dangerous between these superstitious people leaded by fanaticism & intolerancy but dangerous only for the beginning: — afterwards it is safer and better.

... after having lived two years in these Countries & having heard so much of the more remote Countries, I think it very proper the Society might expect my return before they send out another Traveller for the Northern Africa. I shall be returning to Europe; but I suppose that will be about 1802, in one of the first Months when I have occasion to go to Tombuctu; if not 3 or 4 months sooner.[1]

On 1 December Hornemann set out on his return journey to Murzuk which he reached on 20 January 1800. He again decided against attempting to travel direct to Katsina by way of Agades because of continued turbulence in the desert. Thanks to the influence of the Basha of Tripoli, he was able to make friends with a Shereef of Bornu whom he arranged to accompany to his country in a few weeks' time. On 6 April he wrote to Banks that he was that evening joining a caravan which was leaving for Bornu where he proposed staying till September when

[1] *D.T.C.*, xi, 326.

he hoped to complete his journey to Katsina. 'Consider this letter as the last for this year, or perhaps as the last before my arrival at some port on the coast of Africa.' It was in fact the last letter to be received from Hornemann.

At the annual general meeting of the African Society held in May 1800 the safe arrival of Hornemann's journal of his travels between Cairo and Murzuk was reported, and abstracts from it were read. It was also reported that all his Majesty's consuls in Africa had been instructed to pay any drafts drawn by him, 'and also to receive him with friendship, if he should return by any of the places at which they reside'.[1]

At the next annual meeting, in June 1801, it was reported that an opportunity to send another explorer into the same field had been rejected lest the Committee should 'incur any possible interference, improvident communication of parties, or clash of enterprise, which might compromise his [Hornemann's] safety, or hazard the success of so promising an undertaking'.[2] Hornemann's *Journal*, translated from the original German into English, was published as part of the *Proceedings* for that year.

The *Journal* was well received by the public, but the *Edinburgh Review*[3] made it an excuse for a venomous attack on the African Association. The article was, as we shall see, mildly critical of Hornemann's work, but its venom was mainly directed against the Association's secretary, Sir William Young. It condemned Young's Introduction to the *Journal* as a 'laboured and pompus panegyric upon the institution', a verdict which it is not easy to reject. 'While the Society', it continued, 'instead of leaving its deeds to speak for themselves, continues to sound forth its own praises in studied eulogiums, we must be excused for stopping to examine, a little more nearly, those achievements, to the magnitude of which our attention is thus forcibly turned. ... But, to whomsoever belongs the merit of the success which has hitherto accompanied Mr. Horneman, we can scarcely allow, that his discoveries have been so important, as to justify the vaunting style of the Secretary; or that he has hitherto done more, than give a very fair promise of succeeding in the subsequent part of his expedition.'

In his ire Banks turned to Henry (later Lord) Brougham who had been closely associated with the *Edinburgh Review* since its foundation and who knew personally the author of the attack. 'I communicated your opinion on the review of Horneman's Journal to the author and

---

[1] *Proceedings*, II, 21.   [2] Ibid., II, 26.   [3] Vol. I (1802), 1814 edn., 130–41.

the other Critics who compose our sanguinary tribunal', Brougham replied, 'I also added my own in the same terms — they all agreed that, if the slightest disrespect was meant to the celebrated body under whose patronage Mr. Horneman pursues his adventures, the article deserved suppression. The author declared that such a thought never entered his head, and that he levelled his criticism not at all against the African Association, but against the secretary at whom he has conceived some ill will. . . . I urged the apparent tendency of some passages to evince a disrespect towards the Society. . . . He persisted, however, in his plan of criticism, refused to modify the article in the 2nd Edition.'[1]

v. Murzuk to Bokani

On 12 January 1802 Banks wrote to W. G. Browne that Hornemann's 'two years will elapse next April; & from that time I shall be in hopes of seeing him daily; he is an excellent observer, &, if he succeeds, will fill up a vast blank in the Geography of Africa'.[2]

Banks's expectation that Hornemann would appear near the date he had so haphazardly predicted, for which there was little justification, was not to be realized. Years passed without any news of the explorer. Indeed, nothing was heard until the end of 1804 when, as Sir William Young told the Association at its annual general meeting in the following June: 'Mr. Macdonogh, long time Consul at Tripoli, on the 21st of December last, meeting me at the table of Sir Joseph Banks, mentioned that he had, when at Tripoli, received accounts from a very respectable Moorish merchant, of Jussuph, or Horneman, having been well at Cas'na about the month of June, 1803, and that he was there highly respected as a Marabout, or Musselman saint.

'Scarcely two years have elapsed since Horneman, according to this account, was known to be safe and well; and we must not yet forego the hopes of receiving from himself, an account of the interesting tract of country which he had then reached, and of his observations made, successively at Cas'na, at Houssa, and at Tombuctoo.'[3] It would seem that up to this time, no less than three years after Hornemann had been expected to return, the length of his absence was thought to be the measure of his success.

Not until the 1808 meeting of the Association was there any sign of anxiety about Hornemann's fate, but even then it was very slight. The chairman, the Earl of Moira, told the meeting: 'It may be thought

[1] *D.T.C.*, XIII, 306–9.   [2] *D.T.C.*, XIII, 4.   [3] *Proceedings*, II, 363.

proper, and probably is expected, that your Committee should say something with regard to the situation of your highly esteemed traveller, Mr. Horneman; the Committee wish that it was in their power to give any satisfactory information on that interesting subject; but your Committee have only received very imperfect information with respect to Mr. Horneman; all that is positively known is, that at the time he left Mourzouk, which is now at the distance of seven years, he was in perfect health, and in full confidence that he should be able to accomplish the wishes of the Association; but whether he is detained by the governing power of the country to which he is gone, and which is thought to be not improbable, or he has fallen by accident or disease, is perfectly unknown to your Committee; but though totally ignorant of his actual situation, your Committee is not without some gleam of hope, founded on some uncertain reports, that he may still be in safety, and at some future time may be able to return to his anxious employers.'[1] We unfortunately know nothing about the 'uncertain reports' which continued to nourish the unabated optimism of the Committee.

A year later hope had begun to fade. 'Some few circumstances relating to your traveller, Mr. Horneman', declared Lord Moira, 'have been laid before your Committee, but of so vague and uncertain a nature as to afford no great hope of a successful termination of his important undertaking, but at the same time not so absolutely unfavourable as to extinguish every hope of his return to his friends and to his country.'[2]

No more was heard of Horneman until early in 1817 when a Captain Smith,[3] 'employed in surveying the northern coast of Africa', visited the antiquities of Ghirza, in the hinterland of Tripoli. 'It was on this journey', we read, 'that in the course of conversation, the bey of Fezzan told Captain Smith that, about seventeen years ago, an Englishman accompanied him on an expedition to the southward of Fezzan, died on the road in consequence of a fever, and was buried near Aucalas. The time and place exactly correspond with what has been surmized of the fate of the unfortunate Horneman.'[4]

About a year later Captain Smith, accompanied by the renegade Scot Murad Rais,[5] and Hanmer Warrington, the British Consul-General who in later years was to show himelf so good a friend to ex-

---

[1] *Proceedings*, II, 417, 418.   [2] Ibid., 420.
[3] He was in fact Captain W. H. Smyth, afterwards Rear-Admiral. In his book *The Mediterranean* (London, 1854), there are two brief references to Horneman (pp. 490, 492).
[4] *Quarterly Review*, XVII (1817), 319.   [5] See p. 27n. 4 above.

plorers, had an audience of the Bashaw of Tripoli whom he questioned about the fate of Hornemann. The Bashaw confirmed the report of his death. 'He fell ill at Houssor [Hausa]', he said, 'in the dwelling of a Tripoline merchant established there, and resuming his travels before he was perfectly recovered, relapsed, and died at Tombutoo.'[1]

A few months later the explorer Captain F. G. Lyon passed through Tripoli on his way to Fezzan. In Fezzan he had the good fortune to meet a man who had accompanied Hornemann from Murzuk to Nupe where, in the town of Bokani, and in the house of one Ali el-Felatni, he had died of dysentery. 'Our informant', wrote Lyon, 'gave the following account of his having accompanied Horneman from Mourzouk to that place. They first became acquainted in Fezzan, from whence they went together with a large Kafflé [caravan] to Bornou, when they separated. After Horneman had resided three or four months there, they again met in a Kafflé going to Kashna, and associated much together. The people became greatly attached to Horneman, on account of his amiable deportment and skill in medicine; and he was generally considered as a Marāboot.[2] After a short time they proceeded with another party of merchants to Noofy, living together in the house of a man named Ali, of the tribe Fellata. It was Hornemann's custom while on his journeys after quitting Fezzan, to note down the bearings of every tree, mountain, or village, he saw; by which means he might be more easily enabled to know his road again without a guide. His intention was to go on through Dagomba to Ashantee, which is forty days' journey to the southward. When our merchant left Noofy, he was in good health and spirits, and had not experienced any difficulties; but this man, on arriving in Kashna, heard that Horneman had died of dysentery, a few days after their separation.'[3]

Five years later this report of Hornemann's death was confirmed to Captain Hugh Clapperton by two Fezzan merchants whom he met in Kano and who had been with him when he died. 'Both Hat Salah and Benderachmani', wrote Clapperton, 'had been with the late Mr. Hornemann at the time of his death. They travelled with him from Mourzuk

---

[1] *Quarterly Review*, XVIII (1818), 372. In a letter dated 2 Sept. 1818 Warrington told Sir Thomas Maitland, the governor of Malta, that 'Respecting Mr. Horneman's Papers Instruments &c. they were delivered by the Minister and Mourad Reis to Mr. Mc Donough a Gentleman attached to the British Consulate (surgion).' See also Warrington to Lord Bathurst, 16 April 1821. P.R.O., F.O. 76/15. These papers and instruments must have been sent back to the coast by Hornemann before he left Murzuk for Bornu. See p. 107 below.

[2] See p. 36n. below.

[3] Captain F. G. Lyon, *A Narrative of Travels in Northern Africa* (London, 1821), 132.

to Nyffee, where he died of dysentery, after an illness of six days. He passed himself off as an English merchant, professing the Mahometan faith, and had sold two fine horses here. At my instance, Benderachmani sent a courier to Nyffee, to endeavour to recover Mr. Hornemann's manuscripts, for which I offered him a reward of a hundred dollars; but, on my return from Sackatoo [Sokoto], I found the messenger come back with the information, that Jussuf Felatah, a learned man of the country, with whom Mr. Hornemann lodged, had been burned in his own house, together with all Mr. Hornemann's papers, by the negro rabble, from a superstitious dread of his holding intercourse with evil spirits.'[1]

Those two short extracts from Lyon and Clapperton are all we know of Hornemann's travels after he left Murzuk. They tell us where he died but leave us in doubt about how he got there and the date of his death.

He evidently travelled to Bornu with the caravan which, as he told Banks in his letter of 6 April 1800, he was joining that evening, and appears to have carried out his intention of staying there till the following September, at the end of the rains. Again according to plan, he travelled from there to Katsina with a caravan of merchants along a well-established trade route. His onward journey to Nupe must have been made easy for him by the singularly happy accident that some of the Fezzan merchants with whom he was travelling and whose friendship he had secured were bound for the same country.

Nineteen years after Hornemann's arrival in Katsina Lyon's informant, who had accompanied Hornemann to the south, said that the usual route from Katsina to Nupe was through Yandakka, Zurmi, Zamfara, Dufun Mafara, Talata Noma, Bakura, Gandi, Birnin dan Gada, Sokoto and 'Mifferadaati',[2] 'whence several small towns are passed until Noofy'. That may well not have been the route in the days when he travelled with Hornemann. In one respect it certainly was not: Sokoto had not yet been founded.

It is evident that the success with which Hornemann made his way from Katsina almost to the coast of Guinea was due to his remarkable gift for winning the friendship of the people of the country. What might have proved the most difficult part of his journey, through the Hausa country in which later explorers encountered endless frustrations though little danger, was perhaps for him the easiest. The Fezzan

[1] Major Denham and Captain Clapperton, *Narrative of Travels and Discoveries in Northern and Central Africa*, 2 vols. (London, 1826), II, 264.
[2] Unidentified.

merchants with whom he travelled were evidently bound for Rabba, the great market on the Niger which, as the Landers learnt, was carrying on a regular trade with Fezzan in salt, textiles and other manufactured goods,[1] which they probably exchanged for slaves. Not only was Rabba in Nupe, which Hornemann so much wanted to reach, but it had a ferry across the Niger on which converged trade routes from the south and west. At Rabba he would be singularly well placed to continue his journey westwards along one of the great kola nut trade routes leading to the hinterland of Ashanti and thence to Timbuktu, the final goal of his ambitions. That he might have achieved, had he lived, what would have been the most remarkable journey in the history of African exploration is suggested by the Landers having heard of an Arab who was about to set out from Rabba to Timbuktu.[2] This was the very journey on which Hornemann had set his heart. With Arabs to travel with he would probably have found it practicable.

But Hornemann, alas, was not destined even to reach the Niger. Bokani, where he died, was only a day's march from Rabba. That he was staying in the house of a Felatta or Fulani is not surprising. Although four years had yet to pass before the Fulani conquered Hausa they were already well established as immigrant settlers throughout its length and breadth, and among the pagan Nupes they constituted an intelligentsia to whose houses foreign traders, like Hornemann's friends, would naturally have been drawn. It seems likely that the military conquest of the country by the Fulani was the occasion of Hornemann's host and all his papers being burnt by the outraged Nupes.

It is not possible to determine with any certainty the date of Hornemann's death. He probably left Bornu in September 1800, as he had expected, and would have reached Katsina in October. He had intended spending a little time there and probably did so for the merchants with whom he was travelling would themselves have had much to occupy them in so important a market. As the rains, which make travel in Hausa almost impossible for trading caravans for several months in the year, were not due to break till April they did not prohibit a stay in Katsina. It is nearly a month's journey from Katsina to Rabba so it is improbable that Hornemann reached the neighbouring town of Bokani

---

[1] Richard and John Lander, *Journal of an Expedition to the Niger*, 3 vols. (London, 1832), II, 290, 313.

[2] 'Among the Arabs', they wrote, 'is a famous Sheikh who, we understand, will set out in a few days on a journey to Timbuctoo' (*Journal*, II, 290).

till the end of the year. But his friends would almost certainly have wanted to reach Rabba in time to do their business there and get back to Katsina, if not to Bornu, before the rains broke in April and closed the roads. Indeed one of them, Lyon's informant, had already set out on his return journey before Hornemann's death. All these circumstances point to his having died very early in 1801.

According to Clapperton's informants Hornemann, at the time of his death, was travelling 'as an English merchant professing the Mahometan faith', which suggests that his disguise had been partially penetrated and that he had ceased to pretend that he was an Arab. Lyon's informant, on the other hand, said that 'he was generally considered as a Maraboot', which he certainly would not have been had it been known that he was a European.[1] It may be that Clapperton's friends were merely being wise after the event. Clearly, however, Hornemann had not weakened in his resolve to travel as a Moslem.

A resolute determination to accomplish what he intended to achieve was Hornemann's outstanding characteristic. He did precisely what he set out to do. From the first he had made up his mind to get to Katsina and from there to Nupe. It is difficult to doubt that had he lived his iron will would not have carried him on to Timbuktu. His truly remarkable journey from Egypt to within 300 miles of the coast of Guinea, wholly along routes hitherto untrodden by Europeans since Roman times, would however not have been achieved had not his resolution been matched by his capacity for winning the confidence of the people he met on the road. But these two gifts, though essential to successful exploration, are not enough in themselves. If the fruits of exploration are to be gathered to the full the explorer must also have an enquiring and acquisitive mind. This Hornemann signally lacked. In describing him as 'an excellent observer' Banks was sadly mistaken. Hornemann's account of his journey from Cairo to Murzuk is an arid document from which we learn next to nothing of the people through whose countries he travelled. Never could it have been said of him, as

[1] On this point Dr. Cabot Briggs comments as follows: 'It is not wholly inconceivable that Hornemann was accorded a quasi-maraboutic status even when known to be a European, and so may have been referred to commonly as a marabout. The story of Aurélie Picard, the daughter of a French gendarme who married the head of the Tidjania brotherhood and established the great zaouia at Kourdane (some forty miles west of Laghouat) is evidence in this connection. For Aurélie remained openly Christian until just before she died in 1933, over sixty years after her marriage. And yet during these intervening years she exercised great influence in Moslem circles by virtue of her personal prestige as well as that of her maraboutic husband. Like Hornemann, she had a kind of forceful, efficient and materialistic personality which appeals strongly to Moslems.'

Sir William Young wrote of Mungo Park, that he 'not only designated the route in *country* but in *men*'. Twenty printed pages sufficed to tell all he had to say about Fezzan, one of the most interesting districts in northern Africa as those who followed in Hornemann's footsteps — Lyon, Denham, Oudney and Barth — were to make abundantly clear. When presented with an opportunity for spending some months in Murzuk and making a thorough study of the surrounding country and its people he withdrew to Tripoli rather than 'stay in such a miserable place . . . the most disinteresting Town I ever saw'. Nor had he the imagination to realize that much of what was daily passing before his eyes might interest his employers. Like W. G. Browne, he reported caravans arriving in Cairo from Sennar, Darfur and Fezzan, but whereas Browne recorded the trade-goods they carried Hornemann did not mention them. It is not from Hornemann, but from Lyon, that we hear of his having travelled from Tripoli to Murzuk with so important and influential a friend as the Bey el Noba.

Hornemann's weaknesses naturally did not escape the critical reviewer of his *Journal* in the *Edinburgh Review*, to which reference has already been made. He found it 'rather singular' that the explorer gave no description of Murzuk, where he had spent so much time. 'Unfortunately', he continued, 'he has neglected to give any narrative of the journey from Mourzouk to the coast, although this tract of country is as little known as that between Cairo and Fezzan, and can scarcely be less interesting.'[1]

Allowances must be made for Hornemann's youth and the possible shortcomings of the training that he had received at Göttingen. He was obviously interested in geology and, judging by the space he gave to the antiquities of Siwa, also in archaeology. But these were interests of little value to his undertaking.

Hornemann, alas, was not of the stuff that makes a great explorer. Much as we may wish that the papers burnt in the hut at Bokani had survived, it is doubtful whether they would have added greatly to human knowledge.

Where Hornemann failed was in not realizing that for the explorer to reach remote and unexplored places was not in itself enough, that that was only the means to an end — the gathering of information. He would probably have made a fine leader of an expedition composed of men of learning who would have supplemented his splendid courage, resolute determination and capacity for making friends,

[1] *Edinburgh Review*, 1814 edn., I (1802), 134.

with the more sophisticated gifts so essential to successful exploration.

Nevertheless, to have accomplished so great a journey across so vast and unexplored a region without a companion to support him was one of the great achievements in the history of geographical discovery, for which his name will always be deservedly honoured. It was tragic that his early death prevented his turning a remarkable journey into a truly astonishing one.

vi. Hornemann and the Niger

Mindful that the main object of his travels was to discover the middle Niger, Hornemann closely questioned everyone he met who was likely to be able to throw light on the problem of the river's course. As the African Association had repeatedly found, enquiries of this kind tended towards most misleading conclusions. It is no blame to Hornemann that his contribution to the problem served only to confuse the issue. Piecing together the often contradictory information he was able to gather, he concluded, correctly, that the Niger flowed to the south of Kebbi and Nupe. From that point he was led sadly astray. From Nupe he gave the river a north-easterly course 'into the district of Burnu where it takes the name of Zad [Chad]', confusing it with its great tributary the Benue, flowing south-west into the Niger not far south of Nupe. An Egyptian traveller well acquainted with Wadai and Darfur told Hornemann of a river flowing to the south of these two countries, no doubt with the Shari and Bahr el Arab in mind, which very naturally led him to conclude that this river was in fact the Niger flowing to join the Nile. This was confirmed to him shortly before he left Murzuk for Bornu by a man who had been to Darfur and told him that 'the communication of the Niger with the Nile was not to be doubted'.[1]

But no harm was done to the cause of science. Major James Rennell, F.R.S., the most illustrious geographer of the day, wholly rejected the possibility of a junction of the Niger with the Nile. Was it probable, he asked, 'that the Niger, after running about 2250 British miles in direct distance from its source, should have arrived at a lower level, than that of the countries adjacent to the heads of the Nile?'[2]

Rennell had his own theory about the termination of the Niger. His efforts to reconcile what the old Arab geographers had said about the interior of Africa with modern discovery and native report had led him

---

[1] See p. 110 below.　　　[2] Hornemann, *Journal*, 170.

to declare that 'on the whole, it can scarcely be doubted that the Joliba or Niger terminates in lakes, in the eastern quarter of Africa; and those lakes seem to be situated in Wangara and Ghana'. He believed that here, somewhere in the region of Hausa and Chad, in what he called the 'sink of North Africa', the waters of the Niger became so widely dispersed that they were completely lost by evaporation.[1] Hornemann's report that the Niger flowed eastwards as if heading for the Nile seemed to Rennell to provide fresh evidence of 'the termination of the Niger, by *evaporation*, in the country of Wangara'.[2]

There was one most valuable aspect of Hornemann's work to which neither he nor his employers appear to have attached any importance. This was his revelation of the vast extent of the international trade which in those days flowed north and south, east and west, across northern Africa. That Murzuk was an entrepôt for trade extending north to Tripoli and Tunis, east to Cairo and Darfur, west to Fez and Timbuktu, and south almost to the Guinea coast, and that in Fezzan there were traders who knew all these markets, failed to arouse a flicker of interest.

---

[1] Mungo Park, *Travels in the Interior Districts of Africa* (London, 1799) lxxvii. Rennell was led to this conclusion by his erroneous belief that the Wangara which Leo Africanus had placed in Hausa was the Wangara which Edrisi had described as 'surrounded by the waters of the Nile'. Not only were they different, but they were only two of several Wangaras in West Africa where, as Denham wrote, 'all gold countries as well as any people coming from the gold country ... are called Wangara' (Denham and Clapperton, II, 85).

[2] Hornemann, *Journal*, 163.

BIBLIOGRAPHICAL NOTE

The Journal of Frederick Horneman's Travels from Cairo to Mourzouk, translated from the German text, was first published in the *Proceedings* of the African Association for the year 1801. It was republished in London in 1802 by G. and W. Nicol, Booksellers to his Majesty, Pall Mall.

At the annual meeting of the Association in May 1804 the Secretary reported:

'Soon after the presentation of a copy of Frederick Horneman's Journal to the First Consul of France, by order of this Association, at its General Meeting, 1802; the book was by order of the Consul translated into French; and Mr. Langles, a Member of the National Institute, who was the editor of the work, and had added to it a learned essay on the Oasis of the ancients, in *his note* on our original preface, explanatory of the views and purposes of this Institution, says, "the above important considerations, so well set forth and explained, deserve the attention of our government, and of every Frenchman who is a friend to his country, and to science: may a noble spirit of emulation, induce us to form an *African Society in France*, which shall correspond with that in Great Britain. — above all, may the members and agents of the two Institutions so act in concert, as to render their discoveries of general advantage to science, to their respective countries, and to mankind at large".

'Immediately ensuing the publication of Horneman's Travels in French, and the above proposal and exhortation of Mr. Langles, a society was established at Paris, intituled "*La Société de l'Afrique interieure, et de Découvertes*"[1] The French edition of Hornemann's *Journal*, translated from the English edition, was published in Paris in 1803 under the title *Voyage de F. Hornemann dans l'Afrique Septentrionale*, edited by L. Langlès who added an appendix from his own hand entitled *Mémoire sur les Oasis, composé principalement d'après les auteurs arabes.*'

In 1895 a German edition of the *Journal* was published in Hamburg, edited by Adolf Pahde, under the title *Der erste deutsche Afrikaforscher (Fr.K. Hornemann, geb. 1772, gest. 1801)*.

The present edition of the *Journal* is a reprint of that of 1802, with corrections which collation with the German edition of 1895 (presumed to have been from Hornemann's original text) showed to be necessary. These corrections are mostly of a minor nature, some of them due to mistranslation and others to misprints. The Appendix, however, has been greatly reduced. Sir William Young's *Observations on the Country and Antiquities of Siwah*, Major James Rennell's *Geographical Illustrations*, William Marsden's *Observations on the Language of Siwah* and the *List of Members* of the Association, have all

---

[1] *Proceedings*, II, 326.

been omitted because, valuable though they may have been to contemporary readers, today they are of little interest.

Hornemann's *Journal* was written in German, but his letters to the Association, most of them addressed to its President, Sir Joseph Banks, were invariably written in English, of which he was no great master. The Association published some of his letters but before doing so they rendered them into correct English. In the following pages the English rendering of his published letters has been retained, but quotations from his unpublished letters are exactly as he wrote them.

Some of the footnotes in the original edition have been omitted. Those that have been retained are marked with an asterisk, thus *, while those of the editor are numbered.

The following abbreviations have been used in the footnotes:

Proceedings	*Proceedings of the Association for Promoting the Discovery of the Interior Parts of Africa*, 2 vols. (London, 1810).
D.T.C.	*Banks Correspondence*, Dawson Turner Collection of copies of Correspondence of Sir Joseph Banks.

THE JOURNAL

of

FREDERICK HORNEMAN'S TRAVELS,

from

CAIRO TO MOURZOUK,

the

CAPITAL OF THE KINGDOM OF FEZZAN,

IN AFRICA

in the years 1797–8.

LONDON

Printed by W. Bulmer and Co.
Cleveland-Row, St. James's;

FOR G. AND W. NICOL, BOOKSELLERS TO HIS MAJESTY,
PALL-MALL.

1802

INTRODUCTION

The Society, instituted in the year 1788, for the purpose of exploring the Interior of Africa, in pursuing their *great* design, adopted *wise* and certain principles of procedure: they inquired, and then examined; they sought intelligence, and then directed research: their progress has been answerable to the just system of their pursuits and perseverance; and the Society, from the epoch of 1798, have been enabled to direct their efforts for further discovery, on data from actual visitation and experiment.

A volume of the transactions of the Society, printed in the years 1790-92, sets forth in detail, such communications respecting the Interior of Africa, as might be collected on inquiry from British Consuls; from the recital of Negro, or Moorish traders; or from that of Shereefs and others, who had passed with the caravans on religious pilgrimage, in different directions between Mecca and the various and remote stations of Mahomedans in Africa.

Those communications were, at the time, most interesting and useful; they afforded at once the incentive and the direction to further inquiry; they opened new objects to commercial enterprize, and new matter for scientific speculation, on the productions of nature, and the manners and conditions of society, in a quarter of the globe hitherto unexplored; further, they pointed out the road, and facilitated the means, of ascertaining the truth of each account, and of estimating its importance and advantages by actual visitation and experiment.

Be it allowed, that the narrators spoke of what they had heard, as well as of what they had seen; let it be granted that they were mostly ignorant, credulous, or partially informed; and that, distinctively and in detail, the accuracy of their representations was little to be depended upon; yet on points wherein their accounts agreed, they merited attention and regard; they *together* opened a general view of the society, and of the country; and afforded matter of such reasonable conjecture and inference, as might warrant and direct the course of further investigation. Reflecting on these and other relations made by unenlightened men, it appears, that as the great continent of Africa, amidst its seas of sand, occasionally shews its Oasis, or fertile isle, rising in each desert; so, in analogy to the face of the country, does the blank and torpid mind of its people, display occasionally notes of intelligence and philanthropy; rich spots of genius, and partial scenes of improved social establishment. Having passed whole regions sterilized by apathy and ignorance, the result of superstitions, prejudice, and oppression, the enlightened traveller comes to a sudden view of some rich field of character, and contemplates with delight the free-born spirit and sagacity of the Tuarick of Hagara,[1] and the ingenuity and benevolence of the Houssan.[2] To unfold and disseminate these germs of civilization, is surely a noble task! What description of men and country can be more interesting? whither could the refinement of arts? whither could enlightened philosophy better tend, to humanize and improve? whither could the spirit of trade better direct its course? As we speculate on the projected intercourse, the noblest views open to the mind, anticipating reciprocal advantages: in the dispensation of intelligence and the arts of peace, carrying therewith complacent manners to rude and ferocious nations; and in a full compensation to the enlightened adventurers, from new materials of ingenuity and of commerce, and from new subjects of scientific inference, extending the advancement of human knowledge in all its branches.

The communications in question, operating on the minds of intelligent Members of the African Society, and giving a spur to the curiosity and enterprize of the agents they might employ, formed a suitable and necessary PREFACE to the undertaking and efforts for practical discovery, and for ensuring the advantages thence to be derived.

The compilation of various informations respecting Africa, had thus an intrinsic value, as affording premises of inquiry, and as giving encouragement and direction to adventure.

But further, and even immediately, wisdom and sagacity will extract truth from accounts, however contradictory, and useful and certain inference, from documents the most ambiguous or incomplete.

Efforts of rude ingenuity often suggest not only improvement but discovery; the rustic forms a lever to raise the mass, and the sagacity of the mechanic applies it to ascertain the weight.

Science often works with effect on the loose and disjointed materials which ignorance has heaped together; compares, arranges, and connects their substances and forms; shews in their matter, construction, or decomposition, new uses; derives new informations, and adds to the stock of human inventions and knowledge.

Were it necessary to illustrate such position by example, the writer

---

[1] The Tuareg of Ahaggar. [2] Hausa. See p. 117 below.

would refer, as a special instance, to the elucidations of Major Rennell on the communications in question: to that most accurate and acute philosopher and geographer, the details have afforded matter of enquiry and deduction of the highest import to science. By analysis, and a comparative view of accounts given of journies and places, in reference to the plans of D'Anville, and other geographers; to modern travels; to ancient expeditions; to descriptions of ancient writers; and above all, to those of the father of history, Herodotus; Major Rennell hath corrected the map of Africa, with a learning and sagacity which *hath converted conjecture into knowledge*; and on experience of those who have explored parts of that great continent, given confidence to each future traveller who may visit its remotest regions.

Had the proceedings of the Society stopped here, and its work been confined to the compilation above alluded to, and to the comments of Major Rennell, the usefulness of its institution would have been acknowledged by posterity.

But happily the Journal of Mr. Park's travels to the Niger, and that of Mr. Horneman's journey from Cairo to Mourzouk, will fully shew, that the attainments of the Society are no longer narrowed to the mere rudiments of discovery, which tradition and ingenious inference, alone before supplied.

Even under the inauspicious circumstances of wars and revolutions which from nearly the date of the establishment of the Society, have spread desolation far and wide, and in the year 1798, reached to the very capital of Africa; their chosen emissaries have surmounted all the dangers and difficulties, which these events superadded to the ordinary risk of enterprise.

It should not be omitted, that the traveller, (whose work is now submitted to the public,) was further indebted to the liberal and enlightened spirit, which directs the genius of truly great men to foster useful arts and sciences amidst the horrors of war; and give orders to the armies under their command, to forbear all molestation of the emissary from even an hostile country, whose intentions and pursuits are directed to objects of common value and concern, to the nations of the world at large.

Under such patronage and protection from the General Bonaparte, and with his special passport and safeguard, Frederick Horneman safely reached the caravan passing from Mecca, and pursued, and accomplished his journey from Cairo to the kingdom of Fezzan; which from the general resort of caravans to its capital, Mourzouk, may be considered as the proper post of direction and outfit, for his further travels to the remotest regions of Africa.

In planning the routes of Park and of Horneman, the Society availed itself of former communications, sagaciously discriminated the proper path of research, and have to exult in the success of each adventure. These emissaries have explored roads which shortly mercantile adventure will, and must enter. In this new race of commerce, shame indeed would it be to our national councils, could it possibly be supposed that from the default of patronage and support of Government, our commercial people may lose the start for a priority of factories and establishments of trade, and permit other nations to usurp the vantage ground which British enterprise, under the auspices of a patriotic and enlightened, but private institution, shall have explored, marked out, and prepared for them.

By Mr. Park's discoveries, a gate is opened to every commercial nation to enter and trade from the west to the eastern extremity of Africa. The navigable parts of the rivers Gambia and Niger are not so far distant, but that great facilities of trade may thence be derived, aided by the establishment of intermediate stations and points of intercourse. A considerable traffic is carried on by the natives for ostrich feathers, drugs, ivory, and gold, even without such advantage. On due directions and exertions of British credit and enterprise, it is difficult to imagine the possible extent to which the demand for our country's manufactures might arrive, from such vast and populous countries in the bosom of which *gold*, the great medium of commerce, is readily found; and which would be sought for and brought into circulation with new avidity and success, in proportion as objects for the exchange, became known, desirable, and necessary to the people.

This subject has already been recommended by the Society, to the attention of Government; and on the return of peace, it is not doubted, but it will be treated with a consideration and regard, suitable to the important interests which it involves.

When the thorny track of a Park or a Horneman is become the beaten road of the merchant, advantages of another sort will quickly follow; and the intercourse extend to the instruction of the naturalist and philosopher, to the promotion of civilization, and to the increase of the general stock of human knowledge and happiness.

Contemplating such accomplishment of the wise and benevolent purposes of their Institution, the patriotic members of this Society cannot but look back with exultation to the hour of its establishment, and they will with satisfaction recapitulate its means and progress, towards such happy termination of their labours.

Of those who transmitted accounts which they had received, concerning the people and country of Africa, Mr. Ledyard and Mr. Lucas were specially employed, with the further intent of progress into the heart of the country; for the purpose of ascertaining the truth of these recitals, the correcting them on personal information, and the elucidating, on actual survey, any future plan for turning the knowledge thence derived to account.

Mr. Ledyard died at Cairo, ere his eager and enterprising spirit could even start towards its object; Mr. Lucas, deterred by impending difficulties and dangers, proceeded not further than to Mesurata, seven days journey S.E. of Tripoly; there collected informations from the Shereef Imhammed, and traders of Fezzan, and then measured his road back to Tripoly; and shortly after returned to England.

The Society, with that persevering spirit which ever distinguishes manly minds, engaged on sound principles, and for noble purposes, were not appalled by the death of one emissary, or the failure of another.

They sought out and appointed a new traveller, and to take a new road. Mr. Ledyard was to have penetrated from the East, Mr. Lucas from the north; Major Houghton was appointed in the year 1790, to sail for the mouth of the Gambia, and to traverse the country from west to east; Major Houghton arrived on the coast of Africa November 10, of that year, immediately commenced his journey, ascended the Gambia to Medina, 900 miles (by the water-course) distant from the mouth of the river, and thence proceeded to Bambouk and to the adjoining kingdom of Kasson; where, in September 1791, he unfortunately terminated his travels with his life, near the town of Jarra. Mr. Park, who was engaged in the service of the Society, in 1795, more successfully followed the route of Major Houghton, and further explored to the banks of the Niger, to Sego, and to Silla, the first of that great line of populous and commercial cities, dividing the southern from the northern deserts of Africa; and the very existence of which, for centuries past, hath been rather matter of rumour than of information; and been made the subject of philosophic romance,* in default of authentic account and description.

The informations of Mr. Park were communicated to the Society at their annual Meeting in May 1798.

* By Bishop Berkeley.

The year 1798 will ever be noted, as the memorable epoch, when the researches of this Society announced to the world the course of the Niger, from west to east; and, after the distance of 2300 years, corroborated the testimony of the Nasamones, and accounts of Herodotus, contested during that long period by ancient and later writers, and ultimately rejected within the century past, by the learned D'Anville. But further, the settlements on its fertile shores, are by the informations of Park, derived from inquiries so near to the source, as now greatly to be depended on; at least so far, as to give assurance of objects of commerce and learned inquiry, that will amply repay further research. The just motto of the Society is, *'quod non peractum, pro non inchoato est;'* its exertions and perseverance answer to it, and it is to be congratulated that the task is now easy, its accomplishment assured.

The writer of this Essay, not presuming to graft addition or observation on the intelligent and authentic Journal of Mungo Park, ventures a single comment, of import to the Society, and in justice to its agent.

Mr. Park has not only designated the route of *country* but of *men*. He hath marked the districts of population covering the great belt of land intersecting Africa from west to east, and at the same time hath noted the distinctions of Moor and Negro, in manners, prejudices, and government. He hath thereby given to the Society information of the *viaticum* of character and accomplishments proper and necessary to ensure the success of *their future agents*: he hath pointed out the roads to districts and cities of the greatest interest, and at the same time hath shewn the means of securing entrance and hospitable reception.

The Society hath availed itself of the intelligence; and the new emissary, Mr. Horneman, hath given his lesson full effect in an expedition which is the subject of the present Volume.

Of the further progress of this accomplished traveller, the Editor forbears to intimate design or suggestion.

The season of mere expectation and conjecture is gone by. It were idle indeed at this period of actual discovery, to hazard surmise for future correction on experiment.

At the outset of the Society instituted for the purpose of exploring the Interior of Africa, it might have been proper to set forth, in glowing colours, all that was rumoured, and all that might be expected; well were general reports and ingenious inferences suited to rouze curiosity, to excite adventurous spirit, and to give a spring to the first movements and purposes of the Institution.

Such incentives are no longer necessary; and knowledge actually acquired, demands, in the future display, merely accuracy and precision, as the guides to further success.

The Society is confirmed in its purpose, and assured of its objects and of the means of attainment.

Its travellers will not in future rush on with zealous but unadvised curiosity; or hesitate as in the dark, and on unfounded apprehensions; but, disciplined and educated, proceed with a spirit corrected and confirmed by knowledge and precaution, towards certain purposes and ends.

An adventurer may yet fail; but it is presumed the adventurer cannot, unless from failure of the funds and resources of the Society; which, in this great and opulent country, it would be a calumny on the generosity and patriotism of its people, for one moment to anticipate as possible.

Yet let it be remembered, that the extent of our undertakings can only be commensurate with our means.

Expense and charge attend our present inquiries; and even a more advantageous extension of our researches apart, demands of much beyond what our actual numbers and contributions can furnish, will be necessary to ensure the effect of national advantage, and turn to public account the successful experiment of an enlightened and patriotic, but not numerous, Association.

The Society cannot condescend to solicitation; nor is it necessary: it will suffice, that, emboldened by success, they suggest to their countrymen, that, under proper patronage, and with the means of extending their researches, *the conclusion will be of advantage*, to Great Britain — to Africa — and to the World.

W. YOUNG.
Secretary to THE AFRICAN SOCIETY.

PREFACE TO THE JOURNAL

GIVING SOME ACCOUNT OF MR. FREDERICK HORNEMAN; OF THE PREPARATIONS FOR HIS VOYAGE; AND OF EVENTS PREVIOUS TO HIS LEAVING CAIRO.

★

At the time that Mr. Mungo Park, engaged in the service of the Society instituted for the purpose of exploring the Interior of Africa, was prosecuting discoveries eastward from the river Gambia, it was thought proper to extend their researches in another line of direction, and engage an emissary to explore that great Continent, proceeding westward from the city of Cairo.

Early in the year 1796, Mr. F. Horneman offered himself to the Committee of the Society for this service; he appeared to be young, robust, and, in point of constitution and health, suited to a struggle with different climates and fatigues: in his manner and conversations he displayed temper, acuteness, and prudence: he was well apprized of the dangers and difficulties of the enterprise he was to engage in, and shewed a spirit and zeal for the undertaking, which strongly recommended him as a proper person to be employed for the carrying it into effect.

The Committee accordingly engaged his services; and observing in him such foundation of good ordinary education, as further attainments might readily be engrafted upon, they sent him, at the expense of the Society, to Gottingen; there to study the rudiments and writing of the Arabic language, and, generally, such sciences as (in the result of due application of the knowledge acquired), might render any account of his future travels more interesting and useful to him employers, and to the public.

F. Horneman pursued the requisite studies for several months with great assiduity, under the tuition of Professors Blumenbach, Heeren, Hoffman, Tyschen, and Heyne; and in May, 1797, returned to England, properly instructed for his intended voyage. He was then introduced to a general meeting of the Society, when his engagement was approved of, and he was directed to proceed to Egypt with all convenient dispatch.

Passports from Paris were applied for, and granted, permitting him to pass through France; and in July, 1797, he left London on his way to Paris.

He was furnished with letters of introduction to several persons of literary distinctions in that capital; and, on arrival, his reception was liberal and friendly, and proportionate to the lively interest which was every where taken in his scheme of enterprize, and in the means of promoting its success. He was invited to a meeting of the National Institute. The first members of that learned society tendered their patronage, encouragement, and assistance: Mr. Lalande furnished him with copies of his 'Memoire sur L'Afrique.' Mr. Broussonet recommended him to Mr. Laroche, appointed Consul for Mogadore; and by this latter gentleman's means he made a further and most useful acquaintance with a Turk of distinction (a native of Tripoly), then resident at Paris. This Mussulman entered into the motives and plan of his travels with a liberal approbation, and a zealous interest in the success; which was little to have been expected from one of such persuasion and character. He gave Mr. Horneman letters of introduction, strongly recommending him to the friendship and protection of several leading Mahommedan merchants at Cairo, who were in the habits of trade with people of the remotest regions of Africa; and he added his own advice, and instructions for the journey.

Thus provided, Mr. Horneman, in August, left Paris for Marseilles, where he embarked the end of the month, and arrived at Alexandria the middle of September: he staid at Alexandria but a few days, and then went to Cairo, where he purposed residing some time, to study the language and manners of the Mograbins, or western Arabs, with whom he was to associate in his future travels: His own letter will best describe his further progress.

(TRANSLATION)

Cairo, August 31, 1798

Sir,

In my last letter I mentioned my intentions of leaving Cairo about the end of May. The plague beginning to rage in the month of April, it became a proper and necessary precaution not only to defer my journey, but absolutely to shut myself up in my house. My zeal for the undertaking I have engaged in, would have led me to break through this confinement and leave the city, with a view to join the merchants at their place of rendezvous, whence they were directly to depart for Fezzan, had not obstacles arising from the difficulty of procuring the necessary credits for my equipment prevented my immediate procedure.

As soon as from abatement of the pestilence, I could safely go abroad, I met and renewed my acquaintance with several of the caravan, who remained in the city, expecting the return of others from Mecca. A French commercial house, on whom I had no letters of credit or other claim to confidence, than what arose from private friendship and esteem, having handsomely offered such advance of monies as I might require, I was enabled to prepare for my journey, and set out with this caravan, as soon as complete and ready for departure. All these designs were suddenly frustrated by the arrival of the French on the coast of Egypt. Those who formed the caravan at Cairo quickly dispersed; that from Mecca coming to join it was not yet arrived; myself and other Europeans were seized and confined in the castle, rather as a place of refuge from the indignation and fanaticism of the populace, than as a prison, and we remained there until the arrival of the French at Cairo.

Soon after their coming, I made acquaintance with two of their learned men, Berthollet and Monge,[1] they liberated and presented me to the Commander in Chief, and he received me with every mark of attention and goodness. His regard for science, and esteem of learned men are too well known to render it necessary for me to expatiate on these high qualities. He promised me protection, he offered me money or whatever was requisite to my undertaking, and he directed the necessary passports to be prepared for me.

I lost no time in seeking out my friends, the merchants of Fezzan, and renewing my connections with them. Gradually as the public tranquillity became assured, they returned, one by one into the city, till the whole were again assembled; and fifteen days have now passed, since we have been making preparations for our final departure, actually fixed for the day after tomorrow.

Commonly those who engage in an extraordinary enterprise, consider means yet more extraordinary, as requisite to the success of the undertaking; my opinion, and therewith procedure will be founded on directly the contrary proposition. The plan which I have chalked out for my journey will be simple and easy to pursue. You shall have it in a single line, 'it is to travel as a Mahommedan merchant of the caravan.' I am assured that under such character, I can travel with the same surety as the natives of the country.

Many of the caravan having been at Mecca, are aware that there are numbers of good Mussulmen from various countries who speak not Arabic, and who have different usages and customs; and thus simply attaining a knowledge of certain religious ceremonies and prayers, there is no difficulty in passing generally as a Mahommedan; for as to a certain less equivocal criterion of a personal nature, the delicacy of Mahommedan manners precludes any danger of inquiry.

---

[1] Claude-Louis Berthollet (1749–1822) and Gaspard Monge (1746–1818), the one a scientist and the other a geometrician, were among the *savants* who had accompanied Bonaparte for the purpose of establishing French culture in Egypt.

To travel as a Christian, will perhaps be impracticable for at least five years to come, for it is incredible how deep and strong an impression the expedition of the French has made on the minds of the pilgrims to and from Mecca: dispersed to their several homes they will carry an aggravated prejudice against Christians far and wide, and to the very heart of Africa.

Should it be objected to me, that I risk a similar fate with that of Major Houghton, by travelling as a trader, my answer is, 'that by travelling as a Mahommedan trader, I shall never travel alone; and with those too of the caravan, considered as one of the least of its merchants.'

In respect to my astronomical instruments, I shall take special care never to be discovered in the act of observation; should those instruments, however, attract notice, the answer is ready, 'they are articles for sale;' nor is there fear that I should be deprived of them, whilst master of my price. My comrades know the value of gold at least better than myself. In a word, the merchants of our Fezzan caravan, are men of wealth, integrity, and enterprise; but Mahommedans, the most prejudiced and fanatic.

I have not yet fixed or methodized my design, as to further journey into the interior of Africa; but I have made acquaintance with a man who has been at Bornou and Cashna, a place, from every account which I can collect, and particularly from the Jalabs, deserving my immediate attention after arrival at Fezzan.

I expect to be at Fezzan by the beginning of November, and I should propose in the next year, setting out for the Agades and Cashna, residing in and exploring those countries during ten months, and then returning *via* Mecca or Senegambia. Should any necessity of the case oblige me to return to Tripoly, I should not consider my tour as complete, but (with permission of the Society), hold myself in readiness for a further undertaking.

I will write again from Fezzan, if I can do so without danger; the safest plan that occurs, is to pack up some bale of goods with an ordinary letter of advice in Arabic, making my real dispatch the package or covering of some article of trade.

Pray write to and direct the English Consul at Tripoly, or elsewhere, never to make inquiry after me of the traders from Fezzan, and particularly when conveying any thing from me consigned to you. These people are of a very jealous and inquisite temper, and any inquiries made after me by a Christian, might raise a thousand suspicions, and prove even of fatal consequence to me.

Nay, should yourselves not hear of me these three years, make no inquiry. Under such precaution, my danger will not be that I travel as a trader and Mahommedan, but such only as results from climate and ordinary perils of voyage in these countries; which I trust successfully to oppose, with a good constitution and strength of body, and with courage and suitable temper of mind.

It remains only for me to recommend to the Committee, the man whom I mentioned in a former letter. I met with the person in question, Joseph

Frendenburgh, who was born in Germany, just on the eve of his intended departure from Cairo for his native country. I engaged and employed him as interpreter; and, pleased with the office, he offered to continue in my service, and attend me in my expedition. He had been ten or twelve years past forced to embrace the Mahommedan religion; had three times made the voyage to Mecca, and spoke perfectly both the Arabic and Turkish languages; in short, he was precisely the man that suited me. The connection with him will ensure me character and confidence from others, and indeed, without him, I should scarcely be able to pursue my journey, without actually embracing and professing Mahommedanism myself, I now well know him on ten months experience, and in just reliance on him, have no apprehension of the calamity incident to travellers, of being robbed by their servants.

I shall consign to him the care of my camels and my horses, (for we merchants of the caravan all go armed, and on horseback,) he will further have the care of my merchandize, and altogether, I shall have leisure for my inquiries, and for attending to the general objects of my undertaking. The demands of this man are far from exorbitant, and I request of the Society, the attending to a just remuneration of his services, and specially, if in case of my death, he should faithfully preserve my journals and papers, and proceed with them to England.

I have been in some doubt as to the means of sending this letter, but on my request, General Bonaparte has with great goodness, himself condescended to take charge of its safe conveyance.

I hope my next will be from Fezzan, and that after three years, I shall be enabled to give account of the interior of Africa.

I am, &c. &c. &c.

Frederick Horneman

To Mr. Edwards, Secretary to the Society,
instituted for exploring the interior of Africa.

The above letter was transmitted to the African Committee, under the seal of General Bonaparte, who in addition to other marks of favour and protection shewn to the enterprise of Horneman, took on himself the care of forwarding his dispatches, as above stated.

Mr. Horneman's Journal of his Travels from Cairo to Fezzan commences five days after the date of this letter. It was by him written in German, and in that language transmitted to the Committee of the African Society. Under their direction, a translation of it was made by a native of Germany, sufficiently versed in the English language, to render the sense of the original with truth and perspicuity; and, on collating his version, it appears to have been executed with fidelity and care. Some correction of foreign idioms and style was yet required: the

Secretary, in performing this duty of Editor, has been attentive to the preserving not only the genuine descriptions, remarks, and precise meaning of the traveller, but likewise the spirit, and (at the same time) simplicity of narrative which characterizes his Journal; and, it is presumed, that on reference to the original, the translation offered in its present form will *yet* appear to be as nearly literal, as the different idioms and context of the English and German languages will admit of.

Travels in the Interior of Africa

*

CHAPTER I

VOYAGE FROM CAIRO TO AUGILA

SECTION I

To Ummesogeir

The merchants of Augila had appointed their rendezvous to be held at *Kardassi*,[1] a village in the vicinity of Cairo; where I joined them on September the 5th, 1798, and leaving that place the same day, in about an hour we reached the great body of the caravan, which yearly returns from Mecca through Cairo and Fezzan, to the western countries of Africa. The caravan was waiting for us at a small village called *Baruasch*:[2] we halted at some little distance from the pilgrims, and encamped until the next morning: when the monotonous kettle-drum of our Sheik awakened us before rise of the sun, with summons to proceed on our journey.

I had not under-rated the difficulties of the journey; I was aware that many must arise, especially affecting myself, never having before travelled with a caravan, and being little acquainted with the customs and manners of those who composed it. We had travelled from daybreak till noon, and no indication appeared of halt or refreshment, when I observed the principal and richest merchants gnawing a dry biscuit and some onions, as they went on; and was then, for the first time, informed, that it was not customary to unload the camels for regular repast, or to stop during the day-time, but in cases of urgent necessity. This my first inconvenience, was soon remedied by the hospitality of some Arabs who were riding near me, and who invited me to partake of their provisions.

Soon after sunset, our Sheik gave the signal for halting; and we pitched our tents.

My dragoman, or interpreter, might, even in Europe, have passed

[1] Kirdasah.
[2] Abu Rauwash. Both Kirdasah and Abu Rauwash lie to the west of Cairo on the road running north-west from Giza.

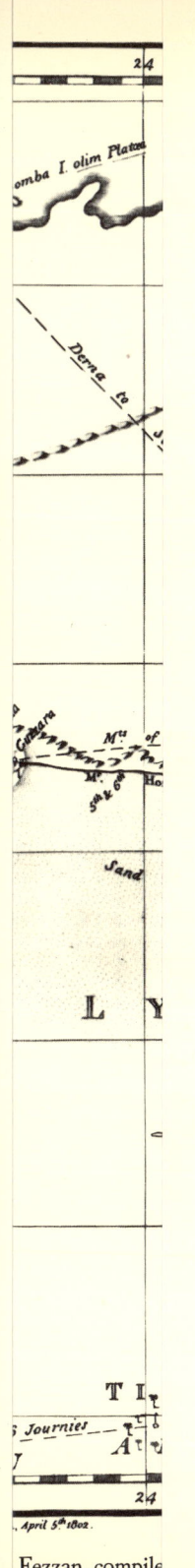

for a good cook; and from remains of the provision which our hospitable friends at Cairo had supplied, was preparing an excellent supper, when an old Arab of Augila, observing his preparations, and that myself was unemployed, addressed me nearly as follows: 'Thou art young, and yet dost not assist in preparing the meal of which thou art to partake; such, perhaps, may be a custom in the land of infidels, but is not so with us, and especially on a journey: thanks to God, we are not, in this desert, dependent on others, as are those poor pilgrims, but eat and drink what we ourselves provide, and as we please. Thou oughtest to learn every thing that the meanest Arab performs, that thou mayest be enabled to assist others in cases of necessity; otherwise, thou wilt be less esteemed, as being of less value than a mere woman; and many will think they may justly deprive thee of every thing in thy possession, as being unworthy to possess any thing: (adding sarcastically,) perhaps thou art carrying a large sum of money, and payest those men well.' This remonstrance was not thrown away. I immediately assisted in every thing that was not beyond my force; and proportionally gained on the good opinion and esteem of my fellow-travellers, and was no longer considered as a weak and useless idler in their troop.

The next morning we set out early, and after a march of four hours, arrived at *Wadey-el-Latron*. The signal had been made to halt, for the purpose of collecting fresh water, when a troop of Bedouins appeared at some distance in front, and created great alarm in our caravan. Our Sheik, or leader, had acquired, and deserved, the veneration and confidence of his followers, as much from his known prudence and valour, as from his dignity of Iman. He immediately ordered us to occupy the spot affording water, and himself, with about twenty Arabs and Tuaricks, advanced to reconnoitre the ground where the Bedouins had appeared; they had now retreated wholly out of sight, and we had time to cook and fill our water bags. We could not, however, consider this as a proper or safe station for the night; accordingly at four o'clock we proceeded on our march; and camped at about eight in the evening at the foot of a sandhill, which we descended in indescribable disorder, created by the late alarm; — making no fires, and using every precaution to avoid notice or discovery of our retreat.

The next morning, September 8th, we entered the Desert, which may be considered as the boundary of Egypt; and after travelling thirteen hours, encamped on a tract of land by the Arabs called *Muhabag*.

The ensuing day, our journey was less fatiguing; in four hours and a half we reached *Mogara*,¹ a watering-place on the verge of a fruitful valley.

The water collected for the use of the caravans is carried in bags made of goat-skins, unripped in the middle, and stripped from the animal as entire as possible; those made at Soudan are the strongest and best; water may be preserved in them for five days, without acquiring any bad taste: the bags of an inferior manufacture give an ill taste, and a smell of the leather, from the second day. To render the skins flexible and lasting, they are greased on the inside with butter, and by the Arabs sometimes with oil, which latter gives quickly a rancid taste, and to any but an Arab, renders the water scarcely fit for drinking.

The sixth day we had again a difficult and tiresome journey of twelve hours, without halting; towards the close of our march, the horse of an Arab near me falling sick, and being unable to proceed at the same pace as the caravan, I kept in the rear to attend him, and give such assistance as might be required. On our coming up with the caravan at its evening encampment, the Arab immediately sent by his slave, two pieces of dried camel's flesh, with a proper compliment, requesting my acceptance of the present, as some return for the civility I had shewn. I was in an instant surrounded by a number of meaner Arabs, who eyed with avidity the meat I had received, and on my dividing it amongst them, seemed greatly surprised, that I should so readily part with what, in their estimation, was so great a dainty. Circumstances light and trivial often delineate manners, and characterize nations: the method of equipment, and the means of sustenance which the Arab uses in journeying through these deserts, may furnish a subject of just curiosity, and certainly of special use to such as may undertake a similar expedition.

The Arab sets out on his journey with a provision of flour, kuskasa,² onions, mutton suet, and oil or butter; and some of the richer class add to this store, a proportion of biscuit, and of dried flesh. As soon as the camels are halted and the baggage unladen, the drivers and slaves dig a small hole in the sands wherein to make a fire, and then proceed in search of wood, and of three stones to be placed round the cavity, for the purpose of confining the embers and supporting the cauldron. The cauldron, (which is of copper,) being set over, the time till the water begins to boil is employed first in discussing, and then in preparing,

¹ El Maghra.   ¹ *Cuscus*, see p. 332n. 6 below.

what the mess of the day shall consist of. The ordinary meal is of *hasside*, a stiff farinaceous pap, served up in a copper dish, which, in due economy of utensils and luggage, is at other times used for serving water to the camels: when this pap or pudding is thus served on table, it is diluted with a soup poured on it, enriched or seasoned with the *menschie* dried and finely pulverized. At other times, the dinner consists of flour kneaded into a strong dough, which being divided into small cakes and boiled, affords a species of hard dumplins called *mijotta*. A yet better repast is made of dried meat boiled together with mutton suet, onions sliced thin, crumbled biscuits, salt, and a good quantity of pepper. The meat is at dinner time taken out and reserved for the master, and the broth alone is the mess of his followers. The slaughtering of a camel affords a feast to the camel drivers and slaves. The friends of the owner of the beast have a preference in the purchase; and after dividing the carcase, every slave comes in for a share: no part of the animal capable of being gnawed by human tooth, is suffered to be lost; the very bones pass through various hands and mouths, before they are thrown away. They make sandals of the skin, and they weave the hair into twine.

It is not on every occasion that time can be allowed, or materials found, for dressing victuals: in the anticipation of such an exigency, the traveller provides a food called *simitée*: it consists of barley boiled until it swells, then dried in the sun, and then further dried over the fire; and lastly, being ground into a powder, it is mixed with salt, pepper, and carraway-seed, and put into a leather bag: when it is to be used, it is kneaded into a dough, with just water enough to give it consistency, and it is served up with butter or oil. If further diluted with water, then dates are added to the meal, and it is called *roum*. Such is the food of the traveller when there is a scarcity of fuel or of water; and none can be expended in boiling. I was often, for days together, without other food than this cold farinaceous pap, mixed with a few dates. Onions and red Spanish pepper are the general and the only seasonings of each meal, with the addition of salt.

On the seventh day, after a march of four hours, we reached *Biljoradec*, commonly called *Jahudie*, a term implying that the water is bad, or that other water is not to be found but at a considerable distance.

The three following days, travelling occasionally in the night, we were forty hours in actual journey. On the first of these, (being the ninth day since leaving the vicinity of Cairo,) we reached the chain of mountains which bounded the uniform desert through which we had passed. On the tenth, mounting these hills, I observed the plain on their summit to consist of a saline mass spread over so large a tract of surface, that in one direction no eye could reach its termination, and what might be called its width, I computed at several miles. The clods of salt discoloured with sand lay thick and close, and gave to this vast plain the appearance of a recently ploughed field.

On the summit of this eminence, and almost in the middle of this saline tract, (on computation of its width) I discovered a spring; and the passage of Herodotus occurring to my mind, in which he mentions springs of fresh water on the salt hills, I eagerly made up to its brink. I found it edged with salt: some poor pilgrims attending me tasted the water, but it was so saturated with saline matter, as to be wholly unfit for drink.

On the eleventh day (September the 15th), we came to an inhabited spot; after five hours march arriving at the small village of Ummesogeir.[1]

SECTION II

Observations on the Desert, from the Valley of Natron to the Mountains of Ummesogeir

The Desert forms a natural boundary to Egypt, on the west extending from the *Natron Valley* to the mountains of *Ummesogeir*; to the north, the dreary and barren plain is bounded by a chain of lofty hills, in view during the whole course of the caravan; and to the south, extends a journey, probably, of several days, by the ordinary mode of computation in these countries; but in this direction its limits are not defined, or are not known. The desert consists of waste siliceous sand; which if raised by a strong N. Wind occasions even more painful sensations as a heavy hail shower in the northern parts of Europe.

In this vast tract of sands, petrified wood is found, of various forms and size: sometimes are seen whole trunks of trees, of twelve feet circumference or more; sometimes only branches and twigs, scarcely of a quarter of an inch diameter; and sometimes merely pieces of bark of various kinds, and in particular of the oak, are to be found.[2] Many of the great stems yet retain their side branches, and in many the natural

---

[1] Qara or Un Sogeir, the Karet-am-el Sogheir of W. G. Browne.
[2] Dr. E. A. M. Greiss, Assistant Professor of Botany, Cairo University, confirms that the oak is not among the trees identified in this petrified forest.

timber has undergone so little change, that the circular ranges of the wood are discernible, and especially in those tunks which apparently were of oak. The interior of other bodies of timber was become a petrifaction, shewing no distinctions of grain or fibre, but bearing the appearance of mere stone; though the outward coat and form of the substance clearly denoted the tree.

Several Arabs informed me, that in travelling over this Desert, petrified trees were often found upright, and as if growing in the soil; but I presume, respecting those I did not see, from those I inspected, that they were merely trunks raised by hand, round the base of which the sand had quickly gathered before the winds, and formed a mound, as if heaved up by a root. The colour of the petrified wood is in general black, or nearly so; but in some instances it is of a light gray, and then so much resembling the wood in its natural state, that our slaves would often collect, and bring it in, for the purposes of firing.

These petrifactions are sometimes scattered in single pieces, but are oftener found in irregular layers, or strata, covering together a considerable space of ground.

If there yet remains any trace of a western branch of the Nile, as mentioned by ancient writers, it is probably to be discovered in some part of this Desert. I observed no channel, or vestige of such course of river, on the route taken by the caravan. I would direct the researches of any future traveller specially to the tract of country round where we encamped on the nights when we halted at the foot of the sand hill west of *Wadey-el-Latron*, and in the district of *Muhabag*: these places we reached not till after sunset, and departing before day, I myself had no opportunity of examining the country. The term *Bahr-bella-ma*, commonly rendered *river without water*, by no means designates or points to any specific channel or tract in which any ancient channel may be more probably discovered: for if petrified trees fit for masts, or petrified timbers suited to other purposes of ship-building, said to be found in the *Bahr-bella-ma*, characterize and give the name (as we are told) to the tract of land throughout which they are to be found, then the appropriate translation is not the river, but *sea without water*, for such petrifactions are scattered over the whole Desert. Indeed the general appearance of this vast and barren tract, well accords to the title of *sea without water*; its sandy surface resembling that of a lee-shore, over which the waters streaming before the storm have, on their ebb, deposited timber, or what else was carried on by the tide. I say not wreck of vessels, for I saw no wood that had the least appearance of the tool, or of having been wrought for any purpose of man. Such as, by light observers, have been taken for fragments of masts, are merely trunks of trees of from thirty to forty feet in length, broken and shivered into large splinters, which lying near each other, shew in their forms and grain of timber, the mass they formerly belonged to and composed.

To the north of the Desert runs a chain of steep and bare calcareous mountains, which were in constant view of our caravan travelling at the distance of three to seven miles in like direction. At the foot of these, runs a fertile valley abounding in water, from one to six miles in breadth, and to which we resorted every second or third day for a supply of water: but at the period of our journey, the springs throughout the whole valley were nearly dried up. Only here and there was some water which had sometime collected in pools of several miles in circuit. The water which remained, and run or spread on the surface, was *bitter*; yet digging wells near to these rivulets or marshes, we found water at the depth only of five or six feet, which was sweet and palatable.

SECTION III

Ummesogeir, and further Journey to Siwah

Ummesogeir is situated in a sandy valley stretching into the recess between two diverging branches of the mountain. In the valley thus formed, appear vast isolated masses of rock, on the largest of which the village is built; it is small, and contains few inhabitants, furnishing only thirty men capable of bearing arms. The houses are low, constructed of stones cemented with a calcareous earth, and thatched with the boughs of date trees. I was informed, that some of these buildings covered caves or chambers cut in the rock; probably ancient catacombs. Our camp was pitched at the foot of the rock, among date trees, through which the way leads up to the town. Its inhabitants, poor as they appeared, received us with hospitality; they came down, almost to a man, from their houses, and assisted us in watering our camels, or whatever service was required. Towards evening I walked up to the village by a path of very difficult access. Coming to a kind of marketplace, in its centre I observed bargains making with such eagerness, noise, and altercation, that one should suppose the dealings to be of the first moment; but I soon perceived the sellers to be only a few poor pilgrims of our caravan, and their articles of trade to be merely *henna koppel*, rings of lead or glass, and such like ornaments for women; which, with a little shot and gunpowder, they were bartering for dates: the merchandise on either side was not altogether worth a crown.

The people of Ummesogeir are indeed in every respect poor, depending wholly for subsistence on their dates, which they in part sell to the Arabs of the Desert, and in part carry to Alexandria, and exchange for corn, oil, or fat. Their manners are rude and simple, as might be expected, from a society so small, and separated from every other, by vast tracts of desert in every direction. Thus sequestered from the world, too weak in numbers for attack, and too poor to be attacked, these people derive, from their situation and habits of life, a simple and peaceful disposition. An old man told me, that the Bedouins once attempted to deprive them of their rock, and pittance which the date trees around furnished; and would have succeeded, had not a *marabut* (or holy man) who lies buried in the village, so dazzled the eyes of the invaders, that they could not find the place, though constantly roving round it. A like miracle was hoped for, and (in vain certainly) expected in favour of Cairo, when the French invaded Egypt. The idea of miraculous interposition of this kind appears to have been common to the Oriental nations.

During our stay at this place, the effects of a Twater,[1] who died on the journey were sold by auction. Another man, during our route, was killed by a fall from his camel, pitching with his head on a pointed stone, and which caused his instant death. Two others, poor pilgrims from Mecca, fell victims to the fatigue and difficulties of so long a journey, and for which their scanty means were ill suited, either as to food or rest; and this completes our bill of mortality.

After some days of repose, we proceeded on our journey towards Siwah, distant from Ummesogeir a journey of twenty hours. We soon passed the skirts of the broad sandy valley, and reascended the mountains connected with, and stretching from, those which cover the vale of Ummesogeir to the west. A long and tedious passage over these hills led us finally to a green and fertile valley, towards which, as we descended from the mountain, we perceived people gathering provender for their cattle. Our train of heavy laden camels readily denoted that we were no troop of hostile Arabs; and the people leaving their work, ran to meet and congratulate us on our arrival. They told us that the whole neighbourhood was at peace, and that we might encamp safely and without apprehension. They mounted their asses

[1] A native of the oasis of Tuat in the western Sahara.

and conducted us to a plain west of Siwah, and not far distant from that town, where we pitched our tents.

SECTION IV

Siwah

Siwah is a small independent state; it acknowledges, indeed, the grand Sultan paramount, but it pays him no tribute. Round its chief town called Siwah, are situated at one or two miles distance, the villages of *Scharkie*, (in Siwahian dialect termed *Agrmie*,)[1] *Msellem*, *Menschie*,[2] *Sbocha*, and *Bourischa*.[3] Siwah is built upon, and round, a mass of rock; in which, according to tradition, the ancient people had only caves for their habitation. Indeed the style of building is such, that the actual houses might be taken for caves; they are raised so close to each other, that many of the streets, even at noon, are dark, and so intricate, that a stranger cannot find his way into or out of the town, small as it is, without a guide. Many of the houses built on the declivity of the rock, and especially those terminating the descent towards the plain, are of more than ordinary height, and their walls particularly thick and strong, so as to form a circumvallation of defence to the town within.

The people of our caravan compared Siwah to a bee-hive, and the comparison is suitable, whether regarding the general appearance of the eminence thus covered with buildings, the swarm of its people crowded together, or the confused noise, or hum and buzz from its narrow passages and streets, and which reach the ear to a considerable distance.

Round the foot of the eminence are erected stables for the camels, horses, and asses, which could not ascend to, or could not be accommodated in, the town above.

The territory of SIWAH is of considerable extent; its principal and most fruitful district is a well watered valley varying in breadth of about fifty miles in circuit, hemmed in by steep and barren rocks. Its soil is a sandy loam, in some places rather poached or fenny; but, assisted by no great industry of the natives, it produces corn, oil, and vegetables for the use of man or beast: its chief produce, however, consists in dates, which, from their great quantity and excellent flavour, render the place proverbial for fertility among the surrounding

[1] Aghurmi.   [2] El Menshiah.   [3] Possibly Koreishit.

Arabs of the Desert. Each inhabitant possesses one or more gardens, making his relative wealth; and these it is his whole business to water and cultivate. A large garden yielding all such produce as is natural to the country, is valued at the price of from four to six hundred imperial dollars, there termed *real patacks*. The gardens round the towns or villages, are fenced with walls from four to six feet high, and sometimes with hedges; they are watered by many small streams of salt or sweet water, falling from the bordering rocks and mountains, or issuing from springs rising in the plain itself, and which, for the purposes of irrigation, being diverted into many small channels, expend themselves in the vale, and in no instance flow beyond the limits of this people's territory. The dates produced are preserved in public magazines, of which the key is kept by the Sheik; to these storehouses the dates are brought in baskets closely rammed down, and a register of each deposit is kept.

North-west of Siwah, there is a stratum of salt extending a full mile, and near it salt is found on the surface, lying in clods or small lumps. On this spot rise innumerable springs, and frequently a spring of water perfectly sweet is found within a few paces from one which is salt. North of Siwah, on the road leading to *El-Mota*,[1] I found many of these salt springs quite close to others which were sweet.

It is not easy to ascertain the general population of a place, with so little police, and so little regularity of government as Siwah, unless opportunity occurred of seeing its people assembled at some general meeting or festival. The number of its warriors, however, is more easily known and I was told that they amounted to fifteen hundred; and on such data, further estimate of its population may be made. According to the ancient constitution and laws of the state, the government should be vested in twelve Sheiks, two of whom were to administer its powers in rotation; but a few years past, twenty other wealthy citizens, forced themselves into a share of authority, assumed the title of Sheik, and enlarging the circle of aristocracy, increased the pretensions and disputes for power. On each matter of public concern, they now hold general councils. I attended several of these general meetings, held close to the town wall, where the chiefs were squatted in state; and I observed, that a strong voice, violent action, great gesticulation, abetted by party support and interest, gained the most applause, and carried the greatest influence: perhaps such result is not uncommon in most popular meetings. Whenever these councils cannot

[1] Jebel Mauta.

agree ultimately on any point, then the leaders and people fly to arms, and the strongest party carries the question. Justice is administered according to ancient usage, and general notions of equity. Fines, to be paid in dates, constitute the punishments: for instance, the man who strikes another, pays from ten to fifty *koffas* or baskets of dates; these baskets, by which everything in this place is estimated and appraised, are about three feet high, and four in circumference.

The dress of the men consists of a white cotton shirt and breeches, and a large calico cloth, striped white and blue, (manufactured at Cairo,) which is folded and thrown over the left shoulder, and is called *melaye*. On their heads they wear a cap of red worsted or cotton. These caps, chiefly made at Tunis, are a covering, characteristic of the Mussulman; and no Jew or Christian on the coasts of Barbary is permitted to wear them. At times of festival, the Siwahans dress themselves in *kaftans* and a *benisch*, such as the Arabs commonly wear when in towns.

The women of Siwah wear wide blue shifts, usually of cotton, which reach to the ankles, and a *melaye* (as above described), which they wrap round their head, from which it falls over the body in manner of a cloak.

They plait their hair into three tresses, one above the other; in the lowermost tress they insert various ornaments of glass, or false coral, or silver, and twist in long stripes of black leather, hanging down the back, and to the ends of which they fasten little bells. On the crown of their heads, the fix a piece of silk or woollen cloth, which floats behind. As ear-rings they wear two, and some women three, large silver rings, inserted as links of a chain: their necklace is glass imitating coral; those of the higher class wear round their necks a solid ring of silver, somewhat thicker than the collar usually worn by criminals in some parts of Europe; from this ring, by a chain of the same metal, hangs pendant a silver plate, engraved with flowers and other ornaments, in the Arabian taste. They further decorate their arms and legs, (just above the ancle,) with rings of silver, of copper, or of glass.

I can give no favourable account of the character of the people of Siwah, either from general repute, or from my own observation. I found them obtrusive and thievish. Our tents, and especially my own, were constantly surrounded and infested by this people; and our merchants were under the necessity of guarding their bales of goods, with more than ordinary attention, under apprehension not merely of pillage, but of general and hostile attack.

I was told much of the riches of this people, and should suppose there must be men of considerable property amongst them; as they have a very extensive traffic in dates with different and remote countries, pay no tribute, and have little opportunity of dissipating the money they receive. The policy of the Siwahans leads them to cultivate a strict and close amity with the Arabs to the north of their country, and who occasionally visit Siwah in small troops or parties, and carry on a trade of barter for the dates. Here our caravan disposed of part of its merchandize, receiving in exchange, dates, meat, and small baskets, in the weaving and context of which, the women of Siwah are remarkably neat and skilful, and in the making of which consists their chief employment. Diseases incident to the country and climate, and from which the natives most suffer, are the ague and fever,[1] and opthalmic affections,[2] or disorders of the eyes.

The language of Siwah,[3] whatever words or expressions may have crept in, from various intercourse of people, is not fundamentally Arabic; and this has led me to various conjectures. At first I looked for the root or origin of this language to the East; but on maturer consideration, and from communications with one of the *Tuaricks* from *Twat*, with whom I was in habits of intimacy, I am now satisfied of my former error, and that the language of Siwah is a dialect of that used throughout the great nation of Africa, to which my friend, the Tuarick, belonged, and which may be considered as the aboriginal.

The larger collection of Siwahan words, which I had first made, was lost with other papers, by an accident which I shall hereafter have occasion to mention.

The following list I had from a man of Siwah, whom I afterwards got acquainted with at Augila.

Sun,	*Itfuct*	Horse	*Achmar*
Clouds,	*Logmam*	Horses,	*Ickmare*
Ear,	*Temmesocht*	Have you a horse?	*Goreck Ackmar*
Head,	*Achfé*		
Eye,	*Taun*	Milk	*Achi*
Eyebrow,	*Temauin*	Flesh, or meat	*Acksum*
Beard,	*Itmert*		
Hand,	*Fuss*	Bread	*Tagora*
Camel,	*Lgum*	Oil	*Tsemur*

[1] Probably malaria and bacillary dysentery (shigellosis).
[2] Trachoma was probably the principal one.
[3] The language of Siwa is basically Berber.

Sheep,	Jelibb	Water	Aman
Cow,	Ftunest	Dates	Tena
Mountain,	Iddrarn	House	Achbén
Sabre,	Aus	Houses	Gebeun
Sword,	Limscha	Sand	Itjeda
Mouth,	Ambâ	Cap	Tschatschet
		Catacombs	Tum-megar

SECTION V

Antiquities of Siwah

As we approached the spot destined for our encampment in the Vale of Siwah, I descried to the westward some ruins of an extensive building, a few miles distant from the road, and concluded them to be the same as noticed by a late English traveller, (Mr. Brown,)[1] of whose discoveries I heard first in London, and afterwards, when in Egypt. Circumstances rendered it necessary for me to be particularly on my guard, and to defer any visit to, or actual inspection of, these antiquities, until I had retrieved the confidence of the natives, who, on my very first appearance, (as I was informed,) had taken me and my interpreter, for Christians; and to this supposition they were induced, from our fairer complexion, from our gait and manners, and from our Turkish dresses. When I took advantage of the disturbances at Cairo and its environs, to get introduced as a Mahomedan to the caravan, I could not indeed speak readily, either Turkish or Arabic; but in this, I flattered myself, the assuming character of a young Mamaluke might be my excuse; and I further derived confidence from the experience and abilities of my interpreter, who (a German by birth,) had been forced, twelve years past, to embrace the Mahommedan religion at Constantinople, and whose address and knowledge, I hoped, might preclude, or extricate me from, any consequences of jealousy or suspicion.

Considering the importance of my mission, and the great purpose of exploring the whole of Northern Africa, with which I was entrusted, perhaps it had been more wise and prudent on my part, not to have exposed myself to general intercourse, until better qualified to sustain the character I had assumed; had I so done in the present instance, and abstained from visiting the curiosities of Siwah, and exposing myself

[1] W. G. Browne, the author of *Travels in Africa, Egypt, and Syria, from the year 1792 to 1798* (London, 1806), visited Siwah in 1792.

Antiquities of Siwah

in the novelty of the attempt, to examinations and suspicions, I might have avoided a danger which (as will appear in the sequel) nearly proved fatal to myself, and therewith to the object of my voyage.

Making such candid admission of not having the requisite forbearance, with objects of so just curiosity in view, I proceed to state the course of my inquiries, and the result.

I first visited the ruins of the extensive edifice before observed. I accosted some men working in the gardens near, and questioning them as to what they knew of this building, they answered, 'that in former times Siwah was inhabited by infidels, most of whom lived in caves, but some inhabited these buildings.' One spokesman, pointing to a building in the centre, said, 'tradition tells us, *that edifice* was the hall in which the divan used to assemble; at time of its construction men were stronger than I am; for those huge stones serving as a roof to the fabric, were lifted up and placed there by two men only: there is much gold buried under the walls.' When I then entered into the ruins, I was followed by all the people near, and thus prevented examining the place with any accuracy. On a second visit I was not more successful; and when, after a few days, I returned thither again, some Siwahans directly said to me, 'thou undoubtedly art yet a Christian in thy heart, else why come so often to visit these works of Infidels.'[1] In order to maintain the character I had assumed, I was thus necessitated to abandon any further project of nice examination or admeasurement, and restrict myself to general observations, such as I now submit in detail as they occurred.

Ummebeda (the name given to the site of those ruins by the natives) lies near a village called *Scharkie* or *Agrmie*, between that place and an isolated mountain, on which a copious spring of fresh water is said to rise. The buildings are in such a state of delapidation, that a plain observer, who forms an opinion only from what he sees, and does not accommodate the object in application and conjecture to preconceived notions of a particular structure which he is to look for, and trace out, could scarcely, (I think) from these rude heaps, and mouldered and disjointed walls, suggest the precise form or original purpose of the building when first raised. Its materials might suggest, that it was built in the rudest ages, and when the Troglodytæ of these parts first left their caves, and in their first attempt of building, took their scheme and plan of architecture from their old mansions, heaping rock on rock, in

---

[1] This was because W. G. Browne, who had travelled as a Christian, had also shown deep interest in the antiquities of Siwa. His visit had been much resented, and many of the local inhabitants were openly hostile to him.

imitation of the dwelling places which nature had before furnished.

I ascertained the general bearings of the building by my compass, and found the outward walls constructed with aspects facing the four cardinal points, the aberration being only of twelve degrees, and which might have occurred from variation of the needle. The total circumference may be several hundred yards, and is to be traced out and followed by the foundations of a wall, in most parts visible, and which, from the masses remaining, appears to have been *very strong*. The outward wall, in most places, has been thrown down, and the materials carried away, and the interior ground has been every where turned up, and dug, in search of treasure.

In the centre of this extensive area, are seen the remains of an edifice, which perhaps may be regarded as the principal building, and to which all around may have been mere appendage, and subordinate.

The northern part of this building stands on a native calcareous rock, rising above the level of the general area, within the outer walls, about eight feet. The height of the edifice appears to be about twenty-seven feet; its width twenty-four, and its length ten or twelve paces. The walls are six feet in thickness, the exterior of which within and without is constructed of large hewn square stones, filled up in the interstice with small stones and lime. The ceiling is formed by vast blocks of stone, wrought and fitted to stretch over and cover the entire building. The breadth of each such mass of stone is about four feet, and the depth or thickness three feet. One of these stones of the roof has fallen in, and is broken; the entire southern wall of the building hath likewise tumbled, and the materials have mostly been carried away. But the people have not been able to remove the large fragments from the roof, which their ancestors were enabled to bring from the quarry, and to raise entire to the summit of the edifice. Such are the vicissitudes of art, of knowledge, and of human powers and means, as well as of human happiness and fortunes!

The stones that have fallen, lie sunk, with their surface lower than the base of the yet standing part of the building, and their bottom almost on a level with the area of the great inclosure. The appearance of these fallen stones of the southern wall, leads to a conjecture, that this extremity of the original edifice had its floor or base *lower than that of the northern part*. The entrances to this building are three, the principal one to the north, and the others to the east and west. The inside walls (beginning at half their height from the ground) are decorated with hieroglyphics sculptured in relief, but the figures seem not to have

Antiquities of Siwah

been sufficiently engraved in *alt*, or *salient*, to resist the ravages of time and weather; and in some places they are wholly mouldered and defaced, and especially on the ceiling.

On different parts of the wall appear marks of paint, and the colour seems to have been green. I could no where discover traces of the edifice having in any part been lined or inlaid with a finer stone or material. A few paces from the chief entrance, I observed two round stones, of about three feet diameter, in each of which there is a hollow in the middle, as if to receive the base of some statue or other ornament. The general material of which the building is constructed, is a lime-stone, containing petrifactions of shells and small marine animals; and such stone is to be found and dug up in the vicinity.

On examining the country around these ruins, I found the soil contiguous to the foundations of the outward wall on the south to be marshy, and was informed that it contained salt springs. I asked if no remarkable spring of fresh water was to be seen near; and was shewn one, about half a mile from the ruins, which takes its rise in a grove of date trees, and in a most romantic and beautiful situation: It is of sweet water and several small rivulets spring from it. It is not, however, its delightful scene that recommends it to the native of Siwah, but an opinion that it is a specific against certain diseases.

I am conscious that the above description of the remains of antiquity near Siwah, is by far too cursory and incomplete, for any purpose of just and accurate inference; and that it must yet remain a mere conjecture, whether these ruins are those of the famous *Temple of Jupiter Ammon*. It must be obvious, from many points I have adverted to in my description, that I had the site of this renowned temple in view, and that it was a principal object of my research. Circumstances I was under, and of which the reader is already apprised, prevented my pursuing this great subject of just and learned curiosity with the nicety of inspection, and care in the consideration, which I could have wished to employ. Supposing, on reference to ancient writers, the comparison of the buildings not to bear me out in the idea which I entertain; yet on many other grounds I should contend, that Siwah had been a residence of the ancient Ammonites. I draw my conclusion from the relative situation of the country; from the quality of the soil, from its fertility; from the information of its inhabitants, that no other such fruitful tract is to be found any where near; and, in addition to the certainty, at least, that some great and magnificent building once here stood, I derive a further conclusion from the numerous catacombs to be found in the vicinity, and which I shall have occasion more particularly to notice. In regard to the memorable Temple of Ammon, should even my own description of the existing vestiges of building not accurately agree with general accounts of that edifice, yet, notwithstanding, I must continue to hold an opinion, from the general appearance and from the situation of those ruins, that they *may be* remains of the *Temple of Jupiter Ammon*. A delineation and decipher of the hieroglyphic figures, which adorn the inner walls of the building, might be conclusive on this question.

I will further add on this subject, that on inquiry after *Edrisi's Santrich*, no one knew it even by name; but I was told that at a distance of seven days journey from *Siwah*, six from *Faiume*, and some days* from *Biljoradec*, there exists a country, similar to that of Siwah, its inhabitants less in number, and speaking the same language. That region I should take to be the *Minor Oasis* of the ancients. I speak of this place from mere report, and could gain no more accurate, or further account; perhaps it lies among the mountains which traverse the great Desert near *Ummesogeir*, extending towards the south.

I come now to the subject of *various catacombs*, to be found in the territory of Siwah, and which I was enabled more fully to examine, as lying in more sequestered spots, and where I was less liable to observation.

If I well understood my companion, an inhabitant of Siwah, there are four principal places, where catacombs are found. The first, *Belled-el-Kaffer*; the second, *Belled-el-Rumi*; both these terms, denote one and the same thing, namely, 'place or town of infidels;' the third is, *El-Mota*, or place of burial; the fourth, *Belled-el-Chamis*, or *Gamis*.[1] My inquiries were in particular directed to *El-Mota*, situated at the distance of about one mile north-east from Siwah. It is a rocky hill, with a number of catacombs on the declivity, but the most remarkable, are on the summit. There is a separate entrance to each, and the descent inwards is gentle and gradual. The passage from the aperture, leads to a door-way, from which the space of the room is enlarged, and on each side, are smaller excavations for containing the mummies. The stones rising from the threshold are cut in a form that shews a door to have been formerly hung, and to have closed the entrance. The catacombs are of different extent, and each is wrought with great labour and neatness of work, and especially the uppermost, which contains no

---

* The distance from Biljoradec is not clearly expressed in the original.
[1] Khamisa.

traces of any mummy. In others are found various remains. I long, but in vain, searched for an entire head: I found fragments, and especially of the *occiput* in abundance, but none with any investiture remaining; and even in the *occiputs* most entire I could not discover any stain or mark of their once having been filled with *resin*. The cloth still adhered to some *ribs*, but so decayed, that nothing could be further distinguished, than that the stuff in which the mummy had been wrapt, was of the coarsest kind.

The ground in all these catacombs has been dug and explored in search of treasure, and I was told, by my guide, that in every one of these sepulchres gold has been, and is yet sometimes, found at the place where the head of the mummy lay.

There is every probability that entire mummies might be discovered in the catacombs at a greater distance to *westward* of Siwah. I was credibly informed, that besides the open catacombs on the mountains, there are others under ground, and the entrance of which is to be found at no great depth; and that *Biut-el-Nazari*, (houses of Christians, synonymous here to Infidels,) exist on both sides of a long subterraneous passage, forming a communication, between two catacomb-mountains. The catacombs met with on *Gibel-el-belled*, being the hill on which *Siwah* is built, are small, and consist of a little antichamber, leading generally to two caverns where the mummies were deposited. Of these the two most remarkable are two large and high caverns on the north side; the one is twenty, the other sixteen feet square, and both are open to the north.

There are likewise two other caverns, of similar dimensions, but not so lofty, to be seen westward of *Siwah*, and leading to *Augila*; their entrance is low and narrow, and the two excavations are so near, that the partition, as appears from a small perforation, is only ten inches thick.

Quitting the subject of antiquities in the territory of Siwah, I have only to add, that in the nearest plain west of the town, there are other massive remains of some building, but which bear no token or note of remote antiquity, such as may be attributed to the ruins I first described.

SECTION VI

Departure from Siwah. — Journey to Schiacha,
and Danger which the Traveller there incurred

Having remained eight days at Siwah; on the 29th September, at three in the afternoon, we broke up our encampment, and proceeded a three hours march, when we again pitched our tents at foot of a hill. The next day we began our journey late, being delayed till one o'clock, in search of a slave who belonged to a court-officer of the Sultan of Fezzan, and who had absconded from the caravan. Whilst the man was looking for, I set out with a view of inspecting some catacombs which I descried on the neighbouring hills, but was stopped at some distance by a lake of seven or eight miles in circumference, formed at the base of the mountain by the conflux of springs and small pools of water, which the rains at this season had swollen and brought together. Returning to the camp, I took my telescope to examine the appearances I was not enabled closely to inspect, when the first object on the mountain which presented itself to my view was the Negro after whom the search was making. I gave no notice of my discovery, the poor fellow having a good character, and having been driven to the attempt of flight by the extreme severity of his master. I am sorry to say there was little hope of his final escape, the Siwahans having promised to deliver him up. This day we travelled till half an hour after sunset. The next day we marched at two hours before day-break, and halted at nine. The fourth day brought us to the fruitful valley of *Schiacha*.[1]

The mountains by which we travelled from *Siwah* to this spot, are branches of those which I have mentioned as appearing, at all times, to north of our way through the Desert, and often at but little distance. They rise abruptly, and as precipices, from the level ground, and shew a face of mere rock, without the least covering of soil or even of sand. Their appearance, taken together with that of the *sea-sand* which covers the Desert, indicate this vast tract to have been flooded, and at a period later than the great deluge. In the sandy plain below these mountains is seen the surface of a vast calcareous rock, containing no substance of petrifaction, whereas the mountains near consist of limestone, crowded and filled with fragments of marine animals and shells. The strata of all these rocky hills lay horizontal.

Westward of *Siwah*, I found two banks or heaps of calcined shells, some of the size of two inches over. My interpreter told me, that taking his road at some distance from me, he saw a mountain standing singly and unconnected with others, composed entirely of shells. Many such vast isolated mounds are to be seen throughout the whole of this district, and the bed-joints or interstices of their strata of stone (always horizontal), being filled up with reddish, friable, calcareous substance, they often resemble pyramids, and in so exact and illusive a manner,

[1] Scheibat.

that more than once I was deceived into expectation of arrival at such building. The architecture of the ancient Egyptians was of the vast and gigantic kind; and builders of such ambitious temper and stupendous scheme, might readily entertain the idea of transforming a mountain into a pyramid, shaping the huge rock, already in form partly adapted, and casing it with wrought stones on the outside, as they might prefer. Some of the learned have given an opinion, that the Pyramids of *Giza* and of *Saccara*,[1] were not originally erections from the base, but merely hills of earth or stone, shaped and covered by the labour of man. The idea is plausible, though certainly to be controverted, by reasons to be drawn from history, and from other the best sources of fact and argument.

I now proceed to the recital of an event in which I was personally and principally concerned. I shall give the recital in detail, as, in its consequences, being of the highest import to the future safety of myself, and therewith to the progress of discovery which I have engaged in; and, as it has afforded me self-confidence and new encouragement, ever favourable to the success of the enterprize, so will it, I trust, give satisfaction to those who have employed me, inspiring just and well-founded hopes of my finally accomplishing the great purpose entrusted to my care.

The state of quiet and security usually attending our encampments was interrupted, whilst at *Schiacha*, by the arrival of some Siwahans, who, about eight o'clock in the evening, came with intelligence, that a numerous horde of Arabs from the vicinity of *Faiume*[2] were hovering in the Desert, ready to fall upon our caravan. These messengers at the same time assured us, that the people of Siwah had resolved to come to our assistance, and to escort us to the next watering-place; adding, 'that their little army would arrive in a few hours, determined to risk with us every thing in opposing the attack of the Bedouins, whose force they represented as consisting of from 800 to 1000 men. Our leader, the Sheik of the Twaters, immediately assembled the principal people of the caravan, when it was decided not to desert our post, but to await the enemy. Scarcely was our little council broke up, when we heard from afar the braying of some hundred asses, giving notice of the approach of the *Siwahans*. They use this animal on their military excursions, from the advantage it affords of more easily proceeding by narrow and rugged passes among the mountains, and evading or attacking any enemy, who from ignorance of the country, or from the

[1] Saqqâra.   [2] El Faiyûm.

nature of its cattle requiring safer roads, is obliged to confine its march to broader defiles or vallies. Some men were immediately dispatched from the caravan, requiring the Siwahans to halt at half a mile distance from our post. The night passed in disquietude and alarm: each got his arms in readiness, and prepared for a battle on the ensuing day. A little before sunrise, the Siwahans advanced on foot, and gave apprehension of immediate attack. Some *Augilans* rode forward, to inquire their intentions, and were answered, 'that the caravan had nothing to fear': on reporting this to the Sheik, he sent the messengers back, to say he should consider and treat them as enemies, if they advanced a step further. On this message the *Siwahans* halted, formed a circle, and invited some *Augilans* to a conference. During all this time, I remained quiet with my baggage, having sent my interpreter to collect intelligence of what was passing. Seeing him return, and judging from his manner and haste, that he had something of importance to communicate, I ran to meet him. He immediately accosted me with, 'cursed be the moment, when I determined upon this journey; we are both of us unavoidably lost men; they take us for Christians and spies, and will assuredly put us to death.' With these words he left me, and ran to the baggage, where he exchanged his single gun for my double barrelled one, and armed himself with two brace of pistols. I upbraided him with his want of firmness, told him 'a steady and resolute conduct could alone preserve ourselves and friends, and reminded him that his present behaviour was precisely such as to give weight to the suspicions entertained: I further urged, 'that on his own account he had nothing to fear, having for twelve years been a Mahommedan, and perfectly acquainted with the religion and customs; that myself alone was in danger, and that I hoped to avert it, provided *he* did not intermeddle with my defence.' 'Friend, (answered he,) you will never hear of danger: but this time you will pay for your temerity.'

Perceiving that terror had wholly deprived him of the necessary temper and recollection, I now left him to himself, and walked up unarmed, but with a firm and manly step, to this tumultuous assembly.

I entered the circle, and offered the Mahometan salutation, '*Assulam Alckum*,' but none of the *Siwahans* returned it. Some of them immediately exclaimed, — 'You are of the new Christians from Cairo,[1] and come to explore our country.' Had I at this time, been as well acquainted with Mahometan fanaticism, and the character of the Arabs, as I have been since, I should have deduced my defence from the very

---

[1] That is to say, French.

terms of the accusation, and stated that I was indeed from Cairo, having fled from the Infidels; as it was, I answered nothing to this general clamour, but sat down and directed my speech to one of the Chiefs, whose great influence I knew, and who had been often in my tent whilst at *Siwah*. 'Tell me, brother (said I,) hast thou ever before known 300 armed men take a journey of three days, in pursuit of two men, who dwelt in their *midst* for ten days, who had eaten and drank with them as friends, and whose tents were open to them all? Thyself hast found us praying and reading the Koran; and now thou sayest we are Infidels from Cairo; *that is*, one of those from whom we fly! Dost thou not know, that it a great sin to tell one of the faithful that he is a Pagan?' I spoke this with an earnest and resolute tone, and many of the congregation seemed gained over by it, and disposed to be favourable to me: the man replied, 'that he was convinced we were not Infidels, that he had persuaded no one to this pursuit, and as far as depended on him alone, he was ready to return to *Siwah*.' On this I turned to one of the vulgar, who was communicating some of the accusations against me to the people of our caravan. 'Be thou silent, (said I,) would to God, that I were able to speak well the Arabic, I would then ask questions of thee, and of hundreds like thee, who are less instructed in the *Islam* than I am.' An old man on this observed, 'This man is younger than the other, and yet more courageous!' I immediately continued, 'My friend is not afraid of thee, but thou oughtest to have fears of my friend: dost thou know what it is to reproach a man, who lives with sultans and with princes, with being an Infidel?' I was then asked for what purpose we carried Christian papers. I now found that my interpreter had unwarily shewn a passport which I had obtained from General Bonaparte, with a view not to be detained at the French posts through which I was to pass to the caravan. My interpreter at this moment came up, and finding me alive, and the assembly less angry and violent, than when on being first questioned, he had exasperated them by inconsiderate and perplexed answers; he recovered himself, and stood sufficiently composed and collected, whilst I explained partly in German, partly in Arabic, what had passed. Knowing, however, that the paper in question would be demanded, and not choosing to trust to his prudence in the manner of producing it; I went myself for it to the tent, and returning, brought likewise a Koran with me. I immediately tendered the paper to a Chief of the *Siwahans*, who having unfolded it, asked, 'if any bystander could read it.' I could not help smiling at the question, perilous as was my situation. The same question was then put to us, when I answered, 'that we did not understand what it contained, but were told, it would allow us to quit Cairo without being molested.' 'This is the book, (interrupted my interpreter,) which I understand:' and immediately took the Koran from my hand. We were ordered, by reading in it, to give proof of our being truly of the religion. Our learning in this respect went far indeed beyond the simple ability of reading. My companion knew the entire Koran by heart, and as for me, I could even then write Arabic, and well too: which with these people, was an extraordinary proficiency in learning. We had scarcely given a sample of our respective talents, when the chiefs of our caravan, who to this moment had been silent, now took loudly our part; and many of the Siwahans too, interfered in our favour. In short, the inquiry ended to our complete advantage, though not without the murmuring of some in the multitude, who lost the hopes of plunder which the occasion might have afforded.

Thus the character of Mussulman which I had assumed was firmly established, and I shall not be subjected in future, to like inquiries, on which, perhaps, more decisive proofs might be required, and which I could not give. The security of my future voyage is thus assured, and so great an advantage more than compensates for some losses attending the above incident, but which yet I must regret.

During the time I was first in conference with the people of Siwah, and those of the caravan, my baggage was left with my interpreter; who in the paroxysms of his fears, and indeed with no light apprehensions of our bales of goods being searched, took my remains of mummies, my specimens of mineralogy, my *more detailed* remarks, made on my way from Cairo to *Schiacha*, and generally my books, and gave them to a confidential slave of my Arab inmate, to bury them in a bog, of which there are a great number at Schiacha; this was done, and I never afterwards could retrieve them.

SECTION VII

Departure from Schiacha — arrival at Augila

On the fifth day (reckoning by our departure from Siwah), we left Schiatha, and travelled about four hours, when we encamped. The next morning in two hours and a half, we came to a district called *Torfare*,[1] where we halted to collect fresh water: from this place we

---

[1] Bir el Tarfaui.

departed at four in the afternoon of the same day, and continued our march until eight the next morning, through a desert, the level of which was interrupted by numerous sand-hills; at eight o'clock we stopped to refresh, and rested till two o'clock, when we again pressed forward, and continued our march till eight in the morning, when we encamped till one. At one we again proceeded, travelled all night, and till three o'clock the next morning, when the party with whom I travelled, discovered, that during the night, we had wandered from the caravan; we resolved thereon to halt and await the return of day. We placed our baggage by the side of each camel, to be enabled on emergency, to load again with dispatch, and I laid me down to sleep on the sand, with the bridle in one hand, and my firelock in the other, and slept soundly till sunrise.

We now discovered our caravan; and at the same time, that we were not above half a mile from a spot, fruitful and abounding in water. We immediately made up to the place and encamped. The journey from *Torfare* to this spot, was the most disagreeable and fatiguing that in the course of all my travels I had experienced. Both men and cattle were so wearied and exhausted, that as soon as the baggage was unladen, all resorted to sleep. We here reposed the whole day, and the next set forth for Augila, by short marches, (altogether not amounting to more than nine hours travel); we used no haste, as having nothing to apprehend, being now in the country of our friends.

Our entry into *Mojabra*,[1] one of the three places belonging to the dominion of Augila, was solemn and affecting, as the greater part of the merchants of our caravan had here habitations and families. The Bey of *Bengasi*, Viceregent for the Bashaw of *Tripoly*, and at that time resident at *Augila*, sent about twenty of his Arabs to note in writing the burden of the camels, and for which they demanded a small duty. These Arabs then ranged themselves, and formed a right wing to our caravan, drawn up for procession. The merchants who had horses formed the left, and the pilgrims and ordinary Arabs formed the centre, headed by the Sheik preceded by a green flag. The pilgrims marched on singing; and the Arabs made their horses prance and curvet, and so continued until we approached near to *Mojabra*; where a number of old men and children met us, to felicitate and get a first embrace of their sons and relations, whom, on hearing of the French invasion in Egypt, they had given over as lost.

We pitched our tents in a spot adjoining the town, and were

[1] Trigh el Majabra.

most hospitably entertained. The following night I proceeded on my journey towards *Augila*, in company with two merchants, one of whom procured me a lodging on my arrival, it being the intention of the caravan to stop longer than usual at this place.

There are three towns within the territory of *Augila*; Augila, the capital, and *Mojabra*, and *Meledda*. The two last are near to each other, and both about four hours from Augila; *Mojabra* to the south, and *Meledda* to north of the road by which we passed. *Mojabra* and *Meledda* are occasionally comprehended in the general name of Fallo,[1] designating the district.

Augila, a town well known in the time of Herodotus, covers a space of about one mile in circumference. It is badly built, and the streets are narrow and not kept clean. The houses are built of a limestone, dug from the neighbouring hills, and consist only of one story or ground floor. The apartments are dark, there being no aperture for light but the door; and are generally ranged round a small court, to which the entrance of each room faces, for purpose of collecting the more light. The public buildings, comparatively, are yet more mean and wretched. *Mojabra* is of smaller extent, but appears proportionally more populous than *Augila*. The inhabitants of *Meledda* are chiefly employed in agriculture: those of *Mojabra* engage mostly in trade, and pass their lives in travelling betwixt Cairo and Fezzan. The people of *Augila* are of a more sedentary disposition; though some of these too, were with our caravan.

The men of the above places, who engage in the caravan trade, generally keep three houses; one at *Kardassi*, near Cairo; one at *Mojabra*, and a third at *Zuila*, or sometimes at *Mourzouk*. Many have a wife and family establishment at each of these houses; and others take a wife for the time, if the stay of the caravan is longer than usual. The men from their very youth devote themselves to such traveller's life. Boys from thirteen to fourteen years of age, accompanied our caravan the long and toilsome journey from *Augila* to *Fezzan* on foot, or at least seldom mounting a horse. In observing the general character of this people I could not but remark a degradation, self-interestedness, and mean and shuffling disposition, derived from early habits of petty trade, and the manner in which it was conducted, as contra-distinguishing those engaged in this traffic, and those who remained at home.

The men of the country are engaged in gardening and agriculture; but in the last to no great extent. The women are very industrious in

[1] Jalo.

manufacturing coarse woollen cloths of five yards in length and a yard and a half wide, which are called *Abbe*, and are sent in considerable quantities to *Fezzan*. These constitute the chief clothing of this people; they wrap them about their bodies, and without even a shirt or shift under.

Round *Augila* the country is level and the soil sandy, yet, being well watered, is tolerably fertile. Corn is not cultivated in quantity sufficient for subsistence of the people. The Arabs of *Bengasi*, distant about thirteen days journey, import annually both wheat and barley; and this their corn caravan is generally accompanied by flocks of sheep for sale.

The inhabitants of this region can generally speak the *Arabic*, but their vulgar language is a dialect similar to that of Siwah, above noticed.

CHAPTER II

SECTION I

Augila, to the Confines of Temissa

Soon after our arrival at *Augila*, a man was sent off by the chief of the caravan to examine the watering-places as far as the borders of the kingdom of FEZZAN. The precaution became necessary from the increased number of people and camels, now forming this great caravan, and the possibility that, from want of rain or other causes, the springs on the usual route might not afford sufficient water for so large a body. The messenger being ordered to use the utmost dispatch, returned on the twelfth day with the happy intelligence, that water was in plenty, and that he met with nothing to impede our journey.

Accordingly, the 27th October was the day fixed for our departure from *Augila*, and myself and party quitted the town the preceding evening, and encamped in the open air, to be among the first at the breaking up and movement of the caravan. The next morning we set out before sunrise, and proceeded in a direction west by south. Our caravan was increased by companies of merchants from *Bengasi*, *Merote*, and *Mojabra*, in all about 120 men. Many of the inhabitants of *Augila* and *Fallo*, accompanied us part of the way, and, as a mark of honour and attention, pranced their horses and fired their muskets round us. This party had scarcely taken their leave, when an Arab riding to us in haste, gave information, that we were pursued by a large body of horse, and that they were even then close upon our rear. On this intelligence the camels were immediately driven by the slaves and boys to a rising ground, and those who had arms mustered to cover the retreat, and prevent the enemy's irruption and pillage. At the moment we were preparing for action, we were happily undeceived. The horsemen were troops of the Bey of *Bengasi* (then resident at Augila as I before mentioned), and who, hearing the complimentary discharge of firelocks by the friends who had just left us, thought we might have been attacked, and came out to our assistance.

We now resumed our march, and continued it till sunset, each boasting of his prowess, and what feat of arms he had before done, and what he would have done had the Bey's troops been hostile.

The evening we encamped in the open Desert, on a spot devoid of water, and so completely barren, that not even a single blade of herb for our camels was to be found, and we were obliged to feed them with what provender we had with us.

On the *second* day we advanced for twelve hours through the Desert, the plain consisting of soft limestone, sometimes bare, but more frequently covered with quicksand.

On the morning of the *third* day, the scene somewhat altered; detached hills rose here and there, taking from the uniformity of the before level desert. These mounds seemed to derive their origin from a base of calcareous rock, round, and on which the sands had gathered, and been heaped up by the winds, and on some to a considerable height. From this district of hillocks and hills, commences a range of mountains called *Morai-je*, stretching far to ssw, and seemingly also branching towards the north. This day we encamped two hours before sunset, for the purpose of awaiting the return of some *Twaters*, who separated from us about noon, to seek pasture for their camels. Our camp was pitched on the summit of a hill, at foot of which were spread a quantity of petrified shells and marine substances imbedded in a soft limestone.

On the *fourth day* we struck our tents very early in the morning with the view of reaching a particular spot for our next encampment, where fresh water was to be found. The first part of our day's journey we travelled on a continued plain on the heights of the mountain. The ascent from the east had been gentle, but coming to the western declivity, we found the way down most steep and difficult. It is noted by the name of *Neddeek* by the Arabs. The way down is not only steep, but so narrow that the whole caravan was obliged to travel in single file, camel after camel. The perpendicular height of this (almost) precipice was about eighty feet. From the verge of the summit the prospect was most beautiful. A narrow vale, extending far beyond the reach of the eye, was illumined at some distance by the rise of the sun, whose beams slanted over the mountain we had to pass; in regarding the level and brightness of the distant scene, we looked over a fore-ground of craggy rocks, and abrupt and frightful chasms yet remaining in gloomy shade; and the contrast of bright and terrific scene made the stronger impression on our minds, whilst from this awful height we had to meditate on the difficulty and danger of our passage down to the plain. I followed not the narrow track of the caravan, but picked myself out a way down the mountain with some difficulty and risk. Coming to its base, I observed a piece of petrified wood, of about two feet long and eight inches broad; it was the only such fragment I saw in these parts. Forward in the plain to some distance, lay huge stones, or rather rocks. They probably have been there from the time of some great flood, which, on every consideration of what I now and before saw, I must suppose to have inundated these countries, at some distant period, distinctively and subsequent to the deluge mentioned in Scripture. At some distance I cast a look back to the *Neddeek*; its appearance of wild forms of rock broken into or rent asunder, confirmed my idea of irruption of waters, and that the deluge had rushed from the west. Our march was now directed along the valley, skirted by mountains nearly of the same height and form as those we had passed; at length it expanded into a wider plain called *Sultin*, where, at one o'clock, and after ten hours journey we encamped, and with water in plenty to replenish our bags for the ensuing days.

The *fifth* and *sixth* days we journied on through this Desert; for so, from its barrenness and appearance, it may be justly termed, though throughout abounding in springs. The waters I should, however, suppose to be bitter, as the Arabs dig no wells in this district.

The *seventh* day our way lay between ranges of hills, and in the evening we came to a spot affording not only verdure but *trees*, and that to a considerable extent of country; under these trees we encamped, and continued travelling through a very grove the best part of the ensuing day, when our road opened to a Desert chequered with hills, and scabeous calcareous rocks. From one of these eminences I first observed the mountainous region *Harutsch*,[1] so known to and dreaded by travellers. The marvellous narratives of calamity therein suffered, and which had been recited to me on our way; and the black and dreary appearances which the face of the country offered to my view, roused my curiosity, and I pressed on before the caravan to examine a lower mountain, which, like a promontory jutted towards us before the rest. The soil of the desert near was stony, the stones consisting of compact calcareous limestone. The mountain presented the form of an imperfect cone: its strata I take to have lain originally horizontal, as those of the hills passed on our route, but from some convulsion, they are now broken, turned over, and promiscuously confused. The substance of which the mountain consists, on fracture, and as to colour, resembles the ferruginous basalt; and such I take it to be. Range upon range of dreary and black mountains succeed, and form the only prospect!

[1] El Harug.

As the caravan was approaching, I dismounted, and sat me down close to a large stone which formed my table, whilst I partook of such frugal fare as the Arab carries with him on these occasions. When I rose up the caravan had passed the prominence of the mountain and disappeared. The ground, however, being firm, and thence the road to be easily traced, I was under no anxiety; though after half an hour's march, somewhat surprised at not yet discovering my old companions, I took out my spy-glass, when I descried at a little distance four *Moroccans*, whom I rode up to and accosted: they told me that the caravan had already encamped at a short distance from the road, to pasture their camels, and that they themselves were in search of water to satisfy their thirst. I was inclined to be of their party, but was fearful of giving uneasiness to my people by longer absence from the caravan, which, from its fires now kindled, I easily discovered and rejoined.

The *ninth* day we travelled between black and dreary hills; our road meandering through narrow and dismal ravines, now and then spreading to some width, having some grass and even a tree, and sometimes opening to a space of valley, of which the herbage looked fresh, and even luxuriant, from the copious rains which fall in this mountainous region, fertilizing the soil after it is washed down.

Our watering-place consisted of pools of mere rain water from the hills, and was situate at the edge of a valley of about six miles curcuit, shewing not only a rich verdure, but bearing shrubs and trees. Here we saw some *gazelles*, but so shy, that we could not get a shot at them.

We passed our *tenth, eleventh,* and *twelfth* days incessantly almost in march through this dreary solitude; yet we could not expedite our journey as we wished. Sometimes we were obliged to wander from our direct line with the windings of our only path; at other times we were forced to move on slowly and with difficulty, over layers of loose stone for half a mile together: in the course of one of those days, I ventured on a walk to the *south*, accompanied by my Arabian servant and some *Twaters*. We could easily, on foot, outstrip the caravan under all its impediments of march. Every where I found the mountains of like appearance as exhibited to the traveller on the common road, with the only difference that views even more dreary and terrific occasionally caught the eye: it having been matter of course to work and conduct the road along the least rugged vallies.

On the afternoon of the *thirteenth* day, we broke at length from the dark region into an extensive plain. Here we continued on march for some hours, when we came to ranges of low calcareous mountains, and about sunset encamped at the entrance of the defile which leads through them.

On the morning of the *fifteenth* I placed myself among the foremost of the caravan, consisting chiefly of poor pilgrims, hastening to precede the other company, with a view of first quenching their thirst at the spring, which on that day we were to arrive at. On coming to the watering-place, called Ennaté, I perceived a *well* already cleaned and in order, and several *Twaters* lying around. I placed myself near and prepared for breakfast. An old man had laboured a shorter cut across the sand to be sooner at the well; after mutual salutation, I offered him a handful of dates and some meat; these he thankfully accepted, kissing them and rubbing them on his forehead. Putting the provisions down on the ground, he got to the spring, and continued drinking for a considerable time, and recited his prayer *Elham-Dulillah* with great devotion. He told me, that for three days past he had been without his requisite portion of water. This man (as himself told me), was above sixty years old; and this was his third voyage from *Fez* to *Mecca*, without possessing the least means of accommodation for the journey; without preparation of food for his subsistence; nay, even without water, excepting what commiseration and the esteem in which his pilgrimage was held, might procure for him, from the charity and regard of travellers better provided in the caravan.

We reposed the rest of the day on this spot, distant from our last encampment four hours march, and our chief dispatched a messenger to Mourzouk, to give notice of arrival of the caravan on the frontier of the kingdom, and to bear a letter of respect to the sultan from each merchant individually.

And now, on the *sixteenth*, (dating from our departure from *Augila*), we came again to the society of men: a march of nine hours bringing us to *Temissa*,[1] situated within the territory of Fezzan.

SECTION II

Observations on the Region of the Harutsch

The mountainous desert of *Harutsch* is the most remarkable region that came within scope of my observation during this journey; its extent has been stated to me at seven days journey over, from north to south; and at five days from east to west; but in a subsequent voyage from

[1] Tmessa.

Fezzan to Tripoly, I fell in again with a branch or tract of the *Harutsch*, and was there told, that it yet extended further to the *west*. At Mourzouk, too, I was informed of black mountains on the road leading southward to Bornou, on whose heights the climate was of very cold temperature, and whence the people of Mourzouk obtained their iron; and I conjecture that such mountainous tract may be a further branch of the *Harutsch*, though having indeed no positive information or proof of the immediate junction or connection of these regions.

The rugged, broken, and altogether wild and terrific scene which this desert tract affords, leads strongly to the supposition that its surface at some period took its present convulsed form and appearance from volcanic revolution. Its inequalities of ground are no where of great altitude. The general face of the country shews continued ranges of hills, running in various directions, rising from eight to twelve feet only above the level of the intermediate ground; and between which branches, (on perfect flats, and without any gradual ascent of base or fore-ground,) rise up lofty isolated mountains, whose sides are exceeding steep from the very base. A mountain of this description, situated midway on journey over this desert, and north of our caravan road, is by the Arabs termed *Stres*; it has the appearance of being split from the top down to the middle. I was prevented from particular examination of it, but soon, on our caravan halting, had the opportunity of inspecting another of the same kind.

This mountain, I perceived, from the foot to the summit, to be covered with detached stones, such as wholly constitute the lower hills. The small plain from which this mountain rose, was encompassed by rows of hills, such as above described, closely running into each other, and connected as a wall. The flat within was over-spread with white quicksand, on which lay, irregularly scattered, large blocks of stone, of like nature and substance as that generally throughout this desert. With some trouble I procured a sample of the earthy stratum beneath the sand; it seemed to me, at the time, to have the appearance of ashes thrown out from a volcano; but I have since lost the paper which contained the specimen, and cannot further confirm the accuracy of my first observation. In the vicinity of this mountain, I found stones of smaller bulk and a reddish colour, resembling that of burnt bricks; some of these were one-half red, the other blackish; the red part had not the same weight or density, on fracture, as the black: the former is more porous and spongy, and bears a general resemblance to slags or scoriæ.

The stony substance, of which the mass of these mountains consists, varies in colour and density; in some parts heavy and compact, in others having small holes and cavities. These species of stone are intermingled, and I could not discover in either, any extraneous matter or substance.

The stratification or lay of these stones is perfectly horizontal, but often disturbed; parts of the first layer sinking into and mixing with the second below, and the second with the third. Sometimes the strata take an oblique direction; sometimes are promiscuously confused, and sometimes no strata appear at all; and a series of low hills is formed of one solid mass of rock, with fissures in direction to the north. The plain too shews occasionally level rock of the like nature and substance, in parts where bare of sand or soil. The whole of this region of hillocks, hills, rocks, and mountains, is, in parts, intersected by vales, occasionally having water; and though the soil is of white sand, yet it is so far fertile as to produce single trees, and pasturage for beasts; in these productive spots are frequently to be seen the tracks and slots of game. Often, when I thought I could so do without danger of losing my way, I struck into one of the narrow vales running apparently in the same direction as our caravan road; and occasionally led away to defiles becoming more narrow and rugged, I repented my indiscretion, whilst thus separated from my company, and exposed to attack from Bedouins, with dependence for safety on my single sabre and pistols. On regaining the caravan, it yet occurred that my danger had not been great, for what Arab robber could look for a traveller in such a tract, or suppose any hardy enough to wander therein from his troop, excepting, indeed, some wretched Moroccan pilgrim in search of water!

In the course of these excursions, on the side of one of these narrow vales, winding among the mountains, I observed a narrow branch or inlet, towards the termination of which the rocky heights from each side closed, and formed a cavern of about nine feet deep, and five feet wide; and, considering its appearance and situation in this desolate, obscure, and mournful region, I was inspired with feelings, as on viewing the entrance to the subterraneous world, and very passage, *ad inferos*.

My interpreter told me, that at some time when I had taken another path, and when the caravan was travelling about midway through the mountains, he saw a cavern in which the stones to a considerable depth were black, and that under these lay a stratum of white stones. On travelling afterwards from Fezzan to Tripoly, in continuation of the Harutsch, (as I supposed it), I myself observed ranges of basaltic hills, alternate with ranges of calcareous hills. My interpreter brought me a specimen of the white stone taken from the cave himself had seen, but I think was not happy in its selection, it consisting of a mere lump of indurated argillaceous earth, such as often adheres to limestone.

In respect to the many hills, and their curious ranges and direction, the *Harutsch* exhibits a similitude to the excrescences on the bordering mountains I refer to in a subsequent journey; it agrees too in the circumstance of single stones scattered on the surface, which, in the Harutsch, are distinguished as being only of one species or substance, peculiar to the district. There is too a further analogy in the plains formed of bare rock; and in the white quicksand covering other levels, and laying round the mountains, and up their base, though to no considerable height.

Contiguous to the *Harutsch-el-assuat*, or black Harutsch, lies the white Harutsch, or *Harutsch-el-abiat*. The country denoted by this appellation is a vast plain, interspersed with mounds or isolated hills, and spreads to the mountains rising towards Fezzan. The stones covering the surface of this plain have the appearance of being glazed,[1] and so too every other substance, and even the rocks which occasionally rise or project from the level. Among the stones are found fragments of large petrified marine animals, but mostly shells closed up and insolidated. Even the largest of these stones struck or thrown forcibly on others, give a shrill sound, and the fracture presents a vitreous appearance.

The low, bare, calcareous hills which border the plain, are, by the Arabs, comprised in the *Harutsch-el-abiat*; but they are of a nature very different. Of all that I have seen, this range of hills contains the most petrifactions. These mountains rise immediately steep from the level, and the matter of which they are formed is alone friable limestone, in which the petrifactions are so loosely imbedded, that they may be taken out with ease; they consist of petrified conchs, snail-shells, fish, and other marine substances. I found heads of fish that would be a full burthen for one man to carry. In the adjacent vallies are shells in great number, and of the same kind as those found on the great plain, and which, as I before mentioned, have the appearance of being glazed.

[1] This well-known desert phenomenon is caused by wind-blown sand.

SECTION III

Arrival at Temissa, and further Journey

We were yet an hour's march distant from Temissa, when the inhabitants of that place greeted the caravan with welcome and congratulation on arrival. They put questions without number, concerning our health, intermingling wishes for peace in the Arabian stile and manner. The incessant repetition of the same words appeared to me extraordinary, but I was soon give to understand, that it denoted polite manners, according to usage of the country.[1] The more noble and educated the man, the oftener did he repeat his questions. A well dressed young man attracted my particular attention, as an adept in the perseverance and redundancy of salutation. Accosting an Arab of Augila, he gave him his hand, and detained him a considerable time with his civilities, when the Arab being obliged to advance with greater speed to come up again with his companions, the youth of Fezzan thought he should appear deficient in good manners if he quitted him so soon: for near half a mile he kept running by his horse, whilst all his conversation was, How doest thou fare? Well, how art thou thyself? Praised be God thou art arrived in peace! God grant thee peace! How dost thou do, &c. &c.

On our approach to Temissa, the pilgrims arranged themselves with their kettle drum and green flag. The merchants formed a troop, at head of the caravan, and pranced and curvetted their horses as they led on, and in this manner we passed on to our place of encampment near the town, whilst the women assembled without the walls, welcomed us in their Arabian custom with reiterated and joyful exclamation, to which we answered by discharge of our fire-arms; and these compliments continued till we pitched our tents in a grove of date trees.

All was gladness and felicitation this day throughout the caravan, and especially amongst the merchants. Perhaps for years past the caravan had not left Cairo with so gloomy and fearful a prospect as on the present occasion, when an army of Infidels had so suddenly assailed and taken the principal city of Africa, destroyed the ruling power of the Mamelukes, and threatened immediate abolition to the trade for slaves, on which the caravan solely subsists. It was but a few days after our

[1] It may appear surprising that after so long an association with Arabs Hornemann should have found repetitious greetings 'extraordinary'. But Fezzan had acquired many of its manners and customs from the Western Sudan where repetitious greetings are sometimes even more pronounced than in Arab countries.

leaving Cairo, that the appearance of an horde of Bedouins gave alarm to our caravan; indeed it was extraordinary that we should reach Siwah without attack, as the Arabs had of late been so bold, as even to pass the French posts, and rob near to the very capital. Whilst at Siwah, we were apprised of the movements of different hordes of Bengasi and other Arabian tribes; and not far from our road between Augila and the frontiers of Fezzan, we descried numerous vestiges of their depredation, viewing some hundreds of dead camels and beasts of burthen which they had plundered and left, probably from deficiency of water for their support. They had robbed in the neighbourhood, and even made an attack on Temissa, and had waited for us in these parts for a considerable time, till they concluded that, from the conquest of Cairo, our caravan would not this year proceed. Being therefore now in no immediate danger, and our future route laying through the inhabited districts of the realm of Fezzan, our fears at once vanished.

Temissa is at present a place of little importance, containing not more than forty men bearing arms. It is built on a hill, and surrounded by a high wall, capable of securing it against hostile incursion if in due repair, but in many parts the wall is decayed and fallen. I was told there were inscriptions to be discovered on some of the buildings, but I found none, and rather suppose none such ever existed, the ruins consisting of mere dilapidated houses, built with limestone, and cemented with a reddish mortar. These remains, however, shew that the ancient inhabitants of Temissa were more expert in the art of building than the present, who have patched up dwelling places in and among the ruins scarcely so comfortable as our sheds for cattle in Europe.

These people have many sheep and goats. Their only beast of burden is the ass. The place is surrounded with groves of date trees, which furnish the chief subsistence; corn is produced, but in very small quantity.

Having visited the town; on my return to camp, I found there a number of the natives, bartering sheep, fowls and dates, for tobacco, butter, female ornaments, and the coarse woollen stuffs with which the Arabs are generally cloathed. The evening closed in mutual congratulation and festivity, and the younger slaves and boys of the camp made a bonfire.

Our journies from this place being intended to be short, we did not decamp the following morning till half an hour after sunrise, and moved on slowly between date trees, on a generally level ground, interspersed here and there with low hills formed by the wind, which had gathered and heaped a deep sand round some of the trees, so that only the top branches appeared. At two in the afternoon, we came in sight of *Zuila*, and proceeded towards the place destined for our encampment SW. of the town.

SECTION IV
Of Zuila

Zuila being a place of importance in the territory of Fezzan, and the place of residence, not only of many leading and wealthy men, but of relations to the family of the Sultan; we halted at some little distance from the town, and prepared to do the proper honours of our arrival.

The merchants, their pages and slaves dressed themselves in their best apparel; and the *Sheik* ordered his green flag to be borne before him, in honour to the *Shereefs* who live in this place. We had scarcely formed ourselves in procession, when we perceived twenty horsemen, mounted on white horses, with a green flag carried in their centre. It was the Shereef *Hindy*, the principal man of the town, who with his eight sons and other relations, was come out to meet us: at some distance followed a great number of men and boys on foot. They joined our caravan, and we passed together near the town, with huzzas and discharge of muskets, till we reached our place of encampment and pitched our tents.

Many other inhabitants then came out to us, some from curiosity, and some to barter their goods; all behaved with the greatest decorum and regularity; but the family of the *Shereef* was distinguished by its particular complacency and politeness of manners: they wore the Tripolitan dress, but over it a fine Soudan shirt or *Tob*. The dealings of the caravan, on this occasion, were considerable, and especially with the women, who purchased various articles of ornament, in exchange for garden-stuff, milk, and poultry.

Zuila has received the name of *Belled-el-Shereef*, or town of the Shereefs: in former times it was an important place, and its circumference appears to have been thrice the extent of what it is now.[1] Some of the Shereef's family told me, that some centuries past Zuila had been the residence of the sultans, and the general rendezvous of the cara-

---

[1] Zuila was the capital of Fezzan from the seventh to the thirteenth century when the country was conquered by the Kanuri of Bornu who made Traghen their capital.

vans: and even yet the voyage to Fezzan is termed, the voyage to *Sehla*, by the caravan from Bornou.[1]

This little city stands on a space of about one mile in circuit; as in *Augila*, the houses have only a ground floor, and the rooms are lighted from the door. Near the centre of the town, are the ruins of a building several stories high, and of which the walls are very thick; and report says, this was formerly the palace. Without the town near the southern wall, stands an old mosque, little destroyed by time, serving as a sample of the ancient magnificence of Zuila; it contains in the middle a spacious hall or saloon, encompassed by lofty arches behind which runs a broad passage, with entrances to various apartments belonging to the establishment of the mosque. At some little distance further from the city, appear ancient and very lofty edifices, which are the tombs of the shereefs, who fell in battle, at time the country was attacked by Infidels.

The environs of Zuila are level, supplied with water, and fertile. The groves of date trees are of great extent; and its inhabitants appear to pay more attention to agriculture than those of adjoining places.

In the evening we had further proof of the Arab hospitality of yore. A slave of the Shereef's, brought to each tent a dish of meat and broth, and ten small loaves; this most ancient custom the Sheik of the Sultan keeps up and strictly adheres to on arrival of each caravan; soon after, he sent to each of us three small loaves for the morrow's breakfast.

SECTION V

Further journey — and arrival at Mourzouk

We left the hospitable *Zuila* the ensuing morning, and having passed through a grove of date trees, came to an extensive and open plain over which we marched hours, seven and then arrived at *Hemara*;[2] a small village, thin in people, and wretched in appearance, though the country round is most fertile. Here for the first time I was regaled with the great Fezzan dainty of locusts or grasshoppers, and a drink called *luigibi*. The latter is composed of the juice of date trees, and when fresh is sweet and agreeable enough to the taste, but is apt to produce flatulencies and diarrhœa. At first I did not relish the dried locusts, but when accustomed, grew fond of them: when eaten, the legs and wings are broken off and the inner part is scooped out, and what remains has a flavour similar to that of red herrings, but more delicious.

[1] Zuila is still the name by which Fezzan is known in the Western Sudan. [2] Hammera.

The succeeding day we were on march before sunrise; our road crossed a plain, with date trees to the south, among which I descried several small villages. I was till noon separated from my usual party, the Sultan's Sheik of Zuila being pleased to select me as his particular companion. His ordinary clothes were very much worn, and even ragged; he had a cloak, the badge of his high office; he chose to ride with me (as he said) because he deemed it dishonour to ride with the merchants. When permitted to quit him and rejoin my old comrades, I found them in great glee and spirits, at being so near the place where they had houses and families; their gladness, however, soon received alloy, for the officers of the Sultan met us to take account of the bales and merchandize, which had not being usually done till arrival at the gates of Mourzouk; and the merchants had been in the habit of previously disposing of at least a third of their goods, in order to evade the duties. Some however, had contrived to intermingle their baggage with that of the pilgrims, who pay no duties. Rather out of humour with what had passed, our traders of the caravan agreed with a proposal of the Sheik to make a forced march to *Tragen*, where we arrived at sunset.

At this place we reposed the whole of the ensuing day, employed in preparation for honourable appearance before the Sultan, who usually rides out to meet the caravan, in pious respect to the pilgrims returning from Mecca. The Sultan sent forward some camels laden with meat and bread, which were here distributed. The next morning we proceeded, and after eight hours march, pitched our camp near to the chapel and tomb of *Sidibischir*, a holy man of great renown in ancient times, and from whom the village near is likewise named *Sidibischir*. The following day was to be that of our interview with the Sultan. On that day, the *17th of November*, we finished our long and perilous journey, arriving, after a three hours march, in the immediate vicinities of Mourzouk.

The Sultan had posted himself on a rising ground, attended by a numerous court, and a multitude of his subjects.

Our caravan halted, and every person of the caravan, of any importance, dismounted to salute him. With others I approached, and found the sultan seated on an old-fashioned elbow chair, covered with a cloth striped red and green, and placed at extremity of an oval area, round which soldiers were drawn up, of but mean appearance. The Sultan himself wore the Tripolitan vest, and over it a shirt or frock, embroidered with silver, in the Soudan manner. Close to him, on each side, were white Mamelukes and Negro slaves, with drawn sabres;

behind these were six banners, and black and half-naked slaves, holding lances and halberds, of a fashion as old perhaps, as the times of Saladin. We entered the circle by an opening left facing the sultan, and about the middle of the area; according to the ceremonial of his court, we pulled off our slippers, and approached barefoot to kiss his imperial hand. Each having paid his compliment, alternately passing to right or left, and seated himself behind the sultan: the merchants being thus ranged in two equal groups on either side the throne; lastly entered the Sheik of the pilgrims, with his sabre drawn, and kettle-drum, and green flag of Mecca borne before him. The pilgrims followed, chaunting praises to God, who had so far conducted them in safety; and continued their hymns until the Sultan was pleased to dismiss their leader, with a gracious promise of sending his royal present of dates and meat to every tent. This ceremony of audience being over, the Sultan remounted his horse and rode back to the city of Mourzouk, preceded by kettle-drums and banners, and amidst his lance-men and halberdiers; whilst his courtiers, joined by the Arabs of our caravan, pranced and curvetted their horses on each flank of the procession.

CHAPTER III

SOME ACCOUNT OF FEZZAN

The greatest length of the *cultivated part* of the kingdom of Fezzan, is about 300 English miles from north to south, and the greatest width 200 miles from east to west; but the mountainous region of *Harutsch* to the east, and other deserts to the south and west, are reckoned within its territory.

The borderers on the north are Arabs,[1] nominally dependent on Tripoly, but their obedience is merely nominal, and they take each opportunity of public weakness or commotion to throw off the yoke. Fezzan to the east is bounded by the *Harutsch*, and line of deserts. To the south and south-east is the country of the Tibboes.[2] To the south-west that of the Nomadic Tuaricks.[3] On the west are Arabs.

The kingdom contains a hundred and one towns and villages, of which Mourzouk is the capital. The principal towns next in order to the imperial residence are *Sockna*, *Sibha*,[4] *Hun*,[5] and *Wadon*[6] to the north; *Gatron*[7] to the south; *Yerma*[8] to the west; and *Zuila* to the east.

The climate of Fezzan is at no season temperate or agreeable. During the summer the heat is intense; and when the wind blows from the south is scarcely supportable, even by the natives. The winter might be moderate were it not for the prevalence of a bleak and penetrating north wind during that season of the year, and which chilled and drove to the fire not only the people of the place, but even myself, the native of a northern country.

It rains at Fezzan seldom, and then but little in quantity.[9] From November 1798 to June 1799, there was not a single thunder storm; the 31st of January, 1799, there were some faint lightnings without thunder. Tempests of wind are however frequent, both from the north and the south, whirling up the sand and dust, so as to tinge the very atmosphere yellow. There is no great river, nor indeed a rivulet deserving note throughout the whole country. The soil is a deep sand cover-

---

[1] Notably the Meghara and the Hassaouna.
[2] The Tebu or Teda of Tibesti whose range still extends to the vicinity of Murzuk.
[3] The Ajjer Tuareg.   [4] Sebha.   [5] Hon.
[6] Waddan.   [7] El Qatrun.   [8] Germa, the Garama of the Romans.
[9] On the contrary, there are occasionally violent storms which are dreaded for the damage they do to crops and houses.

ing calcareous rock or earth, and sometimes a stratum of argillaceous substance.

Dates may be termed the natural and staple produce of Fezzan. In the western parts of the kingdom some senna is grown, and of a quality superior to that imported from the country of the Tibboes. Pot-herbs, and generally vegetables of the garden, are plentiful. Wheat and barley are suited to the soil and climate, but from inexpertness or difficulties attending the mode of tillage, and generally from indolence of the people and oppressions of the government, corn is not raised sufficient for the inhabitants, and they rely for subsistence on importations from the Arab countries bordering Fezzan to the north.[1]

Very little attention is bestowed on the rearing of beasts. Horned cattle are to be found only in the most fertile districts; and are even there but few in number; they are employed in drawing water from the wells, and are slaughtered only in cases of extreme necessity. The ordinary domestic animal is the goat. Sheep are bred in the southern parts of the kingdom; but the general supply is furnished by the bordering Arabs. The wool is manufactured into *abbes*, or coarse woollen cloths, the general clothing throughout the country; with the meat the very skins are roasted, whilst fresh, and eaten. The horses are but few: asses are the beasts of general use, whether for burthen, draught, or carriage. Camels are excessively dear, and only kept by the chief people, or richer merchants. All these animals are fed with dates or date kernels.

The commerce of Fezzan is considerable, but consists merely of foreign merchandize. From October to February, Mourzouk is the great market and place of resort for various caravans from Cairo, Bengasi, Tripoly, Gadames, Twat, and Soudan, and for other smaller troops of traders, such as Tibboes of Rschade, Tuaricks, and Arabs. The trade from Cairo is carried on by the merchants of *Augila*; that from Tripoly, chiefly by the inhabitants of *Sockna*, and but by few either of Fezzan or Tripoly. The commerce of Soudan, is in the hands of the *Tuarick Kolluvi*,[2] and in particular of the inhabitants of *Agades*; the trade with Bornou is managed by the *Tibboes* of *Bilma*. The caravans coming to Mourzouk from the south or west, bring, as articles of commerce, slaves of both sexes, ostrich feathers, zibette,[3] tiger skins,[4] and gold, partly in dust, partly in native grains, to be manufactured into

---

[1] Owing to the raiding of their crops by desert nomads the Fezzanese never attempted to produce more than was essential to subsistence.
[2] The Kel Owi Tuareg.   [3] Civet.   [4] Leopard skins.

rings and other ornaments, for the people of interior Africa. From *Bornou* copper[1] is imported in great quantity. Cairo sends silks, *melayes* (striped blue and white calicoes), woollen cloths, glass, imitations of coral, beads for bracelets, and likewise an assortment of East India goods. The merchants of *Bengasi*, who, usually join the caravan from Cairo at *Augila*, import tobacco manufactured for chewing, or snuff, and sundry wares fabricated in Turkey.

The caravan from Tripoly, chiefly deals in paper, false corals, firearms, sabres, knives, and the cloths called *abbes*, and in red worsted caps. Those trading from *Gadames*, bring nearly the same articles. The smaller caravans of *Tuaricks* and *Arabs*, import butter, oil, fat, and corn; and those coming from the more southern districts, bring senna, ostrich feathers, and camels for the slaughter-house.

Fezzan is governed by a sultan, descendant from the family of the Shereefs.[2] The tradition is, that the ancestors of the reigning prince, coming from western Africa, invaded and conquered Fezzan about 500 years past. The sultan reigns over his dominions with unlimited power, but he holds them tributary to the Bashaw of Tripoly: the amount of tribute was formerly 6000 dollars, it is now reduced to 4000; and an officer of the bashaw comes annually to Mourzouk, to receive this sum, or its value in gold, senna, or slaves. This officer, whilst in commission, is called *Bey-el-nobe*. On his departure from Tripoly, which is every year in November, he takes all travelling merchants under his protection; and returning from Tripoly to Mourzouk, I shall avail myself of the opportunity.[3]

The present sultan assumes the title 'Sultan Muhammed-ben Sultan Mansur'; and this title is engraved on a large seal, which he applies to acts of authority or correspondence within his realm, but when writing to the bashaw of Tripoly, he uses a smaller seal, on which, instead of the name *Sultan*, that of *Sheik* only, is engraved.

The throne of Fezzan is hereditary: the crown, however, descends not in all cases, directly from father to son; it is the eldest prince of the royal family, who succeeds; and such may be a nephew, in preference to a son who is younger. This custom frequently occasions bloodshed: the son of the deceased sultan may be of sufficient age to govern, though younger than the collateral heir; and having interest and

[1] There is no copper in Bornu. The reference is probably to natron. Hornemann probably confused *natrun* with *nahâs*, the Arabic for copper.
[2] The Karamanlis of Tripoli who were driven out when the Turks reoccupied the country in 1835.
[3] See p. 109n below.

adherents formed by his past high connections and situation, will often be ready to controvert the law of succession, as inapplicable in principle to the case of himself and competitor, equally arrived at the age of manhood and discretion: the question of right is then decided by the sword.

The Sultan's palace (or house) is situate within the circumvallation of the castle or fortress[1] of Mourzouk: he lives there retired, and with no other inmate but the eunuchs, who wait upon him. His Harem is contiguous; he never enters it, but the female whom he at any time wishes to see, is conducted to his apartment. The Harem consists of a Sultana, who, by rules of the empire, must be of the family of the Shereefs of *Wadan* or *Zuila*, and of about forty slaves. These last are often sold and replaced by others, if they do not bear children to the sultan, or do not otherwise endear themselves to him by superior charms and accomplishments.

There is a place set apart within the precincts of the castle, for those who attend on public business, from which a long narrow vestibule leads to a door which opens into the principal apartment of the sultan. The opening of that door, is announced by the beating of kettle-drums, as a signal of audience. The door of audience is opened three times in each day. Those who on account of respect or business, attend for introduction, are conducted by the long narrow passage between slaves, who incessantly repeat, 'May God prolong the life of the sultan!' On coming to the door, the sultan appears opposite, seated on an old-fashioned elbow chair raised some steps, and forming his throne. The person introduced, approaches, kisses the hand of the sultan, raises it so as to touch his forehead, then quits it, and kneels before him. He is permitted to state his case, and address the sultan in ordinary and plain language, but particular attention must be given, that the expressions, 'God prolong thy life;' 'God protect thy country, &c.' be frequently intermingled; and at each presentation, it is customary to offer a small present. It is only on Fridays, or on some solemn festival, that the sultan appears without the castle walls, and then he is attended by his whole court. He goes on Fridays to the great mosque, on horseback: on other days of solemnity or public occasion, he rides on a plain without the town, where his courtiers prance and run their horses round him, and exhibit their skill in equestrian exercises, and in the art of shooting.

The sultan's court or official attendants are, the *kaledyma*, or first

---

[1] Built of the ordinary sun-dried brick of the country, and still standing.

minister; the *keijumma*,[1] or second minister, and the general of his forces; a number of black slaves, and a few white slaves, who are by the Mahometans termed Mamelukes. The *kaledyma* and *keijumma* must both be free-born men; whatever their nominal rank, they at present have but little influence. All the interest and power rests with the Mamelukes, who are mostly Europeans, Greeks, Genoese, or their immediate descendants. The black slaves, are purchased whilst yet boys, and are educated for the court according to their dispositions and talents; some of these too have gained great ascendancy with the sultan.

The apparel of the sultan, on days of state and ceremony, consists of a large white frock or shirt, made in the Soudan manner, of stuff, and brocaded with silver and gold, or of satin interwoven with silver. Under this frock, he wears the ordinary dress of the Tripolitans; but the most remarkable appearance is that of his turban, which, from the fore to the hinder part, extends a full yard, and is not less than two thirds of a yard in breadth.

The revenues of the sultan are produced from certain assessments of tax on all gardens and cultivated lands, and from arbitrary fines and requisitions. The slaves employed in collecting these imposts, are most exorbitant and oppressive, if not bribed. The sultan derives further income from duties on foreign trade, paid by the several caravans. That from Cairo pays from six to eight dollars for each camel load. The caravans from Bornou and Soudan pay two *matkals*,[2] for each slave on sale. He further possesses a territorial revenue, collected from domains of the crown; from salt-pools; from the natron lakes; and from the royal gardens and woods. The present sultan has made great addition to his treasures by predatory expeditions, which he occasionally directs against the *Tibboes* of the tribe of *Burgu*.

The public expenditure consists chiefly in maintenance of the sultan, his court, and palace. The cadi and department of justice, those of the religious order, and the great officers of government, are severally supported from the produce of date-tree woods and gardens, granted as *usufruct* to those holding the respective offices. The princes of the royal family are supported from the proceeds of appropriate territory, and by certain proportions of corn delivered weekly from the sultan's stores, and from occasional exactions on the people, levied by their

---

[1] Both *Kaledyma* and *Keijumma* were Kanuri titles from Bornu where the Lord of the West was called Ngal-ti-Ma (Galadima in Hausa), and the Lord of the South Kaigama.

[2] One *mithqal* or *mitkal* equals about $\frac{1}{8}$ oz of gold.

personal authority, and by means of their slaves. Such oppression is a natural result of the powers of collection, and means of enforcement, and adjudication of right, being vested in each occasional lord of the domain.

Justice is administered by an officer, termed the cadi: his decisions are directed by the Mahometan law, old customs, and established practice; with exception to criminal cases, in which judgment is arbitrary, or referred to the sultan. In the absence of the cadi, his secretary or scribe, performs the office.

The dignity of a cadi, or chief judge, is hereditary in a certain family, ever since the present race of sultans was established on the throne. The sultan, in each instance of demise or vacancy, selects from this family, such individual to fill the office of cadi, as is noted for learning; or in other words, *who can best read and write.*

Besides the cadi, all the princes of the sultan's family, claim a right of jurisdiction, and even of imposing corporal punishments.

The cadi is, at the same time, chief of the clergy, and possesses great influence and authority with the people; the next to him in rank, is the *iman kbir,* or great Iman.

The population of Fezzan is not easily determined. On loose estimate, I should state the inhabitants throughout, at about 70, or 75,000 souls. All of them, without exception, profess the Mahometan religion. The colour or complexion of the people varies; those of the northern parts of the country, for the most part, have a complexion and features, similar to those of the Arabs. In the southern districts, they have mixed with the natives of the great nations bordering on that quarter, and bear a resemblance to the Tibboes and to the Tuaricks. The genuine or indigenous race of Fezzans, may be described as a people of but ordinary stature, and their limbs by no means muscular or strong, their colour a deep brown, their hair black and short, their form of face such as, in Europe, we should term regular, and their nose less flattened than that of the negro.

The mein, the walk, and every motion and gesture of the people of Fezzan, denote a want of energy, either of mind or body. The tyrannic government, the general poverty of the country, and their only food consisting of dates, or a kind of farinaceous pap, with no meat, and rarely with even a little rancid oil or fat, contribute at once to weakness of frame, and dejection of spirit. Even in those parts, where the race may be supposed to be ameliorated by a mixture with the Arabs, there is no energy of character, no industry. Arts and manufactures, will of course supply but a poor and scanty chapter, exhibiting few articles, and no ingenuity: throughout Mourzouk, I could not find one single skilful artificer in any trade or work; indeed, there are no other tradesmen, but shoemakers and smiths. The latter work every metal without distinction; and the same man who forges shoes for the sultan's horse, makes rings for his princesses. The women, indeed, fabricate coarse woollen cloths, called *abbes*; but for the goodness or value of their manufacture the reader may form his own estimate, when told, that the weaver's shuttle is unknown, and that the woof is inserted into the warp thread by thread, and the whole worked solely by hand.

The dress of the people of Fezzan consists of a shirt or frock, made of a coarse linen or cotton cloth, brought from Cairo, and the *abbe* so often mentioned. The middling classes wear frocks made at Soudan,[1] of dyed blue cloth. The richer people and the Mamelukes of the sultan are clothed in the Tripolitan habit, over which they wear a Soudan shirt of variegated pattern and colours, and likewise the *abbe*. The ornamental distinctions of dress are chiefly confined to the head-dress, and to rings on the arms and legs. The lady of a chief or wealthy man of Fezzan divides her hair into seven long curls or tresses; one of these is interbraided with long slips of gilt leather, terminating in a bow; the other six tresses are bound round by a gilt leather strop, and at the end of each is a trinket, which a sketch will best describe.

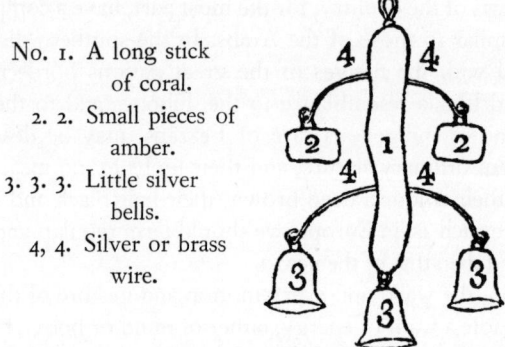

No. 1. A long stick of coral.
2. 2. Small pieces of amber.
3. 3. 3. Little silver bells.
4, 4. Silver or brass wire.

In addition to these ornaments, the Fezzan woman fastens to the top of her head silken cords, on which are strung a number of silver rings, and which hang on each side pendant to her shoulder. The ears of ladies of rank are bored in two places, and in each hole is fixed a thick

[1] In Fezzan Soudan commonly meant Hausa.

silver ring. In ordinary dress they wear nine or ten rings of horn or glass on each arm, four or five of which are taken off on all great occasions, to make room for a silver armillary of four inches breadth. They wear at the same time strong rings of brass or silver just above the ankle bones. The necklace consists of a silk riband, to which are fixed ten or twelve pieces of agate, and in front a round silver plate. The meaner women wear merely a string of glass beads, and curl their hair above the forehead into large ringlets, into which severally is stuffed a paste made of lavender, carraway-seeds, cloves, pepper, mastick, and laurel leaves, mixed up with oil.

The women of Fezzan generally have a great fondness for dancing and every amusement, and the wanton manners and public freedoms which, although Mahometans, they are permitted, astonishes the Mahometan traveller. They dance publicly in the open places of the town, not only in the day-time, but even after sunset. Two or three men stand together with their tambourines; the women immediately form a circle round; the men beat a tune, and those in the circle accompany it with singing and clapping of hands; a girl then advances dancing towards the drummers; the men, as she approaches near, join in the dance and press towards her; on which she makes some steps backwards, and then falls on her back with her body and limbs stiff and perfectly straight, when the women behind catch her in the fall, a few spans from the ground, and toss her in the air, whence she descends on her feet. The men then resume their station in the centre, and a second female dancer repeats the sport, which is successively engaged in by each brisk damsel of the circle.

The men of Fezzan are much addicted to drunkenness. Their beverage is the fresh juice of the date tree, called *luigibi*, or a drink called *busa*, which is prepared from the dates, and is very intoxicating. When friends assemble in the evening, the ordinary amusement is mere drinking; but sometimes a singing girl, or *kadanka* is sent for: *kadanka* is a Soudan word, and answers to the term *almé* used at Cairo.

The song of these Fezzan girls is Soudanic. Their musical instrument is called *rhababe*:[1] it is an excavated hemisphere, made from a shell of the gourd kind, and covered with leather; to this a long handle is fixed, on which is stretched a string of horse hairs longitudinally closed and compact as one cord, about the thickness of a quill. This is played upon with a bow. I was once of a party with *Sidi Mintesser*, the brother of the sultan, at a small house, some distance from the palace,

---

[1] The *imzad* of the Tuareg which is played only by women.

when he ordered a *Kadanka* to be brought, and with whom he soon after withdrew. On her return to the company, she was asked with a significant smile where she had been. She immediately took up her instrument, played upon it, and sung, in the Arabian language, 'Sweet is Sidi Mintesser, as the waters of the Nile, but yet sweeter is he in his embraces; how could I resist?' As a natural consequence of the great freedoms allowed to the sex in Mourzouk, there are more women of a certain description to be found in that capital, than in any other of the same extent and population; and the general character of improvidence, and consequent misery and distress, belong as fully to the frail sisterhood of this place, as of any other.

There are various sorts of venereal disorders prevalent in Fezzan; that imported from Soudan is the worst. The common lues venerea brought from Tripoly and Cairo, is called *franzi*, or the *frank* evil. For the cure of either species they use salts, and the fruit *handal*, (colycinth), as powerful cathartics; and the sores, if any, are at the same time washed with natron water, or dissolved soda. These remedies seldom fail, unless the disease has taken a very deep root.

The other maladies prevalent here are hæmorrhoides, no doubt greatly increased by the immoderate use of red pepper; and a fever and ague, which is particularly dangerous to foreigners. In these disorders there is no remedy whatever known or used but amulets, consisting of certain sentences, transcribed from the Koran, on a slip of paper, which the patient wears about his neck, and in bad cases is made to swallow. Phlebotomy is unknown; but blood is occasionally drawn by means of cupping. As to surgery, I heard there were people at Mourzouk who had sufficient ability to cure a simple fracture.

The houses of the Fezzans are miserably built; they are constructed with stones or bricks made of a calcareous earth mixed with clay, and dried in the sun. No other tools are used in the building but the hands of the labourer. When the walls are completely raised, the friends of the proprietor assemble, and assist him to incrust and cover them with a mortar made with a white calcareous earth. This work too is done only by the hand. The houses are all extremely low, and the light enters by the door only.

As to diet, I never knew a more abstemious people than those of Fezzan. Meat indeed is a food they can at no time abstain from when set before them; but meat is not an article of food with the people in general: to indicate a *rich man*, at Mourzouk, the usual expression is, '*that he eats bread and meat every day.*'

POSTSCRIPT

The particulars above communicated may give some general idea of Mourzouk, and of the people and kingdom of Fezzan. Proposing shortly to return into that country, I may have an opportunity of gaining more satisfactory intelligence, and of enlarging on some points, and of rectifying any mistake in others; I will then draw up for the Society a more full and amended account, having in view the means of conveyance through one of my country-friends, who is going with the caravan to Mourzouk, and proposes returning to Tripoly in May or June 1800, when he will consign my papers to the care of the British Consul.

(Signed) FREDERICK HORNEMAN.

APPENDIX

I

It may be satisfactory to his Employers and to the Public, to receive some further account of Mr. Horneman, on termination of the travels more immediately the subject of his Journal.

By a letter from Mr. Horneman, dated at Tripoly, August 19, 1799, it appears, that on coming to Mourzouk, the end of October, 1798, he was informed that a caravan was preparing to set out for Soudan in three divisions, of which the first was to depart in three days after his arrival. The period fixed for departure of the last division, allowed time for the necessary preparations, and Mr. Horneman had intended to proceed with it on a journey to the Agades and Cashna; but informations he afterwards received induced him to alter his purpose. He was told that the caravan was likely to meet with obstruction or attack in passing through a country of the Tuaricks, then at war with Fezzan; and he observed that the caravan consisted wholly of black traders, from whose intercourse or connection he was not likely to derive either useful consequence or patronage, which might facilitate his friendly reception with the Moors of interior Africa. These and other circumstances induced him to forego the present opportunity, and with the less regret, as, at no distant period, a great caravan was expected from Bornou, with which, on its return, he might travel to the greatest advantage. Whilst remaining at Mourzouk, himself and his servant Frendenburgh were seized with the country fevers: Horneman recovered, but his servant died.

On the re-establishment of his health, Horneman found that some months yet must elapse before the caravan could be expected from Bornou: and in the interval of public resort from the arrival or passage of the caravans, Mourzouk affording no further objects of curiosity or interest, he determined to proceed to Tripoly, for the purpose of transmitting to the Committee of the African Association, such intelligence as he had hitherto collected in their service. He arrived at Tripoly, after a journey of two months, about the middle of August; transacted the business he had in view, and on the 1st December, 1799, set out on his return to Mourzouk, where he arrived January 20th, 1800.

Two letters from Mourzouk have been since received, and at date of writing the last, Mr. Horneman was on *the eve of setting out with the caravan for Bornou*; and with intention from that remote kingdom to prosecute further discoveries to the westward, and in the heart of Africa.

The letters from Mourzouk are as follow:

Sir,   Mourzouk, February 20, 1800

I left Tripoly the 1st December, 1799, and arrived here (the capital of Fezzan) January 20th, 1800 after a safe and good journey, though protracted and slow.[1] I am in the best health, and with fair probability of its continuance.

The route from hence to Soudan, is not yet secure enough for me to undertake proceeding by way of the Agades.

There is now at this place, a Shereef of Bornou, a man of sense, and very much considered by the Sultan of that country. I have made him my friend, and it is in his company I shall depart from this place about the 15th of March for Bornou, whence in the months of August or September, I think to reach Cashna, distant from Bornou about fifteen days journey.

I shall write as often as opportunity offers, that at least some letters may arrive for your information, and the tranquillity of my family.

I remain, with great esteem,
Sir,
Your most obedient,
Frederick Horneman.

Right Hon. Sir Joseph Banks, K.B.
President of the Royal Society, &c.

Mourzouk, April 6, 1800

Sir,
Our caravan is on the point of setting off for Bornou, myself shall join it in the evening.

Being in an excellent state of health, perfectly inured to the climate, sufficiently acquainted with the manners of my fellow-travellers, speaking the Arabic language, and somewhat of the Bornou tongue, and being well armed and not without courage, and under protection of two great Shereefs, I have the best hopes of success in my undertaking.

The Soudan caravan left this place about a month ago; I did well not to join it, as some time past a number of Tibbo were seen hovering, with an intention of attacking that caravan.

Being the first European traveller undertaking so long a journey in this part of the world, *I will not put my discoveries to the hazard, by exposing myself to the casualties of long and unnecessary residence and delays in any one place*, and propose staying no longer at Bornou than till the month of

---

[1] Hornemann travelled, as he had intended, with Mohammed el Mukni, the Bey el Noba, 'collector of the Bashaw's tribute from the Sultan of Fezzan' (F. G. Lyon, *Travels* (London, 1821), p. 3).

September, when I shall proceed to Cashna with the great caravan, which always about that time of the year sets out from Bornou for Soudan.

I cannot yet decide on my further procedure on leaving Soudan, or Cashna, but you may depend on my best intentions and wishes to give full satisfaction to the Society.

Consider this letter as the last for this year, or perhaps as the last before my arrival at some port on the coast of Africa. March the 24th I sent a long letter from Tripoly, and being by a good opportunity, have no doubt of its arriving safe.*

In addition to what I stated in my letter of the 24th March, I have to observe, that in the small-pox, the application used here to preserve the eyes of children, consists of what they term *samsuc*, (tamarinds,) and *zurenbula zigollan*, (onions) and this with good effect, as I am told.

I have more particularly made inquiry respecting venereal disorders, and can confirm what I before wrote, that salts and coloquintida, (in Arabic *handal*) are specific remedies for that disease in this country, and used in the manner I describe.

From every information I can collect, the natives of Fezzan are not susceptible of venereal infection more than once in their lives. It is singular, that notwithstanding there is a great difference as to the nature of this disease, between poxes brought here by the caravan from Soudan, and by those from Tripoly and Cairo, yet never (or at least very seldom) can a man get these two sorts one after the other in the course of his life.

Some days past I spoke to a man who had seen Mr. Brown in Darfoor; he gave me some information respecting the countries he travelled through, and told me, that the communication of the Niger with the Nile was not to be doubted, but that this communication before the rainy season was very little in those parts; the Niger being at the dry period reposing, or *non fluens*.

Not long ago, the same custom was observed at Bornou as in ancient times at Cairo, 'a girl very richly dressed, was thrown into the river Niger.'

Comparing my enquiries as to Soudan, and its communication with the western and south-western coasts of Africa, it must lay generally by the way of Nyffé and Jerba,[1] and be twelve times greater than that between Fezzan and Soudan.

I recommend myself to your remembrance, and assuring you of my great esteem, am,

         Sir,
     Your most obedient,
            Frederick Horneman.

Right Hon. Sir Joseph Banks, K.B.
President of the Royal Society, &c.

* It never came to hand.

[1] This may refer to Jega, about eighty miles S.S.W. of Sokoto which was a market of international reputation in the early years of the nineteenth century. (See H. Barth, *Travels* (London, 1857/58) v. 325.)

Further Account of Hornemann

Mr. Horneman, previous to setting out for Bornou, had availed himself of the intimacies he had formed with intelligent pilgrims and merchants of the Egyptian caravan, and with others at Mourzouk, who were natives of, or had traded to, different regions of Africa, to collect every possible information respecting the countries he was about to visit; and, together with his Journal, transmitted the following results of his enquiries.

II

INTELLIGENCE
concerning the
INTERIOR PART OF NORTH AFRICA

*

SECTION I

Westward from Fezzan, and to the south and south-west,[1] the country is inhabited by the Tibbo, who command also the country from Fezzan towards Egypt, from which it is said to be separated by a large desert. The nearest inhabited places north of Tibbo are Augila and Siwah. On the south they are bounded by wandering Arabs; and on the west beyond Fezzan, by the dominions of the Tuaricks.

The Tibbo are not quite black; their growth is slender; their limbs are well turned; their walk is light and swift; their eyes are quick, their lips thick, their nose is not turned up, and not large; their hair is not very long, but less curled than that of the Negroes. They appear to have much natural capacity, but they have too few opportunities of improving it, being surrounded by barbarous nations, or Mahometans. Their intercourse with the Arabs, to whom they convey slaves, has probably corrupted them; they are accused of being mistrustful, treacherous, and deceitful. The Fezzanians do not travel singly with them, for they are afraid of being surprised and murdered at the instigation of the company with whom they travel. The language of the Tibbo is spoken with extraordinary rapidity, and has many consonants, particularly the L and S. They number thus:

[1] South-east would have been more correct.

One	Trono
Two	—
Three	Agesso
Four	Fusso
Five	Fo
Ten	Markum

Their clothing consists of sheep-skins, which they dress with or without the wool; the former for winter, the latter for summer; but the inhabitants of the principal places, or others, when they go to Fezzan, clothe themselves like the Burmuans, in large blue shirts; their head is wrapt in a dark blue cloth in such a manner, that their eyes only are seen. Their weapons are a lance about six feet long, and a knife from fifteen to twenty inches long, which they carry on their left arm, the sheath being fastened to a ring of leather about three inches wide, which they bear on their wrist.

The Tibbo are divided into several tribes, the principal of which are, the Tibbo of Bilma, whose chief resides at Dyrke,[1] about one day's journey from Bilma. This tribe is a good deal mixed, having established itself forcibly among the Negroes who lived in that district: to this day, the inhabitants of Bilma are mostly Negroes; in Dyrke, on the contrary, they are Tibbo. This tribe carries on a commerce between Fezzan and Burnu, and apparently with great safety to themselves; for they travel in small companies of six or eight men; but on account of their bad character, the slaves of either sex, from Burnu, who have been freed, do not return with them, as the poor people are afraid of being plundered and sold again, or murdered by them.

The religion of the Tibbo of Bilma, is the Mahometan; but it is said they hold it very cheap.

The tribe of the Tibbo Rschade, or the Rock Tibbo, is so called from their houses being built under rocks, and they frequently live even in caves, before which they build huts of rushes in a very coarse manner, for their summer residence. The chief of this tribe lives in Abo; next to which Tibesty is the largest place. The Tibbo Rschade go in multitudes to Fezzan, at which time they clothe themselves like the Tuaricks; however, I have seen several wearing their sheep-skins. This tribe is reported to be good Mahometans.

The Tibbo Burgu[2] are said to be still Pagans: the district which they inhabit, abounds in dates, corn, and grass.

---

[1] Dirki or Dirku. [2] Borku.

A company of Fezzanians having this year been plundered by some of the people of Burgu, as they were travelling from Bergami[1] to Mourzouk, the sultan of Fezzan sent a small army into their country; it consisted of thirty-two men on horseback, seventy Arabs on foot, and about two hundred Tibbos of the Rschade tribe. The Arabs went from Mourzouk into Gatron, fifty-four miles south of that place; to Fegherie[2] thirty-three miles south-south-east of Gatron; then to Abo seven days, and Tibesty three days, in an easterly direction; then to Burgu eighteen days, (reckoning a day's journey eighteen miles.) They stole about two hundred people, the greatest part of whom were sold in Tripoli.

The women of the Burgu tribe, wear their hair in plaits, which hang down from their heads, but the hair on the fore-part of their heads is cut off. The girls are accused of becoming pregnant by their brothers. The slave of one of my friends, who spoke the Tibbo language, assured me, that he had questioned a young woman who was with child, and that she did not deny it.

Farther towards the east lies Arna,[3] the principal place of another Tibbo tribe, at the distance of five or six days.

South-south-west of Augila dwell the Tebabo,[4] who are exposed to the yearly depredations of the Arabs of Bengasi, who go out with the Arabs of Augila, to steal men and dates; and for that purpose, they convey with them several hundred camels.

The distance to Tebabo was stated to me by the Augilarians to be ten days journey, (twenty-one miles per day), and that during the first six days no water is to be found. The most southerly of the Tibbo tribes are the Nomadic Tibbo, who live in the *Bahr-el-Gasel*, which is said to be a long and fruitful valley, seven days journey from Bergami northward.

SECTION II

The west and south of Fezzan is inhabited by the Tuarick, a mighty people, who border south-west on Burnu; south on Burnu, Soudan and Tombuctoo; eastward on the country of the Tibbo and Fezzan; northward on part of Fezzan, and the Arabs who live behind the regions of Tripoly, Tunis, and Algiers; and westward on the great

---

[1] Bagarmi.   [2] Tegerhi.
[3] Arna is today the name of a noble clan of the Tibesti Tebu, whose range is eastern and south-eastern Tibesti.
[4] Tazerbo, today the name of a place, not of a tribe.

empire of Fez and Morocco, of whom a few colonies are found in Sockna, (in the dominion of Fezzan), Augila, and Siwah; in which places the language of the Tuarick is the only one spoken by the inhabitants.*

The Tuarick are divided into many nations and tribes, who all speak the same language; but, by their colour and manner of living, it is probable that they differ widely in their origin. As I will give only certain informations, on this account I confine myself, in the following relation, to the Tuarick of the nation of Kolluvi[1] and the tribe of Hagara.[2] These are thin in growth, rather tall than short; their walk is swift but firm; their look is stern, and their whole demeanour is warlike. Cultivated and enlightened, their natural abilities would render them, perhaps, one of the greatest nations upon earth. Their character (particularly that of Kolluvi,) is much esteemed. The western tribes of this nation are white, as much as the climate and manner of living will admit. The Kolluvians who reached the region of Asben and conquered Agades, and mixed with the nations, are of different colours; many of them are black; but their features are not like those of Negroes. The Hagara and Matkara are yellowish, like the Arabs; near Soudan there are tribes entirely black. The clothing of this nation consists of wide dark-blue breeches, a short narrow shirt of the same colour, with wide sleeves, which they bring together and tie on the back of their neck, so that their arms are at liberty. They wind a black cloth round their head in such a manner that at a distance it appears like a helmet, for their eyes only are seen. Being Mahometans, they cut off their hair, but leave some on the top of the head, round which those who wear no cap, contrive to fold their black cloth, so that it appears like a tuft on their helmet. Round their waist they wear a girdle of a dark colour; from several cords which fall from their shoulders, hangs a koran in a leather pouch, and a row of small leather bags containing amulets. They always carry in their hands a small lance, neatly worked, about five feet long. Above the left elbow, on the upper part of the arm, they wear their national badge, a thick, black or dark-coloured ring, of horn or stone.

Their upper dress is a Soudanian shirt, over which a long sword hangs from the shoulder. The travelling merchants of this nation carry

---

* I have given further particulars on this subject in the account of my journey from Cairo to Fezzan.
[1] The Kel Owi are a tribe, not a nation.
[2] The Ahaggar Tuareg are a confederation, not a tribe.

fire-arms; the others use only the sword, the lance, and the knife, which they carry on their left arm, like the Tibbo, but the handle is finely worked; for they have the art of giving to copper as bright a colour as the English artists, and this art they keep very secret.

They carry on a commerce between Soudan, Fezzan, and Gadames. Their caravans give life to Mourzouk, which, without them, is a desert; for they, like the Soudanians, love company, song and music.

The Tuarick are not all Mahometans. In the neighbourhood of Soudan and Tombuctoo live the Tagama, who are white, and of the Pagan religion. This must have occasioned the report, to which my attention has been called, by several learned men, that there are white Christians in the neighbourhood of Tombuctoo. I am convinced that the fable arises solely from the expression *Nazary* (i.e. Christians), which the Arabs and Mahometans use in general for unbelievers.

The greatest part of the eastern Tuarick lead a wandering life. A place, for instance, under the government of Hagara consists of about twenty-five or thirty stone houses only; but at the time of their markets (which are said to be very considerable), many hundred men assemble there with their leathern tents.

SECTION III

Behind these countries lies Tombuctoo, of which I shall say nothing, as I could not get any well-founded and certain accounts, for there is little intercourse between this region and Fezzan; however, it certainly is the most remarkable and principal town in the interior of Africa.

Eastward from Tombuctoo lies Soudan, Haussa, or Asna; the first is the Arabic, the second is the name used in the country, and the last is the Burnuan name. Of these three names I choose the second, as being the most proper, and understood by the Arabs below Soudan, and all the land southward from Ghaden. The Burnuan name means properly only Kano and Kashna, and the country lying eastward from that region Asna, but incorrectly spoken, it comprehends also Tombuctoo.

As to what the inhabitants themselves call Haussa, I had, as I think, very certain information. One of them, a Marabut, gave me a drawing of the situation of the different regions bordering on each other, which I here give as I received it. (See sketch on next page).

The land within the strong line is Haussa; my black friend had omitted Asben.

These regions are governed by Sultans, of whom those of Kashna

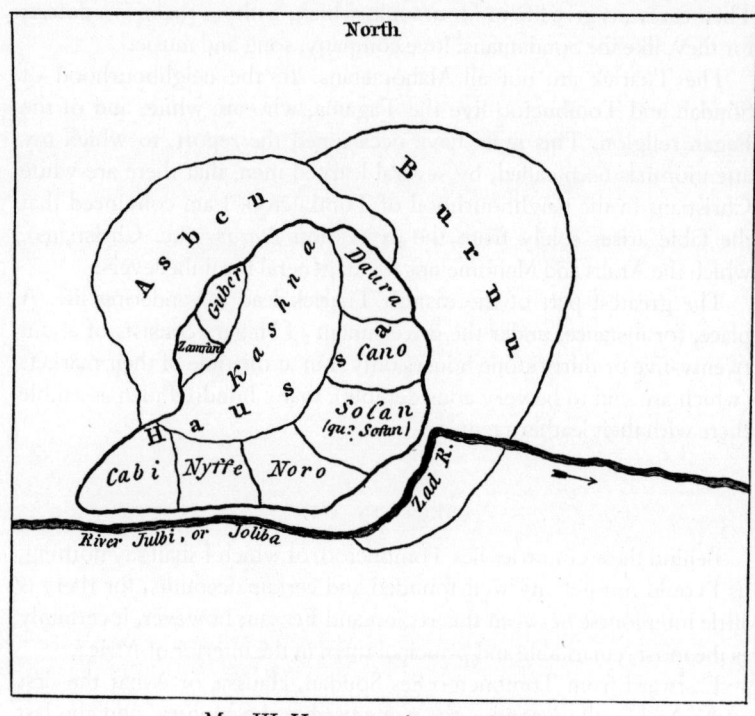

Map III. Hornemann's map of Hausa

and Kano are the most powerful; but they all, (either by constraint or policy) pay tribute to Burnu,[1] except Cabi[2] or Nyffé, their districts being at too great a distance. Guber[3] pays, moreover, a tribute to Asben.[4] Zamfara is united with Guber; the Sultan of the latter having taken possession of it, killed the Sultan, and sold all the prisoners he could take.

The Haussa are certainly Negroes, but not quite black; they are the most intelligent people in the interior of Africa; they are distinguished from their neighbours by an interesting countenance; their nose is small and not flattened, and their stature is not so disagreeable as that of the Negroes, and they have an extraordinary inclination for pleasure, dancing, and singing. Their character is benevolent and mild. Industry and art, and the cultivation of the natural productions of the land, prevail in their country; and, in this respect, they excel the Fezzanians, who get the greatest part of their clothes and household implements from the Soudanians. They can dye in their country any colour but scarlet. The preparation of leather is as perfect as that of the Europeans, although the manner of doing it is very troublesome. In short, we have very unjust ideas of this people, not only with respect to their cultivation and natural abilities, but also of their strength and the extent of their possessions, which are by no means so considerable as they have been represented. Their music is imperfect, when compared to the European; but the Haussanian women have skill enough to affect their husbands, thereby even to weeping, and to inflame their courage to the greatest fury against their enemies. The public singers are called Kadanka.

SECTION IV

EASTWARD from Haussa are situated the dominions of the Sultan of Burnu (i.e. the city). It appears to be much increased since the time of Leo Africanus, as other regions belong to it, which he considered as independent; for example, Wangara, also Edrisi's Cauga, &c. belong to it.

The Sultan of Burnu is reckoned the most powerful in that district; all the neighbouring states pay him tribute. He certainly possesses an extensive tract of land, but he gains more by his authority in the unceasing animosity of his neighbours.

The Burnuans are blacker than the Haussanians, and completely Negroes; they are stronger, and very patient of labour; their constitu-

[1] Bornu.   [2] Kebbi.   [3] Gobir.   [4] Air.

tion is in the greatest degree phlegmatic; they are, altogether, much more rude and uninformed than the Haussanians. Their men are fond of women only of a large size; the Soudanians, on the contrary, prefer those of a slender form.

A paste of flour and flesh is the only food of the Burnuans; the liquor they drink is an intoxicating kind of beer, which is very nourishing. The best natural production of Burnu is copper, which is said to be found in small native pieces. That which is gold in Tombuctoo and Haussa, is answered by copper in Burnu; the value of all their commodities is fixed by pounds of this metal.

Northward from the principal town of that district lies Kanena, which is inhabited by the nation Kojam, so called from their food, which is cow's milk and beef.

Towards the north-east lies Begarmé, the capital of which is called Mesna. Both these territories are dependants of Burnu. Begarmé is famous for its slave trade, perhaps particularly so, as at that place the greatest number of boys are mutilated.

Southward from Burnu lie Margi and Couga;[1] westward, Ungura, [Wangara]; they are under the dominions of governors appointed by the Sultan.

SECTION V

Towards east by north lies Lussi; by the natives it is called Fiddri,[2] and by the people who dwell eastward, Cougu. The dominions of the Sultan of Fiddri are situated round a lake which bears the same name. This realm was formerly one of the most powerful, now it is considerably diminished, by the encroachments of the Sultans of Begarmé and Wadey.[3] The natives live in small huts, which they prefer to houses; they are said to be in a very low degree of civilization. There is not any salt in their country, but they procure it in the following manner: they burn a great heap of straw of *gassab*,[4] gather the ashes and put them in a basket, pour water on them, and collect it as it runs through: this water they boil until the salt settles.[5]

[1] Kuka, the capital of Bornu.   [2] Fittri.   [3] Wadai.   [4] Millet.
[5] Deposits of natural salt are exceedingly rare in the Sudan where an insatiable craving for this essential to human wellbeing often compels people to resort to such crude methods of obtaining it as that described by Hornemann. The principal sources of supply of some of the weaker and more isolated tribes are the ashes of grass, millet stalks and of certain shrubs; cattle dung is another source. The two staples of the ancient trans-Saharan caravan trade were gold, in which the Western Sudan was rich, and salt of which there were abundant deposits in the Sahara, the most famous being Taghaza. El Bekri's statement in the eleventh century that one Western Sudanese tribe, the Ferawi, exchanged gold dust for an equal weight of salt is not wholly improbable.

Towards the south-east of Fiddri lies Metko, a small independent district in a mountainous country. Eastward lies Wadey, which formerly consisted of several small states, but was conquered by the Arabs, who united and made them one realm. The principal language is Arabic; but above ten other languages are spoken in the district. Wandering Arabs occupy the space from Wadey to Begarmé northward.

Eastward from Wadey lies Darfoor; from whence flows a river, the banks of which are very rich in sugar canes: it runs through Wadey, and falls into the lake Fiddri above-mentioned. I had very different accounts of the circumference of this lake, as in the rainy season it swells to double the extent, which, ordinarily, is from four to eight days journey.

SECTION VI

The river that was seen by Mr. Park on his journey to Tombuctoo, flows southward from Haussa. It waters Nyffé and Cabi, where it is called Julbi;[1] and runs eastward into the district of Burnu, where it takes the name of Zad, which means the great water; in some parts of Haussa, it is called Gaora,[2] or the great water.

All the Burnuans and Haussans whom I questioned about the distant regions of this river, agreed in telling me, 'that it ran through the land of Majies, (i.e. Heathens;) by Sennaar: others affirmed that it passes Darfoor, in its course eastward, and flows to Cairo, being one stream with the Egyptian Nile.'

A native of Egypt from Osuit, who had travelled several times to Darfoor, and southward from that place to collect slaves, and lately returned through Wadey, Fiddri, and Begarmé, to Fezzan, informed me, that the river called *Bah-el-Abiad*, is this river. I could get no intelligence about a great inland lake, although I made every possible inquiry.

Besides these two great rivers here described, there are seven small streams in Haussa, which fall into the Julbi near Berva. Northward from Burnu, there is a river which disappears among the mountains, and is said to rush into the earth. All these rivers are very low in the dry season, and swell amazingly during the rainy season. The breadth of the Zad was given me for one mile, (others said two); but in the rainy season, the breadth is said to be a day's journey, (i.e. eight hours).[3] The Budumas always keep themselves in the middle of this stream; they are a very savage, heathenish nation.

[1] Gulbi is Hausa for river.   [2] Kworra.
[3] Hornemann failed to realize that Chad was a lake, not a river. Owing to being very shallow, Lake Chad is subject to wide fluctuations in size.

These few informations are the best that I have been able to collect, on the interior of Africa. In this relation, I pass over men with tails, without necks, and without hair, without land, and living only on the great sea. It would be an easy matter for me to write you many letters on the interior state of Africa; but I might thereby convey information inaccurate or untrue. Besides, am I not returning to England? and if I do return, should I not reserve something new and interesting to plead my excuse for returning?

If I do not perish in my undertaking, I hope in five years, I shall be able to make the Society better acquainted with the people, of whom I have given this short description.

(Signed) Frederick Horneman.

1798

Extracts from a Letter accompanying the above Informations, dated Tripoly, 19th of August, 1799

After a journey of eleven days from Siwah, four of which we travelled eighteen hours each day, through a desert, we arrived at Augila, a small miserable town belonging to Tripoly; and after a journey of sixteen days more, we reached Temissa, the first village of Fezzan. Seven of these sixteen days, I was passing a black rocky desert, certainly the worst of all routes in the world; and which has doubtless been formed by some volcanic revolution. It is called Harutsch, and extend very far to the south-west.

From Temissa, I came by way of Zuila, Tuila, and Tragan,[1] to Mourzouk, (which is also called Fezzan, and by the people of Burnu, *Zela*).[2] Mourzouk is situated in 25° 54′ 15″ north latitude.

With regard to the interior of Africa, I have made all the inquiries possible, and will send you the result of them by the first opportunities. Accept for the present the following notices on that subject.

The river you call Niger — in Soudan, *Gulbi*, or *Gaora*; in Burnu, *Zad*;[3] is a very large river, into which fall more than twelve other rivers. It comes from Tombuctoo, as I am told, runs to the south of Haussa (or Soudan), in the empire of Burnu; here it takes a more southern direction, and falls (at least I could not find a single man who said to the contrary), south of Darfoor into the Nile. There is another river coming from Darfoor, which passes by Wadey and Metho, and terminates in a large lake called *Fiddri*, in a kingdom called by the inhabitants Fiddri; by the people to the east of them, *Cougu*; and by those on the west, *Lussi*. The lake of Fiddri is four days in circumference, but in the time of the rains much more extensive, inundating the surrounding country, which, after the waters are withdrawn, is sown and cultivated.

[1] Traghen. [2] Zuila.
[3] Hornemann believed that the Benue and Lake Chad were parts of the Niger.

Near to *Mesna*, the capital of Bergamé, is another large river; but it is considerable only in the rainy season. Bahr of Gazelles, or *Wad-el-Gazelles*, is not a river, but a long and fertile valley, inhabited by Nomadian Tibbo, whose houses are made of skins.

Burnu is the most powerful kingdom in the interior of Africa. The next to it is the Sultan of *Asben*, who resides at Agades. The kings of the countries of which Haussa consists, all pay tribute to Burnu; these are *Kashna*, *Daura*, *Keeno*,[1] *Sofau*, *Noro*, *Nyffé*, *Gaauri*,[2] *Cabi*, *Guber*, (Zanfara belongs to Guber). Kashna pays every year 100 slaves, &.c. Some of them pay to Burnu and Asben. The king of Asben with the greatest part of his nation are Tuaricks of the tribe *Kolluvi*. Many of the Tuaricks near to Tombuctoo, are white; and another tribe near to Burnu, are also white, like the Arabs of the northern coast of Africa.

Begarmé pays tribute to Burnu; *Ungura*, (doubtless *Wangara*, Leo. Afr.)[3] and *Cougu*, are governed by officers of that sultan.

There is a general opinion of all Burnu and Fezzan people, that Burnu and Fezzan, according to our manner of speaking, lie under the same meridian. Burnu is distant from Kashna 15 days, by travelling very slow 20 fisturnees, or about 330 English miles. Fiddri from Burnu E by N 25 days. The people of Fiddri have no salt in their country, but what they prepare from straw ashes.

A great part of the people of *Wadey*, together with their king, are Arabs.

In the direction of south by west from Augila, distant ten days, or about 200 miles, are the *Febabo*, and some days more to the south the *Birgu*, nations of the Tibbo, whose country is very fine and fertile: they are said to be Pagans. It is singular, that the people of Augila, in speaking of these tribes, make much the same comparison which Herodotus (Melpom. c.183.) does, when speaking of the Ethiopian *Troglodytæ*, hunted by the Garamantes, 'that their language is like the whistling of birds.'

The most interesting nation of Africa, is the *Tuarick*. They are in possession of all the country between Fezzan, Gadames, the empire of Morocco, Tombuctoo, Soudan, Burnu, and the country of the Tibbo. They are divided into several nations, of which the *Kolluvi* in Asben, and the *Hagara* near to Fezzan, are the chief.

Christians and tailed men, I suppose, never will be found in the interior of Africa. The Mahometans call *Nazari* (which is properly the name for Christians) not the Christians only, but also every other people who are not of their religion. Of tailed men I heard no accounts, except from one person,

---

[1] Kano.   [2] Gwari.

[3] Leo Africanus's description of Wangara as a country 'abounding in gold', in striking confirmation of a similar statement by El Edrisi in the twelfth century, made the discovery of Wangara one of the chief objectives of all early explorers of western Africa. They failed because there were several Wangaras. See p. 39n. 1 above.

(but not a *testis fide dignissimus*,) who placed them ten days south of Kano; he called them *Yem Yem*, and said that they were cannibals.[1] In ten months I shall be near to that direction.

I shall now, Sir, conclude this letter, which I hope will find you in good health. I am, &c. &c.

Frederick Horneman.

[1] Throughout the Sudan cannibals, of no matter what tribe, are known as Nyam Nyam, Lem Lem or some similar name. Hornemann's Yem Yem is obviously one of the variants.

The Letters of
Major Alexander Gordon Laing
1824-1826

ABBREVIATIONS

A.R.   Anonymous Report.
B.B.   Papers Explanatory of the Circumstances under which Sidi Hassuna D'Ghies has been accused by the Bashaw of Tripoli of having abstracted the papers of the late Major Laing, *Blue Book*, 1832.
C.O.   Colonial Office.
F.O.   Foreign Office.
P.R.O.   Public Record Office.
R.S.   Royal Society's Archives.
D.T.C.   *Banks Correspondence*, Dawson Turner Collection of Copies of Correspondence of Sir Joseph Banks.

INTRODUCTION

i. *The Materials*

Brief memoirs of Gordon Laing were published in various journals when, after a lapse of two or three years, all doubt about his reported death in 1826 had been finally dispelled. Since then his name and his achievement have been repeatedly noticed in countless works on geographical discovery and African history, but no attempt has hitherto been made to write a definitive account of the journey which was his claim to fame. He consequently became the most neglected of the great African explorers. This was partly because, like Hornemann, he did not survive to tell his tale, and partly because, unlike Hornemann, he left no journal worth publishing; it was also because people lost interest in Timbuktu as soon as they learnt from Caillié, shortly after Laing's death, that it was not even the palest shadow of the city abounding in wealth and architectural glories that they had imagined it to be. The disillusioned British public, whose appetite for tales of discovery was being amply fed from other sources, had no wish to hear more of Laing, who consequently sank into obscurity.[1]

Yet all this time, a century and a quarter of almost silent neglect, the essential documents have been available for study. The last of Laing's letters to survive was one dated Timbuktu 21 September 1826, only three days before he died. How many letters of this tireless correspondent failed to reach their destination we shall never know, but enough survive to make possible the telling of the story of his great journey, except in its closing stages and the culminating tragedy.[2]

Laing had three important correspondents, Colonel Hanmer Warrington, the Consul-General in Tripoli,[3] Edward Sabine[4] and James Bandinel,[5] to one or other of whom nearly all the letters that follow,

[1] *The Quarterly Review*, always ready to find space for news of African discovery, merely mentioned Laing in notices of works by other explorers, Ledyard (XXXVIII, 1828, 100–9), and Clapperton (XXXIX, 1829, 170–4).

[2] Most, but not all, of Laing's surviving letters are printed in the following pages.

[3] Laing numbered the covers of his letters to Warrington, but not the letters themselves. We know from Warrington that many failed to arrive, but how many we do not know because the covers have not survived.

[4] Captain Edward Sabine, R.A. (1788–1883), had already distinguished himself as an Arctic explorer, and in 1861, as General Sir Edward Sabine, he was to become President of the Royal Society.

[5] James Bandinel was at this time a clerk in the Foreign Office. Later in life he was to play an active part in the anti-slavery movement.

apart from his official ones to the Colonial Office, were addressed.[1] Most of these letters owe their survival to their having been addressed to Warrington who, as consul-general, filed them in the official archives. The letters to Sabine and Bandinel were preserved in circumstances to be related shortly.[2]

Laing was also a writer of memoranda. These were often no more than brief notes on odd scraps of paper, but sometimes they were long and careful studies, such as his *Cursory Remarks on the Course and Termination of the Great River Niger*, and his *Notes on Gadamis* both of which are printed at the end of this volume.[3]

With all these papers there are two portions of Laing's journal, but they carry the story of his journey no further than his arrival in Ghadames.[4] They appear to be mere summaries of a more detailed private journal, and to have been prepared and despatched to London as a formal report to the Colonial Office on the progress of the mission. Although they are duller and less informative than Laing's letters they are useful as a check on the latter to which they serve also as an introduction. For this reason, but not without some hesitation, they have been included in this volume.[5]

Hardly less important sources are Warrington's official consular dispatches to the Secretary of State, Lord Bathurst, and the Under Secretary (first Wilmot Horton and later Robert Hay), which, so far as the story of the Timbuktu Mission (as Laing's expedition was called) is concerned, appear to be nearly complete. Unfortunately, however, few of Lord Bathurst's outward letters to Warrington, and none of those to Laing, survive.[6] Their tenor can only be guessed from the replies they elicited.

Most of this material is to be found in two repositories, the Public Record Office and the Royal Society's Archives. The former is naturally much the more important because it includes all the early

---

[1] Laing also wrote to his family in Scotland but we have a copy of only one of his letters to them. It was dated 'Ensala in Tuat, December 8, 1825'.

[2] Of some of these we have only Laing's own copies, or his drafts for them. There are also drafts of other letters but without any record of whether they were sent.

[3] Appendixes II and III respectively.

[4] According to *The Quarterly Review* (XXXVIII, 1828, 109) the journal received at the Colonial Office covered his journey up to his departure from In Salah. As there is no confirmation of this it is possible that his letters from In Salah were wrongly reported to be his journal.

[5] Appendix I.

[6] The present Lord Bathurst has kindly searched his ancestor's papers at Cirencester Park for records relating to Laing, but without success.

nineteenth-century records from the British Consulate in Tripoli of which Laing's letters to Warrington formed part.

But the Royal Society's collection of documents is also important. It includes two of Laing's notebooks, in one of which is an autobiographical sketch carrying the story of his short life up to his departure from the West Indies;[1] the other contains part of the MS. of his published work on his travels in Sierra Leone.[2] More relevant to his journey to Timbuktu are a number of original letters to Sabine and Bandinel, together with copies and drafts of letters Laing wrote or intended to write. With these letters are a number of memoranda in Laing's hand on a variety of subjects. This miscellaneous collection of letters, drafts and memoranda numbers, with the two notebooks, 148 items.

Light on how this collection of papers came into the possession of the Royal Society is shed by two documents in the Society's archives. The first is an undated letter from Bandinel to Sabine; the shaky writing appears to be that of a sick man and may therefore have been written shortly before Bandinel's death in 1849.

James Bandinel to General Sir Edward Sabine:

Dear Sabine,

I send you every scrap which I can find of Laing's hand writing. These consist of memoranda of his wishes as to the direction of his Researches & Journey drawn [?] out I believe at my suggestion, but whether for himself for you or for me to speak to Hay[3] about it, I cannot at this moment recollect.

2. 13 Letters of his own pen [?] to me from the time of his leaving Ensala.

3. Two or three loose notes, which I merely send because I find them at this moment & among the others, & they or some one of them may by chance serve to establish a date — & if they do not, I do not see how they can even have that use, they will not give to you much time or trouble in reading them, or putting them up again.

Yours ever sincerely

J. Bandinel

Return to me these letters when you have done with them.[4]

---

[1] R.S., Laing, vol. 4, 376.   [2] R.S., Laing, vol. 3, 375.

[3] Robert William Hay, born in 1786 and educated at Christ Church, Oxford, started his career in the Admiralty. In 1825 he was appointed Permanent Under-Secretary at the Colonial Office, a post he held with marked lack of distinction until 1836.

[4] R.S., MM., XIV, 143.

Many years later, in 1875, Lady Sabine sent to Robert H. Scott,[1] a fellow of the Royal Society, a packet of Laing's papers which were obviously the property of her husband who was still alive but who had resigned the Presidency of the Royal Society in 1871, at the age of eighty-two.[2] This packet was under cover of the following letter.

Lady Sabine to Robert H. Scott:

13 Ashley Place,
June 29th 1875

Dear Mr. Scott,
 I send you a packet of the late Major Laing's papers. Will you kindly dispose of them for the best. I should think either the Royal Society or the Royal Geographical might be willing to receive them & might probably like to have some among them; others they might destroy.

Very sincerely yours
Elisabeth Sabine[3]

Robert Scott evidently offered the papers to the Royal Society who accepted them.[4]

The Laing papers in the Royal Society's archives include the thirteen letters written to Bandinel and specifically mentioned by him in his letter to Sabine. They probably remained in the latter's hands as the result of Bandinel's death.

How a number of Laing's personal papers, copies of his letters to others, and memoranda of concern only to himself came into Sabine's hands remains unexplained. The collection includes papers which he may have had with him in Timbuktu, but not any of those he probably had with him at the time of his death.

A great part of the Laing records in the Public Record Office belong to a date subsequent to his death, and relate to the diplomatic troubles between Britain and France which flowed from the disappearance of the papers he was presumed to have with him, notably his journals, when, or shortly before, he died. The sordid tale of the alleged theft of the missing papers by the French Consul in Tripoli and the suspected

---

[1] Robert Henry Scott, F.R.S. (1833–1916), was a distinguished meteorologist. He was Superintendent of the Meteorological Office from 1867–1900.

[2] In the meanwhile the papers had been lent to the explorer Heinrich Barth, who had returned them to General Sabine on 8 October 1857, the year in which he published the first three volumes of his monumental *Travels in North and Central Africa* (R.S., MM., XIV, 144).

[3] R.S., MM., XIV, 145.

[4] There is no record of their having been offered to the Royal Geographical Society.

The Materials

complicity of the Bashaw in Laing's murder is only of secondary importance in the history of geographical discovery, and is therefore only briefly outlined in this volume.

Among the Public Record Office papers is a document which, although insufficiently important to be reproduced here, is helpful in trying to piece together the tangled fragments of the Laing story. This is an undated anonymous report carrying the story of Gordon Laing from the date of his arrival in North Africa down to the official enquiry in Tripoli into the mysterious disappearance of his papers after his death. This report, covering sixty-six pages of foolscap, is in two different hands, but from the mis-spelling of local names it seems to be a copy of an original compiled in Africa. It appears to have been written at Warrington's dictation or at least to have been inspired by him. In the following pages it is referred to as the Anonymous Report.[1]

ii. The Problem of the Niger

After the failure of Hornemann's expedition the work of promoting, organizing and financing African exploration was taken over from the African Association by the British government. The immediate need was to complete Park's work by tracing the Niger to its mouth, the situation of which was still a complete mystery and the subject of wild speculation. Thus did the government set its hand to a task which was to take more than a quarter of a century to finish, and which it would probably have quickly abandoned but for fear that some other country — probably France — might reap the rich rewards which, it was believed, surely awaited the discoverer of the interior of Africa. The Niger was thought to be the key to that repository of untold wealth.

There were three likely solutions to the problem of where the Niger ended. It might be the same river as the Nile; it might even be the Congo; or, as the erudite Major James Rennell had declared, it might be lost by dispersion or evaporation somewhere in the heart of the continent. A fourth and seemingly less likely solution, proposed by the

---

[1] Only some of the documents in the Public Record Office have registration numbers, and all such numbers are quoted in bibliographical references. All the Royal Society's records are numbered, and so are the sixty-six pages of the Anonymous Report, thus making precise references possible in each case. The file P.R.O., C.O. 2/20 includes a volume of copies of letters relating to the loss of Laing's journals which Colonel Warrington had especially prepared for the United Service Club, 'the bravest and most honourable of men.'

German geographer C. G. Reichard, that it flowed into the Bight of Benin was rejected on the ground that a range of granite mountains (which no one had ever seen) made its access to the Bight impossible.

Clearly the best way to solve the problem would be to follow the river down to its mouth from where Mungo Park had left it, at Silla or Sélé, just below Sansanding. Accordingly, in 1805, the government launched an expedition, comprising no less than forty-six Europeans with the great Park at their head, for this purpose. It was an utter disaster. Not a soul survived and nothing was learnt.

A few years later, in 1816, the government tried to test the Niger-Congo theory by sending an expedition to each of the two rivers. One, under Captain Tuckey, was to ascend the Congo from its mouth; the other, under Major Peddie,[1] was to attempt from the Guinea coast what had cost Park and his companions their lives. Both expeditions ended in tragedy without any gain in knowledge.

After these disastrous expeditions from the west coast it began to look as though the African Association might after all have been right in pinning their faith on exploration from the north. This, rather surprisingly, found encouragement in the Admiralty. In 1816 a naval commander, W. H. Smyth, was sent over to Tripoli from Malta to inspect and report on 'some ancient architectural relics, which the Bashaw, at the instance of our Consul-general, Colonel Warrington, had recently offered for acceptance of our Prince Regent'.[2] On this and subsequent visits in connection with the relics, which were to come from Lepcis Magna, Smyth learnt enough about the country and its hinterland, and was sufficiently impressed by the friendliness of the Bashaw, Yūsuf Karamanli (whom he credited with far more power and influence than he in fact enjoyed) to conclude that the attempts to explore the interior of Africa from the north should be resumed. 'By striking due south of Tripoli', he wrote in March 1817, 'a traveller will reach Bornu before he is out of Yusuf's influence; and wherever his power reaches, the protecting virtues of the British flag are well known. In fact, looking to the unavoidable causes of death along the malarious banks of the rivers on the western coast, I think this ought to be the chosen route, because practicable into the very heart of the most benighted quarter of the globe.'[3] It is improbable that anything more would have been heard of this suggestion had not the Secretary of the

---

[1] See p. 257n. 2 below.
[2] Rear-Admiral W. H. Smyth, *The Mediterranean* (London, 1854), 473.
[3] Smyth, 487.

Admiralty at this time been the brilliant John Barrow,[1] a man whose influence was felt over a wide field of learning. Among the many subjects on which he was an acknowledged authority was the exploration of Africa on which his advice was generally sought. Smyth's suggestion naturally came to his notice in the Admiralty, received his blessing and appears to have been sent on to the Colonial Office[2] with a strong recommendation that it should be adopted. Many years later Rear-Admiral W. H. Smyth, as the commander had become,[3] proudly claimed that the consequences of his enquiries in North Africa had been 'so successful as to enlarge our geographical knowledge, and to lead to the journeys of Ritchie and Lyon — Oudney, Denham, and Clapperton — and, lastly, of Richardson, Overweg, Barth, and Vogel'.[4]

Smyth's claim appears to have been justified. Only six months after he had suggested exploration from the north a friend of Sir Joseph Banks was planning to reach Timbuktu by way of Tripoli,[5] and in the following year the first expedition from Tripoli was launched. It was led by Joseph Ritchie, who had Captain G. F. Lyon, R.N., as his companion, and its purpose was to cross the Sahara and explore the interior. Ritchie died at Murzuk, and Lyon did not get much further before having to turn back for lack of funds. The latter's enquiries about the Niger led him to the conclusion 'that by one route or other, these waters join the great Nile of Egypt'.[6]

The government, possibly a little penitent at official parsimony having brought the Ritchie-Lyon mission to so abrupt and profitless an end, quickly decided to follow it up with another. Thus was launched in 1821, by the same route, the famous expedition of Dr Oudney, Major Dixon Denham and Captain Hugh Clapperton, R.N., which crossed the Sahara and explored Hausa, Bornu and Lake Chad. It was a great achievement, flooding with light one of the richest parts of the interior of which little had been heard since the travels of Leo

---

[1] John Barrow's appointment was Second Secretary of the Admiralty, a post which he held from 1804 till 1845, with a short break in 1807. He did much to promote Arctic discovery, especially the search for the North West Passage, and was deeply interested in Africa. Outside the field of science, in which his name is still honoured, he is best remembered as the author of *The Mutiny of the Bounty*, first published, anonymously, in 1831.

[2] The Secretary of State for the Colonies was responsible for government-sponsored missions to Africa. The British consulates in the Barbary States also came under his care, but probably only because at this time Lord Bathurst was the Secretary of State for both Colonies and War. In the latter capacity he was required to exercise close vigilance over the tumultuous affairs of the North African littoral.

[3] In 1849–50 Smyth became President of the Royal Geographical Society.
[4] Smyth, 474.   [5] P. 147 below.
[6] Captain G. F. Lyon, *A Narrative of Travels in Northern Africa* (London, 1821), 148.

Africanus at the beginning of the sixteenth century. Nevertheless, the Bornu Mission, as it was called, fell short of expectations by failing to reach the Niger. But Denham and Clapperton (Oudney died near Kano) made exhaustive enquiries about its course and termination. In both Kano and Sokoto Clapperton was told that the Kworra, as the Niger was there called, flowed into the sea in the Bight of Benin.[1] Nevertheless, the map which Sultan Bello of Sokoto had drawn for him showed the river, contrary to what the Sultan himself had said, flowing eastwards and marked 'This is the river of Kowara which reaches Egypt, and which is called the Nile'.[2] This accorded with what Denham had been told in Bornu.[3]

It must have been a grievous disappointment to the two gallant explorers to have to report, on their return to London in 1825, that after travelling for three years they still had no certain knowledge of the course of the Niger. But a surprise awaited them. While they had been away an obscure young Scotsman, an army lieutenant serving in Sierra Leone, had been able to demonstrate convincingly that no matter what course the Niger took it could not possibly be the same river as the Nile. This was the first discovery made by Gordon Laing in a field in which he was soon to rise to fame.

iii. Alexander Gordon Laing: The Soldier

Alexander Gordon Laing,[4] born on 27 December 1794,[5] was the son of William Laing, a popular Edinburgh schoolmaster who had his own private academy. His mother was the daughter of William Gordon of Glasgow Academy. With such a background it was natural for the son, on completing his education at Edinburgh University at the age of fifteen, to start life as a schoolmaster. This he did at Newcastle upon Tyne, but six months later he returned to become assistant to his father in Edinburgh. There he joined the Prince of Wales Edinburgh Volunteers which he found so much to his liking that he decided to forsake teaching for the army. In 1811, his parents having reluctantly agreed

---

[1] Major Denham and Captain Clapperton, *Narrative of Travels and Discoveries in Northern and Central Africa*, 2 vols. (London, 1826), II, 241, 302, 304, 314.

[2] Denham and Clapperton, II, 330.

[3] Denham and Clapperton, I, 198.

[4] He was known to his family as Alexander but signed himself 'A. Gordon Laing'; his wife signed herself 'Emma M. Gordon Laing'.

[5] The year of his birth is usually given as 1793, but in an autobiographical note he says it was 1794 (R.S., Laing, vol. 4, 376).

to let him go, he went out to Barbados where his mother's brother, Colonel (afterwards General) Gabriel Gordon, was serving. There his uncle secured for him an ensign's commission in the York Light Infantry, a West Indian Regiment which he joined in Antigua. Two years later he exchanged into the 2nd West India Regiment and proceeded to Jamaica. There he devloped a tiresome liver complaint which led to his being invalided first to Honduras and from there back to his home in Scotland where he remained for eighteen months, recuperating and, latterly, on half-pay. He had, however, earned the high opinions of his senior officers, and at the end of 1819 was promoted to lieutenant and sent to rejoin his regiment which was then serving in Sierra Leone.

In Sierra Leone, as in all the other European settlements along the west coast of Africa, the activities of the expatriate whites, whether traders, officials or army officers, were still virtually confined to the seaboard, if not to the narrow confines of their trading beaches. This was only partly due to the difficulties of travel in the tropical rain forest of the coastal belt. It was more particularly due to the recently abolished slave trade, the middlemen of which had seen to it that their European customers were denied access to the interior whence they obtained their slaves. By 1821, fifteen years after the abolition of the slave trade in British colonies, it had become clear that there was much to be gained commercially, and also sometimes politically, by establishing contact with some of the more powerful tribes of the interior. At the end of that year Sir Charles MacCarthy, the Governor of Sierra Leone,[1] decided to send a mission into the hinterland to Kambia and the Mandingo country, 'to ascertain the state of the country, the disposition of the inhabitants to trade and industry; and to know their sentiments and conduct as to the abolition of the Slave Trade'.[2] Lieutenant Laing, who had shown great eagerness to explore the interior, was chosen to lead it.

This expedition, and the two others which followed in the same year, took Laing two hundred miles inland through unexplored country to Falaba, the capital of the powerful Soolima tribe, and to the source of the Rokelle River. He ended the year a seasoned traveller and had shown himself to have all the essential qualities of an explorer. He was brave, resolute, acutely observant and, even more important,

[1] MacCarthy's responsibilities were not limited to Sierra Leone. He was 'Governor in Chief of the British Settlements on the Western Coast of Africa, situated between twenty degrees north, and twenty degrees south latitude'.
[2] *Instructions to Lieutenant Laing of the 2nd West India Regiment proceeding on an Embassy to Kambia, and to the Mandingo Country* — January 7th, 1822.

he understood how to handle primitive tribes, whose confidence he secured by a happy combination of firmness and sympathy. As he published an account of these travels in a book,[1] which showed him to be also a skilful narrator, there is no need to dwell upon them here. It is, however, relevant to mention that at Falaba Laing had found himself, so the natives told him, within three short days' journey of the source of the Niger, at Mount Soma, but, to his lasting regret, he had been unable to visit it. This, however, is a matter to which we shall return shortly.

In the following year, 1823, Laing, who had been promoted to the command of a company in the Royal African Colonial Corps, was ordered to the Gold Coast where war had broken out between the British and the Ashantis. In the ensuing twelve months he was constantly in action and a frequent witness of the horrors of savage warfare. He fully lived up to the high standards which his superiors had learnt to expect of him, and was particularly remembered for having volunteered to attempt the rescue of a British sergeant who had been captured by the Ashantis and was held a prisoner in Kumassi. This gallant offer was rejected because it was considered too dangerous.[2]

The campaign took a grave turn early in the following year when the Ashantis overwhelmed a British force led by MacCarthy, whom they captured and killed. Soon after this disaster, Colonel Chisholm, who had assumed command, chose Laing, whose health was causing concern, to return to England with dispatches and to report personally to the Secretary of State on the very serious state of affairs on the Gold Coast. Thus did Laing come under the personal notice of Lord Bathurst.[3]

Laing's active military career was now over except for the slightly acrimonious circumstances of his final departure. These had little to do with his career as an explorer but need recounting here for the light they throw on his character.

In West Africa Laing seems not to have been liked by everyone, and it is probable that he had enemies in high quarters. This would have

---

[1] Major A. Gordon Laing, *Travels in the Timannee, Kooranko, and Soolima Countries in Western Africa* (London, 1825); this work was edited and seen through the press by his friend Captain Edward Sabine, R.A.

[2] *The Annual Register of the Year 1824* (London 1825), 127–8. The British sergeant was murdered.

[3] Henry, third Earl Bathurst, was the real creator of the Colonial Office which he ruled, as Third Secretary of State, from 1812 to 1827. In 1823 the Colonial Office was at 18 Downing Street, a building which no longer exists.

mattered less had he not been ambitious for promotion. He felt that his services in West Africa entitled him to the rank of major but that he was not likely to get it granted out there. So, without reference to his commanding officer, on his arrival in London, in August, he memorialized, or petitioned, the Commander-in-Chief, H.R.H. the Duke of York, for promotion. If it could not be granted, he hoped anyway to be given 'the Rank of Major in Africa only'.[1] This was at first refused, but, after his return from a hard-earned and sorely-needed rest in Scotland, he succeeded, evidently through the influence of Lord Bathurst, in obtaining extra leave direct from the Commander-in-Chief. His commanding officer, Major-General Charles Turner, knew nothing about it till after the leave had been granted.

General Turner had become Colonel of the Royal African Colonial Corps as recently as 1 July, shortly after his appointment as Governor of Sierra Leone in succession to Sir Charles MacCarthy. He had never served in West Africa and was still in London. So he can have known very little of Laing and may well never have met him. But the young Captain's growing habit of trying to get his way by appealing direct to the Horse Guards over his commanding officer's head was creating an antipathy which was shortly to become pronounced. Probably the first warning Laing had of rising resentment was the following letter from the General's A.D.C.:

No. 7 Panton Square.
3rd November, 1824

Sir,
    I am directed by Major General Turner to acknowledge the receipt of your Letter of the 2nd Instant addressed to Lieutenant Glover, extra aide de Camp, wherein you state that His Royal Highness the Commander in Chief has been pleased to grant you leave of Absence during the period of your prosecuting some scientific researches in the Interior of Africa.

    The Major General desires that you will furnish him with your Authority for this communication as he is wholly unacquainted with the circumstances set forth by you and as they are of a Nature which under existing circumstances he could not have expected or approved of
                  I have the honour to be
                        Sir
                Your most obedient
                humble servant,
                            Wm. Ross,
                            Capt. R.A. Corps &
                            Aide de Camp.[2]

---

[1] R.S., 374(La) 59.   [2] R.S., 374(La) 64.

Soon after this news was received in London of the death of Colonel Chisholm who, it will be recalled, was commanding on the Gold Coast. This seemed to Laing to offer an opportunity for promotion which, with the influential assistance of Lord Bathurst, who had befriended him, might be turned to effective account in a fresh assault on the Horse Guards. He accordingly wrote to Bathurst begging his recommendation to the Commander-in-Chief. To this letter, which was dated 12 January 1825, he attached the following record of his services during the previous three years:

In the year 1822 Memorialist performed a Journey of seven Months into the interior of Africa at the request of the late Sir Charles MacCarthy; established friendly relations with many powerful inland Chiefs, and greatly increased the Gold and Ivory trade of Sierra Leone — For this service Memorialist received a letter of thanks and a piece of plate from the Merchants of the Colony.

On the 2nd December 1822, Memorialist saved the American Settlement at Mesurado[1] from annihilation by an army of natives, and secured for it a peace, which it has ever since enjoyed.

On the 26th February 1823, Memorialist commanded the advance guard of the British army at Donquah[2] and with it alone, defeated a large body of Ashantees and Fantees —

After the above affair, Memorialist succeeded partly by negotiation, partly by determined military movement in making allies of the Fantees, among whom he remained for four months, organising them into a force, with which alone, he overthrew and expelled from their country, a large Ashantee Army which invaded it in August 1823.

After the unfortunate defeat of Sir Charles MacCarthy, Memorialist collected the scattered Fantees, and successfully opposed the Ashantees as long as his health permitted him to keep the field; preventing them from crossing the Boosoompra, and dislodging them from the towns on the waterside —

A. Gordon Laing,
Capt. R.A.C. Corps
and Major in Africa.[3]

A comparison of what Laing wrote in this memorandum about his part in the Ashanti campaign with what Major Ricketts, the Brigade-Major of the British force, said about it[4] shows that Laing's was a

[1] Cape Mesurado, where Monrovia now stands, was chosen by the American Colonization Society in 1821 for its first settlement of American freed slaves.

[2] Donquah, or Danquah, was a Fantee town situated about twenty miles east of Cape Coast Castle.

[3] This rank had just been granted him. P.R.O., C.O. 2/15, 209.

[4] Major Ricketts, *Narrative of the Ashantee War* (London, 1831), *passim*.

notably concise, restrained and fair record of what he had done. The anonymous, and therefore less authoritative, correspondent of *The Annual Register*, who had recorded Laing's offer to rescue the British sergeant, also mentioned two different 'gallant and successful' attacks by Laing on a large Ashanti force and a third 'not without considerable loss on his side', the fame of which won over 'most of the Fantee tribes'.[1] Back in April 1821 he had, as we shall see, been very well reported on by the acting Governor of Sierra Leone. In all the circumstances it is not possible to doubt that young Captain Laing was a gallant and thoroughly competent officer. Nevertheless, when a copy of Laing's memorandum reached General Turner in West Africa he denounced it with a venom which must have astonished Lord Bathurst to whom the despatch, dated 9 April 1825, was addressed. This is what he wrote:

I would not fulfil my duty either to your Lordship or to the service, were I not to characterize as unwise, unofficerlike, and unmanly, the conduct of Captain Gordon Laing in this Country. In place of attending to the health and discipline of his Company, his time was occupied in editing a contemptible Newspaper (which I now possess) the columns of which are filled with the most fulsome panegyrics upon himself in prose and rhyme, in magnifying into Armies, a few Wild Negroes in the Woods, deceiving Sir Charles both as to their numbers and quality, also in inflaming the Chiefs of the Ashantees, by foul abuse against the English — Such were his Newspaper proceedings — His military exploits were worse than his poetry, for appalled at the storm he mainly helped to raise, he abandoned and left to their fate, those whom he had brought within it's influence.

Of his Armies nothing more was heard: and I humbly beg your Lordship, in the name of the Regiment, that he may be removed from it — and that we may not be subject to the mortification of his calling us *Brother* Officers.[2]

As Laing had left West Africa months before General Turner had arrived out there, this venomous attack must have been instigated by someone else. It was perhaps someone smarting under the lash of Laing's wit in his 'contemptible newspaper'. As the General was very well liked in West Africa he was presumably a fair-minded man who would not have put his signature to so bitter an attack on one of his officers had he not thought it fully justified. No doubt his excusable irritation at Laing's repeated appeals to the Commander-in-Chief over

[1] *The Annual Register for the Year 1824*, 127–8.
[2] *Ext. of a Dispatch from M. General Turner to the Earl Bathurst dated 9th April, 1825* (P.R.O., C.O. 2/15).

his head, the last of which had secured for him the local rank of 'major in Africa', had predisposed him to lend a ready ear to criticisms of a slightly insubordinate young officer. That they were in fact unfair cannot be doubted. But Laing had a trait which the army has never found it easy to forgive; he was an individualist. Moreover, he was profoundly interested in the country in which he was serving for which the expatriate colonial soldier has seldom been distinguished. It would be unwise to conclude more than that Laing was not a particularly popular officer. The lack of any note of appreciation in Major Ricketts's frequent references to him in his published account of the Ashanti campaign lends colour to this supposition.

There was, however, out in West Africa another young officer with a brilliant career ahead of him who held Laing in great regard. This was Captain Edward Sabine of the Royal Artillery, only six years Laing's senior. Already a scientist of distinction and an accepted authority on the Arctic, he was now engaged on scientific work in West Africa, and was destined to become President of the Royal Society.[1] It was Captain Sabine who edited and saw through the press Laing's book on his travels in the hinterland of Sierra Leone, and to whom we owe the preservation of his personal papers now in the archives of the Royal Society. Had there been substance in General Turner's savage denunciation it is hardly possible that Laing would have been held in such warm regard by an officer of the calibre of Edward Sabine, or that he would have been chosen by Colonel Chisholm to report personally to Lord Bathurst on the troubled situation on the Gold Coast.

iv. Laing and the Niger

'I have had for many years a strong desire to penetrate into the interior of Africa', wrote Laing a few months after he had arrived in West Africa, 'and that desire has been greatly increased by my arrival on the Coast.' The letter from which these words are taken was addressed to Captain Chisholm, Laing's commanding officer, and was dated from Fort Thornton, Sierra Leone, 15 March 1821. Enclosed with the letter was a formal proposal that he should be allowed to attempt to reach Timbuktu, by way of Timbo, at no expense to the government apart from certain equipment he could not afford to buy.

---

[1] He had accompanied two expeditions to the Arctic, in 1818 and 1819, and had been sent to West Africa in 1821. He returned to the United Kingdom in 1823. Sabine Island in the Arctic Circle was named after him.

The latter comprised 'a Good Gun on which I may depend, a Barometer for measuring heights, a Pocket Sextant, an Azimuth for taking Angles, and a Pocket Chronometer which Instruments I should like to be sent out from home, and of a good description'.[1]

Laing's proposal was forwarded to London for submission to Lord Bathurst under cover of the following flattering letter from the Acting Governor of Sierra Leone:

Government House,
Free Town, Sierra Leone;
4th April, 1821.

My Lord,

I have the honor to enclose the copy of a letter handed to me by Captain Chisholm, Commanding 2nd West India Regiment; and addressed to him by Lieutenant Lang [sic] of that Regiment, accompanied by proposals made by Lieut. Laing to penetrate into the interior of Africa, as far as Tombuctoo, by way of Teembo [Timbo].

I have no hesitation in saying, that Mr. Laing is a young Man well calculated in every respect for such an undertaking; of a strong mind, vigorous body, patient of fatigue, with the advantage of a liberal education, which would enable him to make such observations as would not only reflect great credit on himself but be of infinite advantage to the Country.

His motives are no less disinterested, than honorable, and as far as human foresight can divine, he is from his Physical strength and acquirements well calculated to succeed.

In the event of his services being accepted I have to request that your Lordship may be pleased to give directions for furnishing the instruments he mentions as necessary and favor me, by the earliest opportunity, with instructions concerning him,

I have the honor to be
My Lord,
Your Lordship's most obdt. humble Servant,
(sgd) A. Grant,

Acting Governor.[2]

There was no name in all Africa more stirring to the imagination than Timbuktu, and it was one which must inevitably have been constantly in Laing's mind. Mungo Park's travels had not only attracted fresh attention to it, but had shown that the first man to discover Timbuktu would be also the first to discover the middle Niger. It was

---

[1] P.R.O., C.O. 276/53, No. 7.

[2] R.S., 374(La) 46. Captain Alexander Grant was the acting commanding officer of the 2nd West India Regiment.

natural, therefore, for Laing to make Timbuktu his objective, but only as a first step towards completing Park's work.

At this time there was no problem of more absorbing interest to those concerned with unexplored Africa than the mystery of the course and termination of the Niger, and it was one which constantly occupied Laing's mind. He had already tried to contribute to its solution by cross-examining any travelled African he chanced to meet. He recorded the fruits of these enquiries,[1] and published an account of the travels of the more interesting of his informants, notably those of Mohammed Misrah of Alexandria.[2] Like everyone else who had attempted this method, including the African Association, he found it yielded only disappointing results and he was forced to conclude, doubtless to his satisfaction, that exploration was the only way to certain knowledge.

In spite of the strong letter of recommendation from the Acting Governor, Laing's proposal was turned down by the Colonial Office. He was to be told, minuted Lord Bathurst, that as another officer had been appointed to undertake a similar mission into the interior from the northern coast of Africa 'there does not appear at present to be any opening for the employment of Lt. Laing'.[3] As there was no likelihood of Laing's proposed expedition clashing with Oudney's Bornu Mission, to which Lord Bathurst was evidently alluding, it seems to have been made a convenient excuse for rejecting Laing's proposal for which his youth or inexperience may have been the real reason.

Laing was not discouraged. His friend Captain Sabine, already a man of some account in the world of science, was back in London and evidently trying to help, for on 1 February 1822 he wrote to Laing:

Barrow[4] desires me to say, that such is the opinion which is entertained of your qualifications in every respect for African travelling both at the Colonial Office and Admty, that you will find, he believes little difficulty in getting the Government to accede to your further plans — I said £5000 — He replied 'Oh yes they will give that to a person with his experience.'[5]

The nature of the experience which was thought to qualify Laing for a £5,000 government grant is doubtful. He had not yet had any

[1] The Laing papers in the Royal Society's archives include a number of these records (R.S., 374(La) 1–10, 48).
[2] *The Quarterly Journal of Science, Literature, and the Arts*, XIV (1823), 1–16.
[3] P.R.O., C.O. 276/58.
[4] John Barrow would have known Sabine through their common interest in the Arctic.
[5] R.S., 374(La) 47.

experience of exploratory work. He did have some training in the use of astronomical instruments, he knew something about geology in which he seems to have been interested and he was also a first-class draughtsman.[1] In the short time he had been in Africa he had doubtless started to learn one or more native languages for we know that he later became fluent in Mende. But Barrow's optimism did not justify itself.

Laing, as we have seen, was about to gain valuable experience of practical exploratory work which was greatly to improve his prospects of employment by government in that particular field. It was probably on account of his deep interest in the country and his passionate desire to explore the unknown that he was chosen for the missions which occupied him during the greater part of 1822, and from which he returned more determined than ever to make his projected journey. But the emphasis was now frankly on the Niger. On 25 November 1822 he wrote to Sabine in London telling him of his return to the coast and adding:

> As I am still determined on a long Journey into the Interior I wish you wou'd be kind enough to mention me to Mr. Barrow — I have two plans, the most extravagant of which, I think, might cost about £5000 — I shall in my next, submit both [to] your consideration, in the meantime observing, that I am well aware, that thousands of men might be picked out, possessed of far more ability than myself for such an enterprise, men who might set out with great spirit, and equal determination, who might have inclination to attempt as much and strength to execute more, but I doubt much if any one cou'd be found, who has the matter more clearly in view, and who under all circumstances wou'd persecute it with greater firmness and steadiness, and consequently no one who wou'd be more likely to bring it to an honorable and successful conclusion; for this reason — Because I have neither formed the desire of discovering the termination of the Niger from enthusiasm, avarice, or a desire of fame, but from curiosity and a wish to be beneficial in bringing about the civilization of the most ignorant and unfortunate country in the world — You are well aware of my disinterested motives, and it is therefore unnecessary to repeat them here. I shall therefore only state that I expect your assistance in enabling me to gratify this only wish of my heart — I send you a handsome saddle cover, presented to me by the King of the Soolimas, of which I beg your acceptance.[2]

---

[1] In the Public Record Office there is a striking example of the excellence of Laing's cartographical work. It is a map drawn to illustrate his travels in the Sierra Leone hinterland in 1822 (P.R.O., C.O. 276/58, No. 310).

[2] R.S., 374(La) 49.

Laing's chances of realizing his great ambition had much improved. Besides the experience he had gained of travelling in unexplored country he had been signally successful in making a mark in the field of geographical discovery. His journey to Falaba had, as we have seen, taken him close to Mount Soma, the alleged source of the Niger, but he had been prevented from reaching it. Nevertheless he had been near enough to turn his journey to very considerable account.[1]

In 1823 *The Quarterly Journal of Science*[2] reported his safe return to the coast and added:

'The country, thus visited for the first time by an European, possesses a peculiar geographical interest as the source of the mysterious Niger: we understand that the elevation above the sea, as well as the latitude and longitude of the hill of Soma, from whence it derives its origin, have been satisfactorily ascertained by Captain Laing.' This was so. The altitude was such that the Niger could not possibly flow into the Nile.

The announcement of Laing's conclusion that the Niger and the Nile must be two different rivers naturally attracted attention, and probably brought him enquiring letters from men of learning interested in the Niger problem. Among the Laing papers in the possession of the Royal Society there is a rough draft of what appears to be a reply to one such correspondent who had approached him through the Governor, Sir Charles MacCarthy. The draft is undated and we do not know for whom it was intended or whether in fact such a letter was ever sent. But these are not material points. It was probably written some time after Laing's arrival on the Gold Coast at the end of 1822, and certainly before the death of MacCarthy in January 1824. All that really matters is that it is indubitably in Laing's hand. So far as its many corrections, erasures and often illegible interpolations permit, it reads as follows:

Sir — A Memorandum of your's having been put into my hands by His Excellency Sir Charles MacCarthy, I trust I may not be deemed intrusive if I address a few lines to you on the subject to which it bears reference — I have always considered that a knowledge of the height of the Niger's source wou'd be of the utmost importance for that point being once gained, we cou'd to a certainty determine where that river cou'd not finish its course, and consequently save much trouble and expence in the future research after that geographical desideratum — I therefore, in undertaking to conduct a Mission into the Soolima Country, promised myself much satisfaction, in the prospect I had before me of reaching the source of this river and ascertaining its true

---

[1] Laing, 270, 273, 288, 302–5, 323.   [2] Vol. xv (1823), 171.

elevation above the level of the sea; my exertions however were not quite so successful as I cou'd have desired — innumerable obstacles opposed themselves to every advance previous to a severe illness in Falaba which had nearly terminated my existence, and even after my recovery every effort of mine to proceed was unavailing as any exertion in three or four different attempts which I made, were entirely frustrated by the jealousy and superstition of the natives, to say nothing of the barrier which opposed itself, owing to the river taking its rise in a country at War with the tribes to whom I was on a visit — At length I was obliged to content myself with a view which I had of the river & the spot from which it eminates at a distance of about thirty miles; it appeared to me less, but the journey being one of two days I was inclined from that circumstance and from my having seen it & taken its bearings from a lofty mountain in the Soolima country, to allow it that distance from the source of the Rokelle the place from whence I had the second view — The source of the Rokelle is 1441 Feet above the level of the sea by measurement of Barometer,[1] and from the appearance of the ground between the two sources I would not suppose that of the Niger to be 100 feet higher. The question of the Niger uniting with the Nile must therefore be for ever at rest — the elevation at its source not being sufficient to carry it half the distance; to say nothing of the fact that the Nile is higher at Sennaar than the Niger at its source.[2]

In a communication made by me a few days ago to Sir Charles MacCarthy for the information of my Lord Bathurst, I stated this fact (though not so explicitly perhaps as I have done to you) in order to prevent if possible any further missions being set on foot for the purpose of exploring the Niger from Northern Africa, and that his Lordship might be enabled to judge of the propriety of recalling the mission under Major Denman[3] shou'd it be obliged to return again from Morzourk, as it is now very clear that nothing in the way of discovery can be effected from that quarter, and that the attempt is only attended with expense, disappointment, and perhaps the loss of valuable lives — It has long been my wish to explore the course of this hidden stream, & I once made an offer to attempt it, but being unknown to my Lord Bathurst my proposal was not accepted of; I still feel anxious to prosecute research, and trust that the experience I have gained, together with the economic manner in which I conducted the Soolima Mission (not costing Govt. in all 200£) may ultimately procure me the gratification of my wishes — I have never looked for money as a recompense for any thing I might execute, on the contrary it is well known that [2 words illegible] I expended my own in procuring information & in making presents to Chiefs, and I declare that if I had a sufficiency of my own to defray my expenses I wou'd not apply to

---

[1] Eight miles from its source the Rokelle divides into four or five unnamed streams. The source of one of these is 1,900 feet above sea-level, but that of another is only about 1,400 feet.

[2] Sennar is 1,378 feet above sea-level.   [3] Major Dixon Denham.

Government for the smallest assistance in the furtherance of the design which I hope yet to be able to accomplish, the completion of which (after the enormous sums which has been lavished) might be more than ever desired by our Country, as the discovery made by any other power wou'd entail disgrace for ever upon our feeble spirit of enterprise — It is my intention as soon as the Ashantee war is finished, to visit Benin in order to ascertain whether or not advances from that quarter are likely to be attended with probable success, but if it does not offer advantages considerably greater than I at present think it does, I wou'd prefer the route from Sierra Leone, crossing the Niger at Kang Kang [Kankan] and skirting the Sangara country reach Nuffe [Nupe] where I shou'd be guided as to the [2 words illegible] advance by circumstance & information received.[1]

I trust Sir you will receive this letter as I intend it, and that you will neither consider me prolix or tedious upon a subject, which while it is interesting to me I am certain occupies a considerable share of your attention also.[2]

This draft letter was possibly written at about the same time as Laing was making a second attempt to be sent on an expedition to the Niger. On 12 April 1823 MacCarthy, writing from Cape Coast Castle, forwarded to Lord Bathurst a letter from Laing which, although mostly about his late mission to Falaba, ended with these words:

In conclusion, I trust that should Your Excellency feel satisfied with the manner in which I have executed the present Mission that you will be pleased to recommend me to My Lord Bathurst as a person capable of making further research in Africa. — I am anxious to discover the termination of the Niger, and am willing to undertake the enterprize on the same terms that I did the one just performed, that is without regard to emolument or expectation of reward.[3]

In his covering letter MacCarthy wrote:

... it will afford me very great pleasure to be authorized at a future period, to accept of his Services to explore the termination of the *Niger*.
I can state with perfect confidence that to be instrumental in the extension of Science is the only object in the view of that Officer.[4]

These letters were being written and sent off to London at a time when both Laing and MacCarthy were on active service on the Gold

[1] Laing evidently had in mind travelling eastwards through Kankan to Nupe instead of following the much longer route round the great bend of the Niger.
[2] R.S., 374(La) 145.
[3] This is the letter to which Laing attached the admirable map to which reference has just been made.
[4] P.R.O., C.O. 276/58, No. 310.

Coast. With no prospect of an early end to the troublesome Ashanti campaign, there was no question of Laing's early release for exploratory work. It is therefore not surprising that we have no record of what became of his application. That he should have found time during a gruelling campaign in which he was very fully engaged to plan so ambitious an enterprise shows how obsessed he had become with the Niger problem. He had also found time to reach an interesting conclusion about where the end of the river would be found. He had become convinced that Reichard's unpopular theory that the Niger ended in the Bight of Benin was the correct one. He was consequently delighted to hear that the Bornu Mission had searched Lake Chad 'and found *no outlet*, as Mahomed Misrah my priest affirmed — This will entirely upset Mr. Barrow's theory, and as it affords a strong additional proof of the accuracy of the Priest, greatly contribute to strengthen mine, that is to say Reichard's which I conform to'.[1]

v. *The Road to Timbuktu*

Although Laing will always be remembered as the discoverer of Timbuktu, and his expedition was officially known as the Timbuktu Mission, his objective was the Niger. He set out to complete Park's work by discovering the main course of the river and, above all, its termination. The discovery of Timbuktu was his immediate objective, but only as a means to a greater end.

The reader will recall that in the days of Hornemann and the African Association, when it was widely believed that the Niger and the Nile were one, the Hausa city of Katsina, on the flimsiest evidence, was thought to be the key to the middle Niger. Now, on much stronger evidence, the still undiscovered but far more famous city of Timbuktu, which Park had shown to lie very close to the river, was clearly the key. From Timbuktu it should be possible, in spite of what had befallen Park, to follow the Niger to its mouth. At least its middle and lower course was more likely to be traced from there than by groping blindly for it in the wholly unexplored heart of the continent.

The shortest way to Timbuktu from Europe was the caravan road running south from Marrakech.[2] Farther east there was the road through Wargla and Tuat. But there was much to be said for starting

---

[1] R.S., 374(La) 70. He thought the Mission had circled Chad, but it had failed to do so.

[2] This was the route that Giovanni Baptista Belzoni had tried to follow in 1823.

still farther east, from Tripoli. As the northern terminus of the shortest and easiest road to the Sudan — the Garamantian way through Fezzan and Kawar — Tripoli had, since Roman times, been the main gateway to the interior from the north, and the main maritime outlet for the produce of the Sudan, which constituted the life-blood of the Barbary trade.[1] It was because of the ready access which Tripoli gave to the Sudan that Ritchie and Lyon and the Bornu Mission had set out from there, and that Hornemann would have much preferred to do so.

But Tripoli's contact with the Sudan was not confined to the ancient north-and-south road through Fezzan. There was another very old road running south-west through Ghadames and Tuat to Timbuktu. Traversing the Sahara diagonally it was a hard and perilous road and not much used. But difficult though it was — grievously short of water and pasture, and a constant prey to ruthless desert raiders — it was both politically and commercially too important a road to go out of use altogether. Its political importance derived from the link it provided between Timbuktu and the eastern Maghreb, Egypt and Mecca. Originally it owed its commercial importance to the gold trade with Timbuktu, which eventually became the chief distributing centre for the goldfields of Bambuk, but by the nineteenth century this trade had dwindled and was now of small account. Nevertheless the road remained commercially important owing more to its passing through Ghadames than to having Tripoli as its northern terminus.

The oasis of Ghadames, very small and very isolated but abundantly supplied with water, was one of the great entrepôts of desert trade. On it converged caravan routes from Murzuk, Ghat, Kairwan and Tripoli which gave it access to all the great markets of north-western Africa, in both the Maghreb and the Sudan, from Cairo to Timbuktu, and Fez to Kano. Even in Roman times it had been important enough for Septimius Severus to station there a detachment of the Legio III Augusta. Besides attracting to itself traders and pilgrims, going to and from Mecca, from every quarter, it had a small resident commercial community of its own who, with great enterprise, had established themselves in the markets of the south.[2]

It is probable that at the beginning of the nineteenth century no one in Europe knew of the Tripoli-Ghadames road to Timbuktu. In March

---

[1] The staples of the Sudan trade were slaves, ivory, senna, civet and gold.

[2] When, in 1591, the Moors occupied Timbuktu they found that the most flourishing quarter was that of the Ghadamsi merchants (Abderrahman es-Sadi, *Tarikh es Soudan* (Paris, 1900), 222).

1817 Smyth, hearing that Murzuk was trading with Timbuktu, suggested trying to reach the latter by way of Fezzan. 'I think attention ought to be directed to the important object of the Tombuctoo caravans from Mourzouk', he wrote, '... caravans occasionally go from Fezzan, sometimes direct, and at others to Twat, and from thence to Tombuctoo. From every enquiry I really concieve it to be a practicable route.'[1]

So readily was Smyth listened to that only six months later Henry Goulburn, Bathurst's Under-Secretary previous to Wilmot Horton, wrote the following letter to John Barrow:

My dear Barrow,

Lord Bathurst is, as you may concieve, most anxious to forward the project entertained by Sir Joseph Banks' friend, of proceeding to Tombuctoo via Tripoli, and will do every thing that lies in his power to assist him. He will readily authorise the purchase of the necessary presents for the Bey & his son, and will instruct our Consul to urge upon the Bey the fulfilment of his promise & to exert every nerve to carry the enterprize to a favourable issue. Will you therefore concert what is best to be done with Sir J. Banks, & I will be at your orders to execute what you may decide.

Yours ever most truly

Sept. 23rd 1817   Henry Goulburn.[2]

Directly Barrow got this he wrote the following letter to Banks about whose friend's intentions Goulburn seems to have been misinformed:

Admiralty, 8 Oct. 1817

My dear Sir Joseph,

Goldburn[3] only found the enclosed yesterday, which he wrote a fortnight ago. What a fine opportunity now presents itself, if a man properly qualified could be found, and, if you cannot find one, I know not where to look. Pray try to cast about for some person who knows a little Arabic, either in England or the Continent; for we shall not be able perhaps to find another Lord Bathurst at home, or another Basha at Tripoli, so favourable for the undertaking.

I am, my dear Sir Joseph,
very faithfully yours

John Barrow[4]

---

[1] Smyth, 485.   [2] *D.T.C.*, xx, No. 51.

[3] It used to be said, that the popular and high-principled Goulburn first came to be called Goldburn on his appointment as Chancellor of the Exchequer in 1830, to which the nickname appeared to be singularly appropriate. This letter shows that he acquired it at a much earlier date.

[4] *D.T.C.*, xx, No. 50.

Nothing came of this, but in the latter part of the year the Bashaw told Smyth of the more direct road through Ghadames. However, it was not until the end of 1820 that, in a letter to the First Lord of the Admiralty, he drew attention to it by stressing the unrecognized importance of Ghadames, 'a town, I am led to believe, of the utmost importance to travellers in the interior, as being the resort of numerous trading caravans'.[1]

As a starting point for Timbuktu Tripoli offered several advantages to British explorers.[2] One of them was that there was little risk of interference from the French who further west were carving out for themselves an extensive sphere of influence of which they were very jealous. Another, as John Barrow had had occasion to remind Sir Joseph, was the good will of the Bashaw who, through the influence of the Consul, was particularly anxious to help British explorers. A third advantage was the choice of roads which Tripoli offered: there was the ancient Garamantian way as far as Murzuk where there were two alternative roads for the onward journey, either direct to Timbuktu or through Tuat, to which Smyth had drawn attention in 1817; there was also the shorter road direct from Tripoli through the Garian mountains to Ghadames and thence to Tuat which Smyth had reported in 1820.

There was no lack of volunteers to attempt the journey. Late in 1820 or early in 1821 Dixon Denham,[3] before joining Oudney, and, a year or two later, Lyon had offered.[4]

---

[1] Smyth, 494.

[2] In 1821 the Beecheys had met in Tripoli a merchant who offered to take them to Timbuktu in perfect safety. (*Expedition to Explore the Northern Coast of Africa* (London, 1828), 6.) In 1822 Warrington was snubbed by the Colonial Office for having suggested a mission to Timbuktu. Wilmot to Warrington, 3 May 1822. P.R.O., F.O. 8/8.

[3] Denham and Clapperton, I, xvii.

[4] On 21 November 1823 John Barrow, as Secretary of the Admiralty, wrote to Lord Bathurst pressing him to interest himself in proposals from Franklin and Lyon. In regard to the latter he wrote: 'Lyon too is very anxious to go on some land expedition either from Wager Inlet to the mouth of the Copper Mine River to open the road for the fur trade of the Stupid Hudson's Bay people; or to set out with the Caravan to Tombuctoo — He says if the government will give him £1000, he will ask for nothing more, and undertake either. I am very much for encouraging this spirit of adventure and I am sure that the public feeling is for it.' The letter was handed to Bathurst with the following enquiry: 'How does your Lordship feel with respect to sanctioning either Franklin's or Lyon's proposal or both?' To this the Minister replied: 'Lyon's expedition to *Timbuctoo* would interfere with our People now employed. I am *inclined* to Franklin's but should like to hear more of it ... Lyon may be employed elsewhere.' Someone minuted at the foot of the Minister's reply 'Mr. Barrow is very impertinent', while the Minister himself endorsed Barrow's letter, 'You will see I have shown up Barrow to my Daughter.' The words 'Our People now employed' clearly meant Oudney, Denham and Clapperton. (P.R.O., C.O. 324/75, 222, 223).

The Road to Timbuktu

Lord Bathurst rather surprisingly, decided that Laing should take the longer road through Fezzan,[1] but he does not appear to have laid down which of the two alternative routes he should follow from there. Why he so decided is uncertain, but it may have been due to the belief that only once a year did a caravan make the journey from Tripoli to Timbuktu and that it travelled through Fezzan.[2] As we shall see, when Laing got to Tripoli he decided to travel through Ghadames but, owing to political troubles in the Garian mountains, the direct road was closed and he had to make a long detour through Fezzan. Instead of continuing his journey from there direct, according to his instructions, he, still determined to see Ghadames, turned north-west to join the road he had originally decided to follow.

Unfortunately for Laing he was robbed of one of the great attractions that Tripoli had hitherto offered to the explorer. The Bashaw, Yūsuf Karamanli, had suddenly become markedly less anxious to provide the assistance he had afforded the Bornu Mission.

vi. Yūsuf Karamanli

The Karamanli family were of Cologhi origin, that is to say of mixed descent from the union of Turkish Janisseries with local Arab and Berber women. In 1711 Ahmed Karamanli[3] deposed the Turkish Dey, massacred the Janisseries, and established a dynasty that was to rule the country for 125 years. The Turkish sytem of government was preserved, and the precarious economy of the country remained insecurely based on piracy and the slave trade. The country was still nominally part of the Turkish empire and consequently most of the Europeans in Tripoli were protected by the terms of the Ottoman Capitulations of 1761. These conferred on the consuls of the principal European powers privileges which enabled them to protect their nationals against the tyranny of the Bashaws.

The consuls had unfettered jurisdiction over their own countrymen

---

[1] See p. 164n. 2 below.

[2] Lyon had offered to accompany 'the caravan to Tombuctoo', and Laing, as we shall see, was instructed to proceed by 'the Caravan' to Timbuktu. These two references to *the* caravan suggest that in London it was believed that there was a regular annual caravan like, say, the immense *azalai* which yearly set out from Air to fetch salt from Bilma. This was not so. The frequency of caravans travelling between Tripoli and Timbuktu depended on the course of trade and the hazards of desert politics, and was therefore unpredictable. Smyth was probably responsible for this erroneous belief because he was under the impression that there was only one annual caravan (*The Mediterranean*, 492).

[3] His name is sometimes given as Ali.

and, in case of need, they could call on the Bashaw's government to enforce their judgments. Their consulates were inviolate and consequently became sanctuaries for victims of oppression of all races. In times of trouble the consuls of the principal naval powers, notably Britain and France, could coerce the local government, as they sometimes did, by summoning ships of war to demonstrate before the Bashaw's palace.

Although there were, in this small city, eight foreign consuls with these unusual powers the limitations they placed on the sovereignty of the Bashaw were not as great as might be supposed. The Karamanlis were masters of intrigue and skilled in playing off one consul against another, and they found it easy enough to prevent concerted consular action. The Bashaws also had both the duty and the right to provide each consul with two *shawishes*[1] whose duties were to accompany the consul wherever he went, and to keep the Bashaw fully informed about all that was happening in his consulate. An astute Bashaw had little difficulty in holding his own against the powerful foreign consuls, and none was more adept at it than Yūsuf Karamanli.

Yūsuf was a son of Ali, the third Bashaw, and a great grandson of the founder of the dynasty. Early in life he determined not to allow his two older brothers to stand in the way of his succeeding their father. The older one, Hassan, he murdered, and the younger, Ahmed, who in fact succeeded their father but only for a month, he drove out of the country.[2] Thus in 1794 he usurped a throne from which he ruled for thirty-eight years in the same ruthless way that had brought him to the throne.

A cruel and unprincipled tyrant, who never honoured his engagements unless it suited him, Yūsuf was nevertheless the greatest of the Karamanli Bashaws. He had soaring ambitions for his country which he pursued ruthlessly. He used his army to such effect against the ever lawless tribes of the hinterland that his influence was felt, and his name was feared, nearly as far as Bornu.

Intelligent, and endowed with considerable personal charm, he was at home in the company of the foreign consuls, who rose and fell in his favour in accordance with the trend of foreign politics. Early in his reign Napoleon's triumphs in the Mediterranean, notably his capture of

---

[1] The *shawish*, *chaoush* or *chaoux* was a constable, but he was also employed in other capacities, such as guard and messenger.
[2] There is a tradition that Ahmed, like Hassan, was murdered by his brother but, in fact, he died in poverty in Egypt.

Malta and conquest of Egypt, so alarmed the Bashaw that the French Consul quickly acquired a marked advantage over his rivals for influence at court. Later the Bashaw's friendship for the French was cemented by a treaty negotiated between Xavier Naudi, a Maltese emissary especially sent out by Napoleon, and the Bashaw's French-speaking foreign minister Mohammed D'Ghies.[1]

Subsequent British victories in the Mediterranean quickly weakened French influence at court, but it did not wholly give way to the British until 1814 when Colonel Hanmer Warrington was appointed British Consul-General in Tripoli. Great though Warrington's influence became, Yūsuf never allowed him to feel sure of its indefinite continuance. Yūsuf's policy towards the British and French Consuls, the representatives of the two principal naval powers in the Mediterranean, was to play one off against the other. The result was that Anglo-French jealousy and bitterness took deep root in Tripoli and long divided the small consular world of the Bashaw's capital.[2]

vii. Colonel Warrington

In the history of the repeated attempts to penetrate Africa from the north no name recurs more frequently than that of Colonel Hanmer Warrington,[3] a noted personality in the Mediterranean in the first half of the nineteenth century. Deeply interested in the opening up of Africa and unsparing in his efforts to promote it, he placed a number of explorers in his debt.

We know nothing of Warrington's origin and up-bringing, but 1778 appears to have been the year of his birth. In a dispatch to Lord Bathurst of 24 March 1826 he gave the following account of his military career:

At Sixteen years old I entered the Army & served in the Kings Dragoon Guards as Cornet & Lieutenant, & for some time on the Continent, with

---

[1] According to Denham, in 1822 Mohammed D'Ghies, who then had a son Hassuna in London, 'had retired from office some time, on account of a complaint in his eyes. He is a most respectable man, and particularly kind to all European travellers... and so well known throughout Northern Africa, that letters of credit from him are sure to be honoured.' It seems therefore that he had now returned to office (Denham and Clapperton, I, xxi). See p. 20n. above.

[2] R. Vadala, *L'Histoire des Karamanlis; Revue de L'Histoire des Colonies Françaises*, viia (Paris, 1919), 177–288. Seton Dearden, *Introduction* to Miss Tully, *Letters Written During a Ten Years' Residence at the Court of Tripoli* (London, 1957).

[3] He is usually referred to as Colonel Warrington, but he was called Mr by most of his contemporaries, and was so addressed in official correspondence.

which Regt. I returned to England — I then was Captain in the second Dragoon Guards, & after Major in the 4th. Dragoon Guards I then raised & Commanded a Corps of Volunteer Cavalry. I was after Inspecting Field Officer with the Rank of Lieut. Colonel.

When that Service was done away with I was sent to Spain with the rank of Lt. Col., & immediately went on that unfortunate Expedition to Fangarola and Malaga. In the Charge for Retaking the British Guns, I was a Hundred yards in advance of the 89th Regt. and Consequently the first in the French Battery where I had my Horse killed under me, & received Two Balls through my Coat and although unfortunate to others was highly creditable to me — That Service was shortly after done away with and I subsequently returned to England with Dispatches from General Campbell and a Letter from Ballasteros to the Earl Liverpool Soliciting that a Regiment of Cavalry might be formed, paid & clothed by England a Proportion of British Officers & Non Commissioned to be introduced the same as in Portugal & recommending me strongly for the Command.

Your Lordship would not approve the measure unless with the Sanction of the Duke of Wellington, I immediately returned to Spain when I found the Pride and folly of Ballasteros had defeated his views as well as mine.

I am not a little proud my Lord to say in any of the above situations I never even experienced a Censure, & the Testimonials at the Horse Guards are most creditable to me.[1]

Warrington's military service evidently ended with the disgrace of General Ballasteros in 1812. He reappears, unaccountably, as Consul-General in Tripoli[2] in 1814. We know nothing of the intervening period nor of how or why he came to join the consular service.[3]

Gossip has always linked Warrington's name with the Prince Regent, but he is not mentioned in any of the Regent's published or unpublished letters, nor in the Royal Archives are there any letters

---

[1] P.R.O., F.O. 76/20, 1255. According to contemporary Army Lists Warrington's record of service with the army was:

        Cornet, 1st Dragoon Guards 22 October   1794
        Lieut., 1st Dragoon Guards 4 November 1795
        Captain, 2nd Dragoon Guards 19 July   1798
        Major, 4th Dragoon Guards 6 December 1800
        Retired by sale of Commission 15 May   1802

[2] His title was His Brittanic Majesty's Agent and Consul-General to the Regency of Tripoli in the West and all its Dependencies.

[3] We catch a brief glimpse of Warrington at this time in the memoirs of Nimrod, the great sporting journalist of the day. He described him as 'a great ally of mine, being just about my own age, and equally fond of horse-flesh as myself' (C. J. Apperley [Nimrod], *My Life and Times*, ed. E. D. Cumming (London, 1927), 46).

from him to the Regent or to any member of his Household.[1] There is, however, one piece of evidence of a close and unusual association between the Colonel and his future King, which perhaps explains why there is no trace of Warrington in the Royal Archives. It may also account for his being Consul-General in so remote and unfashionable a place as Tripoli. Its source is Pellissier de Reynaud who was appointed French Consul-General in Tripoli in 1850.[2]

On first taking up his post, Pellissier very sensibly made a résumé of everything that he thought interesting or important in the consular archives that had lately come under his care. This important document, which was dated 20 December 1850, remained undiscovered until it was found and published by Augustin Bernard in 1928.

'M. Warrington', wrote Pellissier, 'était un homme passioné, violent, sujet aux surexcitations bachiques et qui prétendait étendre sa prépotence sur tous ses collègues. Il avait épousé une fille naturelle du roi George IV, Jeanne-Eliza Price,[3] et c'est probablement par cette alliance que s'expliquent les ménagements que les ministres avaient pour lui. Il n'habitait pas, comme ses collègues, la ville même de Tripoli, et s'était fait construire une agréable habitation dans la Menchia, au milieu des palmiers de l'oasis. Il faisait de la politique indigène et avait son *sof*,[4] celui des habitants de la Menchia, en hostilité constante avec les citadins de Tripoli.'

At the date of this résumé the British and French viewed each other with considerable dislike, but nowhere was this more pronounced than along the coast of Barbary where bitter rivalry between the two nations for political and commercial advantages had become traditional. They regarded each other with such malevolence that neither could be trusted to be fair about the other. We must therefore be as hesitant to accept what Pellissier said about Warrington as we should be to believe what the latter said of his colleague Rousseau, Pellissier's predecessor. There is indeed need for extra care here because the French government had twice had to transfer Pellissier, first from Mogador and then Malta, because the British had taken exception, on both occasions, to the French Consul being a retired army officer.

---

[1] This was the result of a recent search kindly undertaken by Mr R. C. Mackworth-Young, M.V.O., the Librarian at Windsor Castle.
[2] Augustin Bernard, 'Un Mémoire inédit de Pellissier de Reynaud', *Mémorial Henri Basset*, XVII (Paris, 1928), 79–82.
[3] Mrs Warrington signed herself 'Jane Eliza Warrington'.
[4] In most of North Africa *sof* or *çoff* means a faction, clique or political party. In Morocco the equivalent is *leff*.

Pellissier's career had shown him to be a man of high principles, and all that he said about Warrington (and he said more than what has been quoted here) rings true, and does not conflict with what we know about him from other sources. There therefore appears to be little reason to doubt the truth of what he wrote about Warrington's wife, except that it would have been more accurate to call her a daughter of the Regent than of the King. Moreover, it accords with more than a century of gossip in Warrington's native land and, as Pellissier pointed out, goes far to explain the predominant position which he, neither intelligent nor shrewd, had been able to establish for himself in Tripoli.[1] Perhaps it also explains why he was not dismissed from a post to which he was patently unsuited.

Only three years after Warrington had arrived in Tripoli Smyth was able to report that he had 'acquired a complete influence' over the Bashaw. This was no overstatement for Pellissier, who had no cause to flatter the British Consul or exaggerate his influence, recorded that 'il était plus maître du pays que le Pacha lui-même, qu'un geste de sa part faisait trembler'. Dixon Denham also had a high opinion of Warrington. 'Of this gentleman,' he wrote, 'it is not too much to say, that by his cheerful and good humoured disposition, his zeal, perseverance, and extraordinary good management, we owe, in a great degree, that influence which England possesses with this government far beyond that of any other of the Barbary powers. The English name, in fact, is of such importance in Tripoli, that there is scarcely a point to carry, or a dispute to settle, in which the bashaw does not request the interference of the British consul. . . . But this is not all: the British flag has a peculiar power of protection, and the roof of the English consul always affords a sanctuary to the perpetrator of any crime, not even excepting murder; and scarcely a day passes that some persecuted Jew or unhappy slave, to escape the bastinado, does not

---

[1] There is corroborative evidence of his association with the Royal Family. In 1816, soon after his arrival in Tripoli, he persuaded the Bashaw to offer the Regent the 'architectural relics' from Lepcis Magna which now stand at Virginia Water (p. 130 above). The Royal Geographical Society has a letter, dated 1877, which mentions Warrington losing £40,000 to George IV in one night's play. Finally, on 14 May 1827 a certain V. Martinici wrote from the White Horse, Stafford Row, Buckingham Gate, to R. W. Hay at the Colonial Office as follows: 'Sir, Having been entrusted with the charge of some horses sent from Tripoli by Col. Warrender [sic], with whom I have lived 14 years, for his late Royal Highness the Duke of York and being now upon my return to Tripoli'; he goes on to enquire whether there is any gentleman going to Africa 'as I should much prefer travelling with a gentleman going there' (P.R.O., F.O. 76/22, 2845).

Plate II. Tripoli: The Old English Consulate

rush into the court-yard of the British Consulate[1] for protection.'[2]

This was a strikingly warm, and indeed generous, tribute from a man who must have known that he was not held in any particular regard by Warrington (the Consul having a marked preference for Clapperton with whom Denham had quarrelled). James Richardson, writing after the Karamanli dynasty had been succeeded by the Ottoman pashas, recorded that 'the liberties which Colonel Warrington was wont to take with old Yousef Bashaw, of the Caramanly dynasty, could not now be, in these days of Ottoman politeness, at all tolerated. For a long series of years, and especially during the French war, the Colonel was the virtual Bashaw of Tripoli'. He then relates how one day Warrington, exasperated at something the Bashaw had done, rushed into the court shouting that Yūsuf was a rascal and threatening him with a whip he was carrying. 'The very next day', continues Richardson, 'the Consul and the Bashaw dined together at the British Garden, the Colonel slapping the old gentleman over his shoulder, and drinking wine with him, like two jolly chums. In this way, Colonel Warrington managed to be, what he was called in Malta, *"Bashaw of Tripoli"*.'[3]

These glowing tributes were over-flattering to the Consul, as he himself would probably have admitted. They came from travellers who, being new to the country, were easily impressed by Warrington's local knowledge and dazzled by his engaging personality; these people were also much in his debt for his unsparing efforts to help them, and for generous entertainment under his hospitable roof.

Warrington was indeed influential, at times very influential, but he did not, as these tributes suggest and as Pellissier in later years confirmed, completely outshine all the other consuls. It was not particularly to his credit that the British Consulate was used as a sanctuary for, as the reader will recall, this was a feature common to all the inviolate foreign consulates. That he was in effect the 'Bashaw of Tripoli', as his countrymen alleged, was manifestly untrue, as he himself makes clear. Although he and Yūsuf were at times on very friendly terms, there were long periods when the French enjoyed greater favour at court. A constant embarrassment to Warrington in his relations with the

---

[1] The British Consulate of those days, now converted to a tenement building, stands directly behind the Arch of Marcus Aurelius, at the junction of Sciara Spagnol with the Sciara Hara.
[2] Denham and Clapperton, I, xviii.
[3] James Richardson, *Travels in the Great Desert of Sahara*, 2 vols. (London, 1848), I, 325–6.

Bashaw was the resentment that had been excited all along the Barbary shore by Lord Exmouth's expedition of 1816. Like all other Moslem rules on the coast, Yūsuf had been forced by Lord Exmouth to give up the very profitable enslavement of Christians.[1] About this, wrote Warrington some years later, 'from the year 1818 to 1825 His Highness was continually remonstrating with me'.[2]

An inevitable result of Lord Exmouth's activities had been to restore the French to favour with the Bashaw, and it was several years before they went out of favour again. In 1825, the year with which we are concerned, the Bashaw, acting under Naudi's influence, 'certainly defeated for a short time', wrote Warrington, 'my exertions in favour of the Sardinian flag'.[3] In that same year two official posts in Tripoli were filled by men who did much to undermine further British influence at court. 'I am sorry to inform your Lordship', wrote Warrington to Bathurst on 13 July 1826, 'that for several Months past, I have perceived that British Influence has been on the decline with this Government; and having been constantly at work, to ascertain the true cause, I fear it may be attributed to the appointment of Hassuna D'Ghies as Minister.'[4] This man was the son of the former minister, Mohammed D'Ghies, had been educated in France, spoke French fluently and was a pronounced Francophile. He had been to London, on one occasion apparently in flight from his creditors in Marseilles.[5] From either that or another visit he had been recalled by the Bashaw and seems to have left the country too precipitately to please his London creditors.[6] His experiences there had done nothing to weaken his marked preference for the French.

The second important appointment made in 1825 was that of Baron Rousseau to the post of French Consul-General in Tripoli.[7] Rousseau was an orientalist who quickly became far more interested in the people of the country, and in consequence better informed, than Warrington

---

[1] Edward Pellew, Admiral Viscount Exmouth, was ordered to North Africa in 1816 to secure the release of British subjects who had been enslaved in Barbary. His fleet was resisted at Algiers but when it capitulated each of the Barbary States was forced to abandon this lucrative trade.

[2] P.R.O., F.O. 76/20, 1255, p. 21. [3] P.R.O., F.O. 76/20, 1255, p. 13.
[4] P.R.O., F.O. 76/20, 2716. [5] B.B., p. 51.
[6] On 24 June 1823 Hay wrote from the Colonial Office to Goldschmitt & Co. as follows: 'Sidy Hassuna D'Ghies left this Country, by desire of the Bashaw of Tripoli, in the Month of April, last, and with the avowed intention of returning to Africa' (P.R.O., F.O. 8/12, 74).

[7] Warrington reported Rousseau's arrival in Tripoli to the Colonial Office on 7 August 1825, shortly before Laing himself arrived (P.R.O., F.O. 76/19, 1982).

had ever been. Inevitably Rousseau and Hassuna D'Ghies became close friends to the detriment of British interests generally and to those of Laing in particular.

Laing had the misfortune to arrive at the moment when British influence at court was at its nadir, and that of the French at its peak. But whether, as Warrington hinted and Laing bluntly asserted, the French tried to prevent Laing from starting for Timbuktu is very doubtful. But the Bashaw, who had done all he could for Lyon and a good deal for the Bornu Mission, adopted a very different attitude to Laing for whom he made things as difficult as he could. Warrington clearly no longer enjoyed the powerful influence at court that his countrymen still claimed for him.

Warrington would have been all that his admirers said had his striking personality been matched by his ability which it manifestly was not. He was a naïve and stupid man who frequently caused his masters in Downing Street anxious moments, if not sleepless nights. In June 1825 Lord Bathurst had to warn him to 'abstain as much as possible from all interference with the Bashaw's Relations with Foreign Powers',[1] but there were occasions which drew from Whitehall stern rebukes. It must have been something out of the ordinary that provoked so flowery a passage as the following which is taken from a letter from the Consul to Lord Bathurst in January 1826: 'I have expressed myself warmly, but with deference respect & Gratitude a Beacon which will I trust conduct me with safety into the Haven of Contentment, after having been so nearly wrecked on the Rocks of Your Lordship's Displeasure.'[2] Nevertheless, severe though Bathurst had at times to be with him, Warrington never took his rebukes amiss, nor did he waver in his loyalty to his chief of whom he would permit no criticism. But as years passed he tended to sail closer to the rocks of official displeasure.

In the diplomatic field Warrington's blunders sprang from his ebullient and impulsive nature which at times was also a source of embarrassment to the explorers he so generously befriended. One of the worst victims of the thoughtless stupidity of which he was so often guilty was James Richardson. He had written from Ghadames to Warrington telling him that certain Tripolitan merchants, whom he named and who were under British protection, were financing the slave trade carried on by the Ghadamsi merchants. 'I expressly begged Colonel Warrington', he wrote, 'not to divulge the fact, or my mention

[1] P.R.O., F.O. 76/19, 1720. [2] P.R.O., F.O. 76/20, 1020.

of such a matter, until I was out of the lion's mouth of the slave-dealing interests of this part of North Africa. The Consul, however, deemed it his duty to disregard my request, and to divulge or violate the confidence.' The news quickly got back to Ghadames where it was obvious that the information could only have been laid by Richardson who had the misfortune still to be there. 'I am, therefore, obliged to Colonel Warrington', he bitterly complained, 'not so much for facilitating my progress in the interior, as for increasing my difficulties a hundredfold.'[1]

Warrington, who 'boasted of being able to do anything and everything in Tripoli',[2] was irritatingly prone to minimize the difficulties of exploring the interior of which he himself had had no experience. Before Oudney, Denham and Clapperton's Bornu Mission had been launched Warrington had told Whitehall that 'the road from Tripoli to Bornou was as open as that from London to Edinburgh'[3] and, years later, he told Richardson it was 'as safe as the road from London to Paris'.[4]

On arriving in Tripoli Laing, like every other British visitor, was at once warmly welcomed by the hospitable Consul and his family. They were at this time living at what they called The Garden, and others the British or English Garden, the history of which he gave to Lord Bathurst in a letter dated the 7th February 1820:

> Some time since His Highness granted me a piece of Ground that I might erect a House in the European stile; it is situated about Two miles from the Town with a fine view of the sea & country. I believe the only Instance of a Christian Building in The Three Regencies His Highness gave the regular Deeds with the Power of selling it at any future time.
>
> I have been my own Architect & am not a little vain of the successful attempt. The Garden is about six Acres, sufficient for the Family supply and will be conducive of Health & of the greatest Recreation and Amusement.
>
> In case of Plague I can communicate with the Shipping and carry on the Consular Duty without the smallest Danger my House and Garden remaining in Quarantin.
>
> I have adopted some Mechanical Power to raise water for the supply of the Ground which the Tripolines are much pleased with, & will follow. Certainly the British Cottage is the handsomest & wears the most civilized appearance of anything presenting itself on the approach to Tripoli. It was the British Influence which gained such a Privilege and consequently I offer it to His Majesty's Govt. at the Price it cost me, say between 15 & 2000

[1] Richardson, *Travels*, I, 350, 359.
[2] Richardson, *Travels*, I, 326.
[3] Denham and Clapperton, I, xviii.
[4] Richardson, *Travels*, I, 326.

Plate III. Tripoli: The English Garden

Dollars,[1] altho' it is actually worth 6000 & would have cost 15000 Dollars in any part of England, a Wall of fifteen Feet high encloses the six acres.[2]

Twenty-five years later, after the Garden had been fully developed, James Richardson described it as 'a splendid horticultural development, containing the choicest fruit-trees of North Africa, with ornamental trees of every shape, and hue, and foliage ... The spot ... in the midst of a waste, is now the fairest, loveliest garden of Tripoli'.[3]

Being a man of high principles and deep religious convictions, the Consul made the villa of which he was so proud a stronghold of Protestantism, and every Sunday morning he held there a church service. There too his family appear to have been subject to an iron discipline. They consisted of his wife, a dim figure who never emerges from the background, and an unknown number of children. We know definitely of four sons — George, Frederick, Henry, and Herbert — and three daughters — Louisa, Emma, and Jane.[4] Frederick, the second son, had already left the family by the time Laing arrived; he was probably living in Tripoli where he was much loved by the Arabs who in later years considered him, Richardson tells us, 'one of themselves, and so he is as to habits, manners, and language, and frequently dress'.[5]

Emma, the second daughter, and Laing, quickly fell in love with each other and, two days before he set out for Timbuktu, they were married by her father, in his capacity as consul. In Emma's sad story, to be told later by the documents that follow, her father is not seen to his

---

[1] Throughout North Africa and the interior the so-called Spanish dollar, nominally worth 5s. sterling, was the coin in most demand and so remained up to the present century when it was usually known as the Maria Theresa dollar. It was regularly minted, up to 1962, by the Royal Mint.

[2] P.R.O., F.O. 76/14. The British Garden was close to the sea in the district then called Masheeah (the Menshia of today), stretching along the coast eastwards from Tripoli. It may have been the villa which, late in the century, was known as Hosh Frederik after Warrington's son Frederick, *hosh* (the Turkish *hos*) meaning 'welcome' (H. S. Cowper, *The Hill of the Graces*, London, 1897, 44). According to pencil notes on a watercolour sketch of the villa (Plate III) it had on the ground floor a drawing room and a dining room, both 23 feet × 15 feet, two parlours, the 'Bay Room', and a vestibule. The rooms above corresponded with those below. The kitchen and servants quarters were 30 yards from the house, and the farmyard and stables 100 yards away (P.R.O., M.P.M. 63).

[3] Richardson, *Travels*, I, 16.

[4] There were almost certainly more sons than these, and possibly more daughters. The 'little Osy', to whom Laing frequently refers in his letters, appears to have been a son. It is possible that the 'William' who Warrington told Tyrwhitt, the explorer, had been appointed 'a Cornet in the 11th Light Dragoons' was also a son (P.R.O., C.O. 2/16).

[5] Richardson, *Travels*, 144-5.

best advantage. Although he took great pride in his right to marry British subjects, when the day came to marry Laing and Emma he was suddenly seized with misgiving. Was it possible, he anxiously asked himself, that one day the young couple might find that they had not been legally married? However, he performed the ceremony, issued a marriage certificate and then, in obedience to his Protestant conscience, took very good care that the marriage should not be consummated. All this he reported in a deplorably self-righteous letter to Lord Bathurst.[1]

In the Warrington family circle the stern call of duty seems to have silenced every claim on sentiment and affection. Some months after Laing's parting with his heart-broken wife (two days after the wedding) Warrington wrote to him: 'Your wife dear Emma you may believe me is well & happy as it is her duty to be.'[2]

Laing suffered grievously from his father-in-law's thoughtless stupidity. Months after he had set out he received from Warrington a letter reporting the Colonial Secretary's extreme annoyance at the estimated cost of the expedition having been greatly exceeded.[3] It was a letter which could do little good and was bound to cause distress. The unhappy Laing, who was finding the road to Timbuktu very unlike travelling from London to Paris with which the Consul had compared it, was so hurt that he nearly turned back. Warrington was horrified when he realized what he had done but it was typical of him that he spoilt his letter of abject apology by expressing the wounding hope that Laing and Clapperton might meet and return together.[4] As we shall see in the following pages, and as would have been obvious to a more intelligent man than Warrington, nothing could have been further from Laing's wishes.

We know too little of Warrington to pass judgment on him. It is perhaps mere chance that so much of that little is not greatly to his credit. As a consul-general his services to his country were certainly considerable. Richardson who, as we have seen, had little reason to flatter him, relates now, long after his retirement, so great was the respect in which he was held that it was widely believed out in the desert, in such places as Ghadames and Ghat, that Tripoli either

---

[1] P.R.O., F.O. 76/19, 1725.
[2] R.S., 374(La) 105 (p. 255 below).
[3] P.R.O., C.O. 2/20 (pp. 252, 255 below).
[4] R.S., 374 (La) 105 (p. 255 below). This letter merits the attention of anyone interested in Warrington's complex character. It reveals its weaknesses and also some of its merits not the least of which were his readiness to admit a fault, and his loyalty to Lord Bathurst.

belonged to the British or was under British protection.[1] No one suffered more from the weaknesses of his character than Laing but, to the very end, he held him in warm regard.

viii. *Clapperton and Laing*

Warrington's admiration for Clapperton was a frequent source of irritation to Laing. At times it looked as though he was encouraging the experienced sailor to rob the younger soldier of half what he hoped to achieve.

Laing arrived in Tripoli to find that Warrington had recommended to London that Clapperton, who had only just left for England, should be sent back to Africa to search for the lower Niger from the Bight of Benin. It was a sensible suggestion which, as we know, was successfully carried out, but it was naturally disappointing to Laing who was hoping to do the same by way of Timbuktu. 'I expect to be at Benin by March next', he wrote over-optimistically to Bandinel. 'It might be as well for Govt. to await the result of my attempt before they try any thing from that quarter.'[2]

Far less endurable were Warrington's letters, pursuing him across the Sahara, suggesting that with Clapperton also in the field and likely to meet him *en route*, he would be able to cut short his journey. That of course was the last thing that he, thirsting for glory and confident of winning it, wanted to do. But this never crossed Warrington's mind. 'I have endeavoured', he naïvely wrote to Lord Bathurst, 'to Implant on the mind of Major Laing the cheering Prospect of meeting Clapperton at Sockatoo.'[3] A few months later he wrote to Laing, 'You will certainly meet Clapperton at Youry [Yauri] which I should think will render it unnecessary for you to go to Benin.'[4] A fortnight later he wrote: 'If you recollect I always said you will meet Clapperton at Youry & I think it more than probable now. He is an Honest good fellow & you will find Him so. — When you meet him the course of the Niger is ascertained & I do not perceive the necessity of your going to *Benin*.'[5]

It was exceedingly galling to Laing, engaged on a most perilous

---

[1] This was probably in part due to his having secured, in 1842, the dismissal of an Ottoman Pasha, a blood-thirsty tyrant named Asker Ali. On Warrington's representations the British Government had informed the Porte that if they did not recall Asker Ali the British would remove him by force (Richardson, *Travels*, I, 54, 390; II, 19, 52, 353).

[2] R.S., 374(La) 78. [3] P.R.O., F.O. 76/19, 1722.
[4] R.S., 374(La) 95. [5] R.S., 374(La) 101.

journey, to be told by his father-in-law that he fully expected Clapperton to forestall him in the main object of his journey. Nevertheless, Laing's confidence in himself remained unshaken. 'I understand', he wrote to Bandinel, 'Captn. Clapperton has gone to the Bight to make the long looked for discovery, but he might have saved himself the trouble for the disclosure of that long hidden secret is left to me as I hope to prove by March or April next.'[1] Although the Consul held his son-in-law in very warm regard he appeared to the latter to have put all his money on Clapperton in what had become, so it seemed to Laing, a race not merely to Sokoto or Yauri but to Timbuktu itself. But he, for his part, would take his time which would be more profitable than 'running a race with Captain Clapperton; whose only object seems to be to forestall me in discovery — Shou'd he succeed in reaching Tombuctoo, which I doubt much, I shall have much pleasure in meeting him'.[2]

There are grounds for thinking that Clapperton was jealous of Laing whom he probably regarded as an unwelcome interloper in a field which he wished to reserve for himself. Warrington, who was in fact much more interested in the results of exploration than in who should achieve them, had asked Clapperton, when he was still in Tripoli, to leave him with any information about the interior that might be helpful to Laing who was shortly expected from Malta. That Warrington took the trouble, as he did, to record this request in a letter to Clapperton, then his guest, suggests that he had been instructed to make it by the Colonial Office, and that he had already done so verbally and got an unsatisfactory answer. This is what he wrote:

Sir,
    Having read to you the Contents of a Dispatch from the Right Honble Earl Bathurst of the 7th Dec. last, containing the information of the intention of His Lordship to send out an Officer direct to Tombuctoo to explore the course of the Niger. —
    I beg leave to submit to your consideration the Propriety of your committing to Paper whatever part of that important information you are in possession of which must tend considerably to assist the operations & Labours of Capt. Laing & facilitate the object of the mission entrusted to Him — Prob-

---
[1] R.S., 374(La) 98.
[2] R.S., 374(La) 107. Clapperton had in fact been instructed to proceed from Sokoto to Timbuktu. Lord Bathurst's instructions to him, dated 30 July 1825, read 'You will also, during your stay in Central Africa, endeavour to visit the city of Tombuctoo, provided you shall not have heard that Major Laing had already accomplished that object' (P.R.O., C.O., 2/16).

ably a Sketch of Bello's map would be of the greatest importance accompanied with your opinion & advice & it only rests with me solemnly to assure you on my honor that whatever you may entrust to me will remain an Inviolable Secret with exception of communicating it to Capt. Laing on his arrival.

    With great esteem and Friendly consideration

                        I have the honour to be

                                    Sir,

                        Your Obt. & Faithful Servt.

Lieutenant Clapperton. R.N.   sgd, H. Warrington[1]

Clapperton wrote to Warrington the following day, by when he must have received the latter's written request, but he did not refer to it. This appears to confirm the suspicion that Clapperton had not any intention of helping Laing if he could avoid it.

But when Clapperton got back to London he quickly found that the Colonial Secretary, to whom he looked for further employment, was not prepared to tolerate the pig-headed and selfish attitude he had adopted. In August Laing, who had reached Beni Ulid, wrote to Wilmot Horton[2] acknowledging, in a slightly acid tone, a letter 'transmitting a copy of the opinions and suggestions which Lt. Clapperton had been called upon to furnish for my guidance... their general tenor has been anticipated and acted upon'.[3] The same day he sent Warrington an amusing account of what Clapperton had said and what he thought about it. 'By the bye', he wrote, 'I have received hints from the Colonial Office furnished by Clapperton, evidently wrung from him for my guidance — they amount to this — "I must cordially cooperate with you" — bono "I must wear a plain Turkish Dress" just as "I must be kind and patient with the natives." Tis not my nature to be otherwise "I must not take observations secretly" the sun does not shine in sly corners. "I must not speak disrespectfully of the women" I wonder how he found this out. I might have been a century in Africa & never have made such a discovery — "I must not meddle with the females of the country". Prodigious! "I must have presents to give away". We need not Ghosts to rise from their graves to tell us this.'[4]

---

[1] P.R.O., F.O. 76/19, 1009.

[2] Robert John Wilmot was appointed Under-Secretary in 1821, and in 1823 he assumed the name of Horton. He is chiefly remembered for having authorized the burning of the memoirs of his cousin Lord Byron.

[3] P.R.O., C.O. 2/15, 1986 (p. 234 below).

[4] P.R.O., C.O. 2/20 (p. 236n. 1 below).

Laing unfortunately allowed his natural annoyance at Clapperton's original refusal to help him, which a more sensible man than Warrington would have concealed, to prejudice him unreasonably against a man who had greatly distinguished himself in a field to which Laing himself was a comparatively new recruit. 'I care little for any information that Clapperton cou'd communicate', he wrote to his friend Edward Sabine '... I smile at the Idea of his reaching Tombuctoo before me — how can he expect it? has he not already had the power? has he not thrown away the chance? I cannot think what were his ideas — a man to be within two days of the Niger, and to come back without ever seeing it — I think I may safely aver, that had I been at Sakotoo — the problem wou'd have been long ago solved — and I feel certain that to me the honor of the solution is left.'[1]

ix. Hatita

One of the conditions of Laing's appointment was that his journey to Timbuktu should be made under the guidance of a Targui named Hatita.[2] It was a surprising condition for the Colonial Office to make because at the time very little was known about the Tuareg, and that little was not of a nature to encourage confidence in so remote, wild and predatory a people. Of Hatita himself also very little was known, but it was enough to show that he was an unusual character, by no means typical of his people. Indeed, he was so unusual as to be odd and in nothing was he more odd than in his unaccountable liking for infidel English explorers, unpopular visitors with whom he was associated, on and off, for thirty years. From Lyon in 1820 to Richardson and Barth in 1850, they all knew Hatita.

Hatita, whose full name was Hatita ag Khuden, belonged to the bellicose Ajjer Tuareg of the country round Ghat. James Richardson, who only knew him as a rather tiresome old man, described him as 'an

---

[1] R.S., 374(La) 90 (p. 232 below). Laing had forgotten that he had done the same when he had found himself within three days of the Niger's source.

[2] No copy of Lord Bathurst's instructions to Laing survives so we can only deduct their nature from Laing's own references to them. In his Journal Laing wrote, 'On a careful perusal of my instructions, I observed it to be the desire of your Lordship, that I shou'd proceed through Fezzan to Tombuctoo, either by attaching myself to a Caravan which might travel by that route, or by placing myself under the protection of a Tuarick Chief named Hateeta.' On the other hand, as Hatita had been engaged to accompany Laing long before the latter had arrived in the country, and before the practicability of his joining a caravan had been considered, it is clear that, whether he travelled with a caravan or not, Hatita was to go with him. Colour is lent to this supposition by Laing's references to his instructions in his letter to Lord Bathurst of 18 July 1825 (pp. 228, 348 below).

extremely pacific man in his conduct, and greatly liked for his peacemaking disposition, but he is only a second-rate Sheikh, and has no political influence over Touarick affairs, beyond what the chief of his family enjoys'.[1] Clearly, in his tribe he was not a man of sufficient account to be courted by Europeans for the sake of his influence. One of his services to explorers was to give them a welcome which, in a cruel and hostile land, no one else was prepared to do. He had an equally engaging facility for adjusting himself to strange European ways, and was valuable in protecting his patrons against both insolence, to which as Christians they were frequently exposed, and curiosity, which was everywhere so intense as to make privacy almost impossible. For these services he was of course well rewarded. His ability to win the confidence of successive British explorers, seems to have given him a certain prestige among his own people for although the English were despised as infidels, they were respected for having driven Napoleon out of Egypt. But in his early days Hatita's liking for Europeans did not spring from the rewards it brought him. It appears to have been as disinterested as it was spontaneous. He was proud of being called, as he was throughout much of the Sahara, the Friend of the English or the Consul of the English, and in his old age he even suggested to Richardson, who favoured the proposal, that he should be appointed British Vice-Consul in Ghat.[2] No matter where he was — in his home in Ghat or out on the roads to Murzuk or Ghadames — a message launched from Tripoli into those vaste wastes was sure to find him. He was a personality whom everyone knew, and his name still survives in Air as that of a camel brand used by a colony of his own people, the Ajjer of Ghat.[3]

We first hear of him in 1820. 'Hateeta, a Tuarick of the tribe of Benghrasāta of Ghraat',[4] wrote Lyon of his departure from Murzuk in

[1] Richardson, *Travels*, II, 100, 102.   [2] Richardson, *Travels*, II, 89.
[3] F. R. Rodd, *People of the Veil* (London, 1926), 202. It is probably purely coincidental that Hatita's second name Khuden is more characteristic of Air than of his native Ghat (Père de Foucauld, *Dictionnaire Abrégé Touareg-Français de Noms Propres* (Paris, 1940), 309).
[4] Barth introduces Hatita as 'Hatíta Inek (the son of) Khoden of the Manghásatangh' (Henry Barth, *Travels in North and Central Africa*, 5 vols. (London, 1857–8), I, 182). In Temajegh *inek* means 'mine', not 'son of'. That Barth so interpreted it suggests that he had been guilty of the social solecism of asking Hatita who his parents were. Among Tuareg and Arabs, writes Dr L. Cabot Briggs in a letter to the editor, 'this is considered extremely rude... because to do so suggests that you think he is a bastard.' The Manghásatangh, also writes Dr Cabot Briggs, 'can only be the Imaghasseten, a noble Ajjer Tuareg tribe, which flourished formerly in the neighbourhood of Ghat and along the Ajjer-Ahaggar frontier.'

that year, 'came to take leave of me. He now pressed me very much to promise him, that on my return to Africa, I would pass through his country, of which he is Chief, and take him with me to the Negro land, adding, that if I would bring him a sword like the one I wore, he should be perfectly content. He is the only Tuarick I ever saw, who was not an impudent beggar, or who made presents without expecting a return.'[1]

More than two years later, in April 1822, Denham arrived in Murzuk with a sword sent by the kind and thoughtful Lyon as a gift to Hatita. 'It would be difficult to describe his delight,' he wrote. 'It was shortly reported all over the whole town, that Hateeta had received a present from Said,[2] worth one hundred Dollars.'[3]

During the next three months the Bornu Mission saw a good deal of Hatita, in and around Murzuk and in Ghat to which he accompanied them. Beyond arranging for the hire of camels, which cannot have presented any great difficulty, his services appear to have been unimportant. He had, however, an unusual and pleasing desire to make his patrons a social success, and took pleasure in teaching them how to behave. 'Our friend Hateeta was anxious we should shine', wrote Oudney, 'and read a number of lectures to Clapperton.'[4] To have come across a native so ready, indeed so anxious, to help and advise on social behaviour was an unusual experience in a continent where strange manners excite ridicule rather than sympathy. It was perhaps this rare and engaging characteristic more than anything else that endeared Hatita to successive explorers. Oudney and his companions showed their gratitude by their care and consideration for him when he fell ill, though of nothing more serious than malaria.[5]

It will be recalled that Hatita had offered to accompany Lyon to 'the Negro land', by which he meant Hausa. To Oudney and his companions he declared that 'he could by his influence alone, conduct us in perfect safety to Timbuctoo, and would answer with his head'.[6] These statements, coming from a much respected African, were repeated in London and came to the ears of men like Lord Bathurst, James Rennell and John Barrow whose hearts were set on solving the frustrating problems of African exploration. To such men they appeared to be the words of a prophet, a son of heaven who could unlock every gate that barred the way to the heart of Africa. Thus it came about that Lord

[1] Lyon, 293.
[2] Said was Lyon's travelling name.
[3] Denham and Clapperton, I, xxxi.
[4] Ibid., I, lxxxv.
[5] Ibid. I, lxvii.
[6] Ibid., I, lxi.

Bathurst insisted that Laing, rather than travel alone, should be accompanied to Timbuktu by Hatita.[1]

Hatita was accordingly summoned to Tripoli, but he could not be induced to come. Instead, he waited until Laing had arrived and started on his inland journey, joined him at Ghadames and accompanied him only as far as Tuat. What Warrington did not realize was that there was a good reason for Hatita's reluctance to venture far from his own country. Like all Tuareg, who were feared and hated by their neighbours, he could only have done so at the peril of his life. He could not get to Tripoli without passing through the country of tribes who would not have spared the life of a lone Ajjer Targui.[2] To get from Tuat to Timbuktu he would have to follow an even more dangerous road, controlled partly by the Chaamba Arabs, traditional blood enemies of all Tuareg, and partly by two Tuareg tribes, the Ahaggar and the Ifoghas, both of whom were enemies of his own tribe, the Ajjer.[3]

As the years passed Hatita's charm faded. One day in 1846 Richardson sadly recorded in his diary, 'Today Hateeta did not beg', and he considered him the worst of the Tuareg sheikhs.[4] Hatita had by then become a pathetic old man, 'very tall, thin and attenuated, of extremely feeble frame',[5] mocked by his fellow tribesmen, and bullied by his parasitical relations who made him beg for them. Four years later he had gone still further to pieces. He was 'always begging', and, more serious, 'publicly he was our enemy; but privately he pretended to be our greatest friend'.[6] He was still known as the Friend of the

---

[1] On 7 December 1824 Lord Bathurst, under the impression that Hatita was then in Tripoli, wrote as follows to Warrington: 'I have noticed with much pleasure your reports of the general conduct of the Tuarick Chief Hateeta, who has recently come to Tripoli to place himself under your protection, and as I am much disposed to rely upon the assurances which you have conveyed to me of his fidelity & ability to aid in the measures in progress for exploring the interior of Africa, I have to authorize you to make arrangements for inducing him to remain at Tripoli until the arrival of an experienced Officer whom I intend shortly to dispatch to Africa for the purpose of proceeding direct to Tambuctoo' (P.R.O., F.O. 8/8, 43). This was the first Warrington heard of the intention to send out Laing.

[2] Hatita had been in Tripoli in the previous August. Nearly ten years later Warrington succeeded in persuading Hatita to come again to Tripoli, but only because he was then able to guarantee his safety. This visit appears to have been in about 1833 (Richardson, *Travels*, II, 10).

[3] Although Lord Bathurst intended Hatita to accompany Laing all the way to Timbuktu the Anonymous Report says that 'he had orders not to attend him beyond Tuat'. As there is no hint or indication of who gave those orders, and as it is difficult to think of anyone who would have given them, it seems probable that they were imaginary (A.R.).

[4] Richardson, *Travels*, II, 210, 214.   [5] Richardson, *Travels*, II, 61.

[6] James Richardson, *Narrative of a Mission to Central Africa*, 2 vols. (London, 1853), I, 128, 166.

English[1] a name to which Richardson, for all the hard things he said about him, admits he still in some measure merited. 'Even already', he wrote, 'it may be said that the market at Ghât may safely be visited by British merchants; for although Hateeta may require heavy presents, he will certainly protect them.'[2]

That Hatita should have been spoilt by his patrons was inevitable, but chargeable more against them than him who continued to serve them until the end of his life. Posterity must needs be generous to the memory of a humble desert nomad of sufficient account for his name to recur repeatedly in the annals of geographical discovery for over thirty eventful years.

x. The Story of Timbuktu

The discovery of Timbuktu was to be only a stepping-stone to the discovery of the termination of the Niger, the crowning ambition of Laing's short life for which he was prepared to make any sacrifice. But he was by no means indifferent to Timbuktu, nor unaware of the public esteem that would attach to the discovery of what he liked to call, and perhaps believed to be, the 'far-famed capital of Central Africa'.

For five centuries, if not for longer, Timbuktu had been known by name in western Europe, and for the greater part of that time it had been one of the most famous of the undiscovered cities of the world. In the opinion of many no hidden city was more worth discovering.

Timbuktu owed its fame to the advantages of its geography and to the accidents of its troubled history, for which also its geography was largely responsible. Some time in the twelfth century it rose to importance as a neutral market serving the needs of the diverse peoples of the widely differing countries surrounding it. Although a town of the Sahara, it stood both on a bank of the Niger and in close proximity to the great lakes and swamps of the upper river. It grew to opulence and fame as the meeting-place of merchants who carried their goods on the camels of the Sahara, the oxen and asses and men's heads of the Sudan, and in the canoes of the rivers and lakes. There a strange medley of people, Arabs, Berbers and Negroes, Moslems and pagans, gathered to exchange the salt and dates of the desert for the grain of the savannahs, and the slaves and kola nuts of the forests beyond, and, above all for the gold of the far south, the traffic in which was still as shrouded in mystery as it had been in the days of Herodotus. By the fourteenth century the entrepôt trade of Timbuktu extended nearly from the coast

[1] Barth, I, 191–4.   [2] Richardson, *Narrative*, I, 169.

of Guinea to the Mediterranean where Barbary merchants were bartering the trade-goods of Europe for the gold of the Sudan. This gold carried into the treasuries of western Europe the name of Timbuktu. Thus did Guinea gold and Timbuktu become closely linked in men's minds.

So important a market inevitably excited the cupidity of its neighbours against whose violent incursions Timbuktu had no natural defences. Its history is consequently a record of recurring turbulence as Negroes, Berbers and Arabs fought each other for the control of its trade routes or of the town itself. We are not here concerned with its troubled history, except in a very late phase when Gordon Laing fell a victim to the turbulence which had oppressed it all down the centuries. To that we will return shortly.

Nothing convinced mediaeval Europe of the wealth of the negro countries hidden in the heart of Africa, and of the high standard of culture their *literati* had attained, so much as the spectacular arrival in Cairo of the vast and splendid caravan of Mansa Musa. In 1324 the great Mandingo emperor of Mali had crossed the Sahara, on a pilgrimage to Mecca, and had astonished Cairo by his prodigal display, and lavish expenditure, of gold. When, fifty years later, Abraham Cresques, a Jewish cartographer of Majorca, was drawing his famous Catalan atlas for Charles V, Timbuktu made its first appearance on a map, as *Tenbuch*, closely associated with a conventional representation of the great Mandingo emperor.

With the publication by Ramusio in the middle of the sixteenth century of *The History and Description of Africa* by Leo Africanus Timbuktu reached the peak of its fame. Leo had had the good fortune to visit Timbuktu, on a diplomatic mission, at the beginning of the century when it was the seat of government of Askia the Great. Timbuktu had long been the resort of Barbary merchants, but the visit of a diplomatic mission from so great a potentate as the Shereef of Fez was a compliment demanding special jubilations. The lavish hospitality served its purpose well. 'The rich King of Tombukto', wrote Leo, 'hath many plates and sceptres of gold, some whereof weigh 1300 poundes: and he keepes a magnificent and well furnished court.'[1] Readers of Ramusio never forgot those 'plates and sceptres of gold' but they overlooked or quickly forgot Leo's very fair description of the 'cottages built of chalke, and covered with thatch' of which in fact Timbuktu was composed.

[1] Leo Africanus, *The History and Description of Africa, done into English by John Pory*, ed. R. Brown, 3 vols. (Hakluyt Society, London, 1895), III, 824.

Ramusio's version of Leo was widely read, and in 1600 appeared the famous English translation by John Pory. For nearly three hundred years, until far into the nineteenth century, the maps of the interior of Africa reflected with hardly any change the geography that Leo had described. And all that time when men thought of Timbuktu they pictured it as the city of dazzling opulence which Leo had described.

The illusion, for such it proved to be, was fostered, and indeed nourished, by the consequences to Morocco of the Moorish conquest and occupation of Timbuktu in the late sixteenth century. The merchants of western Europe were astonished by the reports they began to receive from their agents and correspondents in Marrakech. In August 1594 Laurence Madoc reported to his principal in London the arrival from the Sudan of thirty mules laden with gold. But this was only the beginning of a flow which was to amaze the world. A month later Madoc wrote that 'the rent of Tombucto is 60 quintals of gold by the year, the goodness whereof you know.... The report is that Mahomed [the Moorish general] bringeth with him such an infinite treasure as I never heard of; it doth appear that they have more gold than any other part of the world beside.... This King of Morocco is like to be the greatest prince in the world for money, if he keeps this country...'.[1] Five years later Jasper Thomson, another English merchant in Marrakech, reported to London the arrival of 'great store of pepper, unicorn's horns ... and great quantity of eunuchs, dwarfs, and women and men slaves, besides 15 virgins', together with 'thirty camels laden with *tibar*, which is unrefined gold', and which he valued at over £600,000, an immense sum for those days.[2]

During the next hundred years the Moors lost their hold on the Sudan where their corrupt administration was followed by complete anarchy which, synchronizing with the approaching exhaustion of the gold fields, resulted in a greatly diminished flow of gold northwards into Morocco. But it never wholly ceased, and the hold of Timbuktu on the popular imagination remained such that to many its discovery appeared more pressing than the solution of the mystery of the Niger's termination.

To Laing, as to all thinking men, it was apparent that Timbuktu would not come up to popular expectations, but its discovery was

---

[1] Richard Hakluyt, *Principal Navigations* (Glasgow, 1903–5), VII, 99–101; *Purchas His Pilgrimes* (Glasgow, 1905–7), VI, 57–60.
[2] P.R.O., *State Papers, Barbary*, XII.

bound to be a landmark in the history of exploration. So it proved. Its realization made Laing famous, but at the cost of his life.

The inhabitants of Timbuktu were predominantly Songhai,[1] a riverain people whose original home appears to have been in Dendi, far down-stream beyond Gao, the traditional Songhai capital. But seldom in their troubled history had they for long been masters of Timbuktu. Although the city was conquered and occupied by Mandingoes, and Moors, and raided by Mossi, these incursions were mere incidents in an unending struggle with the Tuareg, traditional enemies of the Songhai, who were perpetually raiding Timbuktu for whatever they could squeeze out of its merchants, from gold dust to women. With Tuareg occupying the surrounding desert, both north and south of the great bend of the Niger, danger ever hovered on the horizon; raids were so unpredictable and sudden that it had become the custom to conduct business within doors instead of in the open market. It is astonishing that trade and culture should have prospered over so many centuries in a place which was so seldom free from fear, and where human life and property were perpetually at the mercy of wild desert nomads against whom the town could offer no effective defence.

Laing had the misfortune to arrive in Timbuktu when a wave of fanaticism had been added to the normal secular hazards of the place. This arose from the Fulani or Peuls of Massina, on the upper Niger, having embarked on a *jihad* closely following the pattern of that of their cousins the Fulani of Hausa. At their head was their Ulema, Seku Hamadu, or Sheku Hamadu Lobbo.[2] As a young man Seku had been a disciple of Usuman dan Fodio, the founder of Sokoto and its empire, whom he had accompanied on his victorious *jihad* against the Hausa. On returning to his native Massina, burning with pious zeal, he started preaching religious reform which so alarmed the Arma of Jenne and the Bambara of Massina that they began to persecute him and his disciples. The deep sympathy this excited among the common people impelled him to launch his own *jihad*. Having secured the blessing of his old master, Usuman dan Fodio, the response to his preaching became so great that he was able to rid Massina of the tyrannical rule of the Bambara and, from his headquarters at Bandiagara, to control the

---

[1] With an admixture of Moorish and Tuareg blood.
[2] Hamadu was the son of a Fulani chief, Hamadu Lobbo, who named his son Hamadu Hamadu Lobbo. To the confusion of historians the son came to be called by his father's name, Hamadu Lobbo. Later, he acquired the prefix Seku or Shehu, meaning venerable, a corrupt form of the Arabic *sheikh*. Similarly Usuman dan Fodio had been commonly called Shehu.

country from the Black Volta in the south to Timbuktu in the north.[1]

In August 1826, when Laing arrived in Timbuktu, Seku had probably not yet occupied the town, but that he could and would do so at his convenience was so generally accepted that the sheikh who governed the town did not dare to resist his bidding. It was this that sealed the fate of Gordon Laing. When Seku heard of a European approaching Timbuktu he at once ordered his expulsion. He was to return by the way he had come, and it was to be made clear to him that there could be no question of his returning.

Seku did not take this action because Laing was a Christian, as might have been expected, but because he was a European. Still more surprising, he had done so at the bidding of Sultan Bello of Sokoto, who in 1817 had succeeded his father Usuman dan Fodio as Sarkin Musulmi of Sokoto.

The circumstances that prompted Bello to intervene in the affairs of so remote a country, 600 miles from his own, emerge from Clapperton's accounts of his two visits to Bello in 1824 and 1827, just before and just after Laing's visit to Timbuktu.

The warmth of Bello's welcome to Clapperton on his first visit to Sokoto cooled a little following the white man's talks about the abolition of the slave trade and British plans for the commercial exploitation of the interior of Africa from the coast of Guinea. The foreign merchants of Sokoto, who had considerable influence with Bello, naturally regarded these proposals as a serious threat to their own trade. It quickly became apparent that Clapperton would not be allowed to continue his journey to Nupe, towards the sea, as he had intended. As time passed suspicions grew and it was rumoured that the talk of trade was no less than a cloak for a British plan to seize the country. Bello himself was sufficiently in touch with world affairs to have good grounds for his fears. 'You are a strange people', he told Clapperton, 'the strongest of all Christian nations; you have subjugated all India.' Bello was agreeable to intercourse with England so long as it was by way of Tripoli and the Sahara, but he was dead against a way being opened to the coast where European activities were not of a kind to encourage confidence.[2] Subsequently, however, he relented to the extent that he agreed to an English consul and physician, for whom he had particular need, coming up to Sokoto from the coast.

---

[1] The fertile country of Massina was in a sense the key to Timbuktu which was wholly dependent on it for foodstuffs.

[2] Denham and Clapperton, II, 297, 303, 308, 309, 312–14.

The Story of Timbuktu

On his return in 1827 Clapperton found himself regarded with even greater suspicion. 'If the English should meet with too great encouragement', he was told, 'they would come into Soudan, one after another, until they got strong enough to seize the country . . . as they had done with India, which they had wrested from the hands of the Mahometans.' Before long the common talk was that the 'English intend to take Houssa'.[1]

At this time, before European penetration of the interior had revolutionized the pattern of African trade, commercial intercourse extending from as far as Egypt on the one hand to Fez on the other, and from Tripoli to the coast of Guinea, was traditional in the northern half of the continent. Consequently people were better informed about what was happening in remote countries than they afterwards became.[2] It is not surprising, therefore, to find that with ties of blood and culture, as well as mutual commercial interests, Sokoto and Massina were in very close touch, Timbuktu being predominant in the trade they carried on with each other. Bello's secretary was a Massina man, and someone told Clapperton that Massina and other western countries were 'subject to our Lord the Prince of the Believers, Mohammed Bello'. Seku Hamadu was named as one of Bello's vassals.[3]

Bello's fears of European penetration being what they were, and his relationship with Seku Hamadu being as close as it was, it is not surprising that he cautioned him against Laing, and advised, if not ordered, his banishment from Timbuktu. It was an intervention that cost Laing his life, and scholarship the fruits of a great journey.

xi. Alexander Gordon Laing: The Explorer

It would be unjust to judge Laing by his letters. This is not because we have so few to judge him by (only half a dozen to cover the last eight — and by far the most interesting — months of his fifteen months' journey). Had all his letters survived, and had he written twice

---

[1] Captain Hugh Clapperton, *Journal of a Second Expedition into the Interior of Africa* (London, 1829), 197, 199, 235, 238.

[2] In January 1827, when he was in Sokoto, Clapperton was able to record in his *Journal* a surprisingly good account of the first attack on Laing. 'A small gaffle of Arabs arrived today from Timbuctoo', he wrote, 'one of whom had seen Major Laing, who, he said, had lost his hand in an attack which Tuaricks had made on him and his servants during the night, and that his servants, a Jew and a Christian, had got severely wounded' (*Journal*, 241).

[3] Clapperton, *Journal*, 330–4.

as many, we would still be sadly ill-informed about him and his great journey.

The inadequacy of Laing's letters is due to their having been written without the slightest regard for the needs of his readers. It is not so much that he tells us so little about the people and the country as that he says nothing about the journey or the actual travelling and far too little about himself. We know nothing of how his caravan was organized, what the going was like, when and where he pastured and watered his camels, and what were the hardships of man and beast on that soul-destroying journey. So reticent are his letters that there might have been no hardships, anyway imposed by nature, for all he tells us. And as for himself, we do not know how he passed his days, either in camp or on the march, what and when he ate and drank, what were the calls on his endurance; there is hardly a mention of supremely anxious moments, or of the joy of at last discovering the hidden well, or of finding friends where only enemies were looked for. Without this sort of information no traveller's tale can come to life.

Laing does not even tell us the really important things we ought to know. He wrote a full and adequate account of Ghadames but thereafter, when the journey began to get really interesting, he became so reticent as to be almost dumb, the only lapse being a graphic account of the attack on him in the Wadi Ahennet. Even that was only a half-told tale; 'the detail must be reserved till another period', he wrote, 'when I shall "a tale unfold" of base treachery and war that will surprise you'.[1] Of In Salah, no less important than Ghadames and perhaps more interesting, he tells us next to nothing. Similarly we do not even know whether the months he spent recuperating under the kindly care of El Muktar were passed in an Arab tent, or under a solid roof. At every turn Laing leaves us guessing, and infuriates us with his dullness.

But Laing himself was not dull. Fortunately for his reputation we have his *Travels in Western Africa*, the account he published of his experiences in the hinterland of Sierra Leone in 1822. In that book he fully meets his readers' needs. He tells how his expedition was organized, how he lived and travelled, what the country was like, what people he met and how they behaved to him and to each other; he also records the course of his own feelings, his personal reactions to the varied incidents of travel in a strange and savage land. It is a competent and satisfying book of travel. But Laing could also be a bore.[2]

In Tripoli Laing had doubtless learnt from Warrington to regard all

---

[1] P. 301 below.   [2] See Appendixes I, II and III.

other Europeans, and not a few Arabs, with suspicion. He had, as we have seen, come to share the Consul's conviction that the French would spare no effort to wreck his plans in the hope of forestalling him. After he had set out Warrington had again warned him of the need for secrecy. Tell no one anything, had been his advice, not even the longitude and latitude of the places he passed through. In these circumstances, and not knowing what might befall his letters in the desert or by whom they might not ultimately be read, it would have been natural for him to be very cautious about what he wrote. But this cannot have been the reason for his reticence. 'I am exceedingly cautious', he wrote to his friend James Bandinel, 'as I write particulars to nobody except Smith, Sabine and yourself, to my nearest relations even, my motions are quite unknown.'[1] We do not know what he wrote to Smith any more than we know who Smith was, but we have several of his letters to Bandinel and Sabine, and they are just as uninformative as his more formal ones to Warrington and the Colonial Office. And anyway, letters to his family were not more likely to go astray than those to others. Clearly, then, his extraordinary reticence was not due to the need for secrecy, the need to conceal from jealous rivals what he was doing and the discoveries he was making.

It would be easy to attribute his infuriating reticence to his being a bad letter-writer, but this must be rejected on the grounds that the surviving fragment of his official journal is barren of interest;[2] that he sometimes wrote a very good letter, and that his published work shows him to have fully appreciated what readers, whether of books or letters, wanted to know.

His reticence was certainly deliberate, as indeed is evident from the foregoing quotation from his letter to Bandinel. It probably sprang from his thirst for fame. He was, he knew, engaged on a journey which would make him famous, but the extent of his fame would depend on how the story he would have to tell was presented to the public. The vehicle would be his book which the world would eagerly await and which must be made to astonish it. The less he said about his travels in his letters the less would be known about them, the more eagerly would his book be awaited and the more easily would it astonish. This rather thin argument gains substance from the letter — so far as we know the only letter — he wrote from 'the far-famed capital' itself. In no other way can we account for this queer letter. Despite the greatness of the tale he had to tell, regardless of half the civilized world wanting to

---

[1] P. 295 below.   [2] He kept also a detailed private journal.

know what Timbuktu was like, all he told Warrington, his principal confidant, was that 'in every respect except in size... it has completely met my expectations'.[1] The words are hardly less surprising than the brevity of the comment. It is scarcely conceivable that Laing was not as disappointed in Timbuktu as Clapperton had been in the much less famous Kano, in 1824. 'I felt grievously disappointed', he had written, 'for... I expected to see a city of surprising grandeur.'[2] Laing must have expected far more of Timbuktu than ever Clapperton had of Kano, but he was not going to say so. René Caillié, who was to arrive in Timbuktu about eighteen months later 'had formed a totally different idea of the grandeur and wealth of Timbuctoo. The city presented, at first view, nothing but a mass of ill-looking houses, built of earth'.[3] Laing was better educated and more sophisticated than Caillié, and may therefore have expected less, but that Timbuktu fully met his expectations, except in size, is incredible. He was not going to prejudice the great book of travel he intended to write by allowing it to become known beforehand that Timbuktu had proved an anti-climax.

Before setting out for Timbuktu Laing had shown himself to have the essential intellectual qualities for an explorer, not least an enquiring and acquisitive mind. His book on Sierra Leone and his habit of closely cross-examining travelled Africans for all he could learn from them left no room for doubt about this. They also showed him to be a most painstaking and diligent investigator.[4] He was also an enterprising collector, though not a word of this comes to us from his own pen. Warrington recorded the arrival of a box of 'geological specimens' sent back by Laing from Tuat.[5] Long after his death one of his servants chanced to mention his having sent back to Tripoli an antelope from Ghadames, and a 'curious animal' from Tuat.[6]

It cannot be doubted that on this great journey, with the eyes of much of the civilized world upon him, he was making the fullest use of these qualities to ensure the fame for which he craved. The account he wrote of Ghadames, hard on the heels of his memorandum on the termination of the Niger, shows that he did not waste any time there. He had also turned to good account the long delay in In Salah. To

---

[1] P. 312 below.   [2] Denham and Clapperton, II, 238.
[3] René Caillié, *Travels through Central Africa to Timbuctoo*, 2 vols. (London, 1830), II, 49.
[4] François Jomard, the great French geographer of the day, who had read Laing's book, declared that he had 'proved himself a correct observer', which was a high compliment from such a quarter (Caillié, II, 252).
[5] P.R.O., F.O. 76/22, 2886.   [6] R.S., 374(La) 131.

Sabine he wrote that he had 'collected considerable information here regarding the habits and customs of the isolated inhabitants of the Desart, as well as concerning their position, extent and power, and when you see my Map you will hardly be able to recognise the wonted blank of the Great Desart'.[1] He wrote in the same sense to the Colonial Office adding 'it will be quite beyond my power to forward either chart or detailed Journal till my arrival in Tinbuctoo'.[2] That 'detailed Journal' was the private repository of the mass of information he was accumulating, the writing up of which must have made grievously heavy demands on his time after he had lost the use of his right hand. Between the writing of his letter of 10 July and that of 21 September, almost certainly the last he ever wrote, there was such a marked improvement in his writing that it cannot be doubted that he had recently had a great deal of practice. As it was his habit to write letters only when a courier was available to carry them, and there was no such opportunity at this period, most if not all of the writing he was doing must have been in the journal.

Had the journal of this industrious and acquisitive explorer survived it would certainly have proved to be a work of immense value. It would not have been as encyclopaedic as Barth's great work, for Laing lacked the latter's extraordinary linguistic gifts,[3] nor had he a brain so thoroughly trained in research. But it is highly probable that the journal would have proved much more informative than the work of Denham and Clapperton which still stands high in the literature of exploration. Its disappearance, in circumstances which further embittered Anglo-French relations, was a great loss to scholarship.

Less attractive were Laing's vacillations and his consummate conceit. Time and again we find him, on second thoughts, doing or saying something which a short time before he had condemned in others. He ridiculed searching for the Niger from the north only to become, a few months later, the most ardent champion of this route; he scorned Clapperton for turning back when within a few days' march of the Niger, regardless of having already done that very thing himself; he was no less critical of Clapperton's adoption of Turkish dress which he

---

[1] P. 292 below.   [2] P. 290 below.

[3] We know little of Laing as a linguist. On his first arrival in Tripoli he took lessons in Arabic, and his followers included a Jewish interpreter engaged in Tripoli, Jacob Nahun. We do not know how dependent he was on him, and for how long, but it is significant that when he had got no further than Ghadames, less than four months after landing at Tripoli, he was attempting to write Arabic. Moreover there is no hint of lack of knowledge of Arabic hampering his enquiries after the death of Jacob Nahun.

himself was to adopt only a few weeks later. For a time nothing could shake his conviction that the Niger would be found to flow into the Bight of Benin, but eventually he thought it possible that it flowed westwards into the Atlantic in the neighbourhood of Cape Verd.

In one matter, so long as he remained in good health, he never wavered. This was in his conviction that it was the will of God that he would become the discoverer of the termination of the Niger. He used to boast that 'that long hidden secret is left to me' and he appears to have had no doubt that he owed the special favour of the Almighty purely to his own superior merit. 'I shall do more than has ever been done before', he wrote in the only surviving letter to his family, 'and shall show myself to be what I have ever considered myself, a man of enterprise and genius.'[1]

These weaknesses became more pronounced after the attack in the Wadi Ahennet to which he so nearly succumbed. In spite of his long convalescence under the kindly care of the Arab sheikh he never recovered his mental health and, for all we know, he may also still have been a physical wreck. We have one sure sign that the poor battered brain had begun to fail. On 1 July 1826 he wrote to Warrington that if he failed to reach Timbuktu 'the World will ever remain in ignorance of the place, as I make no vain glorious assertion when I say, that it will never be visited by Christian man after me'.[2] Then there was that last tragic message to his wife at the end of probably the last letter he ever wrote. 'My dear Emma must excuse my writing, I have begun a hundred letters to her, but have been unable to get thro' one.'[3] But Laing must not be judged by what he did and wrote after the Ahaggar so nearly killed him.

Circumstances, rather than failing health, appear to have caused the frequent changes in plans which marked the closing weeks of Laing's life.[4] It may have been physical disabilities that determined him to abandon the Niger project and content himself with discovering Timbuktu. But local politics dictated the uncertainty about where he should go from there. First he decided 'to mount a fleet Mahrie &

[1] Robert Chambers, *A Biographical Dictionary of Eminent Scotsmen*, 4 vols. (Glasgow, 1835), III, 340.
[2] P. 303 below.
[3] P. 313 below.
[4] In In Salah he had, despite his youth, been mistaken for Mungo Park and consequently had become the target of the hatred which the foolish Scotsman had provoked by his indiscriminate shooting at natives as he sailed, or paddled, down the Niger. This had forced Laing to abandon his intention of following the river to its mouth in his own canoe in favour of making the same journey by land.

return to Tripoli'.[1] Then (perhaps as his health recovered), deciding it would be unworthy to retrace his steps, he resolved to follow the river upstream to Jenne, doubtless intending to make his way to country he knew in the hinterland of Sierra Leone whence the sea would be easily reached. When he got to Timbuktu, however, he found that the Fulani of Massina had closed the road to Jenne. Nevertheless, he did not abandon his intention of making for the upper waters of the Niger. He decided to make for Segu Sikoro, far upstream from Jenne. But to reach it an immense detour, by way of Arawan and Walata, was needed. It was on this road that he died.

Laing was born with the two gifts more indispensable than any others to successful exploration. These were courage and determination. He displayed a happy combination of them both on his departure from In Salah. News had come of serious trouble on the road ahead, the last and most dangerous stage of the journey to Timbuktu. The hundred and fifty Ghadamsi merchants with whom he was travelling, people of the country far better able to assess the risks than himself, decided to stay where they were. Laing, the only infidel among them, 'determined upon setting out solus in four days more "Come what will, come what may" '.[2] The courage of this lone Christian, for whom the risks were far greater than for themselves, so shamed the cowardly Moslem merchants that they 'plucked up courage, and this day the whole Kaffila, amounting to upwards of three hundred loaded Camels with a hundred and fifty men well armed, leaves the town of Ensala'.[3] There we see Laing acting in the finest tradition of the great African explorers. The pity is that the loss of his journal, at which he appears to have toiled unceasingly, denied him his rightful place among them.

In the stirring annals of geographical discovery there are few more striking examples of what the human frame can endure, under the compelling discipline of an iron will, than Laing's astonishing journey from Wadi Ahennet to El Muktar's camp. With ten sabre cuts on the head, a musket bullet in the hip, both hands terribly mangled (one almost severed from the arm) and both legs injured, this brave and determined man somehow contrived to cover 400 miles of the worst desert in the world with none to help him but a handful of African attendants.

Laing will always be remembered as the discoverer of Timbuktu. Nevertheless, he was only its re-discoverer, for it had already been visited by several Europeans.

[1] P. 303 below.   [2] P. 292 below.   [3] P. 294 below.

In the fifteenth century the Florentines had secured for themselves a predominant position in the Barbary trade. In a number of African ports, including Tunis and Algiers, they enjoyed a monopoly of the European trade. In Tunis they were also granted the exceptional privilege of trading with the hinterland which, all along the Barbary shore, was usually forbidden to Christians for fear of their becoming interlopers in the trans-Saharan trade. This appears to be precisely what the Portinari, a great Florentine business house, tried to be, for in 1470 they sent a representative to Timbuktu. This man was Benedetto Dei who, having already travelled widely in the interests of his employers, was too sophisticated and probably too exclusively interested in commerce, to be impressed by Timbuktu. All he had to say about it was that it was 'a place situated beyond Barbary in very arid country. Much business is done there in selling coarse cloth, serge, and fabrics like those made in Lombardy'.[1] It may be that at that date Timbuktu had already been visited by Europeans, and that there was nothing remarkable in Dei's journey.

A few years later another European mission reached Timbuktu. This was a party of eight whom the Portuguese sent there from their settlement at Arguin, an island on the west coast lying close to Cape Blanco. That was in about 1487. We do not know how many reached Timbuktu, but only one returned, a certain Pero Reinel who, Barros tells us, was already well acquainted with the Sudan.[2]

In the closing years of the sixteenth century a considerable number of Europeans must have visited Timbuktu. The Moorish army, 4,000 strong, which was sent out from Marrakech in 1590 to conquer Songhai was predominantly European. It was commanded by a Spanish eunuch of whose ten kaids four were Europeans. Most of these men were renegades, prisoners taken either by corsairs or in the battle of Alcazar, who had secured their freedom by becoming apostates. Others, notably the gunners, were probably soldiers of fortune and free men.

But none of these Europeans, from Benedetto Dei in 1470 down to Paul Imbert, the French navigator whom the Moors employed in 1618 to pilot their troops across the Sahara, told the world anything about Timbuktu.

---

[1] Charles de la Roncière, *La Découverte de l'Afrique au moyen âge*, 3 vols. (Cairo, 1924–27), I, 163.

[2] João de Barros, *Da Asia*, 24 vols. (Lisbon, 1777–78), I, 1 Dec., Book 1, ch. 3, p. 29.

Nor did it learn anything from Robert Adams, alias Benjamin Rose, the ship-wrecked American mariner who was captured and enslaved on the west coast of Africa and claimed to have visited Timbuktu. But so far as Timbuktu was concerned he was probably an impostor.[1]

That Gordon Laing was far from being the first European to visit Timbuktu in no way detracts from the credit he deserves for one of the great journeys in the history of African exploration.

As the following letter shows, Laing's personal friends were not slow to recognize the need to pay tribute to his memory:

James Bandinel to Hanmer Warrington:

Copy   Foreign Office, May 24, 1830

My dear Sir,

At the solicitude of Mr. Barrow and Mr. Hay, Captain Sabine has undertaken to make up what account he can of the Life of your and his and my lamented friend Major Laing, with a view to leaving some record to the world of what he was, of the worth he had, and the things he did.

It will much facilitate this undertaking, if you will have the kindness to supply what materials you can for the purpose, in letters to and from Major Laing, in Papers of or belonging to or treating of him, and in any memoranda which you yourself can supply about him. If you will address such papers to Captain Edwd. Sabine, Royal Artillery, to my care, and send them in the Official Bag to the Colonial Department, they will reach Captain Sabine safely, and you will have the gratification of having contributed to having the memorial of one, to whom his memory is very dear, and who is in every way more competent to the task than could be found elsewhere.

                     Believe me &c

                                    (Signed) James Bandinel

Major Warrington

P.S. I have omitted to state that Cap. Sabine, who has already commenced his work, will be ready for the Press by October next.[2]

Nevertheless, despite the eminence of the sponsors of this project and the zeal with which Sabine set about his laudable task, October came and passed, and never, so far as we know, did the proposed biography so much as reach a publisher.

To the lasting credit of the French, in spite of the bitterness which at this time divided them from the British, more especially in Africa,

---

[1] *The Narrative of Robert Adams* (Boston, 1817).
[2] R.S., 374(La) 133.

they were not only the first nation publicly to honour the departed Laing, but the only one (not excepting his own countrymen) to do so for more than a hundred years. In 1829 La Société de Géographie of Paris presented Emma Laing with their Gold Medal in honour of her dead husband.

In 1931 the African Society of London placed a bronze memorial plaque on the house in Timbuktu in which Laing had stayed.[1]

[1] This plaque was unveiled on 9 February 1932 by Monsieur Fousset, Governor of the Soudan Français in the presence of a British Mission (*Journal of the African Society*, XXXI (1932), 282–92).

ITINERARY

Places named by Laing about the identity or precise location of which there is any doubt are shown in italics as Laing spelt them.

Unless otherwise stated the dates are dates of arrival.

I. TRIPOLI to GHADAMES

1825	May	9	Tripoli
	July	7	left Tripoli
			Tagiura
		18	Wadi er Raml
		19	Terhuna
		20	Gabr Doga
		24	Beni Ulid
	Aug.	4	Wadi Scemech
		8	Bir Sèrchet
		9	*under the mountains of Gerza*
		13	*Malhrail*
		15	*Shaba Soudah*
		17	*Lofonsa*
		18	Tamsawa
		21	Agár
		23	El Maharúga
			El Gorama
		24	Gótta
		25	Berghin
		31	*Esser*
	Sept.	2	Bir Mráia
		13	Ghadames

II. GHADAMES to SAHAB

1825	Nov.	3	left Ghadames
		13	Wadi Thakouset
	Dec.	2	In Salah

1826   Jan.   9   left In Salah
                26   Tanezruft
        Feb.   (early) Wadi Ahennet
        April   (?)   *Blad Sidi Mahomed*
        Aug.   13   Timbuktu
        Sept.   22   left Timbuktu
                24   Sahab

CHAPTER I

PREPARATIONS

In August 1824 the British Government was sufficiently concerned about the troubled course of events on the Gold Coast for the Secretary of State to give immediate attention to the young officer who had just arrived in London to report on the Ashanti campaign. We do not know what passed between Lord Bathurst and Captain Gordon Laing at their early meetings, but it was not long before Laing contrived to interest the Minister in his long-cherished scheme to complete Mungo Park's work on the Niger.

Since his appointment as Colonial Secretary in 1812 Lord Bathurst had become deeply interested in exploration, and particularly in the problem of the Niger. It was due to him that the Ritchie-Lyon expedition of 1818 had been launched as a Government enterprise, and that it had been followed up by the Bornu Mission of Oudney, Denham and Clapperton whose return was still awaited. If Lord Bathurst did not recall Laing's earlier approach to him it is improbable that the name of the young captain who had been the first to demonstrate that the Niger could not be the Nile was wholly unknown to him. We may be sure therefore that he lent a ready ear to what Laing had to say, but August was not a propitious month in which to interest a cabinet minister in anything new. It was the time of year when, to the dismay of foreign diplomats, even affairs of state could not stay a general exodus from London to the country.[1] So Laing, we may presume, was told to come back later.

Early in October, after an all too short rest in Scotland, he returned to London to find, if we may judge from the speed of coming events, that in Lord Bathurst he already had an enthusiastic champion. Much as the Secretary of State appears to have favoured Laing's proposal to explore the Niger he did not at all like his idea of setting out from Sierra Leone. Indeed, the record of attempts to reach the Niger from the west coast of Africa was so black that it would have been difficult to justify spending public money on any more expeditions from that quarter. Admittedly the Niger had been discovered from there, but

[1] 'Ministers of State', wrote the American ambassador, 'even Lord Chancellors, can hardly be kept from going' (Richard Rush, *The Court of London from 1819 to 1825* (London, 1873), 323).

when Park had tried to complete his work by following approximately the same route a second time it had cost not only his life but also the lives of his forty-five companions. Before Park, Houghton[1] and after him Peddie[2] had both lost their lives in similar attempts. There could be no doubt that the hinterland of the Guinea coast, which for centuries past had proved, for geographical, political and commercial reasons, almost impenetrable to Europeans, was a barrier to the interior which had better not again be challenged.

On the other hand, it was common knowledge that all down the ages the interior of western Africa, where for a certainty the middle Niger lay, had been readily accessible from Barbary. That Christians could travel the same route as Moslems, that where Africans went Europeans could also go, had been proved by Hornemann and Lyon and, according to reports from Tripoli, also by Oudney, Denham and Clapperton. The chances of success from the north were manifestly greater than from the south. Nevertheless, it seems that Lord Bathurst asked Laing to put into writing, both his reasons for wishing to start from Sierra Leone and his general plans; the draft of a note of this nature in Laing's hand, endorsed 'Memo of Cap. Laing 19 October 1824' survives. It reads:

In the event of my being required to make a Journey of discovery into the interior of Africa, and the choice of a route &c left to myself: I wou'd prefer penetrating from Sierra Leone for various reasons. Firstly because having already travelled a considerable distance in that quarter, I am personally acquainted with many of the most powerful Chiefs who command the road to Timbuctoo, and who have all of them & severally made repeated promises to me of facilitating my Journey to that capital; secondly because I am sufficiently versed in the Mandingo Language to make my way thro' the country without an interpreter; and thirdly because the commercial advantages which I have already obtained for one of our African settlements by prosecuting that route, might be greatly extended at the same time that the object of discovery was in progress.

After reaching the Capital city of Timbuctoo and endeavouring to effect a trading communication between it and the Colony of Sierra Leone, my object wou'd be to pass through the Kingdom of Haoussa, Kashna [Katsina] &c to the Lake of Wangara, Fitri or Belala, and by making the circuit of it, ascertain whether it has an outlet or not — if it has one to follow it to its termination, if it has not to trace upwards the course of the Tsaad which falls into it, & thereby prove if that river is the great Niger on which Park em-

---

[1] P. 7 above.   [2] P. 257 below.

barked[1] — Shou'd this experiment decide that the Tsaad & Niger are different rivers, I shou'd then cross to Nuffi [Nupe], and follow the Niger to *its* termination.[2]

A few months earlier Laing had declared that to look for the Niger from the north would be folly. 'It is now very clear', he had written, 'that nothing in the way of discovery can be effected from that quarter.'[3] Nothing could have been less convincing than his rather petty reasons for wanting to start from Sierra Leone. They certainly did not impress Lord Bathurst who insisted on the northern approach. He appears even to have convinced Laing that it was the right one, for had the latter been induced to adopt it against his better judgment, to accept it *faute de mieux*, he would not have started, as he did, with so profound a confidence in success that it remained unshaken till nearly the end of his perilous journey.

Before the month was out Laing was committed and, to the fury of General Turner, had already got leave of absence from the Commander-in-Chief for some 'scientific researches in the interior of Africa'.[4] These were defined by Captain Sabine in the preface to Laing's *Travels* which he had in consequence to see through the press. 'An opportunity', he wrote, 'unexpectedly presented itself to him, of proceeding under Lord Bathurst's auspices, in the discovery of the yet unknown course and termination of the Niger; an undertaking which, as the reader will perceive, he had long and anxiously desired. It being designed that Major Laing should accompany the caravan from Tripoli to Timbuctoo in the Summer of the present year, his departure from England very early in the year became necessary, and the intervening time was scarcely sufficient for the necessary preparations for the journey.'[5] The speed with which the decision to despatch Laing on his mission was both taken and implemented reflected great credit on the Colonial Office of Lord Bathurst's day. Moreover, it all happened at a

---

[1] Laing's plan was to travel eastwards through Hausa to make a circuit of Lake Chad (his Lake of Wangara). This would enable him to discover whether it had an outlet possibly leading, as some thought, to the Nile. If the lake had no outlet he would turn back and ascend the great river which, according to Hornemann (who called it the Zad) flowed into it. As we have seen, this river was the Benue which flowed neither into nor out of Lake Chad (p. 119 above).
[2] R.S., 374(La) 63.   [3] R.S., 374(La) 145.
[4] Although Laing had been granted the necessary leave by 2 November, and on 7 December the Colonial Office had warned the Consul-General in Tripoli to expect him (p. 167 n. 1 above), his appointment appears to have been dated only from January 1826.
[5] Laing, vii.

moment of great financial stringency when every government department was under pressure to practise the strictest economy, and when the comparatively modest cost of the Oudney, Denham and Clapperton expedition was attracting criticism.[1]

Laing's first task, therefore, was to prepare for Lord Bathurst an estimate of what the expedition would cost. It does not appear to have occurred to either Laing or the Colonial Office that as he had never set foot in North Africa any estimate he drew up of the cost of an expedition launched into the interior from that quarter could hardly fail to be misleading. Had this been recognized from the start much trouble and unpleasantness would have been avoided.

In offering my services to travel in Africa [he wrote], I am free to declare that I have not been influenced by the most distant view to emolument of any kind whatever, but by that desire for prosecuting research which has filled my mind for the last five years, and which has already on a former occasion induced me to sacrifice the one, that I might gratify my inclination in the other. I should feel happy in being placed on a footing with other travellers, but I nevertheless shall be perfectly satisfied to undertake the Journey without any Salary.

... I shall only require two attendants exclusive of my servant, who is a very valuable man, and has already travelled with me in Africa:[2] the other two I should like to be permitted to look out for, as soon as possible, as it may require some time to find such as will answer my purpose, say blacks possessing some acquaintance with the business of a ship carpenter. I estimate their salary at £30 each per annum.

Knowing nothing of the country, he was reluctant to estimate what to allow for subsistence, but suggested 5s. a day for himself and 1s. 6d. for each of his three attendants.

Attached to the memorandum was the following statement:

[1] Nevertheless, in a letter dated only 11 November but which evidently belongs to 1824 Barrow wrote to Wilmot Horton as follows: '... As the expences [of the Bornu Mission] have been so well kept down, I trust Lord Bathurst will allow Capt. Laing to go with the caravan to Tombuctoo, then turn Easterly and make for Bornou as a *point d'appui*. I think now there is no doubt that the Niger falls into the Nile' (P.R.O., C.O. 2/14).

[2] This man was Jack le Bore whom Laing described as: 'Originally a native of St. Domingo, and having entered into the French army as a trumpeter, was present at Austerlitz, and many other of the important victories of Buonaparte. ... He was taken prisoner in a French line of battle ship ... by Sir Alexander Cochrane; after his exchange, he served in almost every country in Europe, and, at the peace, made his way from Denmark to England, whence he volunteered for the late Royal African Corps, in which he served as bugle-major.' His experience of exploration was equally extensive. He had accompanied first Peddie on his disastrous expedition, then, in 1818–19, Staff-Surgeon Dochard to Segu, and finally he had been with Laing to Falaba (Laing, 333–5).

*Probable expense of conveyance to Timbuctoo
for Captain A Gordon Laing and Party*

Purchase of Five Camels	£75.	—.	—
Pay and subsistence of two Arabs to take care of Camels	18.	4.	—
Subsistence for Camels & Expenses at watering places	50.	—.	—
	£143	4	—

N.B. From this deduct the sale of the Camels at Timbuctoo, where I shall have no more occasion for them.[1]

Another annex to the memorandum set out in great detail his estimate of the cost of presents for chiefs 'in his Journey to Timbuctoo and termination of the Niger'.

For Muley Ismael[2] or his Successor, Chief of
the country in which Timbuctoo is situated —

One Double barr^d Gun	£20.	—.	—.
One Handsome Sabre	8.	—.	—.
One silver headed stick	5.	—.	—.
One Lock tie [?] & Twinscrew	—.	13	—.
Two Magazines 8 lbs powder	2.	14	—.
28 lbs assorted shot	—.	12	—.
One Common Watch	3.	3	—.
	£40.	2	—.

Similar, but more modest presents were required for 'El Huide Bakari Chief of Timbuctoo'[3] and 'the Chief of Hawassa' [Hausa][4] at

[1] Beyond Timbuktu he expected to travel by boat down the Niger.
[2] As Muley or Mulai is a Moorish title, it is possible that in Tripoli it was not realized that the Moroccan Moors had abandoned all claim to Timbuktu as far back as the beginning of the seventeenth century. The claim, however, was revived in 1958 when Mohamed V of Morocco alleged that the southern frontier of his country included Timbuktu.
[3] Sidi Mohammed el Muktar, of the powerful Bekkai family, was at this time Sheikh of the Kunta Arabs. (See p. 215 n. 1 below).
[4] Mohammed Bello, the Fulani Sultan of Sokoto whose dominions included the Hausa States.

£29 3s. od. each. Laing estimated the cost of sundry presents 'for numerous unknown chiefs who will be met with on the route, but particularly on the voyage down the Niger', at £299 8s. od. These presents were to include guns, swords, pistols, gunpowder, clasp knives, carving knives, scissors, spy glasses, 20 kaleidoscopes, assorted beads, coral, amber and 20 yards of gold lace.

In another statement Laing listed the instruments he would require: a 5-inch quintant, a 3-inch pocket sextant, a telescope, 3 compasses, a portable barometer, 2 hygrometers, a chronometer and a 'patent lever watch', estimated to cost £120 in all. To this he added 'Outfit for self £50. –. –.'

The memorandum concluded, under the heading Contingencies, with one final request:

I wou'd consider it a mark of extreme liberality in Lord Bathurst, if His Lordship wou'd be pleased to place a reserve of £500 Stg. at my disposal which shall only be touched upon if extreme urgency shou'd render it necessary.

Laing added the following summary in a postscript:

Total original Expence of the Mission.

Presents for Chiefs	£300.	–.	–.
Instruments & outfit	170.	–.	–.
Conveyance to Timbuctoo	143.	4.	–.
Subsistence of Guide	27.	6.	–.
	£640.	10	–.

Annual expenditure of Mission

Subsistence & expences for myself	£91.	5.	–.
Ditto . . . . for party	82.	2.	6.
	173.	7.	6.

Sum to be placed in reserve in case of unforeseen expences	£500.	–.	–.

This estimate was undated but was received by the Colonial Office in December. Its submission seems to have been little more than a

Preparations

formality because Laing was already placing orders, presumably with Bathurst's approval, for the equipment he needed.[1] Moreover, in the also undated covering letter, accompanying the estimate, and addressed to Wilmot Horton, the Under Secretary of State, he wrote that he would 'be ready to proceed to Tripoli at any time & by any conveyance Government may desire'.[2]

He sailed from Falmouth on 6 February and landed in Malta on 3 March. He wrote the same day to Wilmot Horton reporting that he had drawn pay and subsistence for himself and his party of three men which is the first we hear of his having engaged anyone but Jack le Bore. The other two were African boat-builders, Rogers and Harris, presumably from West Africa.[3]

In Malta Laing was able to complete his equipment from the local Ordnance Depot from which he requisitioned rockets, port fires, 'two fusils for attendants',[4] flints, cartridges (blank and ball), etc.[5] But illness — a recurrence of an old liver complaint — prevented his completing his journey to Tripoli as quickly as he had hoped. During his two months' delay in Malta he was buoyed up by encouraging and friendly letters from Colonel Hanmer Warrington, the British Consul-General in Tripoli to which the Bornu Mission had just returned after an absence of three years. 'Denham & Clapperton', Laing wrote to his friend Bandinel, 'have returned — the former has done little, but I understand the researches of the latter in Soudan are most interesting and important — Warrington writes me from Tripoli, that Clapperton

---

[1] Owing to some items costing more than had been expected and to others having to be added, the cost exceeded the very modest estimate. Among the items that had been overlooked were a medicine chest (£29 11s. 2d.), and stationery, etc., including 400 quills (£14 3s. 6d.).
With the payment vouchers is one for £13 4s. 0d. from Joseph Egg for fitting new patent locks to a double-barrelled gun. Egg, of No. 1 Piccadilly, was a fashionable gun-maker (rather surprisingly described in the *Post Office Directory* of the day as Gun & Patent Truss Maker). The bill was almost certainly for converting the gun from the flint-lock to the newly invented percussion system, using a copper cap charged with fulminate, in place of flint and priming powder. This is of interest because on his travels nothing caused more surprise than Laing's ability to fire his gun without a flint. As the converted gun was for Jack le Bore, Laing probably had a new percussion gun of his own.

[2] P.R.O., C.O. 2/15.

[3] If so they must have been engaged long before the expedition had been officially authorized; this would have been consistent with Bathurst's determination to allow nothing to delay the expedition. On the other hand these two Africans might have been recruited in Britain, say in Liverpool, which had a large West African population.

[4] One of his servants, Jack le Bore, had, as we have seen, been equipped with a better weapon in London.

[5] P.R.O., C.O. 2/15, 720.

was informed by *Bello* the Chief of Soudan,[1] that the Niger *terminates in Benin by many mouths* — so much for my hypothesis, but I suppose some one must go down the river to the waterside before a right to a discovery can be established.'[2]

On 3 May he was able to report to the Colonial Office that he expected to embark for Tripoli the following day in H.M. Brig *Ganet*, Captain Bruce. He added that he had heard from Warrington 'who gives me the most flattering prospects regarding my Journey to Tombuctoo — he has sent for the Tuaric Chief Hateeta[3] who is to accompany me on the route, and he was expected to arrive in Tripoli, about the beginning of the present month'.[4]

To Warrington he wrote:

Malta.
April 30th 1825.

My dear Sir,

I was much gratified by the receipt of your kind letter of the 26th Ult.º which I assure you afforded me a great deal of real pleasure — the prospects of my Journey to Timbuctoo held out by you are of the most cheering and enlivening nature, and cannot but contribute much to the happiness of one so devoted to the cause of African discovery and conscious as I am; in fact my dear Sir, my whole thoughts have for the last five years of my life been directed towards that unbroken continent; to develop the secrets of which I have been most desirous of contributing my very humble assistance, being satisfied that by so doing and making our countrymen better acquainted with the capabilities & disposition of its inhabitants, I shall do my part in repairing the injustice they have sustained at the hands of our forefathers in the horrid traffic in slaves — I am truly delighted to hear of the great success of Lt. Clapperton, a success which his persevering industry fully entitled him to — I had long entertained the idea of the Niger terminating in the Bight of Benin, and so marked out its course with pencil on a map in the Colonial Office, the day before I left London — I had formed my opinion on the strength of Ptolemy as ancient authority, and from the information many natives from Haoussa [Hausa] and Yaoore [Yauri],[5] who had come down all the way by water after having been made slaves of by the Goober Foulahs[6] — The information of Bello now, in my opinion, sets the matter entirely at rest, or as nearly so as can be, until the river is absolutely navigated to its

---

[1] Bello was 'Chief of Soudan' to the extent that he ruled Hausa.
[2] R.S., 374(La) 73.
[3] See p. 167 above.
[4] P.R.O., C.O. 2/15, 1178.
[5] Yauri was one of the lesser or banza (bastard) Hausa States and the most westerly.
[6] The Fulani of Gobir, one of the seven principal Hausa States.

embouchure, but I rather apprehend that it will not satisfy Mr. Barrow, who is determined that the Yeou or Schad[1] shall be the Niger.

I shou'd have been with you long ago, but for an attack of illness with which I have been visited here; it is merely a recurrence of a complaint which I contracted during previous excursions in Africa, but from which I apprehend nothing, except perhaps, a good deal of inconvenience — I am recovering fast, and shall leave this about the 10th of May, by which time I hope to be perfectly well, and ready on my arrival at Tripoli to proceed to Gadamis — with every thanks for your kindness, believe me,

My dear Sir,
Yours most obediently,

A. Gordon Laing[2]

[1] The Yeou or Yobe flows into Lake Chad from the west. Had this river been the Niger it would have lent colour to Barrow's theory that the latter would prove to be the Nile.
[2] R.S., 374(La) 74.

CHAPTER II

TRIPOLI: LAING AND THE BASHAW

Gordon Laing arrived in Tripoli on 9 May 1825 and was warmly welcomed by Warrington, who was still waiting for Hatita to arrive from the interior. Laing made a favourable first impression but there were two matters which quickly caused the Consul serious concern. The first was Laing's health which appeared to be so poor that Warrington tried to persuade him to take a doctor with him on his journey; the second, which seems to have caused him equal concern, was the estimate of the cost of the Mission which Laing had prepared for the Colonial Office, without, as the reader will recall, any knowledge of local conditions. Either the estimate would have to be greatly exceeded, for which there was no authority, or Laing's departure, which the Colonial Office insisted should not be delayed, must be postponed pending fresh instructions from London. Unfortunately the Colonial Office had been as insistent on the strictest economy as they had on the need for speed.[1]

The day after Laing had landed Warrington wrote the following letter to Wilmot Horton:

Private Tripoli 10 May 1825

Sir,
    I have always taken the liberty of addressing myself to you under the Term Private, because I could assume a greater freedom of Opinion than Propriety would allow me to do in a Public Dispatch & with your permission I shall continue to do it.

    My Letter to Earl Bathurst of this day & date will acquaint you of the arrival of Major Laing.[2]

    He is both Gentlemanly & Clever & certainly appears most zealous in the cause he has undertaken, altho I much fear the delicate state of His Health, will not carry him through his arduous task — I have strongly recommended to Him to apply himself or to allow me to make application to the Govt. of Malta for a Surgeon to accompany Him.

---

[1] The insistence on speed appears to have been due partly to fear of missing what London believed to be the one and only caravan of the year bound for Timbuktu (see p. 149 above), and partly to fear of being forestalled by the French (p. 197n.4 below).

[2] This was a short letter formally reporting Laing's arrival and the daily expectation of that of Hatita (P.R.O., F.O. 76/19, 1167).

My reasons were the following 1st the Possibility of his dying in which case the object would fail. 2nd. In fever attended with delirium, he would be Incapable of administering what might Preserve his own Life. 3d. The very Name of a Doctor is a Passport to any part of Africa. 4th. The numerous applications for Medicine & advice which would be daily made, would engross too much of his time from the object of the Research. 5th. "Though last not least" on the score of Humanity, as probably thousands or tens of thousands would bless the Name of England. I have read with attention Major Laing's Instructions which probably will be considerably altered when His Lordship sees Major Denham and Lieutenant Clapperton. Major Laing's statement of the Probable Expences is certainly Erronious. — In the late Mission[1] I have always observed & recommended Liberality & Economy & which I am certain is the best Policy, & indeed the only way to ensure a successful result. His Lordships Dispatch gives me no Authority to supply myself with those funds which I may find absolutely necessary to forward the object of the Present Mission. The Confidence invested in me during the late Mission, was in great measure the cause of its success, & I have the satisfaction to know that the strictest Scrutiny of my Accounts (now auditing at Malta) will prove that that confidence in no one Instance has been abused.

When I consider the sums of money I have paid the Bashaw. When I reflect on his Professions of liberality & in the very face of the Travellers asserting that Money He did not want, the friendship & good will of England being His only object, that I must own nothing but the generous feeling which pervades the Colonial Office, could have induced me to pursue a Path so Contrary to appearances. At the moment the Bashaw was Professing such disinterested conduct, a Glance of His Eye & the rubbing together of His Thumb and finger gave strong Indications that He expected something more substantial between them. The Scene was so good & so well acted on his part, that I cannot help smiling at this Moment. On the exit of the Travellers He would frankly say, that as a Sovereign it would not do to speak of Money before Strangers, yet that I must well know these things could not be accomplished without it, & in case I did not accede to His wishes immediately I was certain to have a visit from the Minister or Bethelmal[2] Importuning me to compliance. Now these circumstances have placed me in a very delicate situation. I think it very Probable if not certain that His Highness will in this Instance require some Money to pay (as he will say) Expences, but I shall endeavour to avoid it by telling Him *that I have no Instructions*, & that He had better wait the favorable Representations founded on the Promises of the Travellers.[3]

I shall exert myself to the utmost to get Major Laing off, & that success will

---

[1] The Bornu Mission.

[2] Hadji Mahommed, the Bet el Mel, was a principal minister, probably the Bashaw's treasurer.

[3] Denham and Clapperton of the Bornu Mission (see p. 197 n. 2 below).

attend him I have no doubt. Pray excuse the way I have galloped over this Letter — but with Sentiments of respect & Esteem,
I have the honor to be
your Faithful
& Obt. Servant

Robt. Wilmot Horton Esq.

Hanmer Warrington[1]

In his dispatch to Lord Bathurst reporting Laing's arrival, Warrington had promised to introduce him to the Bashaw at the earliest opportunity and to speed his departure to the utmost. He wasted no time in seeking an audience, an essential preliminary to any sort of progress, but quickly found himself faced with stubborn resistance from the Bashaw in everything to do with Laing. This was to take many weeks to break down. The Bashaw was plainly determined to delay, if not to prevent, Laing's departure for Timbuktu.

This deliberately obstructive attitude may not have been due to either Warrington's loss of favour at court or, as Warrington suspected, to French pressure. It may only have been the attitude which the Bashaw thought would produce the best results so far as he was concerned. Experience had shown him that money was to be made out of European exploration, and he had done very well out of the Bornu Mission. It may well be that he hoped to do still better out of Laing, with the help of a little blackmail. If so the tactics were to prove astonishingly successful.

The following letters record the difficulties with which Laing and Warrington were now faced, and the duplicity of the Bashaw:

Hanmer Warrington to R. Wilmot Horton:

Tripoli 13 May 1825

Sir,

Not being able to see the Bashaw this morning I went to the Castle and had an Interview with Hagge Mohamed Bethelmal. I requested Him to get His Highness to name a day, that I should have the honor to Introduce Major Laing — I was told the Bashaw wished to postpone it till after the present Fast — I informed Him that Major Laing was expected by the British Govt. to leave this as expeditiously as possible. He said that was Impossible as the Bashaw was at War with Haliffa[2] — I told Him that was of no Consequence as we could go by Beneleed [Beni Ulid] avoiding the Gharrien [Garian] altogether — He said that we must wait for Hateeta — I told Him Hateeta

[1] P.R.O., F.O. 76/19, 1191.

[2] Haliffa, Denham's Belgassam ben Khalifa, was the Sheikh of the Jebel Arabs of the Garian mountains, in the hinterland, who were in revolt against the Bashaw (see p. 214 below).

would be certainly here in a few days unless detained purposely[1] — He then said we had better wait the arrival of the other Travellers in England, & the steps England adopted in Consequence.[2] I long suspected his drift & told Him the absurdity of acting in that mysterious manner, Candour & an upright proceeding being the wisest & best Policy — That England would not wish the Bashaw to be out of Pocket, that sooner than suffer Major Laing to be detained here for about four Months I should not hesitate to give his Highness a small sum to enable Him to meet the Expenses — Bethelmal carried that *immediately* to His Highness in his private House. He returned with an Answer that the Bashaw could not think of taking any Money, it would ill become his dignity — I replied I thoroughly agreed with them, & that there could be no obstacle to Major Laing's departure — Bethelmal acknowledged the folly of His Highness, who would not Express his wants & that in consequence of those wants not being complied with would detain Major Laing, thereby defeating the views of England. I desired Bethelmal to tell him that as far as two thousand Dollars I would take it upon myself to give it. He communicated that to the Bashaw & returned with the Answer, 'tell the Consul whatever He does I shall be satisfied with.'

I have therefore written Sir. F. Hankey[3] for the 2000 $ which shall not be delivered till there is a certainty of His departure. In this affair as well as all others I act from the best Intentions, and I trust you will approve of what I have done. I should be sorry indeed, that my fear of the Responsibility should defeat the object of this Interesting Mission & more so that I have got reason to know that the French would endeavour to accomplish it.[4] [formal ending]

Robt. Wilmot Horton Esq.   Hanmer Warrington[5]

[1] Bethelmal knew it was unlikely that Hatita, would come to Tripoli and, as Warrington seems to have suspected, he probably intended to make sure that he would not.

[2] The Bashaw had been promised an extra reward on the safe return of the Bornu Mission. As he was not given anything on their return to Tripoli he was expecting the promised reward after their arrival in England. What he did for Laing would depend on how well he was treated by London. Till that was known he was not going to commit himself (P.R.O., F.O. 76/19, 1419). (See p. 202 below.)

[3] Sir Frederick Hankey was the Chief Secretary of Malta from where the Consul drew his funds.

[4] On 6 December 1824 Giacomo Rossoni, then British Vice-Consul in Benghazi, had reported to Warrington the arrival in Derna of 'two French travellers who have come from Alexandria in mameluke costume' with the intention of travelling 'from Derna to Benghazi, from Benghazi to Tripoli, from Tripoli to Fezzan, and thence to go to Tombuctoo; and the said men are sent by the French Government'. They claimed to have letters of recommendation to both the Bashaw and Warrington. Warrington's comment to the Colonial Office on this report had been 'I shall take good care these French Travellers explore not one yard of the Interior, unless I receive his Lordship's orders to assist them' (Warrington to Wilmot Horton, 21 December 1824, P.R.O., F.O. 76/18, 538). After Laing appeared, references, chiefly by Warrington, to a French mission seeking to forestall the British in discovering Timbuktu became frequent, but, so far as is known, in neither French nor British archives is there any mention of any such mission having been even contemplated.   [5] P.R.O., F.O. 76/19, 1192.

Hanmer Warrington to John Rossoni, British Vice-Consul:

Rossoni,

Tell Bethelmal that I was induced to make a Pecuniary Offer this morning to enable me to Inform my Govt. that Major Laing's departure was fixed.

In consequence of that offer not being agreed to, *I retract*, not having any authority from my Govt. to give one Dollar. Under all circumstances it will be better for me to Inform the British Govt. of the unforeseen difficulties, and probably His Majesty's Govt. will be pleased to try some other Country by whose medium Major Laing can get to Tombuctoo without the same difficulties & obstacles.

H. Warrington
19 May 1825[1]

Keep this as an
Office Document.

I hereby Certify to have Communicated the above order as directed at the time mentioned.

Tripoli 14 Sept. 1825
John Rossoni.

Bsh. V. Cl. & Cor.[1]

Hanmer Warrington to Major A. Gordon Laing:

Tripoli, 23 May, 1825

Sir,

In consequence of what took place at the Audience yesterday I submit to your consideration a rough Sketch of the necessary Expenditure which you will find stated accordingly opposite. Not having received any Authority from the Colonial Office to draw on the Treasury for any sum or sums, it will be necessary to obtain your approbation, & probably it will be advisable that the Bills should be drawn by one of us which will keep the Account with Govt. clearer, & afford the Power of giving Explanation on any Item which may appear to require it. I should recommend that the sum of £2000 is immediately drawn for & sent to the Govt. of Malta & that its proceeds may be sent over here forthwith. In addition to this sum the Bashaw will expect Two thousand Dollars on your departure from Godames, Two

---

[1] P.R.O., F.O. 76/19, 2097. There is much that is unusual in this letter. First, it was not Warrington's habit to date his letters after his signature; the words 'Keep this as an Office Document' are also unusual and, one would have thought, superfluous; finally, in spite of this injunction neither the original of this letter nor a copy was in the consular archives when they were taken over by the Public Record Office; the only copy is that which Warrington sent to the Colonial Office when he was in trouble over the payments he had promised the Bashaw. In these circumstances it is difficult to resist the suspicion that this is a copy of a letter that was never written, but was useful to have on the files.

A rough Calculation of Expences to convey Major Laing & Party to Tombuctoo & the termination of the Niger.

To His Highness before leaving Tripoli		$ 2000	
To have untouched on your arrival at Tombuctoo		,, 3000	
A present to Hateeta to conduct you to Twat	$ 500 ⎫		
Do. to the Sheikh sent by the Bashaw	,, 500 ⎬	,, 1500	
Hateeta's Friend at Twat to take you to Tombuctoo	,, 500 ⎭		
The Moor recommended by Messrs Denham & Clapperton	,, 150 ⎫		
Governor of Godames [Ghadames]	,, 250 ⎬	,, 700	
Small expences unforeseen say	,, 300 ⎭		
To Purchase Camels, Horses, Mules, to arm & clothe camel Drivers, say	,, 1000 ⎫		
Expences from Tripoli to Tombuctoo, say	,, 1000 ⎭	,, 2000	
		,, 9200	
on departure from Godames, to the Bashaw	,, 2000 ⎫		
from Twat ,, ,,	,, 2000 ⎬	,, 8000	
from Tombuctoo ,, ,,	,, 4000 ⎭		
		$ 17,200	

N.B. These sums are certainly large but are in my opinion necessary to ensure success to the Mission as well as your personal safety, and every One of the Africans will expect to make a sort of Harvest of your liberality, & by thus purchase their fidelity, it will leave a lasting Impression of a generous & disinterested Conduct evinced by the English Nation.

             H.W.

thousand on your departure from Twat & four thousand on your departure from Tombuctoo making say the whole amount Seventeen thousand two hundred Dollars.

Altho the amount is large still I conceive we shall not have to call on His Majesty's Govt. for any other sum & it will appear obvious to you that the Bashaw being thus Interested by anticipating the respective Payments at the periods alluded to under the stated circumstances it will give a facility to all your Proceedings & considerably tend to if not ensure the success of the mission.

Altho by the Present calculation you will have 3000 $ untouched at Tombuctoo I should recommend your drawing on me from that Place in Preference to breaking in on that Sum, particularly as no difficulty will attend your obtaining supplies in that way.

I have the honor
to be Sir,
your Obt. & very
Faithful Servt.

H. Warrington[1]

Major Alex[r]. Laing
Tripoli

In his reply to the Consul's letter Laing wrote on 24 May:

although the schedule exceeds considerably the estimate furnished by me to His Majesty's Government yet as the surplus comprises an allowance to the Bashaw, & rewards to guides, which I omitted in my estimate in consequence of my entire ignorance as to their pretensions, I cannot feel any hesitation in giving my full concurrence to the arrangements you propose; more particularly, as under existing circumstances, while the French are making efforts to pluck from England's brow, those laurels to which the latter is so justly entitled, time is to us so precious.[2]

Hanmer Warrington to Lord Bathurst:

Tripoli 24 May, 1825

My Lord,

I have already had the honor to Inform your Lordship of Major Laing's arrival here.

I consider that your Lordships wishes & orders may be comprised under the following Heads. An Expeditious departure, a safe conduct to Tombuctoo and a general adoption of measures to enable us to form a well grounded hope in the ultimate success of this new & most Interesting Mission.

I feel persuaded your Lordship would wish me to pursue the line of Strict

[1] P.R.O., C.O. 2/15. 1455.   [2] P.R.O., F.O. 76/19, 1419.

Economy blended with that degree of liberality, so necessary to uphold the Generous Character of our Great Nation, and so essential to the successful Result of this Important Undertaking, & I have the satisfaction to know that by a steady Perseverance in the above line of conduct the success of the late Mission may be attributed.

I have maturely considered & well weighed the best mode of Proceeding in the Present Instance, and having communicated every circumstance to Major Laing which in my opinion would tend to, or enable me to fulfil your Lordships Orders, & I am happy to say that Under the local Existing circumstances that Gentleman gives His full concurrence in the Arrangement for the departure of the Mission entrusted to His care, who will no doubt convey his opinion thereon by the Medium of his own Pen.

Now my Lord before I enumerate the different mode of Expenditure, I wish to Impress on your Mind, altho' the sum may appear large for this early stage of the Research, still as we have every Reason to believe the first Expence will be sufficient to accomplish the object, I trust it will be thought reasonable, and consequently approved by your Lordship.

It is absolutely necessary to give the Bashaw.		$ 2000
Major Laing to take with him and have untouched at Tombuctoo		3000
Expences from Tripoli to Tombuctoo		1000
To Purchase Camels, Mules, Horses & to arm and clothe Camel Drivers		1000
To Hateeta	500	
The Sheikh sent by the Bashaw	500	
Hateeta's friend at Twat	500	1500
To the Moor strongly recommended by Messrs. Denham & Clapperton[1]	150	
The Governor of Godames	250	
Small Expences say	300	700
		$ 9200[2]

[1] This was the man Laing called Sidi Mahommed Bogoola (see p. 247 below), but, according to the Anonymous Report (p. 29), his real name was Oben Guidah, and he was described as Major Laing's negro servant.

[2] It will be noted that Warrington omitted from this statement the three additional payments that were to be made to the Bashaw: $2,000 on Laing's leaving Ghadames, $2,000 on his leaving Tuat, and $4,000 on his leaving Timbuktu, which would have raised the total to $17,200, as Warrington had already told Laing (p. 199 above). It is hardly surprising that Warrington did not enjoy the full confidence of Downing Street.

Making the Sum of nine thousand, Two hundred Spanish Dollars for which I have this day drawn a Bill for Two thousand pounds Sterling on the Lords Commissioners of His Majesty's Treasury to the Order of the Government of Malta at 30 days sight, which I trust you will be pleased to Order to be paid.

I have received the assurances from the Bashaw that Major Laing & Party shall leave this on or before the 20th of next Month which is fully as soon as we could get the Dollars from Malta in return for the Bill above alluded to.

I am most anxious to expedite His departure as we may shortly expect the French Travellers from the Cyrenaica who may endeavour to Interfere with our arrangements respecting the present Mission. Now my Lord, permit me to say, I have had a most delicate Game to play, as altho' the Bashaw is ever ready to give assurances of the most liberal & disinterested conduct & that the Friendship & good Will of England is His only view still such liberal Sentiments from such a Channel must be considered an Ingenious way of Enhancing His Claim on the British Government, & altho I am the only one who is placed in an unpleasant situation, still it is my duty to state circumstances as they really exist & trust to the generous feeling of the Colonial Office to give Implicit Credit to my Assertions.

Your Lordship's Dispatch of the 30th August 1821 authorized me to hold out to the Bashaw an Assurance 'that if Dr. Oudney or the Gentlemen associated with Him, should be conveyed through His Intervention further into the Interior, in the direction required by the Travellers, and should return from thence in safety, he may rely on the further liberal consideration of His Majesty, in proportion to the distance to which they shall have been so conveyed.'

Allow me also to refer you to the Dispatch of Mr. Wilmot Horton dated 3rd October *1823* giving me the power to promise at a future period a small Equipment of Artillery, & also a Present to Haggi Mohamed Bethelmal and which was I believe offered in consequence of His Highness's conduct in having so readily released the Greek Slaves, therefore it is obvious that the Bashaw has two distinct Claims, & I should strongly recommend a Similar & Conditional Promise being made on the Success of the Present Mission & on the safe return of Major Laing to England, in addition to the $ 10,000

I beg leave to refer your Lordship to No. 1 my Letter to Major Laing,[1] & to No. 2. His answer.[2] Immediately after his departure every particular shall be communicated.

[formal ending]
H. Warrington[3]

Right Honble
The Earl Bathurst K.G.
His Majesty's Secretary of State,
Downing Street,
London.

---

[1] P. 198 above. [2] P. 200 above. [3] P.R.O., F.O. 76/19, 1455.

Warrington wrote to Wilmot Horton the same day:

On my honor everything has been done for the best, & as I feel inspired with a conscientous rectitude of conduct, I am sanguine that the Responsibility I am involved in, will be approved by His Majesty's Government.

I am quite delighted with Major Laing — His Talents are conspicuous, His zeal unbounded, His Gentlemanly manners & honorable conduct I am certain will be duly estimated in any Quarter of the World.

His Health thank God is thoroughly re established & I hope & believe He will be quite successful in his great Undertaking.[1]

Major A. Gordon Laing to Lord Bathurst:

Tripoli in the West
May 24th 1825

My Lord,

In my last dispatch, which I did myself the honor of addressing to Wilmot Horton Esq., Under Secretary of State, I apprised Your Lordship of my arrival in Tripoli, and of the improved state of my health, which is now, (I have much pleasure in stating) completely restored, insomuch, that although this is by far the hottest, and considered by the natives, the least desirable season for traversing the Desert, I shall set out on my Journey with the fullest confidence on the 20th of next Month, the day fixed upon by His Highness the Bashaw for my departure.

In making this arrangement with the Bashaw I regret to be compelled to acquaint Your Lordship that no inconsiderable expence will be incurred by His Majesty's Government, but as I plainly cou'd observe from the cool and hesitating manner of His Highness (who informed me in the most unequivocal language that the door was shut to me unless I opened it with money) that without some pecuniary douceur, particularly as he was so handsomely paid for the last mission (on the successful result of which I beg to congratulate Your Lordship) he wou'd continue to detain me in Tripoli for months upon the most frivolous pretences, I have been reluctantly compelled to accede to the propositions contained in the accompanying letter from His Majesty's Consul General, to whose experience on this side of Africa, as it must of course render him the better judge of what is requisite & necessary, I without hesitation succumb.

I have been the more induced to hazard this responsibility, having been apprised of some communications being made to the Bashaw on the part of the French Government, which it wou'd appear, is jealous of our success, and desirous of being beforehand with us in reaching Tombuctoo, and because I feel that after the great sacrifice of money and life on the part of Great Britain, it wou'd not only much disappoint Your Lordship, but the

[1] P.R.O., F.O. 76/19, 1429.

country at large, to see a rival nation step in and bear away the Palm, particularly at a moment when (as far as human foresight can well divine) it may be said to be actually within our grasp.

A third reason for acceeding to these proposals, and arrangements of the Consul-General, is my full conviction that Your Lordship wou'd not desire, that any expence incurred by the Bashaw in rendering his assistance to the present Mission, shou'd be borne by himself, and although the expectations of the people here much exceed any calculation, the most liberal, that I cou'd have made before I became acquainted with them; yet I am perfectly assured, from my own knowledge of the political relationship in which the Chiefs of Africa stand to one another, that in the opening of a new road (which this decidedly is, every foot of it) the disbursements of His Highness (partly from necessity, partly from the desire so deeply rooted in the breast of all Africans, of manifesting their importance) will be considerable; for on such occasions, as during an election in England, there are certain individuals whose suffrage must be purchased, and who look forward so naturally for the expected harvest, that disappointment on their part, wou'd not only arrest for a time the progress of the Mission, but most probably endanger its ultimate success.

Your Lordship will observe by an inspection of the accompanying rough estimate furnished by the Consul General,[1] that the only expence incurred by me till the arrival of the Mission at Tombuctoo, will be the sum of Two Thousand Dollars, which will include the purchase of camels, feeding &c, fees, dues, customs &c on the road (which are imposed upon, and submitted to by the natives themselves) and the total maintenance of the party: and in order to interest the Bashaw in my speedy arrival at, and departure from that Capital,[2] as also the expeditious conveyance of my dispatches to Tripoli, it has been thought adviseable to hold out to the Bashaw the separate rewards specified at the foot of the estimate[3] of which measure I trust Your Lordship will be pleased to grant your approval — With regard to the three thousand dollars which the Consul recommends that I shou'd have untouched on my arrival at Tombuctoo, I beg to inform Your Lordship, that unless compelled by the most urgent necessity, they shall not be touched upon at all: they shall merely be kept by me in case of need, and if not required, as I hardly expect they will, shall be brought with me to England & returned into His Majesty's Treasury — The other sums of Fifteen hundred and Seven hundred Dollars, as rewards to Hateeta, the Sheikh sent by the Bashaw, a present to the Governor of Godamis &c &c as they were expences that I cou'd not foresee, and yet is quite out of my power to reduce the ideas of extravagance which these people have imbibed from the blind & mistaken liberality of others,[4]

[1] P. 199 above.   [2] Timbuktu.
[3] Warrington had evidently concealed from Laing that he had omitted the 'separate rewards', totalling $8,000, from the statement he had sent to Lord Bathurst.
[4] An oblique criticism of the Bornu Mission.

long before my appearance among them, I hope I shall not incur your Lordship's displeasure by sanctioning; at the same time assuring Your Lordship, that under any other circumstances than that of expecting that the French might anticipate us in this great and highly important discovery, I wou'd have waited for further instructions from Your Lordship.

In the full hopes that Your Lordship will be pleased to approve of my proceedings, and place implicit reliance in my prudent and oeconomical disposal of the funds put into my hands,

[formal ending]
A. Gordon Laing[1]

To The Right Honble
Earl Bathurst. K.G.

On the same day Laing wrote to his friend James Bandinel telling him of the embarrassing position in which he found himself:

I know that after the estimate which I gave in, the sum of Two Thousand pounds for which I have drawn, will surprise them a little at the Colonial Office; but I rather think it will not appear so strange to them as it has done to me as they must have been long air [sic] now informed by experience, of the demands of the Bashaw, & ought I think to have given me some discretionary, or other authority to deal with him — as it is, I am placed in a situation the most awkward & unenviable, fearing that while I am doing my best, I may be subjecting myself to a reprimand, which you must admit, is not a pleasant prospect to look forward to in the interior of Africa. . . . I rather think it has been presumed that as the Journey is as *easy* and *safe* as from *London* to *Edinburgh*,[2] that the expences on the road might be as simply calculated as the price of a *seat in the Mail* or a *passage in a steam Vessel*.[3]

In another letter to Bandinel, dated simply 'May 1825', he wrote:

I have had a good deal of trouble with the Bashaw, and as I have found that the French have been bribing him to keep back the Mission, have been necessitated to oil his palm a little before I cou'd bring him to listen to me. . . . I expect to be at Benin by March next.[4]

[1] P.R.O., C.O. 2/15, 1455. [2] This is what Warrington had said.
[3] R.S., 374(La) 78. [4] Ibid., 79.

CHAPTER III

TRIPOLI: EMMA WARRINGTON

The 20th June, the day on which the Bashaw had promised a start might be made, came and passed with Laing still at Tripoli and no immediate prospect of getting away. Meanwhile both he and Warrington were still worrying over what the Secretary of State would say about the financial affairs of the Mission.

Major A. Gordon Laing to Lord Bathurst:

At the Encampment,
Tripoli in the West,
June, 21st 1825

My Lord,

In my last I had the honor of entering at some length into an explanation of the reasons which led to my incurring the responsibility of an immediate expenditure of Two Thousand Pounds, in lieu of drawing in detail for the sums specified in the Schedules furnished by me to Your Lordship, previous to my quitting London, and I have now to hope with reference to that expenditure, that my conduct will meet with the full approval of Your Lordship, which it shall invariably be my study to deserve.

Pursuant to my intention of leaving Tripoli on the 20th Inst (as I had the honor of intimating to Your Lordship in a former letter) I removed from the town on the 13th Inst. and pitched my tents about two miles distant in the country, in a healthy situation near to the residence of the British Consul,[1] where I am progressively advancing in the completion of my arrangements for departure, and shall be in a perfect state of readiness to set off with the most flattering prospects of success by the first day of July, which has been nominated by the Bashaw in lieu of the earlier date, firstly In consequence of the non arrival of two Sheikhs of Gadamis who are hourly expected, and whose good offices towards the Mission His Highness is desirous of bespeaking, Secondly, In consequence of the necessity which devolves upon His Highness, of making some arrangements for my protection through a part of his dominions, which has lately risen up in rebellion against him[2] — I beg leave nevertheless to acquaint Your Lordship, that as far as either the Consul General or myself are concerned, the Mission might have been in motion yesterday as had been originally intended, and agreed upon — I have been

[1] The British or English Garden in the suburb of Menshia.
[2] See p. 214 n. 1 below.

for the last two weeks past, most anxiously expecting the arrival of Hateeta, the Tuarick under whose care (as stated in Your Lordship's instructions to me) I was directed to place myself for conveyance to Tombuctoo, but I regret to say that he has not yet made his appearance: I have however much pleasure in acquainting Your Lordship, that a letter from him of the most satisfactory nature, reached His Majesty's Consul General yesterday, from the tenor of which I am sanguine in my expectations of meeting with him at Gadamis, or at all events between that town and the Tuarick country, in the course of forty days from this date. Now My Lord, as the day for my departure is so near at hand, and as I feel satisfied that this will be my last communication from Tripoli, unless something beyond the reach of my calculation shou'd in the interim occur, I trust Your Lordship will permit me to take this opportunity of expressing in the strongest manner the high sense I entertain of the extent of the services rendered to me by Consul General Warrington in this important undertaking; and the great satisfaction which I derive in departing upon a Mission, in the interest of which, a person of this zealous activity is so warmly engaged: from what I have been eye witness to since my arrival here, I feel not the smallest hesitation in saying; that I consider protection and safety will be as fully ensured to me, through the medium of Consul General Warrington's exertions and interference, as if I was merely on a tour through the secure districts of my over blessed and happy Country,

[formal ending]
A. Gordon Laing[1]

To the Right Honble.
Earl Bathurst K.G.,
Principal Sec^ty of State.

The letter from Hatita to Warrington to which Laing refers, was dated from Ghat '5th of Shual 1240' [27 May 1825]. According to the translation from the Arabic, Hatita had intended going to Tripoli, as the Consul had directed, but, he wrote, 'I received news from my Country that the Tuarick Hagarah[2] had a Quarrel with the Tuarick of Soudan[3] & the communication was closed so that no Intercourse was kept up between them.

....

If you will send your countrymen[4] to Fezzan I will meet them there & take them through all my Country without any danger'.[5]

[1] P.R.O., C.O. 2/15, 1719.
[2] The Ahaggar Tuareg.
[3] Probably the Kel Owi Tuareg whose range extended seasonally into Hausa.
[4] Laing and his party.
[5] P.R.O., F.O. 76/19, 1722. Hatita, we must assume, employed a scribe.

Hanmer Warrington to Lord Bathurst:

Tripoli 22nd June 1825

My Lord,

I have the honor to Inform your Lordship that my Courier returned on the 19th Inst. and by reference to No. 1. you will be fully acquainted with the cause of delay, as well as the Sentiments of Hateeta.

About one Month since I addressed a Letter to him with Instructions to proceed to Godames, and there wait the arrival of Major Laing, at the same time sending him Thirty spanish Dollars to defray the Expense.

As it is now settled that Major Laing leaves this on the 1st July, and to prevent mistake I shall dispatch a Courier to accompany Hateeta to Godames, if He had not before set off for that Place.

The reasons which induced Major Laing as well as myself to Prefer the road of Godames[1] are simply the following — His getting well introduced to the Inhabitants of Tombuctoo, by the Medium of a Nine years Resident, who is to accompany him,[2] that by pursuing the great line of commercial Intercourse, He becomes one link of the great Chain, and His object not being of a Sinister nature He derives the Influence of such a Powerful connection without exciting one Particle of suspicion or jealousy —

The Godames Merchant will be here today and everything shall be done to Create a favourable Impression on His mind, the Important charge entrusted to him, & the great Interest His Majesty takes in a successful termination of this Mission.

The sooner Major Laing gets beyond the Territory of the Bashaw, the greatest Impediment is removed to the performance of His Interesting Journey, as the unaccountable zest for Procrastination is so implanted in these People, that to eradicate it would be utterly Impossible & certainly if He were to go by way of Fezzan the sickly Season would be passed at Mourzouk.[3]

The road to Godames is unexplored, & every Inch affords an opportunity of establishing the Geographical situation, and assisting Science in various Branches — Under all these circumstances I trust your Lordship will approve of this new Route.[4]

[1] In preference to the direct road from Fezzan to Timbuktu.

[2] Sheikh Babani.

[3] He did in fact go by Fezzan, but he only just touched it and avoided Murzuk which was not what the Secretary of State intended.

[4] The new route through Ghadames was contrary to the Secretary of State's instructions, but to get there the mission had to go a long way round, because the Jebel Arabs were in revolt against the Bashaw and had cut the much shorter direct route. This is clearly stated in the Anonymous Report which reads: 'They [Laing's caravan] proceeded, not by the direct road through the mountains which the Pacha represented as dangerous, owing to the feuds of certain tribes in its neighbourhood, but by the circuitous route of Ben-i-oleed and part of the Fezzan district' (C.O. 2/20, A.R., 2).

I have also received a Letter from Buchaloom,[1] but it is unnecessary to send a copy. No.2. is my Letter to Hateeta, N3 an obligation I have given to enable Major Laing to procure Funds if necessary. No.4 a Recommendation & Guarantee of the Bashaw. No.5. a Guarantee of Mr. D'Ghies & Introduction to his extensive line of Commercial Friends. No. 6 my Account with Maj^r Laing making known to your Lordship the appropriation of the Two thousand pounds every Item of which I trust will be approved of.

Now my Lord permit me to say better arrangements could not have been made, and a fairer Prospect of success could not present itself, & supported by the Enthusiastic Spirit & Indefatigable Exertion of Major Laing I feel as Sanguine as it is possible for Man to do, in the uncertainty of all Human Affairs.

I have endeavoured to Implant on the mind of Major Laing the cheering Prospect of meeting Clapperton[2] at Sockatoo, and I shall give Him a Letter to Sultan Bello.

I have recommended after the time necessary for Recruiting His Health and effecting the object of the Mission, that He should proceed with Expedition and as we may now caculate that *Benin*[3] is His destination I trust in God steps will be taken to convey him from that sickly spot without any delay, as even a weeks Residence there is attended with more danger than His long Journey.

According to my calculation He will be at *Benin* during the Month of January next, about the same time I shall expect to receive His Dispatches from Tombuctoo, & his Dispatches from Tuat in October next.

From the extreme Gentlemanly manners Honorable Conduct, & Sound Moral Principle, which are so visible in Major Laing, that I view him, in the Character of an Old Friend a stimulus which will always assist the execution of a Public Duty —

With every feeling of the highest consideration, & with corresponding Sentiments of Respect,

[formal ending]

Hanmer Warrington[4]

To Right Honble
The Earl Bathurst K.G.,
His Majesty's Secretary of State,
Colonial Department.

[1] This man should not be confused with Denham's Boo-Bucker Boo-Khaloom, 'a merchant of very considerable riches and influence', who accompanied the Bornu Mission to the Sudan where he lost his life in a slave raid. It is possible that Warrington's Buchaloom was the Hadji Ali Boo-Khaloom who also had joined the Bornu Mission.

[2] See pp. 160, 161 above.

[3] By this he meant not the city of Benin but the Benin River, which Laing believed to be the mouth of the Niger.

[4] P.R.O., F.O. 76/19, 1722. A barely legible minute on this letter expresses Lord Bathurst's hope that 'directions will be given to our Ships of War to receive him on Board sh'd he reach the Coast at the period [?] mentioned, ... a Letter sh'd be written to the Admty on this subject'.

Hatita's letter, which accompanied this dispatch, has already been quoted. Warrington's letter to him (Enclosure No. 2), dated 22nd June, read:

Our friend the English Traveller will be at Godames in Thirty days from this day & will wait there ten days for you. I wrote you a month since desiring you to go to Godames, & I sent Thirty Spanish Dollars to pay your Expenses on the Way. I hope you have received it from Buckaloom or the Courier I sent & that you are now proceeding to Godames.

....

If it is possible for you to accompany this Traveller to Tombuctoo my King will feel obliged to you, and you will be most liberally rewarded both now & hereafter. If you cannot go to Tombuctoo yourself we beg of you to go to Tuat, & there place this Traveller in the hands & under the care of some of your Friends who will conduct Him to Tombuctoo.[1]

Laing's letter of credit (Enclosure No. 3) is of interest as an illustration of how, long before the introduction of European banking methods, the internal trade of north-western Africa was financed. The strikingly international character of this trade, necessitating the transfer of funds backwards and forwards across the Sahara, from the great ports of the Mediterranean littoral to remote markets of the Sudan, placed explorers from the north at a great advantage over their fellows who endeavoured to open up less sophisticated parts of the continent.

The following is a translation of the letter of credit Warrington gave to Laing, guaranteed by the Bashaw and his minister Mohammed D'Ghies:

We His Britannic Majesty's Consul General to the Regency of Tripoli hereby authorize the Bearer Major Laing to draw on us for any money which He may require during His journey into the Interior of Africa.

Signed, H. Warrington

In the name of God etc.

---

[1] Warrington also enclosed a copy of a later letter to Hatita, dated 28 May, in which he wrote: 'Should my courier meet you this side Sockna you may as well come on here, but if the other side Sockna you had better proceed direct for Godames and wait there for him.' Sockna is about 400 miles from Tripoli on the road to Murzuk.

To any one who may see this writing in the Interior of Africa, The Bearer of the same an English Officer called Major Laing, if He needs any money to be lent him in his present voyage, those Persons who will so lend him, they will take His Bill for the same which Bill will be duly paid by the Consul here in Tripoli, & we are guarantee for Him.

      Saluting
    date 22 June 1825
    The Slave of God
      Signed, Jouseff Bashaw Caramanli

The bearer of the present the English Traveller, if He is in want of money during his present journey — any of our Friends, & correspond with [correspondents] & those who may have our Funds in hand, they may advance to the said Englishmen all those Sums which He may want & take His Bill on the English Consul in Tripoli, so that it may be paid here.

      Date 14 June 1825
     Signed, Mohamed D'Ghies

Another enclosure with the dispatch (No. 6) was a copy of Laing's account with the Consulate. This shows that the Bashaw had received his initial $2,000, and that Laing's local purchases included, for himself, 11 camels ($295), 2 mules ($146), and 7 waterskins, and as presents 6 brace of pistols (2 brace silver-mounted), 1 sword, 10 gilt-mounted stilettos and 500 pistol flints.

Of greater interest is the following entry, which shows how Warrington sought to ensure that Hatita would meet Laing in Ghadames, and that the latter would be able to get in touch with Tripoli, anyway as far on his way as Tuat:

To the Courier Sala on acct. of his journey to Moorzout [Murzuk], Grat [Ghat] & to return to Godames with Hateeta & then him & his Brother to accompany Major Laing to Tuat & bring His Dispatches down to Tripoli. $40

The credit side of the account shows:

	Tarces
Produce of 2000£ Cashed by the Govt. of Malta & sent here by H.M. Express & by the Tuscan Brig Guerriero.	$ 9142 – 27 – 0[1]

In Tripoli Laing had also to complete the equipment required for the voyage he hoped to make down the Niger. On 25 June he wrote to his

[1] P.R.O., F.O. 76/19, 1722.

scientific friend Edward Sabine: 'I thank you for your hints about sounding, which I shall attend to — I have got a lead and lines made. I am also taking with me tackle for a boat. My sailors are fine fellows, and will prove highly serviceable when I reach the Niger.'[1] In a letter to Bandinel, written the same day, he struck a less confident note: 'I do not like to throw cold water upon any thing, but I can plainly perceive that it will [be] a matter of unusual difficulty to reach Tombuctoo.'[2]

But not all Laing's time in Tripoli had been devoted to perfecting the arrangements for his journey, nor did he find the delay as exasperating as might have been expected. As early as 7 June he had written to his friend Bandinel asking him to buy 'a handsome little cabinet of mineralogical specimens, such a one as will suit a Lady of taste & refinement; also an edition of Brand's Mineralogy & Chemistry,[3] which I shou'd like to have addressed to Miss Emma Warrington. . . . You must not be forming any strange conclusions from this extraordinary request. . . . I am no more than interested, much interested in the young lady in question'.[4] Interest ripened into infatuation and did not go unrewarded:

Hanmer Warrington to Lord Bathurst:

Tripoli 14th July 1825

My Lord,

I have the honor to Inform your Lordship that Major Laing was this morning married to my Second Daughter.[5]

Although I am aware that Major Laing is a very Gentlemanly, honorable and good Man still I must allow a more Wild, Enthusiastic and Romantic Attachment never before existed and consequently every Remonstrance, every Argument, & every feeling of disapprobation was resorted to by me to prevent even an Engagement under the existing circumstance the disadvantages so evidently appearing to attach to my Daughter.

After a Voluminous correspondence, I found my wishes, exertions, Entreaties, and displeasure, quite futile & of no avail, & under all circum-

[1] R.S., 374(La) 81.   [2] Ibid., 82.
[3] The reference appears to be to one or both of two works by William Thomas Brande (1788–1866), chemist and geologist: *Outlines of Geology* (London, 1817), and *The Manual of Chemistry* (London, 1819).
[4] R.S., 374(La), 80. Laing wrote of himself before he was aged eighteen: 'Passionately fond of the fair sex, I had always in my Eye some Dulcima, on whom I used to dote, make verses, and squander away money' (R.S., Laing, IV, 376, p. 2).
[5] It was said that Rousseau's son, Timoléon, and Emma were in love, and that this so infuriated her father that he forced her to marry Laing (L. C. Féraud, 344). There is no supporting evidence, and it cannot be doubted that she was deeply in love with Laing.

stances, both for the Public good, as well as their Mutual happiness, I was obliged to consent to Perform the Ceremony, under the most Sacred, & most Solemn Obligation that they are not to cohabit till the Marriage is duly performed by a Clergyman of the established Church of England, and as my honor is so much involved, that I shall take due care they never be one Second from under the observation of myself or Mrs. Warrington.

Now my Lord I do not conceive a Father can possibly be placed in a more delicate situation, as long as doubts may arise as to the Power and Legality invested in me as His Majesty's Consul General to unite two of His Majesty's Subjects, as Man and Wife, & till that doubt is completely removed I will take good care my Daughter remains as pure & chaste as snow.

I have the honor to submit to your Lordships consideration the Certificate[1] I gave of the Ceremony having been performed by me, in my Official Capacity, and as it is a Question of great Importance I wish to know whether a Marriage so performed is equally binding as if duly Solemnized by a Clergyman of the established Church of England.

At various times under various circumstances, various Marriages have taken place at Algiers and Tunis, but I am not satisfied as to their Legality. May I therefore beg and pray your Lordships opinion on this Most Important & Interesting Question.

[formal ending]
Hanmer Warrington[2]

To The Right Honble
The Earl Bathurst K.G.,
His Majesty's Secretary of State,
Colonial Department

[1] The following signatures of witnesses appear in the marriage certificate: Josef Gomez, Herrador, Consul-General of Spain, J. N. Morillo, American Chargé d'Affaires, John Dickson, Surgeon R.N., H. G. Warrington, Elizabeth Dickson, Jane Eliza Warringtons Jane Elizabeth Warrington, and John Rossoni, the British Vice-Consul.

[2] P.R.O., F.O. 76/19, 1725: A minute on this dispatch reads: 'Copy sent to the King' Advocate 19 Septr. 1825.'

CHAPTER IV

FAREWELL TO LAING

Hanmer Warrington to Major A. Gordon Laing:

Tripoli, 18th July, 1825

My Lord,

Various and unforeseen events have occasioned Major Laings detention so long in Tripoli.

Hateeta will meet him at Godames and it was only three days since that Sheikh Babany arrived, having been prevented passing the Gharian, till His Highness sent about five thousand of His Army to afford him a Safe conduct through Halifa's Territory.¹

On the 7th Inst. We deemed it advisable that the Koffle² should remove from this to Tajura [Tagiura], and there wait till we ascertained whether it could pass the Gharian in safety, or go by the circuitous Route of Beneleed [Beni Ulid], the latter being decided on the Koffle took its final departure this Morning, but will have to wait two or three days at Beneleed for Sheikh Babany, who accompanies Major Laing to Tombuctoo. On the 16th Inst. Major Laing & myself had an audience, & I am happy in saying, handsomer conduct & more satisfactory accounts could not possibly have been Shewn or given.

Altho' Sheikh Babany had not arrived forty eight hours before, He offered in Ten days to leave this for Tombuctoo, but on the Bashaw saying He should only give him Six, it was so arranged.

This Babany has resided at Tombuctoo Twenty two years, & really appears one of the finest fellows I ever saw, with the best tempered & most prepossessing Countenance I ever beheld. He engages to take Major Laing to

---

¹ The warlike 'Arabs' of the Garian mountains, in the hinterland of Tripoli, were more Berber than Arab. The Europeans of Tripoli were in the habit of referring to them loosely as El Gebel or El Jebel (The Mountain), and back in Miss Tully's day they called them Gebeleens or Jebeleens. Although their country lay close to Tripoli they were seldom, if ever, under the administrative control of the Bashaw. This was largely because of the security which their rugged hills afforded them and which some of them turned to even better account by adopting the life of troglodytes. 'The habitations are at the very summit of the mountains,' wrote Miss Tully in 1783, 'not to be easily distinguished but by those who inhabit them, as they are all built under ground in the mountains.... These Arabs are chiefly banditti; and they are never disturbed nor attacked, as the narrow subterranean passages to their houses, where one man may keep many at bay, form a sufficient safeguard to them from the Moors' (Tully, *Ten Years Residence*, 25). At the head of the revolt was Belgassam ben Khalifa, commonly called Haleefa, the sheikh of the Beni Nouïr. There had been a similar revolt, or perhaps it was the same one with Khalifa at its head, when the Bornu Mission arrived in the country in 1822 (Denham and Clapperton, 1, xix).

² Caravan, from the Arabic *qāfila* or *guefla*. Other common transliterations into English are koffle, gaffle and goffle.

Tombuctoo in two Months, & a half, and there pass him over to his particular friend, the Great Sheikh, and Cheif Maraboot Mouckta,[1] who He says has sufficient Power and Influence to pass him in safety to the Sea, either *North West* or *South*, the latter I presume will be his destination, & I trust measures will be so arranged not to detain him at Benin.

When Sheikh Babany has regularly and safely conveyed Major Laing to Tombuctoo & passed Him into the hands of that Chief He will immediately return here, to dispose of his Merchandize and arrange his Affairs & by whom I shall receive Major Laing's Dispatches which according to my Idea will be here in December next. It is Impossible for Matters to stand with a More favorable prospect of success, and the circumstance of Major Laing's Marriage will considerably tend to promote it as His Highness said the day before yesterday, that in consequence of Major Laing being now so nearly related to me, that He would do more than He has ever yet done, & altho' it may appear ridiculous, still I can assure your Lordship the British Consul is a greater Man in the Interior of Africa than in any other Quarter of the World.

N.1 is the Account of Expenditure approved of by Major Laing, since which I have made other payments.

N 2 my Letter to the Governor of Godames and Tuat.

N 3 to the Great Sheikh of Tombuctoo.

N.4 to Sultan Bello. N 5 Recommending Majr Laing as my Son.[2]

Now my Lord I conclude this Dispatch with Prayers & wishes for the success of the Mission which appears to me perfectly certain.

[formal ending]

Hanmer Warrington[3]

The Right Honble
The Earl Bathurst K.G.,
His Majesty's Secretary
of State.

Encl. 3

Tripoli 30th June 1825

To the Sultan of the Kingdom & Territory of Tombuctoo[4] May God Preserve & Protect your Highness etc. etc.

My great & revered Master The King of England wishing at all times to extend his Friendship, & good will to every part of the World, and by His liberal and generous Heart He is always desirous of cultivating, the best Harmony, & the most friendly Intercourse with every great & good

---

[1] This sounds like the famous Sidi el Muktar ben Ahmed of the Kunta Arabs who occupied the desert north of Timbuktu. But as he had died in 1811 the reference is probably to his son Sidi Mohammed el Muktar; the latter was the father of the remarkable Sidi Ahmed el Bekkai who, at great personal risk, shielded Henry Barth against his persecutors in Timbuktu in 1853-4.

[2] Of these four enclosures Nos. 3 and 4 follow. The others are not of sufficient interest to be included.

[3] P.R.O., F.O. 76/19, 1726.   [4] Sidi Mohammed el Muktar.

Sovereign, He therefore sends the Bearer of this an Englishman Major Laing to express His most sincere & friendly sentiments to your Highness.

His Majesty well knowing that your Highness is a good man and a Friend to the stranger, He feels full confidence that your Highness will use His Servant as well as His Majesty would do to your Subjects in any part of the world, and whenever your Highness wishes to have the Powerful Influence of the British Flag in Tripoli, or that your Highness may wish to procure any thing from England, I beg of you to write me well knowing the kind Treatment which my friend & Countryman will receive from your Highness, that it will be Impossible for me to do sufficient to evince my sincere Gratitude & Friendship.

I am informed that there are a number of natural Productions in your Country which will cure various diseases that Human nature is subject to, I therefore trust your Highness will allow the Bearer to collect those specimens which He may require, and should your Highness be in want of a Doctor (which God forbid) I recommend the Bearer as a very good & clever man who understands medicine very well, & can cure most complaints.

My August Master the King of England is very anxious to know where the great river which passes your Kingdom proceeds, & He particularly wishes that your Highness would allow the Bearer to Trace this River in safety through your Territory — & for that purpose He commits Him to your Powerful Protection & friendship.

So God Bless, guard & Protect your Highness is the wish of etc.

Signed, H. Warrington
British Consul General

Encl. 4
Tripoli 30th June 1825

To the Great & most noble Sultan of the Faithful Mohamed Bello[1] Governor Commander in Chief & Captain General to the Great Kingdom & Territory of Soudan. May God Bless and Protect your Highness.

Four Months since I addressed a Letter to your Highness acquainting you that Abdullah[2] arrived safe in Tripoli, after having visited your great Capital — I feel quite delighted with the account He gives of your Country, and above all with the description He gives of your kind, hospitable & generous Conduct towards Him during His stay with you. Abdullah before this has arrived in England & without doubt has delivered your Highness's Letter to my August, beloved & revered Master & King, whose generous Heart & most noble mind will duly appreciate the liberal and disinterested Hospitality which His Servant Abdullah experienced from you.

---

[1] Warrington wrote this letter to Sultan Bello of Sokoto because it was believed that the Niger flowed close to the Fulani capital, and was therefore likely to be visited by Laing on his intended voyage down the Niger from Timbuktu to the river's mouth.

[2] Abdullah was Clapperton's travelling name.

Whatever Abdullah promised and the arrangements entered into will be fulfilled you may be assured, & I think you will see Abdullah before you receive this as I conclude He will go by the Great Sea to Tagara[1] from whence with your Highness's powerful Influence He can be conducted with safety to your Presence.

Abdullah informed your Highness how desirous His Majesty The King of England is to know where the Great River which passes Tombuctoo, & runs through your Kingdom of Soudan, empties itself into the Sea, & He sends the Bearer of this His favorite Servant to ascertain that Interesting point, and as Abdullah received so much Kindness & friendship from your hands I feel confident the same generous sentiments & conduct will be displayed towards this present Traveller who will evince every Gratitude & reward every good Act done to him.

The Present Traveller is well acquainted with Medicine, and any of your Highness's Servants who labour under any sickness will derive much relief by applying to Him.

Your Highness was good enough to promise Abdullah to endeavour to procure the Papers etc. of an Englishman who was lost on the great River some years since — as my good King is very desirous to get these Papers I solicit your Highness if they are not already sent to endeavour to procure them & to give them to the Bearer.[2]

I send your Highness a Brace of English Pistols of the best manufacture, as a small Token of the great regard I have for your Highness, & I shall at all times feel bound to do every thing in my power to serve you; & that God may bless & Protect you, & that each day may add to your Health, Wealth & Happiness. I subscribe myself the sincere friend of your Highness,

(Signed) H. Warrington
British Consul General

Hanmer Warrington to R. Wilmot Horton:

Private. Tripoli 24 July 1825

Sir,

In addition to my Dispatch of the 13th. Inst. I have the honor to inform you that Sheikh Babany leaves this the day after tomorrow for Beneleed where Major Laing waits for Him.

The arrangements of this Mission are excellent, the success so certain, that I feel inclined to congratulate you by Anticipation.

[1] Tagara or Tagra, Bello told Clapperton, was 'a town on the sea-coast, where many Felatahs reside'. The reference was to Idah, the Atagara of the Hausa, which was not on the sea but far inland on the Niger, about fifty miles downstream from the confluence of the Benue (Denham and Clapperton, II, 314).

[2] Mungo Park had lost his life at Busa, on the Niger, in 1806. In March 1824, when Clapperton was in Sokoto, Bello 'Promised to make every exertion in his power' to recover Park's books and papers (Denham and Clapperton, II, 306).

I have mentioned the long residence of Babany (now Governor of Godames)[1] at Tombuctoo where his wife & children still are & that circumstance added to his extreme respectability and Commercial Wealth — He is a great friend of old D'Ghies[2] who has requested me to get the Bashaw to confirm Him in the situation of Governor for His life, which I shall have but little difficulty in doing, after his Conduct merits such a favor.

Babany says that from Godames to Tombuctoo is only 40 days moderate Travelling — that the great Caravan never exceeds 50 — that the last journey He performed in 32 —[3]

He gives the most favorable account of Sheikh & Maraboot Mouckta, of his power, consequence & Popularity — that Bello is a great friend of Mouckta's having been brought up under him —[4]

He says that there is an extensive commerce at Tombuctoo, of English and other European Manufacture that it is brought from the Sea in large Boats which Navigate regularly — That Mouckta can with safety pass Major Laing by Water to the Sea which we have now reason to believe *Benin* — He describes the Power & Influence of Mouckta to be such that without the smallest difficulty He could pass a Traveller North through Morocco to Tangier, He tells me that many of the Natives wear Hats, & dress more in the Costume of Europeans particularly the Bambarrah People.[5] After leaving Godames they pass a Desert of 20 days, but never more than 3 or 4 without Water — they then pass the Territories of Haggi Uniswelside & Amerahash Two Tuarick Chiefs,[6] afterwards they will get to Bonnawaugh[7] the Territory of Mouckta, the Reigning Chief of Tombuctoo which is only 5 days from the latter place.

[1] There is no evidence that he was the Governor in the accepted sense of the word. He may have been the Bashaw's representative to the extent that he had to collect the taxes, but he does not appear to have been a man of authority.

[2] Mohammed D'Ghies, the Bashaw's Foreign Minister (see p. 151 above).

[3] The distance from Ghadames to Timbuktu, through Tuat, cannot be less than 1,350 miles which, according to Babani, no caravan took more than 50 days to cover, that is to say travelling at 27 miles a day which no caravan of loaded camels in such country could possibly have achieved. Babani told Laing (p. 229 below) that the journey took 66 days which meant travelling 20 miles a day. Even that would be unattainable in such country over so long a period for loaded camels.

[4] P. 221 n. 1 below.

[5] As pagans the Bambara of the upper Niger did not wear the turbans and robes familiar to Babani and his Moslem friends. In common with other Sudanese tribes they probably sometimes wore hats made of dried grasses, and it is possible that occasionally European clothes from the coast reached such active traders as the Bambara.

[6] Dr Cabot Briggs suggests that the names of these two Tuareg chiefs were Hadji Yunes uld Sidi and Omar el Hadj respectively. There is no record of a chief of the former name, but there was an Omar el Hadj. This man was the son of a certain Ikhenuken, the paramount chief of the Uraghen, the paramount tribe of the Ajjer Tuareg who at this time probably dominated Ghat and Ghadames and the country in between (letter to the editor).

[7] Dr Cabot Briggs suggests that this might be Ahauagh, a district lying east of Timbuktu and along the left bank of the Niger; it is the traditional home of the Urahgen from where they migrated to Ghat about 300 years ago (letter to the editor).

It appears this is the safest, the nearest road & more frequent Watering places than the road of Tuat.

Major Laing will see Hateeta at Godames & will use his own discretion the distance which He will require Hateeta to accompany Him.

Babany agrees to convey Majr Laings Dispatches from Tombuctoo to Tripoli from 35 to 40 days[1] as the Bashaw has offered 300 to the first Courier — I shall expect these Dispatches the 1st December & Babany himself the first week in January.

I cannot help regretting that Laing has no Companion particularly as the success is so certain. I can assure you, I shall feel the happiest Man living if affairs only turn out, as I have every reason to expect.

It is curious that in the Interior, & in a state of Nature Man should be found so much superior to His own Countrymen on the Coast. — Does the horrid Traffic in the Flesh of their fellow Creatures blunt the edge of the noble but natural feelings of affection & virtue or does their untutored Minds imbibe the Vice & Wickedness of the scum of Christianity?

I am anxious to learn if His Lordship is satisfied with the result of the Bornu & Soudan Mission. The Foreign Prints speak most highly of the Research & give the British Nation every degree of Credit. I think Mr. Adolphe Lenant will have some difficulty to get from Sennaar to Bornu,[2] because the Natives hold the Egyptians with Horror & view every one as a Spy who comes from thence as two Expeditions have within these few years been sent in a Hostile way — the reason the six Mamelukes who arrived here from Sannaar by way of Cordofan Wadey [Wadai] &c. &c. were permitted to pass, was that they were flying from Egypt & seeking an Asylum in the Hospitality of the Natives. At the present Moment the road is open from Bornu to Sennaar — & I am inclined to believe the Shad[3] is the sourse [sic] of the Nile — The Sheikh must now know if there is an outlet.

[formal ending]

Hanmer Warrington[4]

Rbt. Wilmot Horton Esqure
His Majesty's Under Secretary of State

[1] That is to say from 41 to 47 miles a day over a distance of not less than 1,650 miles. Even a fast *mehri* or riding camel could not have approached such a speed over a far shorter distance.

[2] Adolphe Linant de Bellefonds was distinguished as both an explorer and an engineer. At this time he had but very recently been engaged by the African Association to explore the upper Nile. The following letter from Warrington to Lord Bathurst, dated Tripoli, 24 July 1825, throws some light on what was proposed for him, and explains how it became so quickly known to Laing: 'I have the honor to acknowledge your Lordship's Dispatch of the 8th Ultmo,' it read, 'and conformable to your orders I shall address the Sheikh El Kanemy [of Bornu] recommending in the Strongest manner possible Mr. Adolphe Lenant [sic] to His Protection Hospitality and best Offices' (P.R.O., F.O. 76/19, 1730). In 1827 Linant ascended the White Nile to $11\frac{1}{2}°$ N, some distance further south than Sennar.

[3] This in spite of having presumably learnt from Denham and Clapperton that there was no outflow from Lake Chad.   [4] P.R.O.,F.O. 76/19, 1727.

Hanmer Warrington to Major A. Gordon Laing:

Copy.   Garden 24 July 1825

My dear Sir,

I had an Audience yesterday with his Highness & strict to his word he was ready to compel Babany to depart, but the latter not being ready, & from his urgent Solicitations I have allowed him to remain till Thursday next, when positively we shall leave this — It would have been an easy matter for me, with the Bashaw's authority to have insisted on his departure but in my opinion it would have been bad Policy, as any rigour, & in my way of thinking unnecessary, might be retaliated on you when *He* could exercise the authority of a Bashaw.

A favourable impression being made of your wish to accomodate your Conduct at the commencement of the journey, will not be forgotten, depend on it, and after all as these three days are a Religious Feast of the Biram,[1] none of the Kaffle wou'd wish to travel[2] — on Sunday you may expect us certainly[3] after which you will find no other delays between this & Tombuctoo, & if it were not for the hot weather, you would find it a journey of pleasure neither danger nor difficulty presenting themselves — I send some News Papers — so God Bless you &

Believe me ever
Faithfully,

(signed) H. Warrington[4]

Major Laing.

Hanmer Warrington to Major A. Gordon Laing:

Copy. H.W.   Tripoli 27th July 1825

My dear Sir,

I accompany this with my Letters to the Governor of Godames and Tuat, as also to the Sheikh of Tombuctoo & to Sultan Bello — likewise my Circular introducing you as my son, which if you think will be of service you can shew each of them.

Babany seems firm in his opinion, as to the certainty of the mission being well received and attended with every success. I am glad to find He is so anxious for Expedition and that he calculates that in two months & a half that you will arrive at Tombuctoo & that Maraboot Mouckta can forward you to Benin — He says large Vessels navigate the River & communicate with the

---

[1] The feast that follows the fast of Ramadan.

[2] This letter clearly shows Warrington's weakly indulgent attitude to Babani which can only have been due to his being afraid of him. It seems that he wanted Laing to be the same.

[3] Warrington had intended to ride out to Beni Ulid to bid Laing a final farewell.

[4] R.S., 374(La) 86.

Sea and that Mouckta can send you safe down in these large Boats. They do not carry sails and do not hoist any as such a novel appearance would excite curiosity & suspicion and the Natives would flock down to the Banks to see such an uncommon sight, whereas if you go in the Boats of the Country they will excite no wonder or attention as the Natives cannot know they contain the English Mission. It appears that Mouckta and Bello are great friends, the latter having been brought up under the former.[1] I should recommend your intimating to Babany the more money you are obliged to pay at Tombuctoo the less will be left for him otherwise he will be endeavouring to gain a certain Popularity at your Expense by representing the necessity of giving large sums. Probably he may wish you to return with him from Tombuctoo be prepared to resist that. D'Ghies showed me a most handsome dress for the Queen of Tombuctoo,[2] I wish you had taken something of the sort. By the French paper which I send, it appears the English have decided on a settlement at Benin[3] and I am of opinion that you will meet Clapperton at Socatoo [Sokoto] or Youry. You are indeed a most fortunate man. Such Immortal Credit and Renown seldom falls to the lot of man particularly neither danger of difficulty attending your journey — Pay particular attention to your health particularly for the first Month. August will be nearly gone I think it likely before you quit Godames and then the Climate will be improving hourly. God Bless & Protect you,
     Believe me ever Faithfully
           (signed) H Warrington[4]

Major Laing

Hanmer Warrington to Major A. Gordon Laing:

Private   Tripoli 27 July 1825

My Dear Laing,
 For the last twenty four hours I have had such an argument with myself whether I am to mount my horse tomorrow Morg. & accompany Babuny to Benoleet. Inclination is a strong advocate in favour of the measure, because I should have the selfish consideration of taking you by the hand, and enjoying a few days of your conversation — On the other hand ought I to be the means of detaining having already been so much longer than you expected, and as the animals are all fresh you would certainly wish to be off.

---

[1] It would seem from this that when Babani talked of Sidi Muktar, he really meant Seku or Shehu Ahmadu, the Fulani Ulema of Massina who was now virtually, if not actually, master of Timbuktu. Seku had started life as a disciple of Shehu Usuman dan Fodio, the father of Bello whom he probably knew well (see Introduction, p. 171 above).
[2] There was, of course, no such person.
[3] The French were misinformed. Benin retained its independence until it was occupied by British troops, after bitter fighting, in February 1897.
[4] P.R.O., F.O. 76/19, 2141.

There is another point on which nature betrays a weakness, and let the Journey of a friend be far or near the farewell shake of the hand is always most unpleasant and I always endeavour to avoid it. Added to these I have neither Public of [sic] Private business, or indeed one word to say that I cannot commit to Paper therefore under all considerations I think it better not to go, in which I hope you will agree with me. Therefore with every blessing, with every prayer & the cordial wish of my Soul, I bid you goodbye & may the same all merciful God, who has safely conducted you through the dangers of the field as well as the most unhealthy Climate, continue his most bounteous Protection & watch over you during this most Important and interesting Journey. As far as the Eye can see and the mind can reason there is not the smallest danger or even difficulty; the fine Arrangements of the Mission & the Equipment of the Koffle all bid well for the most successful termination. Whenever your Imagination transports you to Tripoli to the object most dear, let the reflection be fraught with Consolation Comfort & Contentment, and recollect every Mile (altho' your Travelling South makes a little Paridoxical [sic]) will bring you nearer & certainly sooner to dear Emma. She has always experienced the greatest affection from her family and her present situation will entitle her to additional attention & kindness, therefore on that head feel happy & cheerful. I expect the Packet by the 7th Augt. and shall have a Courier ready So God Bless you. Mrs. W. Jane & the whole family with heart & soul wish you success.

Ever affectionately

(signed) H. Warrington[1]

Hanmer Warrington to Major A. Gordon Laing:

Tripoli 27th July 1825

My dear Sir,

Yesterday Old D'Ghies sent to me & requested me to call on him as he had something particular to say. He told me that Babany was much in want of 400 $ and unless He could get it he must sell some of his Merchandize and said it would be a great accommodation if we would advance that sum and he would repay you in Godames — As he approved of the Contract and as matters stood in the fairest point of view, I did not hesitate to enter into an obligation which you will find by reference to [word illegible] An hour after I sent Rossoni with the Contract to get signed by Babany & the Bashaw having already affixed my signature. . . .

After a Consultation between Bashaw, Babany & Bethelmal, the latter informed Rossoni that neither Babany nor the Bashaw would sign No.2 the Contract, but that His Highness would merely give his Teschera[2] to pay

---

[1] R.S., 374(La) 88.
[2] In Arabic a *tadhkira* (Turkish *tezkere*) meant a permit or authority.

Girvenelly[1] the *3000* $ and that his Highness would not be answerable for any *act of God* which if agreed to on my part would be holding out a reward, in case anything happens to you, I therefore have plainly and distinctly informed His Highness that should you not reach Tombuctoo from any circumstance whatever, we shall call upon him to pay the 1000 $ as well as the *3000* $ that Teschera were of no use, as the Flag would have justice & the Merchant would take my word, therefore I sent Rossoni with No.3. a written Message, Finding so much Trick & Humbug, I have thought proper to revoke that part of No.1. Binding myself to give a Bill, & it now rests entirely with you, if you advance Babany the *400* $ and if you are so inclined you had better have the Teschera made payable two days after your arrival at *Godames*, & not Tombuctoo. If you find Babany not act up to your wishes, you have only to Intimate to him that you will report his conduct to me. Babany is a fine fellow, with a Generous & disinterested Countenance but recollect He is an Arab or Moor therefore Trick, low cunning & a disposition to cheat you in every way, you may expect, & under those circumstances you must endeavour to get on as well as you can, & I may add Lying also is a ruling passion, be prepared, but do not let him suppose you entertain such an opinion. God bless & protect you & that success may attend you is the Prayer of Yours

       Faithfully,

            H. Warrington[2]

Major Laing.

Before many weeks had passed Warrington learnt that his fear of Lord Bathurst's reactions to the mounting and unauthorized cost of the Timbuktu Mission was fully justified. He appears to have received a warning of what to expect for on 5 September, before the arrival of the Secretary of State's dispatch, he wrote to Wilmot Horton, the Under Secretary:

A successful Termination of this Mission & to render certain the Personal safety of Major Laing has been my ardent wish & exertion, & if I have exceeded the expectations of His Lordship in pecuniary matters, you may believe me of the absolute necessity to ensure the two points which both Honor & Duty bid me strictly to attend to.[3]

Four days later the storm burst with the arrival of Bathurst's dispatch of which, unhappily, no copy survives. It was evidently more

---

[1] This is the first of several references to Gerolamo Girvanelli, who appears to have been a merchant in Tripoli, perhaps a Maltese.
[2] R.S., 374(La) 89.
[3] P.R.O., F.O. 76/19, 2146.

censorious than even the apprehensive Consul had expected. The task of trying to placate the infuriated Minister was made doubly difficult by having now to admit that the financial position was even worse than he had dared to admit, and that since then he had entered into further secret commitments. Happily for him, however, the Bashaw was accommodating.

Hanmer Warrington to Lord Bathurst:

Tripoli 10 Sept. 1825

My Lord,

I was this morning honored with your Lordship's Despatch of the 5th July.

As I shall address a separate Letter on the subject of the poor Maltese who was compelled to change His Religion, I shall pass that affair unnoticed in the Present.

That my Letter of the 13th May[1] should have caused Your Lordships Displeasure I sincerely lament & certainly not expecting your Lordships animadversion I felt it the more, but the only consolation I have is the conscientious reflection that my actions have been for the best, & that a successful termination to the Bornow Mission is attributable to those actions, and as far as my Office is concerned, I cannot divest myself of the Idea that the expenses were very moderate, as Independent of the £5000 given the Bashaw the Mission did not expend £1,000 per Annum.

With regard to the Timbuctoo Mission, I can assure your Lordship that nothing but absolute necessity could have induced me to adopt the measures I did & which were approved of by Major Laing, and as your Lordships disapprobation is so strongly marked by the Payment of the 2000 $ that you may easily Imagine what my apprehensions are when you know of our having agreed to give His Highness *8000* $ more.[2]

My dilemma was great, and my Situation this morning when I received your Lordships Dispatch was most unpleasant, and the only course left for me,[3] was to go openly to His Highness, & tell Him that as the 2000 $ had been disapproved of, that the subsequent Payments could not be made, at the same time using every Argument to induce the Bashaw to continue His good offices, so as to prevent the return of the Mission.

His Highness received me in His usual kind and liberal way, & without any hesitation said to shew His friendship to me He would relinquish the 8,000 $ & that He would pay all the expenses and your Lordship will see His Sentiments which were subsequently written to me.

---

[1] See p. 196 above.   [2] See p. 201n.2 above.
[3] This reads as though Warrington was acting on his own initiative. In fact he was doing as ordered by Lord Bathurst (P.R.O., C.O. 2/20, A.R. 4).

The Present which Major Laing & myself agreed to give Babane to conduct the Kaffle to Tombuctoo, I have been fearful of mentioning as well as the Secret Present to Bethelmal of 1000 $ & now I shall propose to Major Laing that we shall jointly sustain the loss, as the only alternative to prevent the return of the Mission, so that we have every reason to believe Major Laing has ample means to complete this Interesting Undertaking, the whole Expense being the 2000 £ already drawn for.

I am also extremely sorry I should have given an Opinion as to the necessity of a Medical Man accompanying Major Laing, & altho' I regret having so given it, still the necessity of it I am certain of, & trust in God subsequent Events will prove my Error in judgement.

Your Lordships Orders & wishes are now so clear that it would indeed be Culpable in me to transgress a Second time, & as I always have, I shall always endeavour to merit your Lordships approbation.

I verily believe His Highness will have to pay the whole 8000 $ & if it were double that sum He would have relieved me from my unpleasant situation.

[formal ending]

Hanmer Warrington[1]

The Right Honble The Earl Bathurst K.G.

Hanmer Warrington to Major A. Gordon Laing:

Tripoli 24 Sept. 1825

My dear Laing,

No Courier having yet arrived announcing your having safely reached Godames, is the cause of much anxiety to me, & you may easily Imagine to poor Emma.

....

... I have Dispatched two Couriers for Godames which I hope you have received before this — The last by Hateeta's Servt. who took your July Letters — by which you will perceive they are very severe on me at Home, but when censured for doing my duty & forwarding the great object of this Undertaking with I may say a certainty of success & what is *as much* with

---

[1] P.R.O., F.O. 76/19, 2097. Received 17 October 1825. This dispatch is endorsed: 'Express Ld. Bathurst's satisfaction at finding that the Bashaw or his representative has consented to forego his claim to the additional Payment which was held out to him by Mr. W, & that the two Presents to which he alludes as intended to facilitate [word illegible] of the Kaffle to Tombuctoo not to be charged to the public account.' The unexpectedly heavy expenditure to which Warrington and Laing had committed the Government appears to have led to increased vigilance in the Colonial Office. On 23 August 1825 R. W. Hay, who had succeeded Wilmot Horton as Under-Secretary, wrote to Sir John Barrow complaining of Clapperton's extravagance in preparing for his second expedition. 'The whole party', he wrote, 'seem to have been totally regardless of expense in compleating their outfit, & as a proof of it, I would particularly instance the Time Piece furnished to each of them, with the names of the Parties engraved upon the watches' (P.R.O., C.O. 324/76, 25).

Personal Safety to you, it resembles a Thunder Storm with its lowering blackness & Portentous Threats, which renders appeal of little avail, therefore bear it we must, & as it cannot last long, I still hope again to have the sun shine of His Lordship's approbation.

Altho' the Treasury is dry to our calls, still do not let that cramp your Operations one Iota. — Your Bills shall be paid by me, to the amount of any thing you may want — Do not therefore feel uneasy on that subject.

You will certainly meet Clapperton at Youry, which I should think will render it unnecessary for you to go to Benin.

The Communication with the sea being established I should conceive Important arrangements will to be made at Tombuctoo as to carrying on a Commerce direct with the Interior, & of establishing a Friendly Relationship with that Place — But these are points for your consideration, & do not let my opinion influence your proceedings, you will now have a delightful climate & we may see you here by the end of March having visited Tombuctoo Youry &c —

When the Augst Mail arrives I shall send another Courier.

Now mark me, do not have any delicacy of drawing on me, as I will pay out of my private Purse. Mrs. W. Mrs. Laing, Jane Louisa &c &c unite in Prayers & wishes, So God bless you & believe me ever

H. Warrington[1]

Hanmer Warrington to Major A. Gordon Laing:

Tripoli, 11 Oct. '25

Extract

You are approaching Tombuctoo under the auspices & Protection of the Governor of Godames whose object is solely to Introduce you to the People, & from His great Respectability & so well known, it must be admitted must carry its full weight & Influence. — You are likewise seconded by Hateeta a Tuaric chief, both of whom are so impressed with the greatness of England, its wealth, liberality & honourable presents & views that the Introduction must be good, & will convince the Natives they have nothing to fear, but much to gain by establishing a friendly Intercourse.

In the end the Niger will be opened to the Navigation of English manufacture.

Clapperton & Pearce sailed in the Brazen Frigate on the 16 August.[2]

As the whole country of Bergherme [Bagarmi][3] is now open to the Sheikh [of Bornu][4] there will be no difficulty to go round the Shad & pursue

---

[1] R.S., 374(La) 95.

[2] Clapperton and his companion Capt. Pearce, R.N., had embarked for the Bight of Benin on 27 August 1825.

[3] Bagarmi was a kingdom bordering on Lake Chad on the south-east.

[4] Bornu at this time was ruled by the famous Shehu (Sheikh) Mohammed el Kanemi under whom it had recently recovered the freedom it had lost to the Fulani in 1808.

its evacuation into the Nile for that certainly must be the case.... If you recollect I always said you will meet Clapperton at Youry & I think it more than probable now. He is an Honest good fellow & you will find Him so. — When you meet Him the course of the Niger is ascertained & I do not perceive the necessity of your going to *Benin*. I think you would do a more Important service to your Country to return to Tombuctoo & to establish a permanent Relationship with that People in commercial Pursuits and get the Name of their Agent at Benin or the mouth of the Niger, so that English manufacture might be consigned to Him, having ascertained the most sellable articles.[1]

Hanmer Warrington to Major A. Gordon Laing:

17 Oct. 1825

Extract

Be cautious of your Latitudes Longtitudes & other Information to whom you Communicate, as every Consul here is a sort of Spy ready to suck the sweets & to transmit the Honey of your Industy to His or their Govt.

In my opinion it is even fair to deceive them, sooner than they should forestall.[2]

[1] R.S., 374(La) 101.   [2] R.S., 374(La) 102.

CHAPTER V

TRIPOLI TO GHADAMES

Major A. Gordon Laing to Lord Bathurst:

Wadey Ramel [Wadi er Raml][1]
July 18th 1825

My Lord,
It is with indescribable feelings of pleasure, that I at length have it in my power to inform Your Lordship of the departure of the Mission[2] which like all preceding ones, has met with its delays, though (it must in justice be admitted) with none of any material or serious importance.

On the 7th Inst. I broke up the encampment which I had formed about two miles from Tripoli, and proceeded about nine miles further to the Eastward to a fine plain near Cape Tajiura, where I again pitched my tents, and after seeing every thing arranged in proper order, I returned myself to Tripoli the following day, for the purpose of taking leave of His Highness the Bashaw, and making the promised arrangements for a safe conduct over the Terhoona [Terhuna] Mountains.[3]

It was not however till the 16th Inst. that I was favored with this interview, which was day after day deferred, in consequence of the non-arrival of the Sheikhs from Gadamis, who had been detained on the Southwestern side of the Garian Mountains until a large escort was sent from Tripoli, to ensure their safety —

The Sheikhs with their Caravan having arrived on the 15th Inst, the farewell interview at length took place on the day following, when His Highness consented in the most handsome and satisfactory manner to my immediate departure, and appointed an escort of one hundred & fifty Cavalry to conduct me as far as Benioleed [Beni Ulid] — His Highness was also pleased to introduce me to one of the Gadamis Sheikhs named Babané, a man about fifty years of age, of mild agreeable manners, & most prepossessing appearance, who is well known and highly respected all along the road to Tombuctoo, to which Capital he has often travelled, and has resided in it off and on for a period of nearly thirty years — He was there twenty years ago when

---

[1] Wadi er Raml lies about twenty-five miles east of Tripoli.
[2] The mission included, besides Laing, his Jewish interpreter, Jacob or Abraham Nahun, who had been engaged in Tripoli (p. 177n.3 above), and his three Africans who had been brought out from England, Jack le Bore, his personal servant, and Rogers and Harris, the two boat-builders.
[3] About forty miles south-east of Tripoli.

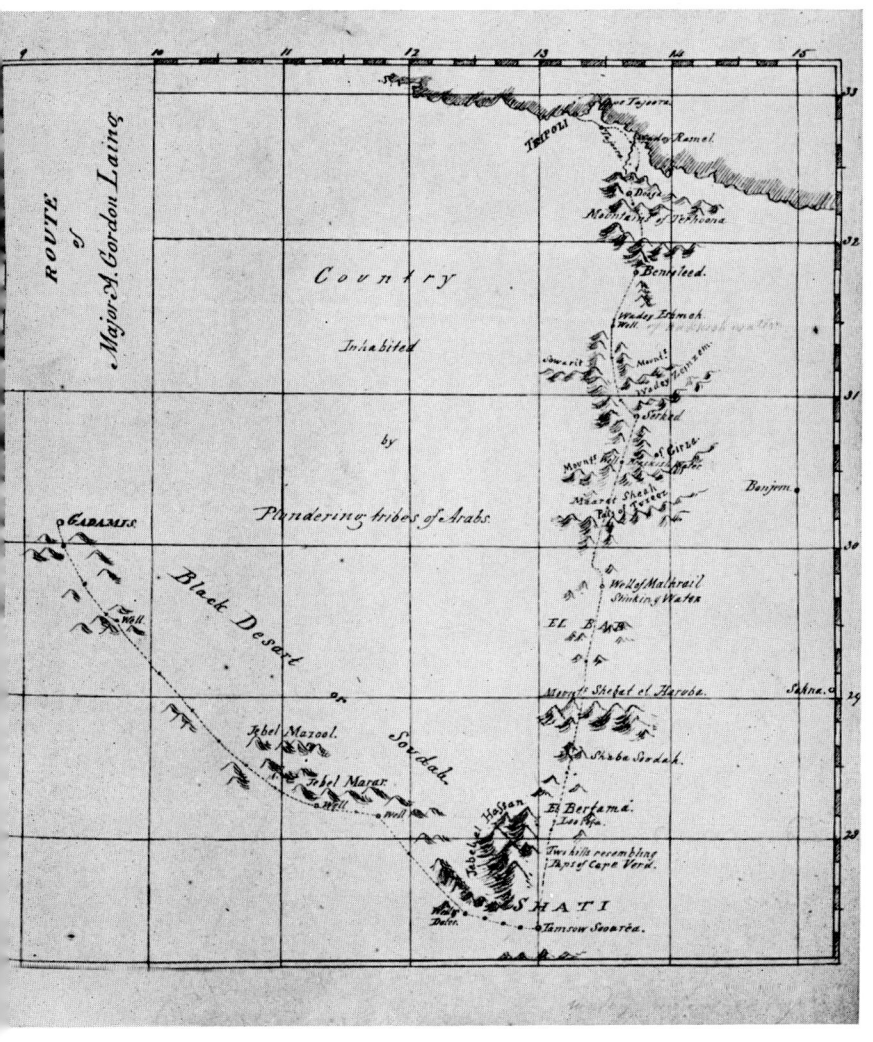

Map. IV. Laing's map of his route from Tripoli to Ghadames

Park embarked at Sansanding,[1] is well acquainted with Jenne,[2] Sego [Segu-Sikoro],[3] & even Foutah [Futa Jallon][4] itself, the names of many of the chiefs of which countries he is quite familiar with and appeared much pleased at my knowledge of them[5] — He seems perfectly confident that I shall be well and cordially received by the authorities of Tombuctoo, and does not apprehend any obstacle to my proceeding to Yaoori [Yauri] by water, as he says that large canoes are constantly flying between that place and Tombuctoo, the length of the voyage being twenty five days.[6] He estimates the journey to Gadamis, at the pace of a camel, to be twenty days; from thence to Twat thirty days, and from Twat to Tombuctoo thirty six days[7] — in all Eighty six or Ninety days. He considers that in the present state of the country, large escorts will be absolutely requisite between Gadamis and Twat, as also between the latter place and Tombuctoo, but he guarantees to pay every expense of that nature, all customs, dues, presents &c on the road, and to conduct me there in safety for the sum of Two Thousand Five hundred Dollars; and as the offer appears to me not only fair but reasonable, considering the present unsettled state of the Country, and the general exhorbitancy of the demands of the people, I have closed with him for that sum, paying him One Thousand Dollars in advance, and promising the remainder on my arrival at Tombuctoo, at the same time, leaving the reward for his services to be a matter of after consideration.

This agreement which has been regularly drawn out and signed by Babané, is guaranteed by His Highness the Bashaw, who, in the event of any casualty occuring to prevent its non fulfilment, returns the money on demand to the Consul General — I have the honor to inform Your Lordship, that I have the more eagerly embraced this arrangement, which appears to promise so well, in consequence of having it in my power to apply to this service, part of the funds which have been placed at my disposal by the proceeds of Consul Warrington's draft on His Majesty's treasury for Two Thousand Pounds, and I now with confidence repeat my assurance, that with the exception of the

---

[1] Sansanding was the great market on the upper Niger at which Mungo Park embarked on his last expedition and from which his last dispatch to reach the Colonial Office was dated 17 November 1805.

[2] Jenne, situated on the Bani, a tributary of the upper Niger, is an ancient town, formerly of great cultural and commercial importance. It owes its survival to a protective screen of rivers and swamps. It is possible that the name Guinea derives from Jenne.

[3] The great Bambara town of Segu-Sikoro, famous in history as the point at which Mungo Park discovered the Niger in 1796, lies about thirty miles upstream from Sansanding.

[4] Futa Jallon is an extensive and hilly country in which lie the sources of both the Gambia and the Senegal rivers.

[5] Laing had learnt these names when exploring the hinterland of Sierra Leone in 1822.

[6] Like most of Babani's statements, this was untrue. It is improbable that there was any through-traffic between Timbuktu and Yauri.

[7] See p. 219 above.

Sum of £73 - 12 - (subsistence and pay for my party for three months, which I shall draw for on the 1st August) I shall not require another farthing independent of what the Bashaw may expect, till my return to England, after the successful termination of the expedition —

I am well supplied with presents of every kind, having at the advice of a Mr. D'Ghiez, a worthy Mahommedan of this place, added considerably to my already ample stock since my arrival in Tripoli — I am also furnished with letters of credit from the above mentioned person, (who has a large Mercantile connexion [?] as far as Tombuctoo) and from the Bashaw, which will prove no doubt of infinite service in case of distress —

I have, I assure Your Lordship, done every thing for the best, and I trust that when Your Lordship observes the real impossibility of adhering to the instructions furnished me,[1] as far as regards my conveyance to Tombuctoo — 1stly In the non-appearance of the Tuarick guide, upon whose assistance I was led to plan such implicit reliance, and 2ndly In the impracticability of attaching myself to any Caravan on a road which Caravans rarely travel, and the necessity which obliged me to form one for myself; Your Lordship will have the condescension to signify your approval of my proceedings, and give me credit for the preservation of the strictest oeconomy; for notwithstanding the great additions that I have been compelled to make (from the causes above mentioned) in Sheikhs, guides, attendants, Camels and their drivers, Mules, Horses &c. I have at length succeeded in comprising the whole expenditure of [word illegible] & subsistence, under the head [?] of three & a half dollars a day from this date — and I am in hopes that as I advance, and leave behind me this territory of extravagance, imposition, and extortion, I shall have the power of reducing it still more, as I hope Your Lordship will perceive by my accounts, which, Please God, shall be transmitted from Gadamis, where I look forward to a few days rest to enable me to make them up.

I have this day reached the place from which this letter is dated — it is about sixteen miles to the Eastward of Tajiura, and separated from the latter place by a desart of burning sand, thrown up into inumerable hillocks by the prevalence of strong Easterly Sirocco winds. Tomorrow morning at daylight the Caravan will proceed to the S.ward towards the mountains of Terhoona; Babané the Sheikh of Gadamis will follow in six days, and will overtake me at Benioleed, where after crossing Terhoona, I have agreed to wait for him — I have for the sake of convenience, as well as to avoid observation in passing through a strange country, adopted the Turkish costume, as have also my three attendants[2] — our dresses are of the simplest and humblest kind, in order not to create Jealousy: and lest it shoud ever be supposed that we attempt to pass ourselves for what we really are not, it is my

---

[1] P. 149 above.
[2] It will be recalled that he had condemned the Bornu Mission for doing this very thing.

intention to read prayers to my three attendants always on Sunday, on which day we shall appear dressed as Englishmen.[1]

[formal ending]

A. Gordon Laing[2]

To The Right Honble
Earl Bathurst. K.G.

Major A. Gordon Laing to Capt. E. Sabine, R.A.:

Benioleed
July 29th 1825
Lat. 31.47 40N. Long. 13– 44–30E[3]
Variation 12° W. Thermom. 104°

My dear Sabine,

Will you allow a few hasty lines to apprise you of my welfare, of my departure at length on the Mission, and of the receipt of yours of 8th of June, after having had an interview with Mr. Clapperton.[4] In a word return you my warmest acknowledgments for your great attention to my interests as well as those of the Mission upon which I am employed, and cannot say enough in praise of your exertions in getting out my book with such empedition after departure.[5] I have read several favourable critiques, but have not seen the Edinburgh, which I understand is very severe and satirical upon me — I find I must expect no mercy from them[6] — *nimporte* they are a set of insolent Lawyers and I heed them not. I arrived here on the 24th and await a Sheikh of Gadamis to proceed on with me — he will I think be here to night, and I shall advance on the 1st of August — by the 20th I shall be at Gadamis, by the 1st October in Twat, and I expect about the middle of November will see me in the far famed Capital of Central Africa — about the 1st of the New

---

[1] Notwithstanding his three attendants—Jack le Bore, and two boat-builders—being Africans.

[2] C.O. 2/15, 1984. This dispatch is marked 'Transmit for Mr. Barrow's perusal'.

[3] The correct reading is 31° 45′ N, 14° 01′ E.

[4] Unfortunately we do not know what Sabine wrote to Laing after he had met Clapperton in London.

[5] This was Laing's *Travels through Timannee, Kooranko and Soolima*, published in 1825, which Sabine had seen through the press.

[6] Laing was misinformed. No notice of his book had yet appeared in the *Edinburgh Review*; moreover, in January it had referred to him approvingly, in a review of another book on West Africa, as 'an officer of merit, who fought with distinction in the commencement of the war' (XI (1825), p. 337). Laing, or his informant, may have been confusing the *Edinburgh* with *The Quarterly Review*. In March (XXXI, pp. 445–73) the latter had published a long notice of Laing's book in which the reviewer had, quite excusably, questioned the accuracy of Laing's estimate of the height of the source of the Niger. 'It is rather too bold a conjecture', he had written, 'we had almost said assertion, to set down the elevation of its source as being "between fifteen and sixteen hundred feet above the level of the Atlantic"' (p. 454). So mild a criticism could hardly be called 'very severe and satirical', but the point was one on which Laing may well have been highly sensitive.

Year, I may probably embark on the Niger, and as I learn from Babané (the Gadamis chief who accompanies me, and who has resided for thirty years off and on at Timbuctoo) that there is constant water communication from thence to Yaouri, the voyage being 25 days I shall most likely by the end of January have visited the spot where the adventurous Park lost his life.[1] Fail not to recommend a Man of War being sent to Benin, I shall be there, Please God, in Spring. I care little for any information that Clapperton cou'd communicate, and you were right in saying you did not think that I wou'd wait for it: I smile at the Idea of his reaching Tombuctoo before me — how can he expect it? has he not already had the power? has he not thrown away the chance? I cannot think what were his ideas — a man to be within two days of the Niger, and to come back without ever seeing it[2] — I think I may safely aver, that had I been at Sakotoo — the problem wou'd have been long ago solved — and I feel certain that to me the honor of the solution is left.

Clapperton reminds me much of Mr. Martin[3] who accompanied Park, remarkably fond of country wine and beer, but I have seen more of that which he states to be made at Morzouk — He amuses me by saying *you must not eat or drink before a Turk* — if so — how is it that I hear the Turks speak so constantly of the quantities which Abdullah (his country name) used to drink — Four bottles of Port wine before dinner whenever he cou'd get it — I am not surprised that Mr. C shou'd not wish to drink before them; such sort of potations wou'd not command respect in any country, much less in a Mohommedan, where the Inhabitants are by religion abstemious. I have received the information communicated by him to the Colonial Office — it is worth nothing, and has been evidently wrung from him — 'I must wear a Turkish dress — and it must be plain — I must be kind and patient with the natives — I must not secretly take observations — I must travel as an Englishman' — I believe is the sum of his suggestions.

My watch goes well — it altered its rate at Malta, and has regularly lost 3″ 5/10 daily since the 13th of April — I have much confidence in it, and I am indefatigable in my observations —

Your's ever
A. Gordon Laing[4]

Captn. Sabine, R.A.

[1] That is to say Busa on the lower Niger.

[2] Here Laing condemns Clapperton for having done precisely what he himself had done when, within three days of the source of the Niger, he had similarly turned back. There were good reasons in each case.

[3] Lieutenant Martyn, R.A., had joined Mungo Park at Goree as his second-in-command and, the last of his companions to survive, had perished with him at Busa. Laing evidently recalled a letter which Martyn had written from Sansanding where he had found 'Whitbread's beer is nothing to what we get at this place, as I feel by my head this morning, having been drinking all night with a Moor, and ended by giving him an excellent thrashing'.

[4] R.S., 374(La) 90.

Major A. Gordon Laing to James Bandinel:

> Benioleed, August 3rd 1825
> 10 clock [sic] p.m.

My dear friend Bandinel,

I am at length thus far (thank God) on my way to the Niger, and its far famed marginal desideratum, which latter I expect to reach in November next at furthest — I leave this place at an early hour tomorrow morning for Gadamis, where the 20th of this month will most likely find me — from all accounts it is a place that will afford me great sources of gratification, in the examination of many antiques and ruins, which my informant says are scattered about with no sparing hand.

I see by the French papers that they consider the great question of the Niger solved, but I differ with that opinion so widely that I have this afternoon drawn up my few ideas on the subject in the shape of a letter which I am forwarding to Lord Bathurst[1] — It is very far from being solved yet — Indeed the Journey of the late Travellers (neither of whom have [sic] ever seen the Niger) only goes to prove that it does not communicate with the Nile, a fact which my measurement of the source of the river had long before established — I have received your kind letter of the 8th June, and am much gratified by its contents — I trust you will continue to write by way of Tripoli as late as by the November packet, after which address to me *Benin via Sierra Leone* — By the way are we to have a colony there?[2] — Now certainly is the time, & to entirely abandon the Gold Coast.

Will you tell Smith,[3] that when I reach Gadamis, and send my despatches from thence, I mean again to memorial for my Majority — It is indeed hard that I shou'd loose [sic] promotion, while others gain it by embarking upon such a service — A Regiment Majority is my right, and I shou'd have got it, had I gone to the Gold Coast; if they refuse that at the Horse Guards, (which I know they will) let them give me Brevet Rank now, and the local rank of Lt. Colonel when I reach Tombuctoo — I shall be very disatisfied indeed if this is not done, not that I care so much about the rank, but because I shall not otherwise be able to divest myself of the feeling of being ill used —

Excuse all this — I write with the paper on my knees by a glimmering lamp, my heads antipodes seated upon *Alma mater* — I shall write you at length from Gadamis — till then believe me Ever your's truly,

A. Gordon Laing[4]

James Bandinel Esq.,
Foreign Office.

---

[1] See Appendix 1. This memorandum was not forwarded to London until Laing had reached Ghadames.

[2] P. 221 above.

[3] In Laing's letters there are several references to 'Smith' but, although he seems to have been an influential friend, it has not been possible to identify him.

[4] R.S., 374(La) 91.

Major A. Gordon Laing to R. Wilmot Horton:

Benioleed, August 3rd 1825

Sir,

I have the honor to acknowledge you letter of the 7th June, transmitting a copy of the opinions and suggestions which Lt. Clapperton has been called upon to furnish for my guidance, and which, I beg you will be pleased to acquaint His Lordship the Earl Bathurst, shall meet with the attention and consideration which is due to them — at the same time I beg to refer to my letter of the 18th Ulto.[1] dated Wadey Ramel, from which it will be observed that their general tenor has been anticipated and acted upon by Sir

Your most obedt.,
Very Humble Servt.

A. Gordon Laing[2]

Wilmot Horton Esq., M.P.,
Under Secretary of State.

Major A. Gordon Laing to Hanmer Warrington:

Benioleed, August 3rd 1825

My dear Sir,

I have the honor to acknowledge all your letters and enclosures by Babané, who made his appearance here at a late hour on Monday night — I feel perfectly satisfied with the agreement, which has been entered into with him, and am perfectly convinced from what I have already seen of this Man, that it will be fulfilled to the very letter —

I am happy that you did not draw a Bill for the four hundred dollars which he requires at Tripoli, and still happier that you left the matter to me: As I am at present situated, I shou'd be unwilling that any further demands are made upon the Government, particularly as I am yet uncertain what may be their sentiments regarding the sums already drawn: as I advance upon my Journey, and have the power of shewing that something has been done, I shall feel less scruple in drawing for whatever may be requisite, meanwhile I have paid the Four hundred Dollars to Babané here, out of the ample funds which I have in hands, and by so doing have made a strong impression with him in my favor, particularly as I have assured him that it has put me to very serious inconvenience, and that nothing but the high respect I entertain for a man of his character and appearance could have induced me so far to have incommoded myself.

We depart from this place to day at 3 p.m., and I expect you shall hear from me at Gadamis, at farthest in the course of another month — Every thing bids fair for my accomplishing this interesting Journey with success, and I feel much pleasure in acquainting you, whom I look upon as the mainspring

---

[1] P. 228 above.   [2] P.R.O., C.O. 2/15, 1986.

of discoveries in this terra incognita, that I am sanguine in my hopes of accomplishing a visit to the far famed Capital of Central Africa, the spot where the adventurous Park lost his life, and the problematical termination of the mysterious Niger, within the space of Six Months —
     I have the honor to be
      My dear Sir,
      Your most obedt,
      Very Humble Servt.
            A. Gordon Laing[1]

Hanmer Warrington Esq.,
Consell [sic] General.

Major A. Gordon Laing to Hanmer Warrington:

          Benioleed ½ past 2 p.m.
          August 3rd 1825

My dear Consul,
 My letter to you must be a very hasty one as Babane has quite taken me by surprise — I expected to have had this afternoon to myself, and to have devoted it to writing to you and my dear dear Emma — but am much much disappointed — Babane has reasons for this sudden departure,[2] which of course it wou'd be absurd in me to call in question — I am under his care, and am determined to be entirely directed by him[3] — I was much disappointed indeed at not seeing you — I had left a great deal unsaid to you, which I meant to have conversed with you upon at Benioleed — I wish much, I indeed wish much you had come — I have this moment received yours of August 1st.[4] I observe what you say, and I fully agree with Pope that 'whatever is, is right' — most fully do I agree with him — but I only do so when the *whatever is*, does not rest with ourselves — had business, illness, or any unforeseen cause prevented you from coming my dear Consul, I shou'd have regretted your absence sincerely, but then I would have said 'whatever is, is right'; however I can not, no (you must excuse me when I say) I cannot think so in this instance, when an argument with yourself was the only cause of prevention — I will say more to you on this subject when we meet six months hence, and when it will give us both more pleasure to shake each other by the hand, than it wou'd have done at Benioleed meanwhile I bestow a thousand thanks for your kind parental attentions to my dearest, most adored Emma — I am equally sorry with you that Clapperton has not shewn a little more of the 'suaviter in modo', but allthough [sic] it

---

[1] P.R.O., C.O. 2/20.
[2] The reason was that he was short of cash and wanted to get to Ghadames as quickly, and as inexpensively, as possible.
[3] Thus from the start was Babani the master rather than the servant.
[4] This letter has not survived.

may do him no good in a certain way, yet I feel confidant that it cannot, in the slightest degree injure his promotion — It wou'd be hard indeed that a man who *merits richly* the rank of Post Captain for *eminent* services performed, shou'd be refused it, because he is not exactly *cut out for a drawing room* — I hope he may get every thing he can wish or desire, but I am not over anxious to meet him at Yaouri, particularly after what my friend Sabine says of him, and Sabine is as liberal a minded man as ever lived — How differently have I spoken of, and behaved to Clapperton, when I was in England — I always spoke in praise of his enterprise, and pressed his promotion both at the Colonial Office & the admiralty, and my friends used to say I was too disinterested, when I used to declare, that much as I desired to be the first man who shou'd visit Tombuctoo or sail down the Niger, yet I shou'd feel much pleasure on hearing that these objects had been accomplished by Mr. Clapperton, as I considered them due to his steady perseverence & enterprise — All is however left to me now — and I — as I always thought I shou'd, I shall be the man! —

The mean of my observations at Benioleed, allowing your garden to be as laid down in the admiralty tables — is Lat 31° — 47'40" N — & 13°.43'.00" E — but if my Lunar which I took at the Garden is right — & I think it is to be relied on 13°.25'15" E, the Longtitude of Benioleed will be 13°.47'.15" E — Variation 12° W — The difference of time between my Lunar & the time of the Tables being 17^s exactly — With most sincere regards to Mrs. W and the family, believe me

Ever yours sincerely

A. Gordon Laing

I send a large Mail for England — Excuse haste.[1]

Major A. Gordon Laing to Hanmer Warrington:

Wadey Suked[2] August 8th 1825
A hasty line My dear Consul to apprise you of my arrival at this place in Lat. 30°.25 N. — I depart for Gadamis without stoppage at 4 p.m. I am much pleased with my Sheikh, as also with Bogoola — I begin to find out the sterling worth of the latter, and of course to do Clapperton justice — The Marabout[3] of this place has behaved very ill — very ill indeed, and I am desirous that you will acquaint the Bashaw with his conduct as soon as you can — On my arrival here, he made a demand on me for money, which I of course refused — he said, if I did not pay, I must return to Tripoli — that he had nothing to do with any arrangements I had made with the Bashaw —

---

[1] P.R.O., C.O. 2/20. This letter concludes with the postscript so scornful of Clapperton's advice quoted on p. 163 above.

[2] Probably Bir Sèrchet, about sixty miles south of Beni Ulid on the Wadi Zémzem.

[3] A *marabut* could be either a man of reputed sanctity or the tomb in which he had been buried. The latter was sometimes also the house in which he had lived.

I told him, I did not care much which way I went, but having set out for Gadamis I wou'd try to get there; I therefore wished to know if he intended to stop me — he said certainly not, but there were robbers on the road who wou'd — I said that was no business of mine — it was an affair between the Bashaw and the King of England — that I wou'd therefore go forward — finding me determined he has promised me an escort this day at 4 p.m. and has favored me with his valediction — but I heed not a cause [?] given for the *auri sacra fames* — The liberality of former travellers is often thrown in my teeth — but *c est egale* — the money is the Kings not mine, and God knows, whether the sums I have already drawn for, will be approved [?] — I never before met with such a set of greedy vagabonds [?] (for as wandering tribes they may so be styled) — I assure you it cost me nearly 300 $ feasting [?] and fatning them at Benioleed — my funds will soon get below par if I was to encourage such doings, I have therefore in turn thought fit to stop payment — I wish you would acquaint the Bashaw of this, as I understand His Highness has given this very Marabout 250 $ to escort me to Gadamis! Excuse me for being so laconic & inexplicit — I shall write you in full from Gadamis — Kind Remembrance to Mrs. W, Jane, Louisa — Herbert & Osy my little favorite, — God bless you my deal Consul,

      Yours Ever,

         A. Gordon Laing[1]

Major A. Gordon Laing to Hanmer Warrington:

Private   Malhrail[2] on the borders of Fezzan.
         Lat 29–35N — Long –13.50:E
           August 13th 1825

My dear Consul,

As I learn that after the termination of this day's march, three horsemen belonging to the Bashaw who have accompanied me thus far, return to Tripoli, I take up a hasty pen to apprise you that I am all well so far. I wrote you a very hurried and abrupt note from Serked, acquainting you how ill the Marabout of that place had behaved, and I have now to acquaint you further that his subsequent conduct has not in the smallest degree caused me to entertain a more favorable opinion of him. He wished to get a hundred & fifty Dollars from me; and insisted that I should go no further if I did not pay it — this as I before told you I positively refused — when he found me positive he permitted me to proceed, but said as I must go a Journey of six days without water I must hire some Camels from his people and buy some more Gerbies[3] — this I accordingly did — but I must say this *friendly* Maraboot

---

[1] P.R.O., C.O. 2/20.
[2] This well of 'saltish stinking water' has not been identified.
[3] Water-skins, from the Arabic *guerba* (sing.).

has made me pay for them — his people asked ½ a dollar a piece for the Gerbies & two dollars for the hire of each Camel, which he wou'd not permit them to take, but insisted on my paying a dollar for each Gerby and four for each Camel — what cou'd I do? — submit of course — He has behaved in a most extraordinary manner since we left his encampment, having accompanied me with about fifteen of his men, and acting like a madman — he was heard to say, that was he not afraid of the Bashaw, he wou'd put us all to death, and take the money & kaffle to himself, and that if we were not very civil on the road he wou'd do it at all risks — After the first day's march he said four dollars for each Camel was not enough, and that if I did not pay that sum at once, and give more when the Journey was completed the Camels shou'd all go back — I said he might please himself about that, but as it was not my custom to pay for any service till I had seen it performed, I shou'd not begin to alter upon his account — finding me positive he thought better of it, and the Camels were permitted to proceed — but during the whole day, every possible attempt was made to exasperate me and create a Baroofa[1] — At one time his people wou'd lag behind on pretext of their camels being lame, at another, they wou'd cut down the loads, let them fall in the road, and there leave them, threatening to maltreat Roger, Harry[2] or Jack, whomsoever I left in charge — As night came on they commenced irregular firing as we marched along, and as their shot whistled over our heads, several times caused an alarm, it being so dark that we were uncertain whether we were attacked or not — On halting the night before last about ½ past ten — The Maraboot and his guard were missing, a circumstance which incited so much suspicion that one of the Bashaws horsemen came to me, and advised that a good watch shou'd be kept — in the morning we proceeded without having seen any thing of the Maraboot, and it was not till nine (after we had halted) that he made his appearance, galloping down upon us, & firing — My people thought it was an attack, and flew to arms with a promptness and regularity which gave me much pleasure, but as the supposed hostile party drew near, and they were able to distinguish them, they called aloud 'Reis, [Major] it is nothing, it is only the Maraboot' — Upon my honor I was half sorry at the

---

[1] *Baruffa* (Italian) meaning tumult.

[2] Roger and Harry, *alias* Rogers and Harris (p. 228 above), Laing's two West African boat-builders. After Laing's death it was often said that he had a European with him. Bonnel de Mezières mentioned him as an English sailor named Harry (*Le Major A. Gordon Laing*, 4). Laing in fact had no European with him. The belief that he had seems to have arisen from the boat-builders' habit of wearing European dress and to their being, apparently, Christians. Harry, too, was the last to survive. Hassuna D'Ghies, describing the first attack on Laing, said that the suspicions of the Ahaggar 'were, I have no doubt, excited by the appearance of the strangers, who were besides conspicuous from their dress'. This is quoted in the Blue Book with the following footnote: 'Major Laing had not only a Jew in company, whose appearance and dress differed from that of Mussulmen, but a negro dressed in European style and speaking English' (B.B., 109). On one occasion, at least, Laing referred to the Africans, Jack, Roger and Harry, as 'my three English attendants', presumably because they had come out from England (p. 375 below).

discovery, as I had by chance pitched upon the Maraboot as my object of aim, and as I sat on one of my Trunks, had him so fairly covered, that in a few seconds more, he wou'd have paid dearly for his frolic — He leaves me to day thank God — but as we go round by *Shati*,[1] I shall in five days more, be as far from Gadamis as I was this day last month when I was at Tripoli! I shall not reach it till the end of this month — when I shall instantly despatch a courier to you — I believe the Sheikh Babané has written to the Bashaw expressive of his disatisfaction at the conduct of the Maraboot. You must excuse the unconnected manner in which the above is written, as Babané & Bogoola have been in my tent all the time, talking to me about the Journey &c &c — Pray say nothing to Emma about the detention I have met with, as it will only cause her to fret, and to suppose that I may be much longer on the Journey than I expected — which will really not be the case, for Babané assures me that although he is quite a stranger on this road, he knows every foot of ground between Tombuctoo and Gadamis, and that we shall meet with no stoppage there. I believe him really, and he appears so eager to get forward (quite as much as I am) that I expect, in two months after leaving Gadamis, I shall be in the far famed Capital — By the bye — I had suffered a good deal from intermittent fever at Beniolaid, and had a pretty smart attack the morning I left that place. — I am happy to say that I succeeded in overcoming it entirely, & that I am now as well as I ever knew myself to be — (*keep this to yourself also*). Now my Dear Consul I shall conclude this hasty epistle, hardly knowing whether you will be able to make it out or not — I have been so much plagued and interrupted — I do not wish you to say more to the Bashaw about the conduct of the Maraboot, than that I am disatisfied with him, and that I am not pleased at being sent this round about road,[2] after His Highness's promise that I shou'd be forwarded with more expedition — You shall hear from me at great length from Gadamis, when I hope to be able to say to a day about when I shall arrive at Tombuctoo — and I trust my dear Consul, that I shall terminate this mission in a way which will reflect immortal honor upon your Judgement & perseverence in recommending it, and upon my enterprise in undertaking it, as I have done, singlehanded — God bless you my Dear Consul, may God bless and prosper you, and may you ever enjoy that mental happiness which your upright and open disposition so justly entitles you to. — Offer my kindest remembrance to Mrs. Warrington, Jane, Louisa, Herbert and little Osy, and believe me ever

     Sincerely and affectionately
      Your's &c
           A. Gordon Laing

---

[1] The Wadi Sciati leading from Fezzan north-westwards towards Ghadames, which Laing was to follow.
[2] That is to say, by the Wadi Sciati instead of direct through the Garian Mountains.

Remember me if you please to Dr. and Mrs. Dickson, to Mr. & Mrs. Herrador —

By the bye, I like Bojoola more and more every day — he is really a most valuable man — he swears he must see *England*, before he returns *to Tripoli* — a resolution which I encourage in him, though I have my doubts as to the likelyhood [*sic*] of it — As I shall remain only a few days at Gadamis, pray send off a courier with my dear Emma's picture the moment it is done — Don't wait for the packet — the picture is worth to me a million packets.[1]

On an odd scrap of paper is the following note in Laing's hand:

Lofonsa[2]

August 17 1825

We are pushing for the Shati being reduced to one last skin of water. My camels have suffered a good deal. When they have rested these 2 days I shall make for Gadamis by regular days marches of 9 hours a day & hope to reach it about the 1st or 2nd of September. Tis very sultry but I keep my health well, in fact better than any of the party.[3]

[1] P.R.O., C.O. 2/20.
[2] This is not shown on Laing's map and is unidentified.
[3] R.S., 374(La) 94.

CHAPTER VI

GHADAMES

Laing arrived in Ghadames to find the elusive Hatita awaiting him, and he was soon able to report to Warrington 'I have completely won Hateeta's heart with the presents I have given him'. The principal gift was 'from the King of England a fine scarlet Goldlaced Bornouse[1] which delighted him so much, that he gave me his spear & said I will take you safe through Tuarick,[2] & will afterwards go to Tripoli to see my friend the Consul'.[3]

Major A. Gordon Laing to Hanmer Warrington:

Gadamis Sept 13th 1825
8 oclock p.m.

My dear Consul,
 Having sacrificed inclination to public duty, in writing my Official Despatch before I devoted a single moment either to friendship or affection, I now with eagerness take up my pen to make the most solicitous enquiries regarding your welfare, that of Mrs Warrington and the whole family; respecting which I am indeed most anxious, a period of six weeks having elapsed since I have had any tidings from Tripoli — during my long Journey through Fezzan and across the Desart of Soudah,[4] during privations and exposure to a degree of heat, which I am inclined to believe few European constitutions cou'd stand, I consoled myself with the hope that on my arrival at Gadamis I shou'd hear tidings of my dearest most beloved Emma; that I shou'd be made happy in the knowledge that the only object I prize in this world was well — the hope was a reasonable one, I certainly had every right to have expected a Courier by the 13th Sept, but alas how cruelly have I been disappointed — My reflections are cast at fate, not at you My dear Consul, for I know well that long air now you must have despatched a Courier to me — although the unsettled state of the country through which he has to pass impedes his progress — I learn here that the Jebel people have been watchfully looking out for the Kaffle on the road between Serked and Gadamis, and that no longer than three days ago, a party of 130 Cavalry were stationed in the vicinity of a well, where it was expected we were to have rested —

---

[1] A *burnus* is a hooded cloak made of wool or a mixture of wool and camel hair.
[2] That is to say, through the country of the Tuareg which, as we shall see, he was in no position to do.
[3] P.R.O., F.O. 76/19, 2434.   [4] The desert of the Jebel es-Soda.

Bagoola & the Sheikhs say it is as well that we did not come the short road, but I say no — for had we come by that route the Maraboot of Serked wou'd have been obliged to furnish a strong escort[1] — The Courier who carries this will bring me back your answers in sixteen days, after which I shall despair of hearing from you again till I have completed my Journey — few will attempt to travel between Tripoli & Gadamis solus, none will try it between Tuat and Gadamis, and twenty men are not safe between Tuat and Tombuctoo — Every person tells me that this road is very different from that to Bornow [Bornu] — the latter is a regular trading road, under the power of the Bashaw along which a child might travel,[2] but on this there are many conflicting interests, and the Bashaws influence ceases at Gadamis — I shou'd be happy if you wou'd let Mr. Barrow know this, and if you do write to him, pray tell him that I mean to address him by next courier on the subject of the termination of the Niger — I mean to upset all the theories that have as yet sprung from hypothetical imaginations, first by my own theory, and afterwards by practical solutions.

In my official letter I have mentioned the conduct of Bogoola, as I think it not unlikely that I may yet be compelled, howsoever unwillingly, to send him back to Tripoli — I have also stated my uncertainty regarding Hateeta's intentions in an indirect way not exactly wishing to say that I know the cause of this indecision, of course, you are as well aware as I am, that it is on the score of Floos[3] — he hangs back till he knows what I will give him, and I do the same, until an impression which is prevalent here, of my great riches is done away with — By the bye Bogoola has assisted to render this report valid, as also the Courier whom you sent after Hateeta, who told in town that from Tyrwhitt's box[4] containing Sugar Coffee &c which I have received, was only a small supply of *Six thousand Dollars*! If the Roman adage 'Quantum hummi quisque habet in arca tantum fidei' held good in this country, I shou'd have no objection to the prevalence of such a report, but as it is *wice wersa* as Billy Lackaday has it, I took an opportunity this afternoon in presence of Babane, Hateeta, Bogoola and the Courier to open the Box and make an exhibition of its contents — Since I wrote my Official letter I have had a second conversation with Hateeta, who enquired if you had not sent a fine Benish[5] to him, as he understood from the Courier that I was to be the bearer of something of that kind — I replied that I believed you had one for him, but that not being quite certain whether he wou'd go to Gadamis or to Tripoli, you had not sent it — I said that I also had a present for him from the King of England, a fine scarlet goldlaced Bornouse, which delighted him

---

[1] It appears that there was a route running south-west from Bir Sèrchet to Ghadames.
[2] This was of course a gross overstatement, but Yūsuf's influence did in fact extend as far as Bornu.
[3] Probably the Arabic word *fulūs*, meaning small coin or cash.
[4] John Tyrwhitt, now dead, had been a member of the Bornu Mission.
[5] *Benish* is a Turkish word used by Arabs for a riding cloak with long split sleeves.

so much that he gave me his spear, and said, 'I will take you safe through Tuarick, and will afterwards go to Tripoli to see my friend the Consul, and get the Benish, in the mean time I send him Salam yapar'[1] — You must therefore take care to have a Benish ready for him against his return.

Now for Heaven sake My dear Consul, do endeavour to let me hear occasionally from Tripoli — if I can only know that my Emma is well, I will answer for my successful completion of this Journey, but if I am left to conjecture and despondancy, the state of my mind may prove much more prejudicial to the state of my health than the climate of Africa — Give my kindest remembrance to Mrs. Warrington, Jane, Louisa, Herbert and Osy, tell the latter that I am so plagued with flies here, that I wish I had a few of his frogs to eat them — To yourself my Dear Consul I offer my most real and sincere regards, and I trust the sense of your great kindness to me, will become [one] of the last recollections that the memory will loose, that God may bless and prosper you is the fervent prayer of

Yours ever truly

A. Gordon Laing[2]

Hanmer Warrington Esq.,

P.S. May I trouble you to send the animal preserved in this Bottle to Joseph Sabine Esq.,[3]

Horticultural Society
Regent St.
London.

P.S. 2nd.
Both my Official and private letters have been written in such haste that I have not had time to read them over, pray excuse the manner as well as the matter, and make such extracts as you think fit for the information of my Lord Bathurst.

P.S. 3d Jack[4] has just come in and hopes he may send best compliments to the Consul & Mr. George.[5] Shortly after our arrival in quarters, when he saw the number of presents pouring in, Jack observed 'This is fit day to sing Psalms and pray' — This observation gave rise to the following Epigram

Scarce in Gadamis am I seated
E'er Jack my prayer Book brings
And says a Christian when well treated
Te Deum always sings

[1] *Yapar* is Turkish; it is the third person singular of the present aorist tense of a verb meaning to do or make. Thus *Salam yapar* means he makes a *salaam*, or gives greetings.
[2] P.R.O., F.O. 76/19, 2434.
[3] Joseph Sabine, an elder brother of Edward, was at this time Secretary of the Horticultural Society, a post he held from 1810 to 1830 in the course of which he reduced the Society's affairs to chaos, and he left it heavily in debt.
[4] Jack le Bore.   [5] George Warrington.

> Let Heaven I answered grateful see us
> And pray Jack, shou'd you choose it if,
> But though the Journey's been *Te deus* (tedious)
> I will not sing *accusative* —

14th The Sheikh has sent to say the Courier is ready to depart, and I therefore again, and again, repeat, God bless you — My patient is better this morning and in token of his relief has sent me a present of a fat sheep with various other &cs. I expect a long letter from you, and I trust you will tell me exactly how my Emma is — Oh that my anxious mind was at rest — I never never shall subject myself to the pain the tortures of absence again[1] —

Major A. Gordon Laing to Hanmer Warrington:

Gadamis Sept. 13th 1825

My dear Sir,

Having at length arrived in the town of Gadamis after a circuitous Journey of nearly a thousand miles, I hasten to apprize you of the event, as I well know that your anxiety respecting me, must by this time be considerable, particularly as I did not according to promise, send any communication from Shati, which desirous as I was to effect, I found impracticable, in consequence of the enourmous sum demanded by the couriers to whom I made application — We arrived here this morning about nine oClock after a very tedious Journey from Shati, which we quitted on the 21st Ulto: the road has been for the most part a complete Desart, and for the last three days we run very short of water, and entirely so of provisions; and to make matters worse, a provoking Sirocco already of six days duration still continued — in such a situation I verily believe that we shou'd have been happy cou'd we have met with it, to drink

> The gilded puddle
> Which beasts wou'd cough at:

but all difficulties surmounted we are here thank God, and I inform you with much pleasure that our entre [*sic*] and reception has been characterised by every thing that is kind and hospitable — A large deputation met us about three miles from the town, and accompanied us with continued acclamations expressive of the warmest welcome, and although we are not yet two hours in quarters, my house is filled with provisions of every description, and my attendants, my half starved attendants, have at length satiated themselves upon the most substantial viands — with them it is not the time,

> When all the body's members
> Rebelled against the belly......

[1] P.R.O., C.O. 2/20. Received: 16 October 1825.

I have for about an hour been amusing myself with a number of little children who have come out of curiosity to see the Christian, and they seem quite happy at the permission which I have granted them, despite of the orders of their parents to depart, who have naturally enough supposed that they might prove an annoyance to me — I like the innocent play of incipient man in all countries, and it is strange to observe similitude which exists between Turk, Jew, Kafir or Christian before the effects of government or education are felt by the mind — I verily believe that Satan himself (to make no allusion to Milton's paradise lost) was innocent at six years of age —

I have found here the Courier[1] whom you despatched after Hateeta, as also Hateeta himself, but am not exactly certain whether they will accompany me or not — as far as I can at present observe, there is a sort of disinclination on the part of Hateeta on account of my being under the care & protection of the Sheikh,[2] whom he nevertheless acknowledges to be a clever & well informed man, who knows the road well, and who is much respected — I have as yet said little on the subject, being desirous to procure as much information as I possibly can before I make my decision — I have merely told him, that you sent your best wishes to him, and that you hoped he wou'd see me safe through the Tuarick; that I added my own hope that he wou'd do so, to yours, as I had come out from England (where I had heard a great deal of him) expressly to meet him — This seemed to please him, and he made answer, that if he went, he wou'd like to go soon, but we might talk more on the subject in a day or two, when myself and Camels are a little recovered from the fatigue of the Journey we have just performed — As far [as] I am individually concerned I shou'd be happy to depart tomorrow, there being apparently little to interest me here, and as I expect to find little more till I reach Tombuctoo, the country being so provokingly monotonous, but my people who are suffering a little in the abdominal regions from their late aqueous diet,[3] require some rest, as well as my Camels, all of whom are exceedingly thin owing to the privations they underwent in crossing two desarts, one of three, the other eight days Journey, where as little herbage was to be found as in the bottom of a tin mine in Cornwall — besides seven of them are entirely lame, and one rendered so thoroughly useless that I must sell him for whatever he will fetch — This, together with a Mule which died on the Desart, will make up the sum of my pecuniary losses as yet — but I have met with others of a more annoying and perplexing nature in the destruction of instruments, indeed I appear to have been marked out as the very child of misfortune with regard to them, from the very commencement of my Journey, (from my upset in the chaise near Exeter)[4] to the present moment — You are already aware of the loss I sustained in my two Barometers, and had I been in possession of twenty instead of two, they must have all gone to

---

[1] Sala.   [2] Sheikh Babani.
[3] Having run out of provisions they had had, it seems, only water to sustain them.
[4] On his way to Falmouth Laing's postchaise had turned over.

wreck, as their present structure wou'd neither stand the intense heat or Camel shaking to which they are exposed. My Hygrometers are rendered useless from the evaporation of the aether — I am reduced to my two last thermometers, the tubes of the others having snapt by the warping of the Ivory — the glass of my artificial horizon has in many places become so dim (being ground by the friction of the sand which insinuates itself everywhere) as to render an observation a matter considerable trouble, if not of difficulty — two days ago my chronometer stopt, having been previously going very irregularly owing to the extremes of heat and cold to which it has been exposed; and a Camel having unfortunately placed his great gouty foot upon my rifle one night as I lay with it by my side on the ground, snapt the stock in two[1] — but here I shall stop, the catalogue is large enough without noticing minor accidents —

By the next Courier, whom I shall despatch the day before I leave Gadamis, I shall transmit to you my Journal up to that date, a chart of my route, as also two or three sketches of costumes,[2] which I shall request you to forward to the Colonial Office; for the present, as I am desirous to let my arrival here be known with as little delay as possible, I shall leave it to you to acquaint His Lordship the Earl Bathurst with my welfare & reception.

The heat has been almost intolerable since I left you the thermometer at noon standing not infrequently at 120° of Farenheit, which was the more severely felt in consequence of the cold which oftentimes prevailed in the mornings, the thermometer indicating a temperature of 75–68 — and once or twice so low as 62°!! On these occasions I wou'd observe a strong incrustation of nitre on the ground — by the bye this wou'd lead me to make some remarks respecting Lake Schad which Denham says has no outlet, was it not that time is wanting — I shall however take up the subject in my next, meanwhile let me hope that you will persevere in recommending that a traveller may be sent out to encircle it — *a traveller* only, and he by preference a Medical Man, for rely upon it, one will succeed when a dozen wou'd fail — There is no likelihood of its falling in my way, for I am certain that the course of the Niger, which I am directed to follow, will not bring me within thirty Journies of it —

Before concluding, I shall just give you a slight *apperçu* of the character and dispositions of the persons composing my party, with which I am now pretty intimately acquainted, and with which (though it may be very uninteresting) I think it necessary you shou'd be familiarized, in order that you may the more easily comprehend the causes which produce effects that *may* hereafter occur — I wou'd commence with the Maraboot,[3] but it may perhaps be as well to pass him over, as he left me at so early a stage of the

---

[1] This incident was greatly exaggerated by writers of memoirs. For example, the usually staid *D.N.B.* must have astonished its more sophisticated readers by reporting that Laing's 'only rifle had been broken by a charging elephant'.

[2] These have not survived.   [3] The Marabut of Serked.

Journey; and particularly as I shou'd be sorry to say any thing unfavorable of a man who stands high in your opinion, and of whose qualifications a more lengthened acquaintance must have necessarily enabled you to form a better & more correct estimate than I possibly cou'd — my opinion of him I must acknowledge to be unfavorable in the extreme, but at the same time I admit, that that opinion may be extremely erroneous, and I shou'd be sorry if the expression of it should operate otherwise than to induce you to watch him a little more attentively, than a confidence, probably not misplaced, has caused you to do hitherto —

I shall therefore pass on to Babané, who is a man, (to say a great deal in a few words) of the most sterling worth, who is to be found to morrow, exactly as he is to day; he is quiet, harmless, and inoffensive, but a man of infinite determination withall, as I have had occasion to observe on one or two occasions, trifling ones to be sure, but quite sufficient to enable me to form an unfallacious idea — He either is much attached to the English or he is a better actor than Talma,[1] for he has shewn so much apparent friendship and performed such disinterested acts of kindness, not only to myself, but to my three personal attendants, that I must acknowledge the counterfeit to be admirable, if they are not dictated by the genuine feelings of a kind and generous heart — He is a man of mighty importance in Gadamis, being nothing less than its Governor,[2] a circumstance which I was ignorant of till this morning, but which, on being made acquainted with it, you may be assured did not disappoint me — I am lodged in one of his own houses, a very snug dwelling with a fine garden and extensive yard for my Camels &c all of which he is to feed at his own expence during the period we sojourn at Gadamis — He is no advocate for extravagance, but rather recommends the semblance of povery in passing through the country — he thinks it is the surest & safest way of travelling, but in places of importance which we shall have to call at, and where advantage may be likely to arise out of it, he recommends a well timed liberality, and in this respect his ideas correspond exactly with my own — he says the Kaffle is too large, and it is not improbable but I may allow myself to be guided by his opinion in reducing it —

With regard to Bogoola (Sidi Mohamed Bogoola I beg his pardon) I confess myself to be a little at fault — I never liked his appearance from the first, but as I hope I am, at least as I endeavour as much as possible to be, a man free from prejudice, I was willing, nay most desirous to suppose myself in error, and I caught with avidity at the one or two good traits which I fancied I beheld peeping from under a sullen exterior — I endeavoured to persuade myself into a belief that he was a man of worth but in vain; his conduct will not permit me to regard him as either good or useful — I have

---

[1] François Joseph Talma (1763–1826), a French actor who had been educated in England.

[2] Sheikh Babani of Ghadames was in charge of Laing's caravan to Tuat and beyond. He was not Governor of Ghadames.

treated him as a companion, though with becoming distance; at his own request I gave him charge of every thing, and I have often incommoded myself to oblige him, but all to no purpose — When provisions run short, although he knew the cause, and the consequence unavoidable, he was the only man to grumble, saying 'the Consul had promised, that he, his wife and servant shou'd always have plenty to eat' with many other observations very unpleasant for me to hear — he served out corn to his own two Camels every night crossing the Desart, when mine had not a grain, by which improper expenditure the horses & Mules (even the Mule which carried him) were deprived of food Six days before we reached Gadamis, and must have all died, had not the Sheikh sent off a Maherre[1] express to that town for a supply — on our arrival this morning, he left me standing in the Sun, midst a crowd of gazing spectators to get the baggage housed as well as I cou'd, walking off very composedly with his own two Camels, which occupy his sole, his constant care — All this however I cou'd tolerate, I cou'd and in future shall, look after my own baggage, my own corn, my own Camels, but I cannot bear to be accompanied by a man of such an ungovernable temper; he quarrels with every one, and has even made himself disagreeably noxious to that good man Babané, who has complained of him once or twice — the Camel drivers hate him indeed, so much so that one deserted, and the remainder were going to do the same in Fezzan — he has several times struck the poor Jew my interpreter, and one day so unmercifully beat his poor slave, that I was obliged to interfere or I verily believe he wou'd have killed him; as it was, the boy cou'd not walk for several days, & Master Sidi Bogoola told me that as the boy was his property he wou'd cut his throat if he chose!!! Gracious God! How long is the poor unfortunate swarthy native of Africa's interior to suffer from the galling damnable yoke of slavery, how long is he to be exposed to the most unparalleled persecution from that fell passion avarice — how long is paternal, filial and conjugal affection to be sported with, & sacrificed at the shrine of Mammon — oh grant that the retributive day is near at hand — at present the poor unhappy Negroe, with the Merciless Moor on one side for a Scylla, and the expatriating European on the other for a Charybdis, may be compared to the flying fish of the deep, which is exposed to the gormandising gull from above, and the devouring dolphin from below — My hopes for peace and happiness for this long devoted country rest on the Niger being navigable, and having an outlet to the ocean, by which means the Moor will be undersold, and by having no further inducements to cross the burning Desart, be entirely shut out from the interior, and thus an effectual stop put to Slavery on one side — ...

....

Your pardon My Dear Sir for this digression, to return to Bogola — I *believe* him brave, and for that respect him, but I know him to be cruel & for

---

[1] *Mheri*, a fast riding camel.

that detest him — I am certain he behaves differently, with me than with Mr. Clapperton, therefore my observations are not to be taken as any reflection upon that officer's recommendations; he is now in a different situation — with me he has a sure employment — a teskara — like many other men of weak minds he is swelled out with importance — with Mr. Clapperton he was on suffrage, under protection — he was treated with the chivalrous kindness of an Englishman, and has been spoilt — as far as my interest or that of the Mission is concerned, or any thing apart from his own two Camels

> He smells it with a sense as cold
> As is a dead man's nose:

Of Mr. Abraham Nahun my interpreter I may say little, he is extremely willing, tries to make himself useful, but is rarely successful, in fact he is a complete Jackalent.[1]

My Servant Jack you are well acquainted with, and no matter in what garb, he is still honest Jack le Bore — he is a great favorite with Babané, and with every person we meet, except Bogoola —

Rogers is a good humoured rough fellow, is picking up Arabic fast, and is much liked among the Arabs with whom he is always playing —

Harris is a quiet, nobody disturbing sort of Jack Tar, & to any question he answers — Speak to somebody else I don't know your Lingo — His appearance is commanding, and as a fine looking man is much admired —

4 p.m. I have been called away to look at a sick man, for I must tell you that I have attained great celebrity as a Medico — I am now a graduate of Gadamis College — that is to say I have taken the *local* rank of Surgeon, which in *this* country wou'd be of more service to me than that of Major — I made some cures in Fezzan, the fame of which has preceeded me, and though I may not be able to do much good, I shall, like the apothecary who had only two drawers in his shop, one for Magnesia, and the other for money, do little harm; I may like my great predecessor Sangredo,[2] let blood, but I shall keep myself out of *hot water* by not recommending it — The personage whom I have been visiting is an uncle of the Sheikh, in a very deplorable state from dropsy, the abdomen much distended, and the legs much swelled — by the assistance of gentle aperients I shall be able to relieve him, but Astley Cooper[3] himself cou'd not effect a cure — on entering his chamber he saluted me in Mandingo — and on my putting on an appearance of astonishment he said — I know you speak Mandingo, and I know you have been at Tagara,[4] and Wangara — but I find he is not the only one versant in the

---

[1] A Jack-a-Lent was a sort of male Aunt Sally, set up in Lent to be pelted.

[2] Gil Blas was the servant and pupil of Dr Sangrado of Valladolid.

[3] Sir Astley Paston Cooper (1768–1841), a distinguished surgeon.

[4] This Tagara seems to have been in the hinterland of Sierra Leone. It cannot have been the one referred to on page 217 above which had not been visited by Laing and had probably never been heard of by the Mandingo.

Mandingo language here, for on my way home I have had the salutation *ine senne koore beherito* [?][1] good morning, how do you do, from several people —

Being in very great haste I must apologise for this abrupt conclusion, and hastily written letter, therefore in expressing disappointment at not having received any intimation from Tripoli since my departure I shall subscribe myself briefly,

Very obediently yours,

A. Gordon Laing.[2]

Hanmer Warrington Esq.,
H.M. Consul General.

Major A. Gordon Laing to Hanmer Warrington:

Gadamis Sept, 21st 1825

My dear Consul,

As you will hear from me through a more certain & expeditious channel long before this will reach you, I shall enter for the present into no particulars regarding the Mission — and I merely drop you single line to say that having decided upon sending Bogoola back to Tripoli, he will be the Bearer of this — He is a man who may be every thing that he has been represented to be, but to me he has by no means been useful, on the contrary I am inclined to consider him as having been rather a thorn in my side — However to use an old adage '*the least said is soonest mended*' he leaves me to morrow morning so *Bissilama*[3] —

Agreeably to the Teskara, I have purchased a Maherie to convey him back, and have given him a handsome dagger to shew you on his return to Tripoli that we have parted friends, for I can perceive that he stands much in awe of you, and dreads your displeasure — I also send back three of the Camel drivers whom I hired in Tripoli, and one whom at Angelo's[4] suggestion I took with me from Benioleed, they are all extremely good men, and have conducted themselves much to my satisfaction: I send them back simply on account of the reduction which I am making in my Koffle, and because they are not very strong men withall — By way of shewing my high opinion of them, and courting a little the '*aura popularis*', I have given them a new fit out of clothes, and eight dollars a piece over and above their wages, besides provisions &c for the Journey, so that they depart as happy and satisfied as men can well be — With best regards to Mrs. Warrington, Jane and Louisa, believe My dear Sir,

Ever yours truly,

A. Gordon Laing

Hanmer Warrington Esq.

[1] The language of this salutation is unrecognizable, probably owing to faulty transcription, the MS. being very faint.
[2] P.R.O., F.O. 76/19, 2434.
[3] *Bi'ssalama* meaning, in this context, 'wishing you well'.
[4] Angelo Heri was the British Consulate's broker (A.R. 18).

P.S. By the bye I wish you wou'd question Bogoola about the cause of the Maraboot's return to Tripoli — for as yet I am ignorant of it — He had been unwell at Benioleed, but I had cured him, at least so far, that he wanted [?] to go off in the morning (which he was in the habit of doing) and return to quarters late at night. About 2 in the morning of the day after we left Benioleed, he sent [?] to acquaint me that he was sick, and I saw nothing [paper torn] him.

I find on looking over my Accounts [paper torn] Angelo has charged *35* dollars for the first Camel which was bought for the Mission — I have just learned by chance, that Bogoola brought the Camel from Angelo, and paid for it only *18* — If you think this worth looking into, question Bogoola[1] —

Major A. Gordon Laing to Hanmer Warrington:

Gadamis Sept. 25th 1825
6 oclock a.m.

My dear Consul,

I have just seen from the top of my house a small Kaffle leaving Gadamis, and upon enquiring finding its destination to be Tripoli, I have begged that they will wait a moment for a letter — Let these hasty lines therefore serve to apprise you of my good state of health, and of the excellent treatment which I have met with in Gadamis, where every person vies with his neighbour in the continued performance of kind and hospitable acts — You must not be surprised at the long letter which my Dear Emma receives compared with yours for as I make a practice of writing a line or two to her every day, there is of course a packet always ready for her. Bogoola left this three days ago for Tripoli, and by him I sent a letter to you explaining the reason of my parting with him — I found he wou'd not answer my purpose at all, besides his expectations were too large —

I have completely won Hateeta's heart with the presents I have given him, a Rich Gold Laced Burnouse, — a pair of silver mounted pistols, a handsome Dagger, a Mule, & the Gold worked holster which I procured in Tripoli — He is all ready for the route, as is also Sala, & I shall be so (please God) by the time my Courier returns from Tripoli — I have been exceedingly busy since I last wrote — Hateeta sends you *Salam yapar* — With best respects to Mrs. W, Jane, Louisa, Herbert and Osy, believe me,

Ever yours sincerely,

A. Gordon Laing

H. Warrington Esq

P.S. The Kaffle has gone, and I must despatch Jack after it on horseback — I shall despatch a Courier in ten days with my Journal.[1]

[1] P.R.O., C.O. 2/20.

Major A. Gordon Laing to Hanmer Warrington:

Gadamis Sept. 27th 1825

My Dear Consul,

Yesterday afternoon I was greeted at one and the same time by your two Couriers, one bringing my dearest Emma's picture, and the other the packet letters — Babane sends a Courier to Tripoli to night and I must therefore make haste, as I mean to forward my accounts and some other documents to The Colonial Office, as well as answer some private letters — I am agitated by a thousand opposite feelings; love & tenderness on one side; disappointment & indignation on the other: you know the causes which operate in exciting both — No one can regret more than I do, the unhandsome rebuke which you have received from Downing St.[1] after all your exertions, your honorable exertions to assist in promoting the honour and credit of the British nation; no one can feel it more than I do, as I am too sensible that I have been the innocent cause — Had I thought it possible that such mean, such sordid, illiberal ideas cou'd have existed in the fabric of Downing Street, I shou'd have dropt the Mission after the first interview I had with the Bashaw: Wou'd to God I had — I might now have been enjoying the happiness which I hope I deserve, with my dearest Emma in England — Good heaven; have I made such a sacrifice? have I left all that is dear to me on earth to embark upon so thankless an enterprise?! I never looked for, I never cared for reward, and well they know *that* at Downing St. — I might have been a Regimental Major by resigning the Mission — my income as Governor of Annamaboe[2] was £1,000 a year — I sacrificed both promotion and emoluments to serve the good cause of discovery, and ought to have been more liberally dealt with — They may *use*, but they shall *not abuse me* I am determined — I have not yet opened the letter which I find addressed to me from Downing Street, so fearful am I of having my feelings wounded, so tenacious of an insult — for if they have not thought it necessary, or have not been delicate enough to spare you, an old and distinguished servant of Government — what am I to expect, I who am hardly yet known in the world — I am however satisfied of the correctness of my own conduct, I am so sensible that I merit commendation and not censure, that I shall endeavour to care as little for their displeasure, as I now feel I should for their praise — the poor man wou'd not accept the blessing of the Priest, who was liberal enough to offer that, and refuse half a crown — So I care not for the praise of a Government which is not worth Two thousand Pounds — Thank God — 'flamma propriore calesco'. My own feelings, my own conscience shall be my reward — I have now determined to throw up their paultry allowance of a Guinea a day, which I felt myself insulted by the tender of when in London,

[1] No copy of this survives but see p. 160 above.
[2] Anamaboe is on the Gold Coast, a few miles east of Cape Coast Castle. Presumably Laing was in command there for a time during the Ashanti campaign.

and I shall never, never, let me execute what I may, apply for any reward — They cannot reward me for what I have suffered! — I know His Lordship will think that the step of Lt. Colonel will be a most ample reward — I wou'd not accept of it — I must be and shall be '*aut Caesar aut nullus*' —

As to you My dear Consul — whose feelings they have so severely harmed [?] I am at a loss to think in what manner they can ever make reparation — but for your exertions Bornou wou'd have been still unvisited, but for your advice, your endeavours, your disinterestedness, Bello wou'd have been yet a stranger to us — Enormous sums have been lavished in Missions from other quarters, and nothing has been effected — whereas from Tripoli for a few thousand pounds, the secrets of the Interior have been laid open — Is it only when success attends our labours that the expence is to be noticed? If so, let Africa remain unexplored — Let it be as heretofore

> When Geographers on Afric Maps
> With beasts and birds filled up their gaps,
> And oer inhabitable downs
> Placed Elephants instead of towns —

The remarks which your application for a Surgeon have called forth, are not only uncharitable, but unfeeling, and I have difficulty in persuading myself that they can really be the sentiments of the *Principal Secretary of State of the most enlightened, civilised & charitable nation in the world* — By heaven (for I must take an oath) the wildest savage whom we pretend to civilise, wou'd have felt more sympathy for the illness of a countryman, who was to all appearance making a sacrifice of his life for the benefit of others — You know well my Dear Consul — that I never desired a Surgeon, that I detested the bare idea of such a companion, and if His Lordship thinks that under any circumstances I shou'd have required medical assistance to enable me to proceed — he knows not my character or disposition — It is the mind that will bear Laing through — shou'd it fail me, what Doctor cou'd strengthen it? — really this world is made up of such common place matter, that it is painful for a person of mind to exist in it — But let me drop this subject to which, I feel, I have paid more attention than it deserves — I have not yet determined whether I shall *proceed*, or *return to Tripoli*, but I shall let you know in a day or two — it much depends upon the state of my feelings after reading my official letter. Little as I felt disposed to Journalise [?] before, I have a diminished inclination now.

I have a long letter from Denham, who writes in a handsome, gentlemanlike style; Had it [? I] met him, I feel assured I shou'd have been put in possession of much valuable information — He mentions Clapperton's new mission, and the liberal terms[1] — I have no doubt he is finely tied down, and

---

[1] Laing also learnt from Warrington the terms of Clapperton's second appointment to an African Mission. (See p. 259 below.)

I feel assured he will never go beyond Benin! — mark my words — There is no English Consul with an extensive influence there, and I have some idea of the expectations of the Beninites. He and his friend will arrive at the worst season of the year, the season which proved fatal to the enterprising Belzoni[1] — I divest myself of all personal feelings — I care not, on my honor I do not, whether the termination of the Niger is discovered by Clapperton or myself, but I cannot help expressing a hope that he may be prudent enough to return if he finds the bad effects of the Climate lay hold of his constitution, which they undoubtedly will — It was never yet known that a European visited that place without catching fever; the chorus of the Sailors song is rude, but full enough of meaning —

> The Bight of Benin
> One comes out of nine that go in —

Now it wou'd be hard indeed that an enterprising man shou'd loose [sic] his life for a Guinea a day and a hundred Pounds!! — No more at present — I break off abruptly for I have much to do: but shou'd I have time — I may again take up my pen — May God bless you — Kindest remembrance to Mrs. W. Jane, Louisa, Herbert and little Osy,

from yours most sincerely

A. Gordon Laing

Hanmer Warrington Esq.

P.S. Some person (I fancy that fool Angelo) has told Emma that I had fever at Benioleed, and she fancies I am ill although I say nothing — The slight fever I had was so trifling I did not think it necessary to say any thing of it — at present I am as well in bodily health as I ever was, or even wish to be, upon my honor I am, and you may assure her of it in the most positive manner.

P.S. 2d. I have observed Mr. Barrows observations regarding the allowance to Poor Park! I do not consider however that I am to be put on the same scale with either Park or Ledyard — although a man of *enterprise* — I am no *adventurer*, and all I asked of Government was to pay my expences — I do not feel inclined as an Agent of a Government like England to be indebted to the King of Sego [Segu], or any other African Chief for a few shells[2] to save me from starving as poor Park was — and if I do go forward, I shall not appear niggardly or mean, though at the same time I shall have a due and proper consideration for the public purse, which, if at too low an ebb to afford a few thousand pounds, might not be spared [?] at all upon such an undertaking — better by far, that English men shou'd remain at home, than

---

[1] See Introduction, p. 145n. 2 above.

[2] Cowry shells, the common currency in West Africa, had been in use since the eleventh century and probably long before that (El Bekri, *Description de l'Afrique septentrionale*, trad. de Slane (Algiers, 1913), 243). Cowries were imported into Africa from Asia, mostly through Cairo.

come into a country like this to excite commiseration and contempt — I am quite ashamed of the situation in which you have been placed with the Bashaw[1]

Warrington's reply to this letter never reached Laing, but it is of sufficient interest to be quoted here.

Hanmer Warrington to Major A. Gordon Laing:

Tripoli, 22 Nov. 1825

My dear Laing,

The Courier Sala arrived on the 17th Inst. after a long Journey. In future I hope we shall have no difficulty in the communication between this and Godames, as peace is made with Haliefa & His Hostages here.

I shall first answer yours of the 27th. Spt.[2] Your fine feelings & generous disposition I am fully aware of & had I conceived you could have on my rebuke, carried it so far as to make you unhappy I should never have communicated it; as in your passage over dreary Deserts, unknown Regions, & not a Companion to speak to I ought to have been particularly careful not to Introduce a Subject which in some measure would annoy — We must recollect that Lord Bathurst is responsible to Parliament & to the Country for all expenditures & altho the observations were galling, still we must acquit him of any ungenerous or Illiberal feeling towards you or I — I have now been under His Lordship for twelve Years & have invariably experienced everything that was kind Liberal and Handsome. Pray my good Sir, Consider the affair as never to have existed & do not give yourself any uneasiness about it. Indeed Mr. Barrow has explained that business in a truly handsome Manner....

I am truly glad you determined to proceed, had you done otherwise it would have been the ruin to You and to me, as our Enemies would have set us forth in Public View in the horrid Colours which I know neither of us could indure.

I am glad you are pleased & have heard from Denham, no one is more capable of giving information.

Your predictions respecting Clapperton I trust will never be verified. A Man will go through much to kill Him particularly when the Mind is bent on Public good & laudible Ambition which he as well as Yourself possess. May you meet & return to Tripoli together I sincerely hope. It will be to me, a happy and joyful day.

Your wife dear Emma you may believe me is well & happy as it is her duty to be so I am sure you will wish her to be so & that you do not suppose She loves you the less because She is so I have impressed that on her as much as

---

[1] P.R.O., C.O. 2/20. Received 17 November 1825.
[2] P. 252 above.

possible & cautioned her against representations, which cause You to entertain a different belief. It is very Natural She should wish to see You & it is very probable she might resort to every argument to induce You to return, but for Heaven sake do not let Your powerful feelings operate on You so as to adopt a Proceeding which you would for Ever repent.

God bless God Protect and
God Prosper
You my dear Laing is my fervent prayer and Sincere wish
and
Believe me
Most Affectionately

H. Warrington[1]

Emma has seen this letter.

Major A. Gordon Laing to Hanmer Warrington:

Gadamis Sept. 29th 1825

My Dear Consul,

The Sheikh Babané has been to breakfast with me this morning, and has put me into tolerable good humour by saying that in eight days more he will set out for Tuat, and will not despatch the Courier till the day of our departure — my intention of returning to Tripoli is therefore you will perceive abandoned for the present — I had a long argument with myself last night, and I felt too keenly the triumph which my enemies (for I have my share of those miscreants who are jealous of the little reputation I have so hardly earned) wou'd have over me, the exultation of those who wou'd delight to see

> The growing feathers plucked from Caesar's wing
> To make him fly an ordinary pitch —

How delightful it wou'd be to my ears, how pleasing to yours, to My dear Emma's, to hear it remarked — 'This is what we always expected — Laing is a man of fine words, fine promises, but when fairly put to trial his heart fails him' — this wou'd never do; Government may find fault if they please; let us nevertheless put our shoulder to the wheel with double vigour, and shew ourselves above the paltry worldly considerations of reward — we desire nothing of that kind to induce *us* to perform our duty to our Country — Let us go on with our labours with undiminished enthusiasm, and if we can not command, let us at least deserve commendation.

But My dear Consul, while I am writing thus boldly, my heart throbs with sad pulsations on account of my dearest, most beloved Emma — you say she is well and happy — but I fear, I feel, she is not — Good God, where is the colour of her lovely cheek, where the vermillion of her dear lip — tell me,

[1] R.S., 374(La) 105.

has Mr. Herrador,[1] or has he not, made a faithful likeness? — if he has, My Emma is ill, is melancholy, is unhappy — her sunken eye, her pale cheek, and colourless lip haunt my imagination, and adieu to resolution — Was I within a days march of Tombuctoo, & to hear My Emma was ill — I wou'd turn about, and retrace my steps to Tripoli — What is Tombuctoo? What the Niger? what the world to me? without my Emma — Shou'd anything befall my Emma, which God forbid, I no more wish to see the face of man; my course will be run — a few short days of misery and I shou'd follow her to heaven —

I am agitated, but you will bear with me I hope — never since this terrestial ball was formed, was there a man situated as I am — never, never, and may no man ever be so placed again — it requires rather more than the fortitude which falls to the general lot of mortals, to enable me to bear it — I must again entreat that you will

'Bear with my weakness, my brain is troubled' — I must lay down my pen awhile — oh that picture —

---

6 p.m. Excuse my agitation of this morning my dear Consul — I often feel in that way, but thank God, I have not always a pen in my hand at the time — My mind is now tranquilized, and I shall proceed, as I know I have a good deal to say to you, though my head is in such a jumble, that I do not exactly know in what corner of it to search for the subject I wish to introduce — I have broken the seal of my official letter, and have found to my very great surprise *no* reprimand — I am directed merely to send abstracts of my expenditure to the credit office, instead of the Colonial Department, to which I am to be held responsible for *all sums I may* draw upon the Treasury for — This will enable me to perform the Mission with that respectability which is due to the character of my Country, and I shall have little difficulty in passing my account when I return to England — I accuse myself however, for permitting you to draw the Bill which has occasioned all the *Baroofa*, although I can conscientiously declare, that I did not at the time entertain the most distant idea of the excellent measures we had adopted, meeting with disapprobation — and I am yet inclined to think the tide will turn — I *know* that Major Gray expected upwards of 40,000 £ sterling, (to say nothing of the previous expences of that Mission before the death of Major Peddie) without going beyond the French Port of Galam,[2] and I *know* that a Mr. O'Beirne,[3]

---

[1] The artist was evidently Josef Gomez Herrador, the Spanish Consul-General.

[2] The reference is to an unsuccessful mission, sponsored by the Colonial Office in 1816, which attempted to reach the Niger from the Guinea coast. Major Peddie, the leader, died soon after the mission arrived in West Africa. Major Gray later became the leader. Galam was about 400 miles east of St Louis on the left bank of the Senegal.

[3] In 1821 Dr O'Beirne, an army surgeon, had been sent to Timbo, in the Sierra Leone hinterland, to open up a new trade route into the interior.

who went to Timbo distant only 150 miles from Sierra Leone, reduced the finance of the Colony by a sum of 1500 £ — his Mission lasted two months and a half — It is true that I performed a seven Month Journey to Falaba, and the source of the Niger for a sum rather under *a hundred Pounds*, but I was not at that time an Agent of Government, nor wou'd I again attempt a journey under such circumstances — Enthusiasm may lead a man a great way, and it so happened with me — By the bye Gray was a Lieut. when he took charge of the Mission, and for his failure was promoted to the rank of Major, and received a pecuniary reward of Two thousand Pounds besides — Lyon fails, and is made a Commander — Denham & Clapperton perform wonders, much more than they were expected to perform, and are thought to be well rewarded by a single step of promotion — I shall say nothing of myself — but there are very few indeed who know my services, who do not loudly cry out, that I have been ill used — My consolation — tis better to deserve reward, and not obtain — than to obtain without deserving — I have enclosed to you my ideas regarding the Niger; I had written them before I knew of Clapperton going to Benin — when you have read them, seal them and send them as directed to Mr. Horton — I shall be guided by circumstance on arriving at Tombuctoo — but I think my best way will be to cross directly over to the Coast — By so doing I shall find the termination of the Niger if it has a Westerly course,[1] if otherwise, it is not a thing unlikely that it may fall to Clapperton's lot — I am however determined that I shall not go to Benin — Since I have had such corroborative information that it is not a navigable river, I am less interested in the discovery[2] — and since I perceive the commonplace sort of manner in which an officer is spoken of who sacrifices happiness, comfort, society, and secludes himself from the world for the sake of adding to the honor, and Geographical knowledge of his country, I confess myself a little lookwarm [*sic*].

Had I not looked upon the enterprise as a sort of '*la mer à boire*' affair, I shou'd never have thought of undertaking it — I travel now from principle and not from inclination — This packet of letters has made me very low spirited, so much so, that even the natives observe it, and ask what is the matter. I was in hopes I might have been able to forward my Journal up to the period of my leaving Gadamis, but fear now I shall not be able — I have done nothing since the arrival of the Courier; nor do I feel the slightest inclination to begin — I procrastinated, in the hopes that tomorrow I may be better inclined but tomorrow comes, and I feel myself no better disposed.

---

[1] It is surprising that as late as 1825 a man who had studied the Niger so closely should have thought it at all possible that Leo Africanus had been right in giving the river a westerly course.

[2] One of the principal reasons for the wide interest in the discovery of the Niger's mouth was that it was believed that the river was navigable, and would become a great commercial highway into the interior of the continent.

September 30th. I have as yet said nothing of the very handsome and liberal conduct of the Bashaw,[1] which is however no more, than I have always given him credit for: of course it is out of the high respect and esteem which His Highness entertains for you, and any acknowledgement from me, will hardly be worth his acceptance — but I must nevertheless say, that I bestow in the fullest measure my most sincere thanks, together with my assurance that I shall use every exertion personally (Ensh Alla) as well as by letter to open the Eyes of my Government, to the end that they may entertain a proper sense of his generous and disinterested conduct, which I yet hope will meet a due and suitable reward — He has I know been put to great expence in forwarding me to Gadamis, & I am absolutely ashamed when I think of the great presents he has given Babané upon my account — A fine Horse, rich Burnoose, Silk Shirts, Silver mounted Guns, pistols &c — I have nothing with me that can bear competition with them — (*A word extremely private*) The Bashaws authority finishes at Gadamis, and if he wished, he cou'd not now stop me — I cou'd go on with Hateeta if even Babane was unwilling, but the latter is as desirous to go as I am, having a good deal of merchandise with him — His Highness is no great favorite with the people of Gadamis[2] — but that you know is only a word in passing — you are nearly as well aware of that as I am — I have got all my Camel Saddles repaired this morning, and shall be ready to move as soon as the Courier returns from Tripoli — I am always most satisfied when on the road, when resting, I become low spirited and unwell, my mind reverts to Tripoli where I fancy I see my Emma counting the hours of my absence — for heaven sake My Dear Consul, endeavour to keep her spirits, do something to contribute to her amusement — If I can only satisfy myself that she is well and contented, I shall perform my Journey like a Trojan — I expect to get through in the following order with regard to time — Tuat October 28th — Tombuctoo December 10th — where I shall remain till the 1st January when I shall cross the river, and traverse a desart of Ten [?] Journeys, which will bring me to Wangara and the Lake where I presume the Niger terminates[3] — a month more, the middle of February, and I am on the coast, where if I find a Man of War, I shall instantly embark, calling at Sierra Leone, and Gibralter on my return for letters — I mean to write Smith & my friend Bandinel at some length on the subject of expenditure, and on the late illiberal notice which has been taken of it — Clapperton cannot succeed if he has no other allowance than that which you have stated

---

[1] See p. 224 above.

[2] The people of Ghadames had rebelled in 1810 and had not yet forgotten the crippling fine of 20,000 *mithqāls* of gold and 20,000 *maḥbūbs* they had been forced to pay to Yūsuf.

(A *mithqāl* or *mitkal* was about ⅛ oz. gold. A *maḥbūb* was a gold coin of 25 piastres and worth about 6s. to 7s. 6d.)

[3] Laing had come to the conclusion that Rennell and Barrow were, after all, correct in their belief that the Niger did not end in the Bight of Benin.

— adew for the present — Kindest remembrance to all, & believe me —
Ever yours sincerely,

A. Gordon Laing.[1]

Hanmer Warrington Esq.

Major A. Gordon Laing to Hanmer Warrington:

Private.

Gadamis October 5th 1825
Latitude 30° — 07' — 20" N
Longtitude 9 — 16 — 15 E[2]
Magnetic Variation 18° West.

My dear Consul,

I have this day closed my observations at Gadamis, and the above may be looked upon as final, being the result of much tedious labour and application; the Longtitude particularly, to which I have devoted no less than eleven Lunar distances — The position is very different from that laid down by Lyon, but that is not surprising, for I find him further out with places which he actually visited, and am almost led to believe that Master George [Lyon] never troubled himself much with observations — I expected to have been enabled to send my Journal by this occasion, but have met with so much to annoy me, and disturb my mind, that I have given up any idea of the kind, and have resolved upon leaving my notes un-arranged till I have more time, and a greater portion of tranquillity than I am at present blessed with — I intend writing Smith and my friend Bandinel on the subject of expenditure, but shall take no official notice of it for two reasons — Firstly. Because I have not been as yet meddled with, and I have no particular desire to rouse the sleeping Lion, howsoever boldly I wou'd meet him when roused — Secondly. As it is not improbable that I may incur more expence, I wish to plead ignorance of His Lordship's already marked disatisfaction — With regard to Babane, I shall feel much pleasure in paying the amount promised to him myself. I do not see why you shou'd be called upon, or shou'd think of such a thing as to bear half — I shall draw a Bill upon the Lords of the Treasury for the amount, and give it him when he leaves Tombuctoo; shou'd they refuse payment, or rather shou'd they object to it, of course I shall be responsible, and it will then be time enough for me to draw my purse strings, which I shall take care to do in Lord Bathursts own office, after having successfully performed all, & more than they required of me, for the sum of *Two Thousand Pounds* [an illegible Latin quotation]! — By the bye I am not sure whether I mentioned in either of my former letters, that I had entertained reasons for objecting to the Benin termination of the Niger for some time, but did not wish to persuade myself of their validity so long as I

---

[1] P.R.O., C.O. 2/20. [2] The correct co-ordinates are 30°08' N, 9°30' E.

considered the river navigable — I however left a sealed letter in England containing my ideas on the matter, and now have addressed a few remarks to His Lordship, which I leave open for your perusal —[1] I cannot help remarking the singularity of my situation; how many Individuals have I seen depart for the purpose of discovering this mysterious problem — how often have I smiled within myself, and said it was useless — they have all either perished or returned unsuccessful — I have always looked upon myself as the person destined to effect it — and at the very moment that another is going as he expects to the mouth of the river & with ease to snatch the cup from my lip, I find it almost positively to take another course, bending out of the way of others, as if to meet and welcome me — Clapperton may as well have staid at home, if the termination of the Niger is his object — It is destined for me — It is due to me, and neither a Pearce[2] nor a Clapperton can interfere with me — Only take care of my dearest Emma, and Tombuctoo shall be visited, and the Niger explored within a very few months —

> 'I'll be myself the harbinger, and make joyful'
> 'The hearing of my wife' . . . .

Very Private.
By the bye this very quotation brings to mind a subject which has more than once accompanied my thoughts since the receipt of your last letter — Shou'd I perchance *be the harbinger*, shou'd I return to Tripoli *overland* after having done every thing that I intend performing, Shou'd circumstances of any kind bring about such an event — Will you still consider it necessary to keep me to the promise which you have from me in *writing*? (and which wou'd be sacred was it merely verbal) or will you absolve me from it?[3] Do not be offended at my putting such a question — As I merely do it to prevent a disappointment which might take place was I to return to Tripoli without being so liberated; for I made a solemn promise to my Dear Emma, the night of our separation, (that melancholy night which you will well remember,), never again to part from her when it shou'd please God to restore us to each other — Now My dear Consul, unless you will do this, or either accompany us to Malta or Leghorn, where the ceremony may be reperformed, I wou'd not attempt to return by way of Tripoli; but if compelled to recross the desart, wou'd make my way either to Marocco or Tunis — I put the question to you, as one perfectly delicate, being already aware that Dr. and Mrs. Dickson have as yet been united by no stronger tie (as far as ceremony is concerned) than my Dear Emma and myself; I therefore trust that you will understand me, that I ask for the sake of information and to prevent (what might at least be considered) an awkward dilemma hereafter —

To return to other subjects — I have had all my loads rearranged here,

[1] See Appendix II.
[2] Captain Pearce, R.N., Clapperton's companion on his second expedition.
[3] The promise was that his marriage would not be consummated. (See p. 213 above.)

and find I can carry all with ease upon six Camels — my Kaffle is therefore you will perceive much reduced, consisting of my three attendants from England, an Interpreter, *two* Camel Drivers, Six Camels, one horse and a mule — To use a sailors expression I am as closehauled as I well can be now, and cannot well be found fault with on the score of extravagance — By the Courier Sala — whom I despatch as a man upon whom I can depend, I send you a Caftan[1] and Benish, which I intended as a present for the Sultan of Tombuctoo, but which I think now, will be better bestowed upon Hateeta, who will expect something of the kind when he arrives at Tripoli, particularly as I informed him, in answer to his question, that you had such things for him — He does not want money I find, but is exceedingly pleased by the receipt of costly presents — I have given him a very fine Bornouse, sword, Dagger, pair of pistols and a Mule, together with many minor presents which have delighted him — I offered him money, but he declined, saying he did not wish to be paid for his services, but wou'd take twenty dollars to purchase some cloths for some of his people who are attending him — He is a most surprising man quite a *rara avis*. I never yet met with his equal upon *Lybian clay* — 6th October. I have not yet sent off Sala, being desirous to let you know exactly on what day we shall depart from here, and as yet I cannot ascertain that, the Sheikh being rather incommoded by a huge boil on his *head's antipodes*, & being unwilling to name a day. Till he finds himself better — I have made use of all my Esculapean art, and think in three days more, he may stand the jolting of a Camel, but we must wait a little, *et nous verrons* — I cannot help again reverting to the subject of expenditure, the more I think of it, the more unaccountable it appears to me — An active, meritorious agent of Government, who has deserved the highest honors, whose services have been hitherto so highly approved of, to be found fault with because he incurrs an expence of 2000 $ to ensure success. I think I see my Country involved in another war, and fancy to myself an Admiral or General having achieved a great victory, and receiving this kind of Compliment —

We are perfectly satisfied with the victory you have gained, and applaud you for the honor which you have added to the British nation, and although we think *nothing of the number of lives* that have been lost in affecting so desirable an object, yet must express our disatisfaction at the *enormous quantity of Powder and Shot expended* — Bravo, liberal minded, generous cabinet of England I much fear Mr. Huskisson's[2] new plan of the reduction of duties, does not exactly answer —

October *7th*. It is at length finally settled my dear Consul that we are to leave

---

[1] A *caftan* or *kaftan*, Arabic *qaftān*, was a long-sleeved outer garment, open in the front, which in North Africa was considered, when given as a present, a mark of special favour.

[2] William Huskisson, M.P. (1770–1830), was at this time much occupied with finance and trade. In 1827 he became Colonial Secretary and Leader of the House.

Ghadames

Gadamis on the morning of the 13th. I therefore send away Sala tomorrow morning; and as I am in hopes of procuring a guide to take him safe over the Garian, I think you will get my letters within ten days after his departure. I made him a few presents as he has been so long in the country, and have advanced him Twenty dollars to meet his present expences — I have bought a few presents of different kinds from Babane which I understand will prove highly serviceable upon the road, and as I consider it necessary as well as becoming that I shou'd bestow something at the same time with Babane himself, who, I assure you is well supplied with Burnooses, Caftans & Benishes, Trowsers, turbans &c — to the tune of about Two thousand Dollars, all which he says he will be obliged to give away on the road — I have bought from him better Burnooses for eight dollars, and of finer cloth than those which Angelo furnished me with at the rate of fifteen dollars each, and from the little knowledge I have already obtained of the trade of this country, & price of goods, I can plainly observe that the conscientious Jew has made his percentage out of me, as he has often no doubt, done out of you — no matter *'tis done*. I have left my letter to Lord Bathurst descriptive of my Journey to Shati, open for your persual, if you can find time and patience to read 'much ado about nothing' — Whether you peruse it or not, pray seal it, before sending it from Tripoli, as well as the Remarks on the Termination of the Niger, and when you next write, give me your opinion of the latter — By the way talking of writing I think you had better send Sala back to Gadamis instanter, where I shall leave a Tuarick to follow me with such letters as he may bring: Do not I beg of you deprive yourself and family of the newspapers upon my account in future; I am not so anxious about the fate of the Catholic Bill,[1] or a description of the Ladies' dresses at the King's drawing room, as to trouble myself whether I know all about them to-day or six months hence — after you have all finished them, well finished them, from the first advertisment 'For Bombay direct' to the last 'A valuable Freehold Estate', it will be time enough to send them to me —

You are most likely marvelling why I have said nothing of Gadamis, a place which it was expected, wou'd have furnished much matter of interesting description, but I regret that my hopes have been disappointed in this instance as in many others where I have anticipated much — I have visited many different countries within the last thirteen years, and have only met with two places in which the reality met or exceeded expectation: you will perhaps be surprised when I tell you that those two are Malta & Sierra Leone, the former indebted to art, the latter to nature for its beauty.

Gadamis is completely hid from view by the date trees which surround it, and furnish the principal part of the food of the inhabitants — The Town &

---

[1] Four more years of bitter wrangling had yet to pass before Catholic Emancipation became law.

Gardens occupy a space of about four miles in circumference, beyond which every thing is dreary and barren, not an iota of vegetation appearing outside the precincts of the town, which appears to have been built on this isolated spot on account of a large pond of fresh water, which stands in its centre, and which by means of various canals is made to irrigate the thirsty soil, scanty in the extreme, and composed of sand and clay — It is environed by mud walls, in some places not more than five or six feet high, and at intervals are placed small square bastions with *trous de loup* for musketry, a mere mockery of defence — on the western side, about a hundred fathoms distant from the town, are the remains of seven buildings, so dilapidated, and mutilated, that their original form cannot be ascertained[1] — The architecture is extremely rude, and the stones are heaped upon one another in so careless a manner, that I shou'd not have considered them of Roman construction, had I not discovered upon digging around there, several broken sarcophagi, with the buried remains of the dead. In vain has been any search for coins, in vain for any carved tablet; I cou'd not discover a single hewn stone among the ruins, but I understand that a square marble stone upon which are marked some Roman characters, was carried by the Son of the Bashaw to Tripoli, at the time he invaded this unwarlike people[2] — I wish you wou'd enquire about this, and endeavour to see the stone.

These ruins have been extremely useful to the inhabitants of Gadamis, having furnished them with materials to assist in the construction of their houses, which otherwise must have been entirely built of clay: & even as it is there are at least five sixths of them built of the latter tenacious commodity, the stone found in the vicinity being of a crumbling micaceous nature quite unfit for the purposes of architecture, a circumstance which may in some measure account for the rude construction of the ruins already noticed, the stones having no doubt been collected with trouble and brought from a great distance — In so small a space of four miles in circumference, which embraces the town & the whole of the cultivated land belonging to these people, it is to be presumed the former does not occupy a great deal of room, nor does it, although exceedingly populous — the houses being huddled together in the closest order, separated by narrow avenues, which being surrounded by buildings thus, ————[3] with only here and there a small opening to admit air and light, are in many places as dark as the catacombs of Malta, and as difficult to wade through as the Cretan Labyrinth. But my paper is getting short, and my letter is tediously long, you will therefore be glad that I am about to tax your patience no longer by drawing to a conclusion — Requesting therefore that you will say every that I cou'd wish in

---

[1] These were the *Asnam* (*aṣnām* in Arabic means idols, singular *ṣanam*) which look today much as they did in Laing's time (Plate IV). It has been established that these curious structures are Roman tombs.

[2] Yūsuf had sent his third son Ali to crush the rebellion of 1810.

[3] The very rough sketch is too faint for reproduction, but see p. 376 below.

Plate IV. Ghadames: The Asnam
After a sketch by Laing

the shape of remembrance to Mrs. W., Jane, Louisa, Herbert & little Osy, believe me
Ever with much sincerity
Yours truly
A. Gordon Laing.[1]

Major A. Gordon Laing to James Bandinel:
Gadamis October 7th 1825

My dear Bandinel,

    To morrow I despatch a Courier from here, having closed my observations and finished all my Official Despatches; on the 13th please God, I shall again be upon my Camel's back, journeying towards Tuat, which place I may reach most probably by the 1st November — I have been obliged to make a circuit of nearly a thousand miles to get to this place, as on the straight road there were hordes of plundering Arabs laying [sic] in wait for the Kaffle at all the different watering places — I have met a number of Tuaricks here, and among others Hateeta, who accompanies me to Tuat, but it strikes me his influence is not so great as has been represented, nor are the Tuaricks by any means a quiet inoffensive people: they exact very heavy dues from the Gadamis Merchants, and not unfrequently plunder them entirely; indeed I hear such accounts of them that I shall look upon myself as fortunate, if I get through their territories with the loss of half my baggage — I have sent a rough chart of my route & my Journal up to 19th Augt. together with some remarks on the Niger to the Colonial Office, which I hope may give satisfaction. I shall say nothing about my promotion yet, meaning to apply for it from Tuat — they will surely then give it to me, particularly as I might have been a Regimental Major, if I had let the Mission alone — I understand Captn Clapperton has gone to the Bight [of Benin] to make the long looked for discovery, but he might have saved himself the trouble for the disclosure of that long hidden secret is left to me, as I hope to prove by March or April next. My health thank God, continues good, and I feel perfectly confident and equal to the undertaking: On my Journey to this place my constitution was put to the trial, having to endure a temperature of 62° in the morning! and oftentimes 120° Farenheit at Noon!! I was nevertheless not the least affected, and I have therefore, if that is possible, more confidence than ever.

    You will excuse this short letter, as I have a great deal to do, being now a sort of Caleb to my own Mission, and as I wish to address a few lines to my friend Sabine. Remember me kindly to Messrs. Bidwell & Byng, also to the Honble. Hookham Frere,[2] when you perchance may see him, and not forgetting your nephew Le Mesurier.
Believe me with much sincerity,
Your's very truly
A. Gordon Laing

[1] P.R.O., C.O. 2/20.
[2] Perhaps John Hookham Frere (1769–1841), diplomatist and author, and a founder of *The Quarterly Review*.

Mark Gadamis upon your Map in Latitude. 30° — 07' — 20"N — and Longtitude 9° — 16' — 15"E[1]
Sherghi in Wadey Shati by which I went round is very far misplaced by Lyon[2] being in 27° — 25' — 42"N.L. & 13° — 00 — 00. E.L.

Major A. Gordon Laing to Captain E. Sabine., R.A.:

Gadamis October 8th 1825

My dear Sabine,

After a very long and tedious journey by Fezzan and Shati, I reached this place on the 13th Ult. in excellent health, and as I expect to depart from it in five days more on my route to Tuat, I think it not improbable, but I may be in Tombuctoo by the 12th December, perhaps before this letter reaches you — This town of Gadamis stands perfectly isolated in the midst of the black desert of Soudah, nor is there the slightest appearance of vegetation outside of its argillaceous walls — It extends in houses and Gardens a distance of about two miles and a half in length by about half a mile in breadth, and is entirely hid from view by the profusion of date trees, which afford a plentiful supply of fruit and *flies*. The houses are for the most part built of clay or mud, (the stone found in the neighbourhood, being of the crumbling mica formation and unfit for the purpose of architecture) and are of a square shape, extending in straight lines, and forming narrow lanes or allies, which being surmounted by buildings connecting the houses or either side together, thus,[3] are as dark as the catacombs of Egypt, and as difficult to wade through as the Cretan Labyrinth[4] — The Inhabitants are of a very superior cast, and possess a manner exceedingly agreeable; in their conversation they are affable, and exhibit none of that contemptuous hauteur, which appears almost inseparable from the Turk and the Moor. This may probably arise from their peculiar situation; placed in the middle of a desert, in which they wou'd be left to starve if enterprise did not lead them to wander as traders into other countries in order to ensure their safety, they become habituated to politeness, or in other words become men of the world — They are strictly a commercial people, and are perfectly versant in the use of Bills of

---

[1] See p. 260n. 2 above.

[2] This appears to refer to the eastern half of what is now called Wadi el Ajial, running south-west from Sebha to Ubari. Lyon showed it incorrectly on his map running due west from Sebha. But Laing's description of Sherghi as 'in' Wadi Sciati is misleading because it is entirely separate from that wadi and some miles to the south. But according to Lyon's map the whole district used to be called Wadi Sciati, a relevant point which Laing omits to mention (G. F. Lyon, map opposite p. 1).

[3] The drawing, which is similar to that on p. 376 below, is too faded for reproduction.

[4] The town of Ghadames, which has changed little since Laing's day, appears to be composed of houses piled on top of each other to which the only access is by the seemingly subterranean tunnels running beneath them. This curious form of town-planning, which is not peculiar to Ghadames, was adopted in the Sahara as a protection against desert raiders, who found it very difficult to take such a town by surprise or by storm.

exchange, with the gain or loss upon them, calculating the price given for an article in another country, expence of Camel hire, risk &c. with mercantile nicety, and their traffic extends to Marocco, Algiers, Tunis, Tripoli and Misurata on the North, and to Soudan, Tenbuctoo, Jenne & Melli[1] in the South — During the short period I have resided here, I have witnessed the arrival of three Kaffles from Fezzan, Two from Graat, and two from Burnou, making seven in the short space of three weeks — But I have not time to enter into further detail on that head at present.

I have been very indefatigable with my observations, and have determined the longtitude of this place by the means of three, taken at random from Eleven lunar Distances — It is in 30.07 20 N and 9.10 . 15 E, and I have been thus particular in consequence of being obliged to reset my chronometer, which stopt two days before I arrived it — Its rate has altered to a loss of 7" 5/10 daily — Lyon is very far out I am certain in his Longtitude of Mozouk [Murzuk], which I am inclined to think lies not further to the Eastward than 15° — where Major Rennel placed it many years ago — I have sent to the Colonial Office some remarks on the course and termination of the Niger; pray look them over, I was going to say, and give me your opinion, but I shall have proved myself right or wrong before I can hear it — I have an apprehension that Capt. Clapperton will pluck the growing plume from Caesar's wing[2] —

Adieu — God bless you — I hope to see you soon, after the completion of this object which I have so long desired — I hope I may find a man of war in the Bight, as I have no desire to sit down there making signals for several months.

Yours very truly,
A. Gordon Laing.

Kind remembrance to the family in Portland place.[3]

Captain Sabine R.A.

Major A. Gordon Laing to Hanmer Warrington:

Gadamis Oct. 17th 1825

My Dear Consul,

I have at length the happiness to inform you that the Mission will depart from this place at an early hour tomorrow morning, and I shall feel obliged by your acquainting His Lordship the Earl Bathurst of the same — I shall be

---

[1] Mali had long ceased to exist. In the fourteenth century the fame of this great Mandingo empire, of which Niani on the upper Niger was the capital, spread through much of Europe. Leo Africanus was a witness of its decay under Songhai aggression in the early sixteenth century.

[2] Hitherto he had been blindly confident that Clapperton would fail where he would succeed.

[3] R.S., 374(La) 100.

in Twat (please God) by the 7th or 8th prox°, and you may most probably receive my letters from thence by the return of Hateeta about the latter end of November —

I was favored with your's of the 12th Ulto[1] by the arrival of your Courier in the regular period of fourteen days, and I regretted much to learn the disatisfaction expressed by His Lordship, regarding the arrangements made by us at Tripoli, for the furtherance of the Mission: which appeared to me at the time of the most judicious character, certainly, assuming as we had a right to do, the success of the Mission as a matter of importance to the Government, and circumstanced as we were; knowing the attempts which the agents of a rival nation were making, to forestall us in reaching the great goal of all African research, and to wrench from us all the honor we had previously gained by dint of much perseverence, & by the sacrifice of much money & life. I the more regret that our arrangements have elicited disatisfaction; because, as far as I am personally concerned, it wou'd have been infinitely more agreeable to me, to have awaited at Tripoli, the result of a communication with His Lordship, my health having been at the time in a very precarious and insecure state: My feeling & impression was so decidedly in favor of an immediate departure, as the only chance of securing the honor of the discovery to my country, that my personal convenience, or my then critical situation occasioned me not even the shadow of a thought —

There are situations in which Official characters are occasionally placed, which being casual, and unprovided for in their instructions, reduce them to the necessity, how reluctantly soever, of exercising their own *Judgement & Discretion* — In such a situation was you placed, when finding it impossible to forward the mission without a present to the Bashaw, and others, you made to me a proposition; in such a situation was I placed when having no authority to do so, I sanctioned it — I shall now state to you the reasons by which I was actuated —

Firstly then — I saw by the manner & coolness of His Highness the Bashaw, that without a remuneration or gratuity of some kind, the Mission wou'd not be permitted to go far from Tripoli —

Secondly — If the Mission met with detention, which must have been the consequence of a refusal to the Bashaw, and an application to England, His Highness, I felt satisfied, wou'd have forwarded the French Travellers from the Cyrenaica before me, and wou'd have rendered any after attempts of our's needless; at all events of secondary consequence —

Thirdly — When I reflected on the enormous sums which had already been expended in the endeavour to reach Tombuctoo, and the termination of the Niger (for I know pretty well what the Mission of Major Peddie cost, to say nothing of several others) I had every right to consider the success of the Mission as highly important to my Government.

---

[1] No copy of this letter appears to have survived.

Fourthly — A good deal had been already advanced, and expended on account of the present Mission, and the expences wou'd have encreased during the period of waiting for further instructions from England: I cou'd not for a moment anticipate the recall of the Mission; & being satisfied that its recall wou'd be unavoidable if the French Travellers got before me — It only remained for me to consider; whether in sanctioning a further sum of a *Thousand Pounds* and prosecuting the service upon which I was employed, with success — or in failing entirely, & expending the sums for which I was authorised to draw, I was most likely to render satisfaction to my Government: I decided upon the former, and I yet feel satisfied that when His Lordship is made fully acquainted with all the circumstances, the reprimand will be cancelled by an approval of our proceedings — There are other circumstances which I was ignorant of at the time I came to the above decision, which had I known, wou'd have occasioned less hesitation on my part.

The travelling to Tombuctoo is of a very different character from that to Bornoo, the whole road to the latter of which country is under the authority & control of the Bashaw, who (it is a well known fact) cou'd at any time pass a child along it in perfect safety without putting himself to the expence of a single piastre — It did not cost him more to forward the late Mission for which he received £5,000 Sterling — His Highness possesses neither influence nor authority on the road to Tombuctoo, the good will of which always is, and always has been purchased by heavy presents from the different Tuarick Tribes, by the native caravans — I know it to be a fact, that His Highness paid the Maraboot of Serked 150 $ Dollars, a horse & Burnoose to escort me as far as Malhrail, clear of the Jebel Arabs, and I know that he has given the Sheikh Babané the sum of 1,800 $ a rich Burnoose, several handsome silver mounted guns & pistols, besides a valuable Horse, to perform the service of conducting us safely to Tombuctoo — The Tuaricks have heard a good deal of former Missions, and will of course not only expect, but demand more from an English Agent, than a native Merchant; and Babane is so sensible of this, that he has provided himself with presents to the amount of about 3,000 $ to distribute on the road — (I speak positively because I have seen them) — The Tuaricks are a strange people, living mostly upon plunder, or the tribute which they collect: Whatever they demand, must be given them; a refusal wou'd be the signal for plunder & murder; but if once satisfied, they will load your Camels, attend upon you as faithful servants, be your guides & protectors thro' their desert, dreary country — I well remember the words of the Bashaw: 'If you wish to go that road, you must open the door with a silver key', and I find them too true — The expences of the Mission will not exceed the estimate I formed in London as far as myself and party are concerned, but the presents to the Bashaw, Babané, and the various chiefs on the road, ought to be an affair between the Governments, with which I shou'd of course have nothing to do.

This letter is demi official, demi private — and you will just be guided by your own opinion in making what use of it you please[1] — I have brought up my Journal to this date, but have not yet had time to copy it — I have a good deal to say about Gadamis, rather interesting — Take care of my dearest Emma, and do not under any circumstances permit her to despond — I am & shall be safe, and please God, shall soon return. My kindest remembrance to Mrs. Warrington, Jane, Louisa, Herbert and Osy, and that God may bless & prosper you & your whole family, is the fervent & constant prayer of

      Yours ever sincerely

             A. Gordon Laing

Hanmer Warrington Esq.,

P.S. I have written to Smith and Bandinel regarding the notice which has been taken of the expenditure, which really hurts me much[2] —

Major A. Gordon Laing to Hanmer Warrington:

            Gadamis 26th Oct. 1825

My dear Consul,

I have been taken rather unawares by the return of your Courier, who accompanies a Caravan by way of Fezzan, & who has given me very little warning. I shall do little more than apologise for not writing you at greater length, particularly as I wrote you a long letter on the 18th by the Sheikh Habeeb.[3]

The Saharan Arabs have shut up the road to Tuat, and we therefore avoid that place,[4] taking a more direct route to Tombuctoo, at which I now expect to arrive on the 10th Dec. The news of the Schaamba[5] reached us the day on which we were to have left Gadamis, and put a spoke in our wheel — since which Two Maraboots friends of the Sheikh have arrived with an escort, and I believe we shall *really* now go tomorrow or the day after. I send some notes to the Colonial Office, open for your perusal. I have a good many sketches, but none in a finished state — therefore send none — among others I have Babani's wife, a Lady whom I speak of at some length as you will perceive.

I shall write you by Hateeta, who will accompany me within twenty days of Tombuctoo, and by the time you get my letters by him, you may place me for certain in that Capital, and perhaps by February I shall yet be on the other side of this continent — You will perceive my great haste, therefore

---

[1] The tenor of this letter, and that it was in reply to one from Warrington (dated 12 September, no copy of which was kept), suggest that it was written on the Consul's instructions for forwarding to London in justification of the latter's actions.

[2] P.R.O., C.O. 2/20. This letter reached Warrington on 5 January 1826.

[3] This was probably the letter dated 17 October but sent off on the 18th. Habeeb was a sheikh of Ghadames.

[4] They did in fact go to Tuat.

[5] The Chaamba Arabs. (See p. 384 below.)

you will I hope excuse me — With kindest remembrance to Mrs. Warrington, Jane, Louisa, Herbert & Osy — believe me My Dear Consul,
Ever your's sincerely,
A. Gordon Laing

Remembrances to Dr. and Mrs. Dickson.[1]

Since his first arrival in Ghadames Laing had become increasingly aware of the difficulties he must expect on the road to Timbuktu. 'Every person tells me', he had written on the 13th Sept. 'that this road is very different from that to Bournou — the latter is a regular trading road under the power of the Bashaw along which a child might travel but on this there are many conflicting interests. The Bashaw's interest ceases at Gadamis.'[2]

But he was concerning himself less with the dangers that lay immediately ahead than with the problem of where his journey would end, of where he would find the mouth of the Niger. In Ghadames, where there was no lack of merchants familiar with the Sudan, the fruits of his enquiries led him again to revise his opinion on the probable solution to the problem he had set out to solve. On the 24th September he wrote to Wilmot Horton:

... The information which I have received here from many well informed people together with that which I have at former periods collected, leads me to presume that I shall find my way to the Coast of Guinea in tracing the course of the Niger; I should therefore feel obliged if his Lordship will direct application to be made to the Lords of the Admiralty to issue orders to one of the Men of War on the Sierra Leone Station, to call occasionally at the mouths of the rivers Benin and Volta but particularly the latter about the months of April, May and June next. . . .[3]

If Wilmot Horton was surprised to hear that Laing now inclined to think that the Volta might turn out to be the Niger, a possibility that had not occurred to anyone else, he had not long to wait for the explanation, for this letter was quickly followed by another dated 28th September, reading:

With reference to my letter bearing date September 24th 1825, in which I stated that I had reasons for supposing the course of the Niger might lead me to the Coast of Guinea, I have now the honor to enclose *a few cursory remarks*[4] which I have drawn up for the information of His Lordship the

[1] P.R.O., C.O. 2/20.
[2] R.S., 374(La) 95.
[3] R.S., 374(La) 96.
[4] See Appendix I.

Earl Bathurst, & which I offer as an explanation for the request I have made, of a man of war to be placed at my disposal on that coast early in the ensuing year.[1]

On 20 October, just before leaving Ghadames for Tuat, he was able to report to his friend Bandinel an encouraging omen:

I have for some weeks back observed a large Comet in the heavens, and it makes a very rapid progress southward. I regard it as a happy omen — it beckons me on, & binds *me* to the Termination of the Niger.[2]

[1] P.R.O., C.O. 2/15, 189.   [2] R.S., 374(La) 103.

CHAPTER VII

IN SALAH

Major A. Gordon Laing to Hanmer Warrington:

[3 November, 1825,]

At length My Dear Consul, I have it in my power to say that I am on the road to Tombuctoo — The Camels are all loaded, and only wait for me while I give you notice of the event — At length I am off, and please God, shall sleep in the long looked after city, in forty two days more — by the bye I have forgotten to date my letter that you may [be] enabled to make a calculation — it is the *3rd* November — extremely cold & threatening rain — thermometer as low as 43° Farenheit — I suppose — almost freezing on the Desert of Sahara — wonderful indeed are the changes in this land of Ham — In addition to my six Camels, I have hired four Maherries at ten dollars each, from the Maraboot who gives us escort, which will enable us to travel speedily, which, now that I have been able to stir my Sheikh from his own *hotbed*, I find he has every inclination to do — I send back to Tripoli the grey horse and a mule, the Sheikh & Maraboot both recommending it; and as their reasons, which you shall know at another time, are good, I subject myself to be guided by them — I lost one horse at Benioleed & a mule on the road from Shati; I sold the little horse in Gadamis for a [word illegible], the Bay I presented to the Sheikh, and the best mule to Hateeta — thus you have the distribution of my stud — I wrote you some time since by the Sheikh Habeeb, and shou'd he reach Tripoli I beg you will [be] kind enough to treat him with an attention purely political — I received some favors & *salams* in abundance from him during my stay in Gadamis, but it is said, he wou'd have no objection to assist me quietly to the other world if he conveniently cou'd, thinking such an act by embroiling Babane with the Bashaw might help him to the Sheikship of Gadamis — I will however, not vouch for this entirely — I have heard a good deal, and may have suspicions, but no more — he has shewn attention to me & merits a return — I have now to express one regret my dear Consul, and that is that I have not heard in the most distant shape, from Tripoli since the date of my arrival in Gadamis — my mind forebodes nothing ill — I have a strong presentiment that my Dear Emma is well, but it is truly painful to remain so long in the dark. Had I but a single line from her dear hand, I shou'd mount my Camel satisfied, and the impression, that I shall not be made happy with intelligence again, till I emerge from the other side, wou'd be borne with a greater degree of

resignation and fortitude — May God bless you all — kindest remembrance to Mrs. W., Jane, Louisa, Herbert & Osy, and believe me,
      Ever sincerely yours
     (tho' in such haste that I have hardly
     time to say so)
              A. Gordon Laing

Hanmer Warrington Esq.

I have tried to mend my pen —
In twenty days more I shall write you by Hateeta — It will be a very hasty notice, as we shall travel fast — but it will suffice to let you know how matters go — Yours ever

On the cover is the following note in Laing's hand:

I enclose two letters from the Sheikh — Nov. 3rd. Endeavour if possible to let me hear from you and write to me at *Sierra Leone* immediately, by way of England —
 God bless you, as soon as I envelope this, I am off. I think you had better sell the horse & mule for the benefit of the Mission[1] —

    Major A. Gordon Laing to Hanmer Warrington:

        Wadey Thakouset[2] Nov. 13th 1825
      Lat. 28° — 25' — 40"N: Long 8° 07' — 45" E
My dear Consul,
 As it is my intention to send back Hateeta on my arrival at the next well, and as I have an hour to spare to-day before dark, I dipt [?] a hasty pen to apprize you of my welfare. We are travelling along at a fair tho easy rate (from 9 to 10 hours a day) in order to enable our Camels to execute the long dreary Journey — I think I told you in one of my former letters that we do not go by Tuat, in consequence of some reports of an unpleasant nature regarding the perilous situation of the road; but I find that these reports were entirely of a *stockjobbing* nature and only feints of the Sheikh to cover his intention of going the road we are now taking, by which means he avoids Tuat, and the expence to which he wou'd be put in going through that Country — All the presents, therefore, which he shew'd me as intended for that place, are merely the merchandise which he carries to dispose of at Tombuctoo — I shall be able to say more on this subject, when I see more, and shall consequently form no hasty conclusions, but I rather think I shall be obliged to recommend that the Sheikh does not receive more than

[1] P.R.O., C.O. 2/20.
[2] Wadi Thakouset lies about 150 miles south of Ghadames between the Oudian Wan Abelhouda and the O'Gour Farhat.

Two Thousand dollars for the service he performs, as I know that the utmost he has already expended is a hundred dollars, and that, not in cash, but in articles which he received as presents from the Bashaw — In granting the 4,000 $ I had an idea that he wou'd be put to very great expense, and that idea was entertained by me till very lately, but I have many conspiring reasons now for *thinking* otherwise, and when I am certain (which I shall take good care to be before I decide) I shall put in my *veto* to the agreement which was made. In the meantime, perhaps you had better caution Mr. Gervanelli for I rather think the Sheikh brought nothing for *him* to Gadamis, the most of the goods which he had being on Commission for a man in Gadamis named *Hadjé Hand* [?] By the bye, if this man ever goes to Tripoli, I hope you will be kind enough to shew him some attention; he was indeed more than attentive to me in Gadamis, and offered to lend me any money I might stand in need of. I however declined his offer, which I fear I may yet have reason to regret, for I am running very short, the Sheikh having borrowed a great deal from me, and not having it in his power to repay me. I have taken some goods from him in part payment, in the barter of which he has dealt fairly enough, but these goods will not buy my servants a dinner in Tombuctoo — It is getting dark and I must shut my portfolio, for I have no Candles in the Desert. I cou'd write you a volume if I had time, but I fear I must defer most news till we meet, which shall be please God air [*sic*] long — The most of this is taken up with the Sheikh, regarding whom I wish I cou'd speak more favorably, for he is a very innocent harmless man, though needy and avaricious in the extreme.

Nov. 18th. We have halted for the day at a spring of fine water, and a garden from which about a dozen date trees send forth their verdant foliage, peeping from amidst the hills of sand with which they are surrounded, like a few evergreens amidst the snows of December — this garden belongs to a Maraboot of the Hookar tribe of Tuaric who is our guide, and I hope at some future period to bring before your notice & that of my Lord Bathurst the admirable character and conduct of this man. Two days ago a Kaffle of thirty Camels & twelve men which left Gadamis the same day with our- selves, was attacked and captured by a party of the *Hugarin* Tuarics, about twelve miles in advance of us, and this event has so terrified our *Gallant* Sheikh Babané that he has changed his intention, has zigzagged a little more, and now intends steering for *Tuat* by an *unfrequented path* — This is not exactly the way I ought to travel for the sum of four thousand Dollars; I ought to have been placed beyond the reach of risk, and the Sheikh might have brought an escort of twenty men all the way for the sum of four hundred Dollars — instead of which he only has with him two slaves to load and unload his Camels, so that if attacked I have only my own people to depend upon — I carry Hateeta with me to *Tuat*, that you may have late accounts from me, and I hope they may be satisfactory. I fear I am not to hear again from Tripoli — it is truly distressing, but I know that you have done all you cou'd by sending off Couriers.

December 3rd. Ensala [In Salah] in *Tuat* — 27° — 11' — 30" N.E., and 11° — 51' — 15" E. I have much pleasure in dating a few lines to you from this place my dear Consul, where I arrived yesterday afternoon about half past four — my observations to day have given me the above position, by which you will perceive I am much nearer Morocco than I am to Tripoli now, and exactly North of Tombuctoo, from which latter place I am about thirty Journies, though I fear we shall not do it in less than forty in the manner in which we jog on — My Journey just begins to become interesting, and I am not a little pleased when I look at the great improvement I am already making, and contemplate those I shall make in the map of Africa. You must keep up the spirits of my dearest Emma, and allow nothing to create the smallest alarm, if ever you shou'd be six months after the receipt of this without hearing from me, a circumstance which I think by no means improbable, as the Sheikh who I suppose will be my Courier is not famed for expedition — setting out on a journey as the Scotsmen used to do of old for London, expecting to arrive by the will of God in the course *of a month of more.* You must therefore always consider me safe, for it is my destiny to be so, and perhaps you may see me before the Sheikh makes his appearance.

Yesterday was such a day as I have before seen in Africa, but not the present Journey. Upwards of a thousand people of both sexes came out to meet me, and so surrounded my Camel that I had much difficulty in proceeding — I have been in the habit of late of covering my face *à la mode* Tuaric, as a convenient protection against the Sun, and as nothing but my eyes were yesterday visible the curiosity of the multitude was not gratified, and my poor attendants were beleagued with a thousand questions — Is he white? Is his hair like a Turk's? Has he a beard? Can he fire a Gun without flint? — alluding to my rifle, the fame of which has preceeded me, with many other questions regarding the rockets and everything else which I had been seen to possess in Gadamis — I was glad to get into my quarters where I hoped for a little repose, but even there the curious made their way, and absolutely dragged me from the dark chamber in which I was reposing into the open air that they might see me the better; this however did not suffice, and they requested I wou'd oblige them by mounting upon the terraced roof, with which request although reluctantly I complied, and to my surprise found on an adjoining Terrace an assemblage of nearly a hundred women waiting in eager expectation to see me, staring with outstretched neck, and bawling *à pleine gorge* as any thing extraordinary about me attracted their observation — They wished to know if they might come to see me, (for they neither appear to labour under much restraint, nor to possess a great deal of delicacy) but the Sheikh told them no, and seeming much displeased, said if they cou'd not behave themselves, they shou'd not see me again. The rebuke was truly pleasing to my ears, and I took advantage of it to steal from the vulgar gaze — What a sad thing it is to be a Lion — The people here appear of a very superior cast, and the Sheikh, a man of sterling worth — He welcomed me thus — I have long looked for you, I am glad you have come — here is my house for you, and here is my Son, who will attend you wherever you wish to go; look upon the country as your own, and do in it whatever you wish; there is nothing in it too good for you, so you must ask for whatever you desire — shou'd any person annoy or trouble you, *kill* him instantly; I shall be your protection & shall answer for it — I shall remain here for five or six days to rest the Camels, and shall depart on the 10th please God; we shall have plenty of Company, as a larger Kaffila has been waiting expressly for us, and they give the most favorable reports of the state of the road, which is truly satisfactory — every thing seems to favor me, and to bespeak a successful termination — Travelling from this side is a mere journey of pleasure compared *certioris paribus* with that on the other side, and I verily expect to reach Tombuctoo with less trouble, less risk, less fatigue, than I did Falaba in the Soolima country — I despatch Hateeta tomorrow, and shall leave the remainder of this sheet till then — I like Hateeta much, I never met a better man in any country, and certainly never a more disinterested man — Use him according to his deserts my dear Consul, and you will use him well — Shakespeare makes Hamlet say 'Use every man according to his deserts, and who shall escape whipping?' but here he is decidedly in the wrong.

Dec. *4th.* This is Sunday, and I have requested the Sheikh of the Town to grant me a day of rest, but 'tis vain, the people will crowd to see me, and I must of course bear it, Tomorrow we are to rearrange our loads, and on the 10th we shall move on — It will be the middle of January yet before I reach Timbuctoo, and as I am already far beyond it in anticipation, I shall I suppose be in Tripoli in thought, when I arrive at that remote Capital — Rome was not built in one day, nor can the Desert be crossed yet in a Post chaise — I must therefore be satisfied with the conveyance & submit patiently to the delay of the natives — I am as enthusiastic as ever Nigritic research; though I sometimes give the river a left handed blessing, when I think it is the cause of my separation from my Emma; at other times I am more charitable towards it, when I consider that had it not been for the Niger, I might never have been blessed with a sight of the dear object which I prize more than life — Kindest remembrance to Mrs. Warrington, Jane, Louisa, Herbert and little Osy, and believe me My Dear Consul,
    Ever yours most sincerely,
         A. Gordon Laing[1]
Hanmer Warrington Esq.

[1] P.R.O., C.O. 2/20. Received 23 March 1826.

Major A. Gordon Laing to R. Wilmot Horton:

Ensala December 4th, 1825

Sir,

I have much pleasure in dating this letter from Ensala the most Eastern town of Tuat,[1] in which I arrived in safety and in good health at a late hour yesterday afternoon, and was received by the inhabitants with a degree of cordiality, which under any other circumstance might have been considered troublesome and inconvenient: About a mile from the town I was met by upwards of a thousand people of both sexes, and of all ages from the hoary Marāboot 'sans teeth &c' to the infant 'mewling &c in its mothers lap'; and such was the curiosity excited by my arrival in this place, that I was fairly beleaguered by both young and old, all so desirous to procure a near view of me, that it was with no inconsiderable difficulty that my Camel was enabled to pick his steps to the Town through the crowded *'turba faventium'* — I entered Ensala in the costume which I have been lately in the habit of wearing on the road, my person shrouded in my military cloak,[2] and my head covered à la Tuaric as a convenient protection against the morning cold & Meridional rays of the Sun, and as this was rather a shield against the gratification of public curiosity, I had no sooner alighted and seated myself in a dark chamber in the house alloted to me, than a general rush was made from without, in an instant the courtyard was packed as closely as the pit of Covent Garden theatre on a benefit night, and I was under the necessity Nolens volens, of making my appearance in the open air, that I might be seen the better by my visitants — A hundred voices gave me a hundred welcomes, and another hundred asked a hundred questions, which to answer wou'd have been a vain attempt — Where is the Gun that you fire without flint? asked one alluding to my rifle with the copper caps the fame of which has spread far & wide, & has preceded me to Ensala — Where is the fire that you make burn in the water? demanded a second? alluding to the Port fires which they have heard of — where is the fire that you send into the sky? asked a third — Shew me your watch? a fourth, & so on, enumerating everything which I had been seen to possess in Ghadamis.

The Sheikh of the town paid me a complimentary visit this morning, and welcomed me in the following strong language — 'We have long looked for you, I am glad you have come: consider this country and every thing in it as your own: if you wish to walk out my Son shall attend you, and if you see

[1] In Salah is in Tidikelt, not Tuat, but on this point Dr L. Cabot Briggs writes: 'Even today is it not unusual to hear a Targui say that he is "going to Tuat" to buy or sell dates. If you ask him "Where in the Tuat" he will reply "to In Salah".... But In Salah is in the Tidikelt! Marceau Gast and I think that the term Tuat was applied *by the Tuareg* to In Salah by extension, simply because it was controlled by maraboutic Tuatis' (Letter to the editor).

[2] He had evidently abandoned Turkish dress, which, it will be recalled, he had adopted not as a disguise but in order to avoid attracting attention.

In Salah

anything which you desire, ask for it, and it is yours: if any of the people trouble or annoy you, kill them and I shall answer for it.'

We remain here till the 10th Inst. in order to rest our Camels, and re-arrange out loads, after which I expect no further detention on the road, as we accompany a large Kaffle which has been for some time ready to leave this place for Tombuctoo, and has, out of compliment to the Sheikh of Ghadamis, whose arrival they expected, been waiting for him — I think it probable that some considerable time may elapse before I again have the power of giving you any notice of the operations of the Mission, as communication from Timbuctoo Northward, excepting by way of Morocco, is infrequent. I shall however do my utmost to give His Lordship the earliest intimation possible of my arrival at that Capital.

Since my arrival here, I have only had time to take a Meridional Altitude of the Sun, & three sights for my chronometer: by the former I make my Latitude 27°. 11′ — 20″ N & Longtitude 1°.51′. 15″ E — I am not positive that my Chronometer has not altered its rate since I left Ghadamis, and shall not have it in my power to ascertain it precisely for a few days; I have therefore to request that the above Longtitude may not be considered as final, tho I have every reason to suppose it nearly correct, for by the Eclipse of the Moon on the 25th Ulto which I watched with a glass good enough for the purpose, I found the time of my watch correspondent with that of Greenwich, as nearly as cou'd be ascertained by an observation which does not amount to seconds —

Ensala is only twenty five Journies from Morocco,[1] and thirty or thirty five due north from Tinbuctoo —

---

[1] Among the Laing papers there are two scraps of paper recording in Laing's hand the route from In Salah to Fez given to him by 'a Maroccan who seems to know every thing about this country' (P.R.O., C.O. 2/20; R.S., 374(La) 99). The names differ slightly on the two slips which for convenience are here classified as A and B respectively in the following table:

	A	B	
Ensala to	Beremket	Beseemkat	7 days
,,	El Granal	El Grammal	2 ,,
,,	Ulad Ashie	Wad Ashim	1 ,,
,,	Ulad Tit	Ulad Zit	2 ,,
,,	El Hayama	El Hayana	2 ,,
,,	Fir Hir	Fir Hig	3 ,,
,,	Fez		8 ,,
			25

Professor Monod comments as follows on these two lists: 'Ces deux listes de toponymes (entre In Salah et Fez) sont tellement dissemblables qu'on peut croire les mots très déformés et puis, dans ces conditions, il ne semble guère utile (ni d'ailleurs possible) de se livrer à des recherches approfondies risquant de demeurer bien décevantes. On se demande un peu, à voir ses transcriptions, si LAING savait assez d'arabe pour reconnaître les mots,

With reference to my letter of October 26th in which I signified my intention of proceeding with only six Camels, one horse & a mule, I beg to state that I found it necessary to make a slight alteration in the arrangements by purchasing two more Camels, and by sending the horse & mule to Tripoli to be sold for the benefit of the Mission — as I advance into the country I find my expences decrease, and with the exception of a few extras which I hope to have the honor of submitting to His Lordships consideration at a future period, I think it probable that I shall little exceed the Estimate I framed in London under every disadvantage of want of information regarding Barbary —

[formal ending]
A. Gordon Laing[1]

Wilmot Horton Esq., M.P.,
Under Secretary of State.

Major A. Gordon Laing to James Bandinel:

Ensala the most East^y town of Tuat,
December 4th 1825

My dear Bandinel,

I am not yet in Timbuctoo but am gradually drawing near to it:

... My journey now begins to become interesting, and I become more satisfied as I regard my chart, and the improvements I am daily making and contemplate those I shall make, in the unknown Geography of this quarter of the globe — I shall leave this place about the 10th or 12th and shall not of course reach the great Capital before the middle or end of January but that signifies little — I shall do much more, and render my Journey much more interesting by proceeding quietly and coolly through the country, than by running a race with Captain Clapperton, whose only object seems to be to

et les sons qu'il notait: écrire une fois "Ulad" et une fois "Wad" pour le *même* mot donné par le *même* informateur est vraiment très grave. ...

'Il y a un Brinken (peut-être plutôt Bir Inken, Bir-in-Ken, etc.) dans le Tçabit à une distance d'In Salah qui pourrait "coller" pour "Beremket" (?) mais le doublet est "Beseemkat". ...

'A vrai dire, je ne crois pas qu'on puisse tirer grand chose de ces noms. Prénoms "Ulad Ashie" ("Wad Ashim"): si on devait accepter la combinaison "Wad Ashie" cela aurait un sens, mais pas forcément toponymique: "le soir, un oued", tournure fréquente dans les descriptions d' itinéraires: "tel jour, le soir, on arrivera à un oued" (donc a du bois et du pâturage ...).

' "Ulad Tit" et "Ulad Zit" = Oued Ziz? Tout est possible d'autant plus que la route In Salah–Fez passe bien par l'Oued Ziz.

'Par contre Figuig est tout à fait en dehors de la route et il n'y a guère de raisons de voir ce nom dans "Fir Hir" ou même "Fir Hig": est-ce-bien Fir d'ailleurs? "Bir" serait plus attendu. Ou alors ce serait "frig", mal compris, "un campement". ...

'Vous voyez qu'avec de si maigres bases, on ne peut pas aller bien loin.' (Letter to the editor.)

[1] P.R.O., C.O. 2/15, 1590.

forestall me in discovery — Shou'd he succeed in reaching Tombuctoo, which I doubt much, I shall have much pleasure in meeting him, and the information which we shall be able to afford each other, will be highly important, in regulating our future proceedings as to further research — It is my intention on arriving at Tombuctoo to proceed to the Westward as far as Jenné, and by encircling Jinbala[1] to ascertain precisely whether it is really an Island or not; there are also some incongruencies respecting the windings of the river at Jenné which I am desirous by personal observation to reconcile — After having satisfied myself on these points I shall return to Timbuctoo, and make such arrangements for ulterior research, and my return, as may appear to me most advisable.

Tuat is a strange isolated place in the very heart of the Great Desart; it abounds in dates of the most delicious flavor, which indeed constitute the chief part of the food of the inhabitants — It extends in a number of small towns or date plantations to the very borders of Morocco, with which country it has constant communication, and pays tribute to its Sultan —

Like in Ghadamis, every little town has its Sheikh, who is not vested with any supreme authority, but enjoys a sort [of] titulary distinction only — the people are however extremely good natured, orderly, and I may even say polite — they are affable in the extreme, and appear totally divested of any taint of Mahomedan pride — They are I understand commercial,[2] and their appearance bespeaks opulence, every man being well dressed, and the women covered with a profusion of expensive ornaments — The women are far from reserved and have a meretricious manner of conducting themselves, which considerably detracts from the numerous charms which nature has lavishly heaped upon them. Their eyes are dark & keen, and they seem to know for what purpose they were intended, their teeth beautifully white, their complexion rather darker than brunette, and their hair, as black & shining as the plumage of the sable raven — I have only time to add further that although the religion is Mahomedan, the power of the Fetish predominates as strongly as I have [piece torn out of Ms.] met it in the most pagan countries — on this subject I shall have much to say hereafter.

I have written Smith, & requested that he will interest himself about my promotion, when my arrival at Tombuctoo is known; I hope you will be kind enough to interest yourself for me, as I know that your word goes a long

---

[1] Jinbala is a district of Massina lying south-west of Timbuktu, between the Issa Ber and the Bara Issa. The doubt about whether it was an island or not arose from Mungo Park's having written 'The tract of land which the two streams encircle is called Jinbala, (*Travels*, ch. xvi). The doubt was justified because the two rivers do not reunite so as to encircle Jinbala, but the gap is closed by an area of almost permanent inundation.

[2] In Salah owed its prosperity to the Arab Shorfa of Reggan. These Shorfa (singular: Shereef), were active traders and played an important part in the commercial life of the central Sahara. Early in the nineteenth century they moved north-eastwards from Reggan through Aoulef to In Salah which, in Laing's day, they were in process of transforming into an important market (Dr L. Cabot Briggs in a letter to the editor).

way at the Colonial Office — It wou'd be truly pleasing to me on emerging at the other side, to find myself confirmed. In haste I am,
                Yours sincerely,
                              A. Gordon Laing[1]
James Bandinel Esq.

Major A. Gordon Laing to R. Wilmot Horton:

                                    Ensala Dec. 6th 1825
Sir,
    ... With reference to that part of my letter dated Wadey Ramel, July 18th, which relates to the Sheikh Babané under whose protection I travel to Timbuctoo, I have also the honor to state that I have paid him the sum of Fifteen Hundred dollars, which I consider an ample reward both for his services, and disbursements, which latter have not been great, and I have therefore to assure you that His Lordship shall hear no more on this, or any other subject connected with money until the return of the Mission to England — I shall however, regularly transmit to the Colonial, as well as to the Audit Office, quarterly statements of the manner in which the funds I have in hand are appropriated, agreeably with the directions contained in your letter of the 5th July, which I had the honor to be favored with at Ghadamis, and which is the last notice I have from Downing Street,
              I have the honor to be Sir,
                Your most obedt,
                Very humble Servant,
                                    A. Gordon Laing[2]
Wilmost Horton Esq., M.P.
Under Secretary of State.

Major A. Gordon Laing to Hanmer Warrington:[3]

                                          [? 7 Dec. 1825]
My dear Consul,
    Hateeta is now going off, he has been detained by the lameness of one of his Camels, and I have been necessitated to buy him another, which I have done for thirty dollars — I gave him thirty six dollars at Ghadamis, & have paid fifty dollars for his provisions, which with considerable heavy presents that I have found it necessary to present him with, and a great draw which the Sheikh of Ghadamis has several times made upon me, have reduced the state of my *exchequer* to a rather low ebb. We have a long desart to pass without any water on the road to Timbuctoo, and I am necessitated to hire camels and [sic] forty Dollars each to carry water, and provisions for party &

---
[1] R.S., 374(La) 107.   [2] P.R.O., C.O. 2/15, 1591. Received 2 July 1826.
[3] This letter was evidently written in In Salah and probably on 7 December 1825, which was the day before Hatita left for Tripoli.

Camels, this unexpected expence with twenty dollars for every loaded Camel at the port of Timbuctoo[1] will just make me about *par*, and I shall have to find my way back as I can, for I shall not be able to raise a farthing on any teskaras — I forgot to say that it was 23 dollars I gave the Courier Salla — he owed seven to Hateeta, which he nevertheless went off without paying for —

Yours ever truly,
A. Gordon Laing[2]

Major A. Gordon Laing to Captain E. Sabine, R.A.:

Ensala December 8th 1825

Extract

... We shall not leave this place before the 10th when we accompany a large Kaffila of about a hundred Camels which has been collecting here for some time; I must confess that I am very desirous to reach this wonderful Capital [Timbuctoo], as the information which I shall be able to pick up there from persons who have come from all parts of Africa, will not only be of the utmost importance, but will materially serve to direct me in my future researches — I have met with people here, who have been to Senegal, but no one knows anything of our Colony of Sierra Leone or the Gambia. I have got an excellent route to Morocco & Fez from a well informed Moroccino, as also a route to Ghaat & Aghades from hence — The information I get here has puzzled me more than ever regarding the course of the Niger, which must be traced before the various contradictory testimonies can be reconciled — I learn that their [*sic*] are two rivers at Nuffé, one large & another small, and everyone who has been at Yaoori agrees in affirming that during the dry season, the river which runs past it, is fordable, and oftentimes nearly dry.[3]

---

[1] Kabara, on the Niger and about five miles from Timbuktu.
[2] P.R.O., C.O. 2/20.
[3] R.S., 374(La) 109. This reference to the Niger being fordable appears to be an echo of the so-called miraculous crossing of the Niger by the Fulani when fighting in Dendi, about 100 miles upstream from Yauri, in 1809. 'When we came to this river', wrote Sultan Bello, 'the river was obedient to us so that we forded it. Again we crossed it a second time, on our going and on our return the water did not pass the soles of our feet' (*Infaku'l Maisuri, apud* E. J. Arnett, *The Rise of the Sokoto Fulani* (Kano, 1929) 97). Barth describing the Niger still further upstream, between Tosaye and Gao, found the river so broad that 'it did not at all surprise me to hear from these people than in average years, during the lowest state of the river, it is fordable in several places' (v, 196). Some years earlier Capt. Hill of the Laird-Oldfield Expedition found that at a point as far down as the confluence of the Benue with the Niger the latter was so low that he could walk across it, (MacGregor Laird and R. A. K. Oldfield, *Expedition into the Interior of Africa* (London, 1837), 176).

Major A. Gordon Laing to Hanmer Warrington:

Ensala, December, 13th 1825

My dear Consul,

I have at length been able to accomplish the grand object of having a quiet hour to myself in Tuat, by nailing the door of the house in which I am quartered, and thereby excluding the multitude of curious and troublesome visitors, who have really intruded upon me hitherto without mercy — I have always looked upon *patience* as the first and greatest of virtues, and every day convinces me of the truth of my position: the man who possesses it not, has no business in Tuat, and had I not been gifted at a very early age with the blessing of reflection, I must have made a very indifferent African traveller....

....

In my last I threw out some hints respecting the Sheikh Babane, whom I did not consider, as acting up to the spirit of the agreement which he entered into with you at Tripoli, a copy on which you were kind enough to send to me at Benioleed. This circumstance has caused me a good deal of uneasiness as well as disatisfaction, for I have in consequence been under the necessity of expending much more than I had anticipated, and the perspective contemplation of a shallow Treasury in the interior of Africa is far from being an agreeable subject to meditate upon — ... suffice it for the present for me to say, that not only have all the expences of presents (with the trifling exception which I mentioned in my former letter) fallen upon me, but a good deal of the actual *subsistence* of his own [Babani's] Kaffilas. On arriving at Ghadamis, he offered to maintain my Camels &c at his own expence.... Disappointed in this expectation, he made me pay for the labour which my own Camels performed, in bringing from the desart the roots of stunted foliage which is the only firewood made use of in Ghadamis — he also saddled me with a thousand other expences, which I, by right of the contract made, had nothing to do with.

Whether he received the Thousand dollars which I paid at Tajiora I know not, or any of the merchandise which Mr. Girvenelli was to advance on account of the promised sum of Three Thousand dollars — but this I have at length found out, that he only brought *fifty* dollars with him from Tripoli, and all the goods were on Commission only —

The most unfavorable part of the transaction is however to be told, perhaps I ought to stigmatise it with the apellation of infamous — for he has given out that he receives *nothing* for the service which he is performing, and which he has been compelled to execute by His Master the Bashaw of Tripoli — an assertion which is calculated to bring myself and Government into disrepute — This discovery was only made by me the day before yesterday, when in conversation with his Son respecting the safety of the road to Tinbuctoo; I said if it is as perilous as you state it to be, why does not the

Sheikh take an escort? The young man looked at me for some time with astonishment, wondering at the assurance (I presume) with which I made the remark, & then replied seriously 'Nsara[1] you ask rather too much. My father has a heavy load upon him in taking you to Tinbuctoo; it has already cost him nearly a *hundred dollars*! — you surely cannot expect him to lay out *his* money for you, and take so much trouble, for no other reason than the fear of the Bashaw — This of course led to an explanation, when the whole secret came out — The young man almost cried with emotion [?] — Four Thousand dollars said he, and Five hundred which you have lent!. we have all behaved very ill to you, thinking you had no right to make such requests of the Sheikh — but we have been all in the dark — Were we to make a road for you to Tinbuctoo with our hands, it wou'd not be too much — Till this moment I thought my Father received no remuneration for his trouble —'

I am exactly situated with regard to disbursements, as if no agreement had been entered into with Babané, and I cannot exactly enforce it, as the Sheikh has not the means of either paying for escorts, or making presents; he has not a farthing, nor can any person imagine what has become of the money he has received — Do you think if probable that the 1000 $ have been hammered into small coin at Tripoli? and that Mr. Giovonelli has put the promise for the 3000 $ to the credit side of the Bashaw's acc^t? I think Rossini might find this out — Babané told me at Ghadamis, that His Highness had made him a present of 2,000 $, and took an oath that he spoke truth, but I have since learned that this was not in Cash, but merely a Garden in Ghadamis, which had reverted to His Highness by the death of a man without issue, & which the Sheikh valued at that sum. . . .

Babane is a quiet, placid, man, and as [word illegible] go among Arabs, a good one: he has ever watched over me with the anxious care of a Father, and if he has not adhered to his agreement, I suppose it to be because he has not the means, rather than because he has not the inclination; but we shall discuss this subject more fully on a future day.

I despatched Hateeta on the 8th with a *Mail*: he informed me before his departure, that he wou'd take the road by Ghadamis, but the people here say that he has gone round by Graat: in either case I presume he will find his way to Tripoli[2] long before this reaches you — He talked about following me to Tuat with letters, but I rather think it wou'd be a useless attempt, as I hope to be well on to Benin, before he cou'd have time to return — Indeed I so much despair of hearing again from Tripoli, that I no longer look back: my whole ideas, my thoughts, my prospects are *'forward'* for I cannot enjoy a moment of happiness till I return — Do not think I despond, or that my enthusiasm which for a while lay dormant, is in the least abated; No, I am still the African traveller, and as eager as ever for discovery, though I lament every moment

---

[1] From the Arabic *Naṣrānī*, meaning a Christian.
[2] Ghat was where he lived and he had, of course, no intention of going to Tripoli.

which my enthusiasm inclines me to devote to it — In former days I used to derive the greatest of earthly enjoyment from living alone: my thoughts took the most fascinating direction, and I had of course to number the seven months I spent in Africa, away from European society, as the happiest epoch of my life[1] — Times are changed, I am now almost afraid to trust myself with the full swing of thought, and for the first time in my life, I express a wish that I had with me a *companion de voyage* — not exactly such a one as you was desirous to procure me from Malta, one who wou'd have been constantly feeling my pulse, and forcing me to acknowledge myself sick against my will:[2] but such a companion as I shou'd have found in my friend George Warrington who I regret, did not accompany me to share the honor which *must* arise out of the accomplishment of such an undertaking. I shou'd have been proud and happy of a companion who wou'd have united with me in saying 'I have not travelled to Tinbuctoo for the sake of any other reward than that which I shall derive from the consciousness of having achieved an enterprise which will rescue my name from oblivion' —

> Tis that which bids my bosom glow
> To climb the stiff ascent of fame
> To share the praise the *just* bestow
> And give myself a deathless name —

Shou'd you have now in your possession, or hereafter receive any letters addressed to me in the interior, pray return them to the Colonial Office, whence I have desired that they may be forwarded to Sierra Leone, to which place I must request of you for the future to address to me — Continue writing to me regularly, and giving me every kind of information which you think will be *interesting to me* — You know there are many subjects to which I am indifferent, therefore do not accuse me of dictating, when I say that I shall be happy if you enlarge most upon matters relating to my Dear Emma, and the Mission upon which I am employed: In both of these subjects we are I believe equally and reciprocally interested — Do not I pray you, omit to apprise me exactly of the state of health of my dearest Emma, whose image ever occupies my thoughts, is ever before my Eyes — I feel in its full force the truly peculiar and delicate situation in which I have left her, and the bare idea is oftentimes nearly sufficient to drive me to distraction: — my only consolation arises from the consciousness that it was necessary to the happiness of us both — If it pleases God to spare us for each other, (and that it will so please Him I have implicit faith) I shall devote the remainder of my life to atone for the unhappiness I have occasioned her, in my future endeavours to render her as happy as it is possible for me to do —

---

[1] This refers to his expedition to Falaba in 1822.
[2] It will be recalled that Warrington had wanted him to travel with a doctor.

Decr 24th. I am sorry to look at the date, and to be obliged to say that I am still in Tuat; this is not exactly what we were led to expect from the words of Babane at Tripoli: I thought, and had every reason to think that my despatches from Tinbuctoo wou'd have been within a few days of your Garden house by this time: It is vain to form any calculation from the words of these people, and as I have been so often deceived, I shall not again attempt it — We are to depart from here on the 27th — the day on which I become 31 years of age, but whether we shall reach Tinbuctoo in thirty, forty, or fifty days, is still a matter of uncertainty — Shou'd Clapperton be so fortunate as to get there about the same time, I think it very likely that I shall face to the right about, and make for Marocco, or else proceed to Aghades,[1] and from thence to Ghaat and Tripoli; and in either of these cases you will most probably see me before you hear from me — Shou'd matters be otherwise ordained, & shou'd any accident interfere to prevent Clapperton's advance, which is far from being unlikely, I shall of course proceed to the Southward by the course of the river; in this latter case, I begin to be very apprehensive from the delays to which I have already been subjected, that I shall be shut in by the rains[2] before I can have time to reach the waterside, and this idea is far from being a pleasant one — I am under no apprehensions of personal risk from climate, but I dread the waste of time — If I do decide upon ulterior [?] research on my arrival at Timbuctoo, you shall have full & correct notice of my intentions from that quarter — I have written a great deal lately & have been immersed in comparisons between the ancient and modern Geography of Africa — I am sanguine enough to think that the results will be interesting, but I have not time at present to transmit them — had I one of the Secretaries which the newspapers were kind enough to attach to me, I might now afford him considerable employment[3]. . . . I intend my Map shall extend, and furnish the most accurate information by far, that has ever been acquired as yet between that Meridian [13° E] and the Atlantic — You must really excuse this writing as well as diction, as it is absolutely painful to hold the pen, the weather being so cold.

Tomorrow being Christmas day, a day which will give rise to many a fine religious sentiment in the heart of a man isolated as I am midst the bigotry of Islamism, I mean to devote it entirely to serious reflections; and as I feel conscious of the turn my thoughts will take, I shall not fail to commit them to paper. . . . To morrow then, I shall not by the arrangements I have made, write to you, and as the following day will be occupied in making preparations for departure on the 27th, I shall now take leave of you for the present

[1] In the south-central Sahara.
[2] Ahead of him was the rainy season, lasting from June to September when travelling becomes almost impossible.
[3] On 11 January 1824 Jonathan Stable wrote to Wilmot Horton that, having heard that the Government was sending out Laing with two secretaries to search for the Niger, he would like to join the mission (P.R.O., C.O. 2/14).

year — wishing you the usual compliments of the season, and praying, that it may please God to spare Mrs. Warrington & yourself to witness many & happy returns —..

Ever yours sincerely,
A. Gordon Laing

N.B. The result of my future or rather my after observations at Ensala, give as follows

$$27° — 11' — 35'' \text{ N. L}$$
$$— 17 — 30 \text{ E L}$$
$$20 — 00 — 00 \text{ Westly variation}$$

Which is final —[1]

Hanmer Warrington Esq.,
Consul General.

Major A. Gordon Laing to Wilmot Horton:

Ensala Dec. 25th 1825

Sir,

Having been rather disappointed in the calculation which I made on my arrival at this place, of leaving it in the course of five or six days, I have the honor again to address you previous to my departure (which will take place (deo volente) on the 30th Inst.) in order to make you acquainted with the causes which have operated towards my detention —

The line of route from Ensala to Temesow,[2] (a well twenty days North of Tinbuctoo, and situated on the borders of the Desart of Azoad) forms as nearly as is possible to determine, the boundary of division between the Hookar (Ahaggar) tribe of the Tuaric and the Ulad D'leim,[3] an extensive Arab tribe whose whole life is devoted to hunting, rapine, and war, and who from their constant vigilance and success in the capture of Kaffilas, are the terror of those, whom the desire of gain induces to cross the Desart of Sāhără: the only check upon these Marauders are the Hookar, with whom they are engaged in constant and bloody wars, and was it not for this check, which they now and then smart under, any attempt to reach Tinbuctoo from this quarter wou'd be at once vain & foolhardy. As it is, all recent efforts at

[1] P.R.O., C.O. 2/20. Received 29 March 1826.

[2] Ti-m-Missao or Timissao is about 600 miles north-east of Timbuktu and to the east of the customary route from In Salah to Timbuktu. The latter runs through Wallen (Ouallen), and across the Tanezruft to Amrénnan, Mabruk and Bu Djébéha. Timissao is about 170 miles east of Amrénnan. The reason for this proposed detour, skirting, but not wholly avoiding, the Tanezruft, may have been political or geographical — unrest or lack of water.

[3] The Ulad Delim, originally a Berber or Moorish tribe, rose to political importance in the eighteenth century by when they were 'one of the most fully Arabized of all the Moorish tribes' (L. Cabot Briggs, *The Living Races of the Sahara* (Cambridge, Mass., 1958), 121–3).

communication with that capital have been attended with failure and disaster the consequence of which has been a suspension of intercourse for nearly a year —

About the month of April last, a rich Kaffila of 150 Camels journeying from hence towards Tinbuctoo was captured by the Ulad D'leim at the well of Temesow, and about a month afterwards a battle took place between the Marauders and the Tuaric, in which the latter proved victorious, slaying sixty five of the Enemy —

Immediately after this event, a party of Ghadamis merchants who had been pent up in Tuat for some time, ventured to set off, thinking to find the road deserted by the Ulad D'leim after such a discomforture: in a few days however they were compelled to retrace their steps in consequence of some very unfavorable reports, and having been apprised on their return of the intended Journey of the Sheikh who is my guide, they did not again care to make another attempt being desirous to take advantage of his advice and experience —

There were some other traders of a different nation, also bound for Tinbuctoo, who returned to Tuat with the Ghadamis Kaffila, intending to await the arrival of the Sheikh, but who, being tired of the delay, at length departed to make the attempt single handed about ten days before our arrival — Several of these unfortunate people returned here on the 16th Inst. desperately wounded, having lost their Kaffila, which was attacked and captured by the Ulad D'leim on the 6th of the Month, who killed several of the party in the act of defending their property —

The Hookar having got intimation of this event, collected together in some force, and pursuing the plunderers, came up with them four or five days after the taking of the Kaffila, when a battle ensued, which has been decisive in the signal defeat of the Ulad D'leim — and as it is now presumed they will not for some time attempt to return to the molestation of the traders, the road has been pronounced open, and secure —

These are the occurences which have impeded my departure from Tuat, and although I have to regret that by such detention the great and ultimate object of my Mission is for a while deteriorated, yet I have to acknowledge myself in a measure repaid, in the information which I have been enabled to glean regarding the Inhabitants of the Sāhără, and their position — My Chart now exhibits the boundaries of Tuat; also those of the separate tribes of the Tuaric, routes from Ensala to Tafilat[1] and Fighig[2] on the borders of Morocco,

---

[1] Tafilelt or Tafilalet, lying about 300 miles north west of In Salah and 175 miles south of Fez is a group of well-watered and fertile oases of which the capital used to be Sijilmassa. In the middle ages, and for long after, this ancient desert market was the northern terminus of the Taghaza-Timbuktu road across the Sahara. After the destruction of Sijilmassa, at the end of the eighteenth century, much of its trade went to In Salah, with which it had long been connected by a caravan road which followed the Wadi Saura.

[2] Figuig is a group of villages lying about 325 miles north of In Salah which Mulay Sliman of Morocco (1792–1822) had seized in 1806, but over which neither he nor his successors succeeded in establishing administrative control.

as also to Ghaat and Aghades; but it will be quite beyond my power to forward either chart or detailed Journal till my arrival in Tinbuctoo, where I shall devote some time to the arrangements of the matter now in my possession: here it is quite impossible, for since the day of my arrival to date, I have not been able to procure for myself a quiet hour, so constantly have I been exposed to the visits of the curious, the importunate, and the sick, to relieve the latter of whom I have much pleasure in saying that my efforts have been attended with considerable success.

As it is my intention to close this letter today, and as I think it by no means beyond the reach of possibility that some accident may yet interfere to prevent my intended departure on the 30th Inst, I shall mark on the envelope the precise date of our quitting the town, that you may have an idea of the time of my arrival in Tinbuctoo, by adding to it thirty five days — I shall also send a short notice of the safety of the Mission by the return of a Mrābot, who accompanies us as far as Temesow, by which time we shall have passed beyond the reach of apprehension from the Ulad D'leim — Shou'd Captain Clapperton be fortunate enough to reach Tinbuctoo before me, or shou'd he arrive there during the period of my stay, I shall advise with him regarding the most advantageous way of employing our future efforts for the benefit of discovery —

And now Sir, I shall most respectfully take my leave of you for the present year, and although it is not exactly customary in an Official letter, yet, situated as I am, in the midst of the bigotry of Mohamedamism, on the anniversary of a day which conferred upon us the inestimable blessing of the birth of the *Saviour of Mankind*, the Glorious Messiah, whose followers, independent of future hopes, bear in this world the stamp of civilization, and pre-eminent superiority; I cannot permit it to pass over without impressing a desire, that you will be pleased to assure His Lordship the Earl Bathurst, with how much sincerity I wish His Lordship all the compliments and many happy returns of the Season. I entertain the fullest, as well as most grateful sense of His Lordship's distinguished patronage, and I tread with pride every step of the Journey, to execute which I have the honor to be employed by His Lordship, who stands pre-eminent as the patron of African research & discovery. Long may His Lordship preside over & give stimulus to such undertakings, and may the present, as well as every future enterprise countenanced by His Lordship, be rewarded with that success which the judgement in their direction, and liberality in their equipment so justly entitle them to, and is so well calculated to ensure to them —

[formal ending]

A. Gordon Laing

P.S. I now, by the result of my observations fix the position of Ensala in
$27° - 11' - 35''$ N L
$2 - 15 - 30$ E L

Mag. Variation 21°. 30′ West
Range of Thermometer 47° — 80°
Average Temp^t { 62°
{ morning 54°
Greatest difference
between Temp & Dew Point. 14°
Smallest diff betn D° & D° 3°
But ever at the highest oscillation of the mercury the atmosphere is cold, or even chilly, arising from the presence of Chloride of Soda, with which the ground is strongly impregnated: This Alkali is continually undergoing chemical changes, forming when acted upon by the rains a solution of Soda and Muriatic Acid (the latter so destructive to vegetable life that the natives cannot rear a single head of grain) and reverting during the solar heat, when the water has evaporated, to dry Chloride of Soda.[1]

Wilmot Horton Esq., M.P.,
Under Secretary of State.

Major A. Gordon Laing to Hanmer Warrington:

Dec. 26th 1825

My dear Consul — I must just add by way of a postscript to my letter of the day before yesterday[2] that I have learned from *Babané himself,* that he did not receive *one dollar* of the money sent from Tajiura, nor a single iota from Mr. Girvanelli on account of the *promised sum of 3000* $ — It is exactly as I thought. This will serve as a clue to you in arriving at the foundation of the transaction, as I shou'd rather it wou'd appear to be discovered originally from that quarter, on account of the poor Sheikh, whose head might otherwise have a strong inclination to take farewell of his shoulders — The presents he received from the Bashaw are no more than the customary annual donation which he [paper torn] receives on bringing to Tripoli the tribute which the town of Ghadamis has agreed to pay — He [the Sheikh] has also told me something about Bet el Mel [?] having advised him not to sign the agreement (a copy of which you sent me) but I cou'd not arrive at any thing certain in consequence of an interruption from some of the people of this very troublesome place. The Sheikh says that if he had got a thousand dollars only, he wou'd have been more than satisfied, and we shou'd have travelled to Timbuctoo in a very different manner from that in which we are now doing — but more of this when I learn more —

Yours ever,

A. Gordon Laing[3]

Hanmer Warrington Esq.,
Tripoli

[1] P.R.O., C.O. 2/15, 1592. Received 2 July 1826.
[2] P. 287 above. This was the continuation of his letter of 13 December.
[3] P.R.O., C.O. 2/20. Endorsed '29 M recd?'.

Major A. Gordon Laing to Captain E. Sabine, R.A.:

Ensala, January 1st 1826

My dear Sabine,

This is the first time this year that I have put pen to paper, and I have much pleasure in devoting the maiden letter to you, much as I regret my incapability to inform you that I am a foot farther on my Journey than when I last had the pleasure of addressing you — The communication between this place and Timbuctoo has for upwards of a year been suspended by the unsafe state of the road, and there are many merchants from difft. parts who have been waiting for six, seven eight and ten months, in the expectation of a favorable moment to commence their Journey; but as I have explained fully in my official to Mr. Horton[1] the causes which have operated towards my detention, it will be unnecessary to enter into a recapitulation here, as you of course now and then pay a visit to the Colonial Office to learn how matters go. About ten days ago the communication was declared open, and the road safe, in consequence of the defeat of the Ulad Dleim by the Hookar Tuaric; and the principal Marabot of Agkabte,[2] under whose direction the Kaffila is to proceed to Timbuctoo, nominated the 30th December as the day of departure; but this order which was music to my ears, has been countermanded in consequence of some rumours of further disturbances, & many of the Ghadamis Merchants seeing no hopes of reaching the intended place of their destination, are now preparing to retrace their steps to Ghadamis — I have been rather taken aback and for a day or two did not exactly know what I shou'd do, but I have at length determined upon setting out solus in four days more 'Come what will, come what may'.

I have much pleasure in acquainting you that I have collected considerable information here regarding the habits and customs of the isolated inhabitants of the Desart, as well as concerning their position, extent and power, and when you see my Map you will hardly be able to recognise the wonted blank of the Great Desart, which is all inhabited, and although the people are chiefly *Rhala*[3] or wandere[r]s, still each tribe has its prescribed boundaries — I have had only one courier from Tripoli since my departure, and I do not expect to receive any more, the road being so very unsafe; I am consequently without any late news, and my Journey appears to partake more of the nature of that of Park's or Horneman's, than that of the late travellers,[4] who had communication with Tripoli along an uninterrupted line of road, and who had the news from England as regularly as the goods [*sic*] folks at Sierra Leone — so much for the Journey to Tinbuctoo, which according to

---

[1] P. 288 above.
[2] Probably Akabli, a small oasis close to Aoulef and midway between In Salah and Reggan. Akabli has long been notable as the home of minor marabutic families of a pronounced negroid character (Dr L. Cabot Briggs in a letter to the editor).
[3] From the Arabic *riḥla*, meaning a journey.   [4] The Bornu Mission.

Mr. Barrow is *far less hazardous than that to Burnoo* — This however is a matter of little moment to me; I have made my mind up to it, and I shall look forward with an anticipation of pleasure to the period of my emerging in the Gulf of Guinea, when if my friends have not forgotten me, I shall enjoy an abundant treat: My health thank God, never was better than at the present moment, and I really think the Journey on the Desert has done me more good than the trip to Cheltenham: I account for it in the strong tone which my stomach has received from drinking the water from the wells, which are so strongly impregnated with Muriate of Lime Soda as to be senisible to the taste. If no accident intervenes I may reach Timbuctoo early in February, where and in its vicinity I shall remain till the beginning of May, visiting Jenne, Goorma [?][1] Hoombaru[2] and Mooshi;[3] when the Niger begins to fill I shall embark for Yaoori, where I think it likely that I shall stop the rains, in order to watch the rise and fall of the river; about the middle of September I shall recommence my Journey, and perhaps reach the waterside[4] about Christmas, an event which will however depend upon the course which the river takes — When you see Bandinel, pray remember me to him, and offer my best respects to your Brother and the family in Portland place — I have got a Lead and line ready, and shall not fail to attend to your directions in sounding the river — If you shou'd be six or eight months after this, without hearing from or of me, pray do not give me up —

                Yours most sincerely

                              A. Gordon Laing

When Denham's work is published,[5] I wish you wou'd tell Murray to send me a copy, as well as of Lyon's[6] to Sierra Leone — The travels of Edrisé, a copy of Ptolemy and Herodotus also, if he can possibly procure them.[7]

---

[1] Gurma is an extensive district on the right bank of the Niger below Say. But Gurma is also the name by which the Songhai call the right bank of the Niger as far upstream as Lake Debo. Similarly over the same distance they call the left bank Hausa. The Songhai carried these terms with them as they moved upstream to beyond Timbuktu from their original home in Dendi which lies between Gurma and Hausa.

[2] Hombori is a mountainous district to the south of Timbuktu and west of Gurma.

[3] Mossi lies west of Gurma and south of Hombori. The Mossi people, warlike pagans who frequently figured in the troubled history of the Western Sudan, were prominent in the eunuch trade owing to their exceptional skill in castration. In 1900 the French ambassador at Constantinople was much embarrassed by the arrival there, then the principal market of the trade, of a number of Mossi eunuchs from the French Sudan (E. F. Gautier, *L'Afrique Noire Occidentale* (Paris, 1939), 139).

[4] That is, the sea.

[5] D. Denham and H. Clapperton's *Travels and Discoveries in North and Central Africa* was to be published later in the year (1826) by John Murray.

[6] F. G. Lyon's *Travels in Northern Africa* had been published in 1821 by John Murray.

[7] R.S., 374(La) 112.

Major A. Gordon Laing to James Bandinel:

Ensala January 9th 1826

My dear Bandinel,

It was not my intention to have written you again from this place, having anticipated a shorter stay, and expecting to have reserved the pleasure of further communication till my arrival at Tinbuctoo... but a day or two before the intended departure, a fresh rumour of the capture of a Kaffila bound hither from Timbuctoo, conveyed a panic into the hearts of the Merchants, who abandoned the idea of attempting the Journey for some time, and entirely upset all my plans — In this dilemma, (finding the transportation of a Kaffila quite out of the question) I proposed to the Sheikh who is my guide, to send back my heavy baggage with my interpreter and two marine attendants to Ghadamis, and placing my papers, instruments and a few dollars upon one Mohree, to mount him, Jack and myself upon other three, and thus attempt the Journey by ourselves, with as much despatch as the fleetness of our Mohree wou'd permit — The Sheikh having given his concurrence of this plan which he considered extremely feasible, agreed to set off with me on the 8th [? 6th] Inst., but we have been spared the attempt, for the Merchants having become acquainted with out determination, have plucked up courage, and this day the whole Kaffila, amounting to upwards of three hundred loaded Camels with a hundred and fifty men well armed, leaves the town of Ensala — I say — thank God — for now there are no more resting places, and if no accident occurs, I must sleep in Timbuctoo on the 9th or 10th of next month.

An extremely ridiculous report has gone abroad here that I am no less a personage than the late *Mungo Park*, the Christian who made war upon the people inhabiting the banks of the Niger, who killed several, and wounded many of the Tuaric, and although at the first blush its statement, you may feel inclined to treat it with the same levity which I did, and smile at the absurdity which cou'd for a moment favor the belief of such a report, yet when I inform you that there is a Tuaric in this place who received a Musket shot in his cheek in a rencontre with Park's Vessel, and who is ready to take his oath that I am the person who commanded it, and when you consider that the great discrepancy in point of time (I being only 31 years of age, and the expedition of Park having taken place 21 year ago) is a matter of no moment among people who do not trouble themselves with investigation, you will regret it as much as I do now, absurd & ridiculous as it may at first appear, for I cannot view without some apprehension the difficulties in which it may involve me in my attempts at research hereafter on the great artery of this unexplored continent — How imprudent, how unthinking; I may even say, how selfish was it in Park to attempt making discovery in this land, at the expense of the blood of its inhabitants, and to the exclusion of all after communication: how unjustified was such conduct! What answer am I to make to the question which will be often put to me? — What right had you, or if it was not you, What right had your countryman to fire upon and kill our people?[1] I fear I shall be involved in much trouble after leaving Tinbuctoo, and I begin to wish that I had nobody with me except my servant Jack, as I shou'd have then less to think of — My two sailors, although superior to the general run of the class to which they belong, are nevertheless exceedingly thoughtless and give me much unnecessary trouble in watching them, for heedless of the dangers which attend such doings in these countries, they will run after the *ladies*, and entail annoyance and inconvenience upon both themselves and me — The only use I intended to make of them was upon the river, but as I now am of opinion that it wou'd be unsafe and imprudent to follow the footsteps of Park, (I mean in a canoe of my own) they cease to be of service to me, and ceasing to be so, become rather a load upon my shoulders — You must not augur any thing unfavorable from this or think that I am in the least affected by the matter which I have related, as the only difference which it makes upon me is a stronger adherence to caution than formerly. I am perfectly assured of success, if it pleases God to spare my life — My health is good, my knowledge of the country & people has been bought by experience, and I feel satisfied (although I may flatter myself in making the assertion) that there is not at present a man being, who is better calculated for the service upon which I am employed — God bless you,

Your's ever truly

A. Gordon Laing

I hope nothing appears regarding me in the Newspapers, excepting such notices as may emanate from Downing St — I am exceedingly cautious, as I write particulars to nobody except Smith, Sabine and yourself, to my nearest relations even, my motions are quite unknown — Remembrance to Byng & Bidwell.[2]

[1] Unfortunately Mungo Park fully merited Laing's indictment.
[2] R.S., 374(La) 113.

CHAPTER VIII

THE FIRST ATTACK

Major A. Gordon Laing to Wilmot Horton:

Desart of Tenezerof[1] [Tanezruft]
January 26th 1826
Lat. 23° — 56 N — Long 2° — 40E —

Sir,

I take advantage of the return of a Tuaric to Ensala, to inform you that the Mission is now within twenty Journies of Tinbuctoo, and beyond the reach of danger from the causes mentioned in my letter of the 25th Ulto.[2] We are now in the Latitude of 23°N and proceeding at the rate of twenty miles per day, over a desart of sand as flat as a bowling green, and as destitute of verdure as Melville Island[3] in the depth of winter; It is about a hundred and fifty miles in breadth, and extends in length from the shores of the Atlantic to the town of Akgades.

The Ulad D'leim were on the look out for us, and at one time we received intimation by means of a Courier mounted on a fleet Mohrie, of their being so near to us, as to excite considerable apprehension on our part, so much so indeed, that I had much difficulty in prevailing upon the Ghadamis Merchants to proceed, and nothing short of my determination to do so alone, prevented the return of the Kaffila to Tuat.

During four days that we were in a constant state of alarm, expecting every moment to fall in with the much dreaded Ulad D'leim, every accacia tree in the distance being magnified or rather metamorphosed by the apprehensive Merchants into troops of armed foes, receiving daily advices from Tuat of the perilous state of the road, my situation was not the most enviable, exposed as I was to the animadversions of the whole Kaffila, for subjecting them and their property to such hazard, when by a little patience in waiting at Tuat, till the road became good, they might all have gone in safety; at length however, meeting by good fortune with a party of friendly Tuaric, who afforded us their protection, Tinbūctoo began to appear within our reach, the Merchant began to calculate his gains, and apprehension having entirely subsided animadversion gave place to a profusion of thanks and benedictions —

[1] For a very valuable account of this district, lying between Tuat and Timbuktu, see Th. Monod, 'Contribution à la connaissance géographique du Tanezrouft', *La Géographie*, LIV (1930) 154–76.

[2] P. 288 above.

[3] Melville Island, northern Canada, is in the Arctic Circle. Its most northerly promontory is called Sabine Peninsula, after Laing's friend Edward Sabine.

I have little time at present to say more, than that my prospects are bright, and expectations sanguine: I do not calculate upon the most trifling *future* difficulty between me & my return to England. On arriving at Tinbuctoo, I shall do my utmost to transmit to His Lordship the whole information which I have acquired in my present Journey, and I am willing to persuade myself that it may be found interesting —

     I have the honor to be, Sir,
      With the highest respects,
       Your Most obedient,
       Very Humble Servant
           A. Gordon Laing

Wilmot Horton Esq., M.P.,
Under Secty of State.

P.S. Jany 27th — I had just finished the above when two Hookgar [Ahaggar] Tuaric arrived at our encampment with accounts that a party of their tribe had fallen in with the Ghazi[1] of the Ulad D'leim yesterday, at a well about thirty miles West from us, & engaged them with advantage, killing several, and taking from them a hundred and sixty two Maheries.

This intelligence is extremely satisfactory, but the Ghadamis Merchants are much afraid that the victors, whose arrival we are compelled to await, will make exhorbitant demands upon them for the service performed —

The weather is now becoming pleasantly mild, the thermometer at Noon averaging 80° Farenheit — to day it stands 85° — Dew Pt. 60°, with a strong breeze from the East.[2]

The fears of Ghadamsi merchants that no good would come of the arrival of the triumphant Ahaggar proved justified. Two months after the last letter was written, Warrington reported to the Colonial Office that a disturbing rumour had reached him.

Hanmer Warrington to R. W. Hay:

           Tripoli 29th March 1826

Sir,
 I have the honor to Inform you that I have received Major Laings Dispatches from Tuat, up to the 27th December,[3] & the following day He was to proceed to Tombuctoo ....
... Hateeta left Him at Tuat, & is now in Godamis. He writes me saying

---

[1] In Arabic *ghāzi* means a Moslem fanatic.   [2] P.R.O., C.O. 2/15, 3020.
[3] So far as we know Laing's last letter from In Salah (Tuat) was dated 26 December. It reached Warrington on 29 March, the date of this letter. No mention was made in that letter of when he expected to leave, but in his letter of 25 December he had twice stated that he intended to leave on 30 December. So either Warrington was mistaken in saying he left on the 27th or he had received a letter from Laing dated 27 December which has not survived.

that there is a *Report* in circulation that the Koffle was attacked by a Band of Robbers on entering the Territory of Tombuctoo — The Bashaw & Hassuna D'Ghies have each received a Letter from Godames mentioning that such a Rumour does exist, & that it comes from Gratt from Hateetas Brother, but no accounts have arrived from Tuat. Now as Tuat is in 27 odd N.L. & about 2 E Lon^{de} the distance to, and the angle by Gratt, precludes the possibility & certainly the probability of the News being true — It is not believed at Godames, It is not believed here, as His Highness assures me if such a circumstance had taken place, & if it had been of serious result, He must have had a Courier with all particulars, & that the Report was either circulated by Hateetas Family to prevent His coming down to Tripoli or from the jealous Intrigue to bring Hateeta into disrepute...... There is certainly a defective Propensity in Human nature to circulate bad news, I therefore beg you will not give any Credit to this Report, should you hear of it by the medium of the News Papers or by any other Channel.

[formal ending]

Hanmer Warrington

R. W. Hay Esq.,
Under Secretary of State,
Colonial Office.

P.S. Laing was reinforced by a very large extra Koffle at Tuat. Be pleased to allow the accompanying Letters to be sent Sierra Leone.[1]

Anxious months passed without Warrington being able to obtain either confirmation or denial of the rumour. At the end of July, however, he had further rumours to report to Downing Street. 'From an Ostrich Hunter who arrived in 9 days from Godames', he wrote to Hay on 29 July, 'I am informed that the Despatches had arrived long since that Laing was well at Tombuctoo & was about to proceed to Youry.' Disturbed at the dispatches from Laing being held up so unaccountably, and at the continued absence of any reliable information about him, he sought an audience of the Bashaw. 'Under all these circumstances', continued his letter, '& dreading some foul & Underhand work, I had an Audience. His Highness told me that He had ordered His Minister to Inform me the Contents of a Letter He had received from Godames this Morning, the substance of which was that a fresh Report was in circulation, that two of the Black Servants had been killed, as well as the Jew, that Babany was wounded & had died, that Laing was wounded, recovered, & had taken Asylum in a Maraboot.'[2]

Two months later, at the end of September, Emma received an

[1] P.R.O., F.O. 76/20, 1258. Received 29 May 1826.
[2] P.R.O., F.O. 76/20, 2719.

undated letter from her husband which mentioned, quite casually, 'I write with only a Thumb & Finger, having a very Severe cut on my fore Finger.'[1] In sending the extract from Emma's letter to Lord Bathurst, Warrington commented: 'It . . . affords reason to credit the Report of the Attack & it is very satisfactory to know that the wound He has received is of no consequence.'[2]

They had to wait till November before hearing what had really happened. On the 3rd of that month, at 10 at night, Laing's camel driver Mohammed (Warrington called him Hamet) arrived in Tripoli with his master's letters to Warrington of 1 and 10 July, and another from Sheikh el Muktar to the Bashaw, but none of these was half as interesting as the story that Mohammed himself had to tell. According to a deposition he made on 5 November, Laing's caravan after leaving Tuat travelled about eight hours or twenty miles a day, making forced marches when in want of water.

We were attacked [he continued] 16 days after leaving Tuat, about 3 o'clock in the morning.[3]

Five days before 20 Tuaric on Mahreis joined the Koffle & continued with them. At the time mentioned these 20 suddenly fell upon the rest of the Kaffle consisting of 45 Persons. The 20 Tuaric had Guns, Swords, spears & Daggers. They attacked Majr. Laing & his part of the Koffle & never molested Babany or any one else. They surrounded Laing's Tents & Baggage & without saying a word fired into them, one ball striking Laing when asleep in the side but with little Injury, they then rushed on the Tents cutting the canvas and cords, on which I raised myself, I received a sabre wound on my Head, which brought me to the ground. They entered Laing's Tent, & before he could arm himself He was cut down by a sword on the Thigh, He again jumped up & received one cut on the Cheek & Ear, & the other on the right arm above the wrist which broke the arm, he then fell on the Ground where he received seven cuts the last being on his neck. During this the jew servt. & Jack ran away. Roger received 1 cut, on each thigh, 1 on his shoulder, 1 on his arm & 1 on his head which killed Him. Harry received a ball which broke his Leg, on which he crawled out on hands & knees to Babany's Tent . . . As the jew run away two Persons followed & with 3 cuts killed Him, & Jack ran to a great distance but in the morng, Laing & Harry being placed on the camels to proceed they discovered Jacks Print in the

[1] P.R.O., F.O. 76/20, 3019.   [2] Ibid.
[3] Laing had left Tuat (In Salah) on 9 January (p. 294 above) so, according to Mohammed, the Ahaggar joined the caravan on the 20th and made their attack on the 25th. But we know from Laing's letter of 26/27 January that as late as the 27th the Ahaggar had not yet arrived though they were expected shortly. The attack therefore seems to have taken place early in February.

sand, which one black man followed & discovered him on a Sand Hill. . . .

We left the Wadey Ahennet where we were attacked at 8 oclock A.M. & travelled to 12 that night. . . .

The Koffle went much faster than Laing, I & Babany's Black Man. We were obliged continually to stop in consequence of Major Laing's wounds being so severe, that he could not proceed — but Babany deserted him & went on with the Koffle with Jack & Harry — at 12 we joined the Koffle. The next day we started together but as the Koffle travelled faster Babany left one to shew the way. Laing, myself, a black man (who Laing gave freedom to)[1] & Babany's servt. followed. We joined the Koffle about 8 at night Laing having suffered much by his wounds. The next day we travelled with the Koffle, & halted at sun set — the last three days saw no one — The morng. following morng. [sic] we set off & arrived at the Watering Place at 4 o'clock, where we remained 2 days. We then travelled 19 days over a Desert without anything occuring of consequence, when we arrived at Mocktar the Sheikh & Maraboot.[2] Mocktar received us very well giving us Rice a Bullock & other things & promised to forward us to any Place. The Koffle rested six days & proceeded to a place call [sic] Arwan. . . . Babany told Laing that they had better stop with Mocktar till he recovered & consequently we remained — after 20 days Laing being nearly well He proposed to proceed but Babany recommended to stay a few days for the recovery of the wound on Laing's hand, but in 4 days Babany died of a complaint described as Dysentery. When Babany died Mocktar ordered the Door to be blocked of the room containing Babany's Property & Laing's, till he sent on to Tombuctoo for Babany's Nephew who had been before with them, but not arriving in 19 days Major Laing asked Mocktar to allow him to separate & take His things which was granted but after 10 days more the Nephew arrived & found all right. The Nephew remained 27 days & then proposed to set off with Laing to Tombuctoo. Mocktar said that the Nephew might go but that Laing's Life should not be endangered again. That He would take Him in safety to Tombuctoo & bring Him back too. A violent sickness appeared which detained Laing — Mocktar died, Jack & Harry also — Young Mocktar promised to take Laing to Tombuctoo, & bring Him in safety to Tuat for 1000 $ which was agreed to Majr. Laing saying He had no money but would pay in other things which He had & was to set off in 16 days when I left. Mocktar distant from Tombuctoo on makries [sic] 5 days — Not any danger going as He does. Major Laing said he would be in Tripoli in Six months from the time I left him. . . .

Laing desired me to mention 'that on the night previous to the attack He fired at a crow passing over a Lake & Babany then told him not to reload His Gun, because there was no danger' & Babany one day before the attack

[1] Bungola.

[2] To get to Muktar's Laing must have had to cover not less than 400 miles, a truly astonishing achievement for so grievously wounded a man.

took the belts & Gun Powder from me & the other black man & gave them to the 20 Tuaric. But Laing did not tell me to mention that part, but objected at the time to Babany's giving Powder & the Belts to the 20 Tuaric'.[1]

Laing himself, with characteristic restraint, gave a far less stirring account of the ordeal he had been through.

Major A. Gordon Laing to Hanmer Warrington:[2]

Blad Sidi Mohamed[3]
May 10th 1826.

My Dear Consul,

I drop you a line only, by an uncertain conveyance, to acquaint you that I am recovering from very severe wounds far beyond any calculation that the most sanguine expectation could have formed, & that to morrow please God I leave this place for Tinbuctoo, which I hope to reach on the 18th; I have suffered much, but the detail must be reserved till another period, when I shall 'a tale unfold' of base treachery and war that will surprise you: some imputation is attachable to the old Sheikh [Babani], but as he is now no more I shall not accuse him: he died very suddenly about a Month since, and there are some here who look upon his demise as a visitation: be that as it may, he has by this time answered for all. Since the robbery committed by the Tuaric, I have been very badly off for funds: I have succeeded in getting a small advance of 270 Timbuctoo Mitkallies (which by the bye are a dollar each in value) from the Nephew of the Sheik, who is a remarkably fine young man, & who has shewn me much attention all along, but more particularly since the death of his uncle. As he will carry my dispatches from

---

[1] P.R.O., F.O. 76/20, 3172. See also 76/20, 90 for another version.

[2] For reasons the letter explains, its handwriting is not recognizable as Laing's.

[3] Bled Sidi Mohammed would be easier to locate with certainty if we knew whether it was an encampment or a village of permanent buildings. Barth (I, 570) identifies it with Hillet e Sheikh Sidi el Muktar about 130 miles north of Timbuktu, which had been the home of Sidi Mohammed's noted father, Sidi el Muktar ben Ahmed, the powerful Sheikh of the Kunta Arabs who had been master of all this part of the Sahara. Professor Monod, who has made a characteristically careful study of this question, takes a different view. 'CHEIKH SIDI MOHAMMED est enterré à Bou-el-Anouar, donc là où il a vécu.... Or, nous savons qu'il avait fondé là 'un petit village, dont on voit encore les ruines, et fait forer un puits' (MARTY, 1920, p. 69). A Bou-El-Anouar, lieu de pélerinage, sont enterrés aussi son père CHEIKH SIDI-L-MOKHTAR et 3 de ses frères, ZEYN al-ABIDIN, SIDI HAYB ALLAH et SIDI HAMOUA LAMIN. Je considère comme tout à fait possible, pour ne pas dire plus, que le 'Blad Sidi Mohammed' est Bou-el-Anouar, (que vous ne trouverez pas sur les cartes, mais mesurez entre 15 et 20 Kms N E du puits d'Aneschag qui lui est sur toutes les cartes, et dont la position est: 18°42′07″ N et 1°02′04″ W G.). (Letter to the editor.) Barth's suggested itinerary for the route Timbuktu–Bled Sidi Mohammed is unhelpful as not all the places he names can be identified and his distances are manifestly wrong (IV, 454). There appear to be no grounds for questioning the accuracy of Professor Monod's proposition.

Tinbuctoo you will have an opportunity of seeing him, when I shall recommend him to your best notice and attention — When I write from Tinbuctoo I shall detail precisely how I was betrayed & nearly murdered in my sleep,[1] in the mean time I shall acquaint you with the number and nature of my wounds, in all amounting to twenty four, eighteen of which are exceedingly severe — To begin from the top, I have five sabre cuts on the crown of the head & three on the left temple, all fractures from which much bone has come away, one on my left cheek which fractured the Jaw bone & has divided the ear, forming a very unsightly wound, one over the right temple, and a dreadful gash on the back of the neck, which slightly scratched the windpipe:[2] a musket ball in the hip, which made its way through my back, slightly grazing the back bone: five sabre cuts on my right arm & hand, three of the fingers broken, the hand cut three fourths across, and the wrist bones cut through; three cuts on the left arm, the bone of which has been broken, but is again uniting. One slight wound on the right leg, and two d⁰ with one dreadful gash on the left, to say nothing of a cut across the fingers of my left hand, now healed up. I am nevertheless, as I have already said, doing well, and hope yet to return to England with much important Geographical information. The map indeed requires much correction, and please God, I shall *yet* do much, in addition to what I have already done, towards putting it right.

So much is official, & I shall feel obliged by your sending a copy of it to Lord Bathurst, as I write with my left hand with much pain and difficulty and shall not upon that account communicate till my arrival at Tinbuctoo. Private. I have many charges of complaint against the memory of the old Sheik, all of which you shall know in due time; he has never repaid the 400 $ he borrowed from me at Benioleed; he bore no expence of any sort upon the road, and when I was laying without expectations of living, he took my best gun, sent it to Tinbuctoo & *sold* it for a hundred dollars, the original cost in England — I write to no one but you; May God bless you all: I dare not yet trust myself with my feelings, for which reason I have not attempted a line to my dearest Emma: I shall make the trial at Tinbuctoo; & in the mean time remember me with kindest love & beg her to think nothing of my misfortunes, for all will yet be well

Yours ever truly
A. Gordon Laing[3]

[1] Wadi Ahennet, where the attack took place, cannot be identified precisely, but it presumably lay in the district of Ahennet, which lies about 150 miles south of Tuat.

[2] Robert Chambers, who published most of this letter in his memoir of Laing, and who had access to Laing's letters to his family, adds a footnote to the effect that 'windpipe' 'should read Spine' (*Eminent Scotsmen*, III, 342).

[3] P.R.O., C.O. 2/20. Received 28 August 1828. Although this letter took over two years to reach Tripoli, the next two, dated 1 and 10 July 1826, were delivered on 3 November following.

The First Attack

Major A. Gordon Laing to Hanmer Warrington:

Azoad[1] July 1st, 1826

My dear Consul,

With a mind sadly depressed with sickness, sorrow, and disappointment, I lift an unwilling pen to acquaint you that I am no further on my Journey than when I last addressed you,[2] having been detained here on the most frivolous pretences, and in the most annoying manner, in fact in such a way that I have for some time past, regarded my situation as that of a Captive. About the time I last wrote you, when I was preparing (as I expected) to set off for Tinbuctoo, a dreadful malady something similar to yellow fever in its symptons, broke out in this place, & I was detained to afford assistance to the sufferers with my Medicines: Nearly half the population have been swept away by its ravages, and among others Sidi Mohtar himself, the Mrabot & Sheikh of the place; his loss I much regret, for he had taken a considerable interest in my situation, & had promised to forward me to Mooshi;[3] which I regret to say his Son neither possesses the disposition nor the power to do — While attending Sidi Moohtar, I was seized with the malady myself, and for nine days lay in a very helpless & dangerous state, without any attendance for poor Jack was taken ill at the same time, & the surviving sailor never was of much service to himself nor to any body else; my fever yielded at length to the effects of blistering & calomel, but poor Jack's proved fatal, and he breathed his last on the 21st Ulto. I cou'd have ill spared him at any time, but never less so than at the present, and I shall long have to acknowledge, that to 'take him all in all I ne'er shall look upon his like again' — On the 25th the Sailor was taken ill, & died on the 28th, so that I am now the only surviving member of the Mission and my situation far from being agreeable.

I have now obtained permission to proceed to Timbuctoo, but it is at the expence of every thing I have got, but I had no alternative, and I consented because I am well aware that if I do not visit it, the World will ever remain in ignorance of the place, as I make no vain glorious assertion when I say, that it will never be visited by Christian man after me. — With Timbuctoo my research must for the present cease, as I have no funds to carry me further: it is therefore my intention, as soon as I possess myself of such information as I desire, to mount a fleet Mahrie & return to Tripoli: I hope Clapperton has succeeded in settling the point of the Niger's termination, if not, I know how it may be done & I shall have no objection to undertake it, from a very

---

[1] Azoad, or Azawad is a district lying about a hundred miles north of Timbuktu and south of Arawan.

[2] The letter to which Laing refers is missing, but he may still have been at Bled Sidi Mohammed. See p. 307 below.

[3] Possibly Mossi, south of the Niger.

different quarter & on a very different scale — but I have not time to say more at present as it is now getting dark, & I did not get intimation of the Kaffila leaving this to morrow early, till a late hour this afternoon — I shall be in Ghadamis please God, early in Nov. when I expect to be greeted by a Courier from Tripoli — send me plenty of news — papers, a little tea & Sugar, & some sort of a tin tea pot; also half a dozen pair of stockings & about four hundred dollars, for I am now without a stiver, and shall be obliged to get credit in Tuat — Communicate the above to my Lord Bathurst: I shou'd like to have written to His Lordship, if the Goths [?] had given my proper notice — I have hardly day light enough to say God bless you all —

Your's ever,
A. Gordon Laing[1]

Major A. Gordon Laing to Hanmer Warrington:

Azoad, July 10 1826

My dear Consul,

The sudden departure of the bearer of this, my only remaining follower from Tripoli,[2] leaves me as much in the lurch with regard to time as when I wrote you on the 1st Inst, allowing me in fact little more than to state the circumstances under which he departs — I never desire to speak ill of any man, much less of one who has received a wound in my service, and shall therefore just say that the bearer followed my Camels from Tripoli to Azoad without my having reason either to commend or find fault with him materially: for the quantity of sleep which he could endure, & for laziness he has been most remarkable, and had it not been for two men whom I hired at Ghadamis (one of them worth his weight in Gold) I might have been obliged to load my Camels myself for all that he cared — So much for character, now for the circumstances under which he leaves —

Soon after my arrival here, he evinced a very strong desire to go to Tripoli as Courier for me, in order as he said to give you all the proper news respecting me, as I was unable from the mangled state of my arms to do it myself. Now as I thought this a very desirable arrangement, as well as a *spirited* offer on his part, I at once agreed, and applied to Sidi Mohamed at the *bearers request* to furnish him with a good man who might steer him clear of the Tuaric as far as Tuat, but Sidi Mohamed refused saying that he was desirous I should see Tinbuctoo before I communicated with Tripoli — To make a long story short, I soon discovered that the offer of the bearer originated in selfishness and fear, and not with the most distant view of serving me, for he dreaded the Journey from hence to Tinbuctoo, which is said to be pregnant with danger, and Mahomed never famed for the courage of the Lion [?], had

---

[1] P.R.O., C.O. 2/20. Received 3 November 1826.
[2] Mohammed, one of Laing's camel drivers, and the Hamet of the Anonymous Report.

no desire to be taken for a christian a second time. The day on which the Kaffila by which I last wrote you left, when I was in a very weak state, having barely succeeded in overcoming the severe fever by which I had been assailed, while as yet the corpses of my poor Jack & the sailor were hardly cold, the bearer unmindful of all laws of humanity, came to me and said he wished to go to Tuat along with the Kaffila — You very naturally conceive the proposal staggered me, and you may as naturally suppose that I refused, but on reflecting next day my usual way of thinking recurred, and despising the services of any man who gives them unwillingly, I told him he might go by the first opportunity that offered, which has most unexpectedly turned up to day, one of the late Sheik's sons going suddenly to Tuat to endeavour to make some pacific arrangements with the Tuaric for the passage of Kaffilas — I blame no man for taking care of his carcase, so in God's name let him go — Notwithstanding all I have said he is a very safe man to travel with, and if he does little good, he wou'd not do any harm in a hundred years, for he is innocence itself, therefore I do not wish you to find any fault with him, tho' I have considered it necessary to put you in possession of the above facts — I wish him to be paid up to the 24th of this month at the rate of 10 $ p. month, which sum I promised him after he received the wound from the Tuaric — he has received from me since we left Tripoli in all fifty two dollars, which with the advance made him in Tripoli you will of course deduct — I have given him a Mohree, provisions &c, so that he departs like a Sultan. There has been sad work at Timbuctoo lately, the Tuaric & Foolahs fighting for the sovereignty, but it is supposed to be now nearly at an end[1] — Please God I shall leave this after the feast of the Byrom,[2] which is now only six days off — I am recovering rapidly, but am subject to dreadful pains in my head arising from the severity of my wounds — Love to my dearest Emma, whom may heaven bless — & may God bless you all — In the hopes of a speedy meeting believe me

Ever yours truly
A. Gordon Laing
signed with my right hand
Tinbuctoo Mitkallies are $\frac{1}{4}$ $ each[3] —

Major A. Gordon Laing to Hanmer Warrington:

Monday[4]

My dear Consul,

On the eve of my departure for Tinbuctoo I drop you a single line which I hope may reach you before you settle with the Camel Driver, whose

---

[1] See p. 171 above. [2] The feast of Biram which follows the fast of Ramadan.
[3] P.R.O., C.O. 2/20. Received 3 November 1826.
[4] The date of this letter is uncertain but it was obviously written soon after the previous one, dated 10 July.

villainous conduct is really deserving of some punishment[1] — When I found the Sheikh of this place determined in appropriating to himself the property of the Mission, I put into Mahomed's hands two small bags containing each 200 $, that they might be the better concealed by being put into his basket: on the day of his hasty departure, I received from him the bags & without counting the contents, locked them in the box which contains my instruments, the key of which I carry about my person — A few days after his departure I thought proper to count the money, from having received positive proof of his having robbed me in other ways, & found that he had extracted 20 dollars from one bag & 10 from the other — I had missed one of my handsomest mounted pistols, without suspecting who cou'd have taken it, but yesterday an [?] Arab showed it to me & took his oath that he bought it from Mohamed for ten Mitkallies! I have also been shewn knives, forks, beads, snuff boxes, looking glasses without number &c — which I know to be mine, that the villian has been selling, at the time I was so ill with fever that it was presumed, expected, and hoped, that I wou'd die — I had detected him in many thefts before, but did not wish to give him quite so bad a character as he deserved. His mode is when accused, to utter Wallahis in abundance, & finish with a flood of tears, for which you must be prepared — You will be the best judge whether he ought to be punished for such conduct or not,

In haste, ever yours
A. Gordon Laing[2]

When the camel driver Mohammed set out on his return journey to Tripoli on 10 July, Laing, according to Mohammed's deposition, was still at Muktar's, or Bled Sidi Mohammed, as Laing called it. Therefore, although only Laing's letter of 10 May had been dated from there, and his later ones from Azoad (a large district in which Muktar's may well have been situated), it seems probable that Laing had remained in that one hospitable spot from the time of his arrival in April, as a grievously wounded man, until his departure some time in July. It cannot be doubted that he owed his survival to the kindly treatment he had received there from El Muktar and, on his death, from his son.

In his letter of 1 July to Warrington, Laing complained of having been detained 'on the most frivolous pretences, and in the most annoying manner, in fact in such a way that I have for some time past, regarded my situation as that of a Captive'.[3] Knowing as we do Laing's impatient

---

[1] Fortunately for Mohammed this letter did not arrive until over two years after the previous one.
[2] C.O. 2/20. Received 28 August 1828.   [3] P. 303 above.

and intolerant nature, it is not surprising to find, as we shall in the next chapter, that he was being kept back purely in his own interests.

Laing's letter dated simply 'Monday' was written on the eve of his departure for Timbuktu, and evidently fairly soon after his previous one of 10 July, the day Mohammed left him. The latter had said that his master had been due to leave for Timbuktu 16 days later, and it looks, rather surprisingly, as if he had been about right. Mohammed had also said that Muktar's was only five days by fast riding camel from Timbuktu where, we know, Laing arrived on 13 August. But Laing can hardly have been sufficiently recovered to travel at that pace. These circumstances all point to his having set out late in July, or very early August.

On this, the last, stage of his great journey he was accompanied by, or (more correctly) under the care of, Alkhadir, Babani's nephew. This man, it will be recalled, had been with Laing at the time of the attack in the Wadi Ahennet, but when his uncle and the explorer had stayed behind he had gone ahead with the rest of the caravan to Arawan and from there to Timbuktu. He had rejoined Laing when young El Muktar had summoned him back after the death of his uncle.

The following extract from a report on Laing's death which was sent to the Bashaw by a correspondent in Timbuktu a good deal later, accords with Mohammed's testimony. It was dated 21 Saffar 1244 (30 Aug. 1828), and read:

Sheik Babani ... arrived at the residence of the Sheik Mohamed Mochtar and brought with him an English Christian who was so dangerously wounded as to be on the point of death. In consequence of this the Sheik Babani remained with him two months at the Sheik Mochtar's but his, Babani's, fate came, and he died. After his death the Christian continued at the Sheik Moktar's two months more when that pious man also was translated to his Lord's Mercy. His son then succeeded him and conveyed the Christian under the care of some of his friends to the Governor of Tombattu Prince Osman Ben Ahmed.[1]

[1] R.S., 374(La) 130.

CHAPTER IX

TIMBUKTU

Laing had now reached the most critical stage of his journey, and it is small wonder that the last of his followers from Tripoli, the camel driver Mohammed, had decided to turn back. As we shall now see, Laing himself was under constant pressure to do the same.

The second half of 1826, with the Fulani of Massina about to seize the town, was no time for any stranger to visit Timbuktu, and for a Christian it was courting disaster. This was probably clear to the young Sheikh el Muktar who, regardless of self-interest, was as anxious as his father had been to protect the lonely Christian who had for so long sheltered under the hospitable family roofs. All efforts to persuade Laing to turn back inevitably failed, although he was probably still a very sick man with an excellent excuse to give in. Laing's resolution was matched by the kindness of his host, whose influence ensured for him a friendly welcome to Timbuktu and the same disinterested help and advice.[1]

Some years later, in circumstances recounted elsewhere in this volume,[2] Hassuna D'Ghies prepared for the British Prime Minister, Lord Goderich, a long report on what had happened to Laing. This report, which was compiled in the light of what information D'Ghies had been able to collect from African sources, must have been written within six years of Laing's death, that is to say when the closing events of his life were still clearly remembered, any way in broad outline, by witnesses of them.

This is what D'Ghies wrote:

Sheikh El Mouktar is not only virtuous and powerful, he is learned also and clear-sighted.... My present purpose is not to give this sort of information and I mention these facts only to show that Sheikh El Mouktar is, from his exhalted station, his understanding, and his honour, the more likely to ascertain and correctly to declare the truth.

---

[1] An outstanding characteristic of the Sudanese, to which every explorer of Western Africa paid tribute — from Ibn Battuta in the fourteenth century to Park and Barth in the nineteenth — was their hospitality. It was their extraordinary kindliness to strangers that particularly distinguished them from the cold and brutal desert tribes. But, as the El Muktar family had shown to Laing, even among the latter there were exceptions, but they were very rare.

[2] P. 338 below.

The father of the present Sheikh, not only received the travellers with kindness, but entertained them with hospitality for several months. There it was that Babany, the conductor of the expedition, died of his wounds.[1]

When by the care bestowed upon him, Major Laing recovered from those he had received, and pressed his departure for Timbuctoo, the present Shaik, who had now succeeded by the death of his father to his station, endeavoured to dissuade him from his design, representing to him the danger incurred by an European, from the bigotry of the tribes, the uncertain state of the country about Timbuctoo, and the fact that Timbuctoo had passed under the influence of Bello Chief of the Fellatah or Foulah [Fulani].[2] Seeing, however, that his guest was determined to depart, he sent him to Timbuctoo with a large escort, commanded by one of his own relations.

The letter of Hamed Labou[3] seems already to have arrived there. Shortly afterwards, nevertheless, from respect to Shaik El Mouktar, the traveller was kindly received at Timbuctoo by the principal people of that place.

Major Laing appears to have remained at Timbuctoo several weeks. Of his proceedings there I have little other knowledge than what is derived from the document brought to Tripoli by Al Khadir,[4] and afterwards by Mahommed El Fezzany.[5] He was in want of money and endeavoured to procure it from the persons with whom he had become acquainted. He did not at first meet with any success, but upon producing my father's letter of credit ... the same persons ... advanced the money. One other fact I have heard, viz. that all these persons being notables of Timbuctoo, united with Al Khadir, in the endeavour to dissuade Major Laing from travelling any other road than that by which he had come. It was represented to him that as he had come to Timbuctoo and found an asylum there through the protection of the Shaik El Mouktar, the most prudent course was to depend upon the same protection for his return, that all others were full of peril.[6]

René Caillié, who arrived in Timbuktu in April 1828, naturally enquired about Gordon Laing, but travelling as a Moslem and fearful of his disguise being discovered, he was unable to make exhaustive enquiries for fear of arousing suspicion of his too being a Christian. He

[1] Laing, on the other hand, said he died of the epidemic which resembled yellow fever (p. 303 above).
[2] Sultan Mohammed Bello of Sokoto.
[3] Hamed Labou, or, as he was more usually called, Hamadu Lobbo was now dead and had been succeeded by his more famous son Seku Hamadu, the disciple of Usuman dan Fodio of Sokoto. The reference here is clearly to Seku Hamadu. His letter follows.
[4] Babani's nephew. See p. 313n. 1 below.
[5] Mohammed el Fezzani had been a servant of the explorer John Tyrwhitt. He had been told about Laing's death when he was in Tuat.
[6] P.R.O., F.O. 76/33. *Papers Explanatory of the Circumstances under which Sidi Hassuna D'Ghies has been accused by the Bashaw of Tripoli of having abstracted the Papers of the late Major Laing*, 110, 111.

attributed the kindliness shown to Laing by the people of Timbuktu to the cosmopolitan character of the commercial community. 'This toleration', he wrote, 'may be accounted for by the fact, that the Moors who reside at Timbuctoo come from Tripoli, Algiers, and Morocco, and that, being in the habit of seeing Christians in their own countries, they are less liable to be offended at their worship and their manners. ... Thus it may easily be conceived that the major was free to inspect every part of the town and even to enter the mosques.'[1]

Caillié also learnt something of how Laing passed his time in Timbuktu.

> It would appear [he continued] that after he had made himself completely acquainted with Timbuctoo, he wished to see Cabra [Kabara] and the Dhioliba [the Joliba or Niger]. But had he left the city in the day time he would have incurred the greatest danger from the Tooariks, who are continually roaming about the environs of Timbuctoo, and whose attack he had too much reason to remember. He determined to set off during the night. This was wise, for though the Tooariks dared not touch him while he staid in the town, they would have wrecked [sic] their vengeance on him had they caught him beyond its limits, and murdered as well as robbed him.
>
> Taking advantage of a dark night, Major Laing mounted his horse, and, unaccompanied by a single native, reached Cabra, and even it is said, the banks of the Dhioliba without accident. On his return to Timbuctoo, he ardently wished, instead of proceeding to Europe by the desert, to travel by Jenné and Sego, ascending the Dhioliba, whence he might have reached the French factories on the Senegal. But no sooner had he communicated his plan to the Foulahs established on the borders of the Dhioliba, (a great number of whom had resorted to Timbuctoo, on hearing of the arrival of a Christian) than they all declared they would never suffer a *nasarah* to set foot in their territory, and if he made the attempt, they warned him that he would have cause to repent it.[2]

They had in fact already taken steps to ensure that Laing's progress was blocked. Almost simultaneously with his arrival in Timbuktu the following letter from Seku Hamadu, the Fulani Sheikh, was delivered to the Governor.

To the Governor Othman Ben Al Khaid Abu Bukr,[3] and those who are his brothers in office.

---

[1] René Caillié, II, 81.   [2] Caillié, II, 81, 82.
[3] This man, the sheikh of Timbuktu, was the Osman of Caillié who described him as a negro. He was probably of Arma blood because the Arma, descendants of the Moorish conquerors of Timbuktu by intermarriage with the people of the country, became the ruling aristocracy when the Moors abandoned the Sudan early in the seventeenth century.

To give you to know, that having heard that a Christian traveller desires to visit our country, but not knowing whether he is arrived or not, (at Timbuctoo) you are to endeavour to prevent his entry, if not already come, and if he is come, endeavour to send him away, and take from him all hope of returning into our dominions. For I have just received a letter from Bello Danfoda,[1] full of wholesome advice, by which I am instructed to prevent Europeans from visiting the Musulman country of Soudan. This was *caused by a letter he received from Egypt*, in which the abuses and corruptions the Christians have committed in that country are mentioned, as well as in Andalusia and other countries in former times.[2]

We are fortunate in having also what purported to be a true copy of the letter which Sheikh el Muktar wrote to the Bashaw of Tripoli about Laing's visit to Timbuktu. It translates as follows:

Then it was that he [Laing] entreated us to send him with an escort to Timbuctoo, and to trust him to his fate... then we gave him camels and confided him to one of our cousins, who accompanied him to Timbuctoo without the least disagreeable accident.

About their arrival at Timbuctoo, came the letter of Hammed Ben Mohammed Labbou al Tollany [? Fulani], who possesses and resides upon the territory of Jeuni [Jenne] and that neighbourhood, in which he advises and commands to prevent the passage of Christians who come by sea to the interior of Soudan *from* Timbuctoo and *from* all places under their dominion.

He adds that this hindrance is ordered by the Sovereign of the faithful Sultan Mohammed Bello, who gives him to understand the intention of the Christians, and says that Soudan is feeble, and that the consequences of these visits of the Christians will be mischievous, and the cause of perpetual war.

Then at the arrival of this order, the chief persons of Timbuctoo were embarrassed between obedience to the order of their new Sovereign, and the consideration they had for our recommendation. In order to reconcile the two interests, they permitted him to remain at Timbuctoo about a month, without allowing him to pass by water, until he met with the enemy of God and his prophet, Hamed Ben Abayd Ben Rachal El Barbuchy, who persuaded him that he was able to conduct him to Arawan, from thence in order to embark at Sansandyng, and thence to continue his road to the great ocean.[3]

Before setting out for Arawan Laing wrote the following letter to Warrington:

[1] Sultan Bello was a son of Usuman dan Fodio.
[2] P.R.O., F.O. 76/33, *Sidi Hassuna D'Ghies*, 113.
[3] P.R.O., F.O. 76/33, *Sidi Hassuna D'Ghies*, 112. Laing was given the choice of returning to Tuat or continuing his journey to Bambara (A.R., 20).

Major A. Gordon Laing to Hanmer Warrington:

Tinbuctoo Sept. 21st 1826

My dear Consul,

A very short epistle must serve to apprise you, as well as my dearest Emma, of my arrival at & departure from the great Capital of central Africa, the former of which events took place on the 13th Ulto, and the latter will take place (Please God) at an early hour to morrow morning. I have abandoned all thought of retracing my steps to Tripoli, & came here with an intention of proceeding to Jennè by water, but this intention has been utterly upset, and my situation in Tinbūctū rendered exceedingly unsafe by the unfriendly disposition of the Foolahs of Massina, who have this year upset the dominion of the Tuaric & made themselves patrons of Tinbūctū, & whose Sultan has expressed his hostility towards me in no unequivocal terms, in a letter which Al Kaidi Boubokar the Sheik of this town received from him a few days after my arrival — He has now got intelligence of my being in Tinbūctū & as a party of Foolahs are hourly expected Al Kaidi Bouboker, who is an excellent good man, & who trembles for my safety, has strongly urged my immediate departure, and I am sorry to say that the notice has been so short, and I have so much to do previous to going away, that this is the only communication I shall for the present be able to make. My destination is *Sego*,[1] whither I hope to arrive in fifteen days, but I regret to say that the road is a vile one and my perils are not yet at an end, but my trust is God Who has hitherto bore me up amidst the severest trials & protected me amid the numerous dangers to which I have been exposed — I have no time to give you my account of Tinbūctū, but shall briefly state that in every respect except in size (which does not exceed four miles in circumference) it has completely met my expectations — Kabra [Kabara] is only five miles distant, & is a neat town, situated on the very margin of the river — I have been busily employed during my stay, searching the records in the town,[2] which are abundant, & in acquiring information of every kind, nor is it with any common degree of satisfaction that I say, my perseverence has been amply rewarded — I am now convinced that my hypothesis concerning the termination of the Niger is correct —

May God bless you all; I shall write you fully from Sego, as also My Lord

---

[1] As Laing himself explains, he could not take the direct road to Segu because it lay through Massina, the country of his sworn enemies, the Fulani. But it is not easy to see why he should have first set out for Arawan, over 150 miles in nearly the opposite direction. He probably intended to travel from there to Walata, and thence to Segu, which would have involved a journey of 700 miles to reach a place half that distance away. There were certainly shorter routes which avoided Massina, but they were probably not much used. He may have been advised, or perhaps compelled, to make the long détour through Arawan by Othman, the sheikh of Timbuktu, because he would be more secure on that much-used road than on any other, and able to travel in company.

[2] See p. 333 below.

Bathurst, & I rather apprehend that both letters will reach you at one time, as none of the Ghadamis Merchants leave Tinbūctū for two months to come —

Again, May God bless you all, My dear Emma must excuse my writing, I have begun a hundred letters to her, but have been unable to get thro' one; she is ever uppermost in my thoughts, & I look forward with delight to the hour of our meeting, which please God, is now at no great distance. —

Your's ever truly

A. Gordon Laing

P.S. On the order of 270 Mitkallies which I gave Alhader [Alkhadir][1] he has been unable to make up 85, which he will return to you when he presents this: he is a very good young man, and has behaved well to me, a circumstance with which I hope you will acquaint the Bashaw[2] —

It was seldom that Laing left any place as soon as expected. His departure from Timbuktu was an exception, but he did not start till 3 p.m. on 22 September, accompanied by his two servants, Bungola (the negro whom he had liberated)[3] and an Arab boy. Mohamed ben Abayd either started with him or caught him up later. This man, a fanatical Sheikh of the Berabich tribe who controlled the road to Arawan, is more usually known as Ahmadu Labeida. The Sheikh of Timbuktu was said to have entrusted Laing to his care. They travelled in company with a caravan of Arabs who were probably bound for Morocco.[4] Here we can resume the story which El Muktar told to the Bashaw:

They departed from Timbuctoo together. When they reached almost halfway, this guide ordered his negroes to seize the traveller in a cowardly manner, and to put him to a cruel death.[5] . . . After this shocking action he searched his baggage. Every thing of a useless nature, as papers, letters, and books, were torn and thrown to the wind, for fear they should contain some magic, and the articles of value were retained. This is the faithful history of

---

[1] This letter and that of 10 May were brought back to Tripoli by Alkhadir (P.R.O., C.O. 2/20, A.R. 23).

[2] P.R.O., C.O. 2/20. Attached to this letter is a note in Warrington's hand reading:

'From Major Laing to Consul Warrington dated 21st September at Timbuctoo, Being the first Letter ever written from that place to any Christian.

H. Warrington.'

[3] P. 300 above.

[4] See p. 318n. 1 below. According to Mohammed M'Goram Laing had made friends with merchants from Fezz in Timbuktu.

[5] This was on 24 September.

the circumstances. He who adds to or takes from these particulars does not declare the truth.¹

It is permissible to doubt whether in fact El Muktar wrote to the Bashaw quite as the latter alleged, for it is improbable that a Moslem sheikh writing to a Moslem potentate would have so deprecated the death of a Christian.² Nevertheless, the manner of Laing's death was sufficiently confirmed in broad outline in later years to show that what little El Muktar was said to have written did not depart very far from the truth.

Two years after Laing's death Bungola got back to Tripoli where, on 1 September 1828, he was cross-questioned about the murder by Warrington who made the following record of what he said:

What is your name? — Bongela.
Were you servant to Major Laing? — Yes, and produced the following paper:

> 'Azoad July 23, 1826
> 'I promise to pay Bearer Bungola the sum of 6 Dollars per month from the 15 Dc. 1825 'till my return to Ghadames.... A Gordon Laing.'

When did you enter the service of Major Laing? —
From Tripoli, as I went with Bungola,³ Major Laing's conductor.
Were you with Major Laing at the 1st attack? —
Yes, and wounded (shewing his head).
Did you remain with Major Laing at Mocktar's? —
Yes.
Did you accompany Major Laing to Timbuctoo from Mocktar's? —
Yes.
How was Major Laing received by the natives of Timbuctoo? —
He was received well.
How long did he remain in Timbuctoo? — About two months.
Did you leave Timbuctoo with Major Laing? — Yes.
Was Major Laing obliged to leave Timbuctoo? —
Major Laing wished to go.
Who went with you? — A Koffle of Arabs.
In which direction did you go? — The sun was on my right cheek.

---

¹ P.R.O., F.O. 76/33, *Sidi Hassuna D'Ghies*, 112.
² Moreover, earlier in the letter he had called the murderer 'the enemy of God and his prophet'. At this time the Bashaw was much on the defensive because he was suspected by the British of being an accessory to the theft of Laing's papers and perhaps even to his murder. He therefore wanted to present both himself and his correspondent as being well disposed towards Christians.
³ Obviously Babani is here meant.

Timbuktu

Did you know where you were going? — To Sansanding.

Did you see any water, and did you proceed without molestation the 1st day? — We did not see water nor were we molested. We travelled from 12n to about Ashe.[1]

The same question the 2nd day? — We saw no water, were not insulted, travelled from day light untill 12 o'clock.

The same question the 3rd day? — We saw no water, passed unmolested during the day, but at night the Arabs of the country attacked and killed my Master.

Was the attack on the Koffle or only against your Master? — I do not know.

Was any one killed besides your master? — I was wounded but cannot say if any were killed.

Were you sleeping alongside your Master? — Yes.

How many wounds had your Master? — Cannot say, but all with swords, and in the morning saw the head had been cut off.

Did the person who had charge of your Master commit the murder? — Sheikh Barbush who was the person who accompanied the Reis killed him being assisted by his black servants by many cuts of sword when asleep.

What did the Sheikh then do? — He went on to his Country. An Arab took me back to Timbuctoo.

What property had your Master when he was killed? — Two camels. One carried the Provisions the other carried my Master and his Bags.

Where were your Masters papers? — I was so stunned with the wound I never thought of the papers.

Were the papers brought back to Timbuctoo? — I dont know they were in a skin or portfolio.[2]

As Bungola was the only eye-witness of Laing's death whose account has survived at first hand, great weight attaches to his evidence. At the time of his cross-examination by Warrington he was in fear of, and much under the influence of, the Bashaw and D'Ghies; therefore any evidence he gave about Laing was suspect. As the Bashaw and D'Ghies were in no way implicated in Laing's death, but knew that Warrington suspected otherwise, their only interest in what Bungola had to say was to make sure he told the truth. In these circumstances it would appear probable that he did so. But in several respects what he said was in direct conflict with other contemporary and near-contemporary accounts of what happened. Although none of these was first-hand evidence they call for a critical examination of Bungola's testimony.

[1] From the Arabic *ishā*, meaning nightfall, one of the hours of the ritual daily prayers.
[2] R.S., 374(La) 131.

Every statement he made in the course of his cross-examination which can be checked is correct except that he said Laing had spent two months in Timbuktu, a slight overstatement which cannot in fairness be held against so unsophisticated a witness to whom time meant very little.

But when in 1910 F. J. Clozel, the Lieutenant-Governor of Haut-Sénégal-Niger requested A. Bonnel de Mezières to enquire into the circumstances of Laing's death and the disappearance of his journals, a somewhat different account of his death emerged.

Bonnel de Mezières had the good fortune to find an old Berabich, eighty-two years of age, who was a nephew of Ahmadu Labeida by whom he had been brought up, and who had frequently told him the story of how he had killed Laing, and pointed out where he had done it.

According to this man, Laing went ahead of Labeida, accompanied by his two servants, following the road to Arawan. About thirty miles from Timbuktu they came to a place called Sahab,[1] where they rested in the tenuous shade of an ethel or delib tree (*Balanites aegyptiaca*).[2]

Suddenly four horsemen appeared. They proved to be Labeida, a certain Mohammed Faradji uld Abdallah, and two others. Labeida rode up to Laing and called on him to renounce his faith and turn Moslem. When he refused Labeida ordered his men to kill him. But they hesitated, 'La belle attitude du major leur en impose encore.' However, when the Sheikh insisted two of his men seized Laing's arms, and Labeida plunged his spear into the defenceless man's chest. Faradji finished him off and then cut off his head. They also killed the Arab boy.

All Laing's possessions, including his papers, were straightway burnt for fear of their alleged magical properties, the exceptions being his money which the four Berabich divided between them. Labeida's share of the booty was 'une breloque en or ... qui figure un petit coq', which in 1910 was still in the possession of a certain Mohammed uld Mohammed, a grandson of Labeida.

The two bodies were left unburied at the foot of a tree. Later in the day a passing Berabich, Brahim uld Omar uld Salah, of the Ulad Sliman, stopped and buried them where they lay.

It will be noted that there were marked differences between Bungola's testimony and what Bonnel de Mezières' investigations revealed.

---

[1] Sahab, or Es Seheb, is not shown on the 1:1,000,000 map, but it was midway between the two wells, Agonegifal and Aouessy Ould Ali, or, writes Professor Monod, 'plus exactement entre la Tayert Tui Equelhaye et l'Elb Tabegane, à environ 50 Km. au Nord de Tombouctou' (Letter to the editor).

[2] This was more probably an *atil*, *Maerua crassifolia*.

The former said the attack was at night when Bungola was sleeping beside his master and that the attackers had used swords. The latter's account, at second-hand and nearly a hundred years after the event, described an attack by day when Laing was resting under a tree, a demand that he should renounce his faith and, on his refusal, the plunging of a spear into his chest. Had Laing died in the manner described to Bonnel de Mezières how came Bungola to be wounded and the Arab boy killed? Only by their having attempted to protect their infidel master which, from Bungola's silence, clearly they did not. It would have been astonishing if they had. That Laing's two servants suffered with their master from the thrusts and slashes of the attackers' swords is consistent with a night attack, but not with a daylight one when the white man would have been singled out. Moreover, a night attack was typical of the country as Laing had found, almost at the cost of his life, in Wadi Ahennet.[1]

Bonnel de Mezières found the two skeletons buried where he had been shown; after examination by medical officers in Timbuktu, who confirmed their alleged identity, a European adult and an Arab youth, the skeletons were buried in the local European cemetery.[2]

The evidence collected by Bonnel de Mezières and the testimony of Bungola are so much at variance with other accounts of Laing's death, besides not agreeing with each other, that some have doubted whether the two skeletons exhumed from under the tree at Sahab were really those of Laing and his Arab boy, and therefore whether Sahab was in fact the scene of the crime.

Bonnel de Mezières' informant related where the murder took place to which Bungola's testimony gives only the clue that it was on the third day out from Timbuktu. Sahab was about thirty miles from Timbuktu which is not inconsistent with Laing's having reached it only on the third day for he had started late on the first day. Bungola's testimony, therefore, does not conflict with that of the assassin's nephew in this respect.[3]

---

[1] The statement of the murderer's nephew that Laing had been killed only after he had refused to turn Moslem was just the sort of gloss, in the interest of respectability and self-justification, that might be expected.

[2] A. Bonnel de Mezières, *Le Major A. Gordon Laing* (Paris, 1927), 17–25.

[3] The conflicting evidence of others cannot however be wholly ignored. Mohammed M'Goram, like Bungola, had said Laing was killed on the third day out from Timbuktu, but El Muktar had said the scene of the murder was 'halfway' to Arawan, or about ninety miles out from Timbuktu. Mohammed el Fezzani had said it was 'half a day' out from Timbuktu and had occurred at midday. Caillié was apparently five or six days out from Timbuktu and close to Arawan when he was shown where Laing had

In all these circumstances we may conclude with very little doubt, but not of a certainty, that Bungola testified truthfully. From this flows the conclusion that Laing died at Sahab late at night on 24 September 1826.[1]

been murdered. But as a Berabich sheikh pointed out in recent years to Monsieur E. J. Paris, common sense was against his being killed very far from Timbuktu, 'Pourquoi attendre d'arriver si loin pour le tuer?' asked the Sheikh, 'Mon parent voulait déjà le faire dans la ville, mais il préféra, à cause des notables, attendre sa sortie de Tombouctou. Il campait dans la plaine située non loin et au nord de l'actuel puits de Lembeidir, et eût vite fait de rattraper l'Anglais' (Professor Th. Monod in a letter to the editor).

[1] From time to time relics of Laing have been reported. Caillié, less than two years after Laing's death, wrote: 'A Moor of Tafilet, who belonged to the caravan, had for his share of the spoil a sextant, which I was informed might be found in the country. As for the Major's papers and journals, they were scattered among the inhabitants of the desert. During my stay at Gourland, a village of Tafilet, I saw a copper compass, of English manufacture. Nobody could tell me whence this instrument had come, and I concluded that it had belonged to Laing' (Caillié, II, 83). These two references to Tafilet are a strong indication that the caravan which Laing was accompanying was bound for Morocco. This is as might have been expected because, as we know from M'Goram, he had made friends with Fezz merchants in Timbuktu.

In 1880 the Austrian explorer Oskar Lenz reported that the Berabich sheikh of Arawan had a number of Laing's possessions, including 'numerous bottles of medicine, clothes and underwear, written books and 45 Spanish Duros in money' (Lenz, *Timbuktu*, 2 vols. (Leipzig, 1884), II, 93).

CHAPTER X

THE SEARCH FOR LAING

The Sahara, in spite of its vast extent and the paucity of its inhabitants, was a region in which there were few secrets. A constant source of surprise to students of Saharan history is that in this tremendous desert everyone seemed to know what everyone else was doing. This was because the trading caravans, which traversed the desert in every direction, carried with them the local gossip of all the places they visited, from the great peripheral markets down to the smallest oases in the heart of the desert. In the early nineteenth century nothing caused more gossip than the passage of a European. Always a rare and notable event in desert life, it was now becoming less unusual and this, as we have seen, was giving rise to suspicions and disturbing thoughts. Consequently the fate and activities of European explorers were subject to increased vigilance and had become even greater sources of gossip, Thus in Tripoli, on which so many caravans converged, desert gossip was a frequent source of information, albeit and inevitably very unreliable, about both Laing and Clapperton though vast distances separated the two. So it was not very long before rumours of Laing's death began to reach the ears of the anxious Warrington family.

The anxiety about Laing, to which the accounts of the attack on him in the Wadi Ahennet had naturally given rise, were rendered more acute by the lack of later news. Warrington's exaggerated ideas of the extent of the Bashaw's influence, which he believed extended at least to Timbuktu, had led him to suspect that the Bashaw either knew what was happening to Laing, and was deliberately concealing it, or, that he could quite easily find out if he wanted to. Incensed at the unbroken silence, Warrington made the chance visit of any British naval vessel to Tripoli an opportunity to put pressure on to the Bashaw. As in fact the Bashaw did not know what had happened to Laing and naval pressure consequently produced no results, Warrington began to attribute sinister reasons to his continued silence.

At last, however, at the end of March 1827 the Bashaw sent him a letter which he had received from a certain Mohammed el Washy, undated but apparently addressed from Ghadames:

To His Highness The Bashaw saluting &c:

Respecting what you have written me, regarding the Christian & desiring me to send to Inquire about Him & to obtain certain news I prepared every thing to set off, & Provision I had sent on, & we intended to start in the morning, when there arrived some People in the Eveng. from Tuat, by which I received a Letter from my Friend, mentioning that the Christian was Dead after His arrival at Tombuctoo who came with the son of Sheikh Mocktar & after their arrival the Felata took Tombuctoo, & demanded that the Christian should be sent away, otherwise they would Plunder the Town. — when the People of Tombuctoo found that the Felata were determined to have Him, they assisted Him to escape & gave Him a Man to conduct Him to Banbarra, the Felata hearing this followed Him on the road & Killed Him. This is the true news, & come from God.[1]

Warrington forwarded a copy of this letter, and of less important documents, to the Colonial Office under cover of the following letter:

Hanmer Warrington to Lord Bathurst:

My Lord,   Tripoli, 31st March 1827

I have the honor to refer your Lordship to Nos. 1 & 2 being Copies of Two Letters His Highness's Minister brought to me this morning. — In the Evening arrived my Dragoman & Jacob (Clappertons late Servant)[2] who placed in my hands Nos. 3[3] & 4 the latter being evidently meant as their justification for having quitted their Post —

It is indeed my Lord sad news, & although not confirmed to the full extent I do fear it is but too true, — but I pray to almighty God that it may prove otherwise.

The extreme bad Faith, unjustified & I may add truly treacherous conduct of this Bashaw, we may attribute the murder of as Brave an Officer, as Loyal a subject & as good a man as great Britain can Boast of. With your Lordship those are points sufficiently strong to call forth every feeling of Regret,

---

[1] P.R.O., F.O. 76/22 1315.   [2] The Bornu Mission's mess steward.

[3] Enclosure No. 3 was an undated Letter to Warrington from Hamet el Habeeb reading: 'I inform you that some People have arrived from Tuat, & in Tuat arrived People from Tombuctoo who brought Letters from the Ghadamsins in Tombuctoo, saying that the Reis [Major] had arrived there conducted by the son of Mocktar, in which place He remained some time, when a Letter came from the sultan of the Felata in the west ordering the Christian to be sent away, otherwise He would do something against them. When they heard that they sent away the Christian, accompanied with an Arab of the Brabesh to conduct Him to the city called Arwan & from there to Bambarra & after the Felata over took them & killed Him. This news came by the caravan that arrived at Tuat but in the Letters written to the People of Ghadames no mention is made of His being killed as the letters were written 6 months & 10 days since. This is the news I hear of the Reis which I am sorry for but it is a business of God.'

independent of being deprived of that Information England ought to have had without the loss of such Blood. —

To substantiate such my accusation, I commence by the unnecessary journey which the Bashsaw gave Major Laing in the first Instance to Godames —

The 3000 $ Merchandise & the 1000 $ in cash which the Bashaw purloined deprived Babany the Power of taking Major Laing in safety to Tombuctoo by hiring an Escort sufficiently strong, the avowed Purpose for which the sums were given —

For having Intercepted Laing's Dispatches in various Instances I am certain. . . .

Is it not strange that when He was compelled to fly for safety, He should have quitted His Protector enstead of retreating to the Ground on which He had so long remained in safety, altho' I apprehend not at Liberty — From His Letters to His wife we know others are missing & had He not sent His Servant[1] down we should have been deprived of all Information.

Babany not having proceeded in July last according to the solemn Promise of the Bashaw, the days were even fixed for His reaching Godames, Tuat, Mocktars, Tombuctoo & His return with Major Laing. He enlisted into our Service & stampt His engagement by receiving some Money & clothes from the British Flag. . . .

The detention of Major Laing at Mocktars must have been at the Instigation of the Bashaw, as after He knew of it, there was ample time to communicate & I am certain He did but not in the way He ought.

It appears that the numerous Dispatches that I sent never arrived at Godames & most probably the Couriers who were paid & Dispatched in various Instances, from my Office never got beyond the Castle[2] . . . so that the minister knowing the English Language has enabled this Government to know the contents of every communication to & from the perusal of the latter, I make no doubt caused the non delivery. . . .

H.M.S. Pelorus arrived to remind the Bashaw England expected good Faith & that He would take decided steps. His solemn Promises were given but no decisive steps taken. H.M.B. Cameleon came renewed & solemn Promises but nothing done.

H.M.B. Alacrity arrived, Promises again made without being respected in any shape.

After the Expense which has been incurred, after the sacrifice of such a valuable Life (for I fear it much) I cannot reconcile it with my way of thinking, that such Interesting & Scientific Labours should be subject to every Ignominious purpose of such People, who now I am confident possess those valuable Papers.

If we demand the Production or the full amount of all & every expense of

---

[1] Mohammed, the camel driver. [2] The Bashaw's palace.

the Mission we shall obtain the one or the other. Indeed I consider that as the surest & only mode of Preserving the Life of Clapperton. —

If it were intimated that should He die in any way, we shall call on the Bashaw to pay every expense because that it was on the promised good Faith of the Bashaw, & His Influence in the Interior that caused Him being sent. I have already made a Grave Remonstrance & I have reason to believe this Govt. bitterly repents.

Sheikh Buttabel says that by a Letter from Sheikh el Kanemy dated 2 months since that Clapperton was safely arrived at Kano.[1]

If my Lord I have expressed myself too freely & too warmly I crave your Lordships Indulgence

[formal ending]

H. Warrington

To. Right Honble.
The Earl Bathurst K.G.,
His Majesty's Secretary
for the Colonial Department.

P.S.
... Although I have good reason to charge this Govt. with bad Faith. Although I entertain great apprehension for the safety of Major Laing, I must also say I conceive there is less reason to believe He is murdered than we had last year.

It is now merely report conveyed by such numerous channels. From Bambarra it was brought to Tinbuctoo, transferred to another conveyed to Tuat, told another who brought it to Godames & from thence to Tripoli.

H. Warrington[2]

Hanmer Warrington to Lord Bathurst:

Tripoli 20th April, 1827

My Lord,

I have the honor to Inform your Lordship that I have had this Day an audience on the subject of Major Laing & Capt. Clapperton.

I told the Bashaw it had been always my study during my residence here to promote the most Friendly Understanding but in the present Instance the bad Faith was so obvious that I was compelled to submit every particular to the consideration of your Lordship.

I alluded to the 3000 $ merchandise altho' subsequently the Bashaw paid. Still it deprived Laing taking a strong Escort. I also reverted to the 1000 $ given for the same Purpose but not repaid.

---

[1] Clapperton had arrived in Kano in July 1826, eight months before this letter was written.
[2] P.R.O., F.O. 76/22, 1315.

I asked the Bashaw if He had reason to believe the Report. He replied He had no other reason than its being merely a verbal report.

I mentioned that as Mocktar had written Him in such friendly Terms announcing the safety of Laing, would He not have written likewise had any thing unpleasant taken place — He said He thought He certainly would. —

I informed His Highness that altho' Mocktar had treated Laing well, still He could be considered little better than a Prisoner, & from the friendly Letter I could not reconcile it in my way of thinking, such Professions with such a mode of Acting —

I mentioned the violation of His Highness's solemn Promise to send Babany's Brother in July last & with [MS. mutilated] particulars made known to your Lordship.

I accused Babany with Treachery to Laing in the former Attack in having supplied the Robbers with Powder Ball &c. In having desired Laing not to reload His Gun & Pistols the night before the Attack & above all for having remained a silent spectator during the Attack without rendering any assistance whatsoever....

I produced a Book of the address of Letters being 24 independent of Mrs. Laing & my own — most of them delivered into the hands of Mr. D'Ghies to be forwarded & He assured me they had been sent to Tinbuctoo but that I found they had not even arrived at Godames & unless they were produced with seals unbroken I could not believe otherwise than Mr. D'Ghies had opened them. I accused them of bad Faith in not having caused Laing's Dispatches to be delivered — We well knew many were missing & indeed it would be madness to suppose He had been silent so long when opportunity was offered for writing.

I noticed the solemn Promises made when the Pelorus arrived, but nothing done. — A Repetition of those Promises made when the Cameleon came, assurances the most solemn made that those Promises had been performed when the Alacrity arrived, all of which I found evasive & untrue — To these accusations His Highness found it difficult to reply, but by further Promises which I fairly told Him I could not believe till I found realised.

I said that Mr. D'Ghies being Present, I should also accuse Him of bad Faith respecting the cloth delivered to His Brother to be sent to Soudan....

I accused the Minister of bad Faith on other points & proved them. The Bashaw replied that Hassuna must indeed be a bad man & an ungrateful one, as I had saved Him from being exiled. Fear & confusion was strongly evinced by D'Ghies & anger by the Bashaw. I therefore requested His Highness not to punish Him in consideration of the respectability of His Family....

On my return to the Office Hassuna came & cried like a child & actually supplicated my Forgiveness & Protection on His Knees — I told Him it was my Religion to return good for Evil, & however shameful His conduct had been, that my Influence should be exerted in His favor, altho' I could not transact business with Him any longer — and in consequence my Vice

Consul accompanied Him to the Castle with my Intercession as before expressed.

Bethelmal has given me His word (which is better than the whole Regency) that every thing shall immediately be adopted to ascertain every particular & afford every support.

[formal ending]

H. Warrington

The Right Honble.
The Earl Bathurst, K.G.
His Majesty's Secretary of State.

P.S. 21 April. Hagge Mohamed this morng. assured me He sends to Tuat about Laing & Mourzouk about Clapperton. Hassuna had been with me soliciting that I would obtain Permission for him to learn this — I told Him that was Impossible, as if the British Govt. demanded the Production of the Letters, the Bashaw would answer that with my Intercession Hassuna had quitted the Country.

H. Warrington[1]

Hanmer Warrington to R. W. Hay:

Tripoli 24th July 1827

Sir,

I have the honor to Inform you that I communicated with His Highness that Letters had been received from Sierra Leone of the 14th April & at that date not any unfavorable accounts had arrived respecting Major Laing and as no confirmation had been received here I was sanguine in belief of the Report being unfounded —

The Bashaw replied 'I never believed it from the beginning,' which is also satisfactory but certainly a few days will clear up these unpleasant Reports as a Koffle is expected.

I have this day written the Sheikh El Kanemy, as well as Clapperton, a Native of Bornou leaving this to morrow Morning.

[formal ending]

Hanmer Warrington

R. W. Hay Esq.
Under Secretary of State
Colonial Department.
Downing Street.

28 July. The Ghadames Koffle is arrived with the first Sheikh — One and all deny the Truth of the Report — No one believes at Ghadames that any thing happened to Laing a Second time & they are positive the Report is unfounded.

[1] P.R.O., F.O. 76/22, 2306.

It originated with a Tuarick who told another Person on His leaving Ghadames to circulate the sad Story — Now this Tuarick arrived in Ghadames in the middle of Febry. consequently it is hardly possible for the news to have been conveyed the distance — Sheikh Habeeb says that the Tombuctoo Koffle must be in Ghadames now, & please God we may receive good news yet.

H. Warrington[1]

Hanmer Warrington to Lord Goderich:[2]

Tripoli 5th August 1827

My Lord,

I have the honor to refer your Lordship to No. 1 a cruel and Shameful Paragraph, misleading the Public mind, and reopening the lacerated feelings of the friends of Major Laing.

N. 2. is a Letter addressed to Sir Frederick Hankey which I have requested Him to Insert in the Malta Gazette.

If the Author invented the News he deserves to be exposed, if he really received it He has an opportunity of saying who He is, and by what Channel He gained the Information.

It was reported to me the day before yesterday that Letters had arrived, in consequence I asked His Highness and Hagge Mohamed who denied it. At nine o'clock last night I sent my son Frederick to Buthabel who immediately said a Person had arrived from Timbuctoo.

I have this Morning been actively employed & I submit No. 3 to your Lordships consideration being the substance of my Inquiries.

The Account seems to remove every Probability of the first news being true and should Laing have actually got safe to Sonsunday (Parks Sansanding) He can not be more than 400 Miles from Port St. Joseph on the Senegal the French Settlement[3] or He may go down the Gambia to Sierra Leone or to Benin, all those Roads being open to Him.

If your Lordship should receive any News of Major Laing I should esteem it a particular favor for the earliest Information as I am truly interested in His Welfare & Success,

[formal ending][4]
Hanmer Warrington

Oct. 3rd 1827   Tripoli   Encl. 1.

The Etoile contains the following account of the Death of Major Laing & His Companions.

[1] P.R.O., F.O. 76/22, 2891.

[2] Lord Goderich was now Secretary of State for War and the Colonies.

[3] St Joseph, on the Senegal a little above the confluence of the Falemé, was established by the French in 1698 as their first outpost in the Sudan.

[4] P.R.O., F.O. 76/22, 2892.

They write from Sickhara[1] Tripoli on the 5th April — Major Laing whose Tragical fate had been announced has actually fallen a victim to His Courageous Perseverance, not however untill after He had visited the famous City of Tombuctoo. The Pacha of Tripoli has communicated this Intelligence on the Authority of a Letter which His Vassal the Governor of Ghadames wrote to apprise Him of the event & which Letter reached Him in less than 15 days being conveyed by an Extraordinary Courier.

The British Travellers who were at first stated to have fallen under the weapons of the Robbers in the Territory of Touatt, had then been only wounded, so that after having escaped this first danger, through the Philanthropy of a maraboot they at length reached Tombuctoo; Shortly after their arrival in that city the Fellans which Powerful & Warlike Tribe now reign exclusively over the immense Deserts of Central Africa appeared to the number of 30,000 & Imperiously demanded the Travellers should be given up to them in order that they might put them to Death and thereby prevent the Christians from availing themselves of the Information to be gained, their means & from penetrating some day these remote Countries to enslave the People.

— Such are the Expressions of the Sheikh of Ghadamis in His Letter to the Pacha. The Prince commanding at Tombuctoo refused to give up the Strangers who he had received with benevolence & in order to with draw them from the Enmity of their Persecutors whose resentment He was at the same time unwilling to provoke — He sent them off secretly to Banmbara escorted by 15 Horsemen from His own Body Guard, but being speedily overtaken by a Party of Fellans who had rapidly pursued them on hearing of their Escape. The unfortunate Laing was mercilessly strangled with all His companions — Such was the Tragical end of the Intrepid traveller who was the first to Penetrate into the Precincts of this mysterious city the object of so much solicitude & the knowledge of which is still likely to escape the best directed Inquiries as according to all appearance there is no hope of recovering the Papers of the unfortunate Laing — Meanwhile the Fellans whose ambition is equal to their Ferocity availing themselves of Majr. Laing's arrival at Tombuctoo & the species of protection He had received there seized on that city & imposed an annual Tribute which the Inhabitants unable to offer resistance are in future to pay, for having as it is said, made themselves accomplices in the Project of Invasion meditated by the Infidels. These last accounts have been communicated by a Tripolitan Sheikh who has long resided at Tombuctoo. He declares that there exists a very Interesting History of that City which carries back its foundation to the year 510 of the Hegira A.D. 1116 & the author of which is Sede Hamet Barba a native of

---

[1] This should have read Sukkara. Sickhara, or Sukkara, was at this time the name of the residence of Baron Rousseau, the French Consul (B.B. 33).

Arawan a small Borough of the Kentis [? Kunta] Country a Considerable Colony of the Sultan[1] —

Hanmer Warrington to Sir Frederick Hankey:

Encl. 2
Tripoli 2d August. 1827

Sir,

A worthy friend & honorable Colleague told me this morning that he had been informed that His Highness's Minister was the Author of the Paragraph which appeared in the 'Etoile' respecting Major Laing.

I repaired to the Castle & His Highness took the Affidavit of the Minister stating that he was not the Author nor did he believe one word in the said Paragraph. I then put the following questions to the Bashaw who answered in his usual Frank & Manly way:

Questions	Answers
Does you Highness believe that Major Laing has fallen a Victim?	Report said so but I never believed it.
Has Your Highness's Vassal the Governor of Ghadames given any other information than is known to me which caused him or You to believe it?	I gave the original letter to You & you well know that letter was merely founded on Report.
Did the Governor of Ghadamis or any other Person write to say that fifteen horsemen were sent from Timbuctoo to accompany Laing to Bambara & that he was strangled as well as them?	That letter does not mention one word of it and no other news has been received.
Have these accounts been communicated by a Tripoli Sheikh who had long resided at Timbuctoo?	He is not a Tripoli Sheikh who wrote the Letter I gave you & I know not if he were ever at Timbuctoo.

[1] This was a fairly accurate translation of the report that had appeared in *L'Étoile* of Paris of 2 May 1827 (Appendix v). The final word 'Sultan' should have read 'Soudan,' and the concluding sentence of the original was omitted. No special significance appears to attach to these departures from the original. Shortly after the publication of this report, on 30 July 1827, François Jomard, the eminent French geographer, wrote, 'Le rapport imprimé dans *l'Étoile* est faux, et il est fâcheux que le correspondant de Tripoli ait propagé une nouvelle si affreuse pour les amis du major Laing' (*Bulletin de la Société de Géographie*, VIII (1827), 180). Jomard was in touch with London and knew that Warrington doubted the truth of the report.

Questions	Answers
Does he declare that there exists a very interesting history of that City which carried back its foundation to the year 510 of the Hejira (A.D. 1116) & the author of which is Sede Hamet Baba a native of Arawan a small Borough of the Kentis Country a considerable Colony of the Sultan?	I never heard of it in all my life, and never heard of the name except my Mameluke Hamet Baba who has been 30 years in my service but never in the interior of Africa.

The numerous applications that have been made to me to know the truth of the said Paragraph & the honorable interest and good feeling from every quarter which has been so strongly manifested induces me to lay these simple Facts before a generous Public who can & do feel for a meritorious Officer & enterprising Traveller & who ought not to be imposed on to gratify the feelings of Folly Interest or ambition.

[formal ending]

H. Warrington

The third enclosure with Warrington's letter of 5 August summarized the results of his inquiries which, although mostly a repetition of old rumours, gave slight encouragement to the fast fading hope that Laing still lived. In Timbuktu, it was reported, 'they heard of His safe arrival at Sonsunday [Sandsanding] distance from Tombuctoo 30 days by land & 20 by water.... There was in the first Instance a Report at Timbuctoo of Laing being killed, but was not believed'.[1]

Warrington, who had been keeping the Bashaw under constant pressure to obtain information about Laing, reported to Lord Goderich on 1 October that the Bashaw 'had sacredly promised that in Thirty days, He would communicate Intelligence from Laing & Clapperton, which time is merely taken to save the credit of His Highness'.[2] At the end of the month, however, there arrived in Tripoli a certain Mohammed el Fezzani from Bornu who reported that on his way he had heard that Laing had been murdered but did not believe it. El Fezzani had been in the service of the late John Tyrwhitt, and was consequently known to Warrington who had a high opinion of him. Warrington,

[1] The final paragraph read: 'Some People from Ghadames saw Clapperton safe & well with Bello at Sockatoo about 9 or 10 months since.' Clapperton had reached Sokoto in October 1826 and had died there the following April.

[2] P.R.O., F.O. 76/22, 3511.

The Search for Laing

who is seen at his best in the unremitting energy he put into his quest for Laing, and later for his papers, decided to send El Fezzani to Timbuktu to discover what had become of the lost explorer. But, reads the Anonymous Report, 'so unwilling was the Pacha to take measures himself or to allow of their being taken by others, that one of his Ministers begged Mr. Warrington to detain an English Frigate (Iris) then in the Port till Mahomed should actually have left Tripoli, being certain that obstacles would otherwise be thrown in his way — this advice was acted upon and Mahomed being supplied with money and other things by Mr. Warrington, set off in the beginning of November accompanied by some people dispatched by the Pacha'.[1]

Nine months later, before El Fezzani could be expected back from Timbuktu, Bungola, accompanied by Alkhadir, arrived in Tripoli and gave the eye-witness account of Laing's death already recorded. There could no longer be any doubt about the fate of the gallant explorer.

[1] A.R., 21, 22.

CHAPTER XI

THE MISSING JOURNALS

Laing's fate having been determined, the need was to discover what had become of his journals, a need which the return of Caillié to Toulon in October 1828 made compelling. As even many of his own countrymen doubted the humble Frenchman's claim to have reached Timbuktu there was considerable excuse for the general scepticism with which it was viewed in England. But Caillié might, after all, be proved right and he and his country reap the honour due to Laing and Great Britain. If the journals of the trained and intelligent Scot could be recovered their author's fame as a great explorer would be unassailable and his country's honour saved.

As far back as May 1826, when he was recuperating under El Muktar's care, Laing had said he intended sending his dispatches back to Tripoli from Timbuktu. These would certainly have included his journals because he had Lord Bathurst's instructions to send them back from there. Their carrier, Laing had said, would be Alkhadir, 'a remarkably fine young man'.[1] Yet, at long last, Alkhadir had arrived with Laing's letters[2] but without his journals.

This was a turning point in a quest which had been going on for some months and was to continue, with unabated wrangling between British and French, for several years. It is a long and dreary story which never reached finality and from which none of the principal characters emerged with credit. It is so tortuous and involved that it could not be fairly presented within the compass of less than a single volume, which it certainly does not merit.[3] Indeed, the less said about these shocking wrangles the better, but unfortunately they are too much part of the Laing story to be wholly ignored here. A few pages, however, will suffice to meet their modest claims on our attention.

[1] P. 313n.1 above. When El Fezzani got back to Tripoli in June 1829 he reported that Laing had asked Alkhadir and Mohammed M'Goram, to take his papers back to Tripoli (A.R. 32).
[2] These were Laing's letters of 10 May and 21 September 1826 which, together with the report on the interrogation of Bungola, were published in the January 1828 issue of *The Quarterly Review*, XXXIX, 171–3.
[3] The relative documents number many hundreds and occupy, almost to the exclusion of other matter, three large volumes in the Public Record Office. One aspect of the troubles, covering only half the period, was the subject of the Blue Book which was printed but not published, and ran into about 70,000 words.

Alkhadir denied having brought the journals with him from Timbuktu but this signified nothing. Both he and Bungola appeared to be under instructions from Hassuna D'Ghies, and to be saying no more than he had told them to say. Warrington, we read, 'did not fail to observe upon the extraordinary length of time that the letters particularly that of the 10th May had been upon the road, also that Alkhadir was the bearer of it ... and lastly his coming down without the dispatches, of which Major Laing in that letter expresses an intention of making him the bearer.... His suspicions of foul play were never lulled, and received strength from the pains taken to prevent his intercourse with Alkhadir, and the Negro,[1] both of whom were fed and cloathed by H. D'Ghies but rarely came to the British Consulate, tho' he expressed a wish to take the Negro into his service, both were examined by him and deposed to Major Laing's having papers with him, also to various particulars relating to the murder — yet nothing that could throw a light upon the fate of the papers was elicited from either'.[2]

As it was generally believed that the report of Laing's death which had been published in the *Étoile* had originated with Hassuna D'Ghies, it was inevitable that he should now be suspected of having stolen the journals, probably to serve his close friend Baron Rousseau, the French Consul. By October Warrington had become convinced that this was so, that Rousseau had the journals in his possession, and that 'they would eventually come to light if the demand for their production were persevered in'.[3]

Hanmer Warrington to R. W. Hay:

Confidential   Tripoli 28th October 1828

Sir,
   The Charge is of too Serious a Nature to bring accusation direct but Suspicion is so Strong to justify me writing you confidentially.
   You are aware of the Miserable Intrigue carried on here, and I have cause to suspect the French Consul may have purloined the Papers of Major Laing.
   I ground my suspicion on the following circumstances. About a year since Mr. Rousseau became the Editor of a Paper here termed the *African Investigator*,[4] and under the Head Tinbuctu there appeared the full particulars

---
[1] Bungola.   [2] A.R., 25–6.
[3] It will be recalled that the report published in *L'Étoile* appeared to have been dated from Rousseau's house (p. 326n. 1 above).
[4] A.R., 27.

of the Death of Major Laing,¹ which also appeared in the French Papers.

Now the Bashaw at the time solemnly assured me, that he had no reason to believe the Report, but still Mr. Rousseau was in Possession of the circumstantial fact, which has but lately come to our knowledge. A Dr. Stormont now here heard Mr. Rousseau say the other day that he was about to Publish [? a journal] on the Interior of Africa & that the first number would appear in Paris in a Month. From the nature of the Information therein given you will be able to form your opinion if any Piracy has been resorted to.

At all events it appears somewhat Indelicate and Inconsiderate Publishing on that Head at the present moment, as it must cause suspicion.

If His Majesty attaches any importance to the Papers and is pleased to demand their Production, we shall obtain them I am fully certain.

We know Mr. Rousseau a Man replete in Intrigue and what could be easier than with the connivance of the Minister to intercept the Papers.

Mr. Tyrwhitt's Servt. I sent to Tenbuctu last November & still no tidings of Him and it is probable being faithful to our Interest he may have shared the fate of Poor Laing.²

[formal ending]

H. Warrington³

In the following May Warrington reported to Hay that D'Ghies had a copy of the 'Travels of Bathoute'⁴ and that he was expecting not only a copy of the 'History of Tomboucto' but also the arrival from Tuat of its author 'Sidi Ali Baba d'Arowan'.⁵ At first he had been inclined to ridicule this, not because Ali Baba of Arawan, or more correctly Ahmed Baba perhaps the most famous scholar the Sudan has ever produced) had been dead for over 200 years, but because he did not believe that any African could be interested in the history of his own country. 'Now I will ask', his letter continued, 'is it likely that this Sidi Ali Baba should have examined the Records and written the History of Tinbūctu — Believe me a Bowl of Cuscusou⁶ is more an object of Research to any Moor than such a history.'⁷

¹ Professor Monod's kind endeavours to trace a copy of *L'Investigateur africain* have failed. According to a letter Rousseau published in the *Bulletin de la Société de Géographie*, VIII (1827), 174, the first issue had appeared in July 1827, but 'il nous a été impossible de le publier par la voie de l'impression'. It seems probable that it never was printed.

² The reference is to Mohammed el Fezzani.   ³ P.R.O., F.O. 76/23, 3263.

⁴ Ibn Battuta was born in Tangier in 1304. His visit to the Western Sudan in 1352 concluded a world tour in the course of which he had visited every known Mohammedan country.

⁵ P.R.O., F.O. 76/26, f. 25.

⁶ *Cuscus*, a common Arab dish, is a stew made of grain and vegetables, sometimes with meat added.

⁷ P.R.O., F.O. 76/26, 2006, f. 26. This is probably the first recorded reference to the famous *Tarikh es Sudan* which was a history of the Songhai people, and so covered much

But this report of a history of Timbuktu being on its way to Tripoli seemed to Warrington to have a sinister implication. Could this book, he asked himself, be the one which his imagination had persuaded him Laing had obtained in Timbuktu. He reminded Hay of how Laing had written from there: 'I have been busily employed during my stay searching the Records of the Town, which are abundant and in acquiring Information of every kind nor is it with any common degree of Satisfaction that I say my Perseverance has been amply rewarded.' Unless the Colonial Office had learnt to be surprised at nothing their Consul in Tripoli said, wrote or did, they can hardly have failed to raise their eyebrows at the conclusion he drew from Laing's simple statement about how he employed his time in Timbuktu. 'We are surely justified', was his astonishing comment, 'in believing that Laing was in possession of the History of Tenbuctu.'[1] It was a short step from this unwarranted deduction to the conclusion that whoever possessed the copy of the *Tarikh* possessed also Laing's journals. Moreover, circumstances pointed to the book being destined ultimately for Baron Rousseau.[2] Thus were the fires of controversy fed by the irresponsible conjectures of the British Consul.

Convinced that Laing's journals had reached Tripoli, and that it needed only greater pressure to induce the Bashaw to produce them,

of the history of Timbuktu. Barth, who had discovered a copy in the Hausa town of Gwandu in 1853, reported that 'according to the universal statement of the learned people of Negroland' the author was Ahmed Baba (IV, 407), here referred to as Ali Baba, and sometimes as Hamet Baba. Ahmed Baba, who died in Timbuktu in 1607, was so famous a scholar that in the Sudan they attributed to him any learned work of unknown authorship. Not till the beginning of the present century was it shown by a distinguished French scholar, M. O. Houdas, that the author was Abderrahman es Sa'di, who was born in Timbuktu in 1596. Although the Monnier Commission, which the French Government appointed to report on the British allegation that Laing's journals had been stolen by the French Consul-General, did not know that Ahmed Baba had not written the *Tarikh* it did know that he had been dead for 200 years.

[1] P.R.O., F.O. 76/26, 2006, f. 31. Professor Monod kindly put himself to much trouble in trying to establish whether any of the copies of the *Tarikh es Sudan* in the Bibliothèque Nationale in Paris could be traced to Baron Rousseau. 'En ce qui concerne la Section Orientale du Département des Manuscrits a le Bibliothèque Nationale,' he wrote, 'je me suis informé auprès du Conservateur, M.R. GUIGNARD qui m'écrit (2.4.1962): "Nous n'avons pas trouvé trace de manuscrit arabe provenant du Consul ROUSSEAU".... Mais ce n'est un nouveau mystère, qui ne concerne plus Laing. Ce qui semble certain, c'est qu'aucun manuscrit du Tarikh n'est arrivé à la Bibliothèque Nationale avant la fin du XIXº siècle. Si Rousseau en a eu un... il n'est pas à la Nationale' (letter to the editor).

[2] As indeed it was, and there was no mystery about it. As far back as the previous July the *Bulletin de la Société de Géographie* (x (1828), 41) had published the following extract from a letter from Baron Rousseau: '... j'ai enfin trouvé un assez bon exemplaire des voyages d'*Ibn Bathouta*, et... j'espère être bientôt en possession de l'histoire de Tombouctou par *Sidi Ali Baba D'Arawan*, que j'attends de Touât.'

Warrington struck his Consular flag and refused to communicate further with the Castle. That same month, June 1829, Warrington reported to Hay that he had just met a British subject who for the past five years had been in the service of the Bashaw, whom he had asked whether the *chaus* or messenger the Bashaw had promised to send to Ghadames to enquire for Laing's papers had yet left. The man had replied 'That would be useless as the Papers came down by the Man who brought the Bills,[1] were given to Hassuna and were sent to France'.[2] According to the Anonymous Report, Rousseau had confirmed this to the Dutch Consul to whom he had said, it was alleged, that he had 'sent the history of Timbuctu to France; and that every thing was already in print'.[3]

By this time Warrington had apparently reached the conclusion — as usual, without any apparent justification — that both Laing's death and the theft of his journals had been plotted in Tripoli, and the possibility of the Bashaw's implication still lay at the back of his thoughts. So he perhaps found it a little flattering to his intelligence when, on 27 July, a sheikh 'came to the British Garden, and told the Consul that "the Pacha had given orders to the Head of a Tribe of Arabs to murder Major Laing on his road from Tripoli to Ghedamis" — that "Alkhedir brought the papers down to Tripoli, and gave them to H. D'Ghies", — that "they would not let Alkhedir deliver them to the Consul" — that "he learned all this from a Relation of Alkhedir who slept in his tents when the papers were brought down" '.[4]

A few days later, on 5 August, Warrington got a letter from Dr Dickson, the English surgeon in Tripoli, telling him 'that the Pacha

[1] The bills were ones drawn by Laing on Warrington. The man who had brought them was either Alkhadir or someone he was thought to have handed them to in Ghadames for delivery in Tripoli.

[2] P.R.O., F.O. 76/26, 1969. The Anonymous Report gives the following more detailed account of this incident: 'On the 18th [June 1829] James Briasco, a British subject, commanding one of the Pacha's Vessels reported a conversation that had taken place the day before between one Rais Abdallah, another Tripoline, and himself, both of whom spake of the purloining of the Papers and their transmission to France as a matter of notoriety. Scalaro [Clerk to H. D'Ghies] joined the party and mentioned his having heard the same thing. Briasco then made it his business to enquire about the papers from other Tripolines, and found the belief of their being in France universal. . . .' According to 'one Hadje Boo Ussal, represented as a person who frequented both the Castle, and the House of H. D'Ghies' the papers were sent to France 'by means of the French Consul & H. D'Ghies, who acted with the consent and by order of the Pacha, and the Dragoman of Mr. Wood (V. Consul at Bengazi) said that "some time back he had several times seen the French Consul visiting H. D'Ghies late at night wrapped up in such a way as to disguise himself" ' (A.R., 39–40).

[3] A.R., 38. [4] A.R., 41.

had discovered that the Papers had been delivered by H. D'Ghies to the French Consul, and had sent to Ghedamis for evidence to prove it'.[1]

This was sensational news. If it were true it meant that the Bashaw had turned against Rousseau and D'Ghies, and that the way would now be open for a rapprochement between the British Consulate and the Castle. Warrington's hatred of Rousseau was far too bitter for him to allow any scruples he might otherwise have felt to prevent his embracing so new and so formidable an enemy for the French Consul. It did not take him many days to get the report confirmed.

Hanmer Warrington to R. W. Hay:

Tripoli 10th Augst. 1829

Sir,

I trust you will excuse me not writing you Officially by this opportunity as time will not allow to make up the Documents necessary to prove where the Papers of Major Laing are — Suffice it to say they were brought down last March twelve Months, sold by Hassuna D'Ghies to the French Consul for a deduction of 40 per cent on a large claim He had of say 6000 fr. agst. Hassuna.

The night before last D'Ghies was smuggled from the American Consulate on board an American Corvette[2] dressed as an Officer, & attended to the Boat by the Consul Commander & Officers at 10 o'clock at night — Mohammed D'Ghies has made a full Confession to the Bashaw,[3] & he has taken the Protection of the French Flag with his Brother Seed [?].

The People of Ghadames are here and have set matters perfectly clear as to the Papers.

D'Ghies latterly wrote to Habeeb & Hadeer[4] to escape & in consequence they are gone to Tinbuctoo.

On my honor the Documents are as clear & satisfactory as possible, and should you wish to take any steps with the French Authorities you may safely do it, as I am apprehensive Mr. Rousseau will fly to America also, as soon as he hears His Infamous Villany [sic] is detected. He has not only defrauded the English Government of the journals & manuscripts of Major Laing, but he has stole also Letters to His Wife, to me & my Family — It is really too horrid to continue.

[formal ending]

H. Warrington[5]

R. W. Hay Esq.
Under Secretary of State

[1] A.R., 43. [2] The *Fairfield*.
[3] Directly after Hassuna took flight he was denounced by his brother Mohammed. Hassuna afterwards protested that 'After my departure the accusation was supported by forcing my own Brother at the Sword's point to confess me guilty' (P.R.O., F.O. 76/33, *D'Ghies Statement*, p. 3).
[4] Alkhadir.   [5] P.R.O., F.O. 76/26.

A week later the Bashaw summoned Warrington, Van Breugel, the Dutch Consul, and Angelo Heri, the broker of the British Consulate, to an audience after which the three Europeans put their signatures to an astonishing announcement: 'We, the undersigned, declare, that when in the presence of His Highness the Bashaw, this 12th day of August, 1829, His Highness said "now I think that Hassuna D'Ghies and the French Consul were the cause of the murder of Major Laing"; and this expression was uttered in the presence of Bumais, Mufta, and several blacks.'[1]

The following day Warrington, delighted that the Bashaw should go so far as to accuse Rousseau of murder, sent a copy of the Bashaw's declaration to Hay, commenting in the covering letter that the Bashaw's 'conduct appears so open, honest and candid, that I felt hurt in having ever suspected Him, but Hassuna D'Ghies having made use of the Bashaw's name, hundreds have likewise been deceived, at all events the Infamous Fraud attaches to Messrs Hassuna & Rousseau, and allow me Sir to say, these Delinquents I suspect of having caused the Murder of that Brave Officer, ...

'Under the circumstances, His Highness having removed suspicion, the British Flag is rehoisted under a Salute of Thirty three Guns, and at the time the French Flag was struck & the Consul is about to leave.'[2]

As Warrington had expected, Baron Rousseau went to America and there passed out of the Laing story. But Warrington had yet to fire his last shot in his long-drawn battle with the French Consul.

Hanmer Warrington to the Baron Rousseau:

Sir,   Tripoli, 12 Augt. 1830
I shall not disgrace my pen by addressing such a Convicted Villain and with Infamy will I brand your name to the extremity of this World. I will however Glory in giving you satisfaction and please God sending you before a Tribunal where Treachery & falsehood will avail you nought & where you will answer for your unparallelled Iniquity.
       I am Sir,
         &c   H. Warrington
The Baron Rousseau

Warrington added the following note to the copy of this letter that he presented to the United Service Club:

The above letter was written after I heard the Baron Rousseau was no longer in an Official Situation.

[1] B.B., 7.   [2] P.R.O., F.O. 76/26, 2799.

Having deliberately withheld the last affectionate Letters from Major Laing to his Wife my Daughter (for who can suppose he neglected his promise to write)[1] as well as to me and having distroyed the same, knowing at the time of the horrid Murder, is a Fiendish Insult that no man can tamely endure.[2]

Meanwhile the British Government had taken advantage of the Bashaw's unexpected announcement to press the French to investigate the charges brought against their Consul-General and his friend D'Ghies. This led to the appointment of a commission of enquiry, under the chairmanship of Baron Monnier,[3] which very quickly — perhaps rather too quickly — reached the conclusion that the charges against Rousseau were without foundation,[4] and that it was improbable that the Laing journals had ever passed into the hands of Hassuna D'Ghies.

In France there was seemingly little doubt about the culpability of D'Ghies. In the previous September a Marseilles newspaper had published an article about the Laing papers in the course of which it commented: 'Bientôt une rumeur sourde se répandit que les papiers du *major Laing* avait été apportés à Tripoli par des gens de Ghadames, et qu'un Turc, nommé *Hassouna Dghies*, les avait mystérieusement reçus. C'est ce même Dghies que l'on a vu à Marseille affichant tant de luxe et de folies, offrant aux dames ses parfums et ses schalls, une façon d'*Usbeck* voyageur, moins son philosophie et son esprit. De Marseille il était parti pour Londres, couvert de dettes, en projetant de nouvelles, et toujours escorté de femmes et de créanciers.

'M. *Warrington* se livra pendant long-temps à de persévérants recherches et parvint enfin à saisir les fils de cette horrible mystère. Le *Pacha* ordonna, sur ses instances, qu'on amena de Ghadames les gens qui avait fait partie de l'escorte du *Major*. Le vérité allait enfin être connue, mais cette vérité était trop redoutable pour Hassouna Dghies pour qu'il osât l'attendre. Il se réfugia donc chez le consul des États-Unis, M. *Coxe*.'[5]

In England, inevitably, most people dissented from the findings of the French commission, but so did many people in France where there

---

[1] This, as Laing had told Warrington, was precisely what he had done, but it did not suit the Consul's vindictiveness to remember it. There was little to which he would not stoop to injure Rousseau.
[2] P.R.O., C.O. 2/20, United Service Club volume.
[3] Baron Monnier was an orientalist who had served his country in the Barbary States.
[4] The Duc de Laval to Lord Aberdeen, 8 February, 1830 (P.R.O., F.O. 27/421).
[5] *Le Sémaphore de Marseille*, 12 September 1829.

was little confidence in Rousseau's integrity. Neither side of the Channel was there much doubt about Hassuna D'Ghies's having stolen the Laing papers. 'Our conclusion, we must confess', wrote *The Quarterly Review*, 'is very different as regards both these persons. So far from its being improbable, we think that it is morally certain, that Hassuna D'Ghies, by fraud and perfidy, did obtain possession of the late Major Laing's papers.... But admitting Hassuna to be guilty, what object, it may be asked, could make Baron Rousseau so anxious about getting possession of Major Laing's journals? ... the ambition of publishing the contents of the said papers in his own name. It seems he had already been dabbling in oriental literature, chiefly Arabic, and has been charged, with what truth we know not, of appropriating the labours of a young man in Syria to himself.'[1]

Encouraged by the findings of the Monnier commission, D'Ghies came over to London where he presented himself to the Colonial Office as the innocent victim of the malevolent Warrington but for whose evil influence over the Bashaw he would not have had to flee his country. His hope was to discredit Warrington and persuade the British Government to use its influence to restore him to favour with the Bashaw.

After wasting a great deal of other people's time he was persuaded to put his case into writing. He then produced *A Statement to the Right Honourable Lord Goodrich* [sic] *Secretary of His Britannic Majesty for the Colonies Concerning the Expedition of the late Major Laing to Tumbuctoo and the affairs of Tripoli By the Shereef Mahommed Hassuna D'Ghies late Minister of the Pacha of Tripoli.*[2] This formidable statement, covering, with its supporting documents, 227 pages of foolscap, was a rambling indictment of Warrington, the Bashaw and *The Quarterly Review*. Had it been made public there could never have been any question of D'Ghies being able to return to his country. To none was this more apparent than to D'Ghies himself.

Lord Goderich to Lord Lansdowne:[3]

Downing Street
14 July 1832

Dear Lord Lansdowne,

I have looked over the papers from Hassuna D'Ghiez [sic] which you forwarded to me, but even from a cursory view of them, I am satisfied of the

---

[1] *The Quarterly Review*, XLII (1830), 472. [2] P.R.O., F.O. 76/33, 3224.
[3] Henry Petty-Fitzmaurice, third Marquis of Lansdowne (1780–1863), was at this time President of the Council.

utter impossibility of entering upon the question to which they relate, unless they are made official papers and placed among the records of the Office.

Unless therefore Hassuna D'Ghiez consents to this being done, I shall be under the necessity of returning the papers to him. None of the transactions to which these papers refer, occurred whilst I have held the seals of this Office, and it is quite impossible for me to form any judgment upon the facts of the case, except by comparing the statement he has now drawn up with former communications now in this Office. But at all events it is obvious that I cannot undertake to arbitrate between him and the Quarterly Review, with which I have nothing to do.

I am &c

(signed) Goderich[1]

Even in England D'Ghies did not lack supporters, and some of them were highly placed. This was probably less due to D'Ghies and the doubtful merits of his case than to Warrington's known weaknesses of character. On 10 October 1832 Sir James Scarlett, a former Attorney-General but now a private Member of Parliament, wrote to Lord Goderich:

I own that I entertain a very strong opinion that the honor of the British Government is deeply concerned in having the conduct of its Consul at Tripoli impartially investigated. And I should for many reasons wish this to be done by any other tribunal than the House of Commons, where I believe it will certainly be taken up, even though I should not be a member of it.[2]

Lord Goderich to Sir James Scarlett:[3]

Downing Street
19 Oct. 1832

Copy

Dear Sir James,

I have to acknowledge the receipt of your note of the 11th inst:[4] covering a letter addressed to me by Mr. D'Ghiez under date of the 18th ulto.

I am by no means prepared to say that our Consul at Tripoli may not from excess of zeal for the service of the Govt. and from a very natural eagerness in the pursuit of those persons who have been the cause of his Son in Law's death, and of the abstraction of his Papers, have possibly adopted some erroneous conclusions, & have occasionally acted with precipitation,

---

[1] P.R.O., F.O. 76/33. [2] P.R.O., F.O. 76/33, 2867.

[3] Sir James Scarlett, first Baron Abinger (1796–1844), was at this time Attorney-General.

[4] Scarlett's letter was in fact dated the 10th.

although I must state that after attentive perusal of the various papers which I have received from Mr. D'Ghiez, I am wholly unable to discover what is the actual offence of which the Consul is asserted to be guilty, and which in your opinion, demands the investigation of the House of Commons, if the subject be not taken up by some other Tribunal.

Mr. Warrington is of course legally answerable for any wrong which he may have done to Mr. D'Ghiez, or to any other individual; and if a prima facie case be made out against him, he is equally liable to be called upon to explain his conduct, as in a recent case when he was specifically charged with having made an improper use of his influence to effect the sequestration of Mr. D'Ghiez's Property. But I must own that I do not see upon what grounds I can be expected to condemn Mr. Warrington for having acquired the power of influencing the Sovereign to whom he has been accredited. Still less in judging of the manner in which he has conducted the affairs entrusted to his management, should I be disposed to be guided by the opinion of those persons whose opposition it may have been his duty to overcome, and who as in the present case having lost the confidence of their Sovgn. have now become Mr. Warrington's accusers.

I have already apprised Mr. D'Ghiez that the examination of his papers will require some time, the more so indeed, as common justice requires that I should place Mr. Warrington in possession of the voluminous statement of his accuser, in order that he may have an opportunity of noticing the attacks & insinuations that have been made against his character.

Mr. D'Ghiez has himself greatly lengthened the delay which must thus occur in the consideration of his case, by requiring in the first place that his statement should be received in the character of a Private Communication; but although he may not be alive to the unfairness of bringing charges against an individual without giving the party accused an opportunity of rebutting such charges, I certainly cannot permit such a course to be pursued towards Mr. Warrington.

I am &c

(signed) Goderich[1]

There appears to have been some expectation that D'Ghies would relent, and agree to the publication of his lengthy statement because, in evident anticipation of this, all the relevant official correspondence was printed as a Blue Book.[2] D'Ghies, however, wisely continued to insist on secrecy. His case accordingly lapsed, so far as the British

---

[1] P.R.O., F.O. 76/33.

[2] *Papers Explanatory of the Circumstances under which Sidi Hassuna D'Ghies has been accused by the Bashaw of Tripoli of having abstracted the Papers of the late Major Laing*, 1832 (P.R.O., F.O. 76/33). Although this volume had not been published it was studied by Barth before he set out on his famous journey (IV, 455).

Government was concerned, and the position remained much as Robert Hay had stated in a letter to Sir James Scarlett as far back as 1 April 1830.

> I am afraid [he had written] there is little chance of our securing, at this late period, any portion of the journals of our unfortunate traveller. They have, no doubt, either been destroyed by those who murdered Laing, or have since been put out of the reach of discovery by those in whose hands they have surreptitiously fallen. Still it would be a great satisfaction to know whether D'Ghies has been privy to their recovery from the desert, and has been the channel of conveying them to Mr. Rousseau, the French Consul at Tripoli, as has been alleged by Mr. Warrington, the British Consul at that place.[1]

[1] P.R.O., F.O. 76/33; B.B., 53.

APPENDIX I

Journal of Major A. Gordon Laing[1]

Gadamis, Sept. 20th, 1825.
Latitude 30° — 07' — 20"N
Longtitude 9 — 16 — 15E
Magnetic Variation 18° W.

My Lord,

Having been honored in the month of January last, with an appointment from your Lordship, to proceed into the Interior of Africa direct as far as Tombuctoo, and from thence to follow the course of the river Niger to its termination, I consider it now to be my duty, having arrived at the town of Gadamis, to give your Lordship some detail of my Journey and proceedings thus far.

I took my departure from London on the evening of the 4th February, and on the morning of the 6th. arrived in Falmouth just in time to embark on board H.M. Packet Cygnet, which had already got under weigh; I had been apprehensive that I might lose the opportunity, having been detained several hours on the road by the upsetting of my carriage near Exeter, and was therefore satisfied on getting on board, to regard myself as fortunate, notwithstanding that I was under the necessity of leaving behind one of my servants,[2] who had not yet arrived with the greater part of my personal luggage.

During the month of January I had suffered considerably from an attack of Liver and general derangement of the viscera, a complaint which I had contracted during previous hard and fatiguing service in Africa, but I was now beginning to recover, and the sea voyage proved highly serviceable to my constitution, indeed so fully had I regained my strength and bodily vigour by the time of my arrival at Gibraltar, that I climbed with ease the three pinnacles of the rock, and measured their altitudes above the level of the sea by Barometer, one morning before breakfast; indeed before some of my fellow passengers had well roused themselves from their downy pillows. I landed at Malta on the 3rd. March in as good a state of health, and in as high spirits as I ever remember myself to have been in possession of, fully expecting that

---

[1] P.R.O., C.O. 2/15, 188.
[2] Jack le Bore had been left behind at Falmouth to follow with baggage that had been delayed.

the short voyage had so completely renovated my constitution that I should be able to undergo much, before either climate or fatigue cou'd materially affect me; but alas — how vain are human conjectures, how short is human foresight, how transitory is human happiness — on the 6th April, when joined by my faithful attendant Jack Le Bore who had followed me in the succeeding packet, and for whom I had prolonged my stay in Malta; while in the act of making preparations to depart for Tripoli in a Man of War placed at my disposal by the kindness of Vice Admiral Sir Harry Neale,[1] I was seized with another attack of the Liver of a more serious nature than that by which I had been visited in London, and which seemed to crush in the embryo, the sanguine hopes which were generally entertained of my success — my mind nevertheless remained firm, and although the view in perspective appeared cloudy, cold and cheerless, I nevertheless waited patiently and expectantly for the ray of hope, which after a tedious month appeared, and again gilded my prospects. It would be quite out of place, as well as out of character, for me to make any remarks upon the manner in which Hepatic disorders, and Mercury affect the spirits, yet I may observe that although in general mine have been found less affected by such causes than those of mankind usually are, it required more than my customary efforts to prevent myself giving way to despondancy and despair; indeed such was the extent of my suffering, such the emaciated appearance which I exhibited, that it was considered as a matter of course by those ignorant of the natural energy of my mind, that I must abandon the enterprise entirely! I thank God it has been otherwise ordained, and I may yet live to shew the triumph of the mind over the grosser material.

On the 6th of May I was so far recovered as to be able to embrace the offer of a passage to Tripoli in the Gannet Brig of War Capt. Bruce: The weather was truly mild and pleasant, the breeze a gentle zephyr, wafting us along at a slow and steady rate: on the morning of the 9th we cou'd behold Tripoli from the Main Top, and by two p.m., we were abreast of the town, the Cyrene Corvette Captain Grace, arriving at the same time from Tunis. About 5 p.m. I got the baggage removed from the Gannet to a small schooner sent by the Bashaw to receive it, and shaking hands with Capt. Bruce and his officers from whom I received the most marked and friendly attention, I disembarked amidst the cheers of the crews of both Gannet and Cyrene, who

[1] Vice-Admiral Sir Harry Burrard Neale (1765–1840) was at this time Commander-in-Chief in the Mediterranean.

manned the rigging on the occasion. There are moments in the lives of all men, which amply compensate for years of pain and mortification: this was with me one of these moments; and as my heart throbbed with the most unfeigned gratitude, I silently bestowed my thanks and blessing upon these generous hearted officers who, at a time when my mind was relaxed, and depressed by sickness, hit upon so gratifying an expedient to animate my breast with a spirit of enthusiasm and devotion to the service upon which I was employed and now on the point of undertaking. On placing my foot upon terra firma (which was not until a very late hour, our progress being impeded by the freshening breeze which blew direct from the harbour) I was received by Hanmer Warrington Esq., His Majesty's Consul General, and treated with that friendly hospitality which all preceding travellers from this quarter have experienced in common with myself: — on the following day I took up my abode in a small house in this town, and immediately commenced upon making arrangements and preparations for my Journey.

The Town of Tripoli, having for a background a beautiful mixture of the majestic date, the broad leafed fig, the wide spreading Mulberry and Olive trees, is rather pleasantly situated on a flat promontory close to the waters edge; from seaward it is beheld to the best advantage, appearing from thence both gay and strongly fortified, the numerous Consular flags waving in the pliant air, with the tall spires of the various mosques contributing materially to the former, and the lofty piles of embrasured walls to the latter effect; on landing however this favourable delusion is soon dispelled and Tripoli, like a painted beauty, loses all attraction on a close inspection — gayety vanishes and is lost to the eye, as it travels amid the narrow, irregular dirty streets or rather lanes, and every impression of strength disappears, on an inspection of the ill constructed, misshapen, dilapidating walls. The Castle of the 'Bashaw', an irregular Jail looking pile, is intended (at least it would so appear) by its total detachment from the fortifications of the town, as a strong hold or place of defence against enemies either foreign or civil, who might possess themselves of the latter; but this also is delusion, for a determined foe, with a few pieces of Artillery, battering rams, or even crow bars, might soon and with little difficulty effect an entrance, the walls though lofty, being constructed of small unhewn stones heaped irregularly one upon another, and held together by the presence of a copious incrustation of mortar: Tripoli with all its outward shew, with all its pop gun parade, might be taken with greater ease than a well stockaded Mandingo town. It is indebted to the English pen for more than one description, and upon that account requiring little from me; indeed with the exception of the manners and customs of its inhabitants, which assimilate closely to those of the Turks of other countries, and with which all the world are acquainted, I cou'd perceive little deserving of particular notice: It may not however be entirely out of place to observe 'en passant' that the native inhabitants are quiet, well behaved, and orderly in their demeanour, and invariably conduct themselves towards strangers with becoming politeness and respect. I have to be sure been witness to mirth and revelry at its very *achme* during the continuance of their festivals, but have nevertheless found them harmless withall, and I must in justice to them remark, that I think their conduct towards the Christians has [either — inserted in pencil] been touched with rather too highly a coloured pencil by Captain Lyon, in the account which he has given of a certain scene of wild fanaticism, in the first chapter of his very spirited and highly interesting Journal[1] — or they have altered most wonderfully within a very few years: Were they not the best, the most tolerative of Turks, I am at a loss to conceive how they cou'd permit with common patience the residence among them of the basest and most despicable cast of Christians, for it is to be lamented that the generality of those who have taken up their abode in Tripoli, are of this character: Thefts, robberies and a whole catalogue of crimes, which wou'd merit death or transportion by the laws of any country in Europe, are here committed daily by these vagrants, with an impunity quite surprising: in short they are the very scum, the residuum, the lees of Malta and the states of Southern Europe — a vile collection of

> The ruffian rabble that came down
> From all garrets in the town

The history and intrigues of the court of this place, wou'd no doubt reward the enquirer by affording an ample store of interesting matter: During my short stay I have list'ned to details, which in the hands of a Lewis or a Maturin might be made to rival the Monk or Fredolpho in mystery and romantic horror[2] — Life has been sported with in such a way as to lead one to suppose really that

[1] G. F. Lyon, 9-11.
[2] Matthew Gregory Lewis (1775-1818) was the author of *The Monk*, which was inspired by the *Mysteries of Udolpho* (1794). Charles Robert Maturin (1782-1824) was a novelist and dramatist.

There's nothing serious in Mortality — but with such matters, as it behoves me not to meddle, I shall without further notice of Tripoli or its inhabitants proceed with my narrative.

The circumjacent Country is in a high state of cultivation and extends in fine gardens to a considerable distance: the soil composed of a black loam mixed with sand is richly productive, and yields plentiful crops of corn and barley, as well as every kind of vegetable esculent that industry is disposed to commit to its bosom; nor are the Date,

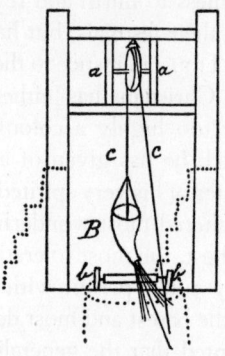

A *dalu*, after a drawing by Gordon Laing

olive, fig and Mulberry trees behind in yielding abundant supplies of their respective fruits. Each Garden in proportion to its extent, has one or more wells, by which it is irrigated and the process of drawing the water is at once ingenious, simple and effective.[1] To a wheel, A (generally about two feet in diameter) moving upon an axis a,a, is suspended a leather bucket or skin, B, with a spout, the mouth of which is held above the level of the surface of the bucket as it is filled, and lowered to us to permit the escape of the water into a tank or receive on arriving above the surface of the mouth of the well, by means of a cord rolling on a cylinder b,b. The bucket is made to ascend by the rotation of the wheel A which is put in motion by the diagonal descent of an ox (to whose neck one end of the rope c.c. is attached) along a plane inclining an angle of about fifteen degrees, and in length exactly double the depth of that at which water is found in the well; the bucket after discharging its contents is lowered by its own gravity, the ox counter-

---

[1] The *dalu* or *dalou*, a common method of raising water in northern Africa.

Appendix: Laing's Journal

marching and retracing his steps along the plain. The bucket may contain about ten Gallons, and is drawn up and emptied once in four minutes: (varying more or less, in proportion to the depth of the water from the surface) not unfrequently there are two buckets to one well, and both of them worked at the same time: when this is the case, and the average length of labour about ten hours, it may be estimated that two men, and two oxen will raise 3,000 Gallons p diem — This method simple as it may be, is better adapted for the country, perhaps than any other that cou'd be devised, the materials made use of being so uncostly and easily supplied; at all events any endeavours at improvement have hitherto proved abortive. The Consul General himself made several scientific attempts with his own well, but with so little success, that he was at length compelled to revert to the Arab practice, and he relates with infinite good humour the reply he got from one of these people who had a garden next to his, and to whom he sent to make an agreement for a supply of water for his drooping plants, 'Tell the Consul' says the Arab 'he has the best well in the country; and if he wou'd do as other people do, he would have no occasion to apply to me.'

It was not till the thirteenth day after my arrival that His Highness the Bashaw condescended to honor me with an audience, a circumstance which caused me some surprise and considerable chagrin, desirous and anxious as I was to commence my Journey, particularly as I had arrived in the fullest expectation of meeting with not only a cordial welcome from His Highness, but of finding him in some measure interested in the success of the Mission. Various were the rumours which were in circulation with regard to the cause of the Bashaw's coolness: one day it was said that His Highness never received anyone during the Rhamadan, which at the time of my arrival was Twenty days old; the next, it was rumoured that His Highness had received a douceur from another Government[1] to throw obstacles in the way of my accomplishing that object which they were desirous of effecting from another quarter; a third day the rebellion which had arisen in the Garian mountains was assigned as the cause of delay, and with every morning's sun fresh conjectures were formed, fresh reports went abroad. This of course was extremely unpleasant to a person situated as I was, and might have caused me considerable uneasiness, was it not that I had implicit confidence in the influence, and ocular proof of the exertions as well as anxiety of the Consul General to for-

[1] By which Laing meant France.

ward the departure of the Mission with as much despatch as possible. At length however on the thirteenth day, the audience was given, and although (from what reason I know not) I cou'd not but perceive great coolness on the part of the Bashaw at my introduction, yet I must acknowledge that I departed from the presence of His Highness much pleased upon the whole with my reception, and fully satisfied that it was his intention to act a fair and straight forward part with me; and although I might be supposed to be rather sanguine and premature in the formation of such an opinion from a single interview with the Chief of a people who, affected by the Government under which they exist, become out of necessity and in self defence adepts in the arts of dissimulation, who can form a deep design in the mind's secret recess and can

'Hide it in smiles and affability'

yet the sequel has proved that I was not mistaken. — On a careful perusal of my instructions, I observed it to be the desire of your Lordship, that I shou'd proceed through Fezzan to Tombuctoo, either by attaching myself to a Caravan which might travel by that route, or by placing myself under the protection of a Tuarick Chief named Hateeta; but as the result of my enquiries at Tripoli, together with the advice of the Consul General (with whom I was instructed to commune) induced me to prefer the route through Gadamis, I shall briefly explain the reasons which influenced my departure in this trivial instance from your Lordship's instructions.

Firstly — I cou'd learn of no Caravan that was likely to start for Tombuctoo by way of Fezzan,[1] nor cou'd I learn that it was a road by which Kaffles were in the habit of travelling.

Secondly. It appeared not improbable to the Consul General, as well as to myself, that on arriving at Murzouk, I might find my advance impeded for some time by the same influence which had impeded former Missions.

Thirdly — Hateeta, the Tuarick Chief, had not made his appearance, and had written to the Consul General to acquaint him that in consequence of some disturbances in Graat he had gone to look after his family.

Fourthly. I was led to understand through the most respectable channels of information that the most frequent communication be-

[1] Starting from Tripoli.

Appendix: Laing's Journal

tween any place under the influence of the Bashaw and the great city of Tombuctoo was from Gadamis.

Fifthly — His Highness the Bashaw promised that I shou'd be accompanied and protected by a Sheikh of Gadamis, who had resided for thirty years off and on at that Capital and had only lately returned from it.

And Sixthly. The offer of letters of credit, both to Gadamis and Tombuctoo, from D'Gheis, a man of much influence in Tripoli, and known as a wealthy merchant, along the whole route that I shou'd be obliged to pursue — withall it was an untravelled road, — a country quite new to the European, and might be expected to afford some novel matter of interest to the inquisitive traveller. But, notwithstanding the many advantages which led to the adoption of this route, and obstacles which operated towards the rejection of the other, there were nevertheless some and indeed considerable difficulties which offered themselves at an early stage of the Journey. The rebellion in the Garian mountains, near which the road to Gadamis lay, was of a nature both serious and determined, insomuch so that the troops which the Bashaw had sent to quell it, had acquitted themselves with rather indifferent success; at least it was so to be understood, from the half smothered reports which here and there prevailed in Tripoli, and the paltry parade of three heads of the disaffected
———— 'on the outward wall',

the only trophies after an engagement in which rumours gave the victory to the rebels — All thoughts of following the route near the Garian were therefore negatived, and one of a more circuitous nature proposed by His Highness, which after a good deal of consideration on the part of the Consul General and myself, was agreed to, on an understanding that I should be at liberty to commence my Journey on the 1st July, taking a direction to the Eastward by way of Benioleed, and thereby avoiding entirely the Garian mountains.

Agreeably with this intention, I quitted my quarters in Tripoli on the 13th June and pitched my tents in a garden about two miles distant in the Country, in order that my people as well as myself might undergo some little preparation, as well as the more readily to get the loads arranged, and the wants of the Mission supplied. These matters occupied rather a longer time than I had at first expected, and although every exertion was employed on the occasion, it was not until the 7th of July that the Camp at the Garden was broken up, when the Kaffle moved to the Eastward as far as Tajoura, distant about nine miles from Tripoli. Here, as there were many small but necessary arrangements to be made, the tents were again pitched on a fine plain in the vicinity of a kind of Lake or Marsh, and near to a fine well of fresh water. By the 10th every thing was in readiness, but I was yet induced to postpone my departure a few days, in consequence of the almost hourly expected arrival of the Sheikh of Gadamis, for whose safe conduct past the Garian, the Bashaw had despatched the greater part of his army. On the 14th a '*dies notetur*' the Sheikh arrived, and on the 16th at my farewell interview with His Highness I was introduced to that most worthy man, whose mild placid expressive countenance, and the *tout ensemble* of whose appearance struck me at once with an impression the most favourable an impression which a further acquaintance has only served to convince me was not erroneous.

> Honest, Good, Sheikh Babuné!
> Who eer o' thee shall ill suppose
> They sair misca' thee.

He agreed to conduct me in safety to Tombuctoo agreeably with terms which your Lordship shall be made acquainted with in a separate communication, and on my informing him that I intended continuing my Journey that very evening, he replied he cou'd travel more expeditiously than me, and that he would overtake me at Benioleed in six days — This matter being duly settled, I thanked His Highness for the great attention he had bestowed upon the interests of the Mission, and taking my leave, accompanied the Consul General to his Garden house, where I partook of a quiet farewell dinner. At a late hour in the evening, I shook that most excellent man by the hand, and mounting my horse took the road to Tajoura, where I arrived about an hour after midnight. The next day was employed in making many necessary arrangements and on the morning of the 18th July at daylight, the camp at Tajoura was broken up and the Journey for the Interior commenced. Whosoever has witnessed the first stroke of the pickaxe at the commencement of some great undertaking, such as a canal or a large dock; or the first stone that is laid of a castle or a building like St. Paul's, must have felt the difficulty in bringing within the scope of the comprehension, the first and last stroke of the work. I entertained something of that kind of feeling this morning, as I contemplated the slow funeral kind of pace at which the Camels moved off, and thought of the distance between the Mediterranean and the Bight of Benin. — Our course lay to the Eastward, over a heavy dreary desert, and the camels appeared to make their way with difficulty over the numerous sand hills, which the force of long continued sea breezes had heaped up in innumerable inequalities — at 5 p.m. we reached a small river named Wady Rumel, shaping its nearly dried up course between ridges of mountainous sand, against which the beaming rays of the Evening sun lingered with a golden splendour truly dazzling — next morning before daylight we recommenced our journey, and, after crossing the bed of the stream, struck off to the Eastward of South, through a flat sandy road covered with long spear grass, and wild thyme; the fragrance sent forth from the latter of which when agitated by the passing Zephyr was both gratifying and delightful. The flat country was covered with many flocks of goats and sheep tended by arabs of the meanest exterior, at the same time happy and contented in their appearance: here and there a party of about twenty with their wives and their children were to be met with surrounding a well, and busy in the employment of drawing water for their flocks, some of which were evidently waiting in parched expectation, while others were emptying with avidity the contents of the wooden troughs, which the shepherds were endeavouring to replenish. About noon we entered upon the bleak looking micaceous hills of Terhoona, and took a last look of the ocean, which they were about to shut from our view — and at 2 p.m. we pitched our tents on a fine plain hemmed in on all sides by gently undulating acclivities — July 20th. Struck our tents at day light, and pursued a path to the Eastward of South along the bed of a dried up river — the road was successively rugged and stony, and the Camels made their way with so much difficulty, that it was thought necessary to halt at Noon, near an old Roman ruin called Dooya [Gabr Doga] to allow them a little rest — the day following we advanced about five miles further to a plain in which were situated a number of Arab huts, where we halted at the accommodation of the Sheikh of Terhoona, who had orders from the Bashaw to furnish an escort of cavalry for the protection of the Kaffle to Benioleed, some danger being apprehended from a party of robbers from Jebel, who it was presumed, might be laying in wait for us on the road, in the expectation of a rich booty. Tripoli is one of those places in which the people, having little employment of their own, are rather apt to busy themselves with the affairs of others, so that it was impossible to conceal any circumstance, no matter how trivial, — from this busy place, reports had gone ahead regarding the immense riches of the Mission, and, as even the few dollars I had, were magnified into so many dubloons, the precaution of the Bashaw was not to be considered an unnecessary one. —

The face of these mountains, although bare, nevertheless exhibits an appearance which may be considered rather beautiful than otherwise, consisting of immense flats, bounded by elevations slightly undulating, like the waves of the sea, a heavy Atlantic swell, covered with herds of cattle, flocks of sheep, Camels and horses grazing in happy tranquillity upon the stinted though fat'ning pasturage. The soil is principally composed of sand formed by the decomposition of red mica, the structure of the mountains being entirely micaceous, in some places shelving with the regularity of a flight of steps.

July 22nd. About noon I paid a visit to the Sheikh of Terhoona, whose temporary habitation was of very simple construction, and cou'd be either put up or taken down in a very few minutes. — A few poles, those in the centre a little longer than the others, supported a covering or roof of very thick coarse cloth, which was equally impervious to the solar rays, or to the pelting storm: the sides were composed of mats, which cou'd be opened or shut at pleasure, so as to admit or exclude the breeze. The furniture, as simple as the hut, consisted of a few Turkish rugs, wooden bowls, pot etc., the matted sides being hung with implements of war, and horse trappings. Here then, thought I, is the dwelling of a chief, with fewer comforts than is [sic] to be found in the hut of a common labourer in England — What an extraordinary animal is man: at times how much, at times how little is necessary for his support and comfort. At 2 p.m. the Kaffle was in motion, by which time to my great surprise, a fine escort of upwards of a hundred Cavalry, and as many Infantry was collected together in these bare and apparently almost uninhabited hills — The ground having become tolerably equal, we were enabled to push on the Camels at so brisk a pace, that by the time the moon set, (a few minutes past 10 p.m.) we had passed over a distance of better than twenty miles, when finding it necessary on account of the darkness that ensued, to make a halt, we stretched ourselves upon mats till about four in the morning, and again took the road with undiminished celerity. — The dawn of morning was ushered in with a few drops of rain, through which the rays of the rising sun sparkled with prismatic splendour; the ground was carpeted with thin herbage of a palish green, and glist'ning with the pearly dew drop, seemed like the smile which chases the tear from beauties cheek — No wonder if on such a morning every heart beamed with gladness. The Arabs appeared in the highest spirits, and as the Kaffle traversed an intensive flat, began to exercise their horses — They would let go their bridles, start off at full speed, take aim, fire, and wheel with an adroitness and dexterity truly admirable: they are however much indebted to Captain Lyon for the appearance they exhibit in this kind of exercise, in one of those elegant plates which embellish his Journal — About 2 p.m. the road became very rugged and unequal, and the soil began to disappear, giving place to hills of mica slate Gypsum and silen, the broken particles of which incommoded the Camels greatly, and impeded our progress, which was now rendered slow and irksome by the presence of a parching Sirocco, which had been blowing for some hours with sultry rigour: —— In the shade of a solitary Accacia tree, under whose branches I stopt to rest awhile, (being in advance of the Kaffle,) the Thermometer stood at 104° — The continued ascent and descent of a succession of lapideous eminences, is at any time a task of dull monotony, but during the presence of a fiery East wind, it becomes intolerably so, the parched burning desolate appearance which is so dismally exhibited every where around, meeting the eye, and exsiccating as it were, the very moisture of vision: it was therefore with no ordinary feelings of satisfaction, that, having arrived on the summit of the last of these stony ridges, we beheld extending beneath us the beautiful Valley of Benioleed, into which we descended about 5 p.m. Here our weary eyes rested with pleasure upon the most refreshing verdure, where the tall stately date trees were waving their pluming foliage in silent majestic grandeur, over numerous thickets of dark green clumpy olives, whose opaque shadows as they stretched gigantically across the vale, and bid defiance to the rays of the evening sun (of whose meridional power, our countenances bore but too convincing testimony) imparted an idea, even a degree of coolness, which to my parched and wearied companions in common with myself was both refreshing and agreeable. By six p.m. the Camels were all unloaded, and the baggage lodged for the night in the Castle of Benioleed for by such a dignified swelling title are designated four square ill constructed walls of stone and clay — On the night of the 1st August, the Sheikh Babuné arrived, and afforded me his assistance during the two succeeding days in adjusting the loads of my Camels: the time previous to his arrival was spent by me for the most part in taking observations for the rate of my chronometer, which I found to remain as at Tripoli with a regular rate of 3″ loss daily, and in endeavouring to acquire a knowledge of the Arabic language, in which I had already made some proficiency. There were reports coming in daily of depredations committed by the Jebel Arabs, who were said to be watching for the Kaffle at all the various watering places on the different roads to Gadamis, and once or twice the whole force of Benioleed was turned out to go in quest of them, but knowing the power of native exaggeration I did not allow these rumours to incommode me much. At one o'clock on the morning of the 4th August we took our departures from Beniolaid, whose beautifully picturesque valley I have already noticed, and whose diminutive dilapidating clay constructed hovels are deserving of the oblivion to which, in turning my back upon them, I consign them. Having cleared the valley we struck off S.S.W. Sy[1] over a stony desert till 11 a.m., when we rested in a valley named Wady Echmed,[2] over which were spread a few detached Accacia, and [blank in text] trees, some of them large enough to afford a kind of shelter from the meridional solar rays; at 4 p.m. we continued our march, and travelling for an hour and a half southerly, arrived at a well of brackish water, where we pitched our tents for the night — The water in this well was obtained with much difficulty, being twenty-five fathoms from the surface.

August 5th. At one a.m. Departed from our bivouac, and proceeded due South, through a wady or valley about a quarter of a mile in breadth, the sides or boundaries marked by a succession of eminencies, rising pyramidaly from their base, but terminating in flat table land, as if regularly pared off with a knife, the consequence of an equal lamellar decomposition. The bed of the valley consisted of stone, gravel and sand, over which were scattered with a sparing hand, some stray patches of wild thyme and long spear grass, with here and there a fine accacia tree, under whose shade some herbage had been permitted to vegetate, but which, by exposure to the Summer heat, had become so arid and brittle, that by pressure from the fist it would make a crackling noise like the kindling of a thorn fire. The heat becoming very intense, we rested from 8 a.m. till 4 p.m., at which hour we again moved along the winding of the valley in a direction averaging S.S.E. till ½ past 7 when darkness compelled us to await for a while the rising of the nearly finished moon, which appearing about midnight, enabled us again to

[1] This probably means 'Southerly'?
[2] This is spelt Echmah on Laing's map. It evidently refers to Scemech.

proceed along the Wady, the course being now about S.E. The bed as in yesterday's march, was composed of stone, gravel and sand, opening out into wide expanses of two or three miles in diameter, resembling large dried up basins or lakes — at 6. a.m. still following the winding of the Wady, we struck off due East, and continued that course for an hour and a half: after which it varied from E by S to SE till ½ past eight, when suddenly turning round the base of a hill, and facing the South, we came upon an Arab encampment, situated in an extensive valley called Serked [Bir Sèrchet], hemmed in by hills of sand stone and Gypsum, in which we pitched our tents; the Sheikh Babane wishing to make some enquiries regarding the relative safety of the different routes to his country. The parched, dried up, yet patriarchal pastoral appearance of this valley, covered with countless flocks of Goats and sheep, caravans of camels etc, and tended by Arabs of a religious order who (as did their progenitors from time immemorial before them) perform in these secluded, solitary regions, the parts of Maraboots, Soldiers, and Shepherds, impressed me with a sort of feeling, which I cou'd not exactly embody — I had either seen or imagined something of the kind before. It was like the feeling occasioned by a visit to an old deserted building whose sombre walls begir'd [sic] with creeping ivy, excited silent veneration — the scene was motionless, cheerless, arid; both animate and inanimate nature appearing equally still; and with the clumps of saffron tinted herbage, on the arenacious soil, seemed like a piece of old fine wrought tapestry, from which the bright colouring had been expelled by the slow yet sure consuming hand of time — The day was sultry in the extreme, at noon the Thermometer stood at 116° Farenheit, a dry Sirocco still breathing along the valley, and increasing in power as the day drew towards a close — at six p.m., it blew a gale, and the atmosphere was rendered dull and heavy by the successive volumes of burning sand which were borne along by the scorching wind, now blowing as if heated by a thousand furnaces — Men and beasts enveloped in burning sand appeared to gasp for breath, and nature seemed as if expiring in a fever — at 9 p.m. Thermometer 107° — We rested in this valley during the 7th and 8th — the Sheikh Babané wishing to enter into some arrangements with the chief Maraboot, for an escort to accompany us the short road to Gadamis; but being unsuccessful in his endeavour to effect such an arrangement, on account of the great avarice and exhorbitant [sic] demands made by the maraboot, we departed on the following morning (the 9th) to make a long curcuit by way of Shati. This was at first a matter of the most serious annoyance to me, being desirous to reach Tombuctoo with as little delay as possible, for from thence I considered the interesting part of my journey to begin, but I had reason to be afterwards satisfied, when informed of the fact that a plundering band of a hundred and fifty Cavalry had been laying [*sic*] in wait for the Kaffle for some weeks, near a well by which it must have passed, if the short road from Serked had been pursued. We rested for the day at 3 p.m. near a brackish well under the mountains of Gerza, a ridge of more various and marked profile than any I had seen since my departure from Tripoli; 10th and 11th passed over extensive plains of sand and gravel, with here and there a few patches of an unwilling vegetation, on the afternoon of the latter day crossed the mountains of Tuyeez, and halted at nine p.m. 12th. On the march at 5 a.m., and crossed valley after valley bounded by regular successions of hills extending from East to West, till 9 a.m., when we stopt at a well of saltish stinking water, so bad indeed that our thirsty brutes at first refused it: this well is called Malhrail, and is situated on the borders of Fezzan.

On the afternoon of the 13th departing from Mulhrail, we continued our march without intermission till 7 a.m. the following morning over a desert of gravel and stone, course as on the preceeding days about S.S.W. — Again on the afternoon we took the road, and after another long journey pitched our tents the next morning in a valley of Sand stone and fine gravel enriched by a number of eminences of a construction singularly regular, with platforms and sloping parapets, resembling a succession of batteries raised by the hand of art under the direction of science. The distance was bounded by some high gloomy looking hills of jetty blackness, which being in the same latitude, are no doubt a continuation of the Soudah or Black mountains laid down by Lyon, but here assuming the name of Shebat el Haruba. ‏شبط الخروب‎ -¹

At noon of this day (the 15th) finding our water running short, and our camels fatigued by the long marches, and fearing our stock, bad as it was, might be expended before we could reach Shati, the Sheik sent off two men upon Maherries, with twenty skins to get them filled at a well which lay before us, at some distance from the straight road: at 4 p.m.,

---

¹ These two Arabic words are interesting as an indication of the progress Laing was making in the mastery of the language. But he still had a long way to go. 'Laing's two Arabic words', writes Professor C. F. Beckingham, 'are meant to be *shabāt alkharrūba*, meaning "the tip of the carob bean". They are very badly written and I should never have guessed what they were intended to be without the help of his spelling in Latin characters just before. I do not think he can have known the alphabet' (Letter to the editor).

we advanced with the Kaffle slowly, and after surmounting one of the heights of El Horuba, descended into a spacious valley of fine sand and gravel, bounded by hills of regular and equal height: about two thirds from the summit of these hills which are composed entirely of sand stone, a straight line is so plainly marked, as to bear the appearance of having been washed by a tide, the valley resembling the bed of a large lake, which a recent ebb had left dry: indeed the whole face of this country, made up of Wadeys and hills, fashioned as if by tides and currents, the strange position of the straggling rocks, the total absence of vegetation, and the hollows with small islets, evidently the receptacle of waters after their retirement from the general level, wou'd almost warrant the conjecture, that at some remote period, it has been entirely inundated — After crossing the valley, we came to some rough irregular broken ground called Shaba Soudah, which we experienced much difficulty in crossing, owing to the darkness of the night — We finished our Journey at midnight, and at the earliest dawn of day on the 16th again pushed forward, but were compelled to stop about an hour after noon, being oppressed by fatigue and thirst — here we expended our last skin of stinking water, and waited with much expectant anxiety for the return of the Maherries which we had sent off for a supply — The lofty hills of Ulad Hassan which here form the western boundary of Fezzan were to be seen in the distance, and as the water to which our people were sent, was to be found on this side of them, we hoped that in the afternoon we shou'd be relieved by their appearance. This gratifying event however did not arrive till midnight, and it is hardly to be conceived how great our disappointment was, when we witnessed the receding rays of the Western Sun, without a drop of water in the whole Kaffle, every one suffering from thirst, and fancying to himself the torture which was in store, during a long tedious, sirocco evaporating night — Having satisfied our thirst, we started afresh in about an hour afterwards, and traversed a surface covered with red and black stones, resembling a country which had been exposed to the action of a general conflagration; at 7 a.m having arrived at a spot on which there was some slight appearance of vegetation, we stopt in order to allow our Camels a little rest and food, both of which the poor patient enduring animals stood much in need of. This spot is named Sasoofa and may again be recognised by two conical shaped mountains resembling the Papo of Cape Verd, bearing about S.W. by W from it.

We left this place at 4 a.m. on the 18th, and halted at 10 — again proceeding at 4 p.m. We kept up a constant march till 9 a.m. the next morning, when we pitched our tents under the shade of some date trees, at Tamsow Soowareea[1] in the fertile valley of Wadey Benioleed, and more thickly studded with the picturesque Date, which seems to flourish here in luxuriant growth upon its parent soil, waving its branches pregnant with clusters of saffron fruit, to the genial warmth of a sultry rip'ning breeze; but from the absence of the thick foliaged olive, which predominates at Benioleed, it exhibits a less varied, less retired, less genial scene. It is nevertheless a place of much beauty, and contrasted with the dry, barren, gravel hills around, cannot fail to be hailed with pleasure by the approaching traveller, who from the period of his leaving the former valley till his arrival here, sees nothing which may be ranked above the dignity of a shrub, with the exception of now and then a solitary accacia tree.

My first care, after the pitching of the tents, was to see my patient hard labouring Camels supplied with plenty of water and hay; after which I was not backward in regaling myself upon the delicious grapes, dates and water melons which this valley affords.

For further remarks upon this place and a general outline of the character and habits of the people, together with the remainder of my journey to Gadamis, I must reluctantly refer your Lordship to a future communication, my time being at present much occupied with matters immediately connected with the progress of the Mission, and a Courier whom I have already detained for two days being on the point of setting out for Tripoli. At the same time I beg to assure your Lordship, that I have been thus minute and perhaps tedious, because I have considered it my duty to be so, and not from any supposition that so monotonous a detail might prove interesting to your Lordship.

[formal ending]
A. Gordon Laing.

Journal continued

from 19th August, 1825[2]

to be left in the Colonial Office till called for by Major A. Gordon Laing

In traversing so vast an extent of barren country as that which I have already described, as unvaried and unchequered in its appearance as

---

[1] Tamsawa. [2] P.R.O., C.O. 2/15, 955.

Appendix: Laing's Journal

the bosom of the wide expansive ocean, the traveller naturally meets with little to excite observation, or call forth remark: — A country deprived of the benefit of moisture from spring or rill, so arid and dried up by exposure to a burning sun, that it produces little for the sustenance of man, is of course but thinly peopled: inhabited by a few tribes of wandering arabs, with whom, as he rarely comes in contact, unless when demands are about to be made on him, he can see little of their character, and certainly by no means the brightest side of it — This has been so exactly my situation, that I shall be very sparing in my remarks particularly as my impression, (which I should be happy to persuade myself is an erroneous one) is far from being favourable, but more especially, as these wandering tribes have been often described by other pens, and by individuals possessing a better knowledge of their character, from long residence among, and repeated personal intercourse with them, than I cou'd possibly obtain in a cursory Journey through the country.

In passing over this dry feverish soil in the most sultry season of the year, as it fell to my lot to do, and observing not a single trace of cultivation between Benioleed and Shati, it wou'd indeed be difficult to form a conjecture as to the manner in which the straggling inhabitants exist, was a person not previously acquainted with it. Nature, even in her most sportive frolics, has made kind and abundant provision for man, whether placed —

> 'Where no summer breeze
> Disturbs the earth or fans the trees',

or whether immured in regions where —

> 'Winter from the frozen North
> Drives his own chariot forth',

Each has his own season of plenty, his hour of harvest when he may lay up against the winter of scarcity, the provision afforded by the summer's wealth. The Arab has his two months of rain, when scattering his corn on the Desert, he soon reaps a hundred fold without either care or attention; and the Esquimaux has his long day in which to supply himself with food and clothing. In the date valleys, and in the vicinity of wells, when by means of irrigation, the ground is rendered productive during the whole year, it is first prepared by a kind of plough or rather toy, which is made to turn it up, or scratch it, to a depth of about two or three inches: this puny machine, which nevertheless answers every purpose for which it is intended, is ridiculously enough drawn by a great, huge, powerful Camel, whose labour might be employed in other ways with much more advantage, an ox or even a *goat* being strong enough to drag the plough. Tamsowa Sooareea, which can hardly be called a town, consisting of a heterogeneous and somewhat detached heap of square mud walls, covered with flat roofs of date branches is entirely hid from view by the numbers of date trees in which it is enveloped, and only forms one of a number of similar Arab residences which extend from East to West along the Wady or Valley of Shati — The soil is of the most thirsty nature, being mostly arenacious and requires constant irrigation from the wells, which are here abundant. This valley is the pride of Fezzan, and is looked upon by the Arab, as he contemplates the clusters of luscious dates, and the buckets of refreshing water which are continually pouring their contents into the resevoirs, as a Land of Milk and Honey, as a terrestrial paradise. 'That is my Country' said one of my attendants exultingly, as the Valley was descried at a distance on the morning of our approach, 'That is my Country, where I cou'd live for ever in the midst of dates and water' — At the moment, I felt almost inclined to wish, that in my own country there was nothing but dates and water, that *my* wants might be as few, and my happiness as easily purchased — Shirghi can however boast of more than Dates and water, as can also the rest of the Wady Shati, producing a sufficiency of corn and cooscooso [cuscus], not only for the consumpt[ion] of its own Inhabitants, but also for the supply of foreign Markets.

The Arabs, both high and low (it has been remarked by some of our travellers) are as if by nature constituted beggars, and I can bear ample testimony to the truth of the assertion; but so natural a reason is assignable for the cause, that were they otherwise, it might reasonably incite surprise, but none certainly that they are. The blind and impolitic avarice of the Government under which they exist, which marks out a man for the bow string or the knife of the assassin, as soon as he is known to be the possessor of riches, at once renders property insecure, and detracts from the natural desire inherent in man of accumulating it, or at least of doing so openly, thus the dread of appearing to possess wealth, in such a state of uncertainty where every man is suspicious of his neighbour, induces the rich man to refrain from ostentatious display, and to conceal what he may possess under the cloak and semblance of

Appendix: Laing's Journal

poverty. In such a state of existence the Miser alone will take upon himself the task and risk of laying up that which, while it subjects him to danger, he can never enjoy. But the majority of the population will be satisfied in having their present wants supplied, and leaving the morrow to shift for itself; but as these cannot always be furnished at pleasure, they are of course compelled to resort to begging, the holders of property following their example to make their wants apparent and conceal their real situation. From an Englishman, whose liberality they have often experienced, they will scarcely beg, asking for a supply of whatever they desire as a matter of right, and with about the same expectation as is evinced by a horse neighing for the corn which he sees approaching him in the hands of his well known groom. A refusal from an Englishman is beheld with astonishment, and even a compliance, unless of the most absurdly liberal nature, is accepted with a thankless appearance of disatisfaction and discontent. Begging arises from two causes, the one from the state of society already noticed, and which I believe to be common through all Africa, the other from the population of a country exceeding the means of employment which it can afford, as at Malta; but in either case, it only requires toleration to take root and flourish: and was it so to happen, that even in industrious England, property was to become equally insecure, and travellers from foreign parts, exceeding it in wealth as much as it exceeds Africa, were to visit it, and scatter comparative wealth with as profuse a hand, as we have perhaps necessarily done, as many mendicants might be found in an English village, as are now to be met with in an Arab encampment.

The Arab must not therefore be received with contempt upon this account, as he is not accessory to the causes which constitute him a beggar; but we must be satisfied in prosecuting our discoveries to be taxed by his importunities, and look upon ourselves as fortunate that he does not proceed in a more summary way.

Departing from Tamsowa on the afternoon of the 21st August, we proceeded to the westward, and in two hours reached another town, village, or whatever it may be called, built more compactly than the former, surrounded with Date and a few fig trees, and irrigated from a large pond two and a half fathoms deep, which is constantly supplied by springs, which are seen to bubble up from its centre. At this place named Agah [Agár], we stopped till the morning of the 23rd, when we again moved slowly westward a little after daylight. In an hour and a half we passed through El Maharoga [El Maharúga], a place of much beauty, the Date and Fig trees being laid out and arranged with great order and taste; and at 10 a.m. we arrived at El Gorama, situated on a hill of sand. That morning at 4 a.m. we passed on to Gorta [Gótta], which we reached at 8. a.m., and on the day following (the 25th) a slow journey of four hours more brought us to Berged [? Berghin], where we remained two days, making agreements for Camels to carry water for us across the Black Desert,[1] which we were now about to enter upon. The country over which we passed and which separates these fertile spots, is a complete stratum of blue mica slate, and white aluminous clay — desolate wastes, which here exhibit the appearance of a recent deluge, there, that of a conflagration, and almost incline the traveller to marvel for what purpose they were created. The habitations which man has erected for himself in the midst of these fertile specks of ground, are of the same description as those of Tamsowa: and upon a close inspection, exhibit a more ruined and desolate appearance than a dilapidated Fantee town of which everyone who has read Mr. Bowdich's Journey to Coomassie,[2] must have a tolerable idea; nevertheless, in the distance, when as yet the formation of objects is as yet incorrectly defined, peeping as these wretched hovels do, from the magnificent foliage of the stately dates, which surround and intersect them, and to which they afford a contrasting shade or back ground, they present an appearance of natural beauty, which the hand of a Nash or a Soane might destroy but cou'd not improve. How careless soever the Arab may be of his domestic comforts, or of the hut which shelters him, there is nevertheless one building on the construction of which he bestows much care; this is the mosque or Maraboot, which stands in the east at some distance from the general Mass. It is sometimes a handsome, but always a neat and decent building, and from its modest appearance and detached situation, surrounded by the graves of those who have in former days offered up their prayers within its walls, commands a feeling of veneration and respect, which the haughty demeanour of its priests wherever they shew themselves, soon causes to subside. At Tamsowa, a man presented himself to me with a severe cut on his head, the flesh being laid open to the scull, to which I applied a remedy, and so much relief, that he followed me to get a fresh dressing daily up to this date. This man sounded my praise as a Doctor at every little place we stopt at, and collected round me so many applicants for medicines and advice, that in my endeavour once to attend to them all, the whole day was expended. Subsequently I never opened *my shop* till towards

---

[1] The Soudah Desert.
[2] The reference is to T. E. Bowdich, *Mission to Ashantee* (London, 1819).

evening, when I was certain that darkness wou'd soon come to my relief — I say to my relief, for I was annoyed by the most absurd applications of some, who fancied themselves sick, or rather wished me to fancy so, in order that they might procure the Englishman's medicines, which they had an idea might contribute to an encrease of their sensual enjoyments, let the dose be what it may — but there were others of a more melancholy stamp, whose relief it was far beyond the reach of man to minister unto: of the former cast, was a healthy robust young man, who desired some medicine to make him stronger, a short man who wished something to make him grow bigger, and a thin one who thought some medicine might make him fatter: of the latter was a poor feeble aged woman within a few days of eternity, to whom I could administer nothing that might in the least benefit her, but gave a potation of Magnesia by way of satisfying her: I pitied her in my heart, but great indeed was my surprise when she enquired in a dying tremulous tone, if the medicine wou'd *help her to bear children*! There was also a man stone blind, who expected I might be able to make his Eyes grow, and another who wished a crippled shrunken leg to be made exactly like the other — but the narration of all this nonsense wou'd be as tedious and annoying, as was the reality to me. On the 25th & 26th of the month, while resting at Berged, the heat was distressingly oppressive, and caused us all to suffer a good deal, the Thermometer for several hours after noon standing at 120° Farenheit in the shade. Water standing in my tent, became more than look-warm [*sic*], the steel scabbard of my sabre so hot as to be absolutely painful to the touch, and the mercury wou'd descend by the application of the thumb to the ball of the thermometer, with as much velocity, as it will ascend by a similar application, in the bleak month of December in England. This great degree of heat produced a deaf'ning, stupid, and heavy sensation of the head, which we one and all experienced. On the 26th the dew point indicated by Hygrometer was as low as 78°, the evaporating force in grains being about 8·67.

August 27th. Left Berged, and proceeding to the Westward for about three hours, arrived at a fine well of fresh water, surrounded with date trees, where we stopt to fill our Gerbies — on the following morning the ground appeared covered with an incrustation of salt, similar to a hoar frost in England in the month of November.[1]

On the 28th at 3 p.m. we departed from this well, and struck off

---

[1] This is a common phenomenon in this region.

N.W. by N. over a desart of black stones, gravel, and sand, interspersed with rocks of red laterite, and continued our journey with little intermission (resting a few hours only during the night and heat of the day) till the 31st when at 10 a.m., we descended into a valley of sand, bounded on the North by an intensive range of high table land called Esser: the ground was strongly encrusted with salt, and the well at which we stopt at noon to refresh ourselves, afforded water of a very brackish taste — Near this well are the remains of an old circular building razed to the very foundation: it measured a hundred and twenty three feet in diameter, and the walls appeared to have been about nine feet in thickness. The weather still continued oppressively hot, and I regretted to observe that Rogers one of my attendants began to exhibit some unpleasant symptons of ophthalmia. During the day I caused him to bathe them in cold water, as often as the movements of the Kaffle wou'd permit, and at night by the application of a little eye ointment to the lashes, and a few drops of Tincture of Opium to relieve the pain, I succeeded in arresting the progress of the disease; but it was not till sometime after our arrival in Gadamis, that a complete cure was effected.

September 1st. At 4. a.m. we resumed our journey, having during the Afternoon of the preceding day replenished our Gerbies. Our course now averaged about W.N.W., though we made but indifferent progress, being opposed by numerous lofty hills of sand, which as we advanced among them, encircled us in terrific inequalities, and reflected from their gilded summits the rays of the morning sun for some time before they reached us in the valley.

The surface of the sand being strongly encrusted with nitre which appears to exude here from subterranean resources, we experienced towards morning during the rapidity of condensation, an unusual degree of cold, which was not removed till the sun had advanced several degrees in his diurnal course, when emerging from behind the shade of a sand hill, which had previously shut us out from his rays, we changed our climate in an instant, leaping as it were from the frosty Caucasus to the sultry Indus. In the course of a few minutes, the Quicksilver rose 30° of Fahrenheit. On the morning of the second day we cleared the sand, and having arrived at a well of good water, we pitched our tents for the day. — This well is called Maraar [Bir Mráia], from being situated near an extensive range of bold table land composed of Gypsum and Sandstone, called Jebel el Maraar — one of my marine atten-

Appendix: Laing's Journal 365

dants remarked that the Desart resembled the sea, and the Jebel el Maraar[1] the coast of Yorkshire. Near this well there are two eminences of sandstone, which are cut and hollowed out into numerous caves and chambers, in which bands of robbers occasionally conceal themselves, and lay [sic] in wait for Kaffles. Hateeta, with fifty Tuarics, once took up their abode here, and captured a large Kaffle from Shati, having first slain many of the Arabs who gave battle, and offered a considerable resistance. The chief of the Kaffle, who was one of Denhams party in the rencontre with the Fellattas, made his escape, having received from Hateeta a severe sabre cut which broke the bridge of his nose.[2]

September 3rd. Departed from this well at 4 p.m. and marched with little intermission till 7. a.m. next morning when the extreme point of the Jebel el Maraar bore due East from us. The ground now varied from broken stones of blue micacious slate, to ridges of drifted sand, with here and there wall sided mountains or rather eminences of slate and sand stone, extending from Nth W. to Sth E in some places in a very advanced state of decomposition. We journeyed in this manner over a dreary black looking country exposed to the fiery breath of a sultry and provikingly steady Sirocco, during seven successive days, reduced on the fifth day to four skins of water, and suffering much from thirst during the two latter. When at length we arrived at a well, only two days from Gadamis. While slowly pacing over these desart, forlorn, black looking plains, these *Lybia deserta*, the eye of the traveller roams in vain over the wide, unvaried superficies in search of some object to rest upon, till at length wearied by a repetition of the bleak and tedious sameness, he is willing to pull one of the folds of his turban over his eyes, and to shroud his head in his Burnoosa, allowing his mind, which refuses to expand upon the exsiccated objects around him, to shrink within itself, and to anticipate in imaginative hope, more genial and enlivening scenes.

[1] Spelt Jebel Marar on Laing's map.
[2] The reference is to Denham's expedition to Mandara in 1823.

APPENDIX II

Laing's *Cursory Remarks on the course and termination of the Great River Niger*[1]

Ghadamis Sept. 28th 1825

Although considerable light has been thrown upon the Geography of Northern Central Africa, by the late gigantic strides of Major Denham and Lieut. Clapperton, yet it cannot be said that their Journey, pregnant as it is with valuable information, has afforded much elucidation towards the solution of that interesting problem, the *Termination of the Niger*, which on the contrary, appears to have become a question more mysterious if possible, and more difficult to unravel by theory than before. — In the following remarks which are intended to consider how far the above Journey has assisted in substantiating, invalidating, or involving in greater uncertainty, either or both of the hypotheses of the day, I trust I may prove myself deserving of the impartiality to which I lay claim, which at all events I am desirous to preserve.

By the ingenious, beautifully, and ably argued hypothesis of the Veteran Rennel, as well as that of Mr. Barrow, which to a certain extent is correspondent with the former, the Niger is made to flow Eastward into the Lake Schad, in a straight line nearly, between the 15th and 16th parallels of North Latitude. In opposition to this, there exists the FACT of Lieut. Clapperton having proceeded to the Southward as far as 13°. N.L. and having met with no river which cou'd be taken for the Niger: there is also the INFORMATION gathered by that enterprising traveller from Bello, the Sultan of Soudan [Hausa], the substance of which I understand to be nearly as follows: — 'The Yeow (the hitherto supposed continuation of the Niger) runs from West to East, to the Southward of Sokatoo, and is *dry, or nearly so* in the Summer. The Niger, or the river which runs past Yaooré, has no connection with the Yeow, but shapes its course to the Southward, and discharges its waters into the Bight of Benin' through many mouths.

This wou'd almost appear conclusive, and the superficial, or little interested reader might be satisfied to consider the question as set at rest; — placed however before the mirror of scrutiny, and compared

[1] P.R.O., C.O. 2/15, 189.

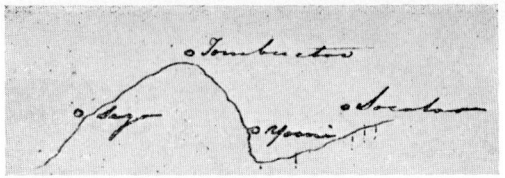

(a) Laing's sketch map of the middle Niger

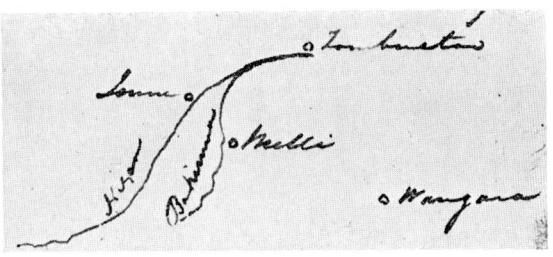

(b) Laing's sketch map of the upper Niger

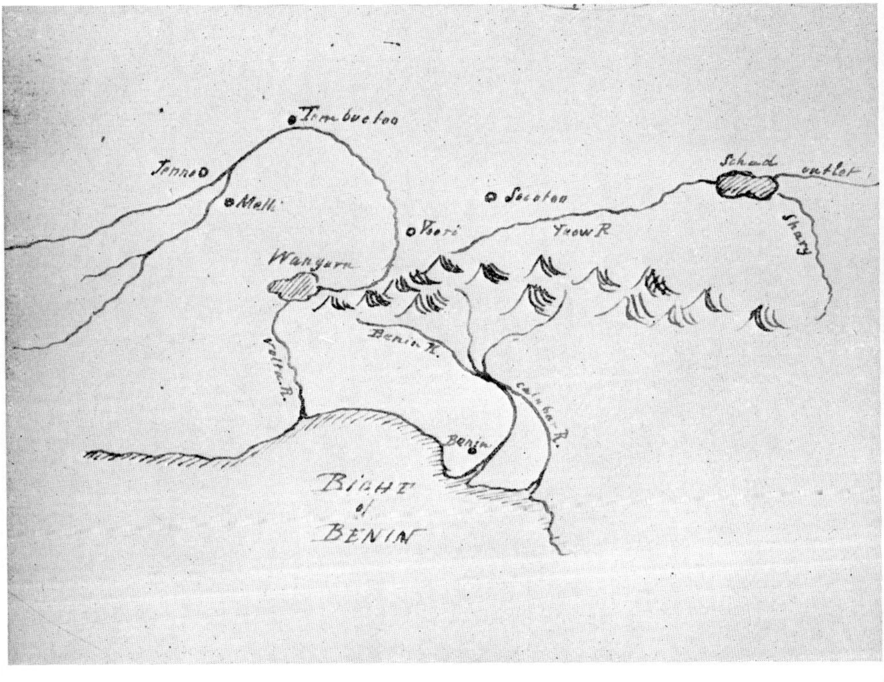

(c) Laing's sketch map illustrating his theory that the Volta was the Niger's outlet to the sea

Map VI

Appendix: Cursory Remarks on the Niger

by the test of other evidence, receiving the FACT only as a sure *datum*, it will be found, as I have already observed, to envelop the matter in clouds of greater mystery, rather than to afford any assistance towards dispelling them — The fact of Lieut. Clapperton having penetrated to 13° N without meeting any considerable river, will first be noticed, and is soon disposed of. It merely shews that if the Niger has an Easterly course, it is not to the Northward of that latitude, but it affords no proof that that river does not pursue such a course to the Southward of Socotoo, as has been stated by Sidi Hamet, the Sheikh Babané and others.

The *information* received by Lt. Clapperton is of a different character, and (if implicit reliance could be placed upon it) wou'd of course be final, but since it is *information only*, gathered from people who are not remarkable for paying much attention to the course of rivers, and as it is more than counterbalanced by corroborative evidence from other & seperate [sic] quarters, received at different times, and in different parts of Africa, upon which perhaps equal reliance may be placed, it must submit to a comparison, and be received only in proportion as it is found to correspond with other statements. Bello may be, and no doubt is, a very superior character, and a man of strict veracity, and had he told Mr. Clapperton that he had traced the course of the Niger HIMSELF from Yeaooré to the Bight, wou'd most assuredly have been entitled to implicit credence; but it must be recollected that Bello is a Sultan, and having never quitted the limits of his own territories, cannot be supposed to speak from personal observation; and superior as he may be when put in the scale with the generality of African Chiefs, & powerful withall, I question whether Geography occupies his attention so much as to induce him to send forth exploratory Missions — he has therefore only related what he has *heard* from his own people, who most probably have *seen the Niger at Yeooré* and only *heard* from others of a large river to the *Southward of Kong* which they have concluded to be the same without troubling themselves with further investigation — I have seen assertions made by natives upon less probable grounds, and such will not appear surprising to those acquainted with them, for it is well known that Geography is not a usual topic of conversation, much less of research among Moors or Negroes.

All my informants in Ghadamis, many of whom have visited both Soudan and Tombuctoo, and among them the Sheikh Babané, who has resided nearly thirty years in that Capital, concur in attributing an easterly direction to the Niger considerably to the Southward of

Socotoo, and mark its course thus:[1] being checked in its progress Southward and making a sudden turn E by N about the 11th degree of North Latitude, by the opposition of some very high mountains: they further inform me, that during the dry season there is very little water in the bed of the river, not sufficient to float a canoe from Tombuctoo to Yeooré; that at the latter town the river is very inconsiderable, and beyond that, where its Southern course is impeded by the mountains, not infrequently becomes dry during the latter end of Summer; but that when swelled by the periodical rains, it forces a passage, rushing with a noise as loud as thunder,* and truly awful to behold. The circumstance of the diminutiveness of the river at Yeooré, is strongly corroborated by the testimony of the Maraboot Mohamed Misrah, (furnished by me to the Quarterly Journal September 1822) who crossed the Niger at Nuffei [Nupe], then a very inconsiderable stream; whereas at Sego, six hundred miles nearer its source, it is as broad as the Thames at Westminster during the dry Season, and increases to such a bulk during the rains, that the report of a musket is inaudible from bank to bank — and indeed all the information which I have received in Ghadamis from people all acquainted with Tombuctoo, is so decidedly in favour of the Western magnitude and navigable importance of the river, that had I been put in possession of it without any previous knowledge of its real course, I am persuaded that I shou'd have fallen into the error with many others, who have ascribed to it an *Easterly* source and WESTERN termination — These assertions of the Western magnitude and Eastern insignificance of the Niger, supported by the authority of Leo Africanus** although it is to

[1] See Map VI (*a*).

* Most likely the place where Park was shipwrecked — I am inclined to believe that the Benin river runs past the base of the other side of this mountain, and that such a near conjunction of the two rivers may have given birth to the idea that the natives entertain, of the white man wishing to open a door in the mountain to let the salt water in upon the country.

** Leo (who has afforded such information regarding Tombuctoo, as to leave no doubt in the mind of the most sceptical, of his having visited that capital) most probably never saw the Niger, but learning that it was to be navigated to the Westward, and not to the Eastward, naturally enough supposed it to have a westerly course: speaking of Kabur [Kabra] the port of Tombuctoo he says '*hic Mercatores ad Jineae, aut Melli regnum navigare cupientes, naves conscendunt*' — Of the course of the river he speaks in doubt, and evidently in the style of a man who has made enquiry, but has not seen '*Alii volunt hunc fluvium suam habere in* [ex] *quodam lacu scaturiem, seseque occidentem versus volvere, donec in Mare Oceanum dilabitur*'. Against its easterly course he reasons '*quod quidem verisimile non est, nam ex oriente navigatur a Tombuto occidentem versus &c &c*' — He has been supposed in error in placing Melli West of Tombuctoo, but he agrees really with the Sheikh Babané, from whose sketch on the sand I have copied the following: [See Map VI (*b*)].

be lamented that they expel all hopes of a commercial nature with the interior regions, in whatever manner, in whatever quarter the river may terminate, are nevertheless interesting, and highly important at the present moment, to those who have favored the hypothesis of its estimated Easterly course, for while it admits the dried up bed of the Yeow, aggreeably with the information received by Lieut. Clapperton, it still holds out the possibility nay even the probability of that river being a continuation of the Joliba, the waters of which are alike absorbed by evaporation during the latter end of the dry season. It may also account in some measure for the various discrepancies which are extant regarding the course of this river, as well as afford a probable explanation of the causes which have so long operated in rendering its termination a matter of such doubt and uncertainty, for had it been a stream swelling in its progress by tributary assistance, as streams generally do, it might have been easily identified in its course by many natives & of information, who have intersected Africa in almost every direction, or at least more certain deductions might have been drawn from their statements, which have from time to time been carefully collected, sifted, and placed before the public inspection.

In the year 1822, when I was within sight of the source of the river Niger, and found its height by Barometer to be about 1600 feet only above the level of the ocean, considering that elevation too insignificant to carry its waters to the Lake Schad, which was at that time supposed to have a more remote easterly situation than the late travellers have proved it to have; and seeing no other probable outlet for the waters of a river which has been considered of such magnitude, I embraced (rather hastily I admit) the hypothesis of Reichard which favors its termination in the Bight of Benin, and being sensible of the great advantages which the interior of this benighted continent wou'd derive from its confirmation, I am free to confess that so long as I entertained hopes of it being a navigable river, I was not overanxious to see the hypothesis overturned, in that instance verifying the old adage of *'Id quod volunt credunt'*. That hope being dispelled by the information already noticed, and the objection which I formerly entertained against the course of the Schad being superseded by the proximity of the Lake, as determined by the late travellers, I shall now state a few objections to the hypothesis, which probably might not deserve so much notice, but for the rather stubborn information received by Lt. Clapperton at

Socatoo. I shall also mention a few circumstances which might almost induce a belief that the river has a termination widely different from any supposition which speculation has yet attempted to form.

I have already stated the reasons which induced me to favor the discharge of the waters of the Niger into the Bight of Benin; and although in making use of the very same reasons which I formerly considered substantiative of such an hypothesis, as arguments against it now, I may be regarded as unsteady, oscillating or fastidious, yet it may permit me to lay the stronger claim to impartiality and attention, more particularly as I argue against a hypothesis which I so much favor in my heart, that I shou'd derive the most infinite pleasure, either in confirming it myself or in seeing it done by others. The elevation of 1,600 feet, although sufficient to propel a stream to a distance of nearly 2,000 miles, as is proved in the case of the Ganges which has a less considerable fall, is nevertheless too insignificant to admit of such an impetuous rush as that by which the currents of the Benin, Calabar, and other rivers, the supposed outlets of the Niger, are ushered into the ocean, which is discoloured during the rainy season for several miles from their mouth by the muddy torrents which they vomit.

It has been thought by some (Mr. Robertson, Mr. McQueen and others) that these rivers cou'd not of themselves afford such a discharge, and must therefore be fed from some remote inland source, which they have naturally enough (as I did in common with them) conceived to be the Niger, particularly after its southerly course at Yeooré was ascertained; but it being now known, or at least presumed, from the evidence of the Ghadamis merchants, that the impoverished state of the bed of this river, cou'd add little to their bulk, it may be inferred that the heavy rains which deluge the Coast of Guinea during three months of the Year viz. June, July & August, and which must collect in voluminous clouds over the mountains which are said to impede the southerly progress of the Niger, are abundantly sufficient for the production of such an effect: besides the channels of the Benin and Calabar rivers do not swell to a greater size than the Volta or Cameroons, which have never been admitted to have any connection with the Niger nor does their periodical rise and fall differ so materially from other rivers on the Coast, as to warrant a belief of their having a more distant source, whereas if outlets for the Niger, they wou'd be at their height in November and December, instead of being in common with the other rivers in the Bight on the decline: Again, the great quantity of alluvial ground along the Coast where these rivers disem-

Appendix: Cursory Remarks on the Niger

bogue [?], is strongly inductive to a surmise, that it is formed by the *debris* and *decomposition* of mountains at no great distance inland brought along and deposited by rapid whelming currents: of the existence of which mountains the slaves from Haossa brought for sale to Benin (hundreds of whom I have examined) bear testimony.

Ptolemy, by far the most accurate of ancient geographers, discharges the river Niger into a Lake called the Lybia Paulus,* and various modern authorities agree in placing a Lake somewhere in the interior to the Southeast of Tombuctoo, where the Lake of Ptolemy is situated — in this existence I incline to think he may prove as correct as Major Denham has found him to be with regard to the Lake Schad, the rivers Yeore and Shary, all of which appear delineated with uncommon accuracy upon his Map.

The slaves from Haossa whom I have examined, all declare, that in coming to the Coast, they have sailed** down the Quorra or Seichie [?] a certain distance; that when it turned *towards the setting sun*, they left it, and walked for several days over *mountains*, when they arrived at *another river*, bigger than the Seichie [?], upon which they were carried to the Salt Water.

Wargee, the Tartar, examined by Mr. Williams at Cape Coast, crossed two rivers on his Journey South from Tombuctoo, one running to THE EAST CALLED JOLIBA, another to THE WEST CALLED QUORRA. Wargee appeared a man of no inconsiderable observation, and was rather communicative than otherwise — he described a voyage to India which he had made in his early days with much accuracy — From a letter of Consul Warrington's dated 28th March 1824, which I was permitted to peruse in the Colonial Office, I copied the following extract — 'A native of Fas describes Yeooré to be about three moons from Burnow [Bornu] towards the setting sun: Part of the Country high mountains — Rivers small and great run from them into the *fresh water sea*, and afterwards into the SALT to the *left* of where the sun sets. He went along the banks of a great river to Burnow, which river runs into the Schad, whence it passes to Bagherné*** [Bagarmi] and

* In Leo's time such an opinion was prevalent, although he did not subscribe to it. '*Sunt preterea, qui dicant jam dictum fluvium in occidente ex quodam monte* [word illegible] *atque orientum versus fluendo, maximum tandem lacum illic efficere.*'
** They are always brought down when the river is full.
*** I have the same information from two men in Ghadamis, as also from a man named Bogoola, whom Denham and Clapperton know well. He describes Lake Schad to be like

enters the Nile. This river takes its rise in *large mountains** beyond Soudan, called El Bouchy [Bauchi]. The river at Yaooré is a *different one*, and runs to the SETTING SUN.' This information is very distinct as far as it goes, and corroborates the statement of Wargu and the Haoossa slaves with respect to the Westerly course of the Niger after passing Yaooré — but it is to be regretted that he has not been made more intelligible with regard to *rivers small and great running from the mountains into the fresh water sea*, & from thence to the Salt. — They wou'd most likely have been ascertained to be those rivers which discharge themselves into the Bight of Benin to the South or *left of where the sun sets*, some of which may previously collect in an inland basin.

[Laing here inserts the following footnote]

Lt. King R.N. has been nearly two hundred miles up the river Benin — he is known at the Colonial Office, & might afford some information, which might be interesting & useful at the present moment.

It has been always understood** that the Niger loses itself in Wangara in a Lake or Marshes;[1] Babané places Wangara S.E. from Tombuctoo exactly in the position of the *Lybia Palus* of Ptolemy, and thus favors a hypothesis which in sketching the course of the river he again contradicts.

But my time is so short, and so much occupied at present with business more immediately connected with the Mission, that I am not permitted to go into detail of evidence at any length, nor to offer refutation to many points that might appear to favor other theories — I may hereafter prove by actual observation the validity of the theory which I have started, which it must be admitted carries with it some degree of probability, and to say the least of it, is entitled to attention.

The whole of the foregoing evidence seems to agree in one particular, viz. the interruption which the Niger meets at about the 11th degree of North Latitude, from whence it may run in any or all of the different directions specified. The evidence of the Haoossa slaves &c is rather against its Southerly progress; there is no evidence to prove, nor is there any to disprove its Easterly course, whereas there are

---

a man's entrails, hard to know the beginning or the end — but says it has an outlet to the sea during the rainy season.

* the Kong no doubt.   ** from the statements of the Moors.

[1] See p. 39n. 1 above.

Appendix: Cursory Remarks on the Niger

three coinciding testimonies (to say nothing of the position of Wangara as laid down by Babané) to prove that it turns towards the setting sun — My present apperçu [sic] of the rivers of Africa are as delineated on the other side:[1] I look upon the Schad or Yeow, and Shary to be the parent streams of the White Nile, and if the Niger has an outlet to the ocean, it may not improbably turn out to be through the Volta, which is a remarkably broad river, and the only one on the Coast of Guinea in which the Hippopotamus is found, an animal common to the Niger.[2]

A. Gordon Laing.

[1] See Map VI (c).

[2] The following extract from a letter written to Sir Joseph Banks by James Rennell on 6 January 1815 is relevant to the theory of the Niger's termination which Laing here propounds:

'I conclude that you do not Credit *Blackey* — Amongst the Causes of doubt, with me are

1 The improbability of the *Joliba*'s penetrating the ridge of *Kong* at all

2 That greater doubt, that it could penetrate such a barrier [?] of mountain without *falls*, or *unnavigable rapids* (Rivers are content with opening a Passage, without caring whether they can carry Boats on their backs, through them)

3ᵈ That Blackey *proves too much*, in respect of his knowledge of Geography:– the river going East, then S. then W. And lastly, that a Slave Merchant at Tombuctoo could find a *cheaper* & *readier* way of sending Slaves to Benin.

'Considering the nature of the rainy Season of the S.W. *Monsoon* of the Coast of Guinea; which corresponds in all its Circumstances with that of India; there is water enough falls to form the rivers in question, on the *south* of the Kong: & soon enough for them to collect in. Moreover, the *Joliba* is far from being, in point of bulk, one of the First Class of Rivers.'

In regard to what Laing writes about the hippopotamus Mr. R. W. Hayman of the British Museum (Natural History) writes: 'The known facts of Hippopotamus distribution in West Africa do not support the view expressed by Laing. This animal is known from Senegal to Gambia eastwards to Nigeria and then through all tropical Africa.

'There are, however, in West Africa gaps in this distribution, particularly in Liberia and parts of the Ivory Coast, so that there might have been some slight grounds, at the time, for Laing's mistaken belief' (Letter to the editor).

APPENDIX III

Laing's *Notes on Gadamis*[1]

20th October, 1825

On the 9th September a little after noon we arrived at a well of brackish water, two days journey from Gadamis, which was indeed a happy relief after the thirst we had experienced during the three preceding days, the scorching Sirocco of a fortnight's duration which at this time of the year is most oppressive, drying up the moisture of our lips as immediately as we were enabled to wet them, with the scanty allowance of water which was left to us. The Camels which had performed seven long journies by day and night without tasting water, were not satisfied till after sunset, although six men were kept in constant employ drawing for them, such was the extent of their thirst.

Next morning we proceeded a short distance from this well, when being met by a party of the Sheikh's[2] friends from Gadamis, and the Sheikh finding himself very unwell, we halted for the remainder of the day. The dress of these people so nearly resembled the Mandingo, that I cou'd not avoid addressing them in that language, which I did involuntarily, being more familiar with it than I as yet was with the Arab, and to my surprise and delight was answered by several in pure Bambarra, of which the former is a slight corruption.[3] They were very communicative and seemed extremely happy to see us, presenting us with some fine bread, Dates, and water Melons, and giving us all the news of the place. Among other matters they congratulated us on our good fortune in having taken the route by Fezzan, as we by that circuit avoided a party of 130 of Jebel Calvalry, who had been laying in wait for us for three weeks past, near a place called Duish only two days from Gadamis, and who being disappointed, had robbed the latter country of a great number of Camels, sheep &c. On the 11th and 12th we journied each day for fourteen hours, and on the morning of the 13th at dawn of day, we beheld the long looked for town of Gadamis, situated like an island in the ocean, in the midst of an extensive barren plain, and enveloped in a green mantle of Date trees — Crowds of well dressed people came out to bid us welcome as we approached, and our reception was truly cordial, decent, & respectable. I desired my

[1] P.R.O., C.O. 2/15, 956.   [2] Babani's.
[3] Sudan languages were widely spoken in the Saharan oases.

three english attendants[1] to dress in White Turkish Shirts, with English trousers; and habiting myself in a light European undress with my blue military cloak, (to which I gave the acting *commission* of a Burnoose) we entered Gadamis as *Christians*, and SUBJECTS OF HIS MAJESTY THE KING OF ENGLAND.

Gadamis is a town of remarkable antiquity, and has been noticed by the traveller Leo[2] as a place of mercantile consequence. There are records extant of its having been a watering and resting place for Kaffles preparing to cross the Desart as far back as three thousand years ago; of it subsequently becoming an encampment, then gradually assuming the appearance of a town about a thousand years before the Hegyra — It is situated in 30°,07′ — 20″N.L., and 9° — 16′ — 15″ E.L.,[3] standing entirely isolated in the midst of the Black Desert of Soudah, about Two hundred and ninety miles distant from the Mediterranean — The scite appears to have been originally chosen, on account of the abundant supply of water afforded by several ponds (one of them of considerable extent, about 108 yards in circumference), which are constantly full, being fed by the guggling [*sic*] of more than a hundred springs: from these the gardens originated by means of numerous canals, which conducting the water first through the town, serve to purify and sweeten it, previous to fertilizing the thirsty soil — The largest of these ponds stands in the centre of the town, and is of sufficient elevation to send abroad its contents without any mechanical help; but from the smaller ones, situated among the Gardens, the water is raised in buckets, with considerable manual labour, as in the Valley of Shati.

The town together with the gardens, occupying a space of about four miles only in circumference, in a triangular form, is enclosed by mud walls seven or eight feet high, with here and there projecting bastions with *trous de loup* for musketry, which are of flimsy construction, and far from being monumental, and as far as they are concerned neither exhibit the appearance nor the reality of strength — Defence with the people of Gadamis, is however a matter of no moment, as

---

[1] See p. 238n. 2 above.

[2] The following is Leo's very brief description of 'the region of Gademes', the Cydamus of Pliny, in Pory's translation: 'This large region hauing many castles & villages therin, standeth southward of the Mediterran sea almost three hundred miles. The inhabitants being rich in dates and all other kinde of merchandise, and trafficking into the land of Negros, pay tribute vnto the Arabians; albeit for certaine time they were subiect vnto the king of Tunis, and the Prince of Tripolis. Corne and flesh are maruellous scarce here' (Leo Africanus, III, 797).

[3] More correctly 30° 08′ N × 13° 15′ E.

their policy which shall be noticed in its proper place, directs a pacific course; otherwise, isolated as they are, in the midst of a desert, in which (excepting within their own walls) neither provision nor water is to be found; they might with no other assistance than that afforded by the dark intricate labyrinths of their closely built town, bid defiance to the combined attacks of all Africa.

The town of Gadamis altho' populous, containing about six thousand souls, occupies a very small space of ground, but is nevertheless kept perfectly clean, and is entirely free from those unsavoury odours, which its confined aspect would lead one to expect, for besides the streams of water which run thro' its lanes, and the conveniences which

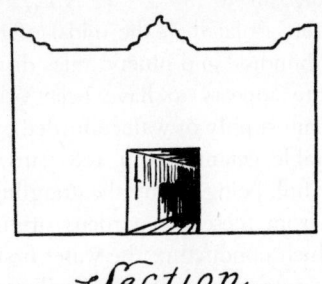

Ghadames: a subterranean passage, after a drawing
by Gordon Laing

every house has within itself, there are public cloacs for the accommodation of the numerous strangers who visit this place from the various distant regions of Africa.

The houses, like those in other Moorish countries, are of square construction with terraced roofs, and only dead walls exposed to view; on either side the narrow lanes or avenues which lead thro' and intersect the town, they are connected by cross buildings, which cover the lanes entirely to the total exclusion of the Sun, and even the light, with the exception of here and there a square opening, like that which admits the light into a subterranean passage, and which is hardly sufficient even at noon, to enable a person acquainted with its intricacies to grope his way. In every attempt of the kind which I made unattended, I invariably became so bewildered that I had to resort to the guidance of some kind Ariadne to extricate me from my difficulties. The interior of the houses exhibits nevertheless a degree of comfort, & occasionally even of elegance, the walls of house being plaistered with considerable

Appendix: Notes on Gadamis

skill, divided into paneling [*sic*] of oblong squares, painted ornamentally, with recesses in which are fixed large pier glasses, which are of the latest fashion, but have been gaudy in their time. There are also niches distributed at intervals, which contain small earthen ornaments, a species of decoration of which they appear as fond as our European Moderns are of their chimney ornaments. The rooms on the ground floor have no other light than that admitted by the doors which open into the square courtyard, but those in the upper stories have the advantage of a skye light. The mountainous darkness of the lanes which lead thro' the town, is sometimes disturbed by large paved court yards into which they open: around these are arranged canopied seats of stone or ornamental clay, upon which the loungers are to be seen reclining during the hours of solar warmth, and conversing upon the news brought by the last Kaffle from some remote part of the Continent, Or (if in front of a mosque, as it sometimes happens) the bigoted Maraboots solemnly discussing texts from the Koran. The Mosques are neat, decorously modest, and entirely free from that gorgeous display of grandeur which in Europe, by a strange anomaly, characterises the edifices dedicated to the worship of the same God, through the medium of a more meek, more humble, more charitable instructor and mediator. The burying grounds are not attached to the mosques, but are situated outside the walls of the town, decently retired, and at a proper distance from the habitation of the living: I have occasionally touched upon the venerated respect which every Turk pays to the manes of his departed relative or friend, but nowhere have I found occasion to admire it more than in Gadamis, where the humblest individual has the place where he measures his length, marked by a commemorative stone, which has consequently caused the extension of the place of sepulture to a most unusual size. Without degrading ourselves, we might borrow much from the decent respectable forms of even the prejudiced Mohamedan; we might teach ourselves a lesson of humility, which whether real or affected, is truly becoming, and is the basis upon which our own inimitable faith, and scale of redemption is founded. Our church yards are either marked by a coldness and deserted frigidity which reflects upon the feeling of the living, or by a pomposity and splendour which honors not the dead, but betrays the vanity of the survivors — in the one instance they are the nurseries of the thistle & hemlock & are avoided by all; in the other, they are the resort of the idle and curious! — How different is the quiet, tranquil, composed appearance of a Turkish burying ground, attended by relatives and friends, who forget not the deceased with the last shovel full of earth which is thrown upon the grave, but who pay to the hallowed spot a variety of endearing attentions — in gathering around a heap of stones, planting a shrub or tree, and in fencing the earthen cup, which is daily filled with water, and serves to quench the thirst of the little feathered tribe, who flock to it, and chirp around it! How widely different the feelings, the ideas which the sight of this attention engenders — it removes in a great degree the horrors of death which are naturally implanted in the human mind, and which are heightened by neglect — and it crushes in the bud the horrid irreligious intent of the self destroyer, who wou'd rush to eternal punishment, to arrest temporary evil.

In my rambles through the town I found three manufactories of common pottery, and the process a rude imitation merely of the method in use in Europe, from whence most probably it has found its way. A few blacksmiths, shoemakers, (the standing mechanics of Africa) with some indifferent tailors, were the only other trades I cou'd see or hear of in Gadamis.

The soil in the Gardens is composed of a hardish clay mixed with sand, which requires so much care and attention to render productive, that it is with considerable trouble that the inhabitants, who are extremely industrious in making the most of their little [two words illegible] and preserve the date trees, which though diminutive in size, and less prolific than those in Shati, constitute the principal part of the food of the slaves, as well as the middling classes. One of my attendants whose remark on approaching Shati I have recorded, observed after we had been some days in Gadamis 'In my country Dates are plenty, even Camels may eat them, but here they are kept under lock and key'. Gadamis in fact produces nothing of itself, and yet perhaps its inhabitants are more rich, generally speaking, than those of any other country in Africa: compelled to become erratic in search of articles which their own country will not afford, they have by their skill in barter, arrived to a mercantile rank, which almost requires to be witnessed to be credited. They calculate with profound nicety the expense of carriage to distant countries, duties or customs, risk, trouble, and the percentage that their goods will bear, and even do business by means of Bills and written agreements or promises — indeed so sensible are they of the advantages which they derive from trade, that rather than fire a single gun in war, they submit to the greatest imposition and taxation in the shape of tribute, which they pay annually to the Bashaw of Tripoli,

Appendix: Notes on Gadamis   379

Jebel Arabs and the Tuaric, from the two latter of whom they are notwithstanding subjected to constant robbery and plunder, but particularly from the latter, who like the Highland Catherans of old absolutely *lift* at times whole caravans of Camels — The people of Gadamis being fully aware that war wou'd shut them out from all commercial advantage, bear all this with patience, pay their tribute for permission to cross the Desart, redeem their camels by the payment of a certain exaction, & accumulate wealth besides. It was this kind of policy which induced them to pay the Bashaw of Tripoli the sum of thirty thousand Mitkalleis about six years ago, instead of destroying the army which he sent to demand it, and which they might have done with half the trouble they took to save it. This army arrived before Gadamis in the most deplorable condition from thirst, and wou'd have been entirely annihilated in a day or two more, had not the Sheikh kindly cut a canal, & permitted the water to flow to them from the ponds in the town — before this was done, some of the Soldiers of His Highness absolutely bartered their muskets for a draught of water. The Bey of Tunis, to whom they paid tribute in the time of Leo, was not so fortunate in his invasion of Gadamis about two hundred years ago. This chief, El Khaidram Dham Sultan of Frikia [Ifrikia] as he was styled, had long received an annual tribute or present from this place, which was suspended for six years on account of some exhorbitant additional demand made by the Bey, of a nature with which the people cou'd not comply: On the seventh refusal, the Bey appeared before Gadamis with an army of 1200 Infantry, 800 Cavalry & two pieces of Artillery, but not succeeding in intimidating the inhabitants into a compliance he attacked the town: The people of Gadamis sheltering themselves among the intricate maze of these condensed [?] buildings, sustained a very trifling loss of six killed and about twenty wounded, whereas the Bey of Tunis left on the field from which he was compelled to retire upwards [*sic*] a hundred slain, double that number wounded, besides his two pieces of cannon.

The attack lasted from nine o'clock in the morning till Assar 3 pm — The Two brass guns have since found their way to Tripoli, and are now in the possession of His Highness the Bashaw.

Gadamis although paying custom or tribute to the Jebel Arabs, the Tuaric, & the Bashaw of Tripoli, acknowledges the supremacy of the latter only, which is an act of wise policy on their part, as they are by such an acknowledgement rendered secure in their trading excursions to Burnoo [Bornu], and Soudan [Hausa], the road to the former of which countries is entirely commanded by the Bashaw, who receives certain customs upon every loaded Camel which passes along it, to or fro. The Sheikh or Governor, who holds his appointment at the pleasure of the Bashaw, also acts in the capacity of an agent for that Chief, collecting & remitting to him all dues, customs &c & retaining for himself a percentage of one tenth. The effects of all persons who die without issue belong to the Bashaw, and constitute the only nominated revenue which His Highness derives from this place, but he will sometimes when pressed for money, as is not infrequently the case with His Highness, make a demand of four, five, or even ten thous^d mitkalleis at a time, which the Sheikh has little trouble in collecting, assigning to every one his proportion according to his known & acknowledged means, & receiving it on the day appointed without a murmur, or disatisfied expression. The average price of land is about a hundred pounds an acre, varying in price from its state of cultivation, number of Date trees, and its proximity to or distance from the wells: Those irrigated from the large pond, which requires no manual labour to supply the water, are considered invaluable: during my stay in Gadamis, a garden of about one third of an acre, irrigated from the large pond, & well stored with full grown date and Fig trees, which had become the property of the Bashaw in the usual manner, was sold for the enormous sum of £2,000 Dollars or a thousand Mitkallies; and its present proprietor assured me that he wou'd not dispose of it for half as much more. When property is so valuable, the greater attention is of course observed in enclosing it, which is done here by mud or swish walls about ten feet in height, small avenues being left to admit of approach.

The climate is generally speaking mild and salubrious, but it is nevertheless subject to sudden variations of temperature, particularly about the changing of the seasons, which are nearly as strongly marked as those in more Northern regions, the proportionate extremes of heat and cold being equally as great. During a Sirocco in Septr I observed the mercury in the thermometer stand at 116° Farenheit in the shade, and on the 23d Octr it fell one morning as low as 58° — but as Augt is the hottest month, and December the coldest, the extremes must be of course more strongly marked, than is even shown by the above observations. After the fashion of the French about thirty years ago, the People of Gadamis rather facetiously divide their year & characterise the seasons in the following manner

Appendix: Notes on Gadamis 381

Three months of Pleasure	Septr / Octr / Novr	When the fruit is ripe & abundant
Three months of Rain	Decr / Jany / Feby	For the growth of grain &c
Three months of Health	March / April / May	A pleasant season, nor too hot, nor too cold
Three months of Heat	June / July / Augt	Cherokes or date winds. People sit down quiet [in] their houses.

Inhabitants. It will hardly be necessary to observe, after the mention of the Mercantile consequence of these people that they are in manner superior to any that I have yet come in contact with in this extensive continent. All Mohomedans possess a dignified though a sullen & haughty deportment, but the peculiar situation of these people, as travellers to distant countries, where a courteous exterior must be preserved by the stranger, the address which is requisite in conducting their rich Kaffles through idle, marauding, and avaricious tribes, has tempered in them this deportment, and rendered them mild in their manner, peacable in their conduct, kind and amiable in their dispositions, of friendly and familiar intercourse & of superior address — Such is the opinion I have formed of these people after a residence of six weeks among them, such indeed have I without a solitary exception found them — my humbler attendants were always received among them with a good natured honest familiar kindness, and on every occasion I perceived from them the most marked respect and attention, which I was proud and happy to perceive, eminated [sic] from no personal considerations or mean sordid motives (as I never was importuned for a present by any native of Gadamis) but from the exalted opinion they had for men of the august Sovereign whom I have the honor to serve, & the character of the country to which I have the happiness to belong — It is true that in passing a bevy of Maruboots once, seated with their Korans in front of a Mosque, I was saluted rather unceremoniously with the undignified appellation of Kafir, which was taken up and re-echoed by some old idle beldams in the neighbourhood; yet I heeded it not. There is much in the solemnity and even in the tenets of the Mahomedan religion to admire, but meakness and forbearance forms no part of it. How cou'd I therefore contemn the illiberal feelings betrayed by teachers of that Faith? when I see them equally prevalent among some of the dissenting preachers of the most meek & charitable religion that ever shone upon sinful man. Let every man regard his own the only true road to heaven, and let him found his hope of future salvation on the moral assistance he renders to others, not in the contempt, or even charitable pity, with which he regards those who dissent from his own acknowledged faith: With regard to the old women who so vehemently re-echoed the ungentle salutation of their pastors, as I have now something to say of their sex generally, I shall only for the present apply to them the french adage: '*Les femmes sont extremes; elles sont meilleurs* [sic] *ou pires, que les hommes.*'

In Gadamis, the women appear to hold a rank superior to that enjoyed by them in any other country in Africa, being generally speaking, relieved from that seclusion and restraint which is imposed by the rigid customs of the jealous turks, and being held in too high estimation to be subjected to the menial and laborious occupations which devolve upon them in the Negro Kingdoms: there are of course exceptions to the above observation, and there are some Ladies in Gadamis, who from the beginning to the end of the year are never permitted to emerge from the houses or prisons, in which their jealous lords think proper to seclude them; but generally speaking it is not so, & it has fallen to my lot to have witnessed some instances of domestic comfort & sociality in Gadamis, where the Lady has appeared & acquitted herself with an ease and propriety, that wou'd not have disgraced European clay — Nay I have even seen so much authority displayed by the female in the presence of her Lord & Master, as to leave a doubt on my mind whether the government in the house was gymcocratic or not — The principal wife of the Sheikh Babané was of this character, and certainly had a will of her own, as verily as any Lady who ever breathed a more northern atmosphere. She seems to regard attention from her husband, and compliance with her wishes as her birthright, and she maintains with determination a sovereign controul over all the domestic concerns of her own dwelling, which is the general residence of the Sheikh, who willingly resigns it to her, seeing it will contribute to his peace and comfort — The females of Gadamis habit themselves on

Appendix: Notes on Gadamis

common occasions in a loose under garment of cotton which crosses the shoulders and inpends as low as the ankle, with a barakan of woollen or cotton which hangs from their head, and in which they envelop themselves like the Roman Ladies with the *palla*; indeed the description of the dress of the latter will nearly apply to that of the women of Gadamis. Ad talas stola, & circumdata palla —

On festivals and other grand occasions, their costume is most magnificent, the *Stola* consisting of rich silk embroidered with Gold, & the *palla* of red cloth edged with broad gold lace, the ears loaded with rings and chains of silver, and the wrists & arms cased in a profusion of manilloes[1] of the same metal. I once admired the workmanship of those which encircled the arms of the wife of the Sheikh, when to my great surprise she pulled them off, & begged my acceptance of them — not expecting such a reply to my expressions of admiration I felt a little confused, and apologised rather awkwardly for declining the present, but she insisted, and enforced the tender by observing that she was tired of them, and she had just been thinking of making her husband give her new ones — I therefore received them with this proviso, that if in three days she cou'd not produce the new set, I shou'd return them; to which she acceeded and on the third day exhibited them in triumph. When I told Babane of the circumstance he smiled, and said — What can I do? she will have her own way — She has to day ordered three sheep to be killed & dried for your provision on the road to Tombuctoo, and when I asked her to give me a small piece for supper, she refused, & enquired if I wished to see the Christian die of hunger.

She had a sort of fiddle with one string on which she cou'd execute some very fair music accompanying it with a voice of little power, but very melodious. I used to pay her frequent visits, and Like that which I have noticed in my journey through Kooranko[2] after becoming a little intimate succeeded in prevailing upon her to amuse me with this instrument, which she wou'd do with becoming and modest propriety, and although sometimes disturbed by the return of her husband, whose expression I used carefully to watch on such occasions, I cou'd neither distinguish restraint on her part, nor disatisfaction on his — on the contrary, Babané seemed both proud and pleased that his wife cou'd contribute to my amusement. These little anecdotes, trifling in themselves, are nevertheless interesting, in as

---

[1] Manilloes or manillas were metal bracelets which were used as a currency in West Africa.
[2] In Sierra Leone.

much as they afford a correct portrait of the state of Society in Gadamis. It gave me infinite pleasure to behold the female rank standing thus high, as it has confirmed a position which I advanced in my former travels, when I saw the low degraded state of the sex, and their total lack of virtue and decency, that the amiability & conduct of women entirely depended upon the estimation in which they are held by the opposite sex. Gadamis appears like one large family, the tranquillity of which wou'd be undisturbed, but for the machinations of a disaffected Sheikh named Habeeb, who is the son of the Sheikh who governed before Babané. This man is in league with the Jebel and Schaamba [Chaamba] Arabs, and oftentimes bribes them & always gives them notice that they may have it in their power to plunder the Kaffles of Babané. It was he who sent the Jebel Cavalry to wait for us at Dursh, and it is he who has apprised the Schaamba of our intended Journey to Tuat. The interior of the town is however so tranquil, that the Sheikh will leave it on his trading excursions for months & sometimes for years, leaving his brother as locum tenens, and it rarely happens that on his return, a single complaint salutes his ear, not even from that source of constant disquietude & annoyance, which agitates most other districts in Africa (perhaps I may extend the observation) viz the intrigues of the sexes.

The Slaves in Gadamis are treated with so much kindness and have so many privileges, that the remark which some have made regarding the condition of the slaves in our West India Islands, *'that Slavery is but a name'* might almost apply here. They are permitted by the savings of their labour to purchase their own freedom which is estimated at fifty Dollars! sometimes an indulgent master will give a slave his whole time to himself, the slave finding himself in every thing, and purchasing his liberty by instalments; at other times by the payment of a certain sum (if unable to make good the whole) he will receive a written document securing his freedom after the expiration of a certain period, and so forth in various ways may a slave become accessory to his own manumission: this it must be acknowledged greatly modifies the pangs of bondage, and affords a powerful incentive to industry. They are permitted at certain periods to indulge in the wild extravagant amusements peculiar to the country from which they have been transported, in the same manner that the West Indian slaves, but particularly those of Jamaica, exhibit at Christmas — at which times the giddy and thoughtless will sometimes squander away, the hard earned savings *'the sair won penny feee'* of the preceeding year. At the end of the *season of pleasure*, when the dates are ripe, they have one particular day, a sort of harvest home, on which they demand from their master the Keys of the date gardens, and pulling the best cluster they can find, in every enclosure in the country, they assemble at night, and have a glorious *festa*. This species of thraldom has existed in the early history of all states, and seems to be by nature attendant upon society in its early stages, but although it is of the mildest description, and although its ancient existence can be proved by annals both sacred and profane, yet such proof can afford no justification or shelter from reprobation, for those who wou'd desire that peacable nations shou'd wage war for the purpose of making prisoners whom they might sell for transportation from their own, their native land. It is a great satisfaction to learn at any time, that the condition of such unhappy people as have been so unfortunate to become slaves, is meliorated by kind treatment, but no argument for encreasing their number; and the pastoral characters in the Idyls of Theocritus, or Eclogues of Virgil wou'd have lost all their sentiment if transplanted from their 'sweet home' to labour at the cane hole or in the sugar house.

There are some ruins to the westward of the town on a piece of elevated ground, of which I give a very hasty outline.[1] They are strongly cemented by mortar, but seem to have been originally of very careless construction, and composed entirely of unhewn stone. I am at a loss to whom to ascribe them — they are decidedly not Turkish, being far beyond the architectural attempts of the people who inhabit the country; and they are too ordinary to be Roman: & I searched in vain for coins or carved stones by which I might obtain a clue to their identity. In digging around, I found some pieces of broken sarcophagi, and came upon a strongly built wall a few feet below the surface of the ground;[2] but as I did not visit the country to search after antiques, and as the people viewed my curiosity with some suspicion, I was unwilling by persevering to give them cause of displeasure. I have no doubt however, that there is a good field here for the Antiquary, and enough to reward his labour, shou'd curiosity lead him to the spot.

[1] See Plate IV.   [2] See p. 264 above.

APPENDIX IV

Emma Gordon Laing

In the background of the Laing story and, because of her sufferings never far from the reader's thoughts, is the tragic figure of his wife. Early in November 1826 she discovered that her father had, as we know, been keeping her in ignorance of much of what Laing had told him in his letters. At about the same time Laing's letter to her father of 1 July arrived, and the Consul's family learnt that he intended to return to Tripoli from Timbuktu. The Bornu Mission's old servant, Jacob, and the dragoman whom the Warringtons called the Marabut, were at once dispatched to Ghadames to meet him. These were the circumstances in which Emma Laing wrote the following pathetic letter to her husband, dated the day Jacob and the Marabut left Tripoli.

Tripoli 10th Nov. 1826

Yesterday my beloved Laing I had the pleasure of closing my letters & delivering them to the Maraboot & Jacob who are now on the road to meet my own adored husband — I now begin to feel some ray of comfort the departure of these people shews me that there is some prospect of my again being restored to happiness which for many many a long month has been a stranger to my bosom — I have this moment by the Consul's desire taken the duplicate of a letter which he has already sent by the Maraboot and by that letter I see that I have been kept in perfect ignorance of all the dreadful cruel reports then [two words illegible] in circulation about you.[1] I do not know whether so doing was cruelty or kindness — Why let me deceive myself with the hopes of your speedy return, the month I first expected you to return in passed away, & disappointed & sickened I looked forward to the next but to be disappointed again — At last the dreadful truth was revealed to me & without being at all prepared for it the blow was most severe — I heard of your wounds of your sickness — the chill of death appeared to pass over me, not a word not a complaint could I utter not a tear would fall from my eyes to relieve the agonising oppression of my heart, I spent the whole night in a state of stupefaction not understanding any thing I heard. The morning dawned, the first object that presented itself to my eyes was your dear picture which hung from my neck, at the sight, my recollection returned to me & I wept over it almost heart broken.

[1] This was evidently Warrington's letter to Laing of 9 November (R.S., 374(La) 120).

Appendix: Emma Gordon Laing

Oh my beloved dearest Laing, alas alas what have you been exposed to, what danger, what suffering, to have saved you one pang I would with joy have shed every drop of blood that warms this heart — Had I been with you in that fearful moment my arms which would have encircled you might for some time have shielded you from the swords of those Daemons — and at last we might have fallen pierced by the same weapon, our souls might have taken their flight together to that land [word illegible] sorrow can never come — My beloved Laing sorrow has laid a heavy hand on your Emma's head & so it has on yours — Alas Laing how cruel how sad has been our fate — Are we destined to endure more misery, or will a kind providence at length pity our unhappiness and restore us to each other — Will you my own idolised husband return to your Emma's fond arms, will you come & repose on her faithful bosom — Will you restore happiness to her torn heart —

Never for a Moment my beloved Laing have you been absent from my thoughts. You have always been present to my imagination waking & sleeping — You will find your Emma the same in heart & soul as when you last embraced her, entirely & for ever devoted to her Laing — God of heaven protect and bless you dearer to me than life — May he guide you in health and safety & may your own dear Emma be cold in death ere she shall again hear tidings of any evil or unhappiness having befallen her idolised husband.

Adieu my best beloved, May heaven soon restore you to the arms of your ever adoring devoted wife,

Emma M. Gordon Laing[1]

From its opening sentence this letter seems not to have been carried by Jacob and the Marabut. How it came to be filed in the consular archives in Tripoli, and thus transferred to the Public Record Office in London, we do not know. A more considerate father than Warrington would obviously have handed so intimate a letter back to the writer, his daughter.

As only one of Laing's letters to his wife has survived it is difficult to resist the impression that his father-in-law was the more favoured correspondent. This may not have been so. But Emma's distress over Laing's death, which was not placed beyond all doubt until Bongula and Alkhadir arrived in Tripoli in August 1828, can only have been rendered more acute by learning at the same time, from his last letters to her father (brought by Bongula and Alkhadir), that he had not written to her at all during the last few weeks of his life.

Whatever sympathy in her distress she may have received her from own family she certainly got none from her husband's. Warrington

[1] P.R.O., C.O. 2/20.

complained to Hay that when he wrote to Laing's father telling him of his son's death he got no reply. This seemed particularly extraordinary to the Consul after what he considered so advantageous a marriage for the son. 'I should apprehend', he wrote, 'in respect of Ancient Pedigree or even Pecuniary Resources that His Family must have been the gainers.'[1] It does not appear to have occurred to him that Emma's ancient pedigree, on one side anyway, might not have profoundly impressed her husband's pious Scottish parents.

Within a few months of Laing's death being proved beyond all doubt a ray of happiness seems to have crept into Emma's life. On 14 April 1829 she was married, by her father, to Thomas Wood, the British Vice-Consul in Benghazi.[2] We next hear of the Woods in Leghorn, in the interests of Emma's broken health. But on 2 Oct. 1829, less than six months after her marriage, she died at Pisa.[3]

Hanmer Warrington to R. W. Hay:

Sir, Tripoli 2 Nov. 1829

I have the honor to Inform you that Mr. Vice Consul Wood returned to Tripoli this Morng. and will proceed to Benghazi by the first vessel.

We are plunged into the deepest affliction, by the loss of as an affectionate Daughter and as Virtuous, and as Amiable a Child as ever lived — but *God's will be done*, and under the decrees of Heaven we must submit.

After the departure of poor Laing from Tuat, all communication for a considerable time ceased, and it is natural to suppose the anxiety and suspence, His poor Wife laboured under — Watchful days and Sleepless Nights first impaired as fine a Constitution ever formed by Nature and the subsequent Tragical events, progressively established a confirmed consumption which has brought my adored Daughter to an untimely Grave — Thus has that Monster of Iniquity the Baron Rousseau sacrificed two Victims to His Diabolical Intrigue — for to my last, shall I conscientiously believe He was concerned in that sad History. . . .

[formal ending]

R. W. Hay Esq. H. Warrington[4]

[1] P.R.O., F.O. 76/26, 1193.   [2] Ibid., 1622.

[3] P.R.O., F.O. 76/25, 2745. It will be recalled that it had been thought that Rousseau's son, Timoléon, had wanted to marry Emma before she became engaged to Laing. In the Anonymous Report there is a footnote reading: 'On the 3rd. March (1828) M. Rousseau actually waited on Mr. W. with a proposal to unite their families by the intermarriage of their children' (A.R., 57). Although at this time there was still a ray of hope that Laing yet lived, Rousseau's object, according to Pellissier, was a second attempt to secure Emma for his son. Warrington was said to have promised his consent but to have broken his promise, and 'le jeune Rousseau expira dans cette attente' (A. Bernard, 81).

[4] P.R.O., F.O. 76/26, 2973.

APPENDIX V

The Report of Laing's death published in *L'Étoile* of 2 May 1827

On écrit du Sukkara-Ley-Tripoli, 5 avril: 'Le major Laing dont on avait annoncé la fin tragique, a réellement péri victime de sa courageuse persévérence, après avoir pu néamoins visiter la fameuse ville de Tombuctou. Le pacha de Tripoli a communiqué cet avis d'après une lettre que le gouverneur de Ghadames, son vassal, lui a écrite pour l'informer de cet événement, et qui lui est parvenue en moins de quinze jours par un courrier extraordinaire.

'Les voyageurs anglais que l'on disait d'abord avoir succombé sous le fer des brigands, dans le territoire de Tonalt [Tuat], n'y avait été que blessé seulement, de manière qu'après avoir échappé à ce premier danger par les soins hospitaliers d'un *marabout*, il s'était enfin rendu à Tombuctou. Peu après son arrivée en cette ville, les *Fellans*, dont la borde puissante et belliqueuse règne exclusivement aujourd'hui sur les immenses déserts de l'Afrique centrale, vinrent au nombre de plus de trente mille, l'y réclamer impérieusement "pour le mettre à mort et empêcher par là, dirent-ils, que les nations chrétiennes profitent des informations qu'il pouvait leur donner sur le Soudan, ne pénétrassent quelque jour dans ces contrées eloignées pour en asservir les peuples". Ce sont les propres expressions du scheikh de Ghadames dans sa lettre au pacha.

'Le prince qui commande à Tombuctou refusa a livrer l'étranger qu'il avait accueilli avec bienveillance, et pour le soustraire à l'animosité de ses persécuteurs, dont il ne voulait pas en même temps s'attirer la vengeance, il le fit partir furtivement pour le Bambara sous une escorte de quinze cavaliers, choisis parmi sa propre garde; mais atteint bientôt après par une bande de *Fellans* qui, informée de son évasion, l'avait vivement poursuivi, l'infortuné Laing fut impitoyablement égorgé avec tous ceux qui l'accompagnaient.

'Telle a été la fin tragique du voyageur intrépide, qui, le premier a pu pénétrer dans l'enceinte d'une ville mystérieuse, objet de tant de sollicitudes, et dont la connaissance échappera sans doute encore long-temps aux investigations les mieux dirigées, puisque suivant tout apparence il n'y a nul espoir de recouvrer les papiers du malheureux Laing.'

'En attendant, les *Fellans*, dont l'ambition égale la férocité, profitant de la circonstance de l'arrivée du major Laing à Tombuctou et de l'espèce de protection qu'il avait trouvée, se sont emparés de cette ville en la taxant d'un tribut annuel que ses habitans, incapables de leur résister, doivent leur payer désormais pour s'être rendus, comme ils les en accusent, complices des projets d'envahissement médités par les infidéles.

'Ces derniers renseignements ont été communiqués par un scheikh de Tripoli qui a long-temps résidé a Tombuctou. Il a déclaré qu'il existe une histoire fort intéressante de cette ville, laquelle en fait remonter le fondation à l'an 510 de l'hégire (1116 de J.C.), et dont l'auteur est Sidi-Ahmed-Baba, natif d'Arawan, bourgade du pays des Kentés [? Kuntá], peuplade considérable du Soudan; on espère pouvoir se procurer cette histoire pour en faire hommage avec les voyages du célèbre Ibn-Bathouta jusqu'à present si peu connus en Europe, à la bibliothèque du Roi.'

BIBLIOGRAPHY

I. Manuscripts

Note. The principal sources of material are marked thus *

PUBLIC RECORD OFFICE

C.O. 2	15*	1825–6	Missions to the Interior.
	16		Missions to the Interior.
	20*		Major Laing's mission to Timbuctoo. Papers relating to his death.

Barbary States

F.O. 8	8	1822–4	Instructions to Consuls, etc.
	12	1822–5	Domestic. Answers to letters.

Tripoli

F.O. 76	14	1820	Consul Hanmer Warrington.
	15	1821	Consul Hanmer Warrington.
	16	1822	Consul Hanmer Warrington.
	17	1823	Consul Hanmer Warrington.
	18	1824	Consul Hanmer Warrington.
	19	1825	Consul Hanmer Warrington.
	20	1826	Consul Hanmer Warrington and Vice-Consul Joseph Dupuis.
	21	1827	Consul Hanmer Warrington and Vice-Consul Joseph Dupuis.
	22*	1827	Consul Hanmer Warrington. Case of Major Laing's mission and various.
	23	1828	Consul Hanmer Warrington.
	24	1828	Consul Hanmer Warrington.
	25	1829	Consul Hanmer Warrington and Vice-Consul Joseph Dupuis.
	26*	1829	Consul Hanmer Warrington. Case of Major Laing's mission and various.
	27	1830	Consul Hanmer Warrington and Vice-Consul J. Fraser.
	28	1831	Consul Hanmer Warrington and Vice-Consul T. Wood.

| F.O. 76 33* | 1832 | Papers Explanatory of the circumstances under which Sidi Hassuna D'Ghies was accused by the Bashaw of Tripoli of abstracting the late Major Laing's papers. |

ROYAL SOCIETY'S ARCHIVES

374(La) 1 to 146*	Sundry letters (drafts and copies) and memoranda by Laing.
Laing vol. 3, 375	Portion of Laing's MS for his *Travels in Western Africa*.
Laing vol. 4, 376	An autobiographical fragment by Laing.

II. Published Journals and other Printed Works

African Society, Journal of the, XXXI (1932), 282–92; XXIX (1929–30), 507.
Annual Register for the Year 1824, The (London, 1825), 124–36.
Augiéras, E. M., *La pénétration dans le Sahara occidental* (Paris, 1923).
Banks Correspondence, D.T.C., vol. xx.
Barth, Henry, *Travels in North and Central Africa*, 5 vols. (London, 1857–8).
Beechey, Captain F. W. and Beechey, H. W., *Proceedings of the Expedition to Explore the Northern Coast of Africa* (London, 1828).
Bernard, Augustin, 'Un Mémoire inédit de Pellissier de Reynaud,' *Mémorial Henri Basset*, XVII (Paris, 1928), 79–82.
Bonnel de Mezières, *Le Major A. Gordon Laing* (Paris, 1927).
Briggs, L. Cabot, *The Living Races of the Sahara Desert* (Cambridge, Mass., 1958).
——, *Tribes of the Sahara* (Cambridge, Mass., 1960).
Caillié, René, *Travels through Central Africa to Timbuctoo*, English translation, 2 vols. (London, 1830).
Chambers, Robert, *A Biographical Dictionary of Eminent Scotsmen*, 4 vols. (Glasgow, 1835), III, 335–44.
Clapperton, Captain Hugh, *Journal of a Second Expedition into the Interior of Africa* (London, 1829).
Cowper, H. S., *The Hill of the Graces* (London, 1897).
Dearden, Seton, Introduction to Miss Tully, *Letters Written During a Ten Years' Residence at the Court of Tripoli* (London, 1957).
Delafosse, Maurice, *Haut-Sénégal-Niger*, 3 vols. (Paris, 1912).
Denham, Major Dixon, and Clapperton, Capt. Hugh, *Narrative of Travels and Discoveries in Northern and Central Africa*, 2 vols. (London, 1826).
Duveyrier, H., *Les Touareg Du Nord* (Paris, 1864).
Edinburgh Review, The, XLI (1824–5), 337; XLIX (1829), 148.

Bibliography

Féraud, L. C., *Annales Tripolitaines* (Paris, 1927).
Gautier, E. F., *L'Afrique Noire Occidentale* (Paris, 1939).
——, *Le Sahara Algerien* (Paris, 1908).
Gentleman's Magazine, The, II (1824), 277.
Geographical Journal, The, II (1832), 1–28, 172–90; XXXIX (1912), 54–7.
Jomard, E. F., 'Geographical Remarks' in R. Caillié, *Travels*, 1830, II.
——, 'Nouvelles du Major Laing', *Bull. de la Société de Géographie*, VII (1827), 203; VIII (1827), 178, 180.
Laing, Major A. Gordon, *Travels in the Timannee, Kooranko, and Soolima Countries, in Western Africa* (London, 1825).
Lenz, Oscar, *Timbuktu*, 2 vols. (Leipzig, 1884).
Leo Africanus, *The History and Description of Africa done into English by John Pory*, 3 vols. (Hakluyt Society, London, 1896).
Lyon, Capt. G. F., *A Narrative of Travels in Northern Africa* (London, 1821).
Martin, P. H., *Les oasis sahariennes* (Algiers, 1908).
Marty, Paul, *Etudes sur l'Islam et les Tribas du Soudan* (Paris, 1920).
Monod, Théodore, *La Géographie*, LIV (1930), 154–76.
Monteil, Charles, *Une cité soudanaise Djénné* (Paris, 1932).
Nelson, Thomas, *A Biographical Memoir of Oudney, Clapperton and Laing* (Edinburgh, 1830).
New Monthly Magazine, The, XXVII (1829), 36.
Park, Mungo, *Travels in the Interior Districts of Africa* (London, 1799).
——, *Travels in the Interior Districts of Africa with an account of a Subsequent Mission in 1805*, 2 vols. (London, 1816).
Pefontan, Lieut., *Histoire de Tombouctou, Bull. du Comité d'Etudes historiques et scientifiques de l'Afrique Occidentale Française* (Paris, 1922).
Quarterly Review, The, XXXVIII (1825), 100–9; XXXIX (1829), 170–4; XLII (1830), 450–75.
Quarterly Journal of Science, Literature, and the Arts, The, XIV (1823), 1–16; XV (1823), 171.
Reichard, C. G., *Ephémerides géographiques* (Weimar, August 1803).
Richardson, James, *Travels in the Great Desert of Sahara*, 2 vols. (London, 1848).
——, *Narrative of a Mission to Central Africa*, 2 vols. (London, 1853).
Richer, A., *Les Oulliminden* (Paris, 1924).
Ricketts, Major, *Narrative of the Ashantee War* (London, 1831).
Rodd, F. R. (Lord Rennell), *People of the Veil* (London, 1926).
Rousseau, Baron, *Bulletin de la Société de Géographie*, VIII (1827), 174.
Sa'di, Abderrahman es, *Tarikh es Soudan*, trad. O. Houdas (Paris, 1900).
Sémaphore de Marseille, Le (Marseilles, 12 Sept. 1829).
Smyth, W. H., *The Mediterranean* (London, 1854).
Société de Géographie, *Bulletin de la* (Paris), X, 41.

Tully, Miss, *Letters Written During a Ten Years' Residence at the Court of Tripoli* (London, 1816).

Vadala, R., 'L'Histoire des Karamanlis'; *Revue de l'Histoire des Colonies Françaises*, VIIa (1919), 177–288.

Young, D. M., *The Colonial Office in the Early Nineteenth Century* (London, 1961).

INDEX

Abbes, 99, 104
Abdullah (travelling name of Clapperton), 216 n. 2
Abo, 112
Abu Rauwash, 58
Adams, Robert, 181
Adelaide, Hornemann sails in, 20
Africa Association, 4, 140, 145; engages Houghton, 7; engages Hornemann, 8, 52; receives proposals from Hornemann, 10; answers Hornemann's proposals, 12–14; agreements with Hornemann, 16–19; hears of Hornemann's travels, 30; discusses Hornemann's fate, 31, 32; publishes Hornemann's *Journal*; purpose of, 45, 50; work taken over by government, 129; engages Adolphe Lenant, 219 n. 2
African Investigator, 331
African Society, memorial to Laing, 182
Agades, 3, 29, 55, 99, 108, 114, 287, 290, 361
Agar, 183, 361
Aghades, see Agades
Aghurmi, 66 n. 1
Agriculture, 82, 346, 359; in Fezzan, 99; in Tripoli, 346
Agrmie, 66, 71
Ague, 69, 106
Ahaggar tribe, 288
Ahauagh, 218 n. 7
Ahmadu Labeida, entrusted with care of Laing, 313
Ahmed Baba, 332, 333
Ahmed el Bakkai, Sidi, 215 n. 1
Ahmed Karamanli, 149, 150
Air (Asben), 165
Akabli, 292 n. 2
Alexandria, 10, 11, Hornemann arrives at 21
Algiers, 113
Ali Baba, *see* Ahmed Baba
Ali Boo-Khaloom, 209
Ali Karamanli, 150
Al Khadir, 335, 387; Babani's nephew, 309; helps Laing, 313; carrier of Laing's papers, 330
Ammonites, 73

Anamaboe, 252
Annual Register, 134 n. 2, 137
Aoulef, 292
Apperley, C. J. (Nimrod), 152 n. 3
Arabs, character of, 68, 103, 360; in caravan trade, 82
Arabic, Laing's use of, 356
Arawan, Laing sets out for, 312 n. 1
Architecture, of Egypt, 77
Arna, 113
Asben, 114; map of, 116; Sultan of, 121, 165
Ashanti, 33, 35, war, 134, 136, 144, 145
Asker Ali, 161
Askia the Great, 169
Asna, 115
Augila, 111, 114, 121
Aucalas, burial of Hornemann at, 32
Augila, 75, desciption of, 82, 83
Aujila, 26
Azoad, (Azawad) 303

Babani, Sheikh, 208, 383; character of, 214; Laing's opinion of, 247; opinion on Niger, 367, 373; leaves Tripoli to join Laing, 217; plans to deliver Laing's letters, 219; trickery of, 222, 223, 300, 323; Warrington's warning to Laing, 223; meets Laing, 228, 350; arrives at Beni Ulid, 353; sudden departure, 235; confidence of, 239; present given to, 259, 282; misunderstanding over money, 284–5, 291; death of, 300, 301, 307, 309; wife of, 382
Bagarmi, 113, 118, 119, 121, 226, 371
Bah-el-Abiad, 119
Bahr-bella-ma, 63
Barh el Arab, 38
Bahr-el-Gasel, 113
Bahr of Gazelles, 121
Baizetil, Captain, 20
Bakura, 34
Baldwin, George (Consul at Alexandria), 19, 21, 22
Bambara, 171; people, 218
Bambouk, 49; Houghton reaches, 7; goldfields of, 146
Bandinel, James, 125, 127, 128, 191, 270;

Index

Laing's letters to, 175; asks Warrington for Laing's records, 181; Laing's letter from Ghadames, 233, 265; Laing's letter from In Salah, 280–2, 294
Banks, Sir Joseph, 8 n. 2, 9, 11, 19, 21, 25, 34, 36, 41, 117, 131, 148; on Africa Association, 4; brings Hornemann to London, 15; obtains passport for Hornemann, 17; rebukes Hornemann, 23; expresses hopes of seeing Hornemann, 31
Barbary, trade with, 3
Bargirmi, *see* Bagarmi
Barrow, John, 140, 141, 166, 181, 188; promoting exploration, 131; letter to Banks, 147; letter to Lord Bathurst, 148; views on Niger, 193
Barth, Heinrich, 37, 131, 165 n. 4, 177; *Travels in North and Central Africa*, 128, 215 n. 1
Bashaw of Tripoli, 5, *see also* Yusuf
Bathurst, Lord, 33 n. 1, 126, 131, 134, 138, 140, 143, 144, 147, 161, 162, 166; Laing asks him for help, 136; chooses Laing's route, 149; instructions to Laing, 164, 167; on Hatita, 167; interest in exploration, 185; insists on another route for Laing, 187; receives Laing's estimate, 188, 230; receives letter from Warrington on expenditure, 200–201, anger at expenditure, 223; informed by Laing of delay, 207–208; letter from Warrington, 208; informed of Laing's marriage, 212–213; rebukes of, 252; receives report of Laing's death, 320–322
Bauchi, source of Niger, 372
Beads, trade in, 23
Bedouin, threatened attack, 59; aggression of, 65, 93; attack Hornemann, 77
Beechey, F. W. and H. W., 148 n. 2
Begarmé, *see* Bagarmi
Belala, 186
Belgassam ben Khalifa, revolt of, 196, 214 n. 1
Belled-el-Chamis, 74
Belled-el-Kaffer, 74
Belled-el-Rumi, 74
Belled-el-Shereef (Zuila), 94
Bello, Mohammed, of Sokoto, meetings with Clapperton, 172; information on Niger, 192; friendship with El Muktar, 221; Warrington writes to, 216–17; Chief of Fulani, 309; warns Sheikh of Timbuktu against Laing, 311

Belzoni, Giovanni Baptista, 145
Benderachmani, 33
Bengazi, 26, 99, 100; Bey of, 81, 84
Benin, 144, 161; Laing's plans for, 232; occupation of, 221 n. 3; relation with Niger, 259 n. 3
Benin, Bight of, 132, 145, 226 n. 2, 259 n. 3, 369
Beni Ulid (Benioleed), 183, 220 n. 3, 351; description of, 358; Laing at, 163, 353; Laing's escort to, 228; Laing's letters from, 231–6; valley of, 358
Benish (riding cloak), 68, 242 n. 5
Berber language, 69
Berged (? Berghin), 183, 362, 363
Berthollet, Claud-Louis, befriends Hornemann, 54
Berva, 119
Bethelmal (Bet el Mel), 195, 196, 322; present to, 202, 225
Bey-el-Noba, 37, 100
Biljoradec, 61, 74
Bilma, 112
Bir el Tarfaui, 80
Bir Mráia, 183, 364
Birnin dan Gada, 34
Bir Sèrchet, 183, 355, Laing at, 236–7
Biut-el-Nazari, 75
Black desert, 362
Blackey, 373 n. 3
Bled Sidi Mohammed, 184, 301 n. 2, 303, 306
Blumenbach, Professor Johann Friedrich, 9, 15, 19
Bogoola, Sidi Mohammed, 201, 304; care for Laing, 174; Laing's opinion of, 240, 247–8; returns to Tripoli, 250
Bokani, Hornemann dies at, 33, 35
Bonduk, 3
Bongula, 387
Bonnawaugh, 218
Bonnel de Mézières, enquiries into Laing's death, 316–17
Boo Bucker (Boo Khaloom), 209
Borku, 112, 113
Bornu, 3, 18, 22, 108, 113, 117, 120, 130, 131; Hornemann in, 34, 109; map of, 116; people of, 117; Sultan of, 117, 226 n. 3; trade with, 99, 379
Bornu Mission, 131, 132, 146, 158, 185, 195, 371; accompanied by Hatita, 166; return of, 191; result of, 219
Boubokar, Al Kaidi, 312

Bourischa, 66
Bowditch, T. E. *Mission to Ashantee*, 362
Brahim uld Omar uld Salah, buries Laing, 316
Brande, William, 212
Briasco, James, account of fate of Laing's journals, 334 n. 2
Briggs, Dr L. Cabot, 36, 218 n. 6, 278 n. 1, 281, 288 n. 3
Brougham, Henry, 30
Broussonet, Pierre, 19
Browne, W. G. 14, 21, 25, 26, 31, 37, 62 n. 1, 70, 71, 110
Bruce, Captain, 343
Bungola, liberated by Laing, 330; credibility of evidence, 315; accompanies Laing, 314; account of Laing's death, 314, 317 n. 3, 329, 331
Burial places, 377
Burnus (hooded cloak), 241 n. 1
Burgu, see Borku
Busa, 105, Mungo Park dies at, 217 n. 2, 232 n. 1, n. 3
Buttabel, reports Clapperton's arrival at Kano, 322

Cabi, see Kebbi
Cabra, see Kabara
Caftan, (garment), 262 n. 1
Caillé, René, 125; investigates Laing's death, 309, 317 n. 3, 318 n. 1; claims to have reached Timbuktu, 330
Cairo, 11, 15, 16, 18, 39, 47, 99; occupied by Napoleon, 24, 54; Hornemann arrives at, 53; plague, 53; Hornemann leaves for Augila, 58; trade of, 51, 99, 100
Camels, 99; cost of, 189, 201, 238; condition of, 245; fast riding, 248 n. 1; Laing hires, 273; care of, 258
Cape Tajiura, 228
caravans, attacks on, 275, 351, 354; Aujila as centre of, 26; between Tripoli and Timbuktu, 149 n. 2; goods carried by, 99, 100; of Mansa Musa, 169; speed of, 218 n. 3; Ulad Delim attacks on, 289, 296
Carthaginians, 8
Cashna, see Katsina
Catacombs, at Siwah, 74
Cathcart, James Leander, 28
Cattle, 99

Chaamba Arabs, 270, 384
Chad, Lake, 38, 186, 187, 219, 366, 369, 371
Chad, River, 116, 119, 120
Chambers, Robert, 302
Chaoush, 150
Chaoux, 150
Charretié, Jean, 17, 19
Chisholm, Colonel, 134; Laing writes to, 138
Clapperton, Captain Hugh, 36, 37, 131, 132, 148, 155, 158, 176, 177, 185, 192, 195, 217 n. 2, 261, 265, 267, 280, 287, 293, 366; Laing's opinion, of 232, 235–6; on course of Niger, 366 et seq.; relations with Laing, 161–4; confirms Hornemann's death, 33, 34; charges of extravagance, 225; sails for Guinea, 226; meets Sabine, 231; return of, 191; second appointment, 253 n. 1; arrives at Kano, 322; welcome at Sokoto, 172; death, 328 n. 1
Cloth, weaving of, 83, 99, 104
Clothing, 112; of Tibbo, 112; of Siwah, 68; of Tuareg, 114
Clozel, F. J., enquiries into Laing's death, 316
Cochrane, Sir Alexander, 188
Colycinth, 106
Commerce of Tuareg, 115; in Fezzan, 99
Congo, relation to Niger, 129, 130
Cook, Captain James, 4
Cooper, Astley Paston, 249 n. 3
Copper in Bornu, 118
Couga, see Kuka, 118
Cougu, 121
Cresques, Abraham, map of, 169
Cuscus, 60 n. 2, 332 n. 6

Dagomba, 33
Dalu, description of, 346–7
D'Anville, 50; plans of, 47
Darfur, 5, 22, 37, 38, 39, 110, 119
Dates, as food, 61, 65, 66; cultivation of, 67, 99; used as fines, 68
Daura, 121
Dei, Benedetto 180
Denham, Major Dixon, 34 n. 1, 37, 39, 131, 132, 143, 148, 155, 158, 177, 185, 195, 255, 293, 366; opinion of Warrington, 154; gives present to Hatita, 166; return of, 191; opinion on Niger, 371

Desert, descriptions of, 62, 84, 86, 351, 352, 353, 354, 359–60, 362; nature of, 364; volcanic appearance of, 89
D'Ghies, Hassuna, 156, 315; hears of attack on Laing, 298; report of Laing's death, 308; accused of bad faith, 323; takes flight, 335; accused of theft of Laing's papers, 331 et seq., 337, 338; statement, 338; supporters of, 339
D'Ghies, Mohammed, 218, 222; helps Hornemann, 20, 29
Dhioliba, *see* Niger
Dickson, Dr and Mrs, 261, 334
Dirki, 112
Donquah, 136
Dress, in Timbuktu, 218; Laing adopts Turkish fashion, 230, 278; of people of Siwah, 68; of women, 383
Drunkenness, 105
Dufan Mafara, 34
Duish, 374
Dyrke, 112

Edinburgh Review, 231 n. 6; attacks Africa Association, 30; criticism of Hornemann, 37
Edrisé, *see* El Edrisi
Edwards, Bryan, 20, 22
Egypt, 21
El Edrisi, 3, 4, 74, 293
El Faiyum, 77
El Gorama, 183, 362
El Harug, 86 n. 1
El Huide Bakari, presents to, 189
El Idrisi, *see* El Edrisi
El Kanemi, 324
El Khaidram Dham, Sultan of Frikia, 379
El Maghra, 60 n. 1
El Maharuga, 183, 361
El Menshiah, 66 n. 2
El Mota (Jebel Mauta), 67, 74
El Muktar, Sidi Mohammed, 189, 215, 221, 300, 301, 303, 306, 309
El Muktar ben Ahmed, Sidi, 215, 301
El Muktar, Sheikh, 299, 300, 306, 307, 309; letter to Bashaw 311; account of Laing's death, 317
El Noba, Bey, 37
Ennaté, 88
Ensala, *see* In Salah
Esser, 183, 364

Faiume, 74, 77

Falaba, Laing's journey to, 142
Falemé, River, 7
Falmouth, 191, 342
Fantees, 136, 137
Ferawi, 118
Fever, 69, 106; Laing suffers from, 239, 254, 303
Fez, 39; empire of, 114; route from Tuat, 279
Fezzan, 5, 32, 33, 37, 39, 47, 53, 55, 83, 84, 89, 115, 119, 121, 146, 348; commerce of, 99; description of, 98; dress of people, 104; government of, 100; Hornemann enters, 26; Bey of, 11; population of, 103
Fiddri, Lake, *see* Fittri
Figuig, 289 n. 2
Fittri, Lake, 119, 120, 186
Florentines, visit Timbuktu, 180
Founad, Shereef, 11
Foutah, *see* Futa Jallon
Franzi, 106
Frere, John Hookham, 265
French, relations with Bashaw of Tripoli, 151; honour Laing, 182; Mission to Timbuktu, 197 n. 4
Frendenburgh, Joseph, joins Hornemann, 25; engagement of, 56, 70; treachery of, 26; death of, 27, 108
Fulani of Massina, 171, 179, 192; prepare to sieze Timbuktu, 308; threats to Laing, 312
Futa Jallon, 229

Gaauri, (Gwari), 121
Gabr Doga, 183; camp at, 351
Gambia, 5, 49; River, 48
Gamis, 74
Gandi, 34
Gaora (Kworra), 119, 120
Garama, 98 n. 7
Garamantian way, 146
Gardens, in Gadamis, 378; in Siwah, 67
Garian, 239 n. 2
Gatron, (El Qatrun), 98
Germa, 98 n. 7
Gerza, mountains of, 183
Ghadames, 99, 100, 115, 121, 146, 176, 183; attacked by Bey of Tunis, 379; character of people, 266, 378–9, 387; climate, 380; distance from Timbuktu, 218; distance from Tripoli, 229; distance to Twat, 229; importance of, 375; Laing's journey to, 228–40; Laing arrives, 241; Laing's

Index

welcome at, 374; Laing's description of, 172, 263–4, 266; Laing writes journal at, 342; Laing leaves, 267; letters from, 241–72; Laing's lodging, 247; Laing's notes on, 374–85; oasis of, 146; position of, 260; ruins of, 385; slaves in, 384; trade of, 267
Ghana, 3, 39
Ghat, 146, 283, 285
Gibel-el-belled, 75
Girvanelli, Gerolamo, 223, 275, 284, 285
Giza, pyramids of, 77
Gobir, 117 n. 3, 121
Goderich, Lord, receives letter from Warrington, 325; letter to Lord Lansdowne, 338–9; letter to D'Ghies, 339–40
Gold, from Sudan, 118; of Timbuktu, 169, 170
Gold Coast, Laing in action in, 134
Gordon, Gabriel, 133
Gordon, William, 132
Gotta, 183, 362
Göttingen, 10, 12, 14, 15, 21, 52
Goulburn, Henry, letter of, 147
Grant, A., letter to Lord Bathurst, 139
Grasshoppers, as food, 95
Gray, Major, 257
Greiss, E. A. M., 62 n. 2
Guber (Gobir), 117
Guerba (waterskins), 237 n. 3
Guinea, trade with, 3
Gulbi, 120
Gurma, 293
Gwari, 121

Habeeb, Sheikh, 270 n. 3, 384
Hadji Mahommed, the Bet el Mel, 195; delays Laing, 196; presents to, 202
Hadji Yunes uld Sidi, 218
Hagara, 114, 121; colour of, 114
Hair styles, 68
Haliffa, *see* Belgassam ben Khalifa
Hamadu Lobbo, 171 n. 2, 309 n. 3
Hamed Ben Abayd Ben Rachal el Barbuchy, 311
Hamet Baba, *see* Ahmed Baba
Hamet el Habeeb, reports Laing's death, 320 n. 1
Hammera, 26, 95
Hankey, Sir Frederick, 197, 325; Warrington's letter to on Laing's fate, 327–8
Harris, accompanies Laing, 228 n. 2, 238 n. 2; Laing's opinion of, 249; wounded, 299

Harug, 26
Harutsch, 86; description of, 88
Harutsch el abiat, 91
Harutsch el assuat, 91
Hassan Karamanli, 150
Hassaouna, 98
Hasside, 61
Hatita ag Khuden, 164–8, 365; character of, 165; opinions of, 165, 166; Laing's opinion of, 277; Warrington sends for, 192, 197; present to, 204, 251, 262; non-arrival in Tripoli, 207, 348; instructed to meet Laing, 208; Warrington's instructions to, 210; meets Laing, 167, 219, 241, 245; Laing decides to send back, 274, 277; departure of, 282, 285
Hat Salah, 33
Hausa, 3, 27, 31, 46, 110, 115, 131, 186; wealth of, 6; Hornemann falls ill in, 33; Kings of, 121; map of, 115, 116; nature of people, 117
Hay, Robert William, 126, 127 n. 3, 154, 181, 225 n. 1; receives rumour of attack on Laing, 297–8; Warrington reports suspicions of D'Ghies, 331–2; Warrington's letter on Emma's death, 388
Heat of desert, 353, 354, 355, 363, 364
Heeren, Prof. A. H. L., 10, 19
Hemara, 95
Henna koppel, 64
Heri, Angelo, 250, 336
Herodotus, 3, 47, 50, 62, 293
Herrador, Joseph Gomez, 247
Heyne, Professor C. G. 10 n. 1, 19
Hindy, Shereef, 94
Hippopotami, 373
Hoffman, Professor F. G., 19
Hofra, 26
Hombori, 293
Hon, 98 n. 5
Honduras, 133
Hornemann, Friedrich, 125, 145; character of, 9, 36, 37; early life of, 8–9; proposals to Africa Association, 10–14; visits London, 15; negotiates with Africa Association, 16–19; engaged by Africa Association, 8; at Gottingen, 52; purchases equipment, 16; instructions, 16, 17, 18, 19; arrives in Paris, 19; engagement of, 52; preparation for journey, 52; leaves Marseilles, 53; helped by D'Ghies, 20; arrives in Egypt, 21; rebuked by Banks, 23; helped by Napoleon, 24, 47,

56; leaves Cairo for Augila, 24, 58; disguises himself as Moslem, 24, 29, 36, 54, 55, 70; plans, 55; route of, 48; arrives at Ummesogeir, 62; leaves, 65; arrives at Siwah, 25, 65; engages Frendenburgh, 25, 70; leaves Siwah, 75; attacked by Bedouin, 77; claims to be a Moslem, 78; arrives at Schiacha, 80; arrives at Augila, 83; arrives at Temissa, 92; arrives at Murzuk, 26, 96; illness, 27, 108; visits Tripoli, 27; returns to Murzuk, 29; leaves for Bornu, 109; last journey of, 108; lack of news of, 31; fate of, 32; death, 33; date of death, 35; papers burnt, 35; results, 37, 38, 39

Hornemann's *Journal*, 43; bibliographical note, 40; French translation, 40; published in Africa Society's *Proceedings*, 30; translation into German, 40

Hornemann, Freidrich Georg, 8

Horses, 99

Horton, R. Wilmot, 126, 163, 188, 191; Warrington writes to, 194, 217–18; Laing's letter to from Beni Ulid, 234; letter from Laing on Volta, 271; Letter from Laing on In Salah, 278, 282, 288–90

Houghton, Major, exploration of Niger, 7; appointment, 49; travels, 49; death of, 8, 49, 186

Houses, description of, 95; in Fezzan, 106; of Tuareg, 115; in Ghadames, 247, 264, 266, 376–7

Hun (Hon), 98

Huskisson, William, 262

Ibn Battuta, 332
Idah, 217
Imbert, Paul, 180
Imhammed, Shereef, 11, 49
Incest, among Tebu, 113
In Salah, 127, 183, 184; Laing arrives at, 273; Laing's welcome at, 276, 278; Laing's description of, 174, 279, 288, 290–91; Laing's letters from, 273–95; route to Fez, 279, 288
Irrigation, 346, 359
Ishmael, Mulai, present to, 189

Jacob, 320, 386
Jaghbub, Oasis of, 26
Jahudie, 61
Jalabs, 55
Jamaica, 133
Janisseries, 149
Jarra, 49
Jebel el Maraar, 365
Jebel-es-Soda, 241
Jebel Mauta, 67, 74 n. 1
Jega, 110 n. 2
Jenne, 229, 281, 312
Jewelry, of Arabs, 68; in Fezzan, 104
Jinbala, 281
Joliba, *see* Niger
Judges, 103
Julbi, River, 116, 119
Jupiter Ammon, Temple of, 14, 26, 71
Jeset ben Abdullah, *see* Hornemann
Jussuph (Hornemann), 31

Kabara (Kabra), 310, 368 n. visited by Laing, 312
Kabur, 368 n.
Kadanka, 105, 117
Kaffle (caravan), 214 n. 2
Kairwan, 146
Kaledyma, 101, 102 n. 1
Kambia, 133
Kang Kang, 144
Kano, 6, 115, 121, 176; Clapperton arrives at, 322; Oudney dies near 132
Karamanli family, the, 100, 149–50
Kardassi (Kirdasah), 58, 82
Karet-am-el Sogheir, *see* Ummesogeir
Kashna, see Katsina
Kasson, 49
Katsina, 3, 6, 7, 11, 13, 15, 16, 22, 24, 29, 31, 33, 35, 36, 55, 108, 121, 145, 186; Hornemann's arrival at, 34; map of, 116
Kawar, 146
Kebbi, 29, 38, 121; map of, 116, 117; river of, 119
Kel Owi, 99 114
Keijumma, 102
Khamisa, 74 n. 2
King, Lt., 372
Kirdasah, 58
Koffle (caravan), 214 n. 2
Kola nuts, 35
Kolluvi, Tuareg, 114
Kong, 367, 372
Koreishit, 66 n. 3
Kourdane, 36 n. 1
Kuka, 118 n. 1
Kuskus, see Cuscus
Kworra, *see* **Niger**

Index

Labeida, accused of Laing's murder, 316

Laing, Emma, 386–88; marries Laing, 212–213; validity of marriage, 261; Laing asks for news of, 286; letter to husband, 386–7; letters from Laing, 178; Laing has news of, 255; hears of attack on Laing, 298; remarriage, 388; death, 388

Laing, Major Alexander Gordon, as explorer, 173–82; character of, 174, 175, 176, 179; courage of, 179; endurance of, 179; inadequacy of, 174; neglect of, 125; opinion of Clapperton, 232, 235–6; opinion on Hatita, 277; opinion of Sabine on, 138; opinion of Tuareg, 269; relations with Clapperton, 161–4; theory of Niger, 142, 178, 258–61; Warrington's opinion of, 203; nature of his journal, 177; army career, 132, 133; explores Kambia, 133; unpopularity of, 135; gallantry of, 134, 137; early explorations of, 133, 134, 136, 141; explores Falaba, 142; asks for promotion, 136; attacked by General Turner, 137; plans, 138, 141; itinerary, 183; preparations for expedition, 185; opinion on route to Timbuktu, 186–7; estimate of expenses, 188–9; equipment, 190, 211–12; engages party, 191; leaves London, 342; arrives at Gibraltar, 342; arrives at Malta, 342; taken ill, 191, 193, 343; sails for Tripoli, 343; arrives at Tripoli, 194; description of, 344–5; meets Warrington, 344; meets Bashaw, 347; suspicions of Bashaw, 347; reasons for choice of route, 348–9; relations with Bashaw, 194–205; estimate of expenses, 195; attempts to delay, 196, 203, 205; expenses of journey, 199, 201; agrees estimate of cost, 200; camps outside Tripoli, 228, 349; meets Babani, 350; informs Lord Bathurst of delay, 207–8; change of route, 208; departure from Tripoli, 208; marries Emma Warrington, 159, 212–13; validity of marriage, 261; leaves Tripoli, 214, 360; letters of introduction, 215–17; route from Ghadames to Timbuktu, 218; plans to meet Hatita, 219; expenses of journey, 223–4; warned of Babani, 223; companions, 228 n. 2; journey to Ghadames, 228–40; meets Babani, 228; adopts Turkish dress, 230; time table 231; at Beni Ulid, 353; use of Arabic, 356; expresses hopes to Warrington, 234–5; letters to Warrington, 234–5; at Bir Serchet, 236–7; complains of treatment, 236, 237; shot at, 238; illness, 239; shortage of water, 240; at Ghadames, 241, 244, 374; meets Hatita, 241; disappointed at lack of letters, 241; threatened attack on, 241–2; letters from Ghadames, 241–72; opens Tyrwhitt's box, 242; reaches mountains of Terhoona, 351; arrives at Wady Rumel, 351; visits Sheikh of Terhoona, 352; at Tamsowa, 360–61; meets Hatita, 245; opinion on companions, 246–9; acts as doctor, 249, 262, 263; comments on Bathurst's rebuke, 252–3, 260; doubts as to course, 253; suffers from fever, 254; has news of Emma, 255; letter on costs, 257–8; buys presents, 263; description of Ghadames, 263–4; on dangers of journey, 265; health, 265; leaves Ghadames, 267; delayed by Bashaw, 268; on costs, 268–9; avoids Tuat, 270, 274; on difficulties of route, 271; arrives at In Salah, 273, 276, 278; letters to Horton, 278, 282, 288–90; letters to Warrington, 273–7, 282–3, 284–91; observations at In Salah, 279; abandons Turkish dress, 278; describes Tuat, 281; plans after Timbuktu, 281; misunderstandings with Babani, 284–5; delayed at In Salah, 292, 294; route, 288; information collected, 292; letters to wife, 178; health, 178, 293; confused with Park, 178, 294; letter to Horton from Tanezeruft, 296–7; first attack on, 173, 178–9, 296–307, 317, 318, 326; cared for by Sidi el Mukta, 174, 200, 307, 323; letter to Warrington, 301–6; left alone, 303, 305; attempt to persuade to return, 308, 309; route to Timbuktu, 149; reaches Timbuktu, 298, 309, 310; on Timbuktu, 171, 176; secretly visits the Niger, 310; threatened, 310; visits Kabara, 310, 312; letter from Timbuktu, 311–12; decides to travel via Segu, 312; via Jenne, 312; death of, 313, 314, 320, 325–6; date of death, 318; Bungola's account, 314; reasons for death, 172, 173; burial of, 316; D'Ghies's reports on his death, 308; enquiries into death, 314–17; report of death in *l'Etoile*, 325–6, 389–90; fears for safety, 318; relics of equipment, 318 n. 1; search for, 318–29, 325; Hassuna D'Ghies

accused of murder, 336; honoured by French, 182; memorial to, 182
Laing's Journals, 342–58; reported destruction of, 315, 316; fate of, 330–41; D'Ghies suspected of theft of, 331 et seq.
Laing's works, *Cursory remarks on the course and termination of the great River Niger*, 126, 366–73; letters of, 123 et seq.; *Notes on Ghadamis*, 126; *Travels in Western Africa*, 174; *Travels in the Timannee*, 134, 231 n. 5
Laing, Willliam, 132
Lalande, Joseph, 19, 53
Lander, Richard and John, *Journal of an expedition to the Niger*, 35
Langlès, L., 40
Lansdowne, Lord, letter to from Lord Goderich, 338–9
le Bore, Jack, 191, 231 n. 1; life of, 188 n. 2; accompanies Laing, 228 n. 2; remains in Falmouth, 342; rejoins Laing, 343; Laing's opinion of, 248; wounded, 299; death of, 303
Ledyard, John, 21 n. 4; engaged to explore Africa, 4–5, 49; death of, 5, 49
Lem Lem, 122
Lenant de Bellefonds, Adolphe, 219
Lenz, Oskar, 318 n. 1
Leo Africanus, 3, 4, 39, 117, 267, 375; on Wangara, 121; on Timbuktu, 169; on the Niger, 258 n. 1, 368
Lepcis Magna, 130, 154
Lernica, 21
l'Etoile, account of Laing's death, 325–6, 389–90
Lisle, Peter, (Murad Rais), 27, 32
Locusts, as food, 95
Lofonsa, 183
Lucas, Simon, 11, 27, 28; engaged to explore Africa, 4, 49
Luigibi, 95, 105
Lussi, 118, 120
Lybia Palus, 371, 372
Lyon, Captain G. F., 36, 37, 131, 146, 148, 166, 293, 345, 353; hears of Hornemann, 33, 34; expedition of, 131; *Narrative of Travels in Northern Africa*, 131; on Hatita, 165–6; observations of, 260, 267

MacCarthy, Sir Charles, 133, 134, 135, 136, 142
McDonogh, Dr Bryan, 27, 28, 31, 33

McQueen, James, 370
Madoc, Laurence, 170
Maghra Hills, 25
Maghreb, slavemarkets of, 6 n. 3
Magra, British Consul, 7
Maherre, see *Mheri*
Mahomed Msrah, 145
Maitland, Sir Thomas, 33 n. 1
Majabra, 26
Majies, 119
Malaria, 69
Malhrail, 183, 356; Laing arrives at, 237
Mali, 3, 267
Malta, Laing ill in, 191, 193
Mamlukes, 24, 102
Mandingo, 133
Mansa Musa, caravan of, 169
Maraar, 364
Marabut, definition, 236 n. 4
Marabut at Bir Serchet, 236, 237–8
Margi, 118
Markets, 64, 93; at Murzuk, 99; at Timbuktu, 168
Marrakech, 145
Marsden, William, 40
Marseilles, 53
Martinici, V., 154
Martyn, Lieut., accompanied Mungo Park, 232
Masheeah (Menshia), 159 n. 1
Massina, 171
Matkara, colour of, 114
Mecca, 24, 54
Medina, 49
Meghara, the, 98
Melaye, 68
Meledda, 82
Mende, 141
Menschia, 61, 66, 159 n. 1
Mesna, 118, 120
Mesurado, Cape, 136
Metko, 119
Mheri, 248 n. 1
Mifferadaati, 34
Mijotta, 61
Misurata, 5
Mithqal, 102 n. 2, 259
Mogora, 60
Mohammed (camel driver), 304; account of attack, 299; steals Laing's possessions, 306
Mohammed Bello, 189 n. 4, 309; hostile to Christians, 311

Mohammed el Fezzani, brings news of Laing, 309; fate of, 332
Mohammed el Mukni, (Bey el Noba), 100, 109
Mohammed el Washy, reports Laing's death, 318–19
Mohammed Faradji uld Abdallah, accused of Laing's murder, 316
Mohammed M'Goram, 313 n. 3, 317 n. 3, 318 n. 1
Mohammed Misrah of Alexandria, 140; on Niger, 368
Moira, Earl of, 15, 31, 32
Mojabra, 81
Monge, Gaspard, 54
Monnier, Baron, 337
Moors, occupy Timbuktu, 146 n. 2, 170, 180
Morai-je, 85
Morocco, 4, 114
Mossi, 293, 303
Moursouck, *see* Murzuk
Msellem, 66
Muckta, *see* El Muktar
Muhabag, 59, 63
Murad Rais (Peter Lisle), 27; investigates Hornemann's death, 32
Murzuk, 13, 32, 33, 36, 38, 39, 47, 88, 96, 111, 120, 143, 146, 148, 267; Hornemann at, 25, 26; his opinion on, 27, 37; palace at, 101; Ritchie dies at, 131; Sultan meets caravan at, 96

Nahun, Abraham, 249
Nahun, Jacob, 177; accompanying Laing, 228 n. 2
Napoleon Bonaparte, helps Hornemann, 47, 56
Nasamones, 50
Natron, Valley of, 62
Naudi, Xavier, 151, 156
Nazari (Christians), 121
Neale, Vice-Admiral Sir Harry Burrard, 343
Neddeek, 85, 86
Nicol, G. and W., 40
Niger, course of, 3, 6, 7, 14, 38, 129, 132, 186, 187, 258, 259, 366, 367; exploration of, 49; fording of, 283; Hornemann's description of, 120; Houghton engaged to explore, 7; Hornemann and, 38; in trade, 48; Laing's attempt to form expedition to, 138 et seq.; Laing visits, 310;

Laing's *Cursory Remarks*, 366–73; Laing's theory, 178, 186, 187, 260, 261; mission of 1816, 257; Mungo Park discovers, 229 n. 3; navigability of, 368, 369; problem of, 129, 232, 233; Ptolemy on, 371; relation to Congo, 129, 130; relation to Bight of Benin, 269, 370; relation to Nile, 142, 145; relation with Volta, 271; Reichard's theory, 145; search for, 3; size of, 368; source of, 372
Nile, Battle of the, 24; relation with Niger, 142, 145; Western branch of, 63
Nioro, Houghton killed at, 8
Noofy, *see* Nupe
Noro, 121
Nupe, 29, 33, 34, 36, 38, 116–19, 121, 144, 187, 283, 368
Nyam Nyam, 122
Nyffé, *see* Nupe

O'Beirne, Dr, 257
O'Gour Farat, 274
Ornaments in Fezzan, 104
Osuit (Asyut), 119
Othman ben Ahmed, 307, 310, 312 n. 1
Oudian Wan Abelhouda, 274
Oudney, Dr, 131, 158, 185, 202; Bornu Mission of, 140; on Hatita, 166
Overweg, 131

Pahde, Adolf, 40
Palla, 383
Paris, 19, 53
Park, Mungo, 52, 139, 145, 254; accompanied by Martyn, 232; death of, 186, 217 n. 2, 235, 368; discovers Niger, 8, 119, 229 n. 3; discoveries of, 23; embarks at Sansanding, 229; Laing mistaken for, 178, 294; route of, 48; *Travels*, 39 n. 1, 47, 49, 50
Pearce, Capt., 226, 261
Peddie, Major, 130, 186, 188 n. 2; death of, 186, 257
Pellew, Edward, *see* Exmouth, Viscount
Pellisier de Reynard, 153, 154
Picard, Aurelie, 36 n. 1
Plague, 53
Portuguese at Timbuktu, 180
Prince Regent, 130, 152–3
Ptolemy, 192, 293
Pyramids, 77; Battle of, 24

Quarterly Journal of Science, The, 142

Index

Quarterly Review, The, accused D' Ghies of theft, 338; mention of Laing, 125 n. 1, 126; notice of Laing's book, 231

Rabba, 35
Real Patacks (dollars), 67
Reggan, 281 n. 2
Reichard, C. G., theory of Niger's course, 130, 145
Reinel, Pero, visits Timbuktu, 180
Rennell, Major James, 6, 39, 40, 47, 166; observations of, 267; on Niger, 7, 38, 129, 366
de Reynard, Pellissier, 153, 154
Rhababe, 105
Rhala, 292
Richardson, James, 131; account of Warrington, 155; complains of Warrington, 157–8; on Warrington's garden, 159; on Hatita, 164
Ricketts, Major, 138
Ritchie, Joseph, expedition of, 131
Rogers, boatbuilder, 228 n. 2, 238 n. 2, develops ophthalmia, 364; Laing's opinion of, 249; wounded, 299
Rokelle, River, 133, 143
Romans, 146; building at Ghadames, 264
Rose, Benjamin, 181
Rosetti, Charles, 5, 21, 22, 23
Ross, Captain William, 135
Rossoni, Giacomo, 222, 285; reports arrival of French mission, 197
Roum, 61
Rousseau, Baron, 156, 212; attacked by Warrington, 336, 388; role in fate of Laing's journals, 331 et seq.

Sabine, Capt. Edward, 125, 127, 128; regard for Laing, 138; tries to help Laing, 140; hears Laing's plans, 141; letters from Laing to, 164, 175, 212, 231, 266, 283, 292; starts Life of Laing, 181; meets Clapperton, 231
Saccara, 77
Sahab, 184; as site of Laing's death, 316, 317
Said (Lyon's travelling name), 166 n. 2
St Joseph, 325 n. 3
Sala, 262; meets Laing, 245
Salt, in desert, 62, 363; stratum near Siwah, 67; methods of obtaining, 118
Samsuc (tamarinds), 110
Sansanding, 130, 325; Mungo Park embarks at, 229

Saqqâra, 77
Sasoofa, 357
Sbocha, 66
Scalaro, clerk to D'Ghies, 334
Scarlett, Sir James, Baron Abinger, 339
Scharkie, 66, 71
Scheibat, 26, 76 n. 1
Schiacha, 76; Hornemann arrives at, 80
Sciati, Wadi, 266 n. 2, 239, 360
Scott, Robert Henry, 128
Sebha, 98 n. 4
Sede Hamet Barba, 326
Segu-Sikoro, 49, 229; Laing makes for, 179, 321; King of, 254
Seku Ahmadu, 171, 221 n. 1, 309 n. 3, 311
Sélé, 130
Senegal, River, 7
Senegambia, 24
Senna, 99
Sennar, 5, 37
Septimius Severus, 146
Serked, Marabut of, 246–7
Shabeni, 6
Shabu Soudah, 183
Shari, 38
Shati, *see* Sciati
Shebat al Haruba, 356
Sheep, breeding, 99
Sheku Hamadu Lobbo, 171
Sherghi, 266 n. 2, 360
Shorfa, 281 n. 2
Sidibischir, 96
Sierra Leone, 133; Laing's travels in, 174
Silla, 49, 130
Simtée 61
Sirocco, 374; Laing's description, 355
Siwah, 14, 22, 111, 114, 120; antiquities of, 70; catacombs of, 74; description of, 66; Hornemann arrives at, 25, 65; he leaves, 75
Slavery, 102, 248, 384–5
Small-pox, 110
Smith, Laing's friend, 233, 270, 281
Smyth, Commander W. H., 8 n. 1; hears Hornemann's fate, 32; learns of Ghadames road, 148; report on exploration, 131; report on Tripoli, 130
Société de l'Afrique interieure et de Découvertes, La, 40
Sockna, 98, 114
Sofau, 121
Sokoto, 34, 132, 162; Clapperton at, 172, 209, 328 n. 1

Index

Soma, Mount, 134, 142
Songhai, 171, 180, 293
Soolima, country, 142; tribe, 133
Soudah desert, 362
Stable, Jonathan, 287
Stola, 383
Stres, 89
Sudan, 99, 113, 115; access to, 146; Bello, Sultan of, 216–17; trade of, 117, 146
Sultin, 86

Tafilelt (Tafilalet), 289 n. 1
Tagara (Idah), 217
Tagara, in Sierra Leone, 249
Tagiura, 183
Tailed men, 121
Talata Noma, 34
Talma, Francois Joseph, 247
Tamsawa, 183, 358, 360, 361, 362
Tamsowa, Laing at, 360–1
Tanezruft, 184
Tarikh es Sudan, 332 n. 7, 333
Tazerbo, 113 n. 4
Tebabo (Tazerbo), 113
Tebu, 98 n. 2, 99, 111, 113
Teda, *see* Tebu
Temesow (Ti-m-Missao), 288
Temissa, 92, 120
Temperature of desert, 246, 353, 354, 355, 363, 364
Tenbuch *see* Timbuktu, 169
Terhuna, mountains of, 183, 228, 230; Laing reaches, 351, 352
Tetuan, 6 n. 4
Tibbo, *see* Tebu
Tibesti, 112
Tidikelt, 278
Timbuktu, 3, 6, 7, 8, 31, 33, 35, 39, 113, 115, 145, 162, 184; dangers of, 308, 309; description of, 176; difficulties of access, 269, 271; distance from Ghadames, 218; early European visitors, 180; history of, 326, 332, 333; importance of, 139, 170; inhabitants of, 171; Laing at, 128, 298, 309, 310; Laing's expectations of, 178; Laing's letter from, 125; Leo Africanus' description, 169–70; Mungo Park fails to visit, 23; road to, 145–9; route via Guinea coast, 186; story of, 168–73; Sultan of, 215 n. 1; trade of, 218
Ti-m-Missao, 288 n. 2
Tmessa, 26
Torfare, 80

Trachoma, 69
Trade, from Timbuktu, 146, 218; in Africa, 48; in Ghadames, 267, 378; of Sudan, 117; with Africa, 3
Traghen, 26, 96, 120
Trees, petrified, 62
Trigh el Majabra, 81 n. 1
Tripoli, 5, 25, 39, 55, 99, 113, 120, 183; as gateway to Sudan, 146; Hornemann arrives in, 27, 108; inhabitants of, 345; Laing arrives in, 194; Laing camps outside, 349; Laing's description, 344–5; Laing's journey from to Ghadames, 228–40; Simon Lucas visits, 5; Warrington's villa at, 158–9
Tripoli-Ghadames road, 146
Troglodytae, 121
Tuareg, 27, 98, 99; attack caravans, 275; clothing, 114; description of, 113, 121; Kel Owi, 99, 121; Laing's opinion of, 269; of Ahaggar, 46; raids on Timbuktu, 171
Tuat, 145, 146, 176; inhabitants of, 281; Laing avoids, 270, 274; Laing's description of, 281; Laing's map of, 289
Tuckey, Captain, 130
Tully, Miss, 215 n. 1
Tum-megar (catacombs), 70
Tunis, 39, 68, 113; Bey of, 379
Turks, in Tripoli, 149
Turner, Major General, 135, 137, 187
Twat, 99, 147, 229
Twater, native of Twat, 65 n. 1
Tychsen, Professor O. G., 19
Tyrwhitt, John, 159 n. 4; box belonging to, 242

Ulad Delim, 288; danger from, 289, 290; defeat of, 292; prepare to attack, 296
Ulad Hassan, 357
Ummebeda, 71
Ummesogeir, 25; description of, 64; Hornemann arrives at, 62; Hornemann leaves, 65; mountains of, 62
Ungura (Wangara), 118, 121
Un Sogir, *see* Ummesogeir
Urahgen, 218 n. 7
Usuman dan Fodio, 171

Vadala, R., *L'Histoire des Karamanlis*, 151 n. 2
Venereal disease, 106, 110
Villages, 64

Vogel, 131
Volta, River, 271

Wadai, 38, 119, 121
Wadey, *see* Wadai
Wadet-el-Latron, 59, 63
Wadi Ahennet, 184, attack at, 178, 179, 299–302
Wadi el Ajial, 266 n. 2
Wadi Echmed, 183, 354
Wadi er Raml, 183, 228, 351
Wadi Shati, *see* Sciati
Wadi Suked, possibly Bir Serchet, 236
Wadi Thakouset, 183, 274
Wadon (Waddan), 98 n. 6
Wangara, 5, 39, 118, 121, 186; Niger empties into, 372
Wargee, the Tartar, 371
Wargla, 145
Warrington, Emma, *see* Laing, Emma
Warrington, Jane Eliza, 153
Warrington, Colonel Hanmer, 125, 129 n. 1, 130, 151–61, 315; and Laing-Clapperton relationship, 161, 162; character of, 157, 160–1; family, 159; early life, 151–2; appointed Consul, 151; army career, 151–2; connection with Royal Family, 153, 154; opinion of Laing, 203; meets Laing, 344; relations with Bashaw, 154, 155; residence of, 158; sends for Hatita, 167, 192, 197; greets Laing, 194; letters to Laing, 191; calculates expense of expedition, 199; instructions to Hatita, 210; marries Emma and Laing, 160, 212–13; writes to Bello of Sokoto, 216–17; writes to Sultan of Timbuktu, 217–18; excuses expenditure, 224–5; offers to pay costs of journey, 226; suggests change of plan, 227; warns Laing of foreign consuls, 227; hears of attack on Laing, 297–8; Laing's letter from Bled Sidi Mohammed, 301–6; fears for Laing's safety, 318; efforts to find Laing, 318–29; reports Laing's death, 320–2; accuses Bashaw of bad faith, 321; hopes of Laing's safety, 325; investigates Laing's death, 327–8; receives confirmation of Laing's death, 329; reports theft of journals, 331–2; reports D'Ghies' flight,

335; attacks Rousseau, 336, 388; attack on D'Ghies, 340
Water, in desert, 64; in Siwah, 67; lack of between In Salah and Timbuktu, 282; salt, 62; result of drinking, 293; shortage of, 240, 357; transport of, 26, 60
Waterskins, 237 n. 3
Weapons carried by Laing, 191; of Tibbo, 112
Wells, 346–7, 365
Wilmot, Robert John, 163 n. 2
Women, of Borgu tribe, 113; position of, 382
Wood, Thomas, marries Emma Laing, 388

Yandakka, 34
Yauri, 161, 192, 283; Laing proposes journey to, 229, 366–8, 371
Yem Yem, 122
Yeow, course of, 366
Yerma (Germa), 98
York, H.R.H. the Duke of, 135
Young, Sir William, 30, 31, 37, 40, 51
Yusuf Karamanli (Bashaw of Tripoli), 33, 100, 130, 149–51, 264, 284, 315; agreement of, 195, 229; castle of, 344; goodwill to British, 148; influence of, 242, 319; meets Laing, 347; relations with Laing, 194–205; Laing's suspicions of, 347; relations with Warrington, 155; presents to, 199, 200, 201, 211; reward for return of Bornu Mission, 197; delays Laing, 196, 203, 205, 268; letter of credit for Laing, 211; confirms rumour of attack on Laing, 298; Sheikh el Muktar's letter to, 311, 313–14; receives letter reporting Laing's death, 318–19; accused of bad faith, 321; Warrington has audience of, 322–4; Warrington's suspicions, 334; accuses D'Ghies of Laing's murder, 336; extracts tribute, 378, 379; rule over Ghadames, 380

Zad, *see* Chad
Zahara, desert of, 5
Zamfara, 34
Zuila, 82, 94, 120; Hornemann enters, 26; description of, 94
Zurmi, 34